VENUE STORIES

Music Industry Studies

Series Editor: Sarah Raine, University College Dublin
Founding Series Editor: Dave Laing†, Honorary Research Fellow at the University of Liverpool and Senior Research Associate at the University of East Anglia.

In recent years, there has been a rapid growth of interest in the music industry, from policy-makers, educationalists, the media and others. This new series aims to satisfy the demand for in-depth knowledge and analysis of all facets of the industry, from recording to live music and the publishing sector. It will include both historical and contemporary approaches and draw on contributions from economics, geography, sociology, legal studies, cultural studies and other disciplines.

Published:

Beyond 2.0: The Future of Music
Steve Collins and Sherman Young

She's at the Controls: Sound Engineering, Production and Gender Ventriloquism in the 21st Century
Helen Reddington

Sounds Irish, Acts Global: Explaining the Success of Ireland's Popular Music Industry
Michael Mary Murphy and Jim Rogers

Forthcoming:

Elements of Music Management
Sally Gross

The Handbook on Music Business and Creative Industries in Education
Edited by Daniel Walzer

VENUE STORIES

NARRATIVES, MEMORIES, AND HISTORIES FROM BRITAIN'S INDEPENDENT MUSIC SPACES

EDITED BY
FRASER MANN, ROBERT EDGAR AND HELEN PLEASANCE

SHEFFIELD UK   BRISTOL CT

Published by Equinox Publishing Ltd.

UK: Office 415, The Workstation, 15 Paternoster Row, Sheffield, South Yorkshire, S1 2BX
USA: ISD, 70 Enterprise Drive, Bristol, CT 06010

www.equinoxpub.com

First published 2023

© Fraser Mann, Robert Edgar, Helen Pleasance and contributors 2023

All rights reserved. No part of this publication may be reproduced or transmitted in any form or by any means, electronic or mechanical, including photocopying, recording or any information storage or retrieval system, without prior permission in writing from the publishers.

British Library Cataloguing-in-Publication Data
A catalogue record for this book is available from the British Library.

ISBN-13 978 1 80050 443 1 (hardback)
         978 1 80050 373 1 (paperback)
         978 1 80050 374 8 (ePDF)
         978 1 80050 407 3 (ePub)

Library of Congress Cataloging-in-Publication Data
Names: Mann, Fraser, editor. | Edgar, Robert, editor. | Pleasance, Helen, editor.
Title: Venue stories : narratives, memories, and histories from Britain's independent music spaces / edited by Fraser Mann, Robert Edgar and Helen Pleasance.
Description: Bristol : Equinox Publishing Ltd, 2023. | Series: Music industry studies | Includes bibliographical references. | Summary: "Venue Stories is an anthology of creative non-fiction that remembers, celebrates and reinvigorates our complex and plural relationship with small and independent music spaces. This is a collection of stories by and for fans, band members, merch sellers, pint pullers, journalists with a freebie, roadies with a backache and sound techs with an earache"-- Provided by publisher.
Identifiers: LCCN 2023015293 (print) | LCCN 2023015294 (ebook) | ISBN 9781800504431 (hardback) | ISBN 9781800503731 (paperback) | ISBN 9781800503748 (pdf) | ISBN 9781800504073 (epub)
Subjects: LCSH: Music-halls--Great Britain. | Concerts--Great Britain. | Alternative rock music--Great Britain--History and criticism. | LCGFT: Creative nonfiction.
Classification: LCC ML3492 .V45 2023 (print) | LCC ML3492 (ebook) | DDC 781.640941--dc23/eng/20230616
LC record available at https://lccn.loc.gov/2023015293
LC ebook record available at https://lccn.loc.gov/2023015294

Typeset by S.J.I. Services, New Delhi, India

For Caroline. Miss you big sis.

Contents

Foreword   ix
EMMA WARREN

Introduction   1
FRASER MANN, ROBERT EDGAR AND HELEN PLEASANCE

1. Peripheral Dancing: The Jazz Rooms, Brighton, 1984   23
   HELEN PLEASANCE

2. Finding the Dirt: Nesh at Elektrowerkz   31
   FRASER MANN

3. Chatting to Jarvis   40
   ROBERT EDGAR

4. Fascinating Rhythms   51
   BETH HUGHES

5. The Bull and Gate, Kentish Town, London, 1987–1989   60
   POLLY HANCOCK

6. Weapons of Bass Destruction   69
   KEVIN NARRAINEN

7. Girls with Guitars   78
   VIM RENAULT AND LENE CORTINA

8. (Princess) Charlotte and her 1980s Offspring, O'Jays   88
   RUTH MILLER

9. The Brewery Arts Centre   98
   PETER ATKINSON

10. 'Nothing Comes Easy': Small Venue Concerts with the Wedding Present   112
    DAVID LEWIS GEDGE AND JON STEWART

11. In Memory of The Standard: Hard Rock in East London   124
    ANNA MARIA BARRY

12. The New Breed: 1990s Mod Revival Scene in Leeds   135
    ABIGAIL GAINES

13	Sitting on the Bench in Leicester's Charlotte ED GARLAND	145
14	Kings Cross, Kentish Town and Kensington Gore via Gallowgate: In Search of the Goldilocks Zone JULIANNE REGAN	153
15	Spiritual Auras: Jungle Venues in Birmingham and the West Midlands, 1993–1997 PENELOPE WICKSON	162
16	The Wheat from the Chaff MATT COLBECK	175
17	More than a Club: The Genius Loci of Eric's PENNY KILEY	185
18	Coming of Age at The Warehouse, Liverpool, 1981 DAWN AMBER HARVEY	194
19	The Rainbow Venues and Swingamajig: Closing the Doors on the Home of One of Birmingham's Favourite Festivals CHRIS INGLIS	200
20	Sold out, Locked out, Power out TOM HINGLEY	211
21	Mothers Club in Erdington ALAN SMITH	218
22	Music Spaces and Music Memory ANNA ELIAS	226
23	Glitter, Rubber Ducks, and Dinghies: The Georgian Theatre and the Teesside Gigging Community in the Early 2010s AMY MCCARTHY	231
24	The Rock Garden: Conversations with My Dad, a Punk-Rock DJ THOMAS JACKSON	238
25	...for a Girl TARRYN WATKINS	248

Final Word MARK DAFYD (Music Venue Trust)	255

Foreword

Emma Warren

The voices in this book offer some delicious nudges into collective memory. After all, many of us have our own personal utopias, and memories of these begin rising up on reading descriptions of The Wheatsheaf in Stoke or Glasgow's Barrowlands. Each culturally undervalued venue is different, but their similarities connect us across time and space.

I have my own favourite places and they span decades: a council-owned civic space that ran under-18s discos in suburban South London; Sankeys Soap in Manchester; or Total Refreshment Centre, aka TRC, on the edge of Hackney in London. In 2019 I wrote and published a book about TRC which was a love letter to all the places like it – unfinished places that are open to new ideas, that allow audiences and artists to grow, and in which the separation between stage and dancefloor is minimised (this isn't always an entirely good thing, as you will read in David Gedge's recollection of having to take their own barrier to pre-festival Wedding Present tours of tiny venues lest an over-excited fan knock the mic stand into his face).

As part of making my book, I ran events and workshops across the country and at each one I asked people to name 'their' TRC – a space that allowed them to become a version of themselves that they believed in. The list was different in Bristol than it was in Kraków, although some names popped up wherever I was – Plastic People, or Antwerp Mansions for example. I began each event by reading out this Roll Call of Honour and asked the audience to applaud all the people that made these places happen – and who continue to make them happen.

The Roll Call of Honour had a remarkable effect. People gathered afterwards to tell me about their spaces, and sometimes they were overwhelmed with feeling. They told me about repurposed cafes, about basements transformed from scratch, and about forgotten youth clubs. They conveyed the independently-minded collective action that is required to create and maintain spaces that focus on cultural profit not shareholder dividends – and the rich community profits that emanate from the spaces. They told me how much these spaces meant to them, and that losing them was like losing a beloved friend.

The writers in *Venue Stories* have the same familial relationship with independent space. They attended gigs, played gigs, drank at the bar, ran the bar, formed bands, or became DJs, producers or promoters. Writers absorbed the music through their moving bodies – or seated ones, in the case of Ed Garland's 'bass bench' where he'd sit and listen with his torso to Doc Scott DJing at Leicester's Princess Charlotte. Other writers explore the different ways the materials in these spaces absorb sound – Penelope Wickson describing how the Victorian bricks in Birmingham venues that hosted early junglist events created a 'more dense, rugged effect'. The sonics reflected the intensity of the music and movement, which itself reflected the intensity of life as experienced by the people in the room. The embodied memory of how it felt to be in these spaces remains even when the detail of what surrounds it fades. Alan Smith's brilliant recollections of Mothers Club in late 1960s Erdington give us a sense of what it was like to be young in the Midlands when your nearby MP Enoch Powell was making Rivers of Blood speeches, and how much the social context required a spatial response.

Venue Stories allows us to see some of the threads that connect these environments: that they amplify local culture and can even build it from the sticky floor up, creating space where seeds can be sown and new possibilities emerge. That they tend to be easy-access and welcoming, with free aspects that make them accessible even for the youngest or the brokest and the underage. Zines often spring up, like dandelions.

Peter Atkinson's essay on the Brewery Arts Centre in Kendal shows how having the right people in even an unpromising space can form 'the productive nucleus' of an independent scene – the right people often involving a certain richness across age, interests and demographic. Other contributions describe mutable spaces that generate new stop-offs on the national touring circuit and allow audiences and bands to grow, and to continue growing once they've gained national success through contact with the rootsiest part of music culture. They allow people to see artists at their first gigs and when they're megastars, as with Dawn Amber Harvey's descriptions of seeing Nick Cave and Mick Hucknall pre- and post-fame in Liverpool. Independent venues are educative: Tom Hingley describes his time rehearsing and playing with Inspiral Carpets at Manchester's Boardwalk as 'a school of sorts for the destitute, the lost and those in need of community, belief and positivity'.

The longer perspective contained in this collection offers a sub-harmonic of hope. Take Thomas Jackson's conversations with his dad, who DJed at the Rock Garden in Middlesbrough in the late 1970s. The Sex Pistols played under the assumed name Acne Rabble, and Motörhead came with an outsized sound rig. But gradually things began to go wrong: the clientele became infected by racist skinheads and closed in 1981, re-opening as The Arena (which has its own remarkable histories). A Rock Garden reunion night in 2010 turned into a regular weekly alternative music event that now happens across different independent venues in Middlesbrough and Teesside. The writer's dad still DJs for these new-school Rock Garden nights, providing a living link between the past and the present. The Facebook groups that emerge from the rubble of beloved venues are a starting point. Like this book, they show we cared. Online memorial groups don't have to become a sad, time-paused metaverse of what once existed. They offer encouragement.

A thousand small Haçiendas must be built.

Author biography

Emma Warren has been documenting culture for decades. She is the author of *Mojo* top ten book of the year *Make Some Space* (Sweet Machine Publishing, 2019), pamphlet 'Document Your Culture', and *Irish Times* book of the year *Steam Down* (Rough Trade Books, 2019). Her journalism appeared in *The Face*, *Guardian*, and *Fader* and she spent six years working on youth-run publication *Live Magazine*. She has a monthly show on Worldwide FM.

Introduction

Fraser Mann, Robert Edgar and Helen Pleasance

As the editorial team for a previous collection – *Music, Memory and Memoir* (2019) — we sought to establish some of the ways that text, sound and experience coalesced in the memoir form. Through scholarly work and newly commissioned narratives, we foregrounded the textual nature of personal memory and how various iterations of selfhood organise themselves around music and musical experiences. For us, memoir, and associated acts of creative non-fiction writing, offer a space that 'subverts, challenges and critiques the fantasy of many other historical forms' (Edgar, Mann and Pleasance 2019a: 4). We are not interested in texts that lay claim to authority or singular versions of culture or cultural material. We seek texts and writers that make a virtue of their artifice and relish their instability.

Venue Stories builds on this set of contentions and textual processes. Our engagements with the contributors in this collection have focused on the need to assert the sensory, the half-remembered and the subjective. We seek to celebrate, revise and remember the centrality of independent music space in UK culture and the narratives that it produces. What follows in this text is a series of stories told from a variety of perspectives. These are stories that communicate through the imperfect processes of autobiographical memory as well as more familiar lines of scholarly enquiry, such as historiographical research, critical analyses, participant interviews and cultural provocation. We seek to establish a methodology in which we 'consciously underpin […] critical positions with creative constructions of […] cultural selfhood' (Edgar, Mann and Pleasance 2019b: 181). This creative-critical approach allows for work that sustains academic rigour while exploring and developing subjectivity and the nuances and paradoxes of working with sensory and autobiographical memory. It also speaks to the variety of writing styles included in *Venue Stories*. The result is an anthology of creative non-fiction that remembers and reinvigorates our complex and plural relationship with small and independent music spaces. The editorial team have been speaking and collaborating with musicians, promoters, fans and academics who have a shared passion for such spaces and the musical cultures they contain. Featured here are contributions that blend memoir, essay, life writing, historiography and autoethnography. This is writing that crosses disciplinary lines and blurs distinctions between creativity, reportage and critical analysis. Writers visit celebrated spots, long-forgotten spaces and emergent venues. Whatever the lineage, these are independent, original and wonderfully weird spaces. The stories contain memories of seismic gigs and life-altering raves. They are also mosaic remembrances and recollections. They are funny, heart-breaking, rage-inducing and, sometimes, a combination of all these things. *Venue Stories* foregrounds narratives concerned with musical experiences in specific spaces and the ways in which these experiences shape who we are.

Our role as editors is to bring stories and remembrances together, add shape to them and develop a scholarly understanding of how we can offer an alternative mode of historiography through editorial processes that are akin to the role of the museum curator. Indeed, much has been written about recent shifts in the museum sector and how exhibitions are moving away from strictly material representations of the past towards what Baker et al. refer to as, a 'co-construction of knowledge' (Baker, Instvandity and Nowak 2016: 370). Central to this shift is the collection, arrangement and presentation of narrative that helps 'curators engage with popular music's historical discourses to facilitate an affective connection between museum content and patrons' personal experiences and memories of popular music culture' (ibid.: 371). In museums then, as in this anthology, the curatorial act lies in the selection of narratives and the way they speak to one another. In piecing together singular stories to make a broader meta-narrative, curation (in our case through collaborative editing) is a creative act. Paul Carr claims that 'voices of musicians, audiences, critics, venues, curators and other music industry stakeholders […] form a collective identity, in a series of competing narratives, that are often hidden from mainstream history' (Carr 2019: 13). This text, therefore, illuminates memories and personal histories that often remain overlooked. In *Venue Stories*, our overarching ambition speaks to this gap. Our collection of stories, memories and histories are united by their diversity. It is a diversity that speaks to genre, demography and the spatial. It is also a diversity that addresses the variance in musical experiences through gender and race. Our curation purposefully sets up juxtapositions and contrasts in the way that independent music space has been historically experienced and remembered by different communities at different times.

Nowhere is this narrative complexity more apparent than in the experiences of women in music spaces. Despite the progressive stances taken by leading figures in punk, indie, dance and other associated subcultures and genres, music spaces offer examples of what Catherine Strong and Sarah Raine refer to as 'exclusionary practices' (Strong and Raine 2018: 2). Inequalities in access, safety and economic parity are evident in the narratives of promoters, musicians and fans. Hill et al. show that these experiences, particularly those that involve sexual violence, 'significantly impact on musical participation for those that suffer' (Hill, Hesmondhalgh and Megson 2020: 370). In the last decade, alarming testimonies regarding violence, harassment and abuse in small music venues has led to activism in the guise of a 'range of anti-violence organisations focusing specifically on the live music space' (Hill and Megson 2020: 4). Groups have emerged such as Safe Gigs for Women and Girls Against. The latter have campaigned across the media and opened dialogue about 'standing up against sexual assault and misogyny in the live music scene' (Girls Against 2022) while also developing 'valuable educational resources, safe spaces and inclusivity' (ibid.). This work is ongoing and, as Carly Lewis writes of the small venue scene in Toronto, Canada, 'solutions require the whole village – musicians, patrons, booking agents, venue staff – to make a choice against complacency' (Lewis 2019). Several of the narratives in *Venue Stories* stand as evidence of this ongoing discourse.

Penelope Wickson's memories of the jungle scene in 1990s Birmingham are of a masculinist scene in which sexual advances toward female participants are regular. She also, more positively, talks of the significant influence that watching performances of female artists such as DJ Rap had on her own creative career. The three chapters that revisit the Bull and Gate in North London's Kentish Town offer very different perspectives on life at that famous old venue. Kevin Narrainen writes of a performative disinterest in one another offered by surly all-male groups that is occasionally punctuated by booze-inflamed violence. Polly Hancock, meanwhile, explains that the promoter behind the Bull and Gate's HYPE indie night during the 1990s would employ 'girl bands and double acts at the cash-only box office' in an effort to 'look [...] like an indie Hugh Hefner'. That same promoter, in Julianne Regan's chapter, offers a semi-serious marriage proposal. All three of these examples are narrated with the sort of dry and self-deprecating humour that time and intelligence make possible. However, they also make the case for listening to different perspectives as a means of developing dialogue and pressing for change. You must understand the culture and its history to offer meaningful progress. Away from the Bull and Gate, Vim and Lene of PunkGirl Diaries use their chapter to document the opportunities offered to them by punk. This seismic shift created 'participation and action rather than back-seat spectating'. Punk culture 'was freedom, liberation and nurturing of the underclasses, with girls included'. Vim and Lene 'made our own clothes, repurposed stuff from jumble sales and used our kid-comic skills to make zines, posters and artwork'. These, then, were the conditions that made 'a creative and self-determined life seem possible'. Our youngest writer, Tarryn Watkins explores her contemporary experiences as a musician and as a fan. She discusses unwanted sexual attention and male-dominated cultures that leave her isolated and marginalised. However, she also talks of inclusive spaces and the sparks required to make change consistent and sustainable.

The stories in this anthology share a compulsion to bear imperfect witness. Their authenticity lies in their self-conscious artifice. The stories foreground their status as text and documentation. Paradoxically, the textual status is a signifier of experiential authenticity. In Leigh Gilmore's analysis, 'first-person particularities and peculiarities offer [...] corrective readings and to emerge through writing as an agent of self-representation, a figure, textual to be sure, but seemingly substantial, can claim *I was there*' (Gilmore 2001: 9). Acts of writing then, though always rooted in second-hand textual memory, are also acts of testimony or documentation. If there are gaps, then these are the gaps that are owned by the writer. If there is a privileging of the sensory or a foregrounding of present-tense subjectivity, then this is evidence of narrative agency. We do not necessarily learn a material history of the space the writer has inhabited or experienced (although we often do), but we do learn how that space has determined, at least in part, who they are. This shift from the material to the experiential and from the positivist to the textual is central in the aims of *Venue Stories*.

This book, however, is more than just a set of personal accounts. It is also designed to be an archive of spaces and musical communities that are too often ignored or not valued in the same way as so-called 'high culture'. In many cases, the relative marginalisation of independent music spaces has had a dire economic impact, something that has been all too apparent both during and after the coronavirus pandemic. The global health crisis took place alongside a potentially positive period for independent music venues in the UK. In January 2020, the Government announced a 50 per cent cut in business rates for small and mid-sized grassroots music venues while Westminster council granted London's iconic 100 Club full relief under a new scheme put in place to protect independent musical culture. However, these financial boosts were dramatically offset by the nationwide lockdown in March 2020 and by social distancing laws that governed most of the population. According to the Music Venue Trust, at the end of April 2020, more than 500 small venues were 'at imminent risk of being permanently closed down' (Music Venue Trust 2021). Venues, performers and fans organised crowd funders, novel t-shirt designs, ticket pledges and digital performances to secure the future of music venues all over the UK. There was a shared determination to cement the role they play in regional arts and performance scenes. As autumn 2020 moved into winter and second and third lockdowns ground on into 2021, hundreds of venues were still uncertain of their future. At the time of writing, in August 2022, the UK is returning to some semblance of normality. Venues are now finding that property owners and landlords are keen to cash in on spiralling property prices. The Music Venue Trust have now moved their focus to an 'own our venues' campaign to combat such aggression.

What all this rapid change means is that never has there been a more necessary time to celebrate and shout about the value of independent music space. It is an ethical compulsion and an act of cultural significance. Emma Warren, who kindly wrote the foreword for *Venue Stories*, explains in *The Quietus* that 'we can help protect spaces through documentation, as an act of preservation that also supports the growth of future networks and systems. It's always been important but it matters more now, when we're at risk of losing the knowledge accumulated through decades of grassroots venues' (Warren 2019b). Warren's influential pamphlet, *Document Your Culture: A Manual*, offers a toolkit that is 'is designed to help [...] tell the story of a space or a community', 'provoke some forward motion and instigate a little self-enquiry' and 'help [...] locate a story, an angle, and to decide how you'll tell it' (Warren 2019a). It is an urgent call to arms for communities and groups that are unlikely to have a traditional storytelling platform. The pamphlet's introduction makes this imperative clear when explaining that, 'stories create a long view. We lack this because most people find themselves in these spaces during a very specific period of their life, usually in youth [...] Stories can act as blue plaques' (ibid.). This is activism through text and is an ethical approach to culture, heritage and narrative. The pamphlet and our collaborations with Emma Warren have provided significant cornerstones for much that we are attempting in *Venue Stories*.

Popular Music Studies

We have made conscious attempts to examine the position of *Venue Stories* and its methodologies and objectives in relation to current debates regarding the disciplinary parameters of popular music studies. With such a dynamic field, it is difficult to pin down concrete terms and conditions for the way in which these endeavours are defined. Of course, this is no bad thing. The fluid nature of music, memory and experience requires a set of enquiries that shift and twist in response. Creating models that have movement built into their core is vital to the ongoing success (and existence) of our work. This success is made possible by embracing interdisciplinarity. Wright et al. make this requirement clear when they write of 'popular music scholars' analyses and interpretations [that] are enriched by an interdisciplinary toolkit of theories, methods, and discourses' (Wright, Coddington and Mall 2021: 4). This scholarly pluralism and multiplicity make possible 'a dedicated effort to move our discourse out of specialist circles, look for wider resonances and solidarities across music scholarship as a whole, and envision future scholarship that is relevant and responsive to a wide array of audiences' (ibid.: 6). Lee Marshall adds that popular music studies is 'inherently interdisciplinary with significant input from sociology, cultural studies, musicology, ethnomusicology, literary studies and others' (Marshall 2011: 155). The benefit of this methodology lies in recalibrating how 'listeners create musical meaning through their position within a discursive framework that gives them the tools to make sense of the sounds they hear' (ibid.: 159). Both examples here mention tools. There is a distinctly utilitarian tone which suggests that making sense of our experiences of music and how they shape both selfhood and broader social issues is something of a puzzle or problem. Only pragmatic and collaborative solutions will help the work we do make any palpable and tangible progress.

The editorial team for *Venue Stories* have backgrounds and specialisms in creative writing, film studies and literary studies. These areas are in themselves interdisciplinary in contextual, analytical and theoretical terms. The question we are faced with at the outset of a project such as this one involves the transferability of our own toolkit in discussing musical experiences. We are also faced with 'the slippery interface between the abstractions of sound and the narrative processes made possible in language' (Edgar, Mann and Pleasance 2019b: 198). Sonic experiences lie beyond language and, short of onomatopoeia (a clunky tool if overused), there are very few strategies for capturing sound through creative or critical writing. However, that does not mean that we cannot use other modes. The material world that surrounds sound in the guise of t-shirts, posters, record sleeves and ticket stubs provides an 'extra-musical turn' (ibid.: 199) which can anchor musical narratives. Also connecting several of our chapters is that music spaces are often the site of epiphany. Foundational and transformational experiences take place in subcultural spaces and our writers negotiate and navigate the significance of these experiences through the twin filters of memory and text. Because of this approach, epiphanies work in two ways. Firstly, there is the account of the epiphany as a lived experience but secondly, and perhaps in a more complex fashion, there is a discussion about the process of epiphany itself. In this way, the various guises of narrative voice operate as self-aware. The writer tells a story but also assesses and analyses their own storytelling. The epiphany is then both an important moment in time and a piece of textual artifice. Carolyn Ellis et al.

examine this curious double bind by arguing that such 'epiphanies reveal ways a person could negotiate intense situations and effects that linger like recollections, memories, images and feelings long after a crucial incident is supposedly finished' (Ellis, Adams and Bochner 2011: 275). This narrative plurality feeds into the stories we tell about music and musical experiences. The music is both central and peripheral. Our subjectivities are led by our stories and memories, and we understand music through this process. In *Venue Stories*, the significance of epiphany is evident in Fraser Mann's chapter in which he discusses the sensory overload involved in raving in the Elektrowerkz venue in North London. The chapter's epiphany lies in finding, after a long search, the experiential version of dance music which has thus far only been a second-hand phenomenon. Ed Garland, meanwhile, discusses the way that the material make-up of the Charlotte in Leicester operates as a wondrous amplifier and intensifier of Doc Scott's jungle. Three decades earlier, Alan Smith's experiences of late 1960s counterculture in the Mothers Club in the Birmingham ward of Erdington are a gateway to a new way of thinking, living and listening. Anna Elias moves from indie performer to music therapist in her chapter and finds that the two roles share remarkable synchronicities. Understanding these examples is made possible through narrative and imperfect storytelling.

Rachel Carroll and Adam Hansen claim that what 'surrounds and makes possible music [...] and conditions how we experience what such music sounds like, is writing' (Carroll and Hansen 2014: 6). They go further in stating that 'the contexts of music's consumption matter, and these contexts include consumption in or through writing, language and words' (ibid.). These comments suggest that language and narrative, linear or otherwise, provide a way to navigate some of the subconscious, corporeal and deeply held memories associated with sound. Of course, narrative does not necessarily provide a teleological answer to the question of how we understand ourselves through music. Such a thing is not even desirable in our field of work and would undermine the fluidity and dynamism that we value. However, it is a start. It is a way to bring divergent modes of thinking, feeling and experiencing together. Cláudia Guerra and Ana Oliveira insist that 'connections between musical and literary culture, and also between thought and creation [...] open a rich dialogue between two fields of culture and language' (Guerra and Oliveira 2019: 129). That this interplay is dialogical and open ended is key to resisting unnecessary closure or didacticism. Indeed, Jack Hamilton speaks of the central role of public engagement in popular music studies and its focus on 'bridging the divide between the university and the public in order to educate people who are outside our classrooms and scholarly networks' (Hamilton 2021: 30). Again, engagement such as this is not a case of those in scholarly roles teaching those outside of the academy, it is much more of an open exchange. As Hamilton states, if we 'ignore work done outside of the academy either unconsciously or consciously [...] we risk creating adversarial relationships with interlocutors with whom popular music scholars should be forging alliances and kinships, not least of all because our field would not exist without them' (ibid.: 32). It is here that *Venue Stories* sits. We see this collection as an act of public participation rather than one of simple engagement.

The genesis and development of this collection took place during the most severe months of the initial Covid lockdown in the UK. These restrictions meant that much of our usual academic networking was not possible. There were no chats over coffee at conferences, no corridor summits on campus, and all of us had our hands full with the rapid switch to an entirely new way of teaching. Rather than physical separation being an obstacle, however, it created an opportunity to reach beyond the usual and familiar voices through social media (mostly Twitter) and via video chats on Zoom. The results of this interaction are evident in the biographies of many of our contributors. Alongside industry veterans like Tom Hingley, Julianne Regan, Jon Stewart and David Lewis Gedge, we have work from music therapist Anna Elias, sixth form teacher and drum and bass DJ Penelope Wickson, media production specialist Kevin Narrainen, photographer and teacher Abigail Gaines, art historian Anna Maria Barry and the team behind the innovative and influential PunkGirl Diaries blog, Ruth Miller and Polly Hancock. That is not to say that there are no academic voices. We have chapters from Matt Colbeck, Peter Atkinson, Alan Smith and Ed Garland who are all specialists in humanities subjects. However, in *Venue Stories* they are very much writing in a hybrid voice. They position themselves as fans who take an academic and enquiring approach to their own experiences and subjectivities. The same can be said of the most experienced writers in our collection such as Dawn Amber Harvey and Penny Kiley. Despite their years of experience working to specific briefs and deadlines, here they too take a more esoteric and fluid stance in their stories. There are also voices from much younger writers. Doctoral students Amy McCarthy and Tom Jackson are just beginning a career as literature specialists and Beth Hughes and Tarryn Watkins are learning their trade as creative practitioners. This range of backgrounds means that the text is presenting many stories that speak to music spaces as a plural and ever-changing cultural experience.

Text and Memory

Such textual acts are shaped in imperfect ways. Much of this process comes about through memories of music. Music sociologist Tia DeNora writes that, 'we do things to music [...] work, eat, fall asleep, dance, romance, daydream, exercise, celebrate, protest, worship, mediate and procreate' (2000: 7). It is embedded in what she calls the 'everyday' to the extent that 'music articulates social life and social life articulates music' (ibid.: 5). Consciously and unconsciously, music has an influence on the ways that we present and position ourselves in social relations. Whether that is as part of a musical scene or tribe, through shared love for a particular artist or genre or simply through the social rituals that are sound tracked by music, we cannot escape its power. DeNora confirms that this relationship extends to 'how people compose their bodies, how they conduct themselves, how they experience the passage of time, how they feel in terms of energy and emotion' and that this is the case when talking and thinking 'about ourselves, about others, and about situations' (ibid.: 17). Music also helps to shape our interior world and our private understandings of selfhood. In Lauren Istvandity's ground-breaking examination of music and autobiographical memory, *The Lifetime Soundtrack*, she argues that the everyday experience of music referred to by DeNora means that music 'enters our consciousness without invitation and often without a means to control it' (2019: 4). As such, it is formational in shaping experience and, crucially for this collection, how we remember and narrate those experiences. Istvandity goes on to make clear connections between memory and identity construction. For her, we understand who we are by revisiting and narrativising incisive moments and episodes in both our childhood and our adult life. That so many of these moments are accompanied by music means that 'our engagement with music is linked to our sense of self, and we do our best to remember what it is that make us who we are by reflecting on moments that are important to us' (ibid.: 6). Crucially, the movement from memory to narrative is self-aware. The stories we tell about ourselves through our music (and about our music through our selves) are usually up front in their artifice. The mechanics of narration become a way in which we can engage in 'ongoing reconstruction of past encounters rather than a faithful replication of an individual's experience' (ibid.: 18). Music is a 'dynamic medium' (ibid.: 16), which means that our stories, our narrative shapes and our developing autobiographies are in flux and are plural.

The nature of memory formation raises questions about the relationship between music itself and the experience of music in a space. 'Autobiographical information associated with musical melodies is evoked when we hear relevant music or when we are engaged in conversation about music or episodes and events in our life in which music has been important' (Jänke 2008). Therefore, and at a biological level, there is an intrinsic link between music and environment via the triggering of episodic memory, in this case via music. This process suggests that the experience of hearing music itself has a less specific location in terms of memory; it is possible to remember melody, lyrics, etc. as a function of semantic memory but its value is in its evocation of experience within a given location. 'Episodic memory for musical information will be referred to here as the capacity to recognize a musical excerpt (whether familiar or not) for which the spatiotemporal context surrounding its former encounter (i.e., when, where, and how) can be recalled' (Platel et al. 2001: 731). This is different from the recollection of music in and of itself and in abstraction from experience.

The recollections that exist within this collection, then, implicitly foreground experiential memory and this manifests itself as spatio-temporal complexes in terms of memory and associated narrative construction and reconstruction. In essence, music in and of itself has the capacity to function in abstract. Music as connected to an experience where there is a relationship to time and space is crucial. Venues serve to provide a memory function in which experience is contained, a referent is fixed and where music becomes a trigger to recollect a memory of and/or in that space.

Whilst the above discussion concerns memory function in respect of the individual and their recollections of their past, the venues that are being discussed stand outside individual memory as well as intersecting with it. We might define this duality as a form of cultural and individual intertextuality, where our authors' memories start to intersect with ours by virtue of the totemic function of particular venues. It doesn't even matter that a venue no longer exists; the fact that it has been experienced by a number of people who recollect it from an individual perspective provides a level of social and cultural provenance. Collective memory functions in relation to the individual memories that contribute to the narrative recounting of the whole. This complex system leads to a multiplicity of memories in a variety of time sequences which themselves may, or may not, overlap.

When putting together this collection, such multiplicity was central to our planning. We know from our own experiences that no two tellings of the same musical event are the same, even when coming from a single source. This narrative openness is at the heart of our work. Our approach is always to embrace plural and creative configurations of uncertainty and ambiguity. Dates of gigs, prices of pints and the precise time signatures being employed by a band reworking their material cannot always be remembered accurately.

Even when they can, these sorts of details rarely make for good storytelling or function in the formation of identity and self-knowledge. Istvandity, in her introduction to *Remembering Popular Music's Past*, argues for recognition and the documenting of remembered narrative and memory as it is a 'precarious resource' and 'without its collection and preservation, knowledge otherwise untraceable may be lost permanently' (Istvandity et al. 2019: 3). The importance of narrative and memory is central in our collection. The music spaces under discussion are precarious in terms of economics and cultural weight. In too many cases, their disappearance from our towns and cities also means that they are precarious in terms of heritage, and broader, public and cultural memories. So, in collecting and curating memories and narratives, we see this work as an alternative to the certainties of positivist historiography. We are building a resource that is strengthened by its subjectivity and variance. Indeed, several of our chapters involve the same venues (The Bull and Gate in Kentish Town features three times) remembered and narrated from very different perspectives. This variance, we argue, underlines the value of this work. Multiplicity, plurality and divergence mark our stories and our memories of music space. Georgina Born suggests that understanding shared experiences of music spaces requires the stories of 'many human subjects' (2013: 19). Their 'gathering [...] constitutes a novel set of social relations' and their 'experiences of music and sound are variant [and] mediated by subjectivities, corporealities, locations and movements' (ibid.). Such variables mean that each narrative offers unique perspectives that foreground the limitations of memory as explored in self-conscious textual processes.

Sensory Spaces

The stories contained within this collection share two key components: the spatial and the sensory. These are components that intertwine, overlap, and continually shift. Musical experiences in music spaces rely on these elements in their recounting. We have asked our writers to foreground them in their work, so it is appropriate to now spend some time discussing them. Clearly, a collection of stories about music venues speaks to the spatial but it is important not to underestimate the complexity of this issue in both practical and conceptual terms.

This complexity is first manifest in the variety of spaces that are being documented, recollected and discussed in this collection. If there is a conceptual spatial discussion to be had, it is driven by a real space of (often) bricks and mortar and with physical dimensions which then shape experience. The variety of venues available for live musical performance or musical experience presents some challenge with there being (in theory) very little formal delineation in narrative terms between, say, a stadium and the back room of a pub. However, the various chapters in this book do share commonalities in terms of the recognition of the importance of certain forms of space. There is an equivalent narrative discourse (Genette 1983) in the recounting of experiences in the form of small and independent venues being discussed here. In Genette's narratology there is a fundamental relationship between what is being said and how it is being said. In the chapters included in this collection there is a relationship between what is being said and where it is located. In terms of the spatio-temporal complexes, as a core element of narrative communication, the form of venue has a function.

Founded in 2014 the Music Venue Trust (MVT) is a charity that was established to 'protect, secure and improve Grassroots Music Venues' (Music Venue Trust 2022). Their mission statement makes clear 'the essential role these venues fulfil, not only for artist development but also for the cultural and music industries, the economy and local communities' (ibid.). Their values, activism and strong media presence in part inspired the production of this book, so it is useful at this stage to examine the way that they categorise small venues.

> We define the cultural and social importance of a Grassroots Music Venue (GMV) by testing its reputation, role and activity against six criteria:
>
> 1. Elephant Test. Musicians and audiences in the town/borough/city think that is the Grassroots Music Venue.
> 2. Focus on cultural activity as its main purpose and its outcomes. [...]
> 3. It is a music business, run by music experts. [...]
> 4. It takes risks with its cultural programme, and that risk taking is the ignition system of the engine that is the UK music industry. [...]
> 5. A Beacon of Music and key generator of night-time economic activity. [...]
> 6. Plays nicely with others. [...]
>
> A Grassroots Music Venue displays some or all of these characteristics, dependent upon factors such as location, economic climate, or seasonal variations. (Music Venue Trust 2021)

The MVT go on to recognise that there are different strata to grassroots music venues where attitude and approach are much more important than audience capacity. This is a more useful working definition than the rather amorphous notion of 'independent' with concomitant issues of what constitutes independence; from whom and what? What is clear though is that there is often independence from large corporate backers and, with this, financial security. The irony being that often what makes these venues beloved and memorialised is their quirkiness and character and it is these characteristics that also make them financially vulnerable. This paradox is reflected to an extent in the submissions to this collection where the emphasis is on the venue as independent and individual as it relates to the person recounting the experience of the space. This is not to say that the small venue is unique in aesthetic terms. As many of the chapters in this collection demonstrate, there is a loose aesthetic unity which transcends time and geographical location. This notion is most evident in the range of chapters which discuss 'toilet venues' but is evident in the engagement with other spaces. Sam Whiting explores this shared aesthetic in respect of Bourdieu's concept of cultural capital:

> [S]mall venues walk the line between various systems of power, not by partitioning them, but by disguising their engagement with one – the project of remaining a financially sustainable business – within their mastery of another – as a decidedly niche space of cultural production, blurring the distinction between intrinsic and instrumental forms of value and bringing any binary understanding of these value-forms into question. (Whiting 2021: 560)

The transcendence of time is important and again is reflected in the commentary in these chapters. It would be all too easy to view the contributions to this book as a form of memorialisation with venues being signifiers of heritage as much as the reconstructed Cavern Club or an episode of *Downton Abbey*. Many of the chapters within this book are looking to a continuum where present experience is equated to the past. Time is 'out of joint' but rather than this experience resulting in a haunting of the spectre of halcyon days of small venues there is a celebration of their currency (Fisher 2015). The spectre that haunts this book is of the potential for venues to close; this risk emphasises the importance of the value of these spaces, whether that is the longevity of Eric's, the Adelphi or the Forum or the emergence of a new venue such as the Crescent in York. The form of venue discussed is supported by the BBC Radio 6 Music annual Independent Venue Week (IVW); the banner proclaims it is about 'Celebrating the spirit of independence and the culture of live music'.

> Independent Venue Week is a 7-day celebration of music venues around the country and a nod to the people that own, run and work

> in them, week in, week out. These venues give artists their first experience of playing live in front of an audience. They give fans somewhere to get up close to artists that one day, may well be playing stadiums and festival main stages. They also provide those wanting a career in music, off the stage, the chance to learn their craft up close in a small venue.

This statement is central to the conception of spaces considered in this collection. Proximity is central to artists and to fans and often to the relationship between the two. This intimacy implies a sense of space rather than a specific set of dimensions; rather, that everything is within reaching distance. Proximity is also crucial in relation to communities. This importance is emphasised in the IVW's reference to the local: 'Independent Venue Week is unique in that it is a nationwide initiative with a completely local feel'. This statement captures the national network that is forged through the interconnections between venues. These relationships are signified in a variety of complex and intersecting ways. Many of the chapters reflect on how a particular band or scene will tour spaces of a similar sort with the space lending its aesthetic to the band and vice versa. The names of these venues become known from gig listings and slip into myth. Venues can also be connected through a loose sense of look and occasionally even scent.

> By championing these venues, we are able to highlight why they are so much more than just places for live music – they are cultural hubs for learning, creativity, arts and culture more widely connecting people in their local community of all ages, backgrounds, abilities, genders, skills and walks of life. These venues, all local businesses, are the backbone of the live music scene and Independent Venue Week recognises all that they have done to create some of the most memorable nights of the past so they can continue to do the same in the future. (Music Venue Trust 2021)

This recognition leads to a question central to the conception of this collection and which is explored through the common elements they share. In the variety and subtle differences in the spaces explored in the following pages, what fundamental things do they have in common?

In the humanities, the spatial turn has been hugely influential, and it is the work of Henri Lefebvre that offers a good starting position. In his now canonical text, *The Production of Space*, he quickly reveals the ubiquity of discourse around space and the shifts towards the spatial, away from the temporal or linear. Experiences of space are discussed in terms of 'physical, mental [and] social' (1991: 11) systems and the spaces themselves are 'occupied by sensory phenomenon' (ibid.: 12). For *Venue Stories*, the flexibility offered by such an approach works well in terms of understanding narrative and its relationships with lived and remembered experience. Crucially, Lefebvre rejects singularity and embraces multiplicity; 'space considered in isolation', he argues, 'is an empty abstraction' (ibid.: 12). This concept is key for working with the range of writers that are featured in our collection. Limiting ourselves to singular iterations of spatial discourse would leave yawning gaps in understanding the role of venues in personal, political and social lives.

Lefebvre organises his analyses of space into a conceptual triad. It is important, however, to make it clear that the three categories are porous. They bleed into each other and overlap. Their interdependence is what makes each of them operate. The first of these categories he terms 'spatial practice'. It is a site of production and reproduction and is 'lived directly before it is conceptualised' (ibid.: 34). From such immediacy, 'the spatial practice of a society is revealed' (ibid.: 38). Key to understanding spatial practice is the centrality of the body and of sensory perception. Any gig goer or raver will tell you that the primary memory of their night out is one of sensory stimulation. The heat, the volume, the smell of your fellow punters, and the metallic tang of your overpriced lager all form and shape spatial memories and how they are narrated. Indeed, Lefebvre makes clear that 'spatial practice presupposes the use of the body: the use of the hands, members and sense organs' (ibid.: 40). It is 'the realm of the perceived' (ibid.: 40) which means that our spatial experiences happen before we employ language to impose order on them. As a result, narratives of such experiences are disordered and in flux. In this collection, we foreground this complexity and celebrate such uncertainty. The process of telling a story is laid bare.

The second and third components of the conceptual triad consist of 'representations of space' and 'representational spaces'. These near homonyms are made distinct by a juxtaposing sense of singular order and plural complexity. Representations of space exist in conceptual design and careful mapping. They sit in architectural plans or city blueprints and communicate a sense of dominance and control. Representational spaces, however, are 'directly lived through [...] associated images and symbols' (ibid.: 39). These are artistic spaces that comment on their own shape and invite multiple readings of their functionality. Lefebvre associates them with resistance and subculture. They are spaces in which 'the imagination seeks change' and where 'artists and [...] writers and philosophers [...] describe and aspire to do more than describe' (ibid.: 39). The dominance imposed through representations of space is resisted, both in material terms and through potential and radical change, by those who embrace 'less coherent symbols' (ibid.: 39). This, of course, is where the small and independent music venues that make up the content of this collection fit best. While we are not idealistic enough to see music venues as some kind of utopian vision, free from the trappings and pitfalls of late capitalism, they are at least somewhere where the art usually comes first. The mechanics and economic necessities work around the music. They have their own shifting and changing dynamics. The crowds are simultaneously well versed in the unwritten spatial codes and capable of making each night a unique event, free from design and pre-ordained structure. The stories that come out of such spaces are equally dynamic. They celebrate movement and contradictory retellings. They take various positions within the venues and offer perceptions and memories that are specific to their own place within these complex spaces.

Bennett et al. speak of 'rich experiential settings in which music is consumed' and that the music itself 'plays an important role in the narrativization of space' (2017: 2). Multiplicity and multi-dimensional complexity are in evidence here, too. The writers that we are working with make music, consume music and remember music. Their narratives are situated at the temporal moment of production and at a variety of material and symbolic distances. They bring experiences to music that shape their response to it and, in a curious double bind, the music shapes the way such experiences are remembered. This makes for fascinating and self-aware storytelling. Sound, space and memory combine in what Nedra Reynolds describes as 'acts of writing that are enacted not in stable, always-the-same places but within a shifting sense of space, in the betweens, in thirdspace' (2007: 4). For this editorial team, this is self-conscious in our work. Our initial conversations with writers and practitioners made clear that process, multiplicity and incompleteness were the qualities that we valued above all else. What this means is that we must be open to writing that shifts and shakes in multiple forms, modes and genres that stretch the definitions associated with life writing and creative non-fiction. The self is also situated within broader narratives about culture and cultural spaces. Our disparate collection of writers is united here by their love of musical space and experiences of them. Gig rooms, toilet venues, back rooms, raves, clubs and all the other myriad of spaces used to enjoy loud music are as central to British culture and subculture as they are to the construction of selfhood. Our collection attempts to acknowledge this by moving between the personal and the panoramic in ways that are surprising, contentious and unexpected. Material culture, the imagination and the memory have equal weight in these contributions and how they are written. As a result, we hope to offer histories of music space that are precarious, plural and dynamic. This collection aims to provide a home for such history writing.

Stories as Archive

Venue Stories itself can be thought of as a kind of venue. In putting this anthology together, we are hosting a single space where disparate personal accounts of attending music venues in the UK, over the last forty or so years, can be housed and preserved together. We are creating an archive. All acts of archive creation are political, as the archivists make decisions about what is worth adding to a society or culture's archival record and, just as importantly, what is unworthy of this record and will disappear without a trace into a lost past. Archiving is an act of privileging particular events, places, people and stories over others. As Randall C. Jimerson has asserted about archives, 'This power places them near the centre of debates over history, memory and meaning' (2003: 91). This debate is also at the centre of *Venue Stories*. By archiving certain memories, and the experiences with which they engage, we are asserting their historical significance.

There are two aspects of this process that are worth considering: the content of these stories and the form in which their writers have recorded them. Both these aspects illuminate further our contribution to what Jaume Aurell and Rocio G. Davis, in their discussion of the convergence of history and autobiography, have called 'the diversity of contemporary approaches to the past' (2019: 504). The content of these stories is of historical significance. We are positioning *Venue Stories* as a text that gives 'access to both individual and collective pasts' (Aurell and Davis 2019: 504). By archiving these stories, we are asserting the historical significance of all the activities in and around music venues that they narrate – however ephemeral they might seem. The significance of small music venues has already been outlined in our discussion of the Music Venues Trust, and its characterisation of 'the cultural and social importance of a Grassroots Music Venue' (Music Venue Trust 2021). The stories in this collection bear witness to the role that music venues have played in the social life of the UK over the historical period covered. It is striking how historical identities emerge both within individual chapters and between them. By housing disparate stories in the same archive, resonances and echoes emerge.

Dawn Amber Harvey's chapter takes readers back to The Warehouse in Liverpool in the 1980s. It evokes how this venue provided a space for young people to escape from the daily hardships of being unemployed or working on the government's Youth Training Scheme for very low wages. It provides an insight into the collective past of Thatcher's Britain. Beth Hughes's chapter lands readers just a decade later in the York and London of the 1990s. Her journey through indie and dance venues of the decade reveals a turnaround in the emotional world of venue goers. They are riding a wave of optimism and excitement, which culminates around the election of the Blair government in 1997. The details in both Harvey's and Hughes's accounts give a sense of the lived experiences and sensibilities of what are now understood as two distinct political eras. Elsewhere, Chris Inglis and Ruth Miller, through the insider knowledge of being there, show how venue owners, managers and event organisers navigated by-laws and bureaucracy to bring about strange and unexpected musical assemblages in Birmingham and Leicester respectively. Both accounts reveal how human agents negotiate systems of power to make things happen.

The 'emotional turn' has been noted by Katie Barclay (2021: 457) across a range of social science and humanities disciplines. She suggests that: 'The relationship between culture and the body is at the heart of many of the methodological discussions within the field' (ibid.: 458). This is clearly a discussion that is at the heart of *Venue Stories*. Music venues are the sites of both heightened cultural and heightened bodily experiences. Barclay's reference to Mark Seymour's notion of the 'emotional arena' (Seymour 2020: 460) clarifies why an engagement with human activity in and around music venues can elicit new historical insight. Seymour's approach:

> Seeks to take account of how different social arenas within a given culture provide spaces for different forms of emotional expression, behaviours and associated power dynamics; this contributes to a broader and growing conversation about how space and place are part of emotional experiences. (ibid.)

Textual exploration of music venues, as specific sites of frequently subcultural activity, can be particularly articulate in relation to developing an understanding of social power dynamics. In many of the stories here, music venues are the arenas where new cultural formations come into being.

Writing Memory

This potential brings us on to an explanation of why we have foregrounded memory writing in *Venue Stories* as the most appropriate form through which to turn material and emotional experiences of venues into narrative. As outlined earlier, we have sought to assert the importance of the sensory, the half-remembered and the subjective in the forms that these stories are told. We are intellectually convinced that memory writing in its many forms makes a unique and important contribution to historical knowledge through an understanding of the emotional dimensions of historical experience. Barclay identifies one of the key difficulties in the study of the history of emotions as finding an 'access point to emotion' (2021: 459). She very rightly points out that, 'Most historical sources are texts, objects or the material world, rather than living and emoting bodies' (ibid.).

Our turn to memory writing, in various forms, serves to provide texts in which emotional experience is privileged. Such texts are predicated on writers giving textual expression to their experience of being a living, emoting body. The emotional turn has led to an interest in textual forms, such as memory writing, that engage with lived experience.

Kalle Pihlainen, in his discussion of autobiography and history, argues that an examination of these two forms of 'past writing' illuminate 'the complex role of experience [...] and the ways in which it may manifest in texts or even be produced in readers' (2019: 618). Conventional historical writing can be understood, philosophically, as hermeneutic – concerned with interpretation; while autobiographical forms, including memoir, can be understood, philosophically, as phenomenological – concerned with experience. The two genres use different modes to engage their readers. We are happy to contribute to a paradigm shift in historical writing, from the hermeneutic to the phenomenological, to understand the role – and importance – of experience in human knowledge. We are aware that texts that foreground lived experience are not simplistically mimetic of real lived experience. But their textual strategies allow readers an access point to the emotions and experience being narrated.

The phenomenological mode of memory writing in *Venue Stories* allows readers to experience, textually, the sweat, sticky floors, loud, joyful noises and shadowy recesses of the venues herein. Readers will rub up alongside frequenters of the many different venues. In doing so they will begin to understand why all these disparate, disjointed and plural experiences matter and are worth recording as history.

References

Aurell, Jaume, and Rocio G. Davis. 2019. 'History and autobiography: The logics of a convergence'. *Life Writing* 16, no. 4: 503–511. https://doi.org/10.1080/14484528.2019.1648198

Baker, Sarah, Lauren Istvandity and Raphaël Nowak. 2016. 'Curating popular music heritage: Storytelling and narrative engagement in popular music museums and exhibitions'. *Museum Management and Curatorship* 31, no. 4: 369–385.

Barclay, Katie. 2021. 'State of the field: The history of emotions'. *History* 106, no. 371: 456–466. https://doi.org/10.1111/1468-229X.13171

Bennett, Andy, et al. 2017. *Music, Space and Place: Popular Music and Cultural Identity*. London: Routledge.

Born, Georgina, ed. 2013. *Music, Sound and Space: Transformations of Public and Private Experience*. Cambridge: Cambridge University Press.

Carr, Paul. 2019. 'Introduction to the special issue: Lost musical histories—Curating and documenting local popular music-making in the UK'. *Popular Music History* 12, no. 1: 5–14.

Carroll, Rachel, and Adam Hansen, eds. 2014. *Litpop: Writing and Popular Music*. Surrey: Ashgate.

DeNora, Tia. 2000. *Music in Everyday Life*. Cambridge: Cambridge University Press.

Edgar, Robert, Fraser Mann and Helen Pleasance, eds. 2019a. *Music, Memory and Memoir*. New York: Bloomsbury.

Edgar, Robert, Fraser Mann and Helen Pleasance. 2019b. 'Music, memory and memoir: Critical and creative engagement with an emerging genre'. *Journal of Writing in Creative Practice* 12, no. 1–2 (2019): 181–199.

Ellis, Carolyn, Tony E. Adams and Arthur P. Bochner. 2011. 'Autoethnography: An overview'. *Historical Social Research/Historische sozialforschung* 36, no. 4: 273–290.

Fisher, Mark. 2015. *Ghosts of My Life: Writings on Depression, Hauntology and Lost Futures*. London: Zero Books.

Genette, Gérard. 1983. *Narrative Discourse: An Essay in Method*. Vol. 3. Ithaca, NY: Cornell University Press.

Gilmore, Leigh. 2001. 'Introduction: The limits of autobiography'. In *The Limits of Autobiography: Trauma and Testimony*, 1–15. Ithaca, NY: Cornell University Press.

Girls Against. 2022. Girls Against. 9 August. https://www.girlsagainst.co.uk/about

Guerra, Paula, and Ana Oliveira. 2019. 'Heart of glass: Gender and domination in the early days of punk in Portugal'. In *Contemporary Popular Music Studies: Proceedings of the International Association for the Study of Popular Music 2017*, ed. Marija Dumnić Vilotijević and Ivana Medić, 127–136. Wiesbaden: Springer.

Hamilton, Jack. 2021. 'Across the great divide: Popular music studies and the public'. *Twentieth-Century Music* 18, no. 1: 29–44.

Hill, Rosemary Lucy, David Hesmondhalgh and Molly Megson. 2020. 'Sexual violence at live music events: Experiences, responses and prevention'. *International Journal of Cultural Studies* 23, no. 3: 368–384. https://doi.org/10.1177/13678779198917

Hill, Rosemary Lucy, and Molly Megson. 2020. 'Sexual violence and gender equality in grassroots music venues: How to facilitate change'. *IASPM Journal* 10, no. 1: 3–21.

Independent Venue Week. 2021. Independent Venue Week, 20 December. https://www.independentvenueweek.com/about/

Istvandity, Lauren. 2019. *The Lifetime Soundtrack: Music and Autobiographical Memory*. Queensland: University of the Sunshine Coast.

Istvandity, Lauren, Sarah Baker and Zelmarie Cantillon, eds. 2019. *Remembering Popular Music's Past: Memory-Heritage-History*. London: Anthem Press.

Jänke, L. 2008. 'Music, memory and emotion'. *Journal of Biology* 7, no. 6: Art. 21. https://jbiol.biomedcentral.com/articles/10.1186/jbiol82

Jimerson, Randall, C. 2003. 'Archives and memory'. *OCLC Systems and Services: International Digital Library Perspectives* 19, no. 3: 89–95. https://www.emerald.com/insight/content/doi/10.1108/10650750310490289/full/html

Lefebvre, Henri. 1991. *The Production of Space*. Trans. Donald Nicholson-Smith. Oxford: Blackwell.

Lewis, Carly. 2019. 'Music venues tune in to #MeToo'. *Herizons*, January 2019: 6ff.

Marshall, Lee. 2011. 'The sociology of popular music, interdisciplinarity and aesthetic autonomy 1'. *British Journal of Sociology* 62, no. 1: 154–174.

Music Venue Trust. 2021. 'Grassroots music venue (GMVs): Definition'. 20 December. https://musicvenuetrust.com/resources/grassroots-music-venue-gmvs-definition/

Music Venue Trust. 2022. 'Music Venue Trust – Our mission'. 11 August. https://www.musicvenuetrust.com/team

Pihlainen, Kalle. 2019. 'Experience, materiality and the rules of past writing: Interrogating reference'. *Life Writing* 16, no. 4: 617–635. https://doi.org/10.1080/14484528.2019.1633251

Platel, Hervé, Jean-Claude Baron, Béatrice Desgranges, Frédéric Bernard and Francis Eustache. 2001. 'Semantic and episodic memory of music: A positron emission tomography study'. *Neuroimage* 6, no. 13: 727ff.

Reynolds, Nedra. 2007. *Geographies of Writing: Inhabiting Places and Encountering Difference*. Carbondale, IL: SIU Press.

Seymour, Mark. 2020. *Emotional Arenas: Life, Love, and Death in 1870s Italy*. Oxford: Oxford University Press.

Strong, Catherine, and Sarah Raine. 2018. 'Gender politics in the music industry'. *IASPM Journal* 8, no. 1: 2–8.

Warren, Emma. 2019a. *Document Your Culture: A Manual*. London: Sweet Machine Publishing.

Warren, Emma. 2019b. 'Why documenting your culture is an act of resistance'. *The Quietus*, 3 September.

Whiting, Sam. 2021. 'The value of small live music venues: Alternative forms of capital and niche spaces of cultural production'. *Cultural Sociology* 15, no. 4: 558–578.

Wright, Brian F., Amy Coddington and Andrew Mall. 2021. 'Looking towards the future: Popular music studies and music scholarship'. *Twentieth-Century Music* 18, no. 1: 3–11.

Author biographies

Fraser Mann is Senior Lecturer in Literature at York St. John University, UK. He is a specialist in American writing with particular interests in conflict, testimony, and trauma. He has published research on a range of literary figures such as Ernest Hemingway, James Jones and Norman Mailer. He also works on music writing in the form of creative non-fiction and co-edited the Bloomsbury edited collection *Music, Memory and Memoir* (2019). His creative writing can be found on the *Twistin' My Memory, Man* blogspace. His teaching interests include American Studies, autobiography and twentieth- and twenty-first-century war writing.

Robert Edgar is Professor of Writing and Popular Culture in the York Centre for Writing based in the School of Humanities at York St John University, UK. His publications include *Screenwriting* (Bloomsbury, 2009), *Directing Fiction* (Bloomsbury, 2009), *The Language of Film* (Bloomsbury, 2010 and 2015), *The Music Documentary* (Routledge, 2013), *The Arena Concert* (Bloomsbury, 2015), *Music, Memory and Memoir* (Bloomsbury, 2019), *Adaptation for Scriptwriters* (Bloomsbury, 2019), and *Thomas Hardy and the Folk Horror Tradition* (2023). He is co-editing the *Routledge Companion to Folk Horror* (2023) and *Horrifying Children: Hauntology and the Legacy of Children's Fiction* (Bloomsbury, 2024).

Helen Pleasance is a Senior Lecturer in Creative Writing at York St John University, UK. She has written on the Moors murders, the spectral form of memoir and music memoirs. She is currently working on a hybrid family memoir about the women in her family and needlework.

1 Peripheral Dancing: The Jazz Rooms, Brighton, 1984

Helen Pleasance

Venue: the place where something happens

Trust me. I remember, just about, how to get us back there. It's somewhere I still frequently return to in memory, after all. It is a Saturday evening in Brighton. 1984. Let's say it is early autumn, just past dusk. The sea is churning pebbles on the beach. There is a chill in the air and my coat is pulled over a shimmering cocktail dress I found in a charity shop in Hove last weekend. I'm feeling a little bit Diana Ross, even if to the naked eye I am a plump blonde. You have dressed down, but it doesn't matter, we both have our dancing shoes on.

We turn off the front, down the street that has the chip shop on the corner. You know, the one that's got tiles decorated with tropical fish on the back wall behind the fryer. That's right – *Ship St*. We will go down Ship St. I can never quite remember how far along it is to the building we are heading for. Don't worry, though, we will hear it. Music – raucous trumpets, a clattering piano, high hat and saxophone will chase each other up the stairs and pull us down to the basement venue. Before you know it, we will have stowed our coats, bought a drink and found a space on the edge of the tiny dance floor. Our bodies will feel their way into the grooves of the music: Art Blakey, Dexter Gordon, Tito Puente, Duke Ellington, Celia Cruz, Jimmy McGriff. We know these names pre-date us, and like that they bestow an aura of the past on us. We take them for our own. It is still early. The night is before us and there is plenty of room to practise our moves and take in the scene.

We are dancing at the Jazz Rooms, Brighton's hottest new club night and something is about to happen to me. We are heading for the moment that is the destination for all my remembered returns to the club. It is a moment that I turn over and over again in my imagination. Whenever I hear a tune and start to move to its beats and rhythms, wherever I am, part of me is back here on this square of polished floor, on this hazily remembered night. This moment has taken on a life and energy beyond its spatial and temporal confines. I have churned it until it is like one of those smooth pebbles on the beach.

Before we get there, though, let's rewind a little bit further. You need to know more about the cultural wave we have ridden to land us here. Look around, and you will see that the floor is filling up. There is a sartorial range that we know how to read with sharp cultural acuity – as sharp as the creases in the narrow-legged trousers that one dancer has matched with his Fred Perry polo shirt. He bumps up against someone in a vintage Hawaiian shirt and zoot-suit pants. Both are throwing some extravagant moves. There are lots of frocks – floral cottons with wide skirts, tight-fitting velvet and satin. Costume jewellery glints. Those wearing jeans might appear to be casually thrown together but every rip in the denim and label on the back pocket sends out a message.

Back along the seafront in my student house, Dick Hebdige's *Subculture: The Meaning of Style* is sitting on a bookshelf. I'm sure that I'm not the only person on the dance floor familiar with his sociological analysis of self-performance, self-*invention*, in the dress codes of various post-war youth cultures. Brighton is a bohemian university town, after all. In my childhood bedroom in a small town just outside Manchester, there is a stack of *I-Ds*. I devoured this street-style magazine, bought it for several years from the first issue in 1980 onwards. In those early issues it consisted entirely of amateurish black and white photographs of stylish people posing. Under each snap there was a brief caption, listing the items of clothing and their provenance. There were couples in immaculate 1940s garb, complete with victory-rolled hair; hard-core punks with foot-high Mohicans; a young Boy George in a nun's habit. I spent hours in that teenage bedroom, absorbing those low-tech photographs and the typed text between *I-D*'s stapled covers; hungry for those who put themselves together to make a statement out of detritus. I began to put myself together in the same way. The drawer under my bed filled with jumble sale and charity shop finds. My growing collection of earrings was strung up precariously over the bed. *I-D*, as well as Hebdige, is part of what has primed me for the subcultural gazes in which I am caught here on this dance floor, enjoying both looking and being looked at. We are a self-conscious lot, having semiotic fun as we play with signs and codes.

Look beyond the clothes and you will see that nearly everyone is white: 1980s white youth trying on the clothes and popular cultures of the past as we dance to Latin and black music from the 1950s and '60s. This dance music scene looks and sounds like a long way from punk. But that was the starting point for my trajectory here. I imagine it was the starting point for a lot of us.

I'm not really that far removed from the shy and awkward 13-year-old I once was. It was in a northern grammar school in 1978 when I was first transported; whispers of older kids in the dinner-queue, talking about this new thing that was happening. This thing called punk, where girls repurposed kettles as handbags and wore sanitary towels as necklaces, where anyone could start a band and put together a three-minute single. Overnight I went from being an ABBA fan to being a punk. I listened to John Peel's late-night show on Radio One, had heated conversations with my brother about Blondie, The Clash, Buzzcocks and The Undertones (we both preferred 'Get Over You' to Peel's favourite of their singles, 'Teenage Kicks'). It felt like our world was accelerating and expanding as we explored our tastes and preferences. My brother bought me X-Ray Spex's *Germfree Adolescents* for Christmas that year. I gave him *All Mod Cons* by The Jam.

The years that followed were a blur of second-hand clothes, foraged from charity shops and trips to Manchester stores; piercing one ear so I could experiment with plastic spoons, teabags and other oddments as earrings. Poly Styrene (the lead singer of X-Ray Spex) became my first style icon: a Day-Glo celebration of anti-beauty. Musically, I started to follow my (unpierced) punk nose. I went to gigs, made weekly trips to record shops. Reggae and punk were intrinsically entwined – Poly Styrene's first release, prior to X-Ray Spex, was a reggae single. I didn't know that The Clash's 'Police and Thieves' was a cover version. But with punk's DIY mentality it didn't take long to trace it back to Junior Murvin, then Lee 'Scratch' Perry. Another new world began to show itself.

And then the Two-Tone bands, The Specials, The Selecter, Madness and The Beat turned up. I might not have been at Manchester's Free Trade Hall when the Sex Pistols played, but I was at the Apollo in 1979 for the first Two-Tone tour. The fusions of soul, reggae, ska and punk were a joyous embodiment of the cultural melting pots out of which the bands were formed. Of course, I wanted to go back and piece together all their constituent parts. I riffled through the racks of the soul section of HMV and Virgin on Market Street in Manchester on Saturday afternoons. Before too long I had Motown, Stax, Atlantic, northern soul on obscure labels, and Philly in my hands. And my feet were heading towards a dance floor.

By the time I arrived in Brighton as a student at Sussex University in October 1983, I was more likely to be listening to Jackie Wilson than Magazine. Friends sought out Primal Scream and the Jesus and Mary Chain in sweaty, small rooms, or showed off that they knew every lyric of every Smiths' song ever. I was bereft that nobody wanted to come and see Edwin Starr with me behind the anonymous concrete of the Brighton Centre on the seafront.

So, by and by, I found my way to the Jazz Rooms along with other kindred spirits in search of a dance floor. Maybe others had got there via different routes – '70s disco and funk, a bit of Madonna. But I'm sure there were others like me. I didn't know much about jazz before I came to Brighton. But once I was pointed in its direction, I knew how to navigate its contours, find my territory on its map. Which brings us back to this moment in October of 1984 on the edge – a liminal and existential space – of a dance floor. And that is when I see her.

She is alone, a bottle of Sol in one hand, a wedge of lime stuck in the bottle's neck. A slight figure, retro in cotton blouse and skirt cinched in at the waist with a wide plastic belt, she is completely self-contained. Her curling red hair is tied up in a chiffon scarf, forming a big bow on top of her head. It is her clothes that I notice first. I have long been an aficionado of the chiffon scarf and plastic belt. Maybe I see myself in her. She definitely reminds me of Poly Styrene, another woman with a penchant for an extravagant bow in her hair. It might be her clothes that catch my attention, but they are not what make me keep looking.

It is the way she moves. If you only glance in her direction you might be fooled into thinking she is merely swaying; hardly engaged in the music at all. But if you pay her proper attention, as I do, you will see something more in her small movements. They start with precise rotations at the hips, which make their way up her back, through her shoulders and end with flicks of her head; her chiffon bow is an emphatic punctuation mark. Her feet are hardly in it at all. This isn't dancing that draws attention to the dancer. This isn't someone who wants to be seen as being part of the scene. Those hip rotations aren't overtly sexual, either. She is just enraptured by her own musical world; taking the rhythm inside her and letting it course through her body. That's what I see anyway. And it is how I want to dance too; to inhabit a tune the way that she does, to let the music take me somewhere else.

There will be other nights at the Jazz Rooms, through the winter of 1984 and into 1985. It will be featured in *The Face* magazine and the really cool kids from London will start to head there on weekenders to the coast. One night I will dance next to Sadé, as petite and perfect a vision as she is on the cover of *Diamond Life*. Another night it will be Jerry Dammers from The Specials dancing an arm's length away from me. Both of these moments will stay with me. They will become anecdotes I tell of a time that felt like I was on, at least the edge of, a scene. But always, every time I descend the stairs into the club, it will be *her*, the girl on the very cusp of the dance floor, who I seek out, whose movements I will absorb: devour. I will see her no more than half a dozen times, never speak a word to her, nor tell a soul about her. But she will stay with me in a way that I have never tried to put into words until now.

Every time I take to a dance floor, a part of me is also back at the Jazz Rooms with her. Whether it be Latin jazz, house, northern soul or funk, I take a moment to find the rhythm and then my hips start moving. Every other movement, whether up or down (some tunes demand that the feet get involved too) comes from that starting place. Chronology rearranges itself and I am on many dance floors all at once ...

It is a fine summer evening in 1987 and I am at London Zoo, not far from the penguin house. A drum raps for attention from the speakers either side of a makeshift DJ platform. It is a Special Branch club night: Doo at the Zoo. A piano and bass stride in, assertive and muscular. My brother and I exchange a glance. The horns arrive, dirty and joyous, 'Duh-duh-duh-dud-un'. By the time the airy sigh of the backing vocals begins to weave around them, we are sure. We carve a space for ourselves on the improvised open-air dance floor, and the lead vocal comes in, to confirm what we already know. A woman sings in a wistful voice. We are dancing to 'Am I the Same Girl'.

UK label, Kent Records has been reissuing and reframing 1960s soul artists for the last few years, giving post-punk converts like me another route into this musical ocean to find its obscurer shores. *Groovy Ideas* is a recent album release, showcasing Barbara Acklin, and is a current favourite of mine. 'Am I the Same Girl' is its killer track. But this isn't her voice. It is higher, lighter. I can see the same realisation cross my brother's face. He leans towards me, shouts in my ear. 'It's Dusty!'

Oh my God, he's right. It's Dusty Springfield singing, 'Am I the same girl?' and I am joining in. How can I not? I love Dusty; my blonde bob and denim shirt are in part a homage to the cover of *A Girl Called Dusty*. My hips have found the rhythm. It moves sinuously up my back, across my shoulders and down my arms. My hands join in for the chorus, pointing to the stars. I am the Jazz Rooms girl, Barbara and Dusty all at once. 'Am I the same girl? Yes, I am! Yes, I am!' ...

It is a winter night in Manchester in the early 1990s. A northern soul night at Parker's Hotel on Corporation Street. The whole floor throbs, a mass of sweaty, moving bodies. It is a large room but so crammed that owning a piece of the dance floor takes a lot of energy. The dancing is wild. We embody the lyrics of Dobie Gray's 'Out on the Floor' – the dancefloor is definitely where we are getting our kicks. The track changes and, as I feel for the groove, the daytime world melts away. I am no longer a newly qualified teacher, my year already mapped out on a timetable of repeated classes, week after week after week. I am Gloria Jones. I mouth the words as I stab at the air, dramatically enacting the effects of tainted love. Right on the periphery, I can just make her out, still holding her own amidst the ruckus with that familiar turn of the wrist and a flick of the head.

I am performing, in these moments, what autoethnographer, Norman K. Denzin, has termed a 'relived epiphany'. He defines this as an episode 'whose meanings are given in the reliving of the experience' (Denzin 2014: 53). Every time I take to a dance floor – even if, as of late, I am alone and making do with my kitchen and a streaming service – I return to my 19-year-old self and a moment when I appropriated another woman's dance moves. And I appropriate those moves again. Dancing, for me, is still about actively making sense of who I am. Performing is still a kind of self-invention: a little bit Diana, a little bit Dusty, Barbara or Gloria and a lot of that girl I have so idealised over the years. It still feels like there is a clear trajectory from punk and its revelation of joyful, transgressive bricolage: that I could put myself together from whatever bits and pieces I fancied. That moment at the Jazz Rooms in 1984 feels pivotal. It was the moment I found the place where I belong in all the cultural tumult that surrounded me.

But then I find myself back in the upstairs room of a Manchester pub in 2003 and must re-assess this explanation. It is my brother's 40th birthday party. He has hired a soul DJ. I am not sure what tune is playing, but I am dancing. The floor is filling up after the buffet, and my dad joins me on the dance floor. I make space for him, smile. Then I experience a dual shock – that this is the first time I have ever seen my 72-year-old dad dance, and, oh my god, he knows how to hold the music inside himself and just *move* to the beat. Where did he learn to dance like that? I never get a chance to ask him, never see my dad dance again. He died, suddenly and much too soon, in December 2003. I do still catch him, sometimes, out of the corner of my eye, strutting his stuff on the edge of some dance floor.

Postscript One

While writing this chapter I have been slipping between my Word doc. and Google to fact check my fallible memories against the digital archive. Time and time again I am relieved to find they tally up.

Germfree Adolescents and *All Mod Cons* were both released in 1978.

Primal Scream and the Jesus and Mary Chain did both play gigs in Brighton in the early 1980s.

Diamond Life reached number two in the UK album charts in the summer of 1984.

Special Branch did indeed run a club night at London Zoo called Doo at the Zoo in 1987 – there is a recording of one of the sets from it on someone's podcast (sadly it doesn't include Dusty's version of 'Am I the Same Girl').

Parkers Hotel 'was the unusual choice to host soul nights [...] and one or two basement function rooms of Parkers were used for the sixties soul and jazz club until about 1994' (Pubs of Manchester 2013).

The only thing that will not match up is when I type 'Jazz Rooms Ship St Brighton' into the search engine. The information that comes up is this: DJ Russ Dewbury founded this music night in 1987, it moved around various venues in Brighton and settled in Ship St. in 1991 (Rose 2022). However hard I look, I can't find the venue. I was a student in Brighton from 1983–86 and I know I went to the Jazz Rooms on Ship St. during my second and third year there. I remember it so well. I had left Brighton in 1986; I could not have been a regular at a club night there after that. But there is no record that the Jazz Rooms existed in 1984.

Postscript Two

Last year, while sorting through my mum's effects, I found, amongst old photographs and documents, a typed sheet of paper. As I read, I realised it was the best man's speech from my parents' wedding in 1962, a missive from a time before my birth. I scanned down the page and a particular sentence caught my eye. In its account of my parents' love story, it noted, 'a courtship conducted in the jazz clubs of Soho'. I think about my parents, their lives before they were parents.

They met in London in 1960, while training to be probation officers. I imagine their excitement to be part of a new post-war metropolis. I see a longer history of appropriation; I consider again what it means for white people to dance to black music.

Amid ongoing debates about cultural appropriation and the tangled politics of it all, there is a single new moment of meaningful experience where, simultaneously, I hear Dusty Springfield, see my sweet, gentle dad and watch aghast at the wild moves of northern soulers. Through it all I look to another woman dancing on the edge of a dance floor. In all of us there is a yearning for something beyond our immediate worlds and we are joined together in a desire to reconfigure it. I am re-living an epiphany that pre-dates the Jazz Rooms, whatever year in the 1980s that the club began. Trust me.

References

Acklin, Barbara. 1968. 'Am I the Same Girl'. Brunswick.
Acklin, Barbara. 1987. *Groovy Ideas*. Kent Records.
Denzin, Norman K. 2014. *Interpretive Autoethnography*. Los Angeles: SAGE.
Gray, Dobie. 1966. 'Out on the Floor'. Charger Records.
Hebdige, Dick. 1979. *Subculture: The Meaning of Style*. London: Routledge.
The Jam. 1978. *All Mod Cons*. Polydor.
Jones, Gloria. 1964. 'Tainted Love'. Champion Records.
Pubs of Manchester, Past and Present. 2013. 'Parkers Hotel, Corporation Street'. http://pubs-of-manchester.blogspot.com/2013/06/parkers-hotel-corporation-street.html
Rose, Alex. 2022. 'Getting Behind the Groove…with Russ Dewbury'. *Behind the Groove*. https://www.behindthegroove.co.uk/russ-dewbury-interview
Sade. 1984. *Diamond Life*. Epic Records.
Springfield, Dusty. 1969. 'Am I the Same Girl'. Philips.
X-Ray Spex. 1978. *Germfree Adolescents*. EMI.

Author biography

Helen Pleasance is a Senior Lecturer in Creative Writing at York St John University, UK. She has written on the Moors murders, the spectral form of memoir and music memoirs. She is currently working on a hybrid family memoir about the women in her family and needlework.

2 Finding the Dirt: Nesh at Elektrowerkz

Fraser Mann

It is hard to tell your story of raving unless you were an original. The temptation is always to make claims that are a little bit exaggerated. If they don't work, then you just make stuff up. I supervised a dissertation once and the nice young lad said, 'it must have been amazing to have been there, you know in the fields, raving and then legging it from the coppers'. 'Oh yes', I answered and tried to look lost in wistful reverie.

I mean, I'm sure it was. It's just that I wouldn't know. I was too busy playing with my Star Wars figures and figuring out the best spot to put my new John Barnes poster. I remember raves being in the news. I remember the lurid headlines in the reliably toxic tabloids (even as a young teenager I knew that the red tops were liars). I remember a rough approximation of dance music appearing on increasingly weird *Top of the Pops* episodes (I saw Guru Josh doing 'Infinity' last Friday on BBC4. Eccentric with a capital E.) I remember some of the lads in my year at my suburban school talking about the stuff their older brothers and sisters were getting up to around the M25. Acid smiley badges were appearing on school blazers and the back of toilet doors. The naughty kids were talking about 'skins' and 'blowbacks'. I had no idea how to put any of this together in 1989. I was a tubby kid with NHS glasses (a long time before they were Jarvis-ified), two completed Panini sticker albums and a working knowledge of the SodaStream. Not exactly Dreamscape, is it?

But that's not the story I usually tell.

Now I go record hunting. Now I am a bit obsessed with tracing musical histories. Now I like to make cultural spider diagrams. This means that I own lots of old rave tunes (I have 'Labyrinthe' by early '90s Brummie wunderkind Demonik playing as I type this) and that I read lots of books about raving. I know more about it now than I ever did then. I'm also a fan of storytelling. So, when pleasant young students ask me what it was like in the good old days, I can offer something approximating truth. It's just not my truth.

Memory and narrative do funny things to you. As a teenager, I did get into dance culture, but it was by no means my first counter-cultural obsession.

Baggy came first, quickly followed by shoegaze, grebo and Camden lurch. The names were half the fun. I thought dance music was all a bit shit at first. I liked people with guitars. I liked straggly hair, second-hand clothes and scuffed up 8-hole DMs. I liked the Bull and Gate, the *NME* and mosh pits. Raving was for the trendy kids, the show-offs. Raving was for people without scary Scottish Dads. Raving was Es and wiz. It was all a bit scary. Roll ups and cider were about as far as I was prepared to go.

This made me a bit of an outlier with my friends. Sure, we had all started in the same place. Exploring the three racks of indie records in St Albans' Our Price until we had exhausted them. Occasional visits to Rough Trade, travel card in pocket, to buy records by Teenage Fanclub and sneaky peaks into the much scarier Camden Record and Tape Exchange to search for tatty-looking records by obscure bands that would make us look cool when we went to whichever house was parent-free that weekend.

But then we started to diversify. One of our usual trips into London featured a detour through Holloway. My mate Lat stopped at the University of North London to buy tickets for an event at their famous old Student Union cavern, The Rocket. Something called Megadog. Not a band name but an event name. It advertised techno acts with space age sounding names and technical specifications about lights and speakers. This wasn't for me. Where were the bands? Where were the guitars? This was unsettling. My little troop of pals were going to the dark side. There was talk of buying acid. Maybe pills. It was an all-nighter. They would be out all night. All night. 'Exit rave left' for me. I still needed the safety of the 11pm finish and the reassuring rumble of the last train out of King's Cross.

It wasn't that I didn't really like the music. I was and remain pretty open-minded about sounds and will give anything a go. It was more that it was a world that seemed closed off to me. I didn't know where to start. There were so many names and so many of the records didn't even have the names on them. Just logos from record labels that sounded avant-garde and threatening: Rising High, R&S, Planet E, Rephlex, Warp. My increasingly ravey mates were talking about getting 'decks' and hearing '303s'. I was still asking around for a drummer and a bass player for my experimental shoegaze/thrash hybrid.

The epiphany happened in Lat's living room during a half-term holiday. His mum was out at work, so about fifteen of us spent the day smoking roll-ups and sharing three cans of illicit lager in his back garden. He had a new record that was blowing his mind. He had never heard anything like it before. I tried my best to look enthusiastic, but my inside voice was going, 'More techno rubbish, why can't we all just love Mega City Four and Leatherface?' He put it on. It was absurdly good. Mesmerising and strange. Lifting and shifting all over the shop. It was 'Digeridoo' by Aphex Twin. I don't know why this tune hit where others had failed. Maybe the stereo in this house was better than others. Maybe it was the psychoactive impact of half a can of Skol. Maybe it was the thrill of a Tuesday afternoon not in double maths. Whatever. It rocked and I was a changed man.

I got into techno after that. I still loved messy-haired men and women from Stourbridge, Seattle and Boston, but now I also liked producers from Detroit and DJs from south London. I said 'Sorted' and 'Nice one' a little more and 'Where's me jumper' a little less. I even went clubbing once or twice.

Then I went to university in Ripon. Ripon in the middle of nowhere. Ripon surrounded by North Yorkshire farms and populated by local army squaddies. Ripon didn't do raving. Just as I was getting started, I went to a place where clubbing was what you did after the pub and before a fight on the way home. It had two venues. One was called Gio's. One was called Sly's. They were awful. Terrible music. DJs that talked loudly about 'the ladies' and badly parked cars. Free stuff for people willing to be dickheads. Fights, threats and rows. Did I mention the terrible music? The new freedom offered by university was offset by the lack of anything to do with it. So, how did we respond? How could me and my new ravey Uni pals find our groove? Simple really: we did it ourselves. We had parties. We took over the meagre Students' Union sound system and its jumpy decks once a week. We played jungle, drill and bass and gabba. We danced. Other people didn't. People would ask us why we weren't playing the Spice Girls, Oasis or the Grease Megamix. Our eyes rolled in time with the revolving turntable. Failing that we hung out in each other's flats. Overnight essay writing was sound tracked by 909s, bleeps and rumbles. We talked a good rave game. We recycled our handful of clubbing stories over and over again. It was the best we could manage.

But it wasn't actually raving though, was it? It wasn't the sonic chaos we saw in *Mix Mag* or *Jockey Slut*. It wasn't the 'larging it' we knew our mates in big cities were doing. We didn't get to stumble out of a small room as the sun was coming up with our ears ringing and our trainers all fucked up. All of us needed that. We'd been in rave rehearsal for three years, after all. It was time to join in properly. It was time to go to London. It was time to seek out the real rave dirt.

When me and my gang of Uni mates decided to move to London, it was a nervy time. I grew up twenty miles north of London and had always boasted about knowing the streets there like the back of my hand. This was, of course, bollocks. I was as terrified of London as anyone else who'd never lived there. Visiting Camden Market to buy a jacket or Brick Lane for a curry was about my limit. Now I had to rent a flat and find a job there. I had to read the classified ads in *Loot* every morning. I had to use the Tube every day. I had to avoid eye contact with the world and tut at indiscretions. I had to try and be a Londoner.

The job hunt had actually gone pretty well. I got taken on as an Admissions Officer at Goldsmiths College in New Cross. It was a cool place to work. It was still carrying its Charles Saatchi endorsed 'Young British Artists' credentials and my own role as the admin bod for the Fine Art degree meant that I was quite central in bringing in the new batch of Damien Hirsts and Tracey Emins. My colleagues were all young graduates and some of them were bang into their tunes. Dance tunes. I had found people in London who liked dance music. One of them, Jo, had a boyfriend who loved Warp Records. This is where it gets good.

Let me explain.

All us musos love record labels. They are our chief tastemakers. Their appeal is multiple. The music, of course, but also the logo, the sleeve designs, the accumulative cool. These labels have something indefinable about them. This is perhaps their chief appeal. If you are an indie kid into 4AD or a metal fan into Earache, then it's hard to explain why. If someone doesn't get it, then they never will. There's no point explaining it to them. Fellow fans have a telepathic relationship with one another. Two blokes in Sub Pop t-shirts at a gig will know more about each other from a quick nod than any algorithm could ever manage. It's like you have a shared sense of what's what, who's who, and where's where. Some of my proudest moments have been out and about at festivals when someone half smiles and says, 'Nice Ninja Tune t-shirt, mate'. Instant friends for life even though we'll never speak again. This is how I found my new Warp friend Martin.

Down the pub with work colleagues is always an awkward time. This was no different at Goldsmiths. It's nice to natter outside the office, but there is a delicate balancing act to this. A bit pissed is fine. You can show a different side to yourself. Funny, eccentric, maybe a bit odd. Any more pissed is not fine. Nobody wants to see that side of you. Rude, nonsensical, too sweary. It was, in an effort to avoid this very thing happening, that I nattered to Jo's boyfriend, Martin. I had ditched my office shirt for a simple black t-shirt with the Warp Records logo on it. Martin clocked this and quickly we were into a lengthy and engaging chat about all things bleepy. Martin had been a fan longer than me. He had been at early LFO gigs and was on board with the first *Artificial Intelligence* compilation. I was a bit newer to it all. Aphex was my way in and the late '90s release of the timeless *Music Has the Right to Children* by Boards of Canada sealed the deal. I was now working my way around Warp's catalogue and was evangelical about their output and aesthetic. The problem was, I explained to Martin, that there was never anything about Warp in the weeklies. I never knew the Warp news. I never found Warp events. I would scour the daily free sheet *Metro* on the Tube in the morning but all I ever found were shit pub gigs and I'd already been to lots of those. Martin took a sip of his pint and asked if I'd used *Warp Net*.

I didn't really understand the internet then. Still don't. I used it at work to read the football reports at lunchtime but that was about it. Most people were the same. In the early twenty-first century, being online was an office thing. Nobody was connected at home. If they were, it was on dial-up that you had to unplug the phone for. Even then, it was slow and boring. No, home was built around telly and eating. God, I miss that. But Martin told me that there was loads of Warp stuff online. Ways to buy the old catalogue, artist news and interviews. And live listings. Lots and lots of live listings. Lots of semi-mythical Warp artists playing in lots of London venues.

Bingo.

I discovered Nesh. And then rediscovered it every month.

So, let's get the basics in place. Think of this section as the outline and what follows it as the colouring in. I like the colouring in bit, but I am pretty crap at staying within the lines. So, it's important to get some bold black lines down first so you can see what the shape is before I go all Jackson Pollock with the crayons. Nesh was a monthly night that ran over a year and a half in the early noughties. I started going in the autumn of 2000 and stopped going in May the following year. I would have gone to more but the last Nesh I went to was, in fact, the last Nesh. It was housed in the Elektrowerkz, a venue hidden down a little side street behind Angel tube station in the fancy pants part of Islington, North London. It's weird because, from a very young age, I had walked past the entrance to that little side street once or twice a year. I was born with a rare type of glaucoma and have been attending appointments at Moorfields Eye Hospital for as long as I can remember. I would walk from their City Road site up to Angel with my mum after appointments and sometimes in between appointments. It has nicer places to eat, you see. Plus, a good walk is always appreciated after a morning of having your eyes poked about and filled with yellow dye. I still do this walk now whenever I have an appointment. The location of the Elektrowerkz, then, is a kind of multi memory. When I went to Nesh nights, I thought about how funny it was that I'd wandered past here worried about my eyes. Now, when I'm wandering past worrying about my eyes, I think about how funny it is that I used to go down this little side street to go raving.

The Elektrowerkz is the dirt. It's the kind of dirt that only someone who has been to plenty of gigs can truly appreciate. When I tell non-gig people (and I do know some, imagine that!) about the filthy walls or the dark, casualty-filled corners, they visibly shrink away. Why, they wonder, would anyone voluntarily spend time and money in such a space? Tell a raver or a toilet venue aficionado, however, and they nod sagely. Ah yes, they say, you found the dirt. Dirt is a hard concept to get across but it is an essential one for understanding UK music space. It may be that it is increasingly rare, too.

Let's time travel. Dirt venues at the start of the millennium are unkempt, ramshackle, possibly dangerous and always fragrant. They are a blessed relief from the sterile world we spend most of our time in. They are loud, disorientating and genuinely unhygienic. They are subversive and saturnalian. Conversations with friends, strangers and bar staff are half shouted, half frantically gesticulated. The floor is crunchy, sticky and slippery. Drinks come in squishy plastic cups that dump half the booze down your t-shirt if you have to carry more than one. The rest of that t-shirt is stained by sweat and greasy marks from leaning on blackened walls. The venue is full of smokers. The air is thick with tobacco, weed and dry ice. Discombobulating strobes are punctured by little flames appearing here and there. Your B&H cigarette packet's dented and damp but you light up anyway. It's not a healthy place. It doesn't sell wellbeing or juicing remedies. It's not made of glass and steel and foregrounded by happy shiny men and women. The toilets are appalling. It's a shithole and the people in it look unwell. It's too loud and too dirty and it's fucking brilliant.

This is what Nesh was like. The Elektrowerkz is better known as a Goth club. Its Slimelight night dates back to 1987 and has hosted dark royalty on a pretty regular basis. But I was there for Warp's roster. Nesh had the great and the good of the leftfield raving world. It was the cutting edge of the cutting edge. It had famous names and new names. It was where cool journos and nerdy tech heads went. Nesh club nights used all three of the Elektrowerkz floors. The concrete staircase took you up and down from noise to noise. Ravers nodded at one another as they passed. DJs and artists used a set of interlocking rooms. It was loud. So loud. You could feel every bit of you and those around you vibrating. Your innards shook. Discordant sounds, deep bass and shrieks of synth filled every part of this strange space. It was dark. Low lights and strobes were the only real illumination. This is a time before smart phones so glowing screens were absent. Just noise and people and all the dirt. It was gloriously confusing. You could turn up with three or four mates and lose them all instantly. Plans to catch particular sets were abandoned. Other plans to catch other sets were abandoned too. You couldn't quite work out how normal space and Nesh space sat together. This was all unsettling at first. For an inexperienced raver like me this was a bit much. It never got less so. It's more that I learnt to enjoy the confusion. I discovered that once you handed that ticket over on the way in, it was time to suspend the outside and immerse yourself in all that noisy, chaotic dirt.

I need help with telling the next part of this story. I have loads of memories about Nesh nights out but there are three problems with retelling them here. One, it was a long time ago. Two, I was, shall we say, often worse for wear. And three, and most pertinently, I'm an unrepentant bullshitter. There is a danger of recollections getting out of hand. My memory of watching Luke Vibert DJ will morph into me going up there and getting into a one-on/one-off battle with him. Spotting a famous Icelandic singer in the bar will turn into a long discussion about David Attenborough documentaries and getting the scoop on a Sugarcubes reunion tour.

I need some actual details.

This is why I chatted to Greg Eden (on 3 November 2020). He knows plenty about Nesh. Greg worked for Warp for ten years from 1996 to 2006. His career there covered web content (Warp were always well ahead of other labels in this regard), legal affairs and A&R. He signed Chris Clark and Boards of Canada to the label. He was a big part of the team that put together the events. He has been a long-term and active fan of the music. It becomes clear as we chat that the music is what comes first. It's always nice when the things you imagine about an artistic institution like Warp turn out to be sort of true. They hired Greg, he says, because it was easier to 'teach someone law than teach them to love the music'.

Warp relocated from Sheffield to London at the turn of the millennium. Some of their staff were keen to repeat the success of Blech, their 'little back-room night' in Sheffield. It wasn't easy though. Greg explains that 'live events are quite risky things to do and the record label isn't a promoter. You need someone who's got enough passion to really drive an event'. You also need a 'close knit group of people to work with who are young and interested in being involved in that night'. Luckily, this was the case at Warp and 'lots of people chipped in'.

But why that name? My in-laws are all from the northwest and, when they say 'nesh', it is a description of someone who moans about the cold or about their lack of comfort. A whinge bag, I suppose. It is often applied to southerners like me. It's hard to define but it's definitely not a term of endearment. I had always wondered if this was the same for capital N Nesh. I had assumed it was some niche techno term that I didn't know but was too proud to ask about. But no, it was a gang of South Yorkshire folk having a 'sly jab at Londoners for being a bit nesh'. As for the venue choice, I had imagined some type of *Field of Dreams* epiphany as the Warp team explored the Elektrowerkz during the day and visualised the Bacchanalian chaos it promised. But no, that's just me being a bit nesh. It was more that it was in north London near a few of the Warp artists and was 'cheap and available'. Greg does admit that its 'grimy, slightly punk aesthetic felt more of a fit than something that was more blingy or shiny'. But any more than that is over thinking it.

One of the first Nesh nights included a performance from an artist who was rather prosaically billed as 'Chris from St Albans'. I was fascinated by this name in the week leading up to the event. I grew up in St Albans and wondered if I knew him. There were always plenty of blokes called Chris about (as well as blokes called Tom and Stu) and perhaps this was one that I'd had a pint with. It turns out that we've never met but he was in the same school year as my friend's older sister (yeah man, mixing with the rich and famous).

Chris from St Albans would turn into Clark, an artist I've followed for two decades. This was before the release of his debut LP *Clarence Park*. I'd heard nothing like it before. Greg's memories of signing him are pretty funny. 'Warp', Greg explains, 'used to get boxes and boxes full of tapes and CDRs, at least ten a day. Part of my role was to listen to them. Most of them were not very good, or they were average which is actually more depressing'. One artist was pretty persistent and made follow-up calls most days. Nancy the office manager's shout of, 'it's Chris from St Albans' sort of stuck. He played that Nesh night as a new signing and as a way to 'get him on the agenda and raise his visibility a bit'. It worked. I know the sounds on *Clarence Park* well now (the actual Clarence Park was a short walk from my school and is where we used to go to do our lunchtime smoking) but on that night they were brand new. My memory of his performance is of volume and unsettling sonic choices. The opening synth stabs were dystopian. The beats and drum programming were jackhammers. The crowd in the room was pretty sparse at this stage of the evening so I could really concentrate on what was happening. The music was disarming. It was full of textures and ambiguities. Any meaningful or conscious analysis was impossible. You just let the noise hit you. It was dance music. But I couldn't dance. It was music that was doing a number on me. I was a bit frightened but compelled to stay. It was full of such oppositions. This was the dirt. Bad for me. Good for me.

I'm not alone in remembering the levels of volume at Nesh nights. I asked Greg if he has any particular musical memories from the events. It is hard for Greg to pinpoint too many specifics. The nights are all one big mosaic. All that's left is a 'loud sweaty blur'. He does remember being the DJ in the upstairs room though. It is a sensory memory.

> It was a terrifying experience. I'd spent probably a week preparing a set with all my best tracks and vinyl. Then I got on and started

playing the first track and was trying to mix in the second one. I just couldn't hear it. It was so loud in that room. My strongest memory is being in that booth not being able to hear the record I was cueing in. I was feeling the side of my head moving because the headphones I had were so loud that I could feel the magnet moving. But I still couldn't hear them.

I love this story because this is what my memory of the nights is like. I remember bits and pieces. I remember sensations. I remember my girlfriend (now wife) and I trying to use some kind of sign language when screaming in each other's ears failed. I remember bumping into an old school friend and his rather unimpressed fiancé. I really did see Björk in the bar (she even said 'Excuse me' as she squeezed past). I remember a very hammered man falling backwards down the escalator at Angel tube station on the way there one night and about five of us trying to catch him as he tumbled in his Jesus Christ pose. I sort of remember talking to DJ Layla and Plaid but was far too fucked to make any sense of it the next day, let alone now. I remember my friend Angie asking Aphex Twin about his Brit Award nomination as a dozen fanboys looked on in envy. I remember Boom Bip dancing strangely. I remember Bogdan Raczynski looking positively demonic as his sonic assault gained momentum (this is where Greg and I intersect as he told me he was controlling the EQ for this set and whacking up the bass at every opportunity). I remember being permanently confused as to what room I was in and who was playing. I remember getting the first Tube home in the morning. I remember feeling like shit on a plate for about two days afterwards. I know that all of this shaped me as a new Londoner. It shaped the way I saw nightlife. It stuck with me. It was the dirt.

Author biography

Fraser Mann is Senior Lecturer in Literature at York St. John University, UK. He is a specialist in American writing with particular interests in conflict, testimony, and trauma. He has published research on a range of literary figures such as Ernest Hemingway, James Jones and Norman Mailer. He also works on music writing in the form of creative non-fiction and co-edited the Bloomsbury edited collection *Music, Memory and Memoir* (2019). His creative writing can be found on the *Twistin' My Memory, Man* blogspace. His teaching interests include American Studies, autobiography and twentieth- and twenty-first-century war writing.

3 Chatting to Jarvis

Robert Edgar

Time is out of joint. In these difficult times of global pandemics, various economic crises and changing patterns of music consumption, time takes on strange proportions. This is more so for those who frequent a particular form of music venue, not only currently closed but fundamentally and mortally threatened, their survival supported by a committed and fervent fanbase and by the unifying power of the Music Venue Trust. The danger to the existence of small venues is, however, more than economic; it is existential and fundamental (Taylor, Raine and Hamilton 2021). And it's personal. The tradition of the pub or the working man's club being rescued from developers to continue its work is an essential part of their ongoing importance to local communities. Schofield and Miller note that '[v]enues peaked in the 1990s and early 2000s, coinciding with the rise of "Britpop" and "Indie" genres' (Schofield and Miller 2017: 137), although they were built on the site of earlier venues that were often used for other cultural events. Crucially these toilet 'venues are defined as a culture within themselves, unmediated by outside influences of society' (ibid.). The fact that these spaces remain 'unmediated' preserves their independence. They therefore exist on a borderline between the familiar through aesthetic and functional traits, their oppositional quality (which is perhaps more of a distinction of class than counterculture), and places in which youthful rebellion and identification can occur, no matter how old some of the patrons may be getting. Toilet venues have a shared aesthetic which provides a point of connection for music fans across the country. Even more, they provide a place of belonging.

To a particular ilk of music fan, just like me, these venues had a mythic quality that was conferred in the 1980s by *NME* and *Melody Maker* reviews. These publications had become established as icons of a peculiarly British counterculture and carrying one under your arm singled your indie cred as much as your German Army parka and Dr Martens, despite the fact that it was bought from that bastion of capitalism, WHSmith in Doncaster Arndale Centre. To a generation who were hanging out in and outside (their/your equivalent of) Track Records, scouring the listing pages was essential, tracing the name of a band from record shop poster to venue. As more and more people started wearing Stone Roses t-shirts the more the quest was on to find the latest and more and more obscure acts, and these were the people who were listed in those obscure venues in towns that were just out of reach at a transitional age. Mystical names to conjure with: 'The New Adelphi Club' in Hull, 'The Duchess' in Leeds and, perhaps most of all, 'King Tut's Wah Wah Hut' in Glasgow.

The mythic quality of these spaces is in part conferred by their status as sites of cultural resistance, particularly the venues that affectionately became known as the 'toilet circuit'; these are the focus of my consideration and my deep affection. 'Toilet Circuit venues are defined by three core elements: historicism, distinguishable seedy aesthetics, and a compelling sense of community' (Schofield and Miller 2017: 137) – three magical elements. Whilst there is some debate as to the origin of the name and the suggestion that it may be due to the Forum in Tunbridge Wells being a former toilet block, I was always under the impression that the name was bestowed by the sweetly rancid toilets common to all of these spaces.

The beautifully dishevelled appearance of toilet venues is in part what gives them their appeal. There was a bleak miserabilism to be enjoyed by a callow youth in a post-industrial Northern town. The music that went with it was on one level celebratory of the grey streets. I recall feeling as if I spent part of my life perpetually framed in a Ken Cummins photograph with a beautifully bleak Joy Division and Smiths soundtrack playing through the tatty orange foam of a personal cassette player's headphones. But there was also a hopeful side to emergent music in the early 1990s: the house and rave influenced Stone Roses and Happy Mondays. All that was needed was a place where like-minded folk could meet, share their passions and ideally see some of these icons in person. The Toby Jug opened on Doncaster's North Bridge in 1988, or rather reopened and was repurposed as a music venue, despite an evident lack of finance available for any renovation. Any attempts at rejuvenation would have been wasted, partly due to the demilitarised quality of that part of town reeling from the effect of ten years of Thatcher's 'approach' to the North. Whilst a lack of money may have been a significant factor in determining the look of the venue, there was something more fundamental than that: to renovate would have diminished the DIY aesthetic that pervaded indie music. Music historians may cite C86 as the defining moment in the birth of modern indie but in truth there was a continuum where the presence of Joy Division could still be felt and Echo and the Bunnymen and Orange Juice were being played alongside the Inspiral Carpets, Northside and Flowered Up. The fracturing of time and musical genre is not as neat and clear as some historians or our memories might like it to be. In 1989 the 'BYO' opened on the other side of Doncaster's North Bridge opposite 'The Jug', an old warehouse that became an instant draw for Doncaster's rave community. Given the furore in the press about Acid House and rave, the old warehouse had been refused a licence – hence the 'bring your own'. The clientele of The Jug would happily watch an indie outfit ragging their fingers on the strings of their Telecasters before necking a final pint of cider and black and skipping over the road. How much memory people have of the BYO is debatable.[1] The routine was then set: a visit to the 'indie pub', The Castle in the market place, student night at Ritzy nightclub on a Thursday (followed by a couple of hours in the snooker club below), Saturday night at the old warehouse and most other nights watching bands at The Jug. Like everyone else, I formed a band. We were dreadful but it didn't matter, the intention wasn't to hit the charts. This lack of ambition was nothing to do with outsider credibility, it was entirely so we could play at the Toby Jug. We did eventually manage a gig, although initially this was a mid-afternoon Saturday slot where you had to bring your own audience. In time-honoured fashion, I'd followed the biroed instructions badly scrawled on a card in a music shop window. A guitarist 'into the Bunnymen and Wire looking for other musicians'. I should have suspected something was wrong when I met John as he didn't even have a guitar. Mind you, I wasn't a musician so I couldn't complain. We played The Jug and then some local pubs and that's when it fell apart. It just wasn't the same playing at another venue. Nigel, Melvyn, Andy, John and I packed up our instruments and went our separate ways. The important thing was that I had learnt the rules of 'the venue'. 'These venues become established as places of attachment, acceptance and liberation, holding an integral emotional connection [...] to the audience' (Schofield and Miller 2017: 138). As seems customary there is a Facebook group dedicated to the memory of the Toby Jug. A couple of years ago someone posted a beautifully hand-drawn gig list from 1990 including early outings from later musical giants, including Ride and Radiohead. I was there but I have no recollection of them, yet I could still manoeuvre every bump in the felt of the pool table. This personal identification with an aesthetic and 'feel' gives way to something more communal.

I met my partner a decade ago, in part through a shared love of live music. Her earlier life kept her away from the kind of scuzzy toilet venue that I had become so enamoured of. Instead, she had been forced by living at a distance

1. There is an infamous video on YouTube of a couple of patrons gurning beyond the call of duty, about 24 minutes in. https://www.youtube.com/watch?v=IIsZVIbasiA&t=6334s. This is an image more reflective of the times than anything I can think of. Turn off the lights and watch the whole video.

from smaller venues to see bigger performances of bands that had 'made it'. People like U2 and later Oasis and a particular and perpetual favourite, Pulp. However, she too had later found and fallen for the attractions of the small venue. It was natural that our second date was not at a restaurant or theatre but instead at the Brudenell Social Club in Leeds. At such an early stage in a relationship this was great, I knew perfectly well how to handle the environment at least. One of the benefits of the toilet venue is proximity to the stars. We have subsequently seen and been close to groups such as Suede and artists like Johnny Marr and Julian Cope at the Brudenell, but this was our first time there together and I knew how to impress. At the close I wandered forward to the end of the stage and a waiting James Taylor of the James Taylor Quartet ready to buy a signed CD, the perfect gift to impress. Instead, a heavily placed Converse on a crushed plastic pint glass saw me career into the stage, hitting my head on Mr Taylor's organ. Despite my clumsiness the venture was a success. If only I'd been able to get Jarvis Cocker's autograph.

Toilet venues engender community through familiarity; you could play a lowly support slot to an up-and-coming band and make a support slot to an established band with remarkable underground cred possible. This emotional connection then continues as time collapses and as the toilet circuit has endured, with many venues closing and others opening to take their place. In 2018, the Crescent Community Venue opened in York, rejuvenating a threatened working man's club. It is still used by the patrons of old in addition to a new clientele. The value of the toilet venue to the cultural life of a city cannot be overestimated: 'it is essential that strategies make room for bottom-up initiatives, creativity and entrepreneurship. In the conceptualisation of spatial value, we emphasise its multiplicity, as a wide range of grassroots and official actors participate in the valuing of urban spaces' (Hitters and Hitters 2020: 161). On slipping in myself in early 2019, I witnessed the joyful sight of part of the front bar occupied by domino enthusiasts whilst someone was on the newly installed decks at the back treating all and sundry to some obscure techno; both happily co-existing. My partner and I were ecstatic when I heard that this space was opening so close to our house. My own familiarity with these spaces is born out of experience where the memory of the past is a linear one, this being matched by the bands and the form(s) of music played in the venues. This is a common feature of the toilet venue and in particular the function of the 'front bar' afforded by the universal design of the working man's club and where a variety of patrons are likely to rub shoulders in a truly egalitarian fashion. This does happily spill over. We saw Bodega in the new community room of Brudenell Social Club in Leeds in 2018 with its suitably intimate low stage. I recall (with some glee) the New York cool lead singer trying to work out if the gyrating be-sequinned septuagenarians at the front were part of some normcore fan club or not. This mix of fans is a feature of the toilet venue that can only come with time. Fans like me continue to watch new music alongside new fans, a community of people who instinctively recognise each other. On my second visit to the Brudenell I noticed a middle-aged man at the front of the low stage watching the band intently through his spectacles. He's been there, in the same spot at every gig I've been to there since. The specific experiential nature of time in these spaces is part of their vital function. As Baldwin and Keefer note, 'Research demonstrates that life stories with greater temporal coherence, that is, clear causal relationships between events better promote individual well-being' (Baldwin and Keefer 2020: 3073).

My recollection of Bodega becomes blurred in and amongst others, an effect of the continuum offered by the venue. The 'temporal coherence' is one of a perpetual present. The fragility of memory coupled with the prevalence of a vast uncatalogued online archive records of venues, gigs and events leads to a form of personal bricolage. This social media, YouTube-fuelled preponderance of informal gig photos and records collapses time even further (perhaps this has now taken the place of the largely defunct music press). These online informal archives only seek to capture what was already there, a space where you can get close to the band, to meet them (and perhaps even to head butt them). This opportunity still happens with signings and photos at the merchandise table, the democratic nature of performance confirmed in this most personal of fan–performer exchange. The physicality of the space is the antithesis of the large venues and further augments the underground nature of the star; they become ours by proximity and allow us special access.

Relationships of all kinds are forged in these spaces. In 1990, I had an acrimonious break-up of a sort that can only be experienced by adolescents. My ex-girlfriend contacted me out of the blue some weeks later and with a truly shocking message, she had done the worst thing she possibly could. She had written to David Gedge from the Wedding Present and told him how awful I was. A charity gig back home at the temporarily repurposed Ritzy nightclub in Doncaster would afford me the opportunity to let John Peel's favourite writer of love songs know that I wasn't a bad person. Steeling myself and catching a moment at the merchandise table I hurriedly tried to explain the situation. He stopped me mid-flow and simply said, 'Every story has two sides', with a gracious nod. I was absolved. I remember that moment vividly. As one relationship ended a new one formed a seminal moment – the first time that I saw CUD at the Toby Jug. I had first heard their first LP, *When in Rome, Kill Me*, at my mate Simon Cooper's house party when I was seventeen. Some cool older music fans turned up (they were possibly eighteen), they were fans of CUD, and they were from Leeds. To an innocent chap from Doncaster this was the big time. I imagine Simon's memory of the event is different as his parents knew nothing about the party. I went to see him the next day and found him snipping out chewing gum from a section of luxuriant gold shag-pile carpet leaving an obvious bald patch. CUD and other underground bands like the Family Cat and Ned's Atomic Dustbin were, in 1990, foundational and fundamental. Given the intimacy of the space, they were there for us and were playing for us. Some weeks later I saw Carl Puttnam, vocalist of CUD, in the Toby Jug playing pool in a white leather jacket and brothel creepers and I nearly fainted. The devoted fanbase that exists to this day was forged in those moment and in those spaces and continues to this day. The familiarity of the space sweeps that way in favour of something that remains within touching distance. There is, then, an intangible quality about these spaces and their effect on those who understand their unwritten rules; there is something in the air.

Toilet venues reek of authenticity. In established venues this isn't merely a result of history. In 'newer' venues this isn't a mock authenticity or a simulacrum. It is the fabric of the venues that dictates the authentic; these are spaces that have longevity and history to them. This is akin to the discussion of the Arctic Monkeys and the music and video of 'I Bet You Look Good on the Dancefloor' by Mark Fisher. Written in 2013, this piece is typically prescient in terms of the stadium concert behemoth the band became and the 'rock star grunge' associations they forged with Josh Homme. It predicts their self-conscious 1970s nostalgia with *Tranquillity Base Hotel and Casino* in 2018, and 2022's *The Car* sounds like it will follow the same trend. However, in the moment of the recording of their early work there is a question as to whether the setting for their videos with their new wave sound is 'retro' (with all the implications of a conscious look backwards). It would be easy to accept an imperialist history of popular music where Britpop (as an arch and theatrical form) swept away all that went before, using intertextual references clearly and consciously (Oasis with The Beatles, Suede with Bowie, etc.). Many of these bands appeared influenced by the toilet venue scene but were catapulted quickly to the dizzying heights of academies, university refectories or even Knebworth. My partner grew up just far enough away from London to make travelling into the city a difficult exercise and then went to university in a town with no venues. Her experience of live music was the Arena and the festival, and of bands when they had reached the dizzying heights of stardom. Her experience of Pulp was at Glastonbury or Roundhay Park, and my comment that I'd missed seeing them at the Adelphi was met with incredulity (Shelton 2015).

As a student in Hull, I quickly discovered the varied music and club scene, at that time very varied. Steve Lamacq recently commented that 'Hull is overflowing with groups' and this has been true for many years (Lamacq 2017). One toilet venue stands out above all others: the New Adelphi Club. Trying to find the fabled Adelphi was initially tricky. From the street it looks like a small house next to a World War 2 bomb site. This is largely due to it being a small house next to a World War 2 bomb site which now functions as a car park. I first walked in there in 1991; inhaling deeply, I knew exactly where I was. The aesthetic runs deep, a fact that is attested to in the title of the comprehensive history of the New Adelphi Club, *One Man and His Bog* (Smith 2003). Sometime in the mid-1990s the Adelphi Club was renovated (slightly) and the toilets were moved from the side of the stage to now be accessed via a corridor at the side. Seemingly within minutes, someone had crept in and started bravely plastering the high cistern and the urinals with obscure band stickers. I think there may be an anarcho-syndicalist bathroom fitter that kits out venues with pre-stickered fittings; the para-booted plumbers stepping back and admiring their work before slipping a handful of fag-ends carefully in each urinal.

On 19 March 2017, my partner and I saw the Senseless Things play at the Adelphi Club in Hull. When I bought the tickets, I realised that it was almost twenty-five years to the day that I had last seen them in the same venue. I hadn't been back to the Adelphi Club for some years. My partner had never been there before, only knowing it through gig listings. Her surprise at the size, volume and peeling paint was palpable. I quashed her concern for the place with a reassuring note that this was how it had looked for years and it was unlikely the fabric of the building would collapse. It seems that even to the initiated there are some venues that are more toilet than others. Fighting my way to the bar I edged past Ben Harding and what looked like Myles Howell from Kingmaker. Sweat already running down the walls, I looked up at the sound guy stood at the raised mixing desk at the back. 'Hello', he said. 'Hello Jim', I replied. Time had stood still. The intervening years were simply a hiatus and my return there an inevitability. The Senseless Things may have themselves gone on hiatus a couple of decades before, the band members playing with other notable groups (Three Colours Red, Deadcuts, Gorillaz, Muse) but this was too was temporary; they were destined to be back together and back in the Adelphi (Edgar 2019: 14). They were back as if they had never been away. The whole gig is available on YouTube,[2] and you can make out a

2. See https://www.youtube.com/watch?v=QTTeP-LLQ08. This reunion tour is particularly notable as shortly afterwards, in 2021, singer and guitarist Mark Keds sadly passed away, leaving the band forever frozen in time.

well-oiled punter at the front who within seconds of the music starting, took off his shirt and made as if he were going to stage dive. An act that is impossible in that 'intimate' venue, although I have seen people try to do it. I saw CUD perform in the Adelphi just before lockdown in 2020. The same inebriated erstwhile stage diver was at the front, doing what he does at every gig.

As the great Paul Jackson, founder of the venue, commented on receipt of his Music Venue Trust award in 2019, 'on the 1st October I will have completed a 35 years stretch at the helm of my strange but wonderful music venue which has the distinction of looking like a derelict building, both outside and in. Though I have endured numerous periods of being thrown against the wall by officials, I have genuinely loved my work [...] I see my work as being a crusade against mediocrity in music' (Jackson 2019). My most enduring memory of Jacko is him swooping into the toilets (in the Adelphi's original layout for the aficionado) and scooping out the cigarette butts from a blocked urinal with nothing but a handful of paper towels for protection. You have to admire his dedication. To protect itself for the future, the Adelphi has become a place of community significance with Jarvis Cocker as a patron. In return for the favour, Paul Jackson has Jarvis (and Mark E. Smith) pickled in demi johns on the bar.

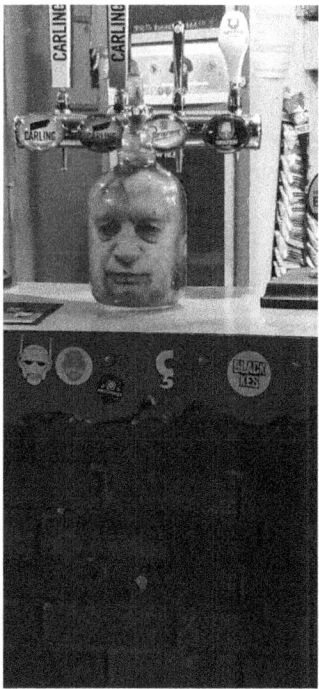

Figure 3.1: Beer taps (photo by author)

The iconic status of the Adelphi is due to its eclecticism as much as to its association with significant musicians and bands – the sort that would now be broadly categorised as post-punk. I have seen Kelzmer bands, comedians, Bill Drummond shining shoes and I even chose it as a location for a performance of a new play as part of the Hull Literature Festival in 2005. Some bands are more recognisable from the toilet venue scene, perhaps carrying the trace memory of an audience who recall them working through those spaces, 'working the circuit'. As economic pressures bite, bands' touring has changed. The increasing popularity (and touring affordability) of acoustic shows utilise the intimacy afforded by many of these venues as well as bringing big acts to intimate spaces. In 2010, I saw CUD play at the Irish Centre in Leeds and some bloke walked past me who looked just like Miles Hunt from the Wonder Stuff. It transpired that it was Miles Hunt from the Wonder Stuff who was providing acoustic support. I nearly fainted.

In 2020 the New Adelphi Club, alongside many other venues, started selling specially commissioned t-shirts and gig posters from iconic performances throughout their history. These artefacts unquestionably feed nostalgia but there is a question about whether it supports a sense of cultural heritage alone. The venue is still there, and the posters have been produced to maintain the existence of the venue given what it currently stands for in its cultural positioning and in terms of contemporary music. Occasionally photographs appear of finely drawn gig listings on the pages of the customary Adelphi Facebook group; a couple of years ago one from 1993 jogged my memory. Emblazoned at the top of the listing was an announcement of local favourites and 'innovative Sheffield package' Pulp who 'looked like they were about to hit the big time'. More than twenty-five years after I first attended the Adelphi my partner and I were sat with a couple of friends, one of whom was an old university acquaintance. I mentioned the poster. 'Great gig', commented my friend, only to be confronted by my blank look. 'Don't you remember chatting to Jarvis in the front bar?' My partner nearly fainted. The frailty of memory evidenced; I spent the rest of the weekend with my popularity somewhat compromised. I doubt I will ever receive absolution.

Figure 3.2: Pulp ad (photo by author)

Many venues have been lost and further economic problems on the horizon mean that the threat remains. As soon as lockdown was relaxed, I was straight back to the Crescent in York and the Brudenell in Leeds amongst many other venues and have been ever since, either watching a performance or sat in the front bar. It doesn't necessarily matter which venue; the rules apply regardless. The man in the specs is still at the front at the Brudenell. Whilst this semi-compulsion isn't really a case of nostalgia, I can deny that there will be, at some point during the evening, a need to visit the facilities and with it a sickly-sweet Proustian rush.

References

Baldwin, Matthew, and Lucas Keefer. 2020. 'Being here and now: The benefits of belonging in space and time'. *Journal of Happiness Studies* 21: 3069–3093.

Edgar, Robert. 2019. 'Hiatus: Music, Memory and Liminal Authenticity'. In *Music, Memory and Memoir*, ed. Robert Edgar, Fraser Mann and Helen Pleasance, 13–24. New York: Bloomsbury.

Hitters, Arno van der Hoeven, and Erik Hitters. 2020. 'The spatial value of live music: Performing, (re)developing and narrating urban spaces'. *Geoforum* 117: 154–164.

Jackson, Paul. 2019. 'MVT's Outstanding Achievement Award 2019 won by Paul Jackson of The New Adelphi Club, Hull!' *Music Venue Trust*. http://musicvenuetrust.com/2019/10/mvts-outstanding-achievement-award-2019-won-by-paul-jackson-of-the-new-adelphi-club-hull/

Lamacq, Steve. 2017. 'Music interview'. *Yorkshire Evening Post*, 12 January. https://www.yorkshireeveningpost.co.uk/whats-on/arts-and-entertainment/music-interview-steve-lamacq-of-bbc-6-music-to-broadcast-from-brudenell-social-club-leeds-607747

Schofield, John, and Dan Miller. 2017. 'The "toilet circuit": Cultural production, fandom and heritage in England's small music venues'. *Heritage and Society* 9, no. 2: 137–167.

Senseless Things – Reunion Warm Up Gig, Hull Adelphi, 19/03/17. 19 March 2017. https://www.youtube.com/watch?v=QTTeP-LLQ08

Shelton, Julia. 2015. 'Rocking around Watford: Trying to find what I was looking for'. In *The Arena Concert: Music, Media and Mass Entertainment*, ed. Benjamin Halligan, Kirsty Fairclough, Robert Edgar and Nicola Spelman, 181–92. New York: Bloomsbury.

Smith, Ian. 2003. *One Man and His Bog*. Hull.

Taylor, Iain A., Sarah Raine and Craig Hamilton. 2021. 'Crisis as a catalyst for change: COVID-19, spatiality and the UK live music industry'. *IASPM Journal* 10, no. 1: 6–21.

Author biography

Robert Edgar is Professor of Writing and Popular Culture in the York Centre for Writing based in the School of Humanities at York St John University, UK. His publications include *Screenwriting* (Bloomsbury, 2009), *Directing Fiction* (Bloomsbury, 2009), *The Language of Film* (Bloomsbury, 2010 and 2015), *The*

Music Documentary (Routledge, 2013), *The Arena Concert* (Bloomsbury, 2015), *Music, Memory and Memoir* (Bloomsbury, 2019), *Adaptation for Scriptwriters* (Bloomsbury, 2019), and *Thomas Hardy and the Folk Horror Tradition* (2023). He is co-editing the *Routledge Companion to Folk Horror* (2023) and *Horrifying Children: Hauntology and the Legacy of Children's Fiction* (Bloomsbury, 2024).

4 Fascinating Rhythms

Beth Hughes

Eyes closed to enhance the beat. I feel my body responding to the music, guided by its rhythm. One ripple in a sea of others, I raise my hands and move in time. Above, a mirror ball twinkles, catching the reflections of the disco lights. They dance rebelliously upon the bunting strung either side of the dance floor. The DJ bends over his decks, head bobbing to the music. Seamlessly, he transitions the Stone Roses' 'Waterfall' into the Pixies' 'Debaser'. Woohoo! This is me at my happiest: liberated, elated and dancing. Completely lost in the moment. It's always been this way.

Well, maybe not quite *always*.

Everyone remembers their first encounter with a nightclub, right? Rewind a few (ahem!) years: Germany, 1988. On a school exchange trip, Mic-Mac nightclub, Bergen, offered my first taste of nights out. In stripy tops, tailored jackets and double denim, we shuffled stilettoed heels to the strains of Tiffany, Falco and S'Express, sipping Coca-Cola from glass tankards. At some point, as the crowd on the dancefloor grew, I managed to lose my inhibitions and somehow forge a bond that would last a lifetime … Me, a DJ and a beat: life-shaping.

A Box of Firsts (York, 1992)

Torrents of students cover the concourse – indie kids, grungers, goths, crusties, rockers, ravers and '80s throwbacks. Locked in animated conversation, they sit at tables, on tables, under tables, in between tables or stand around in groups. From the adjoining dining room, an occasional blast of music drifts through. The DJs are sound checking. This is the ubiquitous university bop – and at York, there's one for pretty much every night of the week. Forming the backbone of our social lives, we have no cause to go anywhere else.

We walk to the bar, sidestepping army boots, cherry-red Doc Martens, Converse One Stars and the occasional Jesus sandal. Drinks in hand, we merge into the crowd: kindred spirits.

The lights dim. The beat breaks through. Time to start the party. 50p and a stamped hand later, we're in. Dining room by day; bop space by night, the hall is high ceilinged and spacious. Already it's packed. People dance in groups, in pairs, and alone. Jumping, shuffling, shape throwing, shoe gazing. Bobbing heads form disjointed lines over the dancefloor, some with hair violently swishing from side to side. As Cobain's naked vocals fill the room, a mosh pit forms near the DJ. In the rising temperature, grungers throw themselves towards one another, revelling in the moment. There's energy – a rawness that penetrates and carries. It feels like we're part of something unique.

This place is a box of firsts: it's the location of my first meeting with my husband-to-be (married 15 years later); the first time I hear Nirvana – the distorted riff of 'Smells like Teen Spirit' reverberating and holding the air; and the first place I really feel the music as I dance – every note lifting me higher and higher.

Indie-pendent Retro-suiting (York, mid-1990s)

Dark walls damp with condensation line this underground labyrinth of nooks and crannies. The cloying scent of vanilla tobacco catches my nose; it will linger tomorrow. A mirror along the corridor displays my hazy reflection – hair – Björked – twisted into tiny buns dotted around my head, and a dress of silver-grey satin, paired with green Converse trainers.

After the summer of my second year, there's a shift, a change. Perhaps encouraged by DJ friends who have recently started up student nights, there's a pull towards town: York beckons. We spread our wings and fly. Toff's Tuesdays and Ziggy's Wednesdays become tradition. Slipping though the throng, we make our way to a corner spot, where friends have grabbed a table. Our coats are added to the pile that is fast becoming a mountain. Squished up against one another, we slug Moscow Mules and Hooch alcopops, and chair-dance in anticipation of *that* tune that will get us up.

The opening riff to Sleeper's 'Inbetweener' cuts through the club. It's on my weekly request list (and yes, tonight is no exception). As the drums kick in, I'm there, dragging a bunch of my friends with me. I love this tune – it's punchy, uplifting, a stark warning of what not to become. Shouting the lyrics to one other, we melt into its melody. And we stay – during Blur's 'Parklife', The Levellers' 'Fifteen Years', Oasis's 'Supersonic', Ini Kamoze's 'Here Comes the Hotstepper' – enjoying the release the music brings.

11pm, we flit from room to room, switching between genres – indie, grunge, dance and, of course, Britpop, whose birth has spawned a pastiche of distinctive lookalikes. With Jarvis retro-suiting and Frischman haircuts, they strut their stuff – Gallagher swaggers perfected – mingling with rockers and ravers. Britpop rides on the wave of Cool Britannia – *Trainspotting*, ladette culture and the girl power of the Spice Girls. In a couple of years, Labour will celebrate its 1997 landslide victory to the tune of D:Ream. It's a great time to be young in Britain. Change is afoot and we feel it. There's a buzz, an uncontained excitement and that reflects in how we party.

Arches of Consciousness (York, mid-1990s)

An indie kid at heart, dance music holds very little interest for me. I mean, I dance to music – just not of the electronic type. Tonight, however, my friend Cate's DJ boyfriend is playing a set at a place in town – and I've agreed to go.

We queue outside the Arts Centre, arms linked to share warmth. The November air is cold, the whisper of our breaths visible under the pool of orange streetlight. This had better be worth it.

'One in; one out,' the doorman says. 'It's full to bursting in there'.

From where we wait, we can hear the fun. Loud chatter and occasional cries of glee emanate through the old church's doorway – wedged open, despite the cold. The first set is in full swing and its steady beat wends its way to our feet outside. Tap, tap, tap, tap. Even the windows buzz in time, their stained glass responding to the echoes of house, fuelling our anticipation.

Inside, the vibe is chilled. Eclectic beats and deep, dirty basslines attract a bunch of regulars. I know some of them from Uni. They're a close knit, underground, dance family. At the bar and around Formica tables, they cluster, chatting, drinking, swapping jokes. The dress code is mixed: Boho-casual – dyed hair, plaited hair, long 'just-got-out-of-bed' hair, jeans, slogan emblazoned t-shirts or long, patterned dresses; Grunge – ponytails, combats, band t-shirts and Doc Marten boots; Distinctly Designer – Calvin Klein, Boss, crisp coloured shirts, beanie hats and slinky dresses – all, of course, dressed down with Nikes; and Fancy Dress – cavorting cowboys, fantabulous fairies – even Elvis makes an appearance!

In the adjoining room, the tempo switches as the second set begins. The melodic tones of trance waft through: ambient and hypnotic. We wander over.

Beneath double-chamfered arches, a hazy fog of dry ice, fags and weed drifts, fragmenting the light. I lean against a pillar, watching the strobes' partial distortion, how their rays douse in light, then just as quickly, cast in shadow. The stone feels cold against my back – I hadn't realised how warm I'd become.

On the dancefloor, a girl in a long purple dress sways from side to side, moving in perfect time. With exaggerated gestures and laughter, a couple – she with short pink hair, he with dreadlocks – walk to the beat, circling each other. Others stand on the dancefloor's periphery, pints in hand, heads nodding. The mood is mellow; waves caressing a shoreline, the calm before the storm.

As the pace builds, the crowd grows. A meandering river that ebbs and flows. And it catches me. Mid-track, there's a lull – a moment of loaded quiet – the beat breaks, then builds, increasing in volume. Moments later we join the dancers, feeling a compulsion to be part of this. The tendrils of trance wrap and cocoon. The music fills the church, travelling upwards and out to the sides, spreading and commandeering every inch of space. As it rises, so do my arms: it consumes me, controls me. Surrounded by smiling faces, I let it. As one, the room moves – the pulsing heart of this cavernous chamber. I haven't experienced this before, this state of euphoric trance. This intensity.

A short while later, I sit on the closed lid of the toilet seat, sipping water. The window's open and a breeze filters through. Outside, the distant rumble of traffic is punctuated with cheering and occasional bursts of laughter. The voice of a girl shouts, 'Get me a kebab. A donner. Large one, with extra chilli sauce'. It feels surreal to hear noises of life outside the womb of the Arts Centre.

When I return ten minutes later, the pace has really picked up. At the helm is Matt, Cate's DJ boyfriend. She dances at his side. With kicking beats of techno house he steers, whipping the crowd into a delirious state of crazy. One tune follows another. The dancefloor is now packed.

Then it comes – a dirty bass line – deep, acidic, intense. Josh Wink's 'Higher State of Consciousness' (the Tweekin' Acid Funk Mix). It starts as a rumble, a beat in the pit of the stomach. A voice, distorted and guttural, seeps into the soul. A break-beating acid base pulls forward, with rash, unrestrained impulsiveness. I follow. It's a ride I can't get off. I don't want to. It's frenzied; I feel every beat, every note. The tune builds to a crescendo – cacophonous layers drawing towards an awe-inspiring climax. I'm buzzing! What a choon!

Four years from now, the Arts Centre, beset by financial difficulties, will close its doors for the last time. It has played a pivotal role for thirty years, enabling opportunities, facilitating friendships and shaping lives. When they sell the building on, remodelling its historical features, tampering with its unique charm, they strip it of its personality, leaving it devoid of soul.

Yet for a while, within its hallowed walls, it felt like God really was a DJ.

Charterhouse Street (London: New Year's Eve, 2000)

Early noughties: the continued era of the Superstar DJ. Glitz and glamour thread through the London club scene. Clubbers want to see and be seen. In their thousands they amass, paying well to hear the live curations of celebrity DJs such as Judge Jules, Paul Oakenfold, Lisa Lashes, Roger Sanchez and Carl Cox. Fatboy Slim recently gathered in the region of 60,000 revellers to his first Big Beach Boutique in Brighton – a resounding success. The next year, however, it all goes a bit Pete Tong, and some worry that it is no longer about the music. Fabric, located in London's edgy Farringdon, is set up to counter this.

In a building formerly used for meat storage, a club is born – one that ignores trends, instead focusing on creating an environment to play the kind of progressive electronica that speaks to them.

I stand in a queue outside it now. The building towers above us, several storeys high. Under a doorway flanked by wide pillars, door staff check tickets, watched over by stone lion heads which protrude from the columns above. The queue moves quickly. Indistinct chatter emanates from inside, overlaid by pulsating beats.

We're separated as soon as we hit the entrance – two directed one way; two the other. Following the curve of the banister upstairs, we bend to the right, expecting to reunite with our friends. No such luck. A wall greets us.

The club is heaving; people close in on every side. There are three dancefloors to explore. As the two of us navigate the labyrinth, we hold hands, knowing if we separate, we may not find each other again. It's minimal, dirty, underground. Exposed brick walls and metal railings exude an urban-industrial vibe with echoes of 1980s warehouse raves. Between rooms, we DJ hop: Craig Richards, Terry Francis, Scratch Perverts and Doc Martin. Hip hop, deep house, tech house, genre-defying mixes, intergalactic space metal and funky basslines with acidic bites. We want to experience them all. Under minimal lighting which shrouds in blue, the DJs play out to an up-for-it crowd. There's no holding back. They've come for one thing and one thing only. Rave rules here. We slip into the surf, taking in the atmosphere. It's buzzing and everyone's so friendly.

In the toilets, fragments of conversation drift.

'He keeps smiling at me. Shall I go for it?'

'Bloody hell. I'm wasted'.

'I've lost it. I had it in my pocket'.

As we re-emerge, we pass a seating area. In corners of darkness, people sit, whispering, kissing, caught up in the lure of the moment. More stairs, another room and we hit the dancefloor. Every beat sends a tremor through my body – I feel it in my legs, along my spine, and all the way up to my head and where my arms punch the air. This is Fabric's infamous bodysonic dancefloor, the first in Europe. Controlled through the bass, low frequencies transmit as vibrations via the dancers' feet into their bodies. I fully feel their effects. Every sense is awakened. Every part of me absorbed by the beat. Looking around, others are too.

The tempo drops, there's a countdown. 10. 9. 8, 7 – it's loud; I've never spent New Year in such a busy place – 6, 5, 4, 3, 2, 1, HAPPY NEW YEAR! We erupt in cheers, shouts. I can no longer see the DJ platform, so many are the raised arms. Then through the sound system comes the unmistakable pulse of Kylie Minogue's 'Can't Get You Out of My Head'. We welcome it with roars of delight, letting its catchy 'la la la' hook carry us higher and higher.

The Beat Goes On (London, early noughties)

Friends of friends are DJs, playing regular sets in and around the capital. Many venues they play in are small, dark spaces. This one lies down a back street in Islington; a pub, sandwiched between a takeaway and a betting shop. We're late and the party's been going a while. As we near, we hear the beat. Windows are open with punters loitering outside, smoking and drinking.

Inside is dimly lit – disco lights hang above the DJ booth, rope lights at the bar. Smoke hovers like mist in the air. Through its amorphous wisps, figures move, silhouetted against ethereal blue. Slipping through the crowd, we get drinks and catch up with friends, who've bagsied a table.

An eclectic mix blasts out – soul, hip hop and techno, with occasional unexpected gems slipped in. The crowd is edgy, bohemian and determined to have fun. Two DJs spin a combination of carefully selected tracks, considering impact, gauging mood. Enthralled, I watch them in action – hands sliding over controls, one tune melting into the next.

As the evening progresses, they ramp up the volume … and techno grips. It urges, it feeds, imbibed by the crowd. Movements become more pronounced, more frantic. Dancefloor faces are fully absorbed in the music – some gurning under the influence of mind-enhancing drugs. In this compelling synthesis of body and sound, there's a distinct lack of pretension. For the hard-core crowd of regulars, these nights are a way of life; an extended family; a home away from home; and part of a culture that has become their normal. With roots in the rave scene of the early '90s, these clubbers are the now thirty-something generation who threw shapes within the revered halls of Manchester's Hacienda, climbed over the fencing to get into Glastonbury, smoked spliffs for breakfast and protested against the Criminal Justice Bill. They transcend the encroaching tropes of middle age. And the party doesn't stop here; it merely changes.

5 o'clock in the morning: the after party. I'm in the living room of a house near Brixton. Drum and bass thrums from the decks in the kitchen. Through

the open doorway, Jez and Tanya jest with DJ friends. They've been dancing pretty much non-stop since early evening yesterday and show no signs of tiring. Other people sit on cushions strewn around the room or chill out on one of the two sofas. Empty cans of lager and bottles of wine litter the coffee table, in its middle a half-eaten bowl of cheesy Wotsits that someone poured lemonade over to see if they would float.

'Thing is,' Maz is saying. 'Thing is [...] you see [...] Jaffa Cakes have different layers – there's one for everyone'.

'You're talking bollocks. It's Hob Nobs. All the way. They dunk and soften. What more do you need?'

'Dunk and dissolve, more like! Jaffas are one of your five a day, mate'.

'You're 'aving a laugh [...]'

In the kitchen, the scent of percolating coffee permeates. I pour myself one then head outside. Dawn's light grazes the skyline nipping at early morning. People sit in deckchairs wrapped in coats and blankets, smoking and chatting. Tobacco smoke mingles with the distinctive whiff of weed. Sometimes these after parties last a whole weekend – people coming and going, transitioning from one house to another. There's dancing, tripping and stumbling, banter, camaraderie, talk about the night before, loved-up hugs, secrets spilled. And a constant beat – which goes on and on.

Around 6:30am, a crimson line appears on the horizon. Pushing up, it ripples across the sky, merging with layers of mauve and cerise. Cerise becomes peach before spreading as ribbons of amber. They lace and embroider. Next, a glimmer – ochre, intense. We watch as the sun escapes, bathing the city in a golden glow. Day is upon us. Yet we don't feel tired at all.

Escapees (York, now)

Eyes closed to enhance the beat. I feel my body responding to the music, guided by its rhythm. One ripple in a sea of others, I raise my hands and move in time: happy, liberated, dancing.

After London and Brighton, I'd moved back to York in 2006 to find the cityscape changed. Bars and trendy cafés had sprung up across the city, attracting a wide clientele. The cluster of streets and lanes in and around Swinegate were now rebranded as The Quarter and the so-called Micklegate Run now extended all the way into town. Tourism had risen significantly which, although great for York's economy and its beautiful diversity of visitors, also brought problems. Homogenous weekends saw a more than generous splattering of hen and stag parties. Although the music scene still thrived, clubs as I'd known them were gone. Small pockets of pleasure could still be found but, with the exception of my kitchen, I was missing a dance home. 'Come to Escape Club,' my friend had said. 'It's in a working men's club. You'll love it – it's your sort of thing'. Working men's clubs and 'my sort of thing' hadn't necessarily been a combination I'd come across before. But rarely one to refuse a dance, I'd decided to give it a go.

The building sat on the road behind the former Odeon cinema, at the end of a tall row of Victorian terraces. From the outside, its split façade was nothing special – red brick upper floors rested over a rendered, cream coloured ground floor which had the distinct air of a 1970s refurbishment. A green sign announced CRESCENT W.M.C. Beneath it, a ramp led up to a plain set of double doors beyond which a handful of older men sat clustered around laminate tables. Clasping pints of lager, they watched a darts tournament on TV whilst a lone member of staff poured a drink for a waiting punter. This was pretty much what I expected of a working men's club but not the night we'd been promised.

To my left, a door opened. Through it, drifted the dying notes of The Smiths' 'What Difference Does it Make'. On the other side a bloke stood at a table, taking money. We paid; he stamped our hands. Then we stepped beyond.

Old Skool reverberated around the room, with forgotten classics from the likes of New Order, The Cure, Depeche Mode transporting me back to the early '90s days of sixth form parties and Uni bops. Disco lights played around the darkened room, casting subtle shades of pink and blue upon the bunting which hung high across the dancefloor. Below, people danced – I mean *really* danced. No posing. No judgement. No pretence. Escape's dress code seemed to be wear whatever you want and (by extension) dance as you want, be who you want. We quickly became converts.

Our friends soon become as addicted as we were. Some affectionately call it 'Middle Aged Disco'. Yet once every couple of months, it feels like we're twenty-something again. It's become something to get excited about, a highlight, a regular social event, *une raison de danser*. Tonight, it's at York's Guildhall, formerly a fifteenth-century meeting place for the city's artisans and merchants. As parents with a distinct lack of pamper time, we've mastered the get-ready-in-ten-minutes challenge. Dress and trainers for me; jeans and t-shirt for him. Babysitters instated, we meet friends at 7pm and head to a city bar. Just after 8, we leave for our ball!

Entrance to the Guildhall is via a wooden gated archway, to the right of Mansion House: the Lord Mayor's official residence. This gate is rarely open – it's hard not to feel excited as we walk down the passage beyond. It's also hard not to be impressed by what we find within the hall. Through an arched doorway, it stretches, long yet not especially thin. We walk under a high vaulted, oak ceiling, supported by two rows of marble pillars which rest on carved stone pedestals. To either side, huge stone windows rise, encasing small panes of leaden framed glass within a latticework of decorative stone. At the far end, backlit by the setting sun, hangs a large, stained-glass window. Through it, streams light, throwing a spectrum of colours into the hall. Below, old meets new, where the DJ booth – Shedonism – sits bedecked in fairy lights. Escape's DJs are chatting within. We wave our hellos and choose our table.

Gradually, it gets darker and the hall fills up. Since its launch, Escape's popularity has increased hugely, mainly through word of mouth. Set lists cover a range of musicians. Not atypical would be Basement Jaxx, Primal Scream, Daft Punk, James Brown, M.I.A., Donna Summer, Groove Armada, The Prodigy, Kraftwerk, Pulp, Underworld, Chemical Brothers, Hot Chip, Stone Roses, The Rolling Stones, The Breeders, as well as occasional splashes of northern soul. Soon the place is a melting pot of activity. And we're in the middle of it. Strobes sweep the room, silhouetting a myriad of dancing figures.

I see a mum friend I haven't seen socially for a while, who shouts, 'I'm out. Look. Pinch me – I'm here!' Another friend, previously an Escape virgin, can't believe how good it is. We sit at the side, chilling out for a while. Perhaps my friend A sums it up the best when she says, 'Escape is just that – a place to escape to, somewhere I leave it all behind to get on that dancefloor and just be me'.

And that makes me think ... From waterlogged floors and sticky seats to euphoric trance and pumping beats, I can't accurately recall the number of clubs I've visited in my life. Yet experiences in these venues help shape us, facilitate friendships, develop our sense of community, invite us in to share something. Each one unique, each one leaving us with a polaroid: a kaleidoscope of places, people, DJs, fashion and music, imprinted in our memories for ever.

So I'm returning now. With my tribe. Back to our spot by the DJ booth. At midnight, this will end. The dying chords of 'I Am the Resurrection' will subside then dissipate. We'll thank the DJs, gather our coats and leave. Not very rock 'n' roll! There are no after parties now. Just chips with lashings of mayonnaise.

Author biography

A recent graduate of York St John University's MA in Creative Writing, **Beth Hughes** is preparing to unleash her first novel on the world. A self-confessed bibliophile with a passion for cooking, she lives in York with her husband, two sons and limitless imagination. An avid partaker of the dance, for Beth, the music never stops.

5 The Bull and Gate, Kentish Town, London, 1987–1989

Polly Hancock

Smaller independent venues are often referred to as 'the toilet circuit' – which is odd because none of them seemed to boast an especially spectacular one. I suppose they could have just as easily been called the 'promoter's dog is asleep on the stage circuit'[1] or even 'the neighbouring taxi firm's radio comes over the PA system circuit',[2] but that would only refer to one particular venue at a time.

Playing gigs around the UK in the late 1980s was a game of rock and roll roulette. Venues could often be intimidating places; sometimes damp, always dark, and often staffed by those who might possibly consider themselves unemployable in any other circumstances. In a world before Arts Administration degrees or health and safety standards, we were all just making it up.

These post-punk venues were cobbled together in the back rooms, basements or the first floors of pubs. Hidden spaces, that seemed like afterthoughts. Rooms that, in their heyday, had hosted family functions with tables laid for blushing brides or grieving widows. Later, these back rooms became the domain of pub bands whose rocking blues jam sessions and Canvey Island twang had, by the 1980s, fallen out of favour. These venues were now in demand by a younger crowd who, inspired by punk, had decided to do it themselves. On the surface, it was all small promoters in miserable venues putting on unheard-of bands for niche crowds and no money. But for anyone who was part of that world, it felt life changing.

These back rooms were altered to accommodate a PA system and a stage, but often still had the hallmarks of the previous pub room incarnation; flock wallpaper now worn thin, its pile scratched off, leaving bare patches and grease stains now a permanent part of the décor. The remnants of the once fashionable and dainty candle bulb light fittings still poked out from the worn-out wallpaper but lacked shades or even bulbs. Whatever the degree

1. The Adelphi in Hull, UK.
2. The Boardwalk in Manchester, UK.

of recent modifications, twenty years of nicotine always laid its greasy veneer over everything. In all these rooms there seemed to be an unmistakable tinge of sadness, and a shiver of a dank, forsaken, unloved space.

The Bull and Gate could easily have been exactly like this, and probably had been in the years before 1979 when the Lynskey family moved in.

Behind the Victorian frontage that hinted at the pub's gin palace past, the Bull and Gate on Kentish Town Road in North London was another pub that had turned its hand to hosting bands. The Lynskeys, Pat and Margaret, liked their pub on the traditional side, which meant engraved mirror backs to the bar, rows of optics, lots of polished wood and furniture heavy enough that it couldn't easily be thrown.

In 1986 Jon Beast had convinced them to let him take over some of the live music nights in the back room. He already had experience in running shows at venues like the Red Rose in Finsbury Park and The Clarendon in Hammersmith but was now looking for somewhere more permanent. Underneath all his exterior bluster and enthusiasm, Jon was quite sensible, he knew how to talk to people and could get things done. Firstly, in an effort to impress, he would have blinded them with a rapid succession of band names, record companies and personal contacts, none of whom they would have heard of. He would have flummoxed them with facts and figures and would have finally charmed them by repeating it all in a way that they would understand. He once told me that he would always refer to any sort of drugs as 'pot' in front of the Lynskeys because that's what he thought they would call them. When he was on form, Jon could persuade anybody of anything; trees were blue, the sky was green, and the new PA system wouldn't be much louder than the one you have in there now.

So, in 1986 the back room of the Bull and Gate became home to the Timebox. Repainted and with a new PA system, it would be the first time the pub had hosted indie bands, and certainly the first time that the Lynskeys had encountered anything like Jon's trademark approach to live music promotion. By the following year, the Timebox was a central pillar of London's indie scene, mostly due to Jon and his infectious, raging enthusiasm. Some weeks it seemed that almost half of the live reviews in that week's *NME* or *Melody Maker* were from Timebox gigs, featuring bands like We Are Going To Eat You, Soho, Zodiac Motel and Junior Manson Slags. Rock journalist, Mick Mercer, remembers.

> Until the Timebox, there was nothing modern going on there [Bull and Gate] and so there was no reason to go. Jon made it a fun, weird place, and I think if there's a degree of humour, then that creates a

charm. There was nothing like that happening in any of the other venues. They probably even had the same bands, but there was no character. (Author interview, 23 February 2021)

What was different about Jon's whole approach was that not only did he genuinely love the music, but he also loved the fun that was to be had in redefining what a small venue could be. His endless chatter and ideas were reflected in everything he produced; from the listings through to his hastily constructed and never quite finished record label, Timebox Records. His photocopied missives were always peppered with news of 'secret gigs' and 'more information to follow' often alongside purposefully childish drawings of himself with the word 'fat' scrawled across the belly. Like we were in any doubt who it was supposed to be. It wasn't long before the 'fat' image and the ongoing self-publicity extended to the stage, and the arrival of his own band, Brian. The premise was that Brian were 'crap' and were always the fixed winners of the occasional Timebox 'No Talent Contest'. These were the evenings where he would fill the bill with other bands that he also thought were 'crap'. He was quite honest about it, and so it became 'a thing', almost a badge of honour to be asked to play. Brian's line-up consisted of guitarist and flatmate Sean, Contenders' bassist Jeff, and whoever else Jon could rope in to make a noise. The songs were bad cover versions that Jon would yelp out half naked from the front of the stage while covering himself in whatever he could find in the convenience shop next door: flour, cleaning items, baked beans and shaving foam. Musician, Gem Archer, recalls: 'It was embarrassing. Do you remember when he ended up in casualty from tipping Fairy Liquid all over himself and getting burns on his back and neck?' (Author interview, 18 January 2021)

Despite this, and Jon's sometimes maddening approach to gig promoting, his ideas and energy elevated the Timebox to a runaway train of up-and-coming bands, some of whom, like All About Eve and Voice of the Beehive, were already on their way to bigger and better things. It was so popular, so successful, and so brilliant, that by the end of 1987 he decided to close it down.

As of January 1988, the Timebox became HYPE, undergoing a sort of Dr Who style regeneration. Still based in the same back room of the Bull and Gate, HYPE was to be Jon's upgraded vision for a new kind of indie club. Instead of the forlorn pub space and the kind of derelict chic upon which he built the Timebox, Jon wanted to spruce up the space and introduce new elements to give both bands and gig goers a fun, sensory overload from the moment they stepped through the door. He went into full Willy Wonka mode.

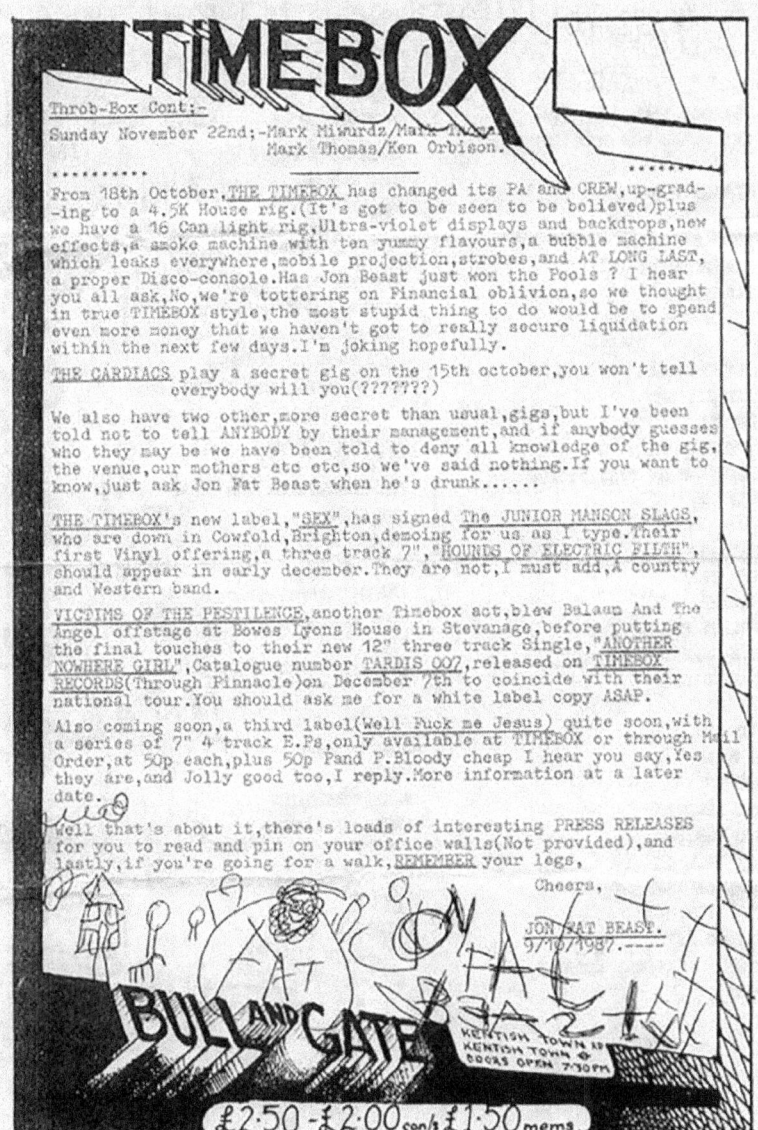

Figure 5.1: Timebox listings handout (photo by author)

The entrance corridor was repainted black, chequered with mirrors, and ultraviolet lights replaced the previously harsh, bright fluorescent tubes. With bubbles, a smoke machine and a bank of flickering televisions installed on the wall nearest the venue entrance, HYPE started to look like a very different kind of club. Inside the venue itself, the whole room had a coat or two of paint, including the floor. The stage was rebuilt and carpeted. Strobes and smoke machines were fixed around the stage. Jon's old habit of booking up to five bands a night apparently wasn't going anywhere, though.

In a way this made a lot of sense. Firstly, nobody wanted to hear a new band for much longer than twenty-five minutes, and many new bands only had six or seven songs to play. What didn't make sense was the constant swapping of equipment on and off the stage to make this happen. Compromises were made where the headlining band would share their kit, and drummers would bring their own snare, pedals and cymbals – the breakable bits.

Not only did Jon have a habit of picking bands, but he also had something of a golden touch when it came to selecting crew and helpers. There were no job ads, no apply within, no CVs or letters of recommendation; Jon simply asked you if you wanted to do something and you either said yes or no. There was some crossover from the Timebox in terms of personnel, including Gem Archer who had pitched in to the revamp and would continue his duties as stage manager once the new club opened: 'I painted that whole floor which was bad enough [...] but those signs! It looked like a cross between Supermarket Sweep and a goth club' (Author interview, 18 January 2021).

Jon had come up with a series of advertising slogans, which Gem had handwritten in permanent marker pen on A2 dayglo coloured card. The signs were hung around the venue, and we never doubted again that every single one of us was a unique individual because 'You Are All Special People' haunted us around every corner.

Figure 5.2: 'You Are All Special People' sign (photo by author)

Jon led the way with a constant stream of ideas, most of which weren't serious – except the ones that were either stupid or dangerous. His humour was infectious, and it inspired a family-like loyalty to those of us in his orbit. Within a month of first meeting him, Jon had asked me and my Popinjays bandmate, Wendy, to run the door. He had a bit of a history of girl bands and double acts at the cash-only box office. Tracy and Melissa from Voice of the Beehive had staffed the post for a while during early Timebox days. He probably knew that it was really disarming to have a couple of girls on the door. Maybe it nipped any potential trouble in the bud, or maybe he thought it made him look like an indie Hugh Hefner. It didn't.

The entry price was £2.50 or £2 with a flyer, and we'd ask everyone who came through the door which band they'd come to see; the bands were paid in proportion to their apparent popularity. Then we'd mark their hand with a UV pen, which would show up under the new lights in the corridor. It all felt purposefully modern, and we could see who'd already paid without giving anyone an ugly inky mark that they might regret in the morning. On a quiet night, we'd have long drunken discussions with interesting regulars including rock journalist and photographer Mick Mercer, Steve Lamacq, Laura Lee Davis from *Time Out*, Fierce Panda's Simon Williams and Andy Ross from Food Records.

HYPE was a world away from the pub at the front of the building in almost every way, except for the L-shaped bar which ran between the two halves. They were also connected via the toilets with a door on each side. Occasionally a pub drinker would mistakenly wander out of the door they thought would return them to the pub, only to find themselves trapped in a black, low-ceilinged corridor full of smoke, lit only by UV and blinking televisions, like some nightmarish Halloween electrical shop. We thought it was cool.

The main go-between, the person who would physically cross these two worlds, was Tommy the glass collector: a man with thick wiry eyebrows and an accent to match. Coming into the venue side of the pub his entrée would always be the phrase, 'Busy tonight', which would be delivered as either a question or a statement. He would still ask 'Busy tonight?' when the crowd in the back bar was so dense that he could barely navigate his tiny frame through the jungle of bodies watching the bands or the over-sized throng around the bar.

Tommy's regular daytime haunts were all within twenty yards of the pub. We'd heard how he would eat at the café at the bottom of Fortess Road every day. He had become so well-known to the owner that, when they had to go away for a few days on a family emergency, they asked Tommy to open up, make tea, toast or whatever he could manage just to stay open. Tommy did as he was asked and for three days over Christmas, the menu consisted of tea, toast and boiled cabbage.

There was a madness to HYPE. And although we probably all felt like observers and the only sane ones there, we all added to it. 'We were all waifs and strays, orbiting around this mad f*cking geezer, Jon Beast,' recalls Gem Archer (Author interview, 18 January 2021).

Bands came and went, except for the ones that came again and there were plenty of those. Thrilled Skinny, The Senseless Things, Shoot, Snuff, and Mega City Four were all regulars. Food Records would often use HYPE to showcase their new signings, because it was somewhere with a buzz that they knew they could pack out for the benefit of a good review. These were the really intense nights at HYPE, when we felt the full pressure of the outside world with managers and record companies breathing down our collective neck. But we were a tight team, with an unspoken trust and a symbiotic way of working. Together we felt like we could do anything: 'When Jesus Jones would play, the venue could step up. Those big gigs never got the better of us' (Gem Archer, Author interview, 18 January 2021).

Jon's habit of employing band members as crew worked well. Not only did we know what bands might need in terms of equipment, but we could also think ahead and were able to guide new or inexperienced bands through the sound-check process in a friendly and helpful way. We were young, we were full of jokes and fun, and carried none of the ingrained cynicism of the old school. We were all on our way up, which might have given the impression that you could come along too, if you wanted.

Even though a number of the bands that played went onto bigger and better things, the majority that played are the ones nobody can remember. Bands that, for whatever reason, never took that enormous leap out of the great unknown. There were heart-stopping bands full of mischief and marvel, and bands that teetered between saving rock music and utterly and totally destroying it. There were the bands with crazy names like Electric Dog Circus, alongside sweet-sounding bands with jangling guitars, floppy fringes and a full rack of desert boots. There were hobby bands made up of office boys who would arrive for sound-checks clutching their shiny new instrument cases. Straight from work, they still wore their Burton's jackets. They would pair them with crisp Fogey jeans whose pockets had never been stuffed with the actual debris of rock and roll: plectrums, dole cards, bus tickets, matches, and someone's phone number drunkenly scrawled on the edge of a crumpled gig flyer.

The Bull and Gate wasn't just about the bands though; it was about everyone who came through the door, and then came back week on week. Mick Mercer recalls:

> The fact that it didn't try to be cool made it more friendly, and that wasn't happening anywhere else. If you had to choose between one place or another, it was always going to be more fun at the Bull and Gate. (Author interview, 23 February 2021)

Over time it wasn't just the venue that got the makeover. Jon re-branded himself as Jon 'Fit' Beast, and started sporting a red tracksuit top, cut his hair and stopped drinking. He binned the Timmy Mallet glasses, lost weight and just when it seemed that he was through the baked beans and the yelping phase, he simply lost interest.

The venue seemed to sense it even before we did. In the corridor, the welcome tape of Jon saying 'You are all special people' and 'Buy more to save more', over what might have been whale noises and lift music, became worn and stopped working. The once obedient bubble machine dripped and vomited its slimy contents all over the floor, and the bulb in the penguin light quietly blew itself out. The only thing Jon seemed to have any enthusiasm for was operating the stage lights. He took to hiding in the lightbox, turning the strobes and smoke machines on full blast during bands, and playing records in-between.

This time, instead of closing the venue, he started to close himself. Within a few weeks he stopped coming in at all, and even as the venue continued to run, it became obvious that he had found something new to pique his interest. Carter USM vocalist, Jim-Bob, tells the story:

> Jon put Carter on at Hype a few times and he'd be up in that box at the top of the back of the venue doing our lights. He had a microphone for some reason and used to insult us through the monitors while we were onstage. When we went on a big UK tour he offered to do our lights every night. I think we said no but he turned up at the first gig anyway. So he became our lighting man and MC. We couldn't afford to pay him so he took a share of the t-shirt sales and used to sell videos he'd filmed of our gigs. He once wrote the Carter logo on strips of toilet roll and sold that. (Author interview, 8 May 2021)

So, Jon had run away with Carter, which felt a bit like he'd run away from the circus to join the circus. Either way, it left the Bull and Gate looking like the dumped girlfriend. I don't think he even said goodbye. You could say that he disappeared, but it felt less dramatic than that because there was no loud bang or theatrical puff of smoke. He just sort of evaporated.

It's true that club nights seem to have a lifespan; audiences mature, fashions change and bands call it a day. Maybe Jon just thought he saw HYPE's expiry date before the rest of us. Meanwhile Carter USM were just starting to see exactly what their new lighting engineer was capable of. Jim-Bob:

> We thought we were a punk band and didn't need a big light show but Jon proved us wrong. He was amazing when he was operating the lights, I loved watching him from the stage. And then he got bored with it and more into just introducing us. His announcements got longer and longer and more bizarre.
>
> We sort of fell out when we were in the pop charts and Jon wanted his name on the posters and his own t-shirts on sale. We parted company but Jon's legacy was there every night with the 'you fat bastard' chants (Author interview, 18 January 2021).

Ultimately the Bull and Gate may have just been an ordinary pub with a good-sized back room, but to London's indie scene of the late 1980s it was a backroom of whirring cogs. More than that it was a community, a springboard for bands and a place to meet. But most of all it was somewhere that weirdness, ultimate loyalty, deafening volume and crazy ideas all triumphed.

Interviewees

Gem Archer – musician. Guitarist with Heavy Stereo, Oasis, Beady Eye, High Flying Birds. Timebox and HYPE stage manager, 1987–1989.
Author interview, 18 January 2021.

Mick Mercer – rock journalist, former editor of *Zig Zag* and regular contributor to *Melody Maker*. Set up the 'Bull & Gate Memories' Facebook group – https://www.facebook.com/groups/160041671013307/.
Author interview, 23 February 2021.

Jim-Bob [James Morrison] – Musician, songwriter, author. Founder member and vocalist of Carter USM.
Author interview, 8 May 2021.

Author biography

Polly Hancock was the guitar half of the Popinjays and co-promoter of the Pop Club at the Bull and Gate (approx. 1991–1993). From 1994 to 2000 she was the live music promoter at the Mean Fiddler in Harlesden and from 2001 has worked in London as a photojournalist. More recently she is co-founder of the blogsite punkgirldiaries.com.

6 Weapons of Bass Destruction

Kevin Narrainen

I imagine most readers are very familiar with the cover art of The Clash's *London Calling*. Paul Simonon smashing his Fender Precision bass at the Palladium in New York City on 20 September 1979 is one of the most iconic images in rock. It's dynamic. It's powerful. It's so full of energy, anger, and emotion. It is the epitome of punk cool. However, it turns out that cool imagery and cool reality are very different things. Learning (and mainly failing) just how hard it is to smash a bass is probably not best attempted in front of a bunch of beer-soaked toilet venue punters.

Utilising a much (MUCH) cheaper instrument and a very large dollop of over-confident stupidity, that is precisely the journey I opted to take across several months and on numerous stages around the capital. An odyssey that would involve blood, sweat, tears, and an inordinate amount of beer. Some of these fluids would belong to me.

I'd joined a friend's band as a bass player. Bass was an instrument I hadn't touched at any point in my musical career. I wasn't worried though. A bass has four strings, right? They must be 66.6 per cent recurring easier to play than a full-blown electric guitar. To a degree, I would still argue this is kind of true, but I would never dream of saying this to the likes of Kim Deal should the opportunity ever arise.

The band I joined was called Ciccone. They were named after Madonna Louise Ciccone with more than a knowing nod to Ciccone Youth, a side project of Sonic Youth. While it would be unfair to say that we were ever as successful as our namesakes, a good number of people did feel the band was one of those 'should've made it' kind of bands. A few independent singles, a Steve Lamacq record of the week, featured videos on MTV2 and a couple of other stations. But we remained no more than yesterday's fish 'n' chip paper. Not that this was still a thing. Even back then.

We all have dreams. These felt quite real at the time. The chance to live the rock 'n' roll life and exist on the road from gig to gig. Emerging only to dish out musical memories to the next generation. Priming the youth with riffs to remember. Junctions in time etched into the very fabric of music itself.

Time for a reality check...

We didn't play places like the Palladium in heady New York City. We were never even close to a sniff of CBGBs. Or New York. We played what is often referred to as the toilet circuit. The smaller venues where you cut your teeth, make your mistakes, earn your stripes. We played countless gigs in settings very few signed bands would even think about visiting.

Playing the toilet circuit in London is largely a thankless task, although usually a fun one too. Dragging your equipment around to play tiny backrooms in places people may well never have heard of, hiring vans, and being fiscally negative. Desperately trying to get your mates to come along for the umpteenth time so you're not playing to a half-empty room. For a bass player, these things are even worse. Your bass amp is always the largest and heaviest piece of equipment. At least a drum kit can be broken into its separate noise-creating elements and distributed between band members.

One such venue was the Red Eye on Copenhagen Street in a hidden corner of North London. Formerly a 1930s pub called the Lord Nelson and (as is so often the case) now converted to flats, it was home to many bands from Snakebite City, a small but popular label that sprang out of the fanzine movement at the time. With a loyal following, it helped the birth and growth of sixth-form common room mainstays such as Mega City Four, The Sweeney and Carter USM, and a whole host of others lost to the mists of time.

The Red Eye was hidden among council estates that, due to redevelopment, are no longer behind King's Cross. Even those that lived in the area could be forgiven for not knowing it was there. Its discreet exterior suggested that windows were an unnecessary luxury. Perhaps the musical escapades inside were better off hidden from the outside world. It was a typical venue: It cost no more than a few quid to get in. The bar looked like it had been squeezed in as an afterthought. And, of course, it only had a tiny space for bands to play.

Unlike many venues, the Red Eye had a stage. On the toilet circuit, this element was often missing. It is odd to play to people when you're not elevated. The height difference usually gives you a sense that you are supposed to be playing and not just blagging it or easily replaced by one of the audience members. Hiding behind a microphone stand has a similar effect. Despite everything that basic physics would have you believe, standing behind that thin metal pole can instill enough separation between you and the audience to make you feel almost grandiose.

There was rarely fewer than four bands on a bill. Often more. More bands usually meant more beer-buying mates. Of course, sometimes mates start to get bored of going to their friends' gigs and you need to build a bit of a following. More bands playing also meant more equipment on stage and, therefore, much less room for rocking out. Consequently, less room on stage and increased chances of knocking something over or bumping into a band mate. This usually meant being as static as possible. Guitar leads fill the floor like the inner sanctum of the pyramid in *Raiders of the Lost Ark* (different kind of Indie though). More room is taken up by my own effects pedals and extension plugs galore. I never bothered to trace leads back to the source of any actual power for fear of seeing exactly how many items were feeding back to a single plug.

And what would be the wisest cherry to balance atop this veritable sundae of electrical cables and sockets? Several pints of beer. There was at least one per member of the band and sometimes more than one just in case you managed to down a pint in between songs. You couldn't expect to play a gig without continuously consuming cheap lager. That I've never been electrocuted or witnessed an electrocution is miraculous. I suppose the desire to drink the beer you've purchased rather than spill it is a powerful force.

On one occasion, my twenty-minute walk from bustling King's Cross felt altered. The Squier Precision bass guitar encased in the second cheapest bass bag in the music shop was heavy. Its weight chafed my shoulders. I'd finally paid it off. It was completely my own property. I'd been buying it from a friend in ridiculously small stages due to my ongoing financial instability. How should I celebrate this momentous turning point in my musical career? This boost in my assets? I had decided that this was precisely the correct time to unleash my inner rock god. Step aside Mr Simonon, it's my time to shine. The hour of bass smashing is upon us. For some reason I decided to be arrogantly flippant with the instrument that had taken me so long to own. Why was I so keen to put this four-stringed beast in danger? I certainly couldn't afford to replace it. Nor could I repair any damage.

A varied mix of bands were on the set that night. As was customary, I dipped between watching the other bands and sinking some beers. The ratio depended very much on the quality of said band. Our turn to play came. My focus during the set was more on my big move at the end of the gig rather than on playing particularly well. The band and I put in a sterling performance all the same. The crowd seemed to be enjoying it too. When they are within spitting distance (an untested theory on both mine and the crowd's part, thankfully), it's easy to tell. It's not just a case of seeing how much they enjoy it, you can pretty much smell it too. Crushed in together like a bunch of music-loving sardines, profusely sweating due to a ventilation system that is either inadequate or entirely imaginary. As their excitement and enthusiasm increase, they act more and more as a single, mad, throbbing entity. All its legs trying and failing to control, connect or coordinate. I suppose collective sardines with legs would struggle to find focus, the tinned idiots.

The Red Eye was small, and we'd started to get a reasonable reception by this point. We didn't have to worry too much about the strange and often repeated arc of intimidation where the crowd avoid a semi-circular area near the front of the stage for fear of being too close to the band. This is largely a London phenomenon; ironically the further you gig from the capital, the smaller the arc is. Large cities may see an uptick in arc-age, but never to the levels regularly seen in London Town. Regional gigs would usually fall somewhere between two extreme categories. The first being that the punters were over the moon that a band were actually playing. Any band. I never felt that this welcome was reserved for visitors; that love of merely seeing a band was given to local outfits too. The other extreme was the slaughtered lamb approach. This combined absolute indifference to your existence while simultaneously communicating a desire to hurt you. The worst case of this was during a support slot to pre-fame Goldie Lookin' Chain in Newport. The audience told us out loud during our set exactly how much they didn't like our music. Or our faces. They also made it clear that they would be more than happy to assist us in separating those faces from the rest of our bodies. For those who are unfamiliar, when the arc does appear all members of the crowd know the rules and manage to maintain a mathematically perfect space away from the band. It would not look out of place in a school textbook: ' ... if the arc of indifference is equal to the volume of the band, then work out how much of the floor has spilt beer on it'. There are rare moments when a particularly drunk person decides to take charge of this area to do something approximating dance. I frown upon this. It takes eyes away from the band.

Back to the set. We were approaching our finale. I can't remember the song, but it had a very punchy ending. In fairness most of our songs ended punchily. It was our thing. I'm getting ready now. I'm adjusting the guitar strap in anticipation of my move. As we hit the note, I thwack my bass extra hard. It continues to ring out as I lift the monster from my shoulder. It's a half-hearted move, really. I can't quite muster the same level of commitment as I'd anticipated pre-gig. As I turn to leave the stage, I hurl the instrument away from me as nonchalantly as you can throw something that weighs several kilos and is half your size. It soars in slow motion. It temporarily gains the power of flight before demonstrating that it is not, in fact, a bird, and it really should continue to obey the laws of gravity just as every other well-behaved instrument in the room seems perfectly happy to do.

As I stated, the room and stage were both far from large. In all likelihood none of this is how it appeared to the audience. There were a few 'oohs' as if a limp back-garden firework had taken off, but most just thought that the bassist was a bit of a stroppy git for throwing his bass. They certainly did not see an iconic, cool, and carefree rock god.

Seconds later, I realized that I had to walk back across the same stage in the opposite direction from which I had so casually flounced to reclaim my now scuffed and slightly cracked bass. Another band were about to play and I could sense that I should kindly take my property out of the way, please. This removed any of the remaining shine. Thankfully the bass was still in working order despite a few war wounds.

The timing for when I did acquire bass 2.0 coincided perfectly with a high-profile band competition taking place at The Garage near the Highbury and Islington tube station. More often, I played upstairs at The Garage in a much smaller room creatively titled 'Upstairs at the Garage'. It's a corridor with a stage at one end on which I have performed many times in various bands. Sometimes this was with a room throbbing with energy and spilling over the monitors. Other times, the audience consisted of one person sat on a chair in the middle of the room. Reading a book.

This competition, though, was in the main venue which was impressively sized. I'd often been in the audience at some of my heroes' gigs like the Flaming Lips, Mission of Burma, Bis and the Afghan Whigs. It felt a bit like walking onto the turf of Wembley Stadium. If, that is, you were in a football team not many people had heard of or had any interest in.

I had a firm plan this time. My new star player was a Purple DeArmand copy with a '60s body. He was match fit. He would debut at our next game. Before then, my friend Mr Squier was going to bow out in a blaze of glory. Or a splinter of glory, perhaps. Pyrotechnics were very definitely off the menu. I'd learnt my lesson and this was going to be the full overhead smash. I'd checked my reference image several times. Wide stance and a considered grip placement. This was going to be beautiful. Barbaric, but beautiful all the same.

One of the worst parts of gigs is the sound check. You're doing a run-through to get levels for the (usually very bored) sound engineer. Everyone populating the room is, by and large, just the other bands on the bill. There's an odd dynamic of acting supportive but really everyone is silently assessing and mentally rating the competition. At this, an actual competition with loads of bands on the bill, there was no sound check. Instead, there was just a quick line check to make sure you were making some sort of a sound. Any resemblance to songs sounding as they should was up to how the engineer felt at the time of the gig itself. When you don't have your own sound engineer, their commitment to your sound is low. Shockingly so, in some cases. The number of bands playing at this encounter also meant that the audience was largely made up of those same bands. Bands whose main interest was very clearly themselves. Few, including ourselves, could be bothered to feign interest in our rivals. This created a weird vibe. The more a band tried to impress, the more a black hole hoovered up any remaining friendliness. Instead of impressing each other, there was a competition to show the most indifference; if there had been a prize for this, the recipient would just have curled their lip and shrugged.

Still, I had bigger, more iconic things on my mind.

After deciding that maybe we should pretend to be interested in other bands and try not to get too drunk (a tough balancing act), our time had come. While negotiating the set, I planned where the big finale would take place. Smashing a bass. I mean, truly destroying it. Not just scraping the paintwork. Doing this takes up an extensive amount of space around your feet and above your head. Neither direction was on my side in this environment. In between each song I subtly nudged a few cables left and right with my feet, creating an area where I could see the floor. I couldn't possibly risk damaging anyone else's stuff, or any more of my own for that matter. Looking carefree and spontaneous was a serious and considered thing. I took a few furtive glances upward too. The onstage lights were not all being used but there were a lot of them. An even wider stance was necessary.

Whatever the final song was, I don't recall. The time of reckoning was upon me. No more mister cheap bass. Rock history was in the making. I located my prepared spot. I widened my stance a touch and hit the final note that my bass would play. Then I swung it. Those of you that have lifted a bass guitar will realise that, despite having two fewer strings than a regular electric guitar, it is significantly heavier when slung around your neck. The diminutive figure of Suzi Quatro looking so effortless is very misleading indeed. If you rotate that same bass to an unnatural position above your head, it becomes even heavier. Having attained this position, and realising the increased weight, I was relieved that the descent to the ground was helped by my friend gravity. My expectations were that the bass would smash wildly, bursting in spectacular fashion. I would be left with the pieces barely held together by the strings. I would end its days of musicality.

That is not what happened.

Instead, the bass bounced back up and whacked my shins. Being hit in the shins is rarely a fun experience especially when it's done by a hefty bass guitar clinging onto its last moments. If the bass had a to-do list for that evening, being obliterated by me was not part of it. I needed to get back on track and I had one weapon left in my arsenal.

Repetition.

Not only did the bass refuse to die, but it also appeared to actively fight back. So as the rest of the band continued to finish the song, I repeatedly smashed my shins into a heavily bruised mess while just about managing to break the bass enough to no longer be playable. I'd fucked it. Not perfectly in any sense. The bass no longer worked, but then neither did my shins or any lingering sense of pride.

As with all epic journeys, we need an epic ending. I'd managed to break a bass on stage. It was not as impressive as I'd hoped, and I had inflicted more injury to myself than the intended victim, but the goal had been achieved.

But only sort of. How could I end here?

I'm not going to pretend that this was thought through, but my next move saw me finding out how much damage I could inflict upon someone else with the bass. A move that surprised me as much as everyone else in the room. Including the person who was the focus of this enquiry.

To play out these events, I now take you to the marvel that is the Bull and Gate in Kentish Town. A short walk from bustling Camden, proverbial capital of the early days of Britpop. The Bull and Gate, along with many other venues, is sadly no longer with us; it's a fancy gastro boozer now. As a venue it had a particularly unusual set up. The stage was a good solid size, and the gig room was too. What made it odd was that this room was separate to the bar.

That's right: in what is an activity that is largely based around the almost non-stop consumption of alcohol, there was no actual way to buy more of your choice of beverage without leaving the room where the bands were playing. This could be an intimidating set up for bands. You needed to convince punters that listening to you play was worth being more than twenty yards from your next beer or leaving the seat you'd managed to secure in the bar room. Your audience could only savour your musical wares knowing full well that, even with a selection of coats scattered on the chairs or someone sacrificed to guard it, your spot would most likely be stolen.

In fact, there were more ways to tempt you away from a gig in this venue than at any other. Some people didn't make it into the venue part of the pub at all. They just continued to drink themselves into a stupor in the main part of the pub which was a lovely old drinking establishment.

If everyone knew what I was about to do (myself included), I feel confident that the bar would have been empty. I'd become quite blasé about the vulnerability of my bass, since demolishing (look, let me have it okay?) the previous incarnation. I'm not sure if the difficulty of its predecessor's demise made me think its successor was somehow immortal, like Christopher Lambert in *Highlander* (this being my second bass somehow makes the *Highlander* comparison a little less relevant). As gigs ended, I would drop it on the floor with little or no care. This grew to be less casual and more and more forceful. I'd started slamming it to the ground. Something had to give. Turns out it was another member of the band.

We were playing a storming set and the room was buzzing and full, which is not a mean feat for an unsigned band at the Bull and Gate. This is the sort of event that can make you get a little carried away. I was certainly jumping around the stage a bit more than I did usually. Physical stage presence was something I had not mastered at this juncture. I tended to be more focused on my fret board. The epitome of shoe gaze in physical stance, if not musical style. This helped with nerves but really didn't make for much of a visual feast. This time, though, I moved around the sprawling stage more than before.[1]

Jumping around the stage was firing off all my rock-god neurons again. As we were approaching the end of our big number, I slipped the strap from my shoulder and, possibly through the adrenaline from the energy in the room and maybe because I may have become a bit stronger though multiple gigs, I held the bass easily aloft. It was like showing off a winning boxing belt, or maybe the WWE Bass Champion title. It was all so much easier than back at the Red Eye. The Bull and Gate also allowed for a real throw. This was everything I was hoping for on my initial step into showmanship. I steadied to hurl my bass beast.

At the last possible millisecond, something snapped in my brain. It triggered the part of me that does incredibly stupid things with little regard for others. I have no idea why, but I threw my bass directly at our lead singer Mick. I did it confidently and efficiently. I turned away as I did it, so I didn't notice my bass had launched with ease and flown unceremoniously across the stage. Unfortunately for Mick, it hit him very squarely and very directly on his head. Clearly none of this was ideal for Mick. He responded by throwing his guitar at me. This seems completely fair. A lot then happened in a very, very short amount of time. The crowd erupted and we bundled ourselves off stage. We weren't even the headliners that night.

Now the Bull and Gate might well have had one of the biggest stages, but the dressing room did not follow the same ratio of square footage. It was a tiny room behind the stage. Maybe that was a good thing. I was able to face Mick immediately and apologise repeatedly, although this will clearly never be enough. To say he wasn't happy is an understatement, but we made up. Thankfully, he was fine. He opted to have at least two more pints and decided

1. It is one of the biggest toilet venue stages, possibly only superseded by the one I graced years later at The Forum in Royal Tunbridge Wells (which coincidentally was previously the largest public toilet in Europe).

to have his head injury checked out the following day. But the white brick walls of the tiny room did have blood spatters on them. Mick's head had been cut and he sported a wound as open as the bar. His shirt was no longer white, either. I felt awful. This made it all the stranger as we emerged from the back room to head to the bar and received multiple pats on the back and congratulations on a great show from random strangers.

Post-gig clear ups are always a bit weird. You're a bit drunk, the crowds (if there were any) have left and the room is once again empty except for abandoned pint glasses and various bits of rubbish. This time, there were also blood stains on the stage. The claret-coloured area where the incident happened was far larger than I thought it would be. I grabbed my pedals and cables and went through the ritual of wrapping them around my elbow to put away in my guitar bag. As the soundman did the same with his gear, he walked over to me. Most soundmen (I don't remember working with a soundwoman during my years as a live performer, but I see no reason to assume they would not be just as grumpy as their male counterparts) don't want to have that much to do with you before or even during the gig and absolutely never, ever afterwards. He tapped me on the shoulder and just said, 'That was the most rock 'n' roll thing I've ever seen'.

I still felt terrible, but I did manage a little, sly smile.

Author biography

Kevin Narrainen has been in and out of bands since the age of fifteen. Despite never taking that first guitar lesson, he has been in enough bands to have received a rock family tree as one of his wedding gifts. He has played multiple instruments (guitar, bass and accordion to name a few) over numerous stages and three continents. He has also worked as a television producer, writer and editor for the last twenty years or so.

7 Girls with Guitars

Vim Renault and Lene Cortina

> Bands with a girl singer, that was acceptable, but it was almost weird to have two [...] and to tell people that we're the guitarists, and that the guitars were the important bit. (PunkGirlDiaries 2020a)

We at punkgirldiaries.com like guitars; we both play guitars and, for some reason, that's been viewed as unusual all through our lives. It's not like guitars were illegal, it's just that until the late 1970s guitars were generally seen as the domain of boys, along with motorbikes, Old Spice and Y-fronts. Meanwhile, girls seemed to have their own separate role within music culture, which was to buy the records and then scream and faint at concerts. For girls, music was a spectator sport. We never thought that we'd end up playing ELECTRIC GUITAR ... with effects pedals, huge amplifiers and people actually watching us at The Garage, the Moles Club, the 100 Club or Rock City. Many of the guitar-playing women that we've interviewed in 2020–21 for our blog have great stories about learning to play, gigging and dealing with the full force of other people's attitudes.

Growing up in the 1970s, we were both vaguely aware of guitar players like Mary Hopkin, Joni Mitchell, and Carly Simon, but those long-haired strummers somehow didn't inspire us much. Girls were just expected to like boy bands – The Osmonds, Bay City Rollers, Flintlock. Screaming at whichever member of the band you 'fancied' was presented as the only way for teen girls to appreciate music. But of course, there are also better things to do when you're a young girl, like bike-riding, den building and drawing our own comics. We knew that we were girls, but as pre-teens it never occurred to us that it should make a difference to our life chances or work ethic.

When we watched TV as teenagers, we started to see the way our lives would go. There in front of us were the viewpoints and truisms of wider society: young women were either 'dolly-birds' or 'women's libbers', and both stereotypes were equally ridiculed. Sitcoms like *The Liver Birds* showed two girls in a flat share, and the comedy centred on their ineptitude and naivety, rather than their independence. We hadn't realised that, at some point, your girl-life would end and you'd be all set for the reality of women's drudgery. The future was portrayed as comfortable, inevitable and beyond question: a few years at the local secondary modern, a couple of years working in an office – which would stop when you got married and had children – followed by a life of cleaning up and caring for people. After twenty years of this, you'd be a fully-fledged old battle-axe ripe for the mother-in-law jokes.

We could have focused on positive role models – Barbara Castle was a politician, Cilla Black had a TV show, and in 1975 Angela Rippon was the first female to be a permanent news presenter on TV – but women with interesting careers were a rarity. And, although we went to all-girls schools, the history of suffragettes, land army girls and pioneering women were neither in the curriculum nor on the BBC. Expectations for most women were low. Worse still, there was little or no mention of guitars.

But then punk happened and we realised that girls can play too. The message that we took from punk was that we had permission to do anything we wanted, and it didn't even have to be done properly. Punk shortcuts permitted us to just get a guitar without worrying that we were yet to play a single note. The punk mindset was all about doing things differently. Seeing Eddie and the Hot Rods play 'Do Anything You Wanna Do' on *Top of the Pops* on 11 August 1977 somehow inspired us both into action, independently, and in different UK towns.

So, we both became punks. Not leather-jacketed, studded and pierced punks, but a more subtle thing; we took on the punk mindset and believed that we could learn to play the guitar, be in a band and play live gigs in our local venues. And then, of course, we started to see the role models. Siouxsie, The Slits, Poly Styrene, The Raincoats, all examples of women who started doing music because of punk, with little training or experience. When punk happened, it wasn't just about the music, it was about participation and action rather than back-seat spectating. It was freedom, liberation and nurturing of the underclasses, with girls included. We made our own clothes, repurposed stuff from jumble sales and used our kid-comic skills to make 'zines, posters and artwork. From this moment, a creative and self-determined life seemed possible. Lene was impressed by her first taste of live punk music.

> The first gig I ever went to was The Adverts at Slough College on 27th October 1979. Apart from the steep learning curve of gig etiquette, which I was still to get the hang of, the most striking thing about the evening was the volume and the spectrum of the sounds. From the guitars and cymbals making my ears jangle to Gaye's bass tones which were rich and punchy and made my insides vibrate. Jostled by the crowd, deafened by the PA and completely terrified by

the pure, raw energy in the room, I knew that this was the only thing I ever wanted to do. (PunkGirlDiaries 2021d)

At first, sitting in your bedroom with a chord book from the library, strumming a nylon six-stringed guitar felt like a step in the right direction. But what we really needed was a blast of amplified noise, and by 1978 we knew that the acoustic's days were numbered. Going electric meant Saturday jobs, chores and saving up for a trip to the local music shop, another very male domain. Even pushing open the shop door demanded self-belief that was both casual and cocky, going against all the expected girl-traits of seeking permission or approval. Music shop staff always studiously ignored you – they'd be busy on the phone or maybe beneath a cloud of wispy smoke, soldering something behind the counter. Staring at the guitars hanging on the wall garnered very little attention. Then, if you asked to see or try a guitar, the bearded man would get it down for you, plug it in, adjust the volume and before handing it over would suddenly play something very complicated, very fast and very loud. Biting his bottom lip and jerking his back, he might as well have been onstage. He might even give you the old, 'you can't beat the Zep, huh?' nod. This was intimidating and made worse by the thought that, in a moment, you might have to play at least two of your three fumbly chords, out loud in the music shop, all in the name of 'trying it out'. In fact, the whole acting casual business was just a defence, a ruse to distract from the plain, hard fact that you couldn't play and were terrified of being judged. Once you'd played in front of the guitar shop man, you would be judged. And then quite possibly ridiculed. It could be a harrowing, raw experience and one way around it was to take a boy with you to test the guitar. He might know even fewer chords than you, but to the guitar shop staff he would be less of a joke candidate and you'd look like 'the girlfriend'.

Another possibility was to find a guitar in one of those junk shops that sold everything. The owner would have no knowledge about any guitars on sale, so it was easier to pretend that you knew what you were doing, and it didn't matter that you only knew three chords and had no technique whatsoever. There was a general belief that you judged a guitar by holding it like a rifle, closing one eye and looking down the neck. We don't know why, but it looked impressive in a junk shop. Having a second-hand guitar automatically made you more of an established guitarist. Sometimes the guitars came with battered, stickered cases and that was perfect to pretend you'd been doing it for years. Vim's junk shop guitar was a 1960s Hofner Galaxie, bought for £30 and now a sought-after vintage model. In 1978, instead of respecting the guitar's heritage and significance, Vim ripped off the white plastic alligator skin cover, painted the guitar black and stuck RAR stickers on it. Then, in her first band, The Devices, Vim played it like a bass guitar in the band: one note at a time.

A common story in the punkgirldiaries.com interviews is the paradigm-shifting shock that comes with guitar amplification. Things that sound basic and boring on a classical guitar can suddenly set your ears alight. Holly Ross of the Lovely Eggs is one of these.

> I wanted to play guitar and sound like all these bands I liked. I had a guitar – a nylon string acoustic – and it doesn't sound like what you hear on records. Then my mum's cousin had an electric guitar and he gave me it when I was 14. I went to the second-hand guitar shop up the road and bought this distortion pedal, plugged it in and [...] shit! It was amazing! I thought, I can't even play a note, but this sounds fucking brilliant. (PunkGirlDiaries 2020c)

Whether the guitar inspires the band, or the band idea necessitates getting a guitar, one thing is certain: making music with other people is one of the best things on the entire planet, especially when you're young, discovering new things and you have loads of spare time. We didn't know about how to network or get a drummer or bass player via those hand-written cards in music shops. For us, forming your first band was like making a last-minute meal, and was conjured up from whatever ingredients were to hand: sisters, school friends, neighbours and people from the youth club were all fair game. They didn't even have to be especially cool. They just needed a similar mindset and enough verve and nerve to carry it off. The resulting bands didn't always have the conventional line-up – another reason for boys to laugh at us. Vim's first band had just two guitars and a recorder. Hagar The Womb started with just three girl singers, when the band was formed in the toilets of the Crass-funded Wapping Autonomy Centre. Guitarist, Stephanie Cohen, explains that they ended up with a short deadline for putting their first gig together when they decided to call out boastful boy punk bands.

> It was a bit of a joke at first – 'Oh we'll do our own band,' but then they said, 'You can play a gig here in a few weeks' time'. So then there was this mad demented rush to try and work out who was going to do what. (PunkGirlDiaries 2021a)

The short deadline and the debating over who's going to play what instrument was particularly common in the post-punk garage band scene. Dolly Mixture's Debsey Wykes started on guitar with Rachel Bor on bass in their first attempt to play, but the two swapped over before playing their first gig.

Again, it was connections between school friends and siblings that enabled the band to happen, as Debsey told us.

> One evening she [Rachel Bor] rang up and said, 'Look, we've got this bass and a guitar, and an amp round here; do you want to come now?' Her brother taught me a couple of chords and she was going to be the bass player – and the next day we gathered up there because he had his drum kit and we had our first rehearsal. That was just the best thing in the world; it was wonderful! It's like you've gone to another country. (PunkGirlDiaries 2021c)

We knew that if we were ever going to get as far as an actual venue with our rag-tag post-punk, then we needed to do some band rehearsals, another thing that our formal education had failed to prepare us for. In our minds we had ideas about how guitarists leap about the stage, strut and thrust confidently, or else they stare into space looking unbelievably cool. They don't sit down, they don't look at their fingers, and the blokes don't have problems about where the strap goes on large boobs. Somehow, we had to get used to performing a number of songs, with each person playing their part and without too much going wrong. For those of us in shared accommodation, there was no alternative but to find a rehearsal space.

Often sited in railway arches or basements, these spaces were inevitably damp, dark and claustrophobic, and were a world away from day-to-day experience. The dirt and the germs which were liberally peppered around these rooms were all part of the rock and roll lifestyle that we were trying to embrace. The rooms were often staffed by under-employed musicians, who were often as grimy and crumpled as the bookings diary they kept at reception. Equipment often included filthy dented microphones, sticky cables, and buzzing amps. Ladies' toilets didn't exist, and the men's toilets are unmentionable.

Vix and Maggie from Birmingham band Fuzzbox told us that the band only did one three-hour rehearsal before playing their first gig.

> Maggie's boyfriend had lent us all this gear, and we would try to tune it to one string, and all the songs were just getting lower and lower [...] Absolutely ridiculous, the things we didn't know [...] We didn't know leads were called leads; we called them wires, and the sound guys were just looking at us in abject horror, they were obviously in sound technician hell, but we worked it out. (PunkGirlDiaries 2021b)

Most bands are sensible enough to do their first gig at a friend's party, a school hall or a private hire where there's a friendly tolerant attitude. But that's not a proper gig. A proper gig is not comfortable; it's where you don't know the people who have organised it, there's a sound engineer you've never met, and the audience doesn't just consist of friends and relatives. To get a gig like this you need to persuade the promoter, do your own advertising, and quickly learn the routines of the sound check and the performance.

Venues always looked a bit sad when you walked into them in good time for your sound check. The scuffs, the sticky floors and stink of the underworld were everywhere. Whether you aimed for cool, enthusiastic or an arsey attitude, there was a lot of waiting and a lot of ritual ignoring going on. Sound checks always seemed to us to be power games, showing off and blokery. Unless you had all the technical language and could play lightning-fast riffs as your instrument was solo-tested, you were quietly but smugly scorned. Lene's band, The Popinjays, experienced this.

> We would get there at 5pm or 6pm and sit there waiting for our turn at sound checks, certain that the soundman who did this job every night of the week had some sort of system and would indicate when it was our turn. We had a tape recorder with drum machine and bass parts, a guitar and two vocal mics. It wasn't difficult; it was exactly the same line up as our then label mates Carter USM had. Before the house lights went off and the doors opened, we asked the soundman about our sound check reminding him that we'd been sitting there for hours already. 'Eh? I thought you were the girlfriends of the last band'. Apparently, we'd been sitting there looking too much like girlfriends, so it was our fault. (PunkGirlDiaries 2021d)

Sound engineering is obviously a skilled job. We've been to gigs in many venues which have a brilliant sound for the audience. Unfortunately, it's often not the case for the women on stage. The general perception amongst those we interviewed was that, in the past, sound guys aimed to make everything as loud as possible without feeding back and would seldom entertain the idea of instruments being turned down to accommodate the singer being able to hear herself. Debsey from Dolly Mixture explained.

> The sound systems were pretty rough in some of those pubs. You just had to hope that you were singing in tune. It was touch and go with the smaller gigs because so much could go wrong. I'd go, 'This isn't working' and they'd go 'Urghh' and stare at you like you're stupid – so I had to learn very quickly. In those days so many people seemed to need to be nasty. (PunkGirlDiaries 2021c)

The 1980s attitude to women and girls in bands always seemed to be extreme. It could be, 'you're rubbish and you shouldn't bother because you don't have a clue' – which we beginner guitarists often perceived. And it could also be, 'you're a goddess and it's so amazing to be in the same room as someone like you'. The singers and beauties amongst us tended to get this reaction, and often someone would want to talk to you before the gig. Fans and friends of the promoter often felt free to barge into the backstage rooms to chat you up or 'interview' you, right at the moment when you were most nervous or having a menstrual crisis. The word 'backstage' can also mean a range of things: from a theatre-style dressing room, with lit mirrors and tea-making facilities, to just a poky back room with a couple of old armchairs. We would often leave the gig venue and go to a more traditional pub that was clean and had proper women's facilities. Miki Berenyi, guitarist and singer with Lush, attracted a lot of fans who were keen to have a chat.

> I realised quite early on, because I would get nervous before playing that I'd have a much better time if I went to watch the other bands. Even when we were headlining at places like the Town & Country, I'd be out the front because I was getting in the mood and not angsting backstage [...] but the difficult part of that is not drinking because that would have been a fucking disaster, and I could never eat before a gig as well [...] then people would come up to you and say they've just bought you a pint of cider. (PunkGirlDiaries 2020a)

Once you get on stage, put the set list down, plug in, swig water and gaze out on whatever audience is there, you're locked into a certain pathway that can be sweet or terrifying according to a number of factors. Alcohol or drugs might act to loosen inhibitions but they're no help at all in getting your fingers to play the guitar accurately – that's mainly down to the practice you've put in and the way your body deals with the adrenaline rush. You're at the mercy of the soundman, the limits of your equipment, and mostly your own nerves. Audiences can help in being warm, supportive and polite, although sometimes heckling, sexism or shouting over the band can galvanise the musicians and make them more determined and sparky. Fuzzbox reported that the frequent 'Get your tits out' comments in the early days strengthened their resolve (PunkGirlDiaries 2021b), and Dolly Mixture, on tour with Madness, developed a 'Fuck you!' attitude when faced with National Front skinheads spitting at them, night after night. Debsey Wykes tells how the band members of Dolly Mixture coped with the onstage nerves.

> You just feel an absolute idiot all of the time, but at the same time you think your band's amazing too, which counteracts that. We did have a tendency, whenever we sang something wrong, we were terrible gigglers. We couldn't help ourselves [...] Some nights everything just conspires to make you laugh. But there were plenty of times we came off stage and wanted to cry too. (PunkGirlDiaries 2021c)

With a bit of experience, bands can try to be more entertaining while staying aloof, or by sneering a rock and roll sneer, but it only works if there are actual people in the audience watching. Your band might not be the headliners, but who's already there at 7.30pm? Girl bands were seen by promoters as the easiest to push around the bill, as Lene found out.

> Touring with the Heart Throbs in the autumn of 1990, The Popinjays arrived at ULU [University of London Union] to discover an extra band had been added, which was all fine until we learned that we would still be going on first, which would be earlier than expected. Last-minute additions may help out with show running times, but they don't sell any tickets. We knew that people would have bought advance tickets to see us, and if we were made to go on early, then our people would miss it. This seemed like a bad deal all round and so we refused to cave in to this 'first on' skulduggery. Negotiations were at a stalemate, so we took our acoustic instruments and ghetto blaster drum tracks outside onto Malet Street where we performed on the steps to more people than were inside the building. We were called 'unprofessional'. (PunkGirlDiaries 2021d)

The main way for girls in bands to succeed seems to be simply to keep on doing it and ignore the critics. This was a hard thing to do if you were self-conscious and had been subject to socialisation into the conventional female roles of the 1970s. We suspect that many of our generation tried it and turned away for proper jobs, normal hours, your own bed and a clean toilet. Those who continued had to be thick-skinned, self-reliant or have especially close relationships with their band, manager or a partner who travelled with them. In the twenty-first century we look back to those girl bands and women musicians playing late 1970s and '80s pub gigs with huge admiration. Our shared memories sound like some kind of marvellous naïve adventure: Enid Blyton with a guitar pedal. Having spoken with so many of the women involved, we'd like to put on record that it was an extremely difficult thing to persist with small venues, bands and touring. It was uncomfortable, challenging and unhealthy at the time, but of course, now great to look back on. Lesley Woods was guitarist and singer with Au Pairs, one of the most important early

'80s post-punk bands. A veteran of the small venue circuit, Lesley quickly got used to the rubbish food, the filthy dressing rooms and the curt sound engineers. Whilst playing in a band for a living was thrilling and full of variety, she doesn't hold with over-romanticising the era.

> People talk about punk as if it was liberating [...] revolutionary. It was a massive cultural phenomenon, but there was also a very dark side to it. There was a lot of drugs [...] and I do remember feeling quite [...] not scared, but it was like being in a zone that's quite dark [...] also it wasn't very fashionable to smile. Most people walked around looking miserable including me because that was what the fashion was [...] downturned mouth and looking quite menacing. (PunkGirlDiaries 2020b)

Books and academic articles are now being written about our era. It sounds remarkable and feisty when we look back to our small-town punk origins; learning to play in garage bands, rehearsal rooms, the college gigs, pub venues and simply trying to make a name for ourselves as musicians. We used to read about Andy Warhol's Factory and think how cool all that 1960s Velvet Underground New York scene must have been, in the same way that younger people now might be fascinated by the punk and post-punk scene. The pervasive low-level abuse and control that we can now spot in so many of our venue stories is all part of what used to be called 'character building'. And yes, our characters have indeed been built. Punk swept away the narrow expectations of what a woman's life had to be. It introduced us early on to 'doing anything you want to do', which has had a life-long positive impact. Without the music, we wouldn't have met so many like-minded people, including each other, and we wouldn't wake up each morning thinking about songs, guitars, bands and how we still need to do more music. We know that our adventure in self-taught guitar-ing is an amazing achievement, and that punk rock got girls out of the doldrums. We're happy to see that generations of women musicians that have come after us are now improving conditions, attitudes and expectations. We can put up with mansplaining and eyerolls; just give us a clean toilet.

References

PunkGirlDiaries. 2020a. 'Interview with Miki Berenyi'. *Blogzine* 3, 15 September. https://punkgirldiaries.com/product/blogzine-3/

PunkGirlDiaries. 2020b. 'Interview with Lesley Woods'. *Blogzine* 3, 15 September. https://punkgirldiaries.com/product/blogzine-3/

PunkGirlDiaries. 2020c. 'Interview with Holly Ross'. *Blogzine* 4, 10 November. https://punkgirldiaries.com/product/blogzine-4/

PunkGirlDiaries. 2021a. 'Interview with Hagar The Womb'. *Blogzine* 5, 8 March. https://punkgirldiaries.com/product/blogzine-5/

PunkGirlDiaries. 2021b. 'Interview with We've Got a Fuzzbox and We're Going To Use It!'. *Blogzine* 5, 8 March. https://punkgirldiaries.com/product/blogzine-5/

PunkGirlDiaries. 2021c. 'Interview with Debsey Wykes'. *Blogzine* 6, 18 May. https://punkgirldiaries.com/product/blogzine-6/

PunkGirlDiaries. 2021d. Unpublished author interviews with each other, 12 October.

Author biography

Punkgirldiaries is **Lene Cortina** and **Vim Renault**. Those are their punk names. Lene plays a red guitar with four pedals and Vim plays a 1970s Fender telecaster with no pedals. They write a blog together, publish colourful printed zines and make punk T-shirts. They're still punk.

8 (Princess) Charlotte and her 1980s Offspring, O'Jays

Ruth Miller

Small cities like Leicester are always trying to attract students, but in 1980, based on what I'd read in the *NME*, I chose Sheffield for three years of no-fee, grant-funded student life. Within a few weeks, I'd seen Siouxsie and the Banshees, the Human League, Dead Kennedys, Echo and the Bunnymen and the Soft Boys and there were plenty of cool record shops, home-grown bands and indie venues to explore. So, when I had to move to Leicester three years later as a postgrad, I thought it was going to be a massive cultural downgrade. 'They'll still be wearing flares in Leicester', my fashion-conscious friends declared. 'With Englebert Humperdinck chest wigs, or maybe Showaddywaddy shoes'.

Leicester simply didn't cut it with live music when I arrived. It didn't seem to have up-to-date bands, or anything beyond folk clubs and council music projects. Leicester Polytechnic booked the big touring bands, but after the gigs there was nowhere to go except the portacabin cafe by the taxi rank. Pubs were mainly for old men and occasionally dancing to the jukebox.

But within a few years, by the end of the 1980s, everything had changed and I was swept up in a Leicester band scene that spread across several small pub venues. One promoter – Andy Wright – turned the Princess Charlotte pub into a thrilling venue for first-time-round touring bands, and he also started O'Jays bar where terrible and fabulous local bands played every night. The shambolic, the under-rehearsed, the revolutionary and the pure art rock of late 1980s Leicester played O'Jays after Andy helped novice landlord, Haz, take over. The two venues were like mother and daughter; both determined to give new bands a chance and take risks with innovative sounds. The Charlotte was a proper pub with some elegance and significance; O'Jays was a naïve but fun mess of a project that drew in hundreds of would-be musicians and under-age kids to create something special and terrible for a few thrilling months. Both venues gave me somewhere to play with my newly-formed band and Leicester became an important stepping-stone to music greatness for the next three decades.

Andy Wright passed away in July 2022, but a few months before that I was able to interview him to get his perspective on the Charlotte's significance as well as finding out why O'Jays bar popped up and inspired so many on the Leicester music scene. The Princess Charlotte was an ordinary city centre pub on the Leicester one-way system close to Leicester Polytechnic (now De Montfort University). There are still metal railings outside – put there to stop drunk people drifting onto the carriageway – but the nearby underpass has gone. In the early 1980s, there was nothing distinctive about the pub when Andy Wright came from Leeds:

> I moved here with my girlfriend, and within four days I got a job as bar manager at the Charlotte. At that point there were no bands playing. I ended up doing the cooking. It was all about the lunchtime market – nice carpets, furniture and stuff, in '85, '86, whatever. It wasn't working out for Garry [the landlord] as a daytime venue for food – financially – so he started booking local bands. Rockin' Ronnie and the Bendy Ruperts were on every Tuesday night, the DTs on a Friday once a month [...] very few bands, but that's how it started. (Author interview with Andy Wright, 14 January 2021)

To someone who was a keen music-press reader, Andy understood which bands were becoming more popular. When bands like The Fall played at Leicester Polytechnic, Andy could see fans walking past the pub or popping in for a pint so he knew that Leicester did have a potential audience for alternative music. Garry Warren, the landlord, was happy to take advice about who to book. Andy recalls:

> He asked me one day, 'Have you ever heard of Alan Vega?' – you know, Suicide, and I'm like, 'Yeah' and he said, 'Do you think I should book him?' and I said, 'Yeah,' because in Leeds I was on the dance floor to Suicide and he was a big deal. '£400?' I said, 'Yeah, bargain'. And he booked it, but sadly only about 12 people turned up. If I'd have done the same thing in Leeds it would have been rammed, but that's how difficult Leicester has been. (Author interview with Andy Wright, 14 January 2021)

When the Princess Charlotte was mainly a lunchtime pub, there was a front lounge and a small back bar. Customers had to go out of the back bar and across the yard to go to the toilet. The first bands played on a tiny stage outdoors, but by the time Andy arrived in Leicester, the yard had been covered over and the stage enlarged to make an indoor gig room. The floor was made of concrete slabs, and, at the end of the night, the double gates would be opened to let people out through the drayman's entrance. Andy says that during his time as landlord, he 'put new slabs on at some point but always slabs. You could just hose them down after a busy one!'

Musician Paul Lunn liked the layout which meant that people drinking in the pub would have to go through the band room to access the toilets:

> We used to drink at the Princess Charlotte. You could pretend you were going to the toilet and go through and have a quick listen to the band that was on. It was like a preview [...] you'd walk in and say, 'I'm just going to the loo', and then you might see that the band's all right, and then pay to go in. (Author interview with Paul Lunn, 26 March 2021)

From 1985, I was a regular gig-goer at the Princess Charlotte and always at the front if the band was well-known. There's something about a small venue where the proximity of the low stage makes it an experience which pops all your senses. At the Charlotte you could see how dilated the guitarist's pupils were, you could watch someone change the drum machine settings, and in 1986 at the best gig ever, I saw close-up how Hüsker Dü played their instruments in a three-way noise perfection. The audience knitted together on these occasions respecting the invisible wall but longing to touch the bands that exhilarated with their rawness.

Maybe that Hüsker Dü gig inspired me to form my own guitar trio, PO! in 1987. I certainly wanted to be seen as a guitarist and not just a 'girl singer' like the indie pop bands of that time, and my songs were punky pop with cutting lyrics. We rehearsed under the railway arches and planned to burst onto the Leicester scene with a big gig at the Princess Charlotte. Andy's insightful booking of touring bands continued, and the venue was often packed but, when there was no headliner, you could get gigs in a kind of self-promotion deal. I persuaded Andy Wright to let us play our debut on Saturday 18 July 1987. The venue hire was £65, and I paid £7 extra to have professionally printed tickets to make us look like one of the big national touring bands and not just a local act.

We set about publicising the gig with a mammoth flyposting campaign to get the band name everywhere. I did radio interviews promising that the gig would be an amazing event because it had proper tickets and hand-painted scenery. Mostly, the plan worked well, and the Princess Charlotte was almost full; people enjoyed our youthful arrogance, and the musical energy distracted from the many mistakes. I'd spent weeks painting the giant dayglo cardboard cut-outs, one to represent each song, and these were hung from the ceiling – a giant guitar, an apple, an eye, a cloud, an ice cream. We almost broke even and had impressed Andy enough for him to offer us future gigs. Afterwards, we sat in the small side room reading the band graffiti that covered the walls and ceiling and felt like we'd made it.

When I called round to arrange another gig with PO!, Andy told me that the brewery was moving him around to manage other pubs. As part of Ansells training, he had to launch and oversee a new pub.

For years, breweries had owned the pubs and tied them to the sole purpose of selling their beer in a drinking culture based around the separate lunchtime and evening sessions. A Monopolies and Mergers Commission investigation concluded that breweries should have no more than 2,000 tied pubs and, at the end of 1989, the Beer Orders would put this into law.[1] In the few years running up to this legislation, breweries knew that they would eventually have to sell off pubs or free them of the brewery tie. As a result, there was a kind of 'last orders' spree for brewery-owned pubs, where monitoring and concerns about cost-effectiveness were tossed aside. Interesting possibilities for small pub venues started due to these changes in laws around pub ownership and management, as Andy Wright recalls:

> The thing is with O'Jays and the Princess Charlotte – they were boarded up pubs. They'd find a new landlord and then six months later, it would fail, and it was boarded up again, so they just left me to it. I was gambling with my own money outside the deal with the brewery. If I agreed to pay somebody four or five hundred quid, it was my money and if I lost, I lost. As long as they got the rent and the beer order, they left me to it forever, to be honest. (Author interview with Andy Wright, 14 January 2021)

As part of Andy's management training with Ansells Brewery, he opened O'Jays bar in September 1988, but after less than six months, he was called back to manage the Charlotte full-time, leaving O'Jays in the hands of Haz, a complete beginner, whose naïve enthusiasm for the venue was surprisingly backed by a 'Why not?' from the brewery. For eighteen months, Haz continued the vibrant, exhilarating and creative scene at O'Jays, extending the music policy of nurturing young bands and having gigs most nights. By the end of the 1980s, Leicester had a buzzing live music scene across a range of venues, mainly due to Andy Wright's influence.

> O'Jays was on my training because it was a boarded-up Ansells pub and it was embarrassing. The brewery wanted to avoid that, so they

1. Monopolies and Mergers Commission, Supply of Beer (Tied Estate) Order 1989, Statutory Instruments 1989 2390 HMSO.

> gave me £2000 to give it a lick of paint and charged me £5 a week peppercorn rent just to get it back up and running. In that time [...] it was just an opportunity to put bands on, which is what I did. At that time, and for a little while after, when Haz took it on from me – I suppose it meant something. Loads of bands played there [...] it was a new little underground pub, and people wanted to play there. (Author interview with Andy Wright, 14 January 2021)

In suggesting the venture, the brewery had some kind of theme pub in mind. In other cities, pubs were being refurbished and styled to attract more affluent respectable couples aged over twenty-five rather than solitary male drinkers. The name O'Jays came from the original plan to style the venue as a soul bar with a different upmarket clientele. But O'Jays quickly took on its own identity and acted as a feeder venue, almost an offspring of the Charlotte, according to Andy:

> The brewery approached me and said, 'What do you think you can do with it?' People convinced me that there was a big market for a soul, Tamla Motown bar [...] I love all that shit, but in Leicester? [...] That lasted about six weeks. And then, 'Fuck this, I'll scrump up some bands!'. Basically, that was the bottom line with that, and then when Garry decided to leave totally, I went back to the Charlotte. (Author interview with Andy Wright, 14 January 2021)

Musician Paul Lunn was in a local band called Dalmatian Rex that rehearsed and played gigs at O'Jays. He has fond memories:

> We started drinking at O'Jays when Andy opened it up and he offered us a rehearsal room. We moved in and a scene started developing with the bands that were there. I think the gigs were mainly free to get into; I can't remember anyone on the door apart from the big, big nights when they had things like Crazyhead on there. [...] The stage was made of pallets and, depending on where you stood, the whole stage would move. If I was playing guitar and put my foot forward to go and sing, the microphone would spin round because the stage was collapsing; the whole place was glued together with gaffer tape. (Author interview with Paul Lunn, 26 March 2021)

As soon as Andy started putting on bands, I went down to O'Jays and booked another gig for PO! The venue was next to a flyover and a large roundabout where very few people would walk about. O'Jays was small with a limited choice of drinks. The size of the building meant that O'Jays could rent out rehearsal rooms above it to bring in some extra money, but making money was never the main aim for Andy:

> I lived very frugally, in one room above the pub. I used to eat the food from the business, and I didn't pay myself a wage [...] I just survived but I elevated something that was closed down to something good, then Haz gave me money and I just put that back into the Charlotte. (Author interview with Andy Wright, 14 January 2021)

By putting on local bands nearly every night, it meant that anyone could get a gig at O'Jays, regardless of ability or appeal. Often there'd be four bands on during one evening and at least two of them would be unlistenable. Nobody lived nearby so noise levels were never an issue at O'Jays. Playing his first ever gig there was Haz Haswell:

> I was working at the university, doing some research and I was in a band. It was my first ever gig [...] playing support at a place called O'Jays, and a load of our friends turned up; it was one of the biggest buzzes of my life! After the gig I went up and spoke to Andy and said, 'Can we have another gig?' and he said they were closing down in about a month [...] 'No-one wants to run it'. So, I said, 'I'll do it'. (Author interview with Haz Haswell, 2 April 2021)

In previous times, the brewery might have been more concerned about the experience and calibre of anyone wanting to run a pub, but as so many of its tired buildings were due to be sold, there were minimal checks. Andy Wright thought it strange and amusing that someone so inexperienced could take on a pub, but he was happy to hand over to Haz so that the scene at O'Jays could continue:

> I wanted to move back to the Charlotte full time and Haz wanted to take the pub on [...] he didn't have a clue about pubs or beer or anything. The thing was, with the pub training, I knew all about that side – how to look after traditional ale and how to clean lines, run a cellar. Of course, Haz turned up in his hippy clothes and said, 'I'll buy the pub off you', and he knew fuck all. (Author interview with Andy Wright, 14 January 2021)

Haz was excited by the possibility that he could actually take on the running of O'Jays, and the speed at which everything then started happening when he did phone the brewery.

> The brewery had one question, 'Are you gay?' 'What an interview question!' I said, 'What's that got to do with anything?' And they said that the last guys who ran the pub before Andy painted it pink and turned it into a gay pub and it was unsuccessful [...] 'so we don't want another gay pub'. It was a bit weird. I needed about £1000 to

buy the fixtures and fittings and the inventory – the beers and spirits. I went to the bank and asked to borrow £1000 because I probably had about £30, and they said yes. (Author interview with Haz Haswell, 2 April 2021)

As Haz only had pub experience as a customer and had not ever served behind the bar or dealt with beer, he asked Andy if he could be trained by him before he moved back to the Charlotte:

Andy said, 'Come down one Tuesday night when there's a band on'. I arrived, and it was absolutely packed. I jumped behind the bar and this old boy came up to me and said, 'A pint of lager, mate'. I was pouring it and it was going everywhere. Eventually I gave a pint to this guy – it was probably about 70p – and he said, 'I haven't got any money' and I thought, 'He's my first ever customer!' – he was just a sweet old guy. I asked Andy what to do and he said to kick him out. 'You'll be bankrupt within a week if you give away free beer'. I was really uncomfortable with that responsibility […] I worked there for just the one night. Andy's good, and he taught me a few things. Then I had to go to court to get a licence. I said, 'Yes I had some – limited – experience at that particular venue'. It was the truth; I had worked there just one evening! And I didn't have a criminal record, so I got the licence. (Author interview with Haz Haswell, 2 April 2021)

The thrill of taking over a live music pub was enormous, but Haz soon found out that running a pub venue also takes a lot of hard work:

Andy had left all the pipes disconnected. I got a delivery of 1000 pints of beer and I thought, 'This is getting even more exciting!' and I connected them up. A lot of the connections are the same, so I had cider coming out the lager, lager coming out the bitter; everything was a complete mess. Being a good bar person is a real skill, I discovered. […] I opened the first week and had a band on that weekend. It was absolutely packed, and I ran out of beer. I had to find somebody with a van and go to another pub, the supermarket or whatever, and buy a lot of tinnies for the following night. (Author interview with Haz Haswell, 2 April 2021)

With at least ten bands playing at O'Jays every week, different crowds emerged. Usually, bands started off playing just to their friends, but as time went on, some of the more established musicians in Leicester started drinking regularly at O'Jays. It was a cool venue, free to get in and people knew that they'd probably witness some terrible bands – which became a source of amusement to them. But there was also the chance of seeing something amazing or significant. Tjinder Singh from Cornershop played his first gig here, when his band was called General Havoc. There were also Leicester bands that had some national recognition and record releases. Haz recalled some of his personal favourites:

> Blab Happy were a very good band; a couple of them used to work behind the bar, Huge Big Massive were great; I don't know how they didn't make it. Company for Henry – they were a two piece. Ada Galaxy [...] then there were some quite young bands like The Ammonites. (Author interview with Haz Haswell, 2 April 2021)

Indeed, a Saturday night gig by The Ammonites usually meant mums and dads dropping off loads of 14- to 17-year-olds. They'd be dressed in colourful vintage clothes ready to take over the bar with wild dancing to the bands and then rapidly weepy drunkenness. Haz's enthusiasm and casual warm-heartedness helped O'Jays to develop a fantastic live music scene in Leicester. He revelled in giving everyone the opportunity to get on stage, and the pub quickly attracted more fans. Andy Wright was not always impressed, though:

> Don't get me wrong [...] I love Haz; he's such a lovely man. But [...] he'd ring me up and say, 'This is broken or that's broken; what do I do?' so I'd have to cycle down to O'Jays from the Charlotte and sort out his gas situation or whatever. I'd walk into the bar, like at one o'clock on a Tuesday lunchtime and there's unicyclists and jugglers there. It was ridiculous – I've loved him ever since – fair play to him. But the pub was filthy. I was trained in a proper pub ethic, that you get up in the morning, clean the pub, because I'd been trained by Ansells in a proper pub environment. But when Haz took it over, he didn't do cleaning. (Author interview with Andy Wright, 14 January 2021)

After just over a year of running O'Jays, Haz was notified that the brewery would be selling the pub, which eventually closed in November 1989. By then, Haz was fed up with living on his own at the pub and had realised that the job wasn't a route to creative freedom and cool music. Rather it was all hard work, admin and a lot of stress. But Haz recognises that the venue and the mini scene around it was significant, and made an impact:

> Something like that's never going to make money, which is why it's so good. It's a rarity that you get the opportunity to be in a community of musicians. Unfortunately, I didn't have a vision; I didn't have a business plan and at the end, there was a 'let's drink the pub dry' party. (Author interview with Haz Haswell, 2 April 2021)

O'Jays was sold to another brewery, which opened a real ale pub without music. Haz then took on another great Leicester music venue pub, The Magazine, which was on the same street as the Princess Charlotte, and that became yet another venue for my band, PO! to play.

Andy Wright ran the Princess Charlotte from February 1989, officially shortened the name to The Charlotte in 1998, and promoted thousands of bands over the years, including Radiohead, Oasis, Coldplay, Teenage Fanclub, Storm Patrol, Arctic Monkeys and many more. One of Andy's strengths was to book a band six months in advance, by which time they'd risen from being unknowns to the front cover of the music press. As a fan it was encouraging to see all the new bands play in Leicester, and as a local band member, there were plenty of chances to play support at well-attended gigs. Throughout all this time, Andy remained a passionate music fan:

> Music can be a lifesaver. There's a thing that goes through most of the people who do music and it's a love thing really; we all connect. For me at the time, I was just going with the flow and having fun. And then even when I took over the Charlotte and it got established and I was booking all these bands that were turning out to be really successful, I still just took it in my stride [...] had a good time, but then went home and looked after my kids. (Author interview with Andy Wright, 14 January 2021)

The printed gig contracts from bands on their first tours who then went on to make it big used to be on display in The Charlotte. You could see a contract for Coldplay playing for £30 or Blur getting paid £50 in the early days and Andy was amused by the interest and prices that collectors are willing to pay for ephemera:

> As time goes on, I see what people post online – it becomes bigger than it actually was [...] but loads of those contracts used to come through via fax [...] I've got reams and reams of fax paper with nothing on them because the ink just fades. Even on the printed contracts, the typewriter ink fades after 25 years and it's just gone. (Author interview with Andy Wright, 14 January 2021)

The joy of attending an exciting, packed gig, and the buzz of playing on stage at The Charlotte and O'Jays are memories that will not fade so easily. Leicester may be a small city, but it's now more significant, with several generations of credible musicians to its name originating from Andy Wright's time as a promoter. The Charlotte, O'Jays and The Mag have all gone, and many of today's small music venues are owned and run independently of breweries.

The 1980s and '90s Leicester music scene was special because the focus was outward and forward-looking. There was a period of experimentation just before the 1989 big pub sell-off where new and young artists developed and refined their music by playing regularly to familiar audiences. The promoters, like Andy Wright and Haz Haswell who created and opened out that scene, allowing so much of it to happen, deserve greater recognition.

Author biography

Ruth Miller is a songwriter, guitarist and singer with PO! and a record label owner – *Rutland Records* (1989–1999). She has recently set up a new label *unglamorous music* working with older women's garage bands. Based in Leicester in the UK, Ruth is also one of the punkgirldiaries.com duo, producing a blog and printed zines.

9   The Brewery Arts Centre

Peter Atkinson

This chapter focuses on the evolution of a young independent music scene within a funded institution. The Brewery Arts Centre's programme featured principal music artists from around the world and two major annual festivals in the mid- to late 1980s. The venue is in the quiet market town of Kendal, a place known as the gateway to the English Lake District and a mere nine miles from Lake Windermere. Kendal is equidistant – approximately 62 miles – from the influential music cities of Liverpool and Manchester and from Leeds whose reputation as a music hub grew in the 1980s. The distance from these urban centres resulted in Kendal's post-punk fans being deprived of their favoured live music in the local area. The scene initially developed around young, local, indie bands, allowing them opportunities to participate and enjoy live performance in an exceptional venue. In the process, the reader is introduced to some of the best band names ever, all from the South Lakeland area. Aye!

From Victorian Brewery to 1970s Arts Centre

The Arts Centre was formed in the premises of the former Whitwell Mark brewery, built in 1853. It was acquired by Vaux Breweries along with thirty tied public houses[1] (pubs) in 1946. The Brewery Arts Centre bars remained tied to Vaux until the 1990s. Brewing at the Kendal building ceased in 1968 and it was put up for sale. The drive and vision of Provincial Insurance Chairman Peter Scott, a social philanthropist whose father had founded the Francis Scott Charitable Trust, was 'pivotal in pushing forward the innovative concept' of the centre (Shenton 2011). It would be supported by Northern Arts Association (of whom Scott was an Executive Member), Westmorland LEA and Kendal Corporation. The proposed principles informing policy stated in 1971 that the new institution should be developed as a Community Centre, rather than an Arts Centre (Paterson n.d.: 8). There was differing opinion over

---

1. In the UK, 'tied' public houses are required to buy all or some of their beer from specific breweries.

the years about the centre's focus as the arts offer on the performance side became aligned with national touring patterns. This factor informs the examination here of the development of the independent music scene in Kendal during the 1980s.

I had attended music nights in the early days of The Brewery and, having returned to the area from away, I ran the bar during the latter half of the 1980s. At this time, the centre was unique. Widely understood to be the best regional arts centre in the country, it provided an outstanding range of events, services and activities. Its unique nature derived from several factors. Firstly, the building itself which was hidden behind the rows of shops and houses on the town's main street. It was approached by an ascending drive leading to a large forecourt which had been landscaped into an attractive garden. The wonderful, imposing, nineteenth-century building was constructed from grey stone with a steep roof and single chimney stack. It had something of the appearance of a church, and yet had clearly been created for an industrial purpose. The conversion of the building resulted in it having a central spine which people would ascend to access the classrooms and studios upstairs. In doing so they passed through a communal café area finished in a rather tacky 1970s real wood style replete with sticky carpet, serving hatch, blackboard menu and chips or salad with everything. The juxtaposition of the old and new, with parts of the building retaining the exposed stone walls and the original wooden beams, along with some of the original planked wooden doors with their clunky latches, gave the building great charm. The centre was enhanced by artefacts from the original brewery which were dotted around to emphasise its heritage. Secondly, The Brewery offered a diverse programme of events and services, to include a broad range of arts and performance classes, two theatre spaces, music, galleries and (sometimes) cinema. The third aspect was the passion and wackiness of its support staff, extensive helpers, volunteers, and punters.

Because the building was not designed as an arts and entertainment venue, there was frequent interaction between audiences attending different concurrent performances in several areas such as the foyer, stairways to upper floors and in the entrance to the theatre (which was outdoors in the courtyard where people would be arriving for other events). The intermingling of different folk gave the middle floor catering and bar area a rich, communal feel with centre users sitting to have a cuppa or meal at lunchtime. The atmosphere was often literally steamy as one entrance was through a modern patio door. Those who did not wish to negotiate the internal system of doors and stairs through the building would enter here in their sodden clothes and be met by a wall of heat generated by the kitchen and existing customers.

Those who attended classes and events in the evening usually took a drink in the characterful Vats Bar, where polite queues would form shortly before 7pm when sessions started. The bar area was so named because it included two original wooden brewing vats that had a small section cut out so that people could squeeze in and sit at round tables inside them. The bar featured a church pew along one wall, wooden tables, and a random selection of wooden chairs (probably derived from various local clear-outs) in front of a long, real wood bar. Various pieces of original brewing equipment and publicity posters were dotted around the room which was usually full of smoke. It was ahead of its time in Kendal in 1985 for, despite being a tied house, the Vats Bar preferred to offer guest real ales rather than the supplier's own. It sold Red Stripe and Coors in cans while pumping out indie, rock, and reggae on the sound-system. It anticipated the modern craft ale bars and was modelled partly on characterful London pubs and partly distinctive Lakeland real ale pubs, such as the Coxswain's Cabin in Bowness (which featured jazz in its cellar bar) and the Old Dungeon Ghyll in Langdale, a climbers' pub which featured live folk music some evenings.

Music in a Unique Environment

Among those enthusiastically entering in early evenings to 'bag a vat' in the mid-1980s were a number of youths, some of whom were involved in the Brewery Youth Theatre, some who were in local sixth forms or colleges, and some who had already left school. This group formed the productive nucleus of an independent scene. Between themselves, a progressive new music officer, and others among the Brewery staff, they were able to create and uphold a vibrant young scene which effectively operated as an independent enterprise. This aspect gave the centre an additional role as a central music venue for a period. It also helped fulfil the centre's original remit as it provided an excellent resource for the local community in addition to generating some welcome extra income.

The former brewery's Grain Store, Sugar Store and Courtyard were converted to art rooms, a gallery and a theatre. Most significantly, a 'Discotheque/Arts Lab' was created in the former Malt Room downstairs. No doubt the founders were picking up on the late '60s London, counter-cultural vibe with this addition and envisaged 'happenings' in Kendal. The Discotheque proved to be the area where cultural changes were most felt as music provision evolved. It was the space in which there was the most engagement with ordinary Kendal folk as the town was short of discos, and it was also hireable as a function room. Sunday lunchtime 'jam' sessions I attended in these early days with school friends were hosted by Bob Dawbarn, a journalist who 'changed the *Melody Maker* in the 1960s into one of the most widely read and influential rock and pop publications' and who founded 'The Raver' column (Houston 2000). A Dixieland Jazz devotee, he played trombone in Mick Mulligan's band in the 1950s alongside vocalist George Melly (George would later often feature in the Brewery's music programme). Bob retired to the Lake District and ran the Brewery bar. As MC for these Sunday jams, he contributed trombone and encouraged local musicians to join in. Dave 'Daisy' Allen, at the time a teenage apprentice tradesperson, would get up and play bass. Dave later moved to Leeds and became a part of Gang of Four. Already the Brewery was a place that inspired creativity and collaboration and a passionate commitment to its inclusive ethos.

Kendal historically had a lively music scene. The Town Hall staged live pop/rock – when Robert Plant played The Brewery in 2000, he remembered that he had performed in that very venue in the 1960s. Numerous pubs also staged live music ranging from rock to country and western, jazz and folk. The Brewery's arrival also created new opportunities. The Malt Room's music provision evolved and by the early 1980s it had become a part of the national touring circuit. Environment-wise, it had a low ceiling with iron pillars (later a severe hazard for moshers) and the rectangular room was partly split by an original stone wall with a cute central arch which accommodated the mixing desk. Parts of the wall on either side had been removed to allow viewing of the stage from the back where a tacky 1970s wood-fronted bar with rattling pull-down grilles had been installed. The floor was parquet with tiles perpetually loosened by beer and other fluids, making heeled footsteps sound like whip-cracks. At the rear of the stage the blue wall was peeling with damp. At the sides of the room, full-length red curtains hid from the music audience's view the storage of the 'good' upholstered chairs to which they rarely had access. These were used for private functions such as weddings, and eighteenth and twenty-first birthday parties. The chairs were upholstered in red, perhaps to discreetly absorb blood stains at such events.

The Malt Room was at the back of the building, and directly underneath the Vats Bar, and so these two areas seemed a world of their own, away from the more respectable core of the centre. Because audiences would go to the Vats for their pre-gig drink, that area would be packed – often servicing both the gig and theatre audience. Attendees could easily hear when the band started below through the old wooden floor and would charge, herd-like, downstairs, often drawing complaints from the adjacent theatre about noises from outside disturbing performances. The Malt Room would also be choked with fumes. The lack of adequate air-conditioning ensured a steamy, humid atmosphere, with moisture dripping off punters and walls alike. The physical and emotional sense of warmth in this idiosyncratic environment was incredible and inspired an eager core audience.

The stage, which was then collapsible, was merely a step high. As a young local drummer in the '80s groups Mirage, Every Man Jack and The Circles observes, 'it felt almost like the audience was on stage with you! There wasn't the same divide'. This feature endures today. The institution has rebranded itself as Brewery Arts and is now led by a CEO who is herself a bassist and an events producer who has delivered projects for the likes of Island Records, Rough Trade and Skint Records (French 2021: 12). The likes of Plant, Taj Mahal, Memphis Slim, Lindisfarne, Buzzcocks, John Martyn, Roy Harper, Humphrey Lyttelton, Courtney Pine, Nine Below Zero, Big Country, Lee Scratch Perry, Slow Readers Club, Sleaford Mods and Tim Burgess have played that one-step-high Brewery stage with the audience as close as hot-breathed lovers.

Figure 9.1: Malt Room bass player (photo by Chris Allen)

In Punk's Aftermath

The Brewery's rise as a music venue coincided with the effects of the punk revolution. Reynolds speaks of the post-punk period from 1978 to 1984 and of the subsequent diversification of British music (2005: xv). This would embrace synthpop, two tone, goth, psychobilly, garage, new mod, Britfunk, Britsoul, British reggae and new pop. Punk, as a fashion, music, social and political phenomenon, showed that things could be done differently in production, distribution, promotion and consumption. Co-orchestrator Malcolm McLaren saw the essence of punk as laying in its 'anti-hierarchical, DIY nature'. A section of South Lakeland's teenage youth identified strongly with this ethos. One, who would eventually play guitar with local independent band The Virgins and others at the venue, recalled in 2021 that,

> The way we saw it, gigs were almost exclusively folk or blues-based and many featured artists who had seen their peak in the 1960s or 1970s: It was a venue for old people and we felt little or no affinity with it. This began to change slowly around the mid-1980s, but we still felt as if we were viewed with suspicion. For example, occasionally, two or three local bands would hire the Malt Room and put a gig on, but there was always the feeling that we were being begrudgingly tolerated by The Brewery, rather than embraced as a valued section of the local community.

Figure 9.2: Martyn of The Virgins (photo by Wayne Baillie)

These youths were also encouraged to seek something different by new, youth-targeted TV shows, particularly *The Young Ones* (broadcast by the BBC in 1982 and 1984) whose creators also had their roots in the DIY turn-of-decade club culture in Soho – in this case, the emerging alternative comedy scene. Also influential in this 'distinct pop cultural epoch' was the development of a fourth TV channel in 1982 which resulted in a liberation in programme-making (Reynolds 2005: xiv). Amongst the array of challenging new titles was Friday evening's adventurous pop-magazine show *The Tube* (Tyne Tees Television for Channel 4, 1982–87). Regional youths identified with the tastes and practices of peers who were consuming and creating new musical forms and artefacts in the major urban centres, but they faced the reality of cultural limitations in their own local areas. Observing the emergent regional hip hop scene in Devon at the very same time, Adam de Paor-Evans notes that regional youngsters craved and consumed an imagery of inner cities – firstly American, and later London – from afar. The 'myth of the urban' was carried to the country as the young regionals aspired to create their own environment and practices (de Paor-Evans 2020). The same happened in Kendal but with different music genres. Those bored teenagers around Kendal who had embraced punk to reject the practices of the past wanted a scene of their own as the Thatcherite '80s kicked in.

Bill Lloyd's Influence

Opportunity was to knock for The Brewery when it appointed a new Music Officer, Bill Lloyd in 1984 and added a new full-time technician with responsibility for the music and theatre spaces. In his forthcoming memoir *The Whispered Waltz* Bill remembers that,

> Because of the age range [of young local musicians] – roughly fourteen to twenty – there was no venue in town available to them for social gatherings or practice or concert. All available venues were either licensed premises, or commercial spaces requiring hire fees, and with noise restrictions. (Lloyd, forthcoming)

The Music Officer gave young local musicians access to the Brewery music stage and provided an environment in which they felt sufficiently accepted and confident enough to begin using it as an independent venue. Bill had a background in arts management, stage managing for major touring acts, hands-on experience as a musician and good local knowledge and contacts. He acknowledges that 'there is no doubt that whatever success I had at The Brewery owed a great debt' to his predecessor 'and the long slog of building up the music programme from nothing' (Lloyd, forthcoming). This included, previously, the creation of the annual Kendal Jazz Festival and Kendal Folk Festival, the latter acquiring significant funding from Legal and General Insurance during the 1980s.

Having a remit to produce eighty gigs a year, along with the two festivals, the range and diversity of The Brewery's musical offering was impressive. However, the average age of the audience was around forty and 'very few people under twenty-five came through the door' (Lloyd, forthcoming). Bill identified with the punk sensibility because of the radical tradition in some folk music. He recalls seeking intelligence amongst Kendal's organic music circle. The proprietor of the nearby Smyth's Records shared his knowledge of both local audience tastes and those of the keen young punk and indie record buyers. Bill's first booking was Billy Bragg, a sold-out gig that remains legendary among the youngsters who attended it. Bragg at the time was making a name for himself with the release of *Brewing Up with Billy Bragg* which was receiving good reviews and airplay on the highly influential BBC Radio 1 John Peel show which championed alternative and non-commercial music forms, particularly indie, and which gave up-and-coming acts a platform. His new political songs such as 'To Have or Have Not' and 'It Says Here' also resonated with the politics of the bitter miners' strike of the time; indeed, he performed benefits for miners, and in the coalfield. The concert thus attracted a young audience, but also an older folk audience who would attend performances by the likes of older political singers such as Dick Gaughan and Christy Moore. Two of the young Vats Bar regulars were indeed delighted to brew up with Billy that evening. Found wandering the street after he failed to source a post-gig cup of tea at his nearby hotel, he accepted an invitation from them for a brew round one of their houses just up the road.

This was the beginning of the period when young local musicians gained access to the Brewery's ample facilities on an unprecedented scale. The Malt Room began operating on a dual level as an independent usage co-existed with the Brewery's official programme. It resulted in a considerable section of the town's young – those with a taste for indie and rock – identifying with the centre as their base. One young drummer from the time notes that the complex had enough space and facilities for them 'to hang out there for hours at a time'. It became a 'go-to place and the hub for many activities' for those at secondary school or college. Bill responded to this, recalling that:

> I set up a regular punk practice night, at which the young aspiring musicians and bands of South Lakeland could meet and talk, swap gear and instruments, and develop their technique and their

repertoire. This group had no money to spare, so they could not afford a ticket or room hire, so there was no admission fee and I gave them the room for nothing. They had no money for drink either, so it was not worth opening the bar on practice nights. Once a week [...] young players and a young potential audience would come through the door and they ran the event themselves, so they felt that they owned it. They bossed the Malt Room and before long they were organising their own concert nights and even a mini festival. (Lloyd, forthcoming)

Strip 'zine, a Liverpool Connection and Bold New Brewery Events

A catalyst for this new productivity was the formation of a local freesheet fanzine, born from the DIY spirit of the punk era. I lived in London during the height of the punk revolution and the post-punk aftermath and was influenced by the creativity of the do-it-yourself approach. Joining with two young habitués of the Vats Bar, one of whom was the same age as the young indie musicians now replacing the older punks on the scene, we created *Strip*. Its name was derived from the inclusion of strip cartoons created by the youngest editor. *Strip* championed the new young local music scene which was unfolding in the area. It enthused local youth through the attention it paid to new emerging bands and by encouraging venues to stage live indie music events. Because I worked for the Brewery, it became associated with the venue to an extent and, while it was embraced by some staff and customers who realised its potential to positively engage young people in creative pursuits, it was viewed with suspicion by others who felt threatened by its independence. Being favourably disposed to the 'zine, the Brewery's new Music Officer noted its reviews and its advertisements for some local venues that were putting on 'alternative' bands. These included the goth-themed Nightmares at the Cross Keys in the village of Milnthorpe and Warton Grange, a hotel in Warton, a small village north of Carnforth, which itself is north of Lancaster. These were both unlikely places to be staging alternative music. To this day, the players and punters from the time still refer to *Strip*. It brought this scene together, energised it and gave those involved the confidence to create a new young environment which had something of the energy and style of the vaunted indie scene in Liverpool and Manchester. The existence of this artefact also provides vital documentation of this neglected piece of Kendal history.

A number of aspiring young musos in South Lakeland used a recording studio – in a remote hamlet near remote Shap – to record demos. *Strip* checked the studio out and learned of their close relationship with Liverpool indie label and shop, Probe Records. *Strip* visited Probe and met the friendly proprietor, Geoff Davies, who raved about his fantastic 'Indie-thrash-punk-Celtic-folk band', as Bill describes them, Gone to Earth (Lloyd, forthcoming). Some sense of bonding would subsequently become apparent between the emergent Kendal young musicians' scene, and Liverpool. It is unsurprising that they should look to that city for a 'myth of the urban'. Manchester in 1985 had not yet mobilised its musical heritage 'in the service of urban regeneration' and its cultural renaissance (Gillespie, Rose and Silver 2021). Liverpool, however, had experienced a 'formidable flowering of new bands' during Roger Eagle's tenure as manager of Eric's club, on Mathew Street, from 1976 to 1980 (Witts 2017: 30). As Witts has observed, this had been very influential upon Tony Wilson's creation of the Factory club, and Factory Records (ibid.). The fertile Liverpool musical environment recommended the city to young people of the Kendal area as a seat of indie authenticity. This seal of approval was enhanced for this group – many of whom shared an intense dislike of the Thatcher government – by the city's militancy in the mid-1980s. During this time, the Liverpool Council refused the vicious cuts to the city's budget made by the Tory government as the city struggled with high unemployment and industrial unrest. The coinciding presentation of 'the Liverpudlian romantic' in on-screen Liverpool dramas by Alan Bleasdale, Willy Russell and Carla Lane at the time added to the city's appeal (Hughes 2020: 13).

Among those bored teenage musicians hanging in the Vats Bar were The Word is Out, an indie unit featuring a charismatic singer (then in the sock manufacturing industry) and a bassist, who was an electrician and would fall asleep sitting in the Vat of an evening after a hard day's wiring. The band was managed by the singer's very capable brother (now sadly deceased) who had a suited job at Peter Scott's Provincial (illustrating the worth of the centre in encouraging creative enterprise). Bill Lloyd read an enthusiastic review of one of their gigs in *Strip* and, observing the coverage and surfacing scene, took a significant step and offered The Word is Out and other local groups a mini-festival to be staged in the Malt Room. The resultant *Futurama* would feature local young groups and be managed by those same youngsters. It was to be one of a series of such events and Bill instructed that the profits from the series should be used to hire a name band to perform. The band would be selected by a public vote organized through *Strip*. The first *Futurama* on 31 May 1985 featured the Barrow band Tier Garden along with The Word is Out, Intensity Field and (another fantastic band name) Dreaming Out Loud, all from the Kendal area. This first event was a magical night. The young performers could barely believe that they were going to take that one small step up and perform on the stage at The Brewery. A couple more in the series were staged before the organisers – led by The Word is Out's manager – had enough money in the kitty to book their chosen name band. The Pogues won the *Strip* vote but their acclaimed album *Rum Sodomy & the Lash*, released in August 1985, charted and up went their fees, significantly past the budget of the young Kendal independent organisers. Second choice was Half Man Half Biscuit. The gig was held on 6 June 1986, just after the Merseysiders' album *Back in the DHSS* and single 'The Trumpton Riots' had topped the Indie charts. The band refused to come on before 10pm because England were playing Morocco in the World Cup and they would watch the game on TV in a pub nearby (it ended 0 – 0). Liverpool's Gone to Earth supported, and 'raised the roof off', Bill Lloyd recalls.

Figure 9.3: Futurama poster (photo by Wayne Baillie)

Kendal's Thriving New Independent Scene

Of this emerging young scene Bill Lloyd writes, 'I had new relationships with the under twenty-five age group. This became important because it opened the door to low budget, low overhead, popular events, publicised by word of mouth' (Lloyd 2023). The support of The Brewery, and coverage from *Strip*, resulted in an assured scene by 1986. With the ability to hire the Malt Room for independent performances, willing parties stepped in to curate their own events featuring local bands. Sometimes organisations would hire the room and stage events of their own. On 14 May 1987, an organisation booked the room and put on Leeds' infamous Chumbawumba. Some of their home fan base trekked across, one of whom apparently had had his collar felt in one of the record shops in town for suspicious behaviour. Ill-feeling amongst the visiting fans caused a riot at the Brewery event, which was shut down. My memory is of a group of fans, who I did not know, stamping around the well-tended Brewery gardens in a circle chanting 'Kill, kill, kill the pigs'. Police duly arrived.

With a small circuit of local venues also staging indie music, the roster of local acts swelled, not necessarily all in the indie genre – some would be described as rock, some as post-punk, punk, garage or psychobilly. These acts included, along with those already mentioned, Big Amongst Sheep, Brothers Grimm, Side FX, The Presence, Cacophony, The Paps, Hot and Horrid (from Windermere), Boat Thief, Every Man Jack, The Circles, The Cuckoos, Freakapotamus, The Cocoons, Rubber Pig Vendetta (another great band name) and The Surfin' Bats (who each had individualised Bat nicknames way before the Spice Girls employed this publicity device ... Bat Power!).

The confidence in this embedded independent scene spawned other developments. Following Bill's example, the Brewery Dance Officer had noted the new hip hop dance trends and formed a young breakdance group. They too were granted their own event at The Brewery in which a legendary local break dancer (now sadly deceased) stunned those present with his head-spinning. In 1990, a group of (mainly) young people were encouraged by the centre director to create the Buzz Club. This was a comedy cabaret club which also featured music acts from the pool of independent local talent including the show's house band, the Tequila Trio and also The Paps (punk), The Circles and Freakapotamus.

The 1990s and Beyond

The arts funding cuts of the Thatcher era impacted The Brewery badly and, by the start of the 1990s, jobs and facilities were under threat and there was some toning down of the programme. The situation was saved by the award of a National Lottery grant and the centre began renovation work in 1996. Two cinemas were built into the hillside behind The Brewery, successfully reflecting the vernacular of the original building and allowing for excellent inclusive access. The Malt Room itself had its central wall removed, allowing much better sightlines. The parquet flooring was replaced and, importantly, the mixing desk console and technical area moved to the back in an enclosed, lockable, space, thus precluding the need to take down the whole rig after every gig. The Vats Bar was extended, retaining the original vats with easier access granted to a patio in a reshaped garden that easily facilitated viewing of summer outdoor music performances. The biggest change was the conversion of the original brewery loading-bay courtyard into an indoor theatre, tripling the audience capacity and including a much larger stage size. Music acts were featured including the likes of Beth Orton, Waterson:Carthy and the Cinematic Orchestra.

Young members of the bands British Sea Power and Wild Beasts – who were formed locally – were attendees at The Brewery. They were well-acquainted with what it offered across the range of musical and social activities, proving that the legacy of accommodating young musicians endures. Many of the youngsters involved in the independent scene described here have done very well for themselves. This is a testimony to the benefits of nurturing the creative instinct and allowing the means for expression and communal involvement. The Brewery celebrated its fiftieth anniversary year in 2022 with a new identity and emphasis on digital production but still includes live music and performance. We wish them the very best of luck. The slogan on the old inherited Leyland Motors clock in the centre's grounds says 'For all Time', which is appropriate for the enduringly positive effect this venue has within its community.

References

de Paor-Evans, Adam. 2020. 'Urban myths and rural legends: An alternate take on the regionalism of hip hop'. *Popular Music and Society* 43, no. 4: 414–425. https://doi.org/10.1080/03007766.2020.1730651

French, Sarah. 2021. 'Behind the scenes'. *Cumbria Life* (June): 10–13.

Gillespie, Tom, Isaac Rose and Jonathan Silver. 2021. 'The housing crisis in Manchester, capital of the "long 90s"'. 24 June. https://www.versobooks.com/blogs/5110-the-housing-crisis-in-manchester-capital-of-the-long-90s

Houston, Bob. 2000. 'Bob Dawbarn: Jazz trombonist and music journalist who was the original Raver'. *The Guardian*, 26 October.

Hughes, Simon. 2020. *There She Goes: Liverpool, a City on its Own. The Long Decade 1979–1993*. Liverpool: deCoubertin Books.

Lloyd, Bill. 2023. *The Whispered Waltz: 40 Years as a Travelling Musician*. Kendal: Lloyd Music Ltd.
Paterson, Anice. n.d. *Recollections: A Celebration of the Brewery Arts Centre*. Kendal: The Brewery Arts Centre.
Reynolds, Simon. 2005. *Rip it Up and Start Again: Postpunk 1978–1984*. London: Faber & Faber.
Shenton, Kenneth. 2011. 'Peter Scott: Businessman and philanthropist devoted to the Lake District and the North-west'. *The Independent*, 26 January.
Witts, Richard. 2017. 'Manpool, the Musical: Harmony and Counterpoint on the Lancashire Plain'. In *Sounds Northern: Popular Music, Culture and Place in England's North*, ed. Ewa Mazierska, 17–36. Sheffield: Equinox.

Author biography

Peter Atkinson teaches Film, Media and Popular Culture at University of Central Lancashire, UK. He has particular expertise, and is passionate about, media representation of the North of England with a strong strand of work on the role of television broadcasting and popular music in generating popular mythologies of the region. Peter has been External Examiner for MA Beatles Studies (Liverpool Hope University) and is a Fellow of the Higher Education Academy.

10 'Nothing Comes Easy': Small Venue Concerts with the Wedding Present

David Lewis Gedge and Jon Stewart

This is an edited version of a dialogue that occurred via Zoom and email during the making of the Wedding Present's *Locked Down and Stripped Back* album in summer 2020.

Jon Stewart: 'Indie' music used to be defined by the type of record distributor. What is it that defines grassroots independent venues?

David Lewis Gedge: Well, as a mathematician, I would say the logical answer is capacity. That is the main thing. A small venue only has a limited number of people and is reducing the amount of money they can make from ticket sales straight away. That then leads on to things such as the stage size. The classic grassroots independent venue, in my mind, would be a small room with a very small stage, often no dressing room, and usually only a small fee because you're not getting the thousands of ticket sales.

JS: Is there a difference in the way you approach that kind of gig compared to, say, a larger venue?

DLG: It's usually more relaxed and a bit friendlier. The promoter's usually there to show you around, you're closer to the audience, and, in general, I think it makes a better concert because the atmosphere's better. It's more intimate and the band can feed off the audience because you're literally two feet away from them. At a larger venue you're thirty feet away and you don't really get the same contact. There's obviously downsides as well because you can be *too* close, especially if there's no barrier. People can fall onto the stage, cause damage, break equipment, and cause injuries. For guitarists and bass players the worst thing that can happen might be that someone jumps on stage and breaks a pedal, but for singers you've got this microphone in your face all the time. Especially as a singing guitarist, because you're stuck there at the mercy of people who just fall into it, with no hands free to hang on to the microphone stand. You kind of have to learn to dodge out the way if you see somebody hurtling towards you. There's been maybe a dozen times where I've actually felt: 'Yeah, I could lose my teeth here if I get this metal projectile rammed into my face'. A barrier can be useful to protect the group, but at the same time, do you really want to fill what could amount to a quarter of the venue with this big, metal structure which doesn't look great?

Because of budget limitations the PA, monitors and lights are also sometimes inadequate. As a musician you notice when they say: 'You can't do that because we haven't got the right number of compressors', or 'We haven't got enough feeds from the desk'. But then, you speak to the audience, and they don't realise that. I think somehow the atmosphere becomes more important. I think they will go to a big gig and be expecting a certain level of sound quality because they're watching more critically and the music is bursting through this huge PA; but then they go to a small venue and it's not so important. A stage backline in the room is probably enough, and with a bit of vocal coming through the PA, people are happy.

JS: The cliché among some bands is that grassroots venues are those that you play 'on the way up' and then also 'on the way down' again.

DLG: To be honest, we never stopped doing them. We have always enjoyed playing those small concerts. In 1992, when we were in the Top 40 singles chart twelve times, we still decided that we wanted to do a small-venue tour specifically. We actually hired a transit van to bring round our own barrier on that occasion, because we knew a lot of those places wouldn't have them. So, yeah, we've never turned our backs on those venues. And they're very useful when you're about to play a festival. It's always nice to play a concert in front of 200 people at a small venue as a warm-up before you play a festival in front of 20,000 people. For example, in Leeds we usually play at O2 Academy, but somewhere like Brudenell Social Club is great because you can do a warm-up show there to a couple of hundred people and it's not going to affect the Academy show. Those same 200 fans will probably go to them both anyway.

Another thing independent venues offer is the opportunity to play in smaller towns. I do enjoy playing outside the Leeds-Manchester-Glasgow-London-Bristol circuit: Milton Keynes or Chelmsford or similar places. Those populations can only sustain a small venue and they often have quite an interesting regional character. It's great that such towns can have venues that attract international artists. You can feel that they're part of a local scene. There are a few examples of that. The John Peel Centre in Stowmarket, the MacArts in Galashiels, the Forum in Tunbridge Wells, the Lemon Tree in Aberdeen, the Craufurd Arms in Milton Keynes, Chinnerys in Southend, the Trades Club in Hebden Bridge. The Trades Club is a good example of one of those places where it can get a bit raucous on a Friday or a Saturday if there's no barrier.

There are two venues which, I think, are great examples of the good and the bad. One is the Wedgewood Rooms in Portsmouth, the other was a place in the East Midlands, which is now closed. What a dive that was! The band didn't like going there because it's such a horrible place. Once we literally had to walk over a broken toilet in the corridor in order to get onto the stage.

JS: ... literally 'a toilet venue'.

DLG: I used to ask Ian Binnington, the promoter at the Wedgewood Rooms, about it. 'How come your venue is so nice? You're both on similar levels in similar towns'. It was purely financial, I think. Ian will pay the bands less but then invest a greater percentage of the profit into the venue. It is always clean, had a nice dressing room, a great PA and lights. Whereas at the other place the staff were underpaid and grumpy, the mixing desk and microphone stands didn't work ... but you got twice the fee so after the show you're thinking: 'Well that wasn't very nice but maybe it was worth it'.

JS: Did you ever play CBGBs in New York?

DLG: I did, yeah, did you?

JS: Yeah. I mean, the toilet *there* ... that was just ...

DLG: Horrible! Yet, in the build up to that concert we were thinking: 'Oh great, we're going to play at CBGBs; this legendary venue!' It was a destination venue. Everyone wanted to go there because of the name. I remember another place like that in Kansas City where the toilet in the dressing room didn't have a door. Everyone could see you.

JS: The better small venues in the USA have stunning PA systems, though. They can sound fantastic!

DLG: That is weird, isn't it? I think maybe they invest more money into the sound. I did notice that; even from going to see gigs – as well as playing them – there.

JS: I think it's possibly because there's less of a drinking culture, as people often drive to and from shows, and more about listening to good-quality music. Some small venues in America have really quirky locations, too: cafes, laundromats, you even played a bicycle shop in Austin, Texas. I wonder if that's because gigs are less boozy in America.

Let's go back to historic venues in the North of England. Were there any small gigs in your area that were particularly important? For me it was the upstairs room of the Hallamshire Hotel in Sheffield.

DLG: Manchester Boardwalk was quite famous. In Leeds we used to play the Royal Park. That was a classic little gig. Nottingham Garage was another. Preston Twang Club. Bradford 1 in 12 Club was always good. It's run by anarchists so there were cheap tickets for unemployed people.

JS: Did you play 'The Square' in Harlow?

DLG: We did, yeah – tiny little place. We turned up once and the support band was supposed to have been Mansun. But they arrived, took one look at the place, and just said: 'We're not playing here. We're not supporting the Wedding Present in this place'. And then they left!

JS: Student Unions played an important role back then because universities would have a stage and crew, so you could do small gigs in nice spaces.

DLG: It was a real eye-opener to play in Europe, too, where so many small venues are state-subsidised, and universities were our equivalent of that at one time. But we played lots of universities, too ... even in the first couple of years, from 1985 to 1987. It was one step up from the small gig circuit with a bit more money and a larger PA, and even if the room was half-empty the promoter wouldn't be tearing their hair out because it's the Student Union budget so they had more freedom to take chances. I was looking at the universities and colleges we've played over the last twenty years and I've got the University of Northumbria, Leeds Metropolitan University, Keele University, Kingston College – that's quite a good place – Liverpool University ... but, I think, the O2 Academy venues have probably kind of replaced those to a certain extent.

JS: Actually, I think a couple of universities are now involved with the O2 Academy brand too, and Academy Music Group now run their venues for them on a commercial basis.

DLG: Manchester University is a good example of that because they've got the different sized venues so they can offer a range, can't they? I guess that's because it's a big city and, as you say, the outside promoters have come in.

JS: We played a few Arts Centres recently and they were great but they're almost too nice – unlike some of the small venues we've already talked about.

DLG: I do love those venues. I actually prefer them because you know, when you arrive, that there's going to be people there to make the PA and the lights work, there's loads of crew, dressing rooms, somewhere to put merchandise, and they're usually in nicer areas that are pleasant and well-lit. But then, for a lot of people, if they were offered the choice of either seeing us at a seedy toilet venue or at a posh arts centre, they'd always go for the first option.

JS: A lot of arts centres are housed in reused spaces such as old churches or theatres. Then again, a lot of small venues are in reused spaces, too, of course. Bedford Esquires is a converted nineteenth-century chapel, Tunbridge Wells Forum was once a public baths, Hull's New Adelphi Club was formerly a terraced house, and Bristol Fleece and Firkin is a historic wool hall with flagstone flooring. That's the venue where you have to sneak down behind the long bar to access the stage area before a show, and then walk back the same way after you've come off stage negotiating the beer taps and boxes of crisps while everyone stares at you.

DLG: The Fleece was the hottest concert I've ever played, I think. It's the only time I've ever played stripped to the waist (laughs). I literally had to take my shirt off because it was just so hot. I thought: 'I can't stand this, I've just got to take this off'. So, I took my guitar and shirt off, and then put my guitar back on. I don't think there's any photos of that one. I'm glad there's not. It was just so hot. It was unbelievable. That's another thing about small venues, isn't it? The lack of ventilation. You're not going to get air conditioning, especially in a little room.

JS: Sometimes there's no toilet backstage ...

DLG: ... you have to push your way through the crowd ...

JS: ... and if you need a wee before you go on, or between the last song and the encore ...

DLG: ... that wouldn't apply to me!

JS: No, of course, because the Wedding Present never do encores.

Have the economics of running a small-venue tour with a band changed over the years, or is it basically the same model as it was when you were doing it before?

DLG: I think we've diversified a bit, mostly in the merchandising department really, but otherwise I think it's pretty much exactly the same model. In the Wedding Present – perhaps because we're all from Yorkshire or something – we saw bands get major deals and suddenly start playing bigger venues and staying at posh hotels and you kind of wonder why, when you think: 'There's absolutely no need to do that. It's your own money'.

I think we've always been very grounded. We've always thought that there's no reason not to just stay at the same hotels we've always stayed at and keep the cost down because, at the end of the day, that'll be money in our pockets. I think that's stayed the same throughout the Wedding Present's existence, really.

What I meant by diversification in the merchandise department is that, in the old days, we'd just take a box of t-shirts into a small venue to sell. I think it was always seen as quite uncool to sell records at a concert because it felt like it was the record shops that should do that, and it was almost a bit embarrassing if you had to sell your own records on your stall. But then we'd go to America and it was totally commonplace.

So, we've definitely extended the range of products to include vinyl and CDs. I don't know whether that's just us, or whether everyone's done that. The decline in income from record sales hasn't been replaced by merchandise, but it certainly helps to address that a little bit. The only problem in small venues is that you often don't physically have enough space in the merchandise selling area if you have a wide range of items.

JS: Do you think that small venues are technically better set up in terms of the stage, and the other practical elements? I've noticed that a lot of equipment has got smaller, which really suits small venues. I couldn't imagine the horror of carting Marshall speaker cabinets around today. Trying to get them up the stairs at the Trades Club or something would just be a nightmare.

DLG: That certainly helps, doesn't it? I think that PAs have gotten smaller, too. I remember at the Royal Park. It wasn't a big room but the PA was enormous! I first noticed that in Japan, actually. When we played in Japan, everything was smaller, and I think that's come here now, hasn't it. Smaller speakers that are still just as powerful. We're all on in-ear monitors now so we don't need wedges anymore, and that gives you a bit more space on a small stage, too.

JS: What's going to happen to small venues after the coronavirus pandemic? It's a difficult time, obviously.

DLG: I'm worried some of them won't survive. If the Wedgewood Rooms went, I'd be quite upset by that because they've done such a good job over the years. The promoter's company is called PVC which stands for 'Portsmouth Venue Campaign'. That's how they started, to establish a venue in Portsmouth, and that venue became the Wedgewood Rooms. I think it's a perfect example of how an independent venue should be.

One thing that's going to be interesting after the pandemic is that no one's played for so long that everybody will want to tour. How will audiences react to that? Will they take it on board because they've been so starved of live music? Or will they be saying: 'I can't go out every night to see all these bands'?

JS: Maybe new small venues will arise after the pandemic, if there's a market.

DLG: That's the question though: is there going to be that market?

JS: Well, I'm very concerned that some important grassroots venues could be lost forever ... but then again, if city centre office spaces and shops become less attractive for commercial use because everyone's working from home, that could provide new opportunities too. The problem with that is the potential for noise issues at brand-new sites, particularly given the amount of residential developments in city centres over the last twenty years.[1]

DLG: Ultimately, I think a lot of it will be driven by the market. You and I grew up when rock music was the only thing. We didn't have the internet, we didn't have computer games, we didn't have millions of TV channels. We listened to the radio, bought records and went to see bands. I think that our age group

1. The 'agent-of change principle' incorporated in planning regulations since 2018 offers some protection for pre-existing venues threatened by noise complaints but will not apply to new ventures that attempt to occupy unused city centre locations after the pandemic (Holmes and Wex 2018).

is probably, to some extent, what small venues are still depending upon. It's almost like: 'All you 50-year-olds should be going out to see gigs'. But people change when they get older. They don't necessarily want to go out as much. And bands aren't the be-all-and-end-all for young people, are they? So, maybe in future there will be a contraction of the market anyway when it comes to small venues.

JS: Habits have certainly changed over the years. People are into a much wider range of music now, and indie guitar seems almost to have become a niche genre again – at least in terms of what young people listen to. I wonder if they are more electronically focused because it's just so much easier to make music with a digital audio workstation? It was the same for us. Learning to strum a guitar was much easier than making music on any classical instrument, and today it's easier to program a computer than to learn the guitar. People gravitate towards the simplest way to be creative. So even in venues set up specifically for bands, many artists are likely to turn up with some form of digital backing tracks and samples. There's plenty of dance clubs with stages too small for a drum kit and backline, so they're not even set up for that. They'll just have a DJ table and visiting artists need carry little more than a memory stick. I wonder if more small venues will have to morph into clubs in order to stay viable?

DLG: If the kind of people who go to gigs are getting older – do they even live in cities anymore? We used to always play Seattle in the States, and it was always a great gig. And then, over the last few years, it's died off a little because the city has become so expensive to live in that people have moved out. Bellingham, which is up the road a little bit, is now a better place to play. I think we've found that here in the UK as well. We do quite well in satellite towns like Aldershot or Guildford; those kinds of places, because people have moved out of the cities. But maybe that's age specific to the Wedding Present. I don't know if that will affect the whole culture around small venues. It would be interesting to hear if young people still go to gigs as much as older people.

Figure 10.1a-c The Wedding Present, Baroeg, Rotterdam, November 2019 (photo by Peter Koudstaal Photography)

Postscript

Since this conversation took place there have been heroic efforts to secure the future of the nation's small venues. The Music Venues Trust #SaveOurVenues campaign has raised more than £4million in donations from over 75,000 people. The Wedgewood Rooms reached its £12,000 target in just twelve hours. Acting entirely true to form, venue manager Geoff Priestley and his staff used their downtime to replace the live room flooring, fix up the roof and redecorate the interior (Broom 2021). After recovering from the devastating floods of December 2015, Hebden Bridge Trades Club saw its income wiped out for a second time in five years, yet was able to secure its future by raising almost £54,000 in 35 days (Hirst 2021). These and other grassroots venues have benefited from additional support via Arts Council England's Cultural Recovery Fund (which made payments in August and October 2020, and in April 2021) and by the Music Venues Trust's 'Revive Live' scheme in late summer 2021. The latter used National Lottery funds to support gigs and tours by well-known artists in small venues across the UK and included a show by Rag 'n' Bone Man at the 250 capacity Tunbridge Wells Forum.

Nonetheless, as some perceptive journalists predicted early on, the Covid-19 pandemic has only accelerated the pace of change in pre-existing economic and social trends (Forsyth 2020; Haass 2020). The ongoing difficulties experienced by so many grassroots music venues exemplify this phenomenon. In March 2021 the Music Venues Trust confirmed that around 200 venues still face an uncertain future and 18 are at risk of imminent permanent closure. Even prior to successive Covid lockdowns, one in three established small venues was under threat, mostly due to noise complaints and high business rates (Davyd 2021a, 2021b; Webster et al.: 2018). So, while it was a real privilege to spend time talking with an artist who has done more than most to support grassroots gigs, it was equally concerning to reflect on how vulnerable these spaces have now become.[2] Thank you to all the people who have created and maintained such distinctive performance spaces over the years. Hopefully, future generations will continue to benefit from their presence.

---

2. The Music Venues Trust website (https://musicvenuetrust.com/) has a wealth of information on the issues facing local independent managers and promoters, and their #SaveOurVenues campaign (https://saveourvenues.co.uk/#/) has details of how you can help.

References

Broom, Chris. 2021. 'How Portsmouth's grass-roots music venue The Wedgewood Rooms is surviving the pandemic'. *The News*, 19 June. https://www.portsmouth.co.uk/whats-on/arts-and-entertainment/how-portsmouths-grass-roots-music-venue-the-wedgewood-rooms-is-surviving-the-pandemic-3279194

Davyd, Mark. 2021a. 'Derby and Sheffield venues removed from Music Venue Trust's Red List: 18 grassroots music venues remain at risk'. *Music Venues Trust*. https://musicvenuetrust.com/2021/03/2-venues-removed-from-crisis-red-list/

Davyd, Mark. 2021b. 'One year of silence: Music Venue Trust's Mark Davyd reflects on the live shutdown'. *Music Week*, 19 March. https://www.musicweek.com/live/read/one-year-of-silence-music-venue-trust-s-mark-davyd-reflects-on-the-live-shutdown/082883

Forsyth, James. 2020. 'This pandemic has put politics on fast-forward'. *The Spectator*, 9 May. https://www.spectator.co.uk/article/this-pandemic-has-put-politics-on-fast-forward

Haass, Richard. 2020. 'The pandemic will accelerate history rather than reshape it'. *Foreign Affairs*, 7 April. https://www.foreignaffairs.com/articles/united-states/2020-04-07/pandemic-will-accelerate-history-rather-reshape-it

Hirst, Ian. 2021. 'Hebden Bridge Trades Club had to reschedule 65 shows five times due to pandemic'. *Halifax Courier*, 23 April. https://www.halifaxcourier.co.uk/news/people/hebden-bridge-trades-club-had-to-reschedule-65-shows-five-times-due-to-pandemic-3211576

Holmes, Sarah and Sara Wex. 2018. 'The "agent of change" principle in the new revised NPPF'. *Womble Bond Dickinson*. https://www.womblebonddickinson.com/uk/insights/articles-and-briefings/agent-change-principle-new-revised-nppf

Webster, Emma, Matt Brennan, Adam Behr, Martin Cloonan and Jake Ansell. 2018. 'Valuing live music: The UK Live Music Census 2017 report'. *Live Music Exchange*. http://uklivemusiccensus.org/wp-content/uploads/2018/03/UK-Live-Music-Census-2017-full-report.pdf

Author biographies

David Lewis Gedge is an English musician best known for his work in influential indie bands the Wedding Present (of which he is the singer, guitarist, principal songwriter, and only ever-present member) and Cinerama. The Wedding Present have had eighteen UK Top 40 singles and seven UK Top 40 albums. A champion of the DIY ethic David has recorded with a diverse range of collaborators, from Steve Albini to the BBC Big Band. Over the last thirty-five years he has played almost 2,000 concerts at venues large and small across the world.

Jon Stewart is guitarist for the platinum-selling Britpop band Sleeper and, since 2019, for the Wedding Present. He is also Course Leader of the Master's in Popular Music Practice at BIMM Institute, Brighton. Previous research publications include work on Robert Johnson, Brian Eno, arena concerts, music memoirs, and YouTube. He is the author of *Dylan, Lennon, Marx & God* (Cambridge University Press, 2022).

11 In Memory of The Standard: Hard Rock in East London

Anna Maria Barry

In the early noughties, Ilford in East London was not the ideal place for a teenage girl obsessed with hard rock. UK garage blasted through school corridors and Burberry prints were more 'in' than band shirts. Luckily, I did not have to go too far to find my people. On Friday nights I dragged my friends onto the 123 bus in search of loud guitars. Our destination? The Royal Standard in Walthamstow.

The night we discovered The Standard was memorable. We had heard rumours of an under-18s rock night, a prospect that sounded way too good to be true. At our (somewhat sheltered) Catholic girls' school, my friends and I were pretty much the only rock fans and our classmates made us feel the difference. We were nicknamed 'The Death Squad'. Though it wasn't meant as a compliment, we scrawled it across our folders and schoolbags in Tippex. In the parlance of high school tribalism at the time, we were 'grungers'. That meant being accused of devil worship and asked to confirm rumours about Marilyn Manson's ribcage on an almost weekly basis (Averby 2020) (if you know, you know). The prospect of meeting other people like us, then, was appealing – not least because there might be *boys* there.

The Standard wrapped around the corner opposite Blackhorse Road tube station. A long, squat building painted pale lemon yellow, it was topped with a semi-circular sign that read 'THE STANDARD MUSIC'. As you walked through the front door, the stage and large dancefloor were to your left (capacity: 300) while the bar was on the right. Tucked behind it was a seating area, filled with crusty sofas in well-worn leather. The walls were daubed with a patchy orange paintjob covered with many layers of band posters and gig flyers. Surrounding the doors to the bathrooms were a series of full-length mirrors – disorientating, I later discovered, after too many pints of snakebite.

We turned up that first night half expecting to be turned away but were instead ushered through the front door into another world. The floors were sticky, the air was thick with cigarette smoke and the bathrooms were revolting. I loved it. We danced in our fishnets to the latest *Kerrang!* hits, high on nothing but Coca Cola and the deafening sound system. I also met my first boyfriend that night. He was someone who appealed to me pretty much solely because he had long hair and said he was in a band (he was not). Whilst our relationship lasted a matter of weeks, my love for The Standard endured and I went back countless times, creating musical memories that my friends and I still talk about nearly two decades later.

Historian Karen Averby has recently charted the history of the venue, tracing its origins back as far as the 1840s when Walthamstow was still a rural town (Averby 2020). She reports that the Royal Standard started life as a beer house that evolved to serve the expanding population as the area became urbanised. Though it hosted a range of events in this early period (judging by newspaper reports, dog racing featured prominently), Averby says it was not until the 1970s that the venue really established itself. Acts who performed at The Standard during this time included Danny La Rue and Mike Reid, but by the next decade rock bands had all but taken over. Some of the most notable acts to appear included Phil Lynott (1984) and Suzi Quatro (1990).

A regular during this period was local musician Mark Venables, who has been in a number of notable metal bands including Airrace (with Jason Bonham) and Di'Anno (with former Iron Maiden frontman Paul Di'Anno.) He says of The Standard: 'For a small venue it [...] attracted a lot of bigger bands that would normally be doing their "smaller" gigs in more upmarket clubs. Instead, they were here in the East End playing in a sticky, smoky, dark pub' (author interview with Venables, May 2021). Venables reminisces about memorable nights, both on stage and in the audience – he was there for the Phil Lynott gig and hung out with him afterwards.

Just as important as these big names, though, were the local bands who cut their teeth at the venue. For some, a gig at The Standard represented the pinnacle of a short-lived musical career, but for others it started them out on a journey that led to shows at bigger venues in London, or even albums and national tours. Local musician Mike Cooper played at The Standard many times with his band Pseudo. He recalls how invaluable the venue was for local bands starting out: 'When I started college and formed my first band we played there so much – and even got paid a few times' (author interview with Cooper, May 2021). This is echoed by Mark Venables who reflects: 'Without small venues we would never have got beyond the rehearsal room, and there would have been no new bands, apart perhaps from those manufactured by record companies' (author interview with Venables, May 2021). He goes on: 'A hard-working young band needs somewhere to play in front of mates and strangers, try out ideas and master their craft, or just jump about and enjoy.

It's an apprenticeship you can't do anywhere else. Small dark clubs are the very lifeblood of live music' (author interview with Venables, May 2021). Groups who played at The Standard before fame include Kula Shaker and an early incarnation of Bloc Party. In other words, the venue was an important part of the music economy.

While I discovered local metal bands at The Standard who I ended up following for years, by the early 2000s it was dominated by tribute bands: Dirty DC, Being Jovi, Limehouse Lizzy, Whole Lotta Led and Guns 2 Roses. The prospect of seeing the original versions of these bands live was slim (Guns n' Roses) if not impossible (Thin Lizzy), so I loved going to hear some of my favourite music played live. Gav Felvus, lead singer of Guns 2 Roses, recalls that The Standard was one of the venues outside of central London that had really made a name for itself, with its 'quirky underground vibe' and mixture of covers and originals bands (author interview with Felvus, May 2021). The latter often supported the former, giving young bands valuable access to the large audiences that tribute bands typically attract.

Nights at The Standard were legendary. Over the years my memories have merged into a kaleidoscopic swirl of images, anecdotes and sensations – with a killer soundtrack. The time we all turned up for an under-18s night to find it cancelled, so had an impromptu party in the car park instead. Dancing with abandon to tracks that now trigger bittersweet nostalgia. The night I flirted with a member of a KISS tribute band, only to be horrified when I saw him without his face paint after the gig (old enough to be my father!). Speakers so loud my ears were still ringing the next day. The ska night, when I skanked with a guy who my best friend maintains was a member of East 17 (they were locals: their band is named after the Walthamstow postcode). Feeling like Penny Lane when I went backstage with my friends' bands only to find a grotesque sofa and some warm cans of Red Stripe. Oh, the glamour! Screeching along to hard rock hits until I lost my voice – I still think of The Standard every time I hear 'The Boys Are Back in Town'. Coming home reeking of cigarette smoke with beer matting my hair. These were the days before smart phones or social media. After particularly eventful nights, we rushed out to get disposable cameras developed. Pouring over blurry snaps, we would relive the action, until next Friday night when we did it all again.

The Standard was used as filming location for both *Peep Show* and *The Inbetweeners*, its distinctive orange walls giving it away. In both series it features as a rough and scuzzy venue, in *Peep Show* renamed 'The Fuck Bunker'. Each show features both someone throwing up and someone embarrassing themselves on stage – two things that happened pretty frequently. Sadly, these episodes are now epitaphs.

In 2011 came the shocking news that The Standard was closing. It was the end of an era. The venue was put up for sale with its owners noting that it represented 'an excellent opportunity for redevelopment' (Binns 2010). In the context of the crazy London property market, it was perhaps inevitable that this sprawling site directly opposite a tube station would eventually be sacrificed to developers. That was ten years ago, though, and at the time of writing the venue still stands boarded up and empty. Initially it was purchased by a company who intended to turn it into a Turkish supermarket, but that never materialised. In 2016, the venue was given a facelift of sorts when it was turned into an installation by artist Al Maser, who covered the entire building in bold geometric patterns. This is as far as the venue's contribution to local culture has gone in the last decade, despite its home in Waltham Forest, recently deemed London's 'Borough of Culture'.

This irony speaks to wider issues. As developers buy up pubs and other landmarks, turning them into blocks of flats and driving up rents, artists are pushed out of previously affordable neighbourhoods. This has famously happened in places like Hackney, once home to a vibrant community of creatives that have largely been forced to move on to cheaper towns and cities (Lewis 2016). Prospective new residents are then sold a vision of the hip new neighbourhood they can move into – but what is left, really, when all of the pubs and venues and artists have moved on? You might be able to find an overpriced flat-white, sure, but can you catch a great unsigned band at the pub down the road? That is less likely these days.

The loss of venues is an issue felt across the musical spectrum[1] and one recently worsened by the coronavirus pandemic.[2] It must be said, though, that alternative venues have been hit particularly hard over the last decade or so. In this context, the closure of The Standard was just another chapter in the ill-fated history of rock and metal venues in London. The legendary Intrepid Fox in Soho (now a Byron Burger), the Ruskin Arms in East Ham (birthplace of Iron Maiden) and Big Red in Holloway are just a few of the venues that have bitten the dust since I last wore fishnet tights. I would struggle to know where to go for some Jack Daniels and a decent jukebox these days.

1. A 2019 report on live music compiled by the Digital, Culture, Media and Sport Committee said: 'In the past decade the UK has seen nationwide closures of music venues, and the sites that remain face a struggle to stay open given rising costs and declining revenues. That poses an immediate threat to the development of the next generation of talent and fans' (House of Commons 2019).
2. Since the pandemic things have only got worse, with the Music Venue Trust reporting that a staggering 556 venues are now at risk of closure (Moore 2020).

This is not just a problem with smaller clubs and bars either. Since I started going to gigs, a staggering number of larger rock venues have closed and nowhere is this more evident than in the area surrounding Tottenham Court Road station. This neighbourhood was once home to four historic venues: the Astoria, LA2, Borderline and Metro, all of which have been sacrificed to the development of London's new Crossrail line. Across the road in Denmark Street, London's famous Tin Pan Alley, the 12 Bar Club was also lost to developers. Now, the site surrounding the tube station has been replaced with a hideous glass monstrosity boasting '60,000 sq[uare] ft of Grade A office space and 8,000 sq[uare] ft of retail' as well as eight (eight!) new homes (Smyth 2021). Sure to make a dent in the housing crisis.

Bands who played The Astoria include David Bowie, Oasis and Radiohead. Nirvana released tracks recorded at the venue on their 1996 live album *From the Muddy Banks of the Wishkah*, while Metallica, Deep Purple and the Arctic Monkeys have all released recordings or footage of their performances there. Going to gigs at The Astoria always felt special because the building had such a heavy sense of history. I remember being in a mosh pit at an Audioslave show, struggling to stay on my feet as Chris Cornell's voice ricocheted around the room. Feeling euphoria tinged with panic, I looked up at the balcony and saw a familiar figure in a black cowboy hat grinning down at me: Motörhead's legendary Lemmy Kilmister. That was just the sort of thing that happened there.

Equally as memorable was the stage door, down a tiny alley to the side of the venue. Here, with other obsessive fans, I waited patiently for autographs and photos with my idols. Once we even befriended a favourite American band and proudly took them on a tour of Oxford Street. It ended with a round of Filet o' Fish burgers at McDonald's (their request). I struggle to imagine quite the same atmosphere in the two new venues that have been promised as part of the Crossrail redevelopment: a paltry consolation prize for all that has been lost.

While the demolition of these venues is a profound loss for live music in London, it also represents a stripping away of our musical history; a critical component of British cultural heritage. In recent years, there have been several high-profile examples of how the history of British music – and rock music in particular – can have a broader cultural impact. For instance, the Victoria and Albert Museum have put on blockbuster exhibitions about both David Bowie and Pink Floyd. The former was, for a time, the museum's most visited exhibition ever. It was seen by more than 1.5 million people at ten venues around the world (Alexander 2016).

This is not just a London thing, either. In 2019, Birmingham Museum and Art Gallery hosted a major exhibition celebrating the 50th anniversary of

Black Sabbath. The show celebrated 'the band, their legacy and the fans'.[3] In Liverpool, The Beatles still generate hordes of tourists who flock to venues like the Cavern Club, while in Manchester, Factory Records nostalgia is practically an industry in itself. (Coincidentally, the original Cavern Club (like the Astoria and its neighbours) was closed because of a new railway line that was being built. The Liverpool venue moved home for about a decade, eventually returning to a site more or less in the original location.) Where will the music fans of the future go to find London's musical heritage? These days those of us who work in the arts are forced to quote these statistics on an all-too-regular basis, but they bear repeating: the arts and culture industry contributes £10.8 billion a year to the UK economy (Brown 2019). People do not come to London to see identikit high-rise office blocks.

Looking back through my collection of old gig tickets, it is not just the loss of so many venues that strikes me, but also how cheap they were. Even large shows at stadiums could cost less than £20: £19.50 for the Foo Fighters at Wembley Arena in 2002, for example. Things have changed dramatically. Of course, the steep rise in ticket prices is symptomatic of a broader change within the music industry. Artists now make the majority of their income from live shows rather than records. This has been the case since online piracy first started to make a dent in album sales (Shaw 2019). Indeed, the internet has changed the landscape significantly. Ticket touts have moved online, where they can (legally) sell tickets at vastly inflated prices. On social media, meanwhile, FOMO (Fear Of Missing Out) drives the fashion-conscious to the latest live music events, where they share pictures of themselves online. There are nearly three and a half million posts on Instagram tagged #FestivalFashion (not to mention #FestivalOutfit, #FestivalMakeup and #FestivalHair!). The atmosphere has changed.

In the last few years, I have been to see several bands including Guns n' Roses and Metallica at stadiums and arenas. Not one of those tickets cost less than £100. Even buying standing tickets is not what it used to be. Being 'down the front' used to involve queueing all day with your friends to grab a good spot as soon as the doors opened. I spent many hours sweltering or shivering outside Brixton Academy, waiting for the Murderdolls or The Darkness. Today, it often means paying several hundred pounds for a 'golden circle' ticket in front of the stage. Who is buying those tickets? Hardcore fans with money, sure, but also corporate clients. I gave up trying to buy tickets for the Rolling Stones several years back, as it seemed you could only purchase 'packages'

---

3. https://homeofmetal.com/event/black-sabbath-50-years

that variously involved boat trips to the O2, dinner at mediocre restaurants or meet and greets with the band. You can't always get what you want.

What is happening, then, is a squeeze from the top and the bottom. At one end of the spectrum, bigger shows with well-established acts are getting more expensive while, at the other, there are fewer places to go and discover up-and-coming bands. With a diminishing number of smaller venues out there, it is harder for bands to work from one end of the spectrum to the other. The Mayor of London's Music Venues Taskforce found that the number of grass-roots live venues in the city fell from 136 to 88 between 2007 and 2015: a decline of 35 per cent (Hann 2017). In our interview, Mark Venables stated: 'I don't know how an upcoming young band […] would get a gig these days, without being on the end of a long waiting list or agreeing to play for nothing (which means at a loss)' (interview with author, May 2021). Indeed, the economic context is hard to ignore. Working-class musicians are hard pushed to make a living from their music in the capital, while those supported by wealthier parents can afford to make a go of it. This problem is by no means isolated to the world of music; the same applies to actors, for example, or curators. Working-class talent is underrepresented across the creative industries, and the problem is only getting worse.

Gav Felvus has been gigging with Guns 2 Roses for seventeen years and has played the many rock and metal venues that have subsequently closed, including both the Intrepid Fox and The Borderline. He reflects that while a lot of venues have shut down, it is 'primarily rock-oriented ones [that] have taken a hit over the last ten years' (interview with author, May 2021). He continues: 'I don't think they are being replaced, at least not in the areas where they were originally based'. Indeed, some venues have migrated from the West End to less central (and more affordable) neighbourhoods. The Intrepid Fox initially moved from its famous home in Soho to Giles High Street in Tottenham Court Road, where it quickly became yet another victim of the Crossrail redevelopment. It then moved on to the Archway Tavern (the interior of which, incidentally, can be seen on the cover of The Kinks' 1971 album *Muswell Hillbillies*) before closing for good in 2014. The club tucked behind the Tavern now hosts the infamous Decadence nightclub, home to London's lovers of hard rock, glam and sleaze. It has itself relocated several times from venues in Soho that have closed.

During the early days of the pandemic came the news that another Soho institution had been forced to close its doors. The Crobar was famous for its jukebox, its bourbon and some of its well-known patrons, ranging from Dave Grohl to Lemmy. Dubbed a 'church to the heavy music community', the bar had been serving music lovers since 2001, with many popping in before or after gigs at the nearby cluster of venues that have since been lost to Crossrail (Leivers 2021). The death of the Crobar was announced in characteristic style when a photo of a gravestone appeared on its Instagram account bearing the words 'CROBAR – SOHO. KILLED BY LANDLORDS. JUNE 2020. RIP' (Daly 2020). The image was captioned: 'fuck the greedy insurance companies, fuck the greedy short-sighted landlords and fuck our brainless government' (ibid.). This anger was shared by metal fans and music lovers around the world.

Reflecting on the closure of so many rock and metal venues, Crobar owner Richard Thomas points to the greed of landlords and the redevelopment of Soho, but also considers broader factors relating to the changing nature of music fandom (interview with author, May 2021). He suggests that 'music used to create tribalism' with dedicated metal fans going out to buy new albums and wearing shirts and patches of their favourite bands. This was certainly my experience as a so-called 'grunger'. These days, Thomas reflects, the 'Spotify generation' tend to be more eclectic in their musical tastes because it is so much easier to explore different genres and artists on streaming platforms. This means that fans might go to a metal bar one night and a jazz bar the next, somewhat diluting the traditional community of fans dedicated to one genre only.

Perhaps it says something that, of all of the acts I used to go to and see at The Standard, none of the original bands are still together while the one going from strength to strength is Guns 2 Roses, who play at large venues around the world. Is this symptomatic of a heavy metal 'canon' solidifying, at the expense of younger bands? This question has been asked by journalist Bryan Reesman. In his 2016 article 'The Slow Death of Heavy Metal', he notes that the 'Godfathers' of rock are getting older (Black Sabbath, Judas Priest) or even passing away (Lemmy, Ronnie James Dio). Coupled with a decline in record sales and a music industry that does not reward originality, Reesman argues that '[t]he game has changed and made it harder for the Next Big Thing to emerge' (Reesman 2016). He asks, 'where do things go from here? Will we see heavy bands on the superstar level of Metallica and Iron Maiden ever again? Will that classic sound become a nostalgic relic relegated to oldies bins? Or will it mutate into something else?' (ibid.). Nostalgia certainly sells. In an interview with the *Financial Times*, Mark Davyd of the Music Venue Trust points out that 'faced with dwindling crowds it makes more sense for venues to put on a tribute act that will bring in a large and boozy crowd' (Hann 2017). These crowds are also older, and more likely to have disposable income.

Richard Thomas is determined to do his part to tackle these problems by providing a new venue for metal fans. In order to save the Crobar, and in light of the outpouring of support for the beloved venue since its closure was announced, he kicked off a crowdfunding campaign that has now raised over £100,000. Thomas is currently on the hunt for new premises. His requirements? The new venue must have room for gigs and it must be central. He rightly feels the importance of retaining a metal venue in Soho – a central location to serve the community and its musicians. Perhaps this community-funded model is one way that venues can look to the future in a hostile climate for live music. It has certainly helped keep some venues alive during the coronavirus pandemic.

And what of The Standard? Plans have been approved to build a towering 'co-living' space on the site of the empty venue. What this essentially means is university-style dormitories with shared facilities. As one councillor pointed out, the plans include only seventeen full kitchens to be shared between three hundred residents (Munro 2020). Underneath this tower block will be a brand-new venue. 'During the day', say developers, this will be a space for yoga, exhibitions, brewery partnerships and vintage markets while '[i]n the evening, the new venue will offer a mix of the best live music, theatre, dance, visual arts and comedy from established and emerging artists, performers and musicians' (The Collective 2020). While the provision of a new venue should be applauded, this vision of a shiny new gentrification station is somewhat soulless and sanitised. The description certainly hits all the right buzzwords (craft beer! vintage!) for the hipsters that developers hope to attract, but I wonder who will be running the venue, what the booking policy will be and whether long-standing locals will have a say in programming. Furthermore, you have to wonder how 300 residents in studio flats will feel about living above a live music venue – is it sustainable? The amps would definitely have to be a lot quieter than they were at the old Standard.

Looking back on the glory days of the venue, Mark Venables says, 'I still hear people to this day talking about [it], along with several other venues that have now achieved iconic status in the memory. Their presence was very important to the rock community. It feels like much of the soul of the scene has gone with their passing'. Will the new Standard restore this soul? Sadly, I doubt it. Our beloved old venue set the bar extremely high. I miss the smoke, the sticky floors and even the crappy bathrooms – but most of all, I miss the music.

References

Alexander, Ella. 2016. 'David Bowie exhibition names the most-visited in V&A history'. *Harper's Bazaar*, 8 November 2016.

Averby, Karen. 2020. 'Charting the history of popular Walthamstow music venue The Standard'. *East London and West Essex Guardian*, 7 November. https://www.guardian-series.co.uk/news/18853128.charting-history-popular-walthamstow-music-venue-standard/

Binns, Daniel. 2010. 'Walthamstow: Music venue owners hopeful of sale'. *The Guardian*, 7 October. https://www.guardian-series.co.uk/news/8439683.walthamstow-music-venue-owners-hopeful-sale/

Brown, Mark. 2019. 'Arts contribute more to UK economy than agriculture – Report'. *The Guardian*, 17 April. https://www.theguardian.com/culture/2019/apr/17/arts-contribute-more-to-uk-economy-than-agriculture-report

Collective, The. 2020. 'A new cultural venue for London: The Collective unveils its plans for Blackhorse Lane'. https://www.thecollective.com/the-journal/a-new-cultural-venue-for-london-the-collective-unveils-its-plans-for-blackhorse-lane

Daly, Rhian. 2020. 'Legendary London rock bar is closing its doors'. *NME*, 20 September. https://www.nme.com/news/music/legendary-london-rock-bar-the-crobar-closing-2757177

Hann, Michael. 2017. 'The fight to save London's live music scene'. *FT Magazine*, 10 November. https://www.ft.com/content/2a399a1a-c345-11e7-a1d2-6786f39ef675

House of Commons Digital, Culture, Media and Sport Committee. 2019. 'Live music: Ninth Report of Session 2017–19'. House of Commons, 19 March, 3.

Leivers, Dannii. 2021. '"It's like a church to the heavy music community": What we'll lose if our metal venues collapse'. *Metal Hammer*, 9 February. https://www.loudersound.com/features/its-like-a-church-to-the-heavy-music-community-what-well-lose-if-our-metal-venues-collapse

Lewis, Jenny. 2016. '"Hackney, I lost you": The London creative priced out of their studios'. *The Guardian*, 28 January.

Moore, Sam. 2020. 'Music Venue Trust launches "Save Our Venues" campaign'. *NME*, 27 April. https://www.nme.com/news/music/music-venue-trust-launches-save-our-venues-campaign-2654484

Munro, Victoria. 2020. 'New plans for The Standard Get go-ahead'. *Waltham Forest Echo*, 11 December. https://walthamforestecho.co.uk/new-plans-for-the-standard-get-go-ahead/

Reesman, Bryan. 2016. 'The slow death of heavy metal'. *Observer*, 15 January. https://observer.com/2016/01/the-slow-death-of-heavy-metal/

Shaw, Lucas. 2019. 'Concerts are more expensive than ever, and fans keep paying up'. *Bloomberg*, 10 September. https://www.bloomberg.com/news/articles/2019-09-10/concerts-are-more-expensive-than-ever-and-fans-keep-paying-up

Smyth, Sharon. 2021. 'M&G, CO-RE get planning approval for 88,000 sq ft Fitzrovia mixed office scheme'. *CoStar News*, 29 January. https://product.costar.com/home/news/shared/361801849

Author biography

Dr Anna Maria Barry is a historian and writer. She completed her PhD at Oxford Brookes University in 2017, writing her thesis on the figure of the male opera singer in nineteenth-century culture. She has since published on a diverse range of topics including Billie Holiday's autobiography and the gothic fiction written by Victorian opera star Sims Reeves. Her current research focuses on death masks in the nineteenth century and has been supported by funding from Princeton University. She is also curating an exhibition of late-Victorian musical portraits at the Royal College of Music in London. Anna often writes features for a range of popular magazines including *BBC Music* and *Who Do You Think You Are?* magazine. She is a life-long fan of rock music.

12 The New Breed: 1990s Mod Revival Scene in Leeds

Abigail Gaines

We weren't 'Absolute Beginners'. We weren't the first, and unlikely to be the last. We were influenced by the past, yet we put our own unique twist on our present and carried that into our future. 'What an age I've grown up in' were the immortal words of Colin MacInnes' hero in his 1959 voyeur novel *Absolute Beginners*, which so cleverly collected the essence of Modernism and put it in print. These were words that still applied to us forty years later. We were a 'new breed'. We were too young to remember the 1980s Mod revival and had witnessed weak media attempts to welcome Mod as a style which clearly missed the target. Our origins were mixed. Our window into the scene was 1990s indie, acid jazz, even lounge music and all that was kitsch. Regardless of the starting point, we found a connection. A portal had been opened. The surface had been scratched. Our eyes were opened, and we liked what we saw. We were the kids of Tom Wolfe's *Noonday Underground*, albeit decades later.

We displayed a spectrum of styles and you could clearly see a range of collective influences, but we also gave the look our own take. Some were reluctant to even take the tag 'Mod', but they were unlikely to deny (somewhere along the path to self-identity) that it was a subculture that had influenced them. Lifestyle choice is what united us. Although clothing styles and musical choices may have differed, what we had in common was an attitude, true dedication and most definitely a look.

For us Mods, the club was still where it was at. It wasn't until 1997 that I first stepped into the building – a night that would ultimately change my life. Eleven o'clock and the doors swung open. A gateway to a happening. Brighton Beach was a club night that ran every Friday night at the Cockpit in Leeds, from 1994 to 2000.

As an indie kid studying at York University, surrounded by peers fully into the late 1990s dance scene, I was ecstatic to meet another who shared my musical influences. Bands we had in common would now be tagged Britpop, but this wasn't the label at the time. Bands such as Pulp, Blur, and Suede could be heard blaring from our university dorms, mixed with The Beatles, The Doors, and The Kinks. We frequented any indie night we could find in York, and it was there that we first saw the iconic Brighton Beach flyer; mesmerising 1960s imagery in red, white and blue. Miraculously our York DJ actually played at Brighton Beach and got us on the guest list for our first visit. We hopped on the train one Friday night, a journey I would not and could not miss every weekend for the next four years. From the train station our fellow travellers headed into the centre of Leeds for the well-known pubs and clubs, whereas we were heading just a short walk from the station – to a location under the railway bridge.

As we approached the club that first time, we saw the spiralling queue along the street under 'the arches', as the area under the railway bridge was fondly known. Those in the line displayed a dazzling plethora of styles. We didn't realise that our guest list status meant we could skip the queue, but in truth I'm not sure I would have wanted to as this would have meant missing the eagerness, the excitement, and the chance to take it all in.

Although the 'big room' was the indie music that I knew and loved, it was in the small back room I discovered a whole new scene that first night. With each step into the room, the years slipped away, and I was plunged back a couple of decades. I was transported to a hip scene with sights and sounds that mesmerized me. The deep rhythms of 1960s R&B, northern soul, garage, psychedelia, jazz, Hammond, boogaloo and more. Not that I knew the names or terms for these aural delights that were soon to become my passion. I watched from near the doorway, unsure whether to enter, convinced that my attire didn't suit. I was already 1960s influenced in the way I dressed, but I could tell there was something very specific about these people; the attention to detail stood out. With each record the DJs played, a different group was attracted to the dance floor. There were slight variations in the way they moved, but none of them like anything I'd ever seen before. I took it all in, both intimidated and in awe. I knew without question that I would be back.

The DJ line-up varied every week, but small-room regulars, Mark Ellis and Lee Miller, played the 45s that first pulled me onto the dancefloor and kept me there. Lee's thing was 1960s R&B and his sets have never been rivalled by any Mod DJ I've come across since. 'Grits Ain't Groceries' by Little Milton (1969) and 'Seven Day Fool' by Etta James (1961). Until my first night at Brighton Beach, I'd never seen the soul shuffle where the dancers' feet barely left the floor, all gliding in glorious coordination but each with a unique quality. The spins, hand claps, the slight kicks. Each dancer lost in their own connection with the music. There may have been a technique, certain moves, but I never learnt them, I just went with the flow and felt the music. My feet just moved and twisted, and it wasn't long until I flicked up my legs and tapped my ankle with my hand in time with the music. I was absorbed. I became a soul dancer. I loved it all. I know that now you can get Northern Soul dance lessons, but my style came from a reaction to the music – perhaps the most authentic method of dancing to the music. My dance moves were what felt right. I loved dancing to it all, but nothing reached me as much as the R&B, and still never has. Styles of dressing went with each type of music. The 1960s soul crowd had a more classic Mod look. Boys were in their sharp suits – narrow-legged trousers, button-down collared shirts, Italian-style bum freezer jackets with three buttons, and French crew haircuts. The attention to detail marked out those who knew from those who wanted to know. The girls had their bobbed or cropped hair, knee-length skirts and shirts or polo necks, flat loafers: shoes for dancing. Then there were those who were influenced by skinhead styles. The coloured socks and matching braces, the Fred Perry, Ben Sherman or Brutus shirts. The skinhead girls with their amazing Tonik skirt suits and feather haircuts.

DJ change and the fast-paced beats of 1960s American garage and British psychedelia sent a new set of dancers whirling onto the floor. More furious, swaying from side to side, hair shaking. Like the craziest swinging scene straight out of my favourite B movies; think *Psych Out* (1968) or maybe even *Valley of the Dolls* (1967). This crowd had longer hair, their clothes a myriad of colours. Girls in short skirts, knee-high boots or dolly shoes. Styles from the early 1960s influenced by the likes of Mary Quant and Foale and Tuffin, and those from the later '60s like Biba and Granny Takes a Trip. Men with their basin haircuts, low-slung hipsters with oversized belts and buckles and Winklepicker shoes with Cuban heels. Pendant necklaces swaying with each and every move. Drawn onto the floor by songs such as 'Save My Soul' (Wimple Winch, 1966), 'Shake' (Shadows of the Knight, 1969), and 'Action Woman' (The Litter, 1967).

I loved all the styles of clothes and soon saw the secret signs that marked out those who knew from those who didn't. I mastered the details. The shape of the toe of your shoe and the size of your heel – it all mattered. Though soul music was at my heart, the swinging '60s style of dress became more my thing. Long hair, short dresses, knee-high boots, but soul dancing. A true postmodern mix. I could 'psych out' with the best. DJ Mark Ellis would perfectly combine an eclectic mix, you didn't have to be into just one type, just one look, just one way of life. His sets cleverly incorporated soul, boogaloo and '60s garage sounds. He seamlessly showed an appreciation for all styles. Totally in love with so many of the songs he played, I was barely off the dancefloor come Friday night. Dee Clark's 'That's My Girl' (1957), Julie Driscoll's 'Indian Rope Man' (1969), Shocking Blue, 'Send Me a Postcard' (1970), Jean-Jacques Perrey,

'E.V.A.' (1970) and even some French yé-yé music such as Jacque Dutronc's 'Le Responsible' (1969).

In addition to the regulars, guests included DJs from Mod clubs across the country, and with them came a new crowd. Mods from London, Sheffield, Newcastle, Birmingham and Manchester all attended Leeds Brighton Beach at times. What intrigued me was how each area seemed to have developed their own unique twist on the style, and certain tracks and style of music were predominant with each scene. We were all Mods but with regional offshoots; all with our own take. Some of the younger Manchester crowd were wildly psychedelic. Girls with drawn-on eyelashes – à la Julie Driscoll and Marianne Faithful – dressed up to the extremes, and boys in striped hipster trousers with basin haircuts.

Brighton Beach in Leeds was the place to be, but it was in fact York where I found someone who was as infatuated by all things Mod as I. Through the quaint, historic streets, I'd spotted a figure with short dark hair with height to the back. The longer sides of her hair framed her face and beneath her heavy fringe lay her large kohl-coated eyes. In the day she wore short A-line skirts, polo necks and leather or suede colourful '60s coats. Her chic style stood out. She was still at Sixth Form when I met her, whereas I was a university student. You'd hear the whispers as she passed by: 'Sixties ... Sixties ...' She'd found her world through music and literature. We soon became friends, kindred spirits. On Friday night we'd head to her house to get ready. Drink in hand, listening to the sounds of the Showmen, 'Our Love Will Grow' (1967) and Tommy Navaro, 'Cried My Life Away' (1964). It was all vinyl; she'd been living the life since her early teens. At school, the other kids just didn't get 'it' – they didn't get her. She stood out and it didn't deter her. As her peers consumed high-street fashion, she sought out the perfect width trousers with Prince of Wales check. She felt no need to fit in with the Topshop tribe. She had mastered style.

Joanna and I would be at Brighton Beach as soon as the doors opened, especially now we were on the small-room DJ's guest list each week. As we were amongst the first to enter, we had the big room all to ourselves. Although this room was mainly where the indie music played and live bands performed, early doors DJ, Dan Guest, would delve into his vinyl 45 collection and play classics such as The Birds' 'Say Those Magic Words' (1966), Spencer Davis Group's 'Looking Back' (1968), and the Mysterians' '96 Tears' (1966) amongst others. Tunes that would help us warm up for the night yet to come.

Dan was also from York and ran a night called 'Into Tomorrow' in the downstairs room of a well-known, popular townie nightclub on a Wednesday. His York audience was a mix of indie kids, Mods, and those who had just rolled into the club after the pubs had kicked out. It wasn't a massive crowd; the upstairs of the club that played chart music was packed, it was just an elite few who filtered into the basement. Dan had the ability to get them all dancing. His music at that night was a perfect mix of sounds of the time such as Cast's 'Sandstorm' (1996), Ocean Colour Scene's 'Traveller's Tune' (1996) and Beck's 'Devil's Haircut' (1996) as well as older stuff like Rolling Stones' 'Paint it Black' (1966), Jimi Hendrix's 'Crosstown Traffic' (1969 UK), the Doors' 'Peacefrog' (1970), northern soul classic 'The Snake' by Al Wilson (1968) and the classic end-of-the-night song that never failed to pack the dancefloor, the Small Faces' 'Tin Soldier' (1966). Dan also played on the soul and scooter scene, and he still does. His weekly nights in York were the perfect warm up for our Friday night Brighton Beach sessions. He probably helped many teens get into the scene, more than he will ever know.

It was early doors in the big room at Brighton Beach, dancing to Dan's tunes, when our Mod friends arrived and joined us on the floor. We never arranged to meet, we just knew we would all be there, and we'd spend the night together on the dancefloor. Our crowd was an eclectic bunch, all twenty-one and under. A mix of art school and university students, and those who'd left school at sixteen. We had the suited and booted Mod types and the kaftan-wearing psych kids. What we had in common was a lifestyle choice, obsession for the minute detail in clothing, a passion for music, and a love of the club night.

We soon began to travel for Mod nights, away from our Brighton Beach home. There was a whole scene – always houses to stay at, clubs to attend and vintage shops to try. The Vault in Brighton hosted a night called Smarties where I first saw the band Quant. Boys with full-on basin style, garage haircuts. Discovering that there were lots of bands and record labels linked to the scene, London soon became 'where it was at' for me and my gang. The one we frequented the most was the Mousetrap all-nighter in Finsbury Park run by a group called the New Untouchables. Upstairs was soul, and downstairs was filled with 'swirlies' who were more into their garage and psychedelic sounds. This was a hard choice for me. I loved both styles. Where Brighton Beach played both in the same room, I found the London scene more divided at that time; people dressed according to the style that went with the music. The early '60s styles were more predominant in the soul room. Girls in over-the-knee skirts or trousers and loafers, tailored shirts, short cropped hair. As you stepped down the stairs you entered a room full of colour with mid- to late '60s fashions predominant. I was a psych kid until the moment you saw me dance to the sounds of Charles Sheffield's 'Voodoo Working' (1961) and Teddy Mack & the Mackinteers' 'Hey Hey Gyspy Woman' (1964). I also loved northern soul classics such as Jimmy Fraser's 'Of Hopes and Dreams and

Tombstones' (1965), so perfect for some of my signature leg kicks and hand claps. In Leeds the styles and sounds worked together, but here in London although all in one club the crowds tended to separate. My main Leeds crowd gravitated downstairs at The Mousetrap, I kept sneaking back up to take in the soul sounds. I wasn't alone, I had the music and other likeminded dancers on the floor around me.

Other London clubs we tried included the Purple PussyCat Club and Blow Up. There was Uptight in Liverpool, Pow Wow in Sheffield, nights like Carnaby Street and later the Hideaway Club in Manchester. In Leeds over the years, nights such as the Lava Lounge and Club 66 were perfect accompaniments to Brighton Beach.

The New Untouchables held a range of bank holiday weekend rallies. Echoing Mods of the '60s they jumped on their scooters and went to seaside towns. These rallies took place in towns such as Brighton, Margate, and Scarborough but the big one was the Isle of Wight each year, something we just couldn't miss. The daytime was for hanging out and people watching, vintage clothes and record stalls. The nights were for clubbing. We'd spend weeks working out our outfits, checking out who'd be DJing and who was going.

Then there were the fanzines. The '80s Mod revival had a range of these publications, and some were still going by the late 1990s. But there were also new ones such as Helen Barrell's *Dansette* and the Hideaway Club's *New Breed*, as well as my own *Sixbeat*. What we wanted to do was share our passion and connect with others who felt the same. The New Untouchable's newsletter was a must. It was there you'd find out about events, shops, and clubs not to miss. I started my fanzine when at university. It was a mix of history, music, club reviews, and a place to write about the current scene. I suppose the fanzine was in some ways a spin-off from my dissertation as I'd chosen to study the original Mods. I read feverishly any books or articles I could get hold of that touched upon the scene, a mix of studies, observations, magazine articles and literature. The university library came up trumps; rarely checked-out books such as George Melly's *Revolt into Style* (1970) and Dick Hebdige's *Subculture: The Meaning of Style* (1979) were renewed over and over again. I was so excited to get hold of a copy of the *Sunday Times* magazine feature from 1962, 'Faces without Shadows' that featured a young Mark Feld (later Bolan). Fervently soaking up each word of Colin MacInnes' *Absolute Beginners* (1959) and Tom Wolfe's *Noonday Underground* (1968), I just couldn't get enough. I'd spent a day a week in the university library, full '60s garb, music on and studying every Mod related book or article I could source. The incredibly high marks I received on my dissertation was either a reflection of my passion and dedication or the fact that my tutors had never come across such highly detailed, somewhat unexplored, social history before.

My fanzine was my outlet for sharing my passion with the outside world. I had to rely on the university computer rooms to type up articles, and a handy glue stick enabled the addition of photos. The smell of the ink and the warmth from the copies are etched into my memory. I had no idea if anyone would be interested, I just wanted to write. I parcelled up a few copies and sent them to the other fanzines I was aware of. A few weeks later, I saw *Sixbeat* mentioned in their review pages and the requests started to come in. Envelopes with little notes and a pound coin or a postal order, at times even foreign notes as Mods from Europe got in contact. I remember writing for other fanzines and one of my articles being published in America. The feeling of knowing there were others who shared your passions was amazing, but despite wanting to shout my love of the Mod scene loud and proud, I opted to write under a pseudonym. However, when Rob Bailey from the New Untouchables started calling me 'Tinx', I realised that I wasn't perhaps as undercover as I'd assumed.

I visited Mod clubs in Barcelona and Hamburg and had contacts all over the world. In the late 1990s, the world was becoming more connected due to the internet. This is how I first 'met' both Nina and Eneida from the Barcelona Mod scene. Nina sent me amazing mixtapes and videos of the soul scene over there, and Eneida ran her own nights. It was fascinating to see adaptations of dancing styles, especially of northern soul which had started out as a purely British scene in the 1970s but had gripped these late teens and young adults in Spain. At the Mod nights on the continent, the looks varied from our own. At the clubs we visited the look seemed subtler for the girls: low-slung coloured or striped hipster trousers, wide belts with large buckles, neat, tailored shirts and slick black bobs or cropped hair. In 2010, I visited the Kit Kat Club in Hamburg. The crowd identified us as British by our 'out there' style as soon as we walked through the doors. We dressed more late '60s with our short dresses and flared sleeves, statement eye makeup and long backcombed hair. It wasn't just the fashion, but the music also varied wherever you went. It is crazy to think that one scene could have such diverse music and songs you'd never heard before. The music may have been from nearly half a century ago, but new floor fillers were always being uncovered.

Vintage clothes shopping was an obsession. Not that we weren't averse to buying new should it have the right style and look or if we could adapt it. The high street's take on Mod and '60s fashion comes into the shops every few years and occasionally some pieces actually get it right. In Leeds, Positively 13 O'Clock behind the Corn Exchange was a regular haunt, and when in London, we'd always check out Portobello market. On rare occasions visiting my family in Lancashire, I uncovered some amazing vintage clothing shops in Accrington and Blackburn – these were treasure troves of wonders. Some Mods would use tailors to get their perfect suits and skirts; the attention to detail was key. It wasn't just clothes and music; it became home decor too. The sights, sounds and styles of the '60s became all-consuming for me – they still are today. At home I went for the more 1960s space-age look: lots of whites, as many dome-shaped Guzzini lamps as I could find. Later my style has taken on a range of mid-century styles and a love for Danish designs alongside British makes such as Ercol, but always influenced by the period I love. Although my clothes, hair and make-up may be less outlandish than they once were, the style and look are always there. I am still hunting for the perfect vintage coat. A wardrobe can never be full enough.

Brighton Beach at the Cockpit in Leeds came to an end in 2000. It didn't hit me too hard as it coincided with changes in my own life. By this time, I was teaching at a secondary school and sixth form college. Originally a history teacher, I couldn't hold back my passions and went on to set up a sociology department, picking a syllabus that included topics such as the sociology of youth subcultures. The textbooks I had access to at the time seemed to get things wrong, missing the mark at times but improving where the writers were part of a scene. What stood out for me were the similarities between the subcultures in terms of passion and approach. Bringing to life subcultures of the past alongside encouraging students to look at what was around them was a way to continue my passion and inspire others to find theirs.

I was still into the Mod lifestyle, but by this time getting out to the clubs did happen, just less often. The fanzine ending coincided with me getting a career; there was no longer a need to write about my passions when I could build them into my teaching. The old crowd went their separate ways after Brighton Beach was no longer a regular thing but bumping into people from the halcyon days at other clubs and the rallies made it all so more special. We were getting older and started to note a new breed emerging, their own take on the style but the same music and way of life. We'd smile knowingly at one another – that had been us once. Deep down, it still was us.

Times changed but the passion remained. In 2004, my boyfriend Andy (now husband) and our friend Paul 'Fuzz' Lowman decided to dust off our tunes and dancing shoes and start 'The Revolutionary Freaked Out Fuzz Club' in York. This was billed as a monthly 'happening' and described in marketing material as 'spinning the finest' in '60s soul and R&B, Hammond, boogaloo, '60s garage, psych and classic '60s floor fillers and whatever else we fancied 'as the night became more deranged'. We filled the room with lava projections and posters of '60s bands and famous faces, '60s films projected onto a wall, accompanied by a mix of the best '60s music. With each one of us bringing with us our different musical influences and backgrounds it meant each of our DJ sets took the night in another direction. The night couldn't be described as 'Mod', but it worked. The eclectic mix of tunes got people on the dance floor and saw us named as a 'night not to miss' in *The Guardian*'s Club Guide.

My sets would include a true mix influenced by the Brighton Beach DJs – pure floor fillers that covered the greats, soul, boogaloo, garage and French '60s yé-yé. Paul Fuzz would delve into the sounds of Black Sabbath's 'The Wizard' (1970) and Terry Reid's 'Superlungs' (1969). Andy was more about classic '60s rock such as the Rolling Stones, Creedence Clear Water Revival and Led Zeppelin. I'd play the classics that had first got me into the Mod scene, the tunes that had dragged me onto the dancefloor the first time I heard them.

Together the mix worked. As Andy was a musician playing on the live music scene, we incorporated bands into the club night. The bands usually ranged from indie to rockabilly, the sounds that perfectly accompanied the retro vibe of the night. Bands travelled from all over to play, including Liverpool's The Cubical, Leeds' Sunshine Underground and York's own The Federals. The club went strong for a few years until we all started to settle down and have families, though the occasional Fuzz Club does happen now and again.

It was at Brighton Beach in Leeds back in the late 1990s that I'd found my tribe. I had watched, learnt, and evolved. The Mod scene would influence everything about my life from that very first night. And while the outside world flits from one underground subculture to another, there is one that always remains inexplicable, a puzzle never to be solved. That's what it is like, a *raison d'être*, incomprehensible to all but those who know. Time is not stagnant, and the Mod scene knows that. Things are always changing and the Mods are too. There are always new generations emerging. Their approach is similar, though different to those who went before. Just like their mod forefathers, they pick and choose from the best, a true diffusion of influences. But beneath it all remains the most important factors of all: style and music. It will always be the clothes, the style, the music, the total life.

References

'Faces without Shadows'. 1962. *Town* magazine.
MacInnes, Colin. 1959. *Absolute Beginners*. London: MacGibbon and Kee.
Wolfe, Tom. 1968. *Noonday Underground* in *The Pump House Gang*. New York: Farrar, Straus & Giroux.

Author biography

Abigail Gaines is a photography studio manager of an award-winning wedding photography business. Prior to this, she worked in school leadership and also taught history and sociology – setting up a sociology department mainly to be able to teach youth subcultures to 17- and 18-year-olds. Abigail lives in her '60s-influenced home in York with her husband and two children. Music is always playing.

13 Sitting on the Bench in Leicester's Charlotte

Ed Garland

The Charlotte was a good place to ponder the relationship between electronic music and trees. This relationship isn't often acknowledged, maybe because acoustic instruments swallow most of the tree-music discussion. Vincent Wozniak O'Connor, for example, points out that makers of certain instruments might favour certain species of tree so much that the tree ends up being named for its sonic properties: 'timber used in traditional Italian violin-making is named "Abeti di Risonanza," or Resonance Spruce' (Wozniak O'Connor 2018). The amount of wood used for speaker-cabinets in sound systems, and the wooden floors and other structures in the interiors of venues, makes me think there ought to be something called 'banging plywood', to acknowledge what this material contributes to our listening experiences.

I might be joking, but I'm not taking the piss. Listen to Jazzie B describe the hugely influential Soul II Soul sessions at the Africa Centre in London on Sundays in the late 1980s: 'as a sound man, what was very important to me was a wooden floor. Lots of people didn't understand that a wooden floor made the music sound ten times better' (in Frost 2020: 69). He doesn't explain the technicalities of why a surface made of sliced and polished tree-parts made loud records more enjoyable; you just have to trust him that the tree-body enhanced his revolutionary musical blends.

The floor in front of The Charlotte's stage was stone. Tiled, rectangular, with a shallow-wave texture, darkened each night by impromptu pastes made of shoe-dirt and spilled drinks. The stone was reverberant: it lubricated long notes and helped higher frequencies to shimmer and swirl.

The Charlotte's mixing desk stood on a platform in the middle of the main room, directly facing the stage, surrounded by a wooden booth, painted black, five feet high, decorated on its outside by A4 posters for recent and upcoming gigs. Built onto the front wall of this booth there was a wooden bench. You could stand on this to get a better view of The Damned, or The Fall, or Lars Frederiksen and The Bastards, or any other band who could reliably fill the venue. At less-well-attended nights, though, you could sit on this bench and feel how it resonated in sympathy with loud low frequencies and made the music sound ten times better.

Eulogies for The Charlotte tend to focus on the guitar-bands who played there before they became too famous to visit 400-capacity venues: Kyuss (fourth ever UK show, 1994, tickets £4), Coldplay (co-headlining with Terris), and Radiohead (where the head of Parlophone records was one of less than ten people in attendance, in the early '90s, in The Charlotte's second room, upstairs, which is now a student apartment) (Gourlay 2014). There were countless others, whose names circulate through The Charlotte's public memorials, in newspapers, magazines, and online forums. Inside the venue, too, the posters for these astonishing visitations were pasted to the walls around the bar, above head-height. You could gawp at the platinum-selling names who would never return to the space where you were and trip up on the awkwardly placed step in the middle of the floor.

But most of The Charlotte's value as a musical space is derived from reasons other than its many brief visitations by pre-fame crooners, shouters, and woe-popes (Woe-pope? Thom Yorke). The two reasons that the thought of The Charlotte's demise is painful to me are these: it hosted a huge variety and quantity of non-legendary events, and it had a wooden bench in front of its mixing desk that made basslines into oscillating objects.

Some lesser-known facts might help to indicate the range of experiences on offer at The Charlotte: in the 1980s, you could eat a free ploughman's lunch to accompany Sunday daytime folk gigs from people like Maurice Coleman. In the late 1990s there was a night called Ultimate Karma, billed as an 'Asian Gay/Lesbian Dance Experience'. Feedback Phil, The Charlotte's sound engineer, cannot remember the name of the best band he ever heard play in the main room (Turnell 2010). And a related detail about the local musical economy – that seems incredible to learn that, as I write this in 2021, after what feels like three thousand years of Conservative government cuts to public services – in the 1990s, Leicester City Council employed a Popular Music Development Officer, and offered one-off grants for bands to purchase equipment, studio time, and promotional materials.

In the early 2000s, The Charlotte sold 'non-stop cheap spirits', and over the years the sweet drinks that contained these cheap spirits spilled onto the square orange tiles on the bar area's floor, thousands and thousands of vodka-and-lemonades and whiskey-and-cokes, sharp ciders and watery beers, flowed out of glasses, across knuckles and forearms, and dripped down to the tiles, where they seeped across the stony rectangles, their residues mopped up the next morning by Jim Robinson, the cleaner.

The combined odour of cloying bleach, spilled drink, and stale cigarettes was the first thing that hit you when you walked in, a smell as loud as the music, the signature smell of what the Reverend Edward Leigh warned his congregation against when he preached a sermon in memory of the woman for whom the venue is named – 'Her Late Royal Highness, The Princess Charlotte of Wales' (Leigh 1817). On the Sunday after her death in 1817, Leigh admonished his mourning congregation: 'you who are addicted to drunkenness, riot, and lust', knowing nothing of the non-stop cheap spirits that would be sold in the building named for her ladyship (A Sermon Preached in the Parish Church of Burbach).

The Charlotte was a dance music venue. In the early 2000s there was Vibronics, a regular dub night; Trisect, a hip-hop/dnb night; and Viroid, a breaks/garage/dnb night. A Trisect flyer looked like this: a computer-cartoon of the Scratch Perverts, crowding two turntables, their hands on fire (artist unknown). A Viroid flyer looked like this: kidney-shaped blobs in various colours from petrol blue to lime green to pale purple to ripe peach, arranged in curves, each blob a different size, adorned at their joining points by bracelets of spheres in fractal chains (artwork by Tony).

Sonic Boom, dedicated to 'cutting edge drum 'n' bass', was up and running by 1998. It started at 10pm and finished at 2 or 3am, and over its decade-long existence it hosted most of drum 'n' bass's main players: Andy C, Peshay, Fabio, and so on. Locals like MC Maveric and APB supported the bigger names. (APB, who you'll find in the same old rave tape-packs as Andy C and Grooverider and everyone else, deserves to be far more widely known as a DJ.) Leicester's healthy d'n'b culture coalesced around DJ SS's Formation label, and 5HQ record shop in the city centre. I moved to Leicester from Manchester when I was eighteen, to study for a BSc in Music Technology at DeMontfort. Sometime in the mid-2000s, when I was in my early twenties, I went to Sonic Boom on my own, to see Doc Scott.

The room was cold, and the sparse crowd formed small groups around the black pillar between the mixing desk and the stage, and against the walls by the fire exit, and in the alcove at the end of the bar, behind and to the right of the mixing-desk bench where I sat. There was very little overt motion in response to the music. As a collective, we manifested the almost-polar opposite of A Guy Called Gerald's image of legendary jungle nights in London: 'as soon as you get in the door, the heat hits you and everyone's just shocking out' (Terzulli and Otchere 2021: 27). At The Charlotte, on this particular night, as soon as you get in the door, the cold hits you and everyone's just milling around.

But this 'milling around' is not a problem, or a failure. The Charlotte was my favourite place to go out on my own, my anticipation peaking as I walked through the long entrance corridor with the ticket desk on the left, hearing the clattering surges of the music on the other side of the walls, enjoying the burst of high and upper-mid frequencies when I opened the doors to the main room on the right of the corridor, and walked straight across the floor to the pale metal bar. This scene repeated itself at other Sonic Booms, where I sat in the basslines of Total Science, Source Direct, and others whose names I can't remember or never learned. Because I always feared the nights would sell out before I got there, I tended to arrive early. I loved the atmosphere of subdued rushing that arose from the people, wearing heavy overcoats, hearing this thrillingly amplified music which is famous for making people want to move, and conserving their energy for when the maximum number of people are present.

To sit on the bench at the front of the mixing desk was to literally sit in the music, to attend to the sound as it moved through the wood under my legs and against my back and through what Julian Henriques calls 'the listening skin' (Henriques 2014: 191). His phrase emphasises the touchable, textural qualities of the beats and basslines that rushed up and out through the femurs, the spine, the chest, the teeth; my solid, liquid, and gaseous molecules; my electrical, chemical, and kinetic processes. Henriques argues that listening skins help us learn how 'auditory propagation is by its nature intensive, without the kind of edges, surfaces, and boundaries that define the visual world' (ibid.). And I think maybe this is true from the perspective of the sound wave itself: it propagates through whatever molecules it encounters, without stopping to note the categorical differences between cold air and warm drinks, or a tiled floor and a shining face. But when we think of music, we have to think of *our perception* of auditory propagation, and this perception always involves more than one of our senses. If we have the senses of vision and touch, then we will always hear music, to some degree, through the edgy, tactile, shimmering world.

Speaker cones, for example, visibly pulse and tremble when they amplify the music directed through them by the DJ, and you can feel how these movements correspond to changes in the air-pressures surrounding your body. The speaker-cone is a visible boundary between the electrical and the kinetic, releasing coded sounds into airy enclosures, where gaseous soundwaves interact with their solid reflections (I did see Remarc play a rave in a swimming pool once, but forgot to check how things sounded immersed in liquid.) The obvious boundaries between walls and floors and their adjacent atmospheres are the boundaries between different rates of absorption, reflection, and propagation: sound propagates through wood at speeds between 3300 and 5000 m/s, for example, while in air it remains around 343 m/s (Wozniak O'Connor, 'Silviphonics', 2018). Then there are all the differences in the timbre of the reflections between different materials, whose various molecular arrangements might be the reason a violin manufacturer favours a certain tree, and why Jazzie B praises the sound of a wooden floor. By making these differences palpable, The Charlotte's bench troubled the idea that sound has no edge, or surface: the sound abruptly changed as soon as you stood up. There was a very definite boundary between what you heard when you stood and what you heard when you sat. As long as I remained seated, with the beats and bass pulsing through me, I could feel what I believed: that I was sat within the music I loved.

Sat on the bench with my hood up, I watched Doc Scott stand at the decks, between the two stacks of speakers at either end of the stage, headphones clamped at an angle across his shaved scalp, so that one ear heard the room and the other monitored the mix. Blue-tinged overhead lights revealed the outlines of his nodding head. Sometimes, briefly, he looked like Marlon Brando's Captain Kurtz.

At this period in his career, Doc Scott was having serious problems with his mental health, involving drug-abuse and self-harm. He sums up his difficulties in an interview: 'I lost myself. As a person and musically' (in Jenkins 2018). He was not enjoying his career as a DJ, which had started in the late 1980s. He describes his friend, the DJ and producer Marcus Intalex (RIP), confronting him at a gig they'd both played: '[Marcus] came up […] saying "what the fuck is this? This is shit!" I couldn't even answer him. I was scrambling around trying to find music that represented me and was just in a mess' (ibid.). He only opened up about these difficulties in 2018. So obviously, as I watched him on the decks in the mid-2000s, I had no idea of his troubles. What I saw was the fluid movement of his hands and fingers making adjustments on the mixer and decks, keeping the tunes in line, his signature precision and blending of complementary tunes, zero clashes or clangs, the aesthetic of smooth progression. I saw a DJ who appeared to be in full possession of his skills, playing to a small but dedicated group of fans.

In barely detectable increments, the milling-around crowd started to move with more energy. Soon, there was a small amount of what Joanna Hall describes in an analysis of drum 'n' bass dance: '[a] static stance where one foot is diagonally in front of the other with weight shifting forward and back. The dancer's focus is often down to the floor or looking around the space with the chin dipped' (Hall 2016: 109). Nobody had gone for the more energetic kinds of dancing yet – no skipping-on-the-spot, no moving arms, no contorted fingers. But that's not to say that anyone who wasn't upright and chin-dipping was not enjoying themselves. I am not sure that dance is exemplified where it is most energetic. There is a great deal of emotion in small movements: tentative responses that are both private and public, self-directed and displayed to the crowd. Head-nods, sways. And these are best seen at sparsely attended events.

Then there was the other kind of dance that happens between a crowd of people in a club and a lone man sat with his hood up: every few minutes, someone would walk over and show me their small square green-glowing phone screen with a message on it like 'can u link any pills?'. Or they'd bend into my ear and shout a request, and I'd shake my head and say something like 'nah, sorry,' and they'd walk away, equally apologetic. Thus, I became a hub of disappointment, as people paused their warm-up dances to come over and ask me for drugs and moved back to their positions afterwards.

The poet Vahni Capildeo names a phenomenon called 'pluralocalism', which describes what can happen when you attend to your presence in a particular location. For example, when you hear bells in a cathedral, 'you're always remembering bells' from the past at the same time as you listen to the bells in the present: 'there are certain ways in which your associations are a real and vital part of what you hear physically' (The Writing Life 2021). Your perception is entangled with the memory of a similar perception, so 'any place that you're in starts to consist of multiple places' (ibid.). Thus 'both memory and anticipation' contribute to our sense of embodiment when we listen (ibid.).

The memories that were alive in me as I sat on the bench went back to the late 1990s, when I heard Doc Scott's classic 1997 mix album, *Breakbeat Experiments*, and became a fan for life. I would emulate his DJing style when I began to make mixtapes at home and had been anticipating seeing him for six or more years. There was also the memory of a sonic fiction: Roots Manuva's 'Inna' from his still-underrated album *Brand New Second Hand*. This slow, bass-heavy track tells the story of a man who goes to a club on his own, and I was always to some extent 'in' it, timestretched across the spaces of memory, whenever I went out on my own. My pluralocalism involved my childhood homes in Manchester and my imaginary homes in other people's music. But also, I was remembering and anticipating my own presence on The Charlotte's stage: around this time, I joined a band called Shy Zandra. I sat behind Michael Liggins on bass and Dan Mattson on guitar and smashed a cheap red drumkit around at the back of The Charlotte's stage, directly opposite the one I occupied at the Doc Scott night.

Electronic music's centres of gravity were shifting. A five-minute walk away, in the basement of a three-floor venue called Sumo, dubstep would emerge at a night called Kontakt. In drum 'n' bass, a new kind of snare was establishing itself. While most snares combined elements of snap, bang, crack, and clang, this new kind of snare was a cousin of the tick and the truncated shush, reminiscent of a sharp chisel stabbed into a block of ice. Some producers started to make tunes with flatter frequency profiles, which DJ Storm would later describe as the kinds of tune that, when they drop, 'they don't drop *around* you'.[1] As the spatial experience of listening to drum 'n' bass changed, the music itself required more storage space. When Andy C and Ant Miles saved all the data for their classic track 'Valley of the Shadows' in 1995, the entire track was 3 megabytes, 'on three floppy disks', whereas in 2021 a single tune may easily use 1 gigabyte of data (Terzulli and Otchere 2021: 51). Tunes hadn't grown to this size when I saw Doc Scott, but they were on their way: I remember being surprised to see CD decks instead of vinyl.

DJ Storm tells a story about Photek: he wanted to make his snares a bit more punchy, so he collected some branches and recorded himself snapping them. She doesn't mention which particular Photek tunes contained these snapping branches, which is another reason why we need to pay more attention to the relationship between electronic music and trees.

While we need to recognise what trees have done for electronic music, we also need to recognise what seats have done for dancing. I've focused on The Charlotte's bench because in my early twenties I had no idea that in my late thirties I would develop an autoimmune disease. This disease has not changed my taste in music, but it has drastically altered my taste in music-venue architecture: I long for a world in which dancefloors have seats, so that I can sit-dance with minimal movements. We do not know what is coming to us, and we should equip our venues to accommodate people whose bodies do not respond well to the call to be upright. And we should accommodate these people in the centre of the action.

When we lost The Charlotte, we lost the only place in town that put seats where the music sounded best. Today, the building is home to a mini supermarket. You enter through the same old doorway, but the interior is entirely different. When I visited recently, I spent a long time in there, trying to conjure up my previous pluralocalism. I think the mixing desk and its bench were roughly somewhere between the drinks-fridge and the noodle-shelves. But the long straight aisles confused my estimations of positions, and the man at the till kept clearing his throat. I bought a large bag of crisps and left without mentioning why I was there.

1. https://www.youtube.com/watch?v=IIzVyzTrzJQ

References

'DJ Storm on Life After Kemi, the UK Rave Scene, and the Internet | Red Bull Music Academy'. 2021. YouTube. https://www.youtube.com/watch?v=IlzVyzTrzJQ

Frost, Jumpin Jack. 2020. *Big, Bad & Heavy*. London: Music Mondays.

Gourlay, Dom. 2014. 'DiS meets Colin Greenwood from Radiohead'. *Drowned in Sound*, 21 January. https://drownedinsound.com/in_depth/4147335-dis-meets-colin-greenwood-from-radiohead

Hall, Joanna. 2016. 'Rocking the rhythm: Dancing identities in drum 'n' bass club culture'. In *Bodies of Sound: Studies Across Popular Music and Dance*, ed. Sherril Dodds and Susan C. Cook, 107–114. New York: Routledge.

Henriques, Julian. 2014. 'Dread bodies: Doubles, echoes, and the skins of sound'. *Small Axe* 18, no. 44 (July): 191–201.

Jenkins, Dave. 2018. '"If I didn't reach out for help, I wouldn't be here today […]" Doc Scott discusses his battle with depression'. *UKF*, 21 June. https://ukf.com/words/if-i-didnt-reach-out-for-help-i-wouldnt-be-here-today-doc-scott-discusses-his-battle-with-depression/22206

Leigh, Rev. Edward. 1817. Pamphlet of A Sermon Preached in the Parish Church of Burbach, in the County of Leicester, on the Sunday after the Funeral of her Late Royal Highness, the Princess Charlotte of Wales. DE1243/523, the Record Office for Leicestershire, Leicester, and Rutland, Leicester, UK.

Terzulli, Paul, and Eddie Otchere. 2021. *Who Say Reload: The Stories behind the Classic Drum & Bass Records of the 90s*. Chislehurst: Velocity Press.

Turnell, Catherine. 2010. 'Leicester legacies: The life and times of The Charlotte'. *Leicestershire Chronicle*. http://leicestershirelalala.com/leicester-legacies-the-life-and-times-of-the-charlotte/

Wozniak O'Connor, Vincent. 2018. 'Silviphonics: Sound in timber'. *Journal of Sonic Studies* 16. https://www.researchcatalogue.net/view/457135/457136/0/0.

Writing Life, The. 2021. 'Julian of Norwich and Biscuits with Vahni Capildeo and Jeremy Noel-Tod'. 29 April. https://www.podbean.com/media/share/pb-sdh3w-10216a0?utm_campaign=w_share_ep&utm_medium=dlink&utm_source=w_share

Author biography

Ed Garland is the author of *Earwitness: A Search for Sonic Understanding in Stories*, a book of essays, memoir, and literary criticism that won the New Welsh Writing Awards in 2018. He recently completed a research PhD at Aberystwyth University entitled 'Sonic Experience in Contemporary Fiction'.

14 Kings Cross, Kentish Town and Kensington Gore via Gallowgate: In Search of the Goldilocks Zone

Julianne Regan

The first gig I attended was Queen at Coventry Theatre in 1975. A satin-clad Freddie Mercury blew my then 13-year-old mind. As a teenager in 1980, I ventured to London with my good friend and gig buddy, Rachael, to see Japan at The Venue in Victoria. The proximity of our hometown meant that we could speed over to Birmingham Odeon on a 20-minute train journey to see bands such as Kraftwerk (my studded wristband was confiscated at the door – clearly, I looked like trouble), Roxy Music, Chic, Duran Duran and the Skids. Rachael and I were in the rear stalls for the Skids, and the view wasn't great. She wondered out loud why people were throwing popcorn at the band. I broke the news that it wasn't actually popcorn, but 'flob'. Even the more salubrious venues were not spared having to host the odd phlegm shower. It's fragments like this – be they ridiculous, spectacular or simply comforting – that come to mind when thinking back over decades of gigs and venues.

An even more regular gig-goer since moving to London at the age of nineteen, I've seen venues I once played turned to rubble and/or luxury flats. My first gig as a performer, as the bassist in Gene Loves Jezebel, was in 1982 at The Venue, Victoria. I found no evidence of David Sylvian and co. in the dressing room; but then, two years had passed.

The cherry-pop of a band's first live performance doesn't always promise to be sweet and juicy, but it should surely be memorable. For my band All About Eve (AAE), the historical rupture happened on 5 September 1985 at a pub venue in Kings Cross, which was then called the Pindar of Wakefield. Bob Dylan sang there in 1962, as this was where Ewan MacColl's 'Singers Club' night was held. Peggy Seeger reminisces that Dylan came across as somewhat underwhelming during his one-song performance (Seeger in Llewellyn Smith 2005). AAE's debut appearance at the venue occurred twenty-three years later, in front of around thirty people, as support to Oxfordshire alt goth band Chatshow. I sang our then entire repertoire of songs, all eight of them, with a sheet of narrow-lined A4 in front of my face, on which my lyrics were scrawled. Of course, I didn't need the prompts; the paper was there as a flimsy shield behind which I attempted to conceal my shyness. At one point, the PA stack fell onto our guitarist Tim's side of the stage, toppling and thudding onto his effects. I can't recall whether it was a WEM Copicat or an Ibanez UE-300 multi-effects unit, but whichever, it was broken – as was the ice. In my handbag (or, more accurately, in my military-style canvas bag), I had my trusty Boss digital delay pedal, which Tim used to get us through the set. Our inventiveness and humility won the audience over, and so, emboldened and paperless, I looked them in the eye.

It was a sultry, sweltering summer night, and mercifully the large ceiling fan was on turbo speed. The headroom wasn't generous, and I watched, with concern, as an audience member held aloft on someone's shoulders miraculously avoided decapitation or, at best, amputation of his jubilantly raised arms. Our first ever live performance was rough-and-ready in a suitably rough-and-ready venue, with no aircon and (apparently) few health and safety standards; but then this was the mid-1980s.

At that time, I lived in Tufnell Park, London N7, where the band was formed. My spartan bedsit in Carleton Road was a mere ten-minute walk away from the Bull and Gate, and we frequently attended gigs there. There was a bar at the front of the building, with the absolutely no-frills auditorium being at the rear.

Simon Williams, founder of Fierce Panda Records and erstwhile gig promoter, describes the Bull and Gate as the 'absolute definition of the toilet circuit' (coldplaychronology 2008: 00:52). There is much scuzzy romance and heartfelt nostalgia associated with this and similar venues, and it is clear they were not only venues but also communities. Crucially, they served as crucibles of creativity, places wherein bands – and friendships – were forged. Would you have liked to have seen the Fields of the Nephilim supported by PJ Harvey's then band Automatic Dlamini in a 150-capacity venue? Well, you could've done so on 7 June 1986 at the Bull and Gate.

We played there on 29 April 1986 as a double headline with And Also The Trees, in our own right on 22 September 1986 and, according to bootlegs, sometime between 17 and 24 October 1986. The gigs were on the venue's 'Timebox' nights.

However, we frequented the venue far more often than we played it, going home with bellies filled with cider and blackcurrant, pockets packed with flyers and sometimes a copy of *The Organ* 'zine stuffed into a bag. There was a sense of anything goes and the fun was innocent. I'll never entirely forgive myself for jumping up on stage with Balaam and the Angel, uninvited, to attempt to sing Black Sabbath's 'Paranoid' with them, while only remembering the first line; but then, alcohol had had a hand in it.

On 3 March 2013, just short of twenty-seven years since our B&G debut, I received an email from Tim Bricheno, AAE's co-founder, co-songwriter and original guitarist.[1]

> Hi JA – A bit of an unexpected one, but The Bull and Gate in Kentish town is closing down as a music venue for good this May and being turned into a gastro pub. I love the old place; so many memories of the gigs we did there. Would you be interested in doing a few of the old tunes with a drum machine, on Friday May 3rd? The promoter thought we would be perhaps interested in playing the last ever Friday night gig together. Obviously I am including Andy in this but thought it best to run it by you initially. Not suggesting a grand reform just a lo-key night out/goodbye BnG thing. Perhaps work up about half a dozen of the more familiar tunes from that era, a few relaxed run-throughs a la Carleton Rd sometime before the gig. Please let me know if it appeals. Hope all is good. Tim.

I replied the next day:

> Hi Tim – Yes, I'd heard about the end of the B 'n' G. Such a shame. As if the world needs another gastro pub. I wish I had your attitude, but I couldn't face it. I haven't been on stage since, oh, 2004? The intimacy of the venue would be terrifying, as would the fact that I'd have to lose about 2 stone before I got on a stage ever again. Seriously. Sorry to be a party pooper. Cheers for now. JA.

Tim's reply:

> Don't be so hard on yourself. We're all 50 now – besides it's all about the voice. Anyway, no probs. I knew it was probably a bit of a long shot so thanks for being so open about it. I totally understand. Tim.

The Bull and Gate is now a place of hot desks, cocktails and Sunday roasts. Its closing gig took place on 4 May 2013. I missed out on making a memory, which for someone so deeply interested in memoir and nostalgia, is particularly regrettable. I don't think I ever lost that two stone either.

---

1. Personal correspondence, 2021, quoted here with permission of Tim Bricheno.

We played in plenty of other small to medium-sized venues during our formative years, many of which I also visited as a punter. They include the aforementioned Pindar of Wakefield (at the time of writing, now the Water Rats), The Broadway basement bar and the Clarendon Hotel Ballroom above it, the Croydon Underground and Finsbury Park Red Rose Club. From a financial perspective, we were reluctant to venture outside of London, resulting in only two of our first twenty-eight gigs being played further afield, namely in Oxford and in Bournemouth. Fairly rapidly, we managed to shimmy up the lubricious pole of the music industry and enjoyed chart success with the song 'Martha's Harbour'. We played a secret gig at the Charing Cross Road version of The Marquee, originally having been founded on nearby Wardour Street, under the not particularly undercover name 'Martha and the Harbours'. Don't ever ask me to write a cryptic crossword.

A community is greater than the sum of its parts, and it is testament to that sense of community surrounding these legendary and beloved venues, that Facebook groups thrive long after their demise, with *Bull & Gate Memories – remembering all who sailed in her musical tidal wave*, and the plainly named *Hammersmith Clarendon* among them. The post-punk/proto-goth/alternative scene of the early to mid-1980s was always about more than just the bands. It was about the fanzine sellers, the flyer distributors, the fly-poster pasters, the audience, and not least, the promoters. One such promoter was the late Jon 'Fat Beast' Driscoll, a large man who sported Deirdre Barlow glasses and often very few items of clothing. He once asked me to marry him. It seems he asked lots of people to marry him. He ran the Bull and Gate's Timebox club, and said of my band, 'I loved All About Eve, they played [the Bull and Gate] a few times...' and said of the wider Bull and Gate phenomena that:

> it was very much a Do it Yourself attitude. We loathed record companies or agents. I used to call Simon Cowell a c*nt twice a week, he was at Phonogram as an A and R man. (Jon 'Fat' Beast interviewed by J. von Sutekh in 2013)

The Red Rose Club in Finsbury Park, which was also used by the Islington Branch of the Labour Party for meetings and functions, was where Jon organised a gig for 4 September 1985. The now legendary cult colossus And Also the Trees were headlining, and we were the support. He had dropped the glitter ball on this occasion and had neglected to hire a PA, resulting in my having to sing through one of And Also The Trees' amps. We were surprised and horrified to discover that this was a dry gig, and the audience was understandably disgruntled. Verbally at least, I was their pain piñata. This was character building, undoubtedly, but the angry young woman I then was took to the stage, greeting the less than throbbing crowd – comprising perhaps fifteen people – with a surly 'Welcome to an abortion!'. The club later became renowned as a comedy venue, but not because of what happened that night.

Ask pretty much any touring artist about favourite venues and Glasgow's Barrowlands (aka the Barrowland Ballroom) is certain to come up. It opened on Christmas Eve 1934, was partially burned to the ground in 1958, and reopened on Christmas Eve 1960. It began life as a dancehall, and many Glaswegians would have met their future spouses there. But behind the blithesome cavorting and courting – or winchin' as it would have been called back in the day – lurked a dark, pernicious presence. A serial killer nicknamed 'Bible John', so named for his penchant for quoting extracts of Scripture to his victims, is believed to have sourced the three women he murdered while attending nights at the Barrowlands, killing each one as he escorted them home. The murders contaminated the venue's reputation, causing it to close in the early 1970s.

It lay fallow and forlorn for much of the time, other than a stretch as a roller disco, until 1983 when Simple Minds decided to use it as the location for the filming of the video to their single 'Waterfront', establishing the Barrowlands as a rock venue. The opening shots of the video are in melancholy black and white, a lone figure calmly and casually kicking through plastic glasses on the wooden floor of the empty venue. The scene is overlaid with the non-diegetic sounds of foot stamping and clapping, as if to herald an encore. The video is then cut with full colour flashes of what appears to be a genuinely delighted and animated crowd, filmed from a stage-eye view. A wide shot then reveals both audience and stage, lightshow and band, resulting in a sense of something resurrective and rhapsodic occurring.

Since 1983, the venue has remained a firm favourite on the gig circuit – not just because of the famed fervour of the Glaswegian audience – and has been documented in song by both Christy Moore and Amy McDonald. Simple Minds pay swaggering tribute to its charm in their 2018 song 'Barrowland Star', with Jim Kerr mining a rich seam of nostalgic belonging, as he sings about days lasting forever and sacrificing yourself for something better. Bowie played there; Iggy Pop played there; it seems like everybody played there. We played four times, but it feels like far more than four because of the lasting impression it made.

Famed for its sprung, bouncy dancefloor and the fantastically ostentatious and massive neon sign across its front, playing the 'Barras' feels like a rite of passage. The daytime, unlit version of the façade, I remember as all silvery greys and soft-hued blues, but on a rainy night, the shimmer and glimmer of its shamelessly enticing signage is reflected in the watery mirror of the Gallowgate pavements. Scottish poet Colin Begg encapsulates the spectacle in his poem 'I Remember Your First Time', as he writes of '...pupils narrowed at lights blazing: Barrowland!!' (Begg 2017). He tells me:

> I was inspired by taking my then-girlfriend, now wife, to her first Barrowlands gig. We'd met about 18 months previously and bonded over a shared love of certain bands. It was also my first gig there after some time away from Glasgow, so I was experiencing the sensations anew. (Personal correspondence with author, 11 May 2021)

The Barrowlands dressing room has an intoxicating air of elegantly faded glamour, with a row of mirrors flanked by a regimented glare of Hollywood-style bulbs. In that room, even under a heavy cloud of self-deprecation, it's hard to resist feeling like a star, even for the briefest of moments, and being in such a glamorous cocoon makes you forget that people are being patted down for knives on their way in. Again, Begg captures the moment:

> Past the louts, through the touts,
> frisked by stout bouncers,
> through the metal detector,
> up the mirrored stair to the bar. (Begg 2017)

In my band's unplugged guise, we've played prettier venues. For example, the neo-Gothic Union Chapel (Islington), the Acorn Theatre in Penzance (a former Wesleyan Methodist chapel), Glasgow's Cottiers Theatre (housed within, again, a neo-Gothic church) and the Leeds City Varieties Music Hall – in all its red and gold Victorian splendour – which some will remember as the venue where the BBC's *The Good Old Days* was filmed. However, for volume, dancing, sweat, and the enthusiastic applause of nigh-on 2,000 people, the Barrowlands has not been bettered.

Although my band kicked off its musical career in small, sweaty pubs and clubs, we managed to rise through the ranks to sport the scalp of the Royal Albert Hall (RAH) on our belts. My colleague Dr Jim Dickinson has also played there with the Scalby School jazz band. It was at the 1985 School Proms and the pupils had travelled from Scarborough for the event.

> I remember having pea soup up in the gods, looking down onto that iconic stage so far below. Me and my friends said that one day we'd come back and headline there with our band. More or less a decade later, we did. Of all the venues we played, this is the most magical – it just seeps musical history from the walls. (Jim Dickinson in conversation with author, 13 May 2021)

In jest, for laughs, we sometimes faux compete in front of our students about the fact that Jim has only played it twice, whereas I've played it three times.

Opened by Queen Victoria in 1871, the Royal Albert Hall is a Grade I listed building resembling a gargantuan terracotta wedding cake and is topped by the largest unsupported glass dome in the world. During World Wars, this immense bubble was used as a landmark by pilots, and consequently the glass panels were temporarily painted black in an effort to thwart them.

Pink Floyd appeared at the RAH in June 1969, and their performance included: '...exploding cannons, keyboardist Richard Wright constructing furniture on stage, and even featured a crew member dressed as a gorilla roaming the audience' (Griffin 2016).

The final straw came in the form of the band setting off a 'huge pink smoke bomb' (ibid.), which resulted in their being handed a lifetime ban. Just as custodial life sentences are rarely for life, Pink Floyd's ban was spectacularly commuted, as they returned to the RAH stage just eight months later.

In April 1990, a well-behaved AAE played three consecutive nights at the venue. We could have played one night at Wembley Arena – currently known as the SSE Arena Wembley – which would have meant playing to 12,500 people, whereas the RAH enabled us to play to 16,500. Had we played Wembley, because of various logistics we'd have made much more money; but maximal isn't always optimal. Our audience members deserved to be gently supported by swanky red velvet seating and to enjoy the spectacle of giant mushroom-like discs looming over them (the fibreglass fungi were installed in 1969 to absorb rogue echoes and improve the hall's acoustics). Our audience also deserved the chance to watch from one of the boxes in either the Loggia, the Grand Tier or the Second Tier. I had no inkling of how to pronounce 'Loggia' at the time but was tutored by a friend who waitressed there some nights, serving drinks, in a white blouse and black tie. Incidentally, you pronounce it as if you're referring to the third album in Bowie's Berlin Trilogy.

The memory of our actual performances is a blur. I felt overwhelmed by the occasion, by the splendour, and by the actual sound of the applause, which was breathtakingly immense yet soft, cushioned, seeming impossibly and unfathomably intimate. The dressing room was clean, tidy and spacious, but not grand. By our third night there, we were composed, and bored enough, to spell out All About Eve on the carpet, in fruit. An after-show event was held in the palatial Elgar room to celebrate the end of our run. As record company executives revelled and fellow band members relaxed, I failed to get past the door, as happy fans kettled me for autographs and chat, telling me that the night had been 'magical'. From outside, I could just about hear a string quartet playing, their music muted, surrounded by the sound of conversational spume, and of networking and hardcore hobnobbing. Eventually, I found my way into the room at the time when the celebration had reached its denouement. Far from being queen at the event, I was a happy and humble worker bee, quite desperate to seek out rewarding nectar in the form of a glass of champagne.

From this performer's perspective, there exists a sweet spot concerning venues, where they need not be too overwhelming and not too claustrophobic, not too sticky-floored, and not too clean, not too soft and velvety, and not too bleakly concrete. A venue such as Glasgow Barrowlands inhabits that much sought-after Goldilocks Zone, alongside previously mentioned repurposed church buildings such as the Acorn Theatre, Cottiers Theatre, the Union Chapel, and in addition, an honourable mention going to Colchester Arts Centre, formerly St Marys At The Walls Church. Neon signs, stained glass windows, wooden pews, wooden floors, high ceilings, dark ale and holy wine; whether congregation or audience, all eyes are to the front where something miraculous is supposed to happen, and sometimes does.[2]

References

Begg, Colin. 2017. 'I remember your first time'. https://scotiaextremis.wordpress.com/2017/02/27/week-fifty-six-the-glasgow-empire-glasgow-barrowlands/

Burchill, Charlie, and Jim Kerr. 2018. 'Barrowland Star'. London: Universal Music Publishing Ltd.

Coldplaychronology. 2008. 'Coldplay – Bull and Gate Gig (1st April 1999)'. 9 March. https://www.youtube.com/watch?v=043l7uni3ocv

Griffin, M. 2016. 'From roaming gorillas to lifetime bans – the Hall history of Pink Floyd and David Gilmour'. https://www.royalalberthall.com/about-the-hall/news/2015/march/from-roaming-gorillas-to-lifetime-bans-the-hall-history-of-pink-floyd-and-david-gilmour/

Llewellyn Smith, Caspar. 2005. 'Flash-back: Bob Dylan'. https://www.theguardian.com/music/2005/sep/18/folk.popandrock

von Sutekh, James 2013. 'The slightly erratic and mildly drunken interview with Jon Fat Beast'. *Plunder The Tombs* blog, 31 March. http://plunderthetombs.blogspot.com/2013/03/the-slightly-erratic-and-mildly-drunken.html

2. Prior to researching for this chapter, it had completely slipped my mind that AAE had also played the RAH in 1988. I'm surprised that something so apparently monumental could fade so completely from memory.

Author biography

Julianne Regan is a founding member of the band All About Eve and is currently involved in musical and audio-visual projects with The Dadaists and also with original All About Eve guitarist and co-writer Tim Bricheno. She was a lecturer in Commercial Music and Songwriting at Bath Spa University. Julianne has also authored a chapter in the *Routledge Companion to Folk Horror* (2023).

15 Spiritual Auras: Jungle Venues in Birmingham and the West Midlands, 1993–1997

Penelope Wickson

> But if we find more to look at in the fire, we also have much to lose by pursuing what we see there [...] and wonder what we can risk, and what we might gain. (Elkin 2017: 89)

In the mid-1990s, I was Icarus, hurtling towards the sun – the flaming orb of the Midlands jungle scene: Birmingham. I was at university in the second city and enraptured by the glorious, thunderous sounds of the breakbeat, the kick drum and snare, and the glistening twinkle of the Rhodes piano. I was transfixed; not by the dank haze of sinsemilla or the cloying, chemical scent of crack, but by jungle's glamour, its excess and warmth. Tom and Jerry's 'Maximum Style' and Ray Keith's 'Dubplate' wrapped their sumptuous sub-frequencies around me. The insistent, chopped-up rhythms of the Amen break and the urgent snippets of sampled sound beckoned.

Of course, the term 'glamour' is subjective. It was first used in the nineteenth century to indicate 'something akin to sorcery or magical charm' (Dyhouse 2010: 1). In order to pass through the doors of The Institute, Paloma's and the Que Club, punters required equal quantities of illusion, panache and guile (Dyhouse 2010: 3). DJ Jumpin Jack Frost, a patriarch of the scene, is familiar with the subterranean collision of criminality and violence and its mollusc-like ability to latch on to musical sub-cultures. He recalls that the gigs in the Midlands were 'very rough' (Frost 2017: 171–72). I sensed this too. Yet undeterred, I was captivated by the drama and intimacy of these three venues. Between 1993 and 1997, they defined my experience of jungle. They were distinct from each other in terms of scale, formal elements, and methods of construction, but were all located on the decaying, industrial edges of the city centre. Constructed in historicist revival styles at the end of the nineteenth century, each had once performed significant civic duties. Secular or spiritual, the function of each building was rooted in the shifting moral values of Victorian Britain. As they metamorphosed into theatres, concert halls and nightclubs, the lingering aura of former glory contributed to their allure. The aesthetic of jungle suited me. I saw similarities between a femininity dependent upon elegance and grace and that of my half-Italian mother. Her hair was always elegantly tied back at the nape of her neck. Her hoop earrings, dark eyes, olive skin and high cheek bones epitomised the poise that I would observe in the dance. My own pale green eyes offset brown hair that was pulled sharply off my face. Nineteen years old, I was an ebullient feline cocooned in a downfilled puffa jacket and protected by steel-toed Caterpillar boots. Luxuriating in sub-frequencies, I sheltered from the frenzy of whistles and horns and the flash of the lighters in dark corners and beneath balconies.

The complex diversity of the culture was welcome. Caspar Melville describes junglism as a 'series of unstable cultural and musical hybrids' (Melville 2020: 151) while Malcolm James emphasises that 'it was a black sound and could not easily be closed down by white identifications of the black other' (James 2020a: 151). He adds that 'racial authentication was error prone, and that disruption was celebrated by black and white producers alike' (ibid.: 151). This is not to deny that negative reactions from the media were underscored by racism. Snax (a former jungle DJ and raver) recalls that it 'was perceived in a negative way compared to say the house music scene' (Snax, conversation with author, 30 August 2020). It was a pariah, described by Bryan Gee as 'the bastard child of dance music' (Gee 2021). The views of the media were echoed by my university peers. I was met with derision which was often sinister and malicious. This confirmed Stephen Gundle's observation that 'glamour is not to everyone's taste […] a surfeit is nauseating' (Gundle 2008: 17). It seemed that revulsion towards the music was intertwined with the identity of the three venues. All were located in transient areas, dressed in the gaudy garb of Victorian historicist revival styles that had long since been regarded as deeply unfashionable. Yet the style and fabric of these venues complemented a sound that was emerging as unique to the West Midlands. The spaces drew attention to jungle sounds distinct from those offered by London.[1]

Undeniably, the capital is where jungle was born. MC Lenni – one of the most important figures in the Midlands underground network – explains the relationship between the two cities in terms of Birmingham's desire to learn:

1. The unique contribution of the West Midlands to the development of jungle is discussed in relation to Jason Ball's Back 2 Basics production and record shop (Terzulli and Otchere 2021: 106–7).

'London started it [...] we had to catch up, but we caught up pretty fast' (in Allen 2013). Lenni's Birmingham based shop, Pure Records, as well as Back 2 Basics in Wednesbury, were critical to the golden era of jungle and showed that the relationship between London and Birmingham was mutually beneficial (Terzulli and Otchere 2021: 106–7). Snax emphasises that Micky Finn 'made his name in Birmingham. In the early days it was so big and important' (conversation with author, 30 August 2020). Equally, MC Majika notes that Jumpin Jack Frost frequently made the journey up and down the M1 to play to the Midlands crowd (in Frost 2017: 119).

Travel, often in the most desirable of vehicles (Audi TT, Mercedes Compressor, Golf GTI), contributed to jungle's mystique. Motorway connections, especially those of the industrial hinterlands of London and the Midlands, were critical to the webs of DJs, producers, clubs, and pirate radio stations that propelled the sound and its culture. Accordingly, it is impossible to grasp the identity of these three venues without placing them in the context of their geography – both historical and contemporary. The Institute was located in Digbeth,[2] a run-down industrial area of central Birmingham, while Paloma's in Wolverhampton was close to the canal and the railway station. The Que Club occupied a more prestigious location at the top of Corporation Street, but this too bordered on less salubrious districts. Caspar Melville notes that 'it is important to remember that Jungle gestated in some of the most socially deprived regions of the UK' (Melville 2020: 218). Indeed, each venue was divorced from the focus of city nightlife, John Bright Street and later Broad Street in Birmingham and the High Street in Wolverhampton. All three touched on significantly neglected spaces which were a long way from being re-generated.[3]

The venues themselves, each once having held a civic function of major importance had transformed, to borrow from Deleuze and Guattari, from 'striated space' to 'smooth' (Deleuze and Guatarri 2015: 179–81). They were spaces that were more akin to the irregular yet compact composition of felt than the uniform, linear construction of woven fabric. They were 'amorphous and non-conformist' (ibid.: 179). These patchwork spaces combined the smooth and the striated and, as Pennina Barnett argues, these are concepts that are 'not set in opposition' but interact in dialectical tension (Barnett 2015: 185).

2. Digbeth is historically an Irish area and many of the buildings (pubs, social centres etc.) catered to this diasporic community and many still do.
3. At the time of writing, regeneration plans for Digbeth are underway. Much of this is stimulated by the arrival of the HS2 railway station.

The Institute

In its past life, The Institute fell into the category of striated space. Its visual symmetry worked with its form.[4] Located at 78 Digbeth Street, The Institute is one of the oldest music venues in the city. Originally built as a Methodist chapel, it opened on 16 January 1908 as an institutional place of worship attached to Carrs Lane congregational church. In 1955, it was taken over by Birmingham City Council and became Digbeth Hall. Undergoing an overhaul in the mid-1980s, it continued to function as a nightclub and concert arena until it was forced to close in 2008.

Although Ethan Edwards at the Birmingham History Forum notes that The Institute was 'synonymous in the development of the British rave music and drum & bass scene', this is an exception (Edwards 2010). The Guardian's *Gig Venue Guide* makes no reference to it as home to huge jungle promotions Pandemonium and Amnesia House, preferring to focus on house and trance events God's Kitchen, Atomic Jam and Sundissential (Langley 2014). Equally, the Guide's author shows little sympathy for its style or history, dismissing it as 'quaint' and 'old' (ibid.). The building was in fact was designed in a Dutch Baroque style, carrying with it connotations of success and aspiration associated with trade and commerce. It was a style entirely appropriate for Birmingham – a city whose success had been rooted in the development of minor industries such as metalwork and jewellery.[5] However, by the late twentieth century, flamboyant, historicist styles were considered crude and tasteless. They drew attention to the city's lack of prestige in comparison with other industrial trading cities Manchester and Leeds. The ornate style of The Institute unsettled *The Guardian*'s correspondent who saw its structure as overly embellished and the interior laden with excessive glass and gold. This disparaging tone amplifies what Yinka Shonibare has termed 'patterns of discrimination' – that is to say, a derisory attitude towards decoration and disgust towards the ornamental driven by a combination of thinly veiled racism, regionalism and classism (Shonibare 2018: 11).

As a raver, I admired its red and white brick contrasts. Its towers broke the skyline, its string coursing delineated its three storeys. I was seduced by the fact that it felt old. The stained wooden floors and unreliable plumbing generated a peculiar atmosphere of decay laced with defiance. There was a suggestion of memory trapped within its walls. The Institute possessed an

---

4. An introduction to the history and architecture of the Digbeth Institute can be found at Birmingham City Council (2021).
5. A thorough consideration of Birmingham's identity as a city of industry and manufacturing is provided by Chinn and Dick 2016.

elegiac mood that was misunderstood by the mainstream media. This is also true of the innovative events that took place there. Inside, the dark corners were complemented by black leather sofas. They provided cover for the night-creatures navigating the burrows and warrens of the jungle nexus. The mood could be tense. Jumpin Jack Frost recalls that he 'was playing out in this club in Birmingham at the height of Jungle and you could sense a dark vibe' (Frost 2017: 197). Frost's intuition was correct – the sleek stylishness masked ambitions and hostility between competing gangs from rival cities. Fridays at The Institute were precarious. One evening, when MC Moose was on the stage, the night was disrupted by a group from Manchester who had 'rushed' the door, bearing machetes (MC Ranski, conversation with author, 29 August 2021). I was able to detach myself from the danger. I held my own and maintained my steely composure; a prerequisite for a junglist. I returned to The Institute again and again.

This was the tenebroso world of Caravaggio. Noble characters, clandestine and sculptural, punctuated shadowed crevices. Lasers shot through hematite depths, luminous green and purple whirled through the sfumato, illuminating the crisp silhouettes of the junglists dressed in black and gold. Mesmerised by the steppers and the rollers, these *spanglers* moved fiercely to the warmth of the pads and the shimmer of distorted vocals and synthesised stabs of Belgian techno, all held together by the lowest sub-frequencies imaginable.

As raver Jack T Ripper remembers, there was 'nothing like Jungle in an old time Baroque theatre' (Jack T Ripper, Twitter message to author, 22 July 2021). Passing through the triumphal arched entrance with its imposing portal, the main auditorium was accessed by a symmetrical flight of curving stairs. The stage was raised, framed by balconies on either side. Such drama was again lost on our *Guardian* reviewer, who felt that the adaptation of a theatrical setting to a forum for dance music was detrimental to the delicate technical finesse of his aural experience. But the issue really seems to be The Institute's flamboyance as he exclaims: 'even the large matching mirrors of the walls are curved' (Langley 2014). I liked this femininity, these flounces and flourishes. But, as Janis Jefferies highlights in her discussion of the abject qualities of excessive ornament, many feel differently: 'the taste for the decorative is pathologised as feminine, as embellishment, as style, as frivolous, as excessive and is therefore constantly repressed' (Skelly 2017: 1). *The Guardian*'s review sharpened my focus on the vilification of jungle in both the dance music and mainstream press and in the conversations I caught in queues, corridors and classrooms.

Despite all this, the nights organised by Pandemonium and Amnesia House were glorious. Once, as I was about to leave, I turned around to witness two immaculately resplendent and self-assured figures descending the stairs. Tall, elegant and composed, I realised that they were DJ Fabio and MC Lenni. Both looked in my direction and one smiled. In a few weeks a phone number would be surreptitiously inserted into my coat pocket whilst I absorbed myself in the dubplates that were being unleashed at Pure Records. The DJs and MCs captured an innate style and charisma that they revelled in and cherished. Bryan Gee remembers a shopping expedition with Frost during which he purchased a fur coat: 'he wore that mink out at Bar Rhumba and he lit up the entire club. He loved his clothes and style' (Frost 2017: 191). However, style and grace are attributes that are rarely bestowed upon jungle. Instead, it was Miss Money Penny's at Bonds in Hockley, touching on the more exclusive Jewellery Quarter and financial district of Birmingham, that was renowned for its strict dress code and 'beautiful people'.[6]

Quest (Paloma's)

Another venue significant to the explosion of jungle in the Midlands was Paloma's nightclub in Wolverhampton where Quest ran for five years from 1991. Its influence cannot be underestimated. Snax explains that 'their lineups rivalled anything coming out of London' (Snax, conversation with author, 30 August 2020). Like The Institute and the Que Club, Paloma's was built at the end of the nineteenth century in a historicist revival style. The Victorian gothic polygonal tower was topped with a pointed spire, gables and chimneys. A local landmark, it was situated on the intersection of Lichfield Street and Broad Street where it formed part of the industrial area's development in the 1880s (Directory of Architectural Ceramics in Wolverhampton 2021). By 1910, John Shaw and Sons occupied the building. It housed their offices and show rooms while facilitating commerce and manufacture – much like a mercantile palace of Northern Renaissance Europe (Directory of Architectural Ceramics in Wolverhampton 2021). The building did not share the same religious purpose as the morally robust Institute or reforming Que Club, but it was just as important to the civic history of the West Midlands. Similarly attached to entrepreneurship in the nineteenth century, general hardware merchants John Shaw and Sons were vitally important to the regional economy of manufacturing – enterprise which was closely linked to craft production. The building appears on an invoice from 1910 and it is believed to possess 'the best Victorian tiled

6. The flashy, aspirational appeal of Miss Money Penny's is described in Pearson (2019). The attendees of the club were known colloquially as 'the beautiful people' by supporters of all types of dance and bass music in Birmingham during the mid-1990s.

hall and staircase in Wolverhampton' (Directory of Architectural Ceramics in Wolverhampton 2021). These yellow, blue and white tiles, their sinuous curlicues framed by warm brown terracotta mouldings, are visible in rare video footage from a Quest night in 1991 (Detonator 2009). Here, Fabio and Micky Finn play to a frenetic audience of ravers energised by the earliest forms of jungle – hardcore and jungle tekno – genres that were often noted for the use of sweeping synth waves, chords and heavy breakbeats. Although the juxtaposition was apparently incongruous, the late Victorian designs complemented the monstrous sounds encased in this fantastical structure.

Pattern was a dominant feature of the Italian fashion popular among junglists in the mid-1990s. Jumpin Jack Frost recounts that 'the Jungle look had started to incorporate Versace, Moschino and Gucci. I had these lovely Versace shirts with patterns all over them' (Frost 2017: 171). There was an unlikely similarity between the ornament and decoration at Paloma's and the type of florid and geometric designs developed by the most exclusive Italian fashion houses at the time. I had a pair of zebra-striped trousers which I would wear low slung on my hips over a pair of Calvin Klein pants with a high waistband. These were accessorised with a pair of Versace sunglasses, or a gold-studded black velvet hairband. Acquaintances at university expressed moral concern regarding the appropriate nature of my dress and similar, if more serious, hostility was expressed towards the jungle community. Quest, in particular, received an invective from *Mix-Mag* in relation to what was perceived to be the widespread use of crack (cited in Martin James 2020b: 58). Consequently, distaste towards my clothing echoed a more sombre discourse which, as Malcolm James highlights, was driven by racism: 'In these panics, Jungle was figured as dangerous and degenerate on black terms' (James 2020a: 63). The Italian fashion became coded as the dress of the British junglist. It had the power to create what Julia Skelly has termed a 'radical decadence' (Skelly 2017: 4). Skelly's concept of the power of excess to purposefully transcend ideological and spatial borders sheds light on the way in which, at a time of increasing hegemonic outrage towards jungle, the use of decoration was empowering. The re-framing of Italian design became a symbol of joy. It was a vital energy and life force. The junglist's sartorial celebration of the swag and the curlicue highlighted the 'means of social and political expression' which Shonibare (2018: 10) believes colour, ornament and pattern are capable of generating.

Speaking inside the venue in 1991, Fabio praised Paloma's for an atmosphere which he placed on a par with his celebrated Rage night (Jungle Drum 'n' Bass 2021). DJ Rap reiterates these sentiments: 'It had a vibe and atmosphere like no other. It was electric [...] the ceiling would be dripping with sweat. It sounds horrible but this was the feel' (*Birmingham Mail* 2021). The experience in Quest was intimate and the visceral intensity created by the pressure of the Victorian interior shaped the way in which sounds were experienced. I felt an intense connection with the rugged reverberation of the low-pass filter as it ricocheted around my body. The lack of sonic polish enhanced the sound of crackling wax, a feature unique to the earlier forms of audio production. Fabio felt that in London 'the bass was cleaner', a sense that correlated with *The Guardian*'s complaint that the acoustics in The Institute were poor due to a 'tendency to blow up the bass so that it frequently obscures details' (Langley 2014). The Victorian brick, tiles and terracotta did not absorb the lower frequencies as effectively as modern materials, instead mirroring them and resulting in a more dense and rugged effect. Yet crucially, it was this less refined sound that distinguished the jungle of the Midlands.[7]

The Que Club

Unlike The Institute and Paloma's, the Que Club received greater acknowledgement regarding its contribution to the development of jungle. *Time Out* states that 'some of the best Jungle and [subsequent] Drum & Bass nights in the UK took place in the massive old venue' (Cook 2021). The building's changing history exposes its transformation from striated space as a place of improvement based on strict moral codes, to a smooth space dependent on the desire for pleasure and enjoyment. It attracted ravers from all over the country who were prepared to climb drainpipes to get inside (DJ Remedee, Twitter message to author, 15 July 2021). DJ Remedee travelled from Norwich with a group of friends in a hired minibus to attend the Que Club.

The Que Club is the largest of these three venues. A Grade II listed building, the enormous Methodist Central Hall, constructed as part of the Temperance Movement, opened as a nightclub in 1989. Its first run lasted until 2002 and then, after a brief hiatus, until 2017 when it closed for good.[8] The main hall

---

7. Birmingham and the Midlands is associated with the genre of 'Jump Up' – a fiercely energetic and dancefloor-friendly style with its roots in the ragga jungle of the 1990s. One of the most important DJs from the Midlands to produce and play 'Jump Up' is DJ Hazard – an original member of Kool FM Midlands who used to work in the Music First record shop in Digbeth. He is now signed to DJ Hype's True Playaz and Ganja Records labels.
8. The historical importance and vulnerability of the Que Club is highlighted by Tappenden 2021. Such is the significance of the Que Club to the history of dance music that it features in a documentary and exhibition curated by Jez Collins who leads the Birmingham Music Archive. More information is available at https://www.birminghammuseums.org.uk/stories/birmingham-the-music-city-an-interview-with-jez-collins.

seated 2,000 and the building contained more than thirty other rooms, making it ideal for promoters and partygoers alike. An amalgam of Romanesque, Gothic and Byzantine styles and methods of construction, the warren of corridors, niches and vestibules surrounded an enormous vaulted central space which was framed by two levels of tiered seating on three sides. The elaborate balconies highlighted this dramatic composition and directed the eye towards the elevated stage accessible on either side by doors and steep flights of steps. The backdrop – an immense organ – acted as a sublime presence in numerous images of the master DJ alone at work on the decks.

Such spectacle, saturated with the spirit of past civic stature, was critical to the musical experience which was at once mysterious and compelling. I watched DJ Rap from high above. She was alone on the stage, and I carefully observed her technique as she cued up each piece of vinyl and acetate. I had, at last, found my ego-ideal. We shared Italian heritage and plumes of dark-brown curly hair piled high upon our heads, a shield for any vulnerability. I was mesmerised as she adjusted the pitch, located the needle in the correct place, steadily brought in a new track and perfectly matched her beats. I wanted her confidence and self-possession to reflect back onto me.

In common with the entertainment and leisure institutions of the nineteenth century, the snaking corridors and hidden corners facilitated voyeuristic and scopophilic relationships. These were predicated on an economy of gender interaction which, at that time, was orientated around the male gaze (see Toppin 2019). MC Scarlett came and sat next to me on the red leather-seated upper balcony, handed me a stage-pass and encouraged me to come and find him later. A tall gentleman, pristinely dressed in classic tailoring, summoned me from the darkness, inviting me for a drink. I didn't bother to find Scarlett. I went home with my stage-pass instead.

Fade to White

By 1997, jungle's moment had passed. Its star had fallen. It was eclipsed by drum 'n' bass, its close but significantly distinct relative.[9] Events were no longer held at The Institute and Paloma's, although the Que Club would continue to stage exceptional nights for a while longer. Planet V/Music First, for example, remained legendary with its on-point line-up and high concentration of sophisticated, innovative music from pioneers such as DJ Die, Roni Size and DJ Krust alongside Ed Rush and Optical. The sound was changing and so was the demographic. Jumpin Jack Frost explains that 'the roughness

9. For a clear account of the difference between jungle and drum 'n' bass and how the genres evolved, see Goldie (2017: 174).

of Jungle started to fade a little. The audience started to change as a result with more white faces appearing at parties' (Frost 2017: 177). Emblematic of this shift was the popularity of a new venue with a new crowd – a crowd that was more reserved, but also more socially and financially mobile. The Custard Factory (the former Birds production plant) was located close to The Institute in Digbeth.[10] However, it projected a very different image through its paradigmatic blank purity of early twentieth-century geometric Modernism. It sat comfortably with this new, more self-consciously intellectual audience.[11] The Rude Boys, Yardies and Fly-Girls had gone.

In contrast, the polychromatic Victorian historicist venues seemed even more vulnerable to distinctions based on class, race, education, and economic status. However, in these irregular spaces, I had felt safer than I had in my hall of residence. In my university accommodation, the rugby team would perform their weekly ritual of going out in their uniform white, vomit-covered boiler suits, unwashed from previous bacchanals, the evidence of drunken weekends embedded triumphantly in the fabric. By 1997, university-based Pro-Session was hosting drum 'n' bass events but refused to book DJs from Kool FM Midlands for fear that they would attract a supposedly undesirable crowd.

10. The Custard Factory represented a contrasting identity to that of The Institute not only aesthetically but also historically and socially despite both buildings in their different ways being synonymous with social advancement. In 1837, the chemist Alfred Bird created an instant custard powder that was free from egg in order to accommodate his wife's allergy. The newly invented sauce was served by accident to friends of Bird and was such a success that the production company Alfred and Sons was founded. By 1902, following the industrial expansion of Digbeth, Alfred Bird opened a new complex in which his custard would be produced. The Custard Factory remained in operation until the 1960s. In 1993 funding was secured to restore the space which was by now in disrepair. Further information and a timeline can be found at https://digbeth.com/about/history. A thorough discussion of the role of the Custard Factory in the origins of the gentrification of Digbeth and its transformation into the cultural quarter of Eastside is located in Porter and Barber (2007). See also https://www.academyofurbanism.org.uk/custard-factory/.
11. The shift from jungle to drum 'n' bass that coincided with the opening-up of the Custard Factory as a creative complex occurred at the same time that Digbeth had been identified as an area for cultural and creative regeneration. This followed on from a desire on the part of Birmingham City Council in the 1980s to rebuild and transform Birmingham city centre, ensuring that its status as a second-order global city was truly reflected in its fabric. The Eastside District Project began formally in 1999 although London-based developer Bennie Gray had acquired the five-acre Custard Factory several years earlier. For a critical examination of the gentrification of Digbeth, a Birmingham City Council led project – in partnership with Advantage West Midlands, see Porter and Barber (2006).

Neither did they want dancers dressed in silver and gold sequins on their stage – the feminine flamboyance of myself and my friend (who had partied with Exodus in Luton) was passé, tasteless and too strongly associated with jungle. For me, the need for excess was nostalgic. Memories were already imbibed with blissful sensations of the halcyon days of jungle – the *jouissance* of the dance. In The Institute, Paloma's and the Que Club, the haptic, the sonic and the visual came together. These were liminal environments, simultaneously *striated* and *smooth*, their 'porous rhythms' and decorated surfaces amplifying a desire for warmth, adoration and acceptance.[12]

References

Allen, Chris. 2013. 'Interview with MC Lenni'. YouTube video, 8.13, 10 September. https://www.youtube.com/watch?v=1T8Jcj-GJk0&t=339s

Barnett, Pennina. 2015. 'Folds, fragments, surfaces: Towards a poetics of cloth'. In *The Textile Reader*, ed. Jessica Hemmings, 182–190. London: Bloomsbury Academic.

Birmingham City Council. 2021. 'The Institute'. https://www.birmingham.gov.uk/directory_record/138087/the_institute

Birmingham Mail. 2021. 'Quest's annual reunion at Wolverhampton's Civic Hall'. https://www.birminghammail.co.uk/whats-on/things-to-do/quests-annual-reunion-wolverhamptons-civic-2589253

Chinn, Carl, and Malcolm Dick. 2016. *Birmingham: The Workshop of the World*. Liverpool: Liverpool University Press.

Cook, Tom. 2021. '15 signs you were on the Birmingham club scene in the '90s'. *Time Out*, 1 March. https://www.timeout.com/birmingham/news/15-signs-you-were-on-the-birmingham-club-scene-in-the-90s-052715

Deleuze, Gilles, and Félix Guattari. 2015. '1440: The smooth and the striated'. In *The Textile Reader*, ed. Jessica Hemmings, 179–181. London: Bloomsbury Academic.

Detonator, The. 2009. 'Quest (Yes Quest) very rare footage from 1991 Part 1', 9.56, 20 August. https://www.youtube.com/watch?v=XZOOJysRXsE

Directory of Architectural Ceramics in Wolverhampton, The. 2021. 'Amar House: Broad Street'. http://www.historywebsite.co.uk/interesting/terracotta/amar.htm

Dyhouse, Carol. 2010. *Glamour: Women, History, Feminism*. London and New York: Zed Books.

Edwards, Ethan. 2010. 'Digbeth Institute (Civic Hall)'. *Birmingham History Forum*. https://birminghamhistory.co.uk/forum/index.php?threads/digbeth-institute-civic-hall.29258/

Elkin, Lauren. 2017. *Flâneuse: Women Walk the City in Paris, New York, Tokyo, Venice and London*. London: Penguin.

Frost, Jumpin Jack (with Andrew Woods). 2017. *Big Bad and Heavy*. London: Music Mondays.

---

12. Malcolm James uses the architectural trope of 'porous rhythms' with reference to the technological sound production of jungle (James 2020a: 79).

Jungle Drum 'n' Bass. 2021. 'Interview with DJ Fabio'. YouTube video, 9.52. https://www.youtube.com/watch?v=aqCw4-rItMA

Gee, Bryan. 2021. 'V Podcast 115'. https://www.vrecordings.com/news/14987/v-podcast-115-bryan-gee-w-illmatika

Goldie (with Ben Thompson). 2017. *All Things Remembered*. London: Faber & Faber.

Gundle, Stephen. 2008. *Glamour: A History*. Oxford: Oxford University Press.

James, Malcolm. 2020a. *Sonic Intimacy: Reggae Sound Systems, Jungle Pirate Radio and Grime YouTube Music Videos*. London and New York: Bloomsbury Academic.

James, Martin. 2020b. *State of Bass: The Origins of Jungle/Drum and Bass*. London: Velocity Press.

Langley, Martin. 2014. 'The gig venue guide: The Institute, Birmingham'. *The Guardian*, 2 September. https://www.theguardian.com/music/musicblog/2014/sep/02/gig-venue-guide-the-institute-birmingham.

Melville, Caspar. 2020. *It's a London Thing: How Rare Groove, Acid House and Jungle Remapped the City*. Manchester: Manchester University Press.

Pearson, Daz. 2019. 'Interview with Jeremy Healy'. *Decoded Magazine*, 11 July. https://www.decodedmagazine.com/jeremy-healy-legends-in-the-park-interview-2019/

Porter, Elizabeth, and Austin Barber. 2006. 'The meaning of place and state-led gentrification in Birmingham's Eastside'. *City: Analysis of Urban Trends, Culture, Theory, Policy, Action* 10, no. 2: 215–234. http://eprints.gla.ac.uk/25333/

Porter, Elizabeth, and Austin Barber. 2007. 'Planning the cultural quarter in Birmingham's Eastside'. *European Planning Studies* 15, no. 10: 1327–1348. http://eprints.gla.ac.uk/25332

Radstone, Susannah. 2000. *Memory and Methodology*. London: Berg.

Tappenden, Roslyn. 2021. 'City planners give go ahead to turn history buildings into flats'. *Culture* 24. http://www.culture24.org.uk/places-to-go/west-midlands/birmingham/art24

Terzulli, Paul, and Eddie Otchere. 2021. *Who Say Reload: The Stories Behind the Classic Drum and Bass Records of the 90s*. London: Velocity Press.

Shonibare, Yinka. 2018. *Criminal Ornamentation*. London: Hayward Gallery Publishing.

Skelly, Julia. 2017. *Radical Decadence: Excess in Contemporary Feminist Textiles and Craft*. London and New York: Bloomsbury Academic.

Toppin, Julia. 2019. '"They're not in it like the man dem": Race, gender and digitilisation in the drum and bass music industries'. MA dissertation, University of Westminster.

Author biography

Dr Penelope Wickson (DJ Tina Irie) is a qualified teacher and art historian. Her work has appeared in the journals *Nineteenth-Century Gender Studies, Italian Studies and Textile History* and she has given papers at major conferences organised by the National Gallery, the Courtauld History of Dress Association and the Association for Art History. Her interest in the intersection of global cultures is mirrored by her love of music. Growing up in the north of England in the late 1980s sparked a deep interest in underground house, hardcore and techno whilst her passion for jungle and drum 'n' bass spans almost thirty years. In 1994, whilst studying History of Art and Italian at the University of Birmingham, she founded its first ever newspaper column to explore the genre. Immersed in labels such as Reinforced, V Recordings and Creative Source, her heart resides in the heady nights of Swerve, Quest and Metalheadz that defined the 1990s. She presents regular radio shows on Imperial Voice Radio, Energy 1058 and Kane FM – playing upfront and contemporary jungle and drum 'n' bass that captures the spirit of the original sound.

16 The Wheat from the Chaff

Matt Colbeck

It's the long, hot summer holidays of 1990. My best mate from school and I are waging guerrilla warfare against his older brother's record collection. It's a risky business (there's a dead arm or Chinese burn hanging over us) but armed to the teeth with C60s, we're locked and loaded. Band posters adorn the walls: James, Carter USM, New FADs, the Stone Roses, the Wedding Present, the Wonder Stuff. Under the watchful gaze of George Best and Méliès's moon (before I even knew who Méliès was), we deftly carry out our raiding party, pirating 7 inches, LPs, EPs and tapes, all the time listening out for the tired footfall of my friend's brother, back from his shift at Alton Towers.

It was in that room and, later, in my own room, listening to our haul, where my music education began and where I discovered one of my all-time favourite bands of my formative years (and still to this day): CUD (the first gig tickets I booked after Lockdown #2 were for CUD in their Leeds hometown). My first encounter with *When In Rome, Kill Me* blew my young mind. Everything about it was fascinating, from the enigmatic cover sporting a decidedly 'unhip' older gentleman (*he* couldn't be in the band, surely?) and lacking any reference to either artist or album title, to the absurd, dramatic segues between the songs themselves and the peculiar, surreal yet parochial lyrics of frontman Carl Puttnam ('Only a Prawn in Whitby', anyone?). And then there was *that* logo with the amusingly uddered 'U'. But the prospect of seeing these rock music heroes of mine perform live seemed remote, living in Stoke on Trent, which hadn't yet developed a cutting-edge music scene. Or so I thought. Instead, I had to satisfy myself with watching CUD's 1990 live performance video, *When At Home, Film Me*, which my friend and I had commandeered through one of our most audacious acts, swapping the video for a VHS recording of *Fletch*, hoping and praying that my friend's brother wouldn't be watching the CUD video that weekend. For those few days, we viewed the performance from Leeds University on a loop through my toploader player, watching the raw power and sauciness of tracks like 'Push and Shuv' and 'Strange Kind of Love' come to life. Will Potter's energetic playing and bestarred shirt, I think, was what kickstarted my desire to be a bassist myself.

Of course, I did go to gigs (the Wonder Stuff, Manchester GMEX, Dec '91; Kingmaker, Wolverhampton Civic Hall, Nov '92; Lenny Kravitz, Birmingham NEC, Dec '93), but these inevitably proved to be a bit of a mission, making the journey to far-flung venues, relying on patient parents willing to taxi us there and back and sit in their car or drink alone in bars around the corner or, worse still, actually attend the gig, an ignominy experienced on both sides of the parent/child divide. If we were lucky, bands would come to the larger-scale, premier venue of the six towns, the Victoria Hall in the city centre of Hanley, but the bands I wanted to see there were few and far between. During my sixth-form college years, I saw a grand total of two acts there: The Levellers in '93 and the Wonder Stuff in '94. Aside from this, it was where I came with my mum and dad (a parental act of broadening my horizons) to watch touring orchestras performing classical works, which was really the meat-and-potatoes of the venue. But it was during my latter years at secondary school and college years that my friends and I discovered an infinitely more modest music venue that would nevertheless have a profound influence upon me: The Wheatsheaf, in Stoke town centre.

Now, a confession. In pitching my idea for this chapter, I had in mind a long-term relationship with the venue, spanning many years and performances. When I came to research and write it, it transpired that most of my experiences and gigs seen there were primarily confined to the two-year period I was at sixth form. And reminiscing about the venue itself (and trying to tally these against the rare photos or videos on the web) revealed certain confabulations regarding the topography of the venue in my mind's eye. So, a disclaimer: many of my memories of The Wheatsheaf itself may well be memory edits or amalgams, *bricolages* of other memories of other venues. As the neurologist David Eagleman points out, 'Our past is not a faithful record. Instead it's a reconstruction, and sometimes it can border on mythology' (Eagleman 2016: 27). What follows, therefore, is a memoir of the memories of feelings I had within a gritty, dingy yet magical music venue which was right on my doorstep.

I first heard about The Wheatsheaf during the winter of '92. I'm not sure why I hadn't come across it earlier. Maybe my ignorance stemmed from my cloistered school-life, attending a small Catholic secondary school in the rural town of Cheadle, only a stone's throw from Alton Towers. Despite the relative insularity, I was lucky to have a group of like-minded, music-obsessive friends and it was because of them that I booked tickets to see the underrated and short-lived indie act, Eat, at The Wheatsheaf. I had first witnessed their pounding combo of swamp blues, funk and hip hop supporting the Wonder Stuff at the GMEX. Ange Dolittle was an electric, charismatic frontman, becoming something of a music icon for me and my pals, *NME* cut-outs of him and the band adorning our schoolboy bedrooms. And so it was, on a cold night in December, that I first set foot in The Wheatsheaf. I met my friends outside the venue, sweatily clutching my ticket, which cost less than a fiver. We waved goodbye to the fleet of dad taxis and headed inside.

Low-ceilinged, dimly lit and freezing cold, it was really nothing to write home about. Like all great grassroots venues, it had that unmistakable aroma: a suggestion of wet dog (if the hound in question had been caught in a downpour of Marston's Pedigree). And of course, there were high-notes of nicotine, a pall of smoke that floated, mid-tank, throughout the venue, filtering the kaleidoscopic light of the Fresnels. Despite spending so many years in smoky, poky rooms, it is almost impossible, today, to fully (re)remember what pubs and clubs were like before the smoking ban. You get a vague sense-memory when someone sparks up at a gig, but this is just an alien smell of a rebellious interloper and comes nowhere near to evoking the general fug of smoke in the venues of yore.

The Wheatsheaf's stage backed onto a whole bank of ceiling-to-floor windows which faced onto the main drag of Stoke, the nexus of a one-way system taking you in and out of town, bordered by run-down buildings and a raised concrete shopping plaza. Standing in front of these windows, with people dotted around us or hanging about the bar in the corner, feet sticking to the floor, we could've just been in a pub. In my memory of attending gigs there, I visualized seeing the activity of the dwindling town unfolding behind the bands, a living, breathing and kaleidoscopically changing back projection. Looking at the odd archive photo or video, however, revealed large chintz curtains covering the windows. Maybe, on occasion, these weren't drawn, and you could look beyond the music to the world beyond and back again; maybe they were always drawn, and I imagined this world. Either way, what struck me and stuck with me was the proximity the acts had to the urban exterior, separated by thin sheets of glass, but also the proximity of audience to the acts: with a small, step-up stage and flimsy barrier, the gap where we ended and the band began was hard to discern.

We were juiced up on Newky Brown that we'd bought with our fake IDs. A kid in school, through his Saturday job at the local leisure centre, had carved out a neat line in selling false gym passes with false DOBs. We shuffled toward the stage. Despite the unfamiliar geography of the venue, the ceremony was the same as any other live music space I had frequented: a fading of the mixtape, a dipping of the lights and the magnetic pull of the barrier had us in its grip as we slid subtly through the closing gaps between shoulders to get to the front. Jammed in tight, now, suffocatingly so, we braced ourselves for the melee as the band started up. Eat were explosive that night. And unlike the hangar expanse of the GMEX, we were virtually on top of the band, and then we were caught in the surge of the crowd, eyeballed at all times by the steely glare of Ange. And like every dive bar or spit-and-sawdust music venue worth its salt, as you sweated, it sweated; as you leapt and stomped and screamed, so did it. From your run-of-the-mill boozer, The Wheatsheaf was transformed, absorbing our euphoria and reflecting it back to us.

We emerged an hour or so later, stepping out once more into reality, drenched, bleary-eyed, ears ringing and basking in the excitement of what we'd just witnessed. The next day loomed like a bad dream, a shattering comedown. It was a school night. I was fifteen. But this gig, in this town (*my town*) and this venue kick-started my passion for live music and indie venues.

The Wheatsheaf was already gaining a reputation as a cherished home for live music when local music teacher and promoter Anne Riddle took over the landlordship in the early 1990s, but it was her vision that led to its expansion and ability to attract big-name acts from across the globe. Her uncanny ability to spot emerging and cutting-edge talent and, more, to lure them to a little town, slap-bang in the middle of the once-thriving, now increasingly faltering and de-industrializing Potteries, was what helped the venue thrive. Green Day, for example, played there a mere four days after their sophomore record *Kerplunk* was released (a record which cemented their reputation among new-wave punk fans). PJ Harvey played The Wheatsheaf, months before her debut album *Dry* dropped. And Radiohead were invited to play there *twice*, while *Pablo Honey* was a mere twinkle in its fathers' eyes, and once before it reached full-term (I still often kick myself for missing these acts even though they had not yet crossed my radar: an anachronistic act of nostalgic masochism). In the early 1990s, Riddle booked Oasis three times – once as second support, once as main support and then as main act in April 1994, four months before the release of *Definitely Maybe*. And it was her ethos of putting on two support acts which also demonstrated her ongoing commitment to showcasing and nurturing new and emerging talent.

Perhaps one of the keys to her success was the fundamental principle of any successful live music venue: a superb sound setup. 'On the ground floor I spent around £200,000 on a new stage and kitting it out with the best PA, sound and lighting equipment', she said. 'It worked really well as bands and artists used to love coming because of the quality of the equipment we had. We always had an in-house sound engineer too' (in Gratton 2019a). And of course, the bands continued to come from far and wide – *seven nights a week*, with as many as twenty-eight acts in a week (ibid.).

In her second year, a further £150,000 was spent on the second floor 'Wheatsheaf II'. Later, in 1997, comedy nights, 'The Wheat N'Chaff Comedy Club', were put on fortnightly. Riddle also collaborated with Peter Cheeseman, artistic director of Europe's first purpose-built theatre-in-the-round, the New Vic in Newcastle-under-Lyme. The idea was to develop the third floor as a space for exploring new theatrical talent and nurturing community theatre. Simultaneously, Riddle was forming links with Staffordshire University, drawing up a 'timetable for students to spend time working with The Wheatsheaf sound engineers' as part of their music technology degrees (ibid.). This strikes me as a very early example of the exciting potential of a 'civic university' whereby the academy explores 'a place-based strategy about how it connects to its local city area and local community'.[1] The fact that Riddle recognised the potential of this interaction between the university and the society in which it sits demonstrates how she was always ahead of the curve, the civic university now widely recognised as a valuable direction of higher education.

For me, back in 1992, despite the deep, visceral impression the Eat gig had made on me, The Wheatsheaf and I didn't cross paths again until just over a year later. I'm not sure why. Perhaps the pressure of GCSE studies, A-level selections (I performed a last-minute reverse ferret, changing A-level choices from Biology, Chemistry and Physics to English Literature, History and Media Studies) and applications to the city sixth form got in the way. But it was while I was at college (moving with my friends from a school of around 400 students to a Further Education institution of around 1,200) that my love affair with The Wheatsheaf reignited. And it was fitting that this rediscovered passion caught and sparked with the band who enflamed my love of music in the first place: CUD. In the years between pirating the record collection of my best friend's older brother and starting sixth form, I had steadily built up a comprehensive collection of CUD vinyl, albums and EPs, bought at Mike Lloyd Music (MLM) in Hanley, both a record store and promoter, as well as a vendor of gig tickets for the city and beyond. So, for CUD to play The Wheatsheaf in January 1994, a few months after I started sixth form, was a real coup.

Built in 1970 and a walking distance to both Stoke and Hanley, our college was a concrete behemoth and the first purpose-built sixth form in the country (Gratton 2019b). At a slight elevation, looming precariously over a vast quarry, it was a brutalist Castle of Otranto. But what times we had there. Cheap hotdogs and burgers from the in-house fast-food emporium, Pat's Pantry; ducking out of history to chain-smoke Marlboro Lights beneath the overhang

1. "What do we mean by civic (local community) engagement and civic university?" https://www.solent.ac.uk/work-with-us/community/public-engagement.

(whatever the overhang overhung was anyone's guess: a concrete ramp which could've been an aborted bike storage facility); playing Pontoon for pennies in the common room or, if you were a high stakes roller, 'Quid Whist'. One of the college's other major advantages was that we could slope off at lunchtime (or, ahem, during periods of General or Business Studies, the compulsory A-levels foisted upon us) and sink cheap ale in The Roebuck near Stoke train station, spinning jukebox discs and shooting pool in the near-empty bar. But we could also make that extra journey into town to The Wheatsheaf and watch bands loading in, and sometimes even blag our way into sound check.

On the day CUD came to town, I ducked out of college twice: once to grab my copy of their latest single, 'Neurotica', from MLM (a record which came with a glow-in-the-dark Virgin Mary which attached to your turntable and revolved as the record played) and second to catch them arrive at the venue, whereupon I got both the vinyl and my beloved 'Rich and Strange' t-shirt signed by the band. I still own the shirt, Carl's sharpie signature still visible, and wear it regularly. It's still quite big on me and I've put on around four stone since I bought it so Christ-knows what I looked like in it back-in-the-day.

Figure 16.1: My 'Rich and Strange' t-shirt

On the CUD band blog, The Wheatsheaf is described thus: 'The venue is snuck between road junctions and car-part shops, and freezing cold. We play to a packed house'.[2] It didn't take long for the room to warm up, for the walls and ceiling to perspire, the interchangeable chants of 'You fat bastard' and 'You sexy bastard', directed at singer Carl Puttnam, almost deafening between songs. For me, it was a dream come true, the physical realization of the video performance I obsessively watched over four years ago while it was briefly, illegally, in my possession. They closed with 'Neurotica', a harder, more metallic offering than previous CUD tracks and it was a blistering rendition, dragging me into my first de facto moshpit.

I emerged for the second time from The Wheatsheaf into another winter evening, sweating, shivering, ecstatic.

From that moment, the rest of my pre-university years were spent playing cards and football at lunchtime and during free periods at college, buying vinyl at MLM, drinking in village pubs and going to gigs at The Wheatsheaf. I would live for the next record to buy, the next gig to see, and to have all this on my doorstep, a short bus or train journey away, was liberating. Looking back, it was a period of my life that was genuinely carefree and which offered so much independence, maybe even more so than my university years which presented their own pressure inherent within the (de/re)construction of identity, the rebooting of selfhood within a new city, a new setting, new friendships. The Wheatsheaf played a massive role in this new-found sense of freedom. Between CUD in January 1994 and leaving for Sheffield University in September 1995, I saw Shed Seven (supported by a little-known group called Supergrass), Kyuss (my gateway drug for QOTSA), Gene (intelligent, musically intricate indie rock), Moist (catchy Canadian grunge; the drummer, at one point, launching drumsticks at some moron who was stood right in front of a pair of wheelchair users), Supergrass (going it alone this time), Skunk Anansie (a sinewy, raging performance) and Bush (memorable, mostly, for the fact that during the gig, my ex-girlfriend and I got back together. It was over again in a matter of months. I still blame the band). It was a fantastic education in music genre and the dynamics of live performance. But aside from the CUD gig, the other real highlight was when I first saw Strangelove play live there. Their music, with its sweeping, cinematic and epic song structures and lead singer Patrick Duff's dark, brooding and disturbing lyrics about depression, addiction and isolation, was a sharp rebuke to Britpop. Together with The The's *Dusk*, NIN's *The Downward Spiral* and The Cure's *Wish*, Strangelove's

2. 'The CUD Story Part 32', Cudband Blog, https://cudbandblog.wordpress.com/the-cud-story-part-32/ (accessed 9 May 2021).

1994 debut album *Time for the Rest of Your Life* formed a safe haven away from the crasser elements of Britpop, and the dick measuring of the Oasis/Blur debate. In 1994, while everyone around me was listening to Oasis (paying a meagre £3 to see them at The Wheatsheaf) I was listening to *Time*, paying £16 (SIXTEEN QUID!) for the CD which MLM had to order in especially for me.

Their performance was astonishing, and I was right up against the barrier, witness to virtuoso musicianship of an intensity I had never seen before, with instrumental improvisation and experimentation which transformed already epic songs into something beyond epic. And all tied together by Duff's mesmeric, fragile yet powerful, warm yet spiky performance, eyeballing the crowd, tearing his hair out (literally) from the trauma of his songs. It was a bleedingly raw show and utterly compelling, solidifying my love for them which I carried through my university years, gobbling up every one of their releases which, despite only putting out three albums, were considerable: the one thing they did have in common with Oasis was their impressive collection of B-sides accompanying every single release.

In reminiscing about the gig, however, I once more began to question my reliability. Did Strangelove *really* play The Wheatsheaf? I couldn't find any record of it on the web. Was it another memory amalgam ... or confabulation? I trawled my mind, excavating impressions of the other times I'd seen them in other venues, superimposing the details of the rooms over my image of The Wheatsheaf: supporting Suede at the Victoria Hall (too big); headlining at Sheffield Foundry (too industrial). Desperate, now, I @-ed Patrick Duff on Twitter, asking if he had any recollection of playing in Stoke. 'Let me have a think man', he replied, and two days later, came back with, 'The rest of the band had gone down the pub and I remember being in the dressing room on my own, turning all the lights out lying on some chairs and listening to Gamelan music really loud till a journalist who was writing a piece about us came in and got totally freaked out'. I was relieved. This was a seminal live music experience in a venue that was so important to me growing up: I *needed* it, somehow, to be real.

Crushingly, Anne Riddle's plans and links with the New Vic Theatre and Staffs University never came to full fruition, despite developing the third floor of the venue and investigating the possibility of acquiring charitable status. In 1998, J.D. Wetherspoon bought the venue from Gibbs Mew PLC, despite the brewery's promise of an option-to-buy once the lease expired. It was also, of course, an early warning of the precarity of the hospitality and live music industries, alongside the might of the chain pubs and the threat that they, big business and the property market pose to small venues, swallowing them up in the pursuit of homogenization, gentrification and profit.

By this time, though, my love affair with the venue, to my shame, had ended, discovering new, bigger venues in my adopted home of Sheffield. I did, however, return to The Wheatsheaf one last time, in 1997, to see John Cooper Clarke in the Wheat N'Chaff Comedy Club. Clarke was fantastic, pipe-cleaner thin, shock of fork-in-the-socket black hair, satchel over shoulder and reading from his trusty book of poems. For me, it was a remarkable meeting with a mythological figure I'd heard about from mum and dad (at this time, books of his poetry were out of print, although I had found a couple of records in the used section of MLM but was never a fan of those poems put to music). I suppose this was a fitting show to end on, a cult figure in a cult venue which, within a couple of months, would close, despite a hard-fought campaign to keep it open backed by, among other musicians, Noel Gallagher who described it as 'a top venue' (in Gratton 2019c).

The late French philosopher Michel de Certeau describes a space as existing 'when one takes into consideration vectors of direction, velocities, and time variables. Thus space is composed of intersections of mobile elements. It is in a sense actuated by the ensemble of movements deployed within it' (de Certeau 1988: 17). This, it seems to me, perfectly encapsulates the nature of the live music venue: a polyvalent space of warm bodies bumping against each other, all engulfed by the unfolding energies of life-changing moments and experiences: some shared; some unique. The Wheatsheaf taught me to love live music but also to appreciate the spaces in which performances take place. Today, Covid has posed another devastating threat to independent venues up and down the country. As the music scene gradually begins to reopen as lockdowns are lifted, it is incumbent upon us, as music lovers, to show our undivided loyalty and support; to help venues (and artists) get back on their feet. For whilst The Wheatsheaf is no longer with us – crushed by the Wetherspoons machine – there are many more like it. Now, more than ever, these venues need us; and now, more than ever, we need them.

References

de Certeau, Michel. 1988. *The Practice of Everyday Life*, trans. Steven Rendall. London and Berkeley: University of California Press.
Eagleman, David. 2016. *The Brain: The Story of You*. Edinburgh: Canongate Books.
Gratton, Adam. 2019a. 'Oasis and Adam Ant – when Stoke's Wheatsheaf ruled the roost for indie music lovers'. *Stoke Sentinel*, 1 September. https://www.stokesentinel.co.uk/news/history/oasis-adam-ant-stokes-wheatsheaf-3266709
Gratton, Adam. 2019b. 'Then & now: Remembering Stoke-on-Trent Sixth Form College, Fenton'. *Stoke Sentinel*, 2 January. https://www.stokesentinel.co.uk/news/history/sixth-form-college-fenton-levels-2360300

Gratton, Adam. 2019c. 'Then & now: Remembering The Wheatsheaf, Stoke'. *Stoke Sentinel*, 19 June. https://www.stokesentinel.co.uk/news/history/music-stoke-wheatsheaf-oasis-2985761

Author biography

Dr Matt Colbeck researches representations of coma and brain injury in literature and media, working with survivors to curate narratives of lived experience. He is the bassist with CreepJoint, featured on Tom Robinson's 6music show. His book, *The Language and Imagery of Coma and Brain Injury*, is published by Bloomsbury.

17 More than a Club: The Genius Loci of Eric's

Penny Kiley

One day in the twenty-first century, a mysterious blog post appeared. It was titled 'More than a club'. It was about Eric's in Liverpool, and the fact that someone had just reopened it: with the original name but without the original ethos.

To be accurate, the blog post (Fulwell 2011) was titled 'Més que un club' (inspired, apparently, by the FC Barcelona slogan). The blog itself was called Gone Midnight but it only ever had that one post. No 'About Us'. No 'Contact Me'. No indication of where it had come from. And it said this: 'In their choice of branding, these would-be revivalists completely miss the essence of what Eric's was about. It was always more than a club'. It went on: 'There was a spirit and a sensibility shared by members and owners alike, the antithesis of "trading off the past"'.

The blog post circulated quickly on Facebook, and it summed up what many of my peers were thinking. It was 2011 and we were approaching late middle age, but we were as angry as any young punks. It was widely assumed that the blog post was written by Pete Fulwell, one of the original club's owners. He's not around anymore to confirm it, but it echoed other phrases he'd used at the time. He shared our outrage about what had happened, but he put it better.

It was thirty-one years since the original club – our club – had closed, and we still cared. Eric's was that sort of place. I'm going to try to explain why.

Toilets

First, some history. For context, in case you missed it or you're southern or young. I'll try and keep it short because there are books. Eric's was opened on 1 October 1976 in an old warehouse building in a Liverpool back street. The first three dates were The Stranglers, The Runaways and the Sex Pistols. The last night was 14 March 1980. The headliners were the Psychedelic Furs and the support was local band Wah! Heat. In between, it was a nursery for a whole generation of pop stars: Echo and the Bunnymen, the Teardrop Explodes, Pete

Wylie, Frankie Goes to Hollywood, OMD, Dead or Alive, Lightning Seeds, The KLF and more. Are you envious yet?

Before that – and very quickly – it got established on the circuit as a major punk venue. When I say major, I don't mean big. We're talking about the toilet circuit. In a typical month (May 1977, for example) you could have seen The Clash, Siouxsie and the Banshees, The Ramones, Talking Heads and The Damned. Are you envious now?

I don't know if toilet venues got their name because they were as small as toilets, as smelly as toilets or because toilets sometimes doubled as dressing rooms (Eric's capacity was 300, and it did have a dressing room, even if it was fairly basic). I do know that the toilets at Eric's were memorable because they were always getting flooded. Not because of the plumbing though; it was due to an underground stream that rose whenever it rained. During the last year at Eric's, I went through a phase of wearing red wellies all the time, because I was skint and couldn't afford new shoes. There were some nights I was glad of them.

People remember the toilets for other reasons. There's always been a lot of reminiscence about having sex in the cubicles. This may have been exaggerated. I didn't notice it happen, but I was shy, and I'd had a sheltered life, so that doesn't prove anything. I remember the Ladies' as less about heterosexual activity and more as the place where we learnt about gender and sexuality and to embrace difference (this, remember, was an era when Tom Robinson's 'Glad To Be Gay' was considered risqué). There were always androgynous boys preening in the mirrors, doing their makeup, primping their hair. For us girls, they were part of the furniture, part of our community. Pete Burns was usually one of them, holding court, captivatingly outrageous.

Pete and his equally outrageous friends – Jayne Casey and Holly Johnson from Big in Japan (the Eric's house band), Paul Rutherford from the Spitfire Boys, Pete's girlfriend (later wife) Lynne – had perfected the art of the pose. Everyone remembers Jayne's shaved head, and Pete's black contact lenses – black all over.

Most of us weren't that extreme, but we found our own ways to express difference. Generally, it wasn't the punk uniform that you saw in photos from London: it was about creativity and playfulness. Julian Cope was right when he wrote in his memoir about London punk: 'It may have started there, but the northern thing seemed far truer to the attitude' (Cope 1994). We liked the word 'attitude'; it felt very rock'n'roll, very New York. Liverpool has never felt English, after all.

You didn't need to pose, but you could if you wanted to. Paul Simpson (the Teardrop Explodes, Wild Swans) would raid his father's wardrobe for demob suits. Julian Cope searched the Army & Navy store for drainpipe jeans and cheap t-shirts. Pete Wylie (at least, until he discovered leather trousers) mostly stuck to the classic rock'n'roll ensemble of leather jacket and jeans, but with props. Famously, he went through a phase of walking around wearing a toilet seat.

Place

> Met Pete [Wylie] and his friends in the students' union and then down to Eric's. I've been in the building while under the name the Revolution Club but tonight it was completely different. I think I'll go again. (Diary entry, 1978)

Eric's was in Mathew Street, hidden away in the no-man's land between the business quarter and the shopping centre, a place of derelict warehouses and flattened wasteland. A lot of the flattened wasteland in mid-1970s Liverpool were World War II bombsites, but the bare-earth car park opposite Eric's had, in fact, been cleared to make way for the Merseyrail underground. There wasn't much to miss. Just an old warehouse with a basement called The Cavern.

Since the heyday of The Cavern (it moved over the road for a few years, to the building where Eric's later had its home), Mathew Street had kept its bohemian spirit. During the mid-1970s, it hosted various theatrical and arty goings-on, presided over by maverick catalysts like theatre director Ken Campbell and the less well-known Peter and Sean O'Halligan.

The queues of young men wanting to see The Runaways in October 1976 probably didn't know or care much about that (there weren't queues for the Sex Pistols: no-one remembers the gig as a big deal). And many members of the new club didn't know or care either. I'd just arrived at Liverpool University and had no idea. As newly born punks we pretended to hate hippies and took no notice of the title 'The Liverpool School of Language, Music, Dream and Pun' written on the warehouse down the road. For the Eric's kids, the building mattered mainly for the Armadillo Tea Rooms and Probe Records round the corner, their daytime hangout. Anyway, we had our own maverick catalysts. Eric's was owned by Roger Eagle, Ken Testi and Pete Fulwell, who loved music and had vision. Roger is the best known because he already had a reputation as a maverick catalyst, but Eric's was his – their – greatest achievement.

Over the years, I have often thought of the phrase 'genius loci' when remembering Eric's. I used to think that Roger was the genius loci (he was definitely a genius, in his own way), until I learnt that it didn't actually mean a person. A genius loci is a spirit of a place. Some people think it's an actual spirit

– a nurturing presence – that watches over the inhabitants. Others believe it's something less tangible: an atmosphere. I believe we had both. As Will Sergeant put it in his memoir *Bunnyman*: "There is supernatural power in the bricks and mortar of the place" (2021: 179–180).

There was definitely a nurturing presence in Eric's. I don't know whether it was through Roger, Ken, Pete, or legendary office manager Doreen Allen, but people took care of others. Even the bouncers were friendly. Innovations like Saturday matinées for under-age fans or putting the headliner on before the last bus departed meant that someone was actually thinking about us.

The club felt like a safe place, and I didn't realize until later how unusual that was. Whether you were female, gay, a matinée kid or a poser, nobody bothered you. Sometimes I went on my own – something that women weren't expected to do in the 1970s – and I was never scared.

For many of us, it was the only place we felt at home: a sanctuary for misfits. People like working-class Pete Wylie (too clever); middle-class Julian Cope (too geeky); shy, southern me (too troubled). Eric's was the only place I could be myself, and the only place where I knew who I was. No-one laughed at what I was wearing. Everyone shared my taste in music. But it wasn't just clothes and music, it was an attitude: an embracing of outsiderism and with it a liberating sense of possibility.

Art school

> *Pete rushed up to us: 'We're on tonight, me and Julian!' Later, there they were on stage, with Paul from the Spitfire Boys, a couple of Big in Japan and various punks. It was a fiasco because the PA wasn't working properly and Paul's Patti Smith vocals couldn't be heard properly, but fun anyway.*
> (Diary entry, 1987)

There's a famous art school exercise: here's an everyday item; think of different uses for it. Here's a brick; it's supposed to fit in a wall; what else might it do? Think of it another way. Here's an 18-year-old. They are supposed to be a square peg in a round hole. What else might they be?

It was only hindsight that showed me how much of an art school Eric's had been. Most of the friends I made through the twenty-first-century reunions turned out to have been at the art school – or art college, as we called it at the time ('art school' was just a musical genre in those days). Many of the women who worked behind the bar or in the kitchen were art students. Deaf School (Big in Japan's slightly older mentors) had been art students and were clearly art school as genre too. For those of us who weren't at the art college, Eric's filled the gap. Years later, Frank Cottrell-Boyce wrote in *The Guardian* that Eric's was, for him, more about the audience than the bands: 'being with people of my own age who were all suddenly aglow with the possibilities of their own creativity' (Cottrell-Boyce 2008).

Everyone remembers Roger's evangelical educationalism. It is why Bill Sykes called his biography *Sit Down! Listen to This!* (Sykes 2012). But music businessman Dave Wibberley also remembers sitting in the Armadillo Tea Rooms 'with Pete Fulwell teaching me about situationism and Dadaism' (Eric's 2019). Nurturing, again.

One of the Eric's legends is that Roger Eagle told his musical protégés to never listen to The Beatles (even though there was a statue of them above the door). There was too much else to listen to anyway, a constant inspiration thanks to the vintage selections on the jukebox and the wide-ranging booking policy. On stage, a roll call of UK and US punk that seems astonishing now (as well as a lot of stuff that wasn't punk: if Roger liked it, it went on). On the dancefloor, a stream of WTF records: dub reggae, rockabilly, electro. (For the record, DJs playing reggae to punks was *not* a London invention.) We absorbed everything; it became part of us. That's why none of the Liverpool punk bands sounded like punk bands, because they were post-punk before punk was even dead.

Ask any old Eric's members now what they remember, and many of them will talk about the records they heard or the bands they saw. But just as many will talk about the way Eric's changed their life. Some of it is obvious. If Julian Cope hadn't (literally) bumped into Pete Wylie at a Clash gig, he might not have become a pop star. If Les Pattinson hadn't embraced the Eric's imaginary-bands movement, he might not have joined a real band (Echo and the Bunnymen) and might still be making boats (actually, I heard recently that he is making boats again). If Yachts hadn't supported Elvis Costello at Eric's they might not have got a record deal with Stiff, and Henry Priestman might not have consolidated his career with The Christians.

But Eric's wasn't just about the ones who became famous. If I hadn't seen my classmate Pete Wylie pick up a guitar, I might not have realized I could choose my own future. Yes, Eric's changed my life, too. I became a music journalist and I married the DJ, Norman Killon. Neither of these lasted – in fact, they both ended around the same time in the mid-1990s – but by then my path in life had diverged enough for me to be myself. Like Roger Eagle, I could say: 'I'm a *southerner* by birth – but a *northerner* by emotion'. And I'm still writing for a living.

It wasn't just about individuals either: it was about the future of music in the city. If Doreen Allen hadn't worked at Eric's, she might not have opened Planet X, a home for a new generation of music fans. If he hadn't watched local bands at Eric's, Phil Hayes (the High Five) might not have spent decades running The Picket, a venue for new generations of bands. Between Merseybeat and Eric's, there had been nothing. That wouldn't happen again.

More than a Club

> *Big occasion – the first Jonathan Richman gig at Eric's. I went in the Beserkely Records T-shirt I got at the Hammersmith Odeon gig last summer, and the Modern Lovers badge Roger Eagle gave me when I went to get my ticket at Eric's.* (Diary entry, 1978)

Eric's was a self-contained world, where normal rules didn't apply. The DJs didn't talk, but they did dance. Norman Killon would line up his favourite record (usually 'Tommy Gun' by The Clash), then jump down and show off his moves on the dancefloor, running back just in time to start the next record playing. When Norman danced, people watched (he still does; they still do). It was a world where I could leave my everyday problems behind: exams, relationships, the fact that I was a student and didn't like students much (except the ones who went to Eric's). All I had to worry about was: how long would I have to queue in the Ladies; would Pete Wylie stand still long enough to talk to me; how close to the front could I get?

Doreen Allen always says that one of the reasons Eric's felt like a club is because they were open in the daytime for selling tickets, and people would just hang around. It felt like a community, a family, even. Of course, it wasn't always one big happy family. Hearts got broken, friendships were made, unmade and remade, as always happens in youth clubs. There were in-crowds and observers. There was a lot of rivalry and attention seeking, but that was one of the good things about the place. It's where 'the scene' came from.

We were proud of that scene. Every week it went up a notch: more new faces, more new records (hot from Probe, where Norman worked), more new bands, more new *local* bands. Even if the bands weren't that good, you could dance, or watch people dance, or just watch people. You would always go with a sense of expectation.

We were proud when Eric's got on television. Granada TV had always been forward-thinking about music, and thanks to Tony Wilson's *What's On* and *So It Goes* slots it still was. (Liverpool's love-hate relationship with Manchester belied the symbiosis in the music scene.) Granada filmed an Elvis Costello gig. The BBC filmed X-Ray Spex for an Arena documentary. If you watch the live footage you can see, behind the bands, the Eric's logo at the back of the stage.

We were prouder still of our homegrown bands. From the start, everyone seemed to be forming bands or, at least, talking about it. Club members became musicians overnight and if they weren't playing gigs they'd be in the audience, heckling. At first, a local band night was likely to be a fun fiasco, but quickly things started getting serious. You don't need the names and numbers: it's all in the history books now. Let's just say that when Pete Frame wrote his 'Eric's progeny' rock family tree in 1980, there were dozens of bands he had to leave out because there wasn't space in his double-page spread (Frame 1993). We saw it happening. Just like the club, they were ours.

When Eric's closed in March 1980, I wrote in the *Melody Maker*: 'You could enter Eric's and feel at home, whatever you looked like. It was a place to escape, belong, to be yourself. And it was the nearest you could get to putting a location on rock'n'roll' (Kiley 1980).

Less than a Club

> *To Lincoln's Inn to see Wah! Heat. The Eric's crowd are there – the youth club's moved – but I don't feel at home like I did at Eric's. And the club's second-best, lacking the rock'n'roll vitality of Eric's that had built up like centuries of worship in a church building.* (Diary entry 1980)

Eric's closed in March 1980, and we were pushed out of the nest before we expected it. Some of us were ready to fly (the first Eric's bands were already too big to play Eric's); some of us less so... We were fledglings, flying in different directions. Which, because of all the different influences we'd had at Eric's, was probably the right result.

Even if we felt lost (and a lot of tears were shed), it would be unfair to say that after Eric's closed there was nowhere to go. One of its legacies was that there were more bands looking for places to play, and more places for them to do so. Eric's member Dave C, who would later run two major Liverpool venues, The Warehouse and Royal Court, started promoting gigs at a small club called Lincoln's Inn ('behind British Home Stores, round the corner from Probe', it said on the flyer). I first went there two weeks after Eric's closed. The same people were there, but there was something missing.

A few months after Eric's closed, the building was opened again. The new owners called it Brady's. It felt like coming home. For about a day. Then it wasn't. The same building was there, but there was something missing. And it wasn't just the jukebox.

It didn't feel like a club. It didn't feel safe (especially at mod gigs). I never knew who the owners were. The people around me didn't feel like members, just audiences; and different ones all the time, because the music had fragmented. This wasn't Roger's intentional eclecticism though, just whatever would pull in the punters: post-punk, mod, two-tone, incipient indie. People stuck to their own subculture and there was no crossover.

It was the same but not the same. The genius loci had flown, and the building was bereft of its spirit. You went there to see bands, but that was all. It was just another toilet venue, no more and no less.

Still a Club

> *There are times when I really miss Liverpool. And there are other times I think, well, I don't actually want to live in a theme park.* (Facebook status update, Penny Kiley, May 2011)

By 2011, Mathew Street had lost its bohemian roots. Gentrification had driven out Probe, and tourism had turned the 'Cavern Quarter' into a bad theme park. The Mathew Street festival, originally (in the 1990s) a giant but slightly quaint Beatles tribute, had become a bank holiday bacchanalia. The warped regeneration of the area had followed a similar trajectory to Dublin's Temple Bar, and the stag parties were moving in.

In this context came the announcement, reported by the *Liverpool Echo*, that 'iconic Liverpool music venue Eric's is to re-open its doors' (Wright 2011). Actually (as we've seen), the doors had already re-opened in 1980, but not under the name Eric's, because, we all believed, that wasn't for anyone else to use. The new owners thought differently: they had resurrected the branding, including the original logo with the words 'World Famous' added. We were furious (Sammons 2011).

I've used 'we' a lot in this piece, not because I would dare to speak for other people, but because when I look back it's with a sense of being part of something larger than myself. In my mind, I remember Eric's as a community.

It still is.

In June 2011, discussing the 'new Eric's' on Radio Merseyside, my friend John D. Hodgkinson (another music writer) coined the phrase 'the Eric's diaspora'. It's still part of who we are. The community is online now, with a Facebook group started in 2014 by Pete Griffiths from the Spitfire Boys. It's offline, too: there have been reunions, new and revived friendships, real-life socialising. We share memories and we support each other (and each other's kids, in the case of teen punk group Yee Loi).

If you asked us (and we do ask each other, sometimes), we'd say how we felt about Eric's and how it changed us. Some of us are still working in the music business or following other creative paths that started back then. But Eric's wasn't really (or just) about career opportunities: it wasn't *what* you became that mattered, but *who* you became. All of us are still touched by the experience, and we all have stories to tell. People say that Eric's opened their eyes and their minds, and not just musically. They talk about learning to value diversity; about a home that made us better people and where we could grow into ourselves; about a sense of alternatives and possibilities – yes, and 'attitude' – that has never left them.

That's why, when I heard about this book, I had to bring my testimony. Here it is.

References

Cope, Julian. 1994. *Head-On*. Cambridge: Magog Books.
Cottrell-Boyce, Frank. 2008. 'We were the guinea pigs of punk'. *The Guardian*, 23 September. https://www.theguardian.com/stage/2008/sep/23/musicals.popandrock
Eric's: Story of a Liverpool Club. 2019. Radio 2 documentary. https://www.bbc.co.uk/programmes/b00bvn83
Frame, P. 1993. *Rock Family Trees*. London: Omnibus Press.
Fulwell, Pete, attrib. 2011. 'Més que un club'. https://gone-midnight.blogspot.com/2011/05/well-well-well-erics-re-opens.html
Kiley, Penny. 1980. 'An undignified death'. *Melody Maker*, 29 March.
Sammons, Angie. 2011. 'Plan to reopen Eric's greeted with anger and dismay'. *Liverpool Confidential*, 10 May. http://old.liverpoolconfidential.co.uk/Culture/Plans-to-reopen-Erics-greeted-with-anger-and-dismay
Sergeant, Will. 2021. *Bunnyman*. London: Constable.
Sykes, Bill. 2012. *Sit Down! Listen to This! The Roger Eagle Story*. Manchester: Empire Publications.
Wright, Jade. 2011. 'Liverpool club Eric's to re-open as music venue'. *Liverpool Echo*, 10 May. https://www.liverpoolecho.co.uk/news/liverpool-news/liverpool-club-erics-re-open-music-3374486

Author biography

Penny Kiley is a former music journalist who began her career as *Melody Maker*'s Liverpool correspondent and token punk rocker in the late 1970s. She was pop columnist for the *Liverpool Echo* for several years.

18 Coming of Age at The Warehouse, Liverpool, 1981

Dawn Amber Harvey

Time has erased from memory the name of the first band I saw at The Warehouse club in Liverpool, but what I clearly recall is the sense of nervous excitement as I climbed the stairs to the entrance, tightly clutching my ticket, scared to death that I wouldn't be let in. It was 1981 and at sixteen years old I was two years too young to be entering these licensed premises. I was utterly clueless, but eager to immerse myself in a new world of adult sights and sounds. School was over and I knew that this was where the next level of my education would begin; I was more than ready for it. I was hungry for the thrill of live music and wanted to move in the circles of the cool people I watched with awe as they floated around the city, from record shop to café bar to night club.

The Warehouse had an unassuming presence – a large brick building in a row of other large brick buildings. There was little to betray what was taking place inside except for the queue where everyone was decked in their goth and punk finest. Appearance was important and the older kids exuded a confidence that I hoped I could fake to pass as one of them for the evening. I was dressed in homemade attire. Long black dress right down to the floor, black lace tights, pixie boots, Siouxsie-style back-combed hair, a big silver cross necklace and armfuls of cheap silver bangles.

You'll be relieved to hear that, thanks to relaxed door staff, heavy make-up and being in possession of a face that I would grow into, I was waved into the venue without so much as a second glance. With my heart racing ever faster, I proceeded through the door and into the main room where a wall of sound hit me. Lively chatter was mixed with loud music from the resident DJ. The air smelled of beer, cigarette smoke and burned hairspray from carefully tended hairdos. This felt like a self-contained little world of its own. Once the door swung shut behind me the outside world ceased to exist. This was *something else*.

You may never have heard of The Warehouse. It was a fairly short-lived music venue that ran at 13 Fleet Street in Liverpool city centre from 1981 to 1983. Its demise came when it suddenly burned down in mysterious circumstances. Sadly, it has been almost entirely erased from the history of Liverpool's music scene, overshadowed by the legacies of Eric's and The Cavern which came before it. Its disregard would appear to stem from the fact that, while Eric's and The Cavern went on to establish musical movements, The Warehouse lent itself to movements that already existed. In the 1980s the tail end of the Liverpool punk scene which had developed in Eric's merged with goth, new romantic and rockabilly. Each of these subcultures had their own looks, their own codes of behaviour, their own music and their own style. I was instinctively drawn to goth. I loved the dark layers of clothing set off with dramatic make up and massive hair. I was particularly keen on a Black Cherry lipstick I got from Woolworths that my grandad liked to tell me made me look as if I'd had a heart attack. I didn't particularly care for the new romantics. I thought they looked kind of soft with their silly frilly shirts and floppy fringes. I imagined myself a bit superior. On the other hand, I was intimidated by the rockabillies. They had a harder look with their shorter, quiffed hair and leather jackets. They also liked to slam dance, which freaked me out. I don't remember any real aggression though, only camaraderie. Any rivalry between camps was just light-hearted fun and all tastes were catered for in the line ups at The Warehouse.

The inside of the venue was one large room with a bar at the side; stage area and dancefloor in the middle; then a DJ and sound booth plus seating sections at the back. The seating areas added a social aspect that could be absent from standard music venues. Here people met to discuss the bands they had seen, swap ideas and make new friends and contacts. This important element expanded the significance of the space. It made it more than a music venue; it was also a cultural meeting point, a part of a network of locations around the city that people visited to escape from the everyday world and explore new ideas. This was Thatcher's Britain, and many young people were either unemployed or, like me, working for a tiny wage on a Youth Training Scheme. I was stuck on a YTS at a sewing factory, making ridiculous, ugly frocks for rich people for a payment of around £12 a week. I hated the job and felt completely alienated, spending each working day surrounded by middle-aged women. I shared an air of disillusionment with many of the youth. Without subcultures we had little else to hold onto. Our futures were unclear, our bank accounts were empty and, without a career or a sense of direction, the experience of belonging to a subculture provided a tribal connection that was a great source of comfort. Musical taste played a fundamental role in subcultural identity and being able to see our musical heroes and mentors play live was hugely significant and inspirational to us as we passed through our formative teenage years. It created memories that would last a lifetime.

It was on the weekends that the city came alive, and on a typical Saturday afternoon a cultural meeting point in the city centre was Probe Records, an independent music store on the corner of Button Street. Cramped and messy, this small store carried an unrivalled stock of obscure recordings by small bands on tiny labels. I spent many a happy hour flicking through the latest vinyl releases and searching for old classics. The counter staff included Pete Burns of Dead or Alive, who never failed to look stunning (and mildly terrifying) dressed in fringed suede shirts with crimped hair and black contact lenses that covered his whole eye. Another popular hangout for the cool and trendy was the underground arcades opposite, on Rainford Gardens, which housed a range of punk and goth clothing stalls. There was also a hair salon called Xtremes, where you could get an extravagant new do, or choose from a selection of 'Crazy Colour' hair dyes to take home for a DIY job. I was a bit too cowardly for this and stuck to a simple black dye from Boots.

At the end of Rainford Gardens, and just around the corner onto the infamous Mathew Street, was the Armadillo Tea Rooms, a café that played a significant part in the '80s Liverpool music scene. It had big wooden tables and a laid-back atmosphere that lent itself to conversation. Bands would meet there to discuss plans and ideas or hook up with managers and promoters. Members of the Bunnymen, Wah! Heat and Dead or Alive would often be seen there, and the rest of us nonentities would gather to eat, sit, and hope for some of their cachet to rub off on us as we watched the world go by. The same faces that frequented this part of town during the day would reappear later at The Warehouse, or at a number of the city's gay clubs and bars, including Jody's and MacMillans, which were much more a part of the countercultural scene than the straight clubs.

Liverpool, at the time, was a fertile breeding ground for exciting new musical talent. The Teardrop Explodes, Echo and the Bunnymen and Orchestral Manoeuvres in the Dark already had hit singles with appearances on *Top of the Pops*, while Dead or Alive and Frankie Goes to Hollywood were chomping at the bit, preparing themselves to hit the big time. For the non-musicians amongst us there was a sense of ownership of these bands; they were 'our' bands from 'our' city, and we shared the joy of their success, which made us all feel a little more glamorous and exciting. The Warehouse showcased many of these local bands and provided a platform for national and international artists. The Ruts, Crass, Theatre of Hate, Dead Kennedys and The Fall crossed its stage, along with the lesser-known bands you would be likely to hear on

John Peel's late-night radio show. There were future stars of television whose early careers also included gigs at The Warehouse. Local lad, Craig Charles, recited political poetry and wound up the audience. Often heckled, he learned to think on his feet and possessed a sharp, sassy wit that always won over the crowd. From out of town, there were evenings with Charlie Higson, later of *The Fast Show*, and his band The Higsons. The Higsons' sound combined elements of funk and punk with an impressive brass section, and their shows were always riotous affairs as the band would goad the crowd, demanding faster, rougher, more enthusiastic dancing. My companion on many trips to The Warehouse was an old school friend, Jan. Jan was a young woman of slight proportions who was constantly knocked over by the rambunctious crowds surging backwards and forwards at Higsons' shows. So, I spent half my time picking her back up again. Curiously, these were among her favourite gigs ever and she couldn't wait for the band to come back again.

Women's Lib(eration) was a big deal in the 1980s and female-fronted, post-punk bands were a popular commodity. Delta 5 made several superb appearances at The Warehouse. Their sound was simple, anarchic, catchy, and combined feminist politics with funky dance grooves. The snot-nosed attitude of their minor hit 'Mind Your Own Business' perfectly conveyed the frustration and discontent of '80s youth, who maintained an anti-establishment stance that had been passed down from the punk generation. My favourites were the Au Pairs, whose political lyrics often challenged the structure of traditional sexual relationships by questioning and subverting roles of male/female power play. Their musical strength came from the powerful voice of their front person, Lesley Woods, who became my lesbian role model. While androgyny and female empowerment were gaining traction in the 1980s, there were surprisingly few dyke icons and Lesley was the first cool, funky and out-and-proud lesbian I encountered. I would stand in the front row, gazing in awe but was far too intimidated to try and talk to her. Many years later I ran a small venue in Hackney (East London) and Lesley contacted me asking for a gig. After nearly dying of shock, I got back to her and we went on to deliver two shows to small but adoring audiences. Now we run into each other in the street and stop for a quick chat. If you'd have told the star-struck teenage me that this would happen they would never have believed you, but they would have been deliriously happy!

Another life-long influence was introduced to me at The Warehouse when Nick Cave's first band, the Birthday Party, rolled into town. This was an evening filled with an electric air of expectation and the place was packed out. I found a spot near the front and the show started off well enough. Nick was charismatic, effortlessly cool and undeniably talented, but he drank a full bottle of

Jack Daniels during the performance and ended the show huddled over in a ball on the stage, screeching and crying into the microphone. At the time I was amused but a little under-whelmed. When I reflect upon it now, I acknowledge that it has been one of the greatest privileges of my life to watch this incredible artist grow into one of the most incredible song writers and musicians of our generation. Over the decades I have returned to see him perform countless times, the venues slowly growing bigger and bigger as he developed his art and expanded his reputation to command larger and larger audiences. He is a master of his craft and accomplished enough to stride out casually onto the stages of stadium-sized arenas where he can hold the audience in the palm of his hand. Somehow, he manages to create a sense of intimacy despite the physical distance between audience and stage. Now it's me who huddles, sobbing, at his shows, rendered speechless by the beauty of his poetry and the nuance of its delivery. This is a genius who could not have developed without those shaky early years in grubby back-street venues. Watching him grow has been a gift.

A rags-to-riches tale nudges its way into the story of the Liverpool music scene in the form of a weird-looking, skinny dude by the name of Mick Hucknall. While they hailed from Manchester, Hucknall's band the Frantic Elevators appeared on the support bill for numerous acts at venues across the city, though there was something about Hucknall that used to annoy people. In fairness, he probably set out to deliberately provoke, but I can remember he was routinely jeered, abused and laughed at by the crowd. He would yell back, furious, humiliated and frustrated: *'One day I'm gonna be a big star and then you'll be sorry. Not with this band but you'll see, one day I'm gonna be a huge star'*. The crowd were having none of it but fair play to him, he did get the last laugh. Hucknall was a textbook example of somebody who wanted success so badly and was driven enough to know that one day he would achieve it. He also understood that there was a lot of hard work to do, and a lot of grit and determination required, so he put himself up on stage night after night, weathering the abuse in order to gain experience and develop. Eyes not in the gutter but focused firmly on the stars. Like many of us he was learning, strutting around the playground like a scrawny ginger peacock, but unlike many of the acts who came and went, he studied hard and graduated from the school of northern night life with an honours degree. He took what he needed and ran with it.

Small music venues have always been essential to allow performers and audiences to grow. Though this is not to suggest that the value of small music venues is a sole possession of the youth. Now in my mid-fifties, I and many of my friends not only regularly attend music venues but some of us continue to work as DJs, promoters, performers and technicians. Those who have chosen careers elsewhere flock back to live music as often as they are able to re-experience the sense of connection that can only be found with bands and in venues. This is the place we call home, where we feel we belong.

The experiences I had at The Warehouse in my teenage years have, without a doubt, contributed to making me the person I am today. The times when I was swept up as part of the crowd, thrilling to loud music and enjoying the abandonment of wild, crazy dancing were not just about discovering music, but beginning the journey towards defining a sense of self. Four decades later, watching any footage of sweaty crowds moshing, punching the air and singing along to their favourite bands can make me well up as I remember the passion and energy of those new and exciting times. Nights at The Warehouse provided liberation from the constricts of childhood and adolescence and set me moving, slowly but surely, and with tottering steps, into a new-found freedom – into adulthood.

Author biography

Dawn Amber Harvey's work has been published in several magazines and on websites, along with an academic journal. Their first book *(Un)Natural Desires: Representations of Homosexuals in Post-War American Literature* was published in 2019.

19 The Rainbow Venues and Swingamajig: Closing the Doors on the Home of One of Birmingham's Favourite Festivals

Chris Inglis

Just to the east of Birmingham's city centre lies the neighbourhood of Digbeth – one of the most heavily industrialised areas of the city, characterised by its abundance of warehouses and disused factories. The area has been continuously occupied since the seventh century and is one of the oldest parts of the city. These days, Digbeth is recognised as quite the trendy neighbourhood, known for its vintage stores, art galleries, and music venues, as well as the Custard Factory complex – set across 15 acres of land, and home to various bars, independent shops, and small creative businesses. Indeed, in 2018, *The Sunday Times* rated Digbeth as the 'Coolest Neighbourhood in Britain' (Bains 2018b).

One of the institutions that contributed to Digbeth's reputation as Britain's coolest neighbourhood was the Rainbow Venues, first established in 2004. Local DJ and producer Tom Shorterz, who has played there, certainly sees it that way:

> When I thought of Digbeth years ago it was just like a barren wasteland of factories and rundown boozers. I think that was what Rainbow did – it landscaped how we see Digbeth now: the cultures there, the coolness of it, the quirky vibe, the vibrance – it's all stemmed from the Rainbow Venues, without the Rainbow Venues we simply would not have this hub, this culture, it wouldn't be there.[1]

1. Quoted in '#educatenotrevocate', available at https://www.facebook.com/watch/?v=1961942547155300.

Located just around the corner from the Custard Factory complex, the Rainbow Venues presented one of the most unique and iconic spaces for live music across the British Midlands. It was a sprawling arrangement of multiple performance spaces which could cater to a whole manner of different events. As I found on the occasions I visited, just taking a few steps from one room to the next could feel like entering a different world. For those in the know, a trip to the Rainbow Venues was considered to be one of the greatest opportunities to enjoy live music. In a part of Birmingham away from the city centre, the Rainbow Venues acted as host to some of Birmingham's most exciting and eccentric events.

These included several of the city's best-loved urban festivals, including MADE, Chapter, Annie Mac's AMP, and Carnival Magnifico, amongst many others. Most notably for the purposes of this chapter, it was also for some time home to the Swingamajig festival – the world's first festival dedicated to the genre of electro swing. Such events took full advantage of the multiple stages and spaces available to them, which included The Warehouse – named and styled after the type of venue that typified early 1990s raves; the Black Box – a small, dingy room suited to more underground styles of EDM; the Roof Garden – a spacious open-air balcony overlooking the rest of the site; and the Car Park stage – the biggest stage, a 5,000-person arena with a semi-permanent Big Top covering it. At full capacity, the entire site could hold up to 25,000 people (Hubzin 2014), and the venue saw over 350,000 visitors a year, employed over 65 members of staff, and contributed over £2 million to the local economy (Frankland 2018).

The history of the Rainbow Venues has been covered in the Birmingham local press. The article reports that it started its life as The Rainbow, a long-standing pub which has existed in some form since as far back as 1767 (Young 2019a). Having been rebuilt during the Victorian age, the building as it currently stands dates back to the 1880s (ibid.). It was allegedly the site of the first recorded attack by the 'Peaky Blinders' gang – on 23 March 1890 (Young 2019b). By the turn of the millennium, the pub was steadily falling into a state of dilapidation, with 'yellow wood-chip walls, world flags on the ceiling and a messy old courtyard with live wires exposed' (Hubzin 2014).

In 2004, the pub was taken over by friends Lee McDonald and Adam Shelton, who were looking for an opportunity to create a new space for raves in the area. As their need to expand and develop continued, the pair gradually began to take over every adjacent space that they could get their hands on; as explained by McDonald, 'as soon as the "To Let" signs went up I would rip them down in the middle of the night and make the call/send the email that day' (ibid.).

This approach helped to transform the deteriorating Rainbow pub into the iconic centre of underground activity that it became, and McDonald and Shelton successfully ran the enterprise for thirteen years, until it was eventually shut down in November 2017.

Teenager Dylan Booth attended the 'Imaginarium' event held at the Rainbow Venues, featuring DJs Hannah Wants and DJ Zinc, on New Year's Eve 2015. Along with four others, Booth fell ill after taking an unidentified amount of MDMA, and was rushed to hospital on New Year's Day, only to end up dying on 3 January (Tyler 2016). This incident became a stain on the Rainbow Venues' legacy.

The damage was further solidified on 29 October 2017 when, at a Halloween event entitled 'The Haunting', 19-year-old Michael Trueman was admitted to hospital after taking MDMA and died the following day (Authi 2017). The drug-related deaths of two young men were shocking. They raised troubling issues about the relationship between music venues and drug dealers active in the clubs.

As a result of the two deaths in as many years, police spokesperson Abdul Rohomon said that they had 'no option but to call for Rainbow's licence to be revoked' (Moore 2017). On 28 November, Birmingham City Council went ahead with this decision, revoking the licence, and closing down the venue. This was an opportunity for the venue to respond to the issue of drugs in the club, as well as identifying what benefits it had brought to the community.

McDonald issued a statement in which he argued that 'the authorities need to acknowledge the huge significance the Rainbow Venues have, to millions of visitors to Birmingham, and what impact [the closure] will have on the city's night-time economy' (Malt 2018). The venue put forward the case to show that the club was concerned for the welfare of its clientele:

> Closing down a club will not stop people from taking drugs, and may put them in more dangerous situations, where specialist medical support is not on hand. [Also, the venue] had invested a lot of money in regenerating warehouse buildings that were previously derelict, and invested profits from its main venue into cultural events less likely to make money. (Ibid.)

On 18 January 2018, the Rainbow Venues officially launched the 'Educate Not Revocate' campaign, in which they formally began the process of appealing the decision, fundraising to cover the costs of legal fees, as well as the rent of the properties whilst it was out of action, and supporting the venue's various suppliers too (ibid.). They also expressed interest in funding a new annual festival, which would draw attention to effective ways to prevent drug use through educational measures, make efforts to save other venues in similar circumstances, encourage young entrepreneurs, and act to change the ways in which authorities view youth culture and the nightlife industry (Frankland 2018).

As a part of the campaign, the venue argued that they 'had very robust policies that West Midlands Police have accepted are more stringent than any other licensed premises in the country' (Rainbow Birmingham 2017), and that closing the venue would '[push] these events back underground [where] there are no measures in place to protect people from harm' (ibid.). Additionally, they argued that 'the future economic success of Birmingham is dependent on the ability to both attract and retain talent […] closing down venues that offer so much to the city is not going to help us achieve this' (ibid.). The campaign was largely centred around a 14-minute video, in which many prominent individuals such as Tom Shorterz and Hannah Wants stated their case for the preservation of the venue.[2] The video received so much initial attention that the website crashed within minutes of it being uploaded, due to the influx of visitors (Probert and Balloo 2018).

After several weeks of campaigning, the Rainbow Venues had successfully managed to raise £24,076 through online donations (Franks 2018), but sadly, all their efforts were not enough. On 21 March 2018, they eventually made the decision to drop all legal action in an effort to minimise any further financial damage (ibid.). This was the final nail in the coffin for the venue. Subsequently, McDonald announced that:

> We are resolute in our commitment to calling for a more progressive approach to licensing through the Educate Not Revocate campaign as announced in January 2018 […] Until the difficult and intimidating climate of licensing in Birmingham and across the UK changes, and the financial and emotional impact that it directly causes on venue owners and licensees is alleviated, we will no longer invest in the city we have previously called home. (McDonald in Franks 2018)

This act of resignation confirmed what many had been fearing, and from this date onwards, the Rainbow Venues – once hailed as 'the city's No.1 dance mecca' (Hubzin 2014) – was no more. The various events and festivals that called the Rainbow Venues home would be forced to relocate, and this was no more pressing of an issue than for the festival due to be held on the upcoming 6 May – Swingamajig.

---

2. Quoted in '#educatenotrevocate', available at https://www.facebook.com/watch/?v=1961942547155300.

Swingamajig

The early 2000s saw the genre of electro swing flourish – the style of which fuses the sounds of the swing era with that of the age of electronic dance music. Known for its escapist attitude and upbeat, lively spirit, electro swing was to become the music of choice for countless partygoers with nostalgic and eccentric tendencies. And despite initially emerging across mainland Europe – primarily across countries such as France, Austria, and Germany – it would see most of the bulk of its development occur in the UK. After several years of steady growth, one of the most significant years for the genre came in 2013. There were several landmark developments that took place in 2013; one of which was the introduction of 'Mayfair Avenue' at Boomtown Fair – the UK's premier festival for underground music. This area of Boomtown was built to cater primarily to the sounds of electro swing, and featured many of the genre's biggest stars, such as Dutty Moonshine, SwinGrowers, and the Parov Stelar Band – without a doubt electro swing's most prominent artist. Boomtown Fair took place from 8 to 11 August, near Winchester; and the following month saw the launch of Maui Waui festival in Suffolk – held on 7 and 8 September, and exclusively dedicated to the genre. These were both significant moments for the evolution of electro swing; yet neither of them could claim to be the first festival with an explicit focus on the genre. That honour will forever be held by Birmingham's Swingamajig.

A one-day event held on 5 May 2013, Swingamajig did not initially take place at the Rainbow Venues. Indeed, whilst that venue was hosting a techno and house event called 'Below', Swingamajig was set up as a kind of street party, on Lower Trinity Street, just outside the front entrance. The festival was founded by members of local band, the Electric Swing Circus – one of Britain's pioneering electro swing acts, who also performed at both Boomtown Fair and Maui Waui that year. In 2012, the Electric Swing Circus, along with DJ C@ in the H@, had founded Ragtime Records – their own label, on which they would release their self-titled debut in 2013 – and saw the creation of their own festival as the next logical step. Both the Electric Swing Circus and C@ in the H@ were to perform at Swingamajig, which was headlined by The Correspondents.

With a capacity of 1,000, and three stages – one for live music, one for DJs, and one for cabaret and other miscellaneous performances – the first Swingamajig was a much more modest event when considering the scale of what it was to become. But the impact of the festival was monumental. Electro swing as a genre had proven that it had the capacity to hold its own in the marketplace of attention, and that it had the power to entertain a festival's worth of people for 15 hours straight. As an attendee, I was blown away by what the organisers had achieved; the level of detail in evoking the swing era through a contemporary lens was phenomenal – through the décor found across the festival site, the stage costumes worn by many of the performers, and the diverse range of performances on show – and the representation of what this genre entailed was something that I had not previously experienced to such a degree.

The following year, the festival saw much expansion, including the addition of a fourth, much larger stage to showcase the headline acts. Still taking place on and around Lower Trinity Street, the 2014 edition was headlined by Molotov Jukebox, fronted by actor Natalia Tena. Of course, this was again rivalled by the Rainbow Venues, which was that year staging the MADE festival, headlined by Annie Mac. Swingamajig moved away from Lower Trinity Street for its third year, instead making use of the various venues within the Custard Factory complex, including Alfie Bird's and the Oobleck. Headlined by Chinese Man, this was by far the most ambitious year for the festival and stands in many attendees' minds as one of the greatest events. The line-up was essentially a who's who of the electro swing world (Chinese Man; The Correspondents; the Electric Swing Circus; Dutty Moonshine; Smokey Joe and the Kid; Mr Switch and many more), and for someone engrossed in the scene, it provided a unique opportunity to see so many of its exemplary acts across a single day. But there was still something problematic about the production of that year's show. Access between the various stages wasn't as streamlined as would have been convenient for the attendees, and there was something of a lack of an overall thematic atmosphere about the place. It wasn't until Swingamajig's fourth event, in 2016, that they uncovered the perfect venue, and it was right on its doorstep all along.

Alfie Bird's and the Oobleck closed its doors in March 2016 (Beardsworth 2016). Like so many other venues featured in this collection, it fell victim to financial difficulties, and like so many other venues throughout the country, it surely deserves a chapter somewhere of its own. This misfortune was not to have an impact upon Swingamajig however, as the formal decision to move to the Rainbow Venues had long been made. Swingamajig's fourth edition was headlined by Balkan Beat Box, the Israeli outfit known for blending Middle Eastern influences with electronica, demonstrating the festival's keenness to branch out beyond electro swing alone; and the event made use of seven of the various spaces. Employing The Arena, The Warehouse, and the Black Box, the attendees were spoilt for choice with the amount of entertainment on offer. There was also a cabaret theatre; a further outdoor stage underneath the railway arches; traditional swing being performed at the accompanying

Night Owl bar; and much more throughout the day and night. Each stage seemed to provide its own unique flavour to the electro swing sound, and as an attendee, the opportunity to move so easily across the site, encountering such variety along the way, ensured that I felt completely spoilt for choice. The festival ran seamlessly, and the Rainbow Venues seemed cemented as a perfect partner.

So it was that the 2017 iteration made use of the very same spaces, with only a few changes here and there, to expand the festival further. The most notable addition was the Vintage Terrace stage, which made use of the Rainbow Venues' roof garden. This was a beautiful space which looked over the whole festival layout, and Swingamajig programmed for several of the more laid-back acts to perform here throughout the day. Another addition of note was the partnership with Scour Records, who were brought in to programme the Black Box stage. Scour brought with them some of the grittier, bass-heavy acts from the scene, and did a fantastic job catering to that end of the festival's clientele. In a blog post in which I detailed the festival's history, I noted that 'in terms of the sheer quantity of fantastic sets, this year probably stands out the most' (Inglis 2020), a statement that I still stand by. And notably, this was the first Swingamajig to feature a repeat headliner. It is perhaps quite poetic, then, that both the first and last Swingamajig festivals to take place in Digbeth were both headlined by The Correspondents: the two-man act whose stage show is characterised by lead singer Mr Bruce's ridiculously outlandish dance moves provided memorable bookends to this era of the festival.

Initially, Swingamajig 2018 was set to be a blinder. The Bristol-based act Slamboree, whose live stage-show can best be described as circo-pyro-gypsy-rave, were booked to headline. Several DJs, such as Duke Skellington and Vourteque, representing electro swing's newfound development in the States, were also booked to come over from America. So, the show was going to be yet another step up from all previous events. With the line-up officially announced on 13 March (Hyland 2018), the festival was counting on the Rainbow Venues' licence appeal being successful; and when this was dropped, they were left with no choice. On 27 March 2018, Swingamajig officially announced that that year's edition of the festival would not be going ahead as planned.

The Future for Swingamajig and the Rainbow Venues

After weeks of frantic organisation, Swingamajig did manage to put together a downscaled replacement event, and even managed to hold it in Digbeth – at the Boxxed warehouse space around the corner from the previously held events. Headlined by part-comedy, part-gospel remix act, Oh My God! It's The Church, the show was a testament to the undying ambition of the festival organisers. Arranged on a shoestring budget, the event was bittersweet, for as admirable a job as the organisers had done – even managing to bring Duke Skellington over from the USA – the cancellation of the festival as originally planned was undoubtedly in the forefront of everybody's minds. Nevertheless, the show was an immense achievement, and ensured that the fans would get a supremely enjoyable event in at least some form that year.

In 2019, Swingamajig returned to a full-scale festival event, but had said goodbye to Digbeth. The year would see many changes, the most prominent of which was the switch to the Birmingham Botanical Gardens as the venue of choice. Based two and a half miles away on the other side of town, not only did this rid Swingamajig of its urban, underground quality, it also allowed the event to become family-friendly for the first time in its history. Headlined by the Hackney Colliery Band, a contemporary brass band from their namesake in East London, the event ran until 11.00pm, before transferring to the Amusement 13 nightclub in central Birmingham for the official afterparty.

Swingamajig 2019 returned the festival to the heights it had achieved at the Rainbow Venues. However, it would never quite achieve the same feel that was unmistakable throughout its time spent in Digbeth. Held in one of Birmingham's more dignified venues, Swingamajig post-Rainbow is a much classier affair – at least with regard to the day-party. The event has evolved to become something which – whilst just as entertaining – is undeniably different, and the memory of the Rainbow Venues is now something to be recalled only by those lucky enough to have attended.

And what of the Rainbow Venues? Losing their licence seemed to spell the end of venue operations for both McDonald and Shelton, who initially renamed their enterprise the Rainbow Events, and decided to return their focus to event promotion (Young 2018) – although this operation appears to have folded as well. The venues themselves were taken over by the Bristol-based event company the MJR Group, who renamed the space as the Digbeth Arena, and began producing events as early as August 2018. Perhaps somewhat reluctantly, McDonald ultimately welcomed this development, stating that 'we have a strong relationship with MJR and could not be happier that they are the company taking the Arena forward into the future' (ibid.). Representing the MJR Group, director of operations Benjamin Newby made the following statement:

> We are honoured and humbled to become part of the innovative and artistic hub that is Digbeth, Birmingham. We have already

started developing great relationships with the business and creative community and look forward to what the future will bring. We recognise the dedicated and inspirational work Rainbow Venues have put into their venues and Digbeth as a whole. We will work hard to continue their passion while adding our own vision and operational standards to the Arena. (Young 2018)

The Digbeth Arena held its first event on 24 August 2018. As part of its 'Skyline Series', Brian Wilson of the Beach Boys performed *Pet Sounds* (1966) in its entirety.

A further postscript for the venue occurred, coincidentally, that same weekend, when the original Rainbow pub was reopened as a cocktail bar by the name of Finders Keepers (Bains 2018a). With plenty of initial excitement, and ambitious plans to refurbish the back room as a space for 'immersive theatre' (ibid.), the project unfortunately fell through after several noise complaints. On 3 January 2019, Finders Keepers formally announced their closure (Finders Keepers Digbeth 2019). Most recently, 25 October 2019 saw the Rainbow pub reopen yet again, following several months of renovations, under its original name (Young 2019a). Coordinated by local events promoter Nikki Taylor, the venue now serves a clientele of reggae lovers, and held its first live event – a Halloween all-nighter, on the 26th.

Whilst the Swingamajig festival and the Rainbow Venues are no longer working in a direct partnership, the golden period of 2016–2017 is seared in the memory of all those who played a part. Personally, I consider myself very fortunate to have experienced this era; the industrial yet vivacious backdrop of the Rainbow Venues, with all its eccentricities and playful delights, provided what I would argue was the perfect venue for the festival. During this time, Digbeth was the centre of worldwide activity for all electro swing – at the time one of the most globally exciting emergent genres. The venue's legacy has to include the devastating deaths of Dylan Booth and Michael Trueman. They stand as salutary evidence of how drug dealers can use music venues as an easy location to trade their wares. That the Rainbow Venues addressed this issue is to their credit. It was an institute which Birmingham locals can be proud to have had as a part of their city. The role it played for electro swing, for Swingamajig, and for the emergence and development of various different styles and subcultures, was one that can genuinely be said to have changed the course of underground music.

References

Authi, Jasbir. 2017. 'Michael Trueman drugs death: Rainbow Venues insists it's a "responsible venue"'. *Birmingham Mail*. https://www.birminghammail.co.uk/news/michael-trueman-drugs-death-rainbow-13852162

Bains, Sanjeeta. 2018a. 'The Rainbow pub in Digbeth reopens as cool cocktail bar Finders Keepers'. *Birmingham Mail*. https://www.birminghammail.co.uk/whats-on/food-drink-news/rainbow-pub-digbeth-reopens-cool-15114364

Bains, Sanjeeta. 2018b. 'This Birmingham neighbourhood has been named the coolest area in Britain'. *Birmingham Mail*. https://www.birminghammail.co.uk/whats-on/whats-on-news/birmingham-neighbourhood-been-named-one-15254789

Beardsworth, Luke. 2016. 'Alfie Bird and the Oobleck closes with immediate effect'. *Birmingham Mail*. https://www.birminghammail.co.uk/whats-on/music-nightlife-news/alfie-bird-oobleck-closes-immediate-11004971

Finders Keepers Digbeth. 2019. *Facebook*. https://www.facebook.com/finderskeepersdigbeth/posts/283043269232517

Frankland, Becca. 2018. 'The Rainbow Venues unveil Educate Not Revocate campaign'. *Skiddle*. https://www.skiddle.com/news/all/The-Rainbow-Venues-unveil-Educate-Not-Revocate-campaign-/37518/

Franks, Richard. 2018. 'The Rainbow Venues withdraws appeal against council'. *Counteract*. https://counteract.co/music/the-rainbow-venues-withdraws-appeal/

Hubzin, Ivica. 2014. '10 Years at Rainbow Venues'. *DJ Mag*. https://djmag.com/content/10-years-rainbow-venues

Hyland, Tom. 2018. 'The 2018 Line Up Poster Has Landed'. *Swingamajig*. https://swingamajig.co.uk/2018-line-poster-landed/

Inglis, Chris. 2020. 'Swingamajig: A Retrospective'. *Chris Swinglis*. https://chris-swinglis.blogspot.com/2020/05/swingamajig-retrospective.html

Malt, Andy. 2018. 'Birmingham's Rainbow Venues launches campaign to help fund appeal against closure'. *Complete Music Update*. https://completemusicupdate.com/article/birminghams-rainbow-venues-launches-campaign-to-help-fund-appeal-against-closure/

Moore, Sam. 2017. 'Birmingham nightclub Rainbow Venues responds after having license revoked'. *NME*. https://www.nme.com/news/music/birmingham-nightclub-rainbow-venues-responds-licence-revoked-2166408

Probert, Sarah, and Stephanie Balloo. 2018. 'Rainbow Venues announces closure of multiple clubs in Birmingham'. *Birmingham Mail*. https://www.birminghammail.co.uk/whats-on/music-nightlife-news/rainbow-venues-announces-closure-multiple-14175146

Rainbow Birmingham, The. 2017. *Facebook*. https://www.facebook.com/therainbowvenues/posts/1905722539443968

Tyler, Jane. 2016. 'Tragic Dylan Booth died after taking ecstasy for the first time at Rainbow Club in Digbeth, inquest told'. *Birmingham Mail*. https://www.birminghammail.co.uk/news/midlands-news/tragic-dylan-booth-died-after-11317741

Young, Graham. 2018. 'New start for Rainbow Arena – and big names lined up to perform'. *Birmingham Mail*. https://www.birminghammail.co.uk/whats-on/music-nightlife-news/rainbow-venues-becomes-digbeth-arena-14341302

Young, Graham. 2019a. 'The Rainbow pub to open again – bringing legendary "peaky blinders" pub back from the dead'. *Birmingham Mail*. https://www.birminghammail.co.uk/whats-on/music-nightlife-news/rainbow-pub-open-again-bringing-17124464

Young, Graham. 2019b. 'This was the first Peaky Blinders attack to take place in Digbeth relived by Carl Chinn'. *Birmingham Mail*. https://www.birminghammail.co.uk/whats-on/whats-on-news/first-peaky-blinders-attack-take-16899038

Author biography

Dr Chris Inglis is a musicologist based in Cardiff, whose research primarily explores the emergence and development of the electro swing genre. In 2019 he received his doctorate from the University of South Wales. He is currently employed by the British and Irish Modern Music Institute in Bristol.

20 Sold out, Locked out, Power out

Tom Hingley

Manchester Boardwalk originally started off as a small venue on Little Peter Street. It opened officially in 1986 as a 100-capacity venue with a relatively low ceiling and narrow sightlines. In the early 1990s, the small gigging space was expanded heavenwards when the ceiling was opened up. This created an extra floor with separate bars and a viewing platform accommodating 200 punters. This made it more of a club venue, hosting events like Dave Haslam's infamous Yellow nights. Six rehearsal rooms were added in the cellar below the concert floor. The building was Victorian and constructed from the raw red brick once at the heart of the sprawling Lancashire cottonopolis. The venue was a painted black room, cold as death when empty but boiling when heated by moving bodies. When it was topped up to the rafters, it hummed with sweet smells of sweat, spilt beer and hedonism. The darkness of the gig room was interrupted by the dazzle of strobes. The preshow queue snaked long around the building and out onto the big city streets.

These were the same streets that, in 1844, Friedrich Engels paced when composing *The Condition of the Working Class in England*. In this book, he described how poor industrial districts in cities like Manchester were made up of factories and slum housing. These areas were hidden behind bourgeoise housing and shopfronts to lend the city a false respectability. Set in tarmacked cobbled back streets, among the ex-cotton warehouses, The Boardwalk was the setting for a burgeoning entertainment and hospitality industry that began to assert itself from the 1980s onwards. This new scene was situated in the Victorian skeleton of buildings that reflected industrial revolutions driven by steam, cotton and, later, electricity. Constructed as a ragged school in Victorian times, the site was a place of study open to destitute kids who didn't attend any other formal education. They would attend on Sundays and weekday evenings.

My first introduction to the building was in 1985. I was rehearsing there with my pre-Inspiral Carpets band, Too Much Texas. At that time, the gig room was a small theatre with cinema seats on a sloping floor. The room was dark, full of dust and in a dilapidated state. You had to step over broken seats and patchy flooring to walk round the room. It was a secret, forgotten place still stuck in its recent past and not yet converted into a modern concert space. It had previously been run as a seedy strip club; the kind conjured up by the Manchester-based television series *Life on Mars*. A small rectangular room, it had a boxy feel with sound bouncing easily off the hard walls. Once it was kitted out as a proper venue, the windows were blacked out behind hardboard and the place seemed much bigger. With a full bar on the left wall adjacent to the stage, it became the ideal starter venue for small bands commencing their push towards stardom.

Between 1985 and 1988 I played quite a few shows in The Boardwalk with Too Much Texas. We lived in Hulme, a local council-estate in the long-demolished Crescents. It was home for a whole bevy of Manchester bands of those years including Big Flame, Rocking Ed and His Rattlesnakes, the Inca Babies, The Membranes, Vee VV, Ignition, and the Desert Wolves. The Boardwalk was one of the cogs in the wheel of the '80s small band scene. We picked up support slots with popular indie names of those years, most notably with the House of Love. I naïvely invited the already famous Guy Chadwick to come and relax in the sewing-room-cum-low-rent-loft apartment I shared with my partner of the time between sound check and show. But he was way too classy and was never going to agree to do that. It is always good to be pushy in art, though. They were mind blowing as a band and we relished the opportunity to open for them.

The Beloved were another up-and-coming band that we supported. They were quite electronic sounding even in 1988. Their big New Order influence meant that their sound was a little too familiar for a Manchester audience, but the integration of guitars, drums and keyboards with gizmos was well realised. The Pastels were another great act and precisely the kind of C86 band that were regularly booked at The Boardwalk. This list of headliners we appeared alongside reassures me that we can't have been all that bad if we were regularly supporting artists of that stature.

You loaded the gear in through the front door and up two flights of steps in this era. Parking on Little Peter Street at that time was already difficult. There were car parks on the site of demolished buildings. One of them stood on the site of the TJ Davidson Rehearsal room where the video for 'Love Will Tear Us Apart' was filmed. Manchester was still post-industrial, dark satanic, semi-demolished mills in the late 1980s. It wasn't the big glass city of skyscrapers you find today. The Boardwalk was a small venue with a capacity of a couple of hundred and had a very low ceiling. It was near enough to clubs like the

Hacienda to have its own gravitational pull for guitar bands. It was easier to fill and had better acoustics than Factory's super club. It was near enough to the Ritz and Venue and close enough to the Hacienda's Whitworth Street West location to provide healthy competition.

The shows that ran at The Boardwalk were promoted by the two local radio stations. BBC Radio Manchester's indie show Meltdown was hosted by Phil Korbel and Alison Bell (a close friend of John Peel) while the independent side was catered for by local record industry plugger Tony Michelides (aka 'Tony the Greek') on his 'Last Radio Show' on Piccadilly Radio. These local shows, as well as the events magazine *City Life*, promoted the Boardwalk shows of the day. It was a vibrant scene.

I next returned to The Boardwalk to play my first Manchester show with my new band Inspiral Carpets (made up of myself, Clint Boon, Martyn Walsh, Craig Gill and Graham Lambert) on 4 March 1989. This time, I was in the headlining band. It was easily sold out and the audience were hungry to see the Inspirals with a new front man. Oldham band The Jerks were supporting. It was fucking mental. This was the big time for me. It was to be the last small-venue show the band did in Manchester in our initial run from 1989 to 1994. The air was electric. Young music fans were crowded from the front of the stage all the way back to the steps below the entrance door. The sound of the indie disco soundtrack battled with the excited throng who were talking, shouting and screaming in anticipation. Sweaty air and damp condensation were running down the walls, down beer glasses, and down foreheads into eyes. The music could be so loud at times that the sensation punched any other thought or emotion out of your consciousness and, along with the alcoholic come-down, you would be feeling the volume for days after the visit.

I was astonished by how different playing there in the support band to a respectable audience of sixty was to being the headliner in front of a breathing, sweating, expectant hulk of two hundred. Two memories come to mind of this particular show in my nascent position as singer in a much more successful band. Firstly, at the end of the gig, I announced to the audience (to the frowns of my much cooler band mates), 'We love you!'. I got told quite correctly not to say that again (I'm still shuddering with embarrassment while typing these words). Secondly, with there being no stage barrier at the show (a rare occurrence in those days), some lad in the crowd grabbed the microphone from me and wouldn't return it. Craig Gill (our late drummer) came to the front of the stage, signalled smiling to the fan to return the mic. When he did, Craig smacked him loudly on the head with it.

I continued to watch shows intermittently at The Boardwalk. A notable one was Oasis's second outing there on 14 July 1992. It wasn't the first time I had seen the band, which was supporting Peter Hook's band of the day Revenge, at the Middleton Hippodrome on 20 April 1992 (in fact the same night as the Freddie Mercury memorial concert). Oasis were supporting a band called Sweet Jesus, but most of the seventy or so attendees who came were there to see them. I think most of Inspiral Carpets attended too, apart from Martyn Walsh. I remember Oasis being brash, loud and heavy sounding. Their finale was 'I am the Walrus'. I'd love to say that I 'got them' and knew they were going to be fantastically stellar both in terms of artistic value and commercial success, but I didn't. That is no criticism of them, it was just early days. I partly went because I wanted to show Noel some support. Our relationship in the Inspirals dynamic hadn't always been that good because (unbeknownst to me for my first three years in the band) before becoming a roadie he had auditioned unsuccessfully to become the lead singer. Once I learnt this secret, I wanted to offer support to his new band. I don't think I discussed with the rest of my band that I was attending. I actually walked the two and a half miles from my flat in Fallowfield to get to The Boardwalk that night.

From 1991, Inspiral Carpets took on the rehearsal room on the top floor that had previously been inhabited by Factory hopefuls the Railway Children. It was directly above the office that the owners Colin and Donald Sinclair and Sue Langford worked from. I retain two memories of the attic room. One was of pouring a boiling kettle on my foot while attempting to make the band a brew. My right foot was a smelly mess and spent weeks wrapped in bandages. The other was of returning from a tour of the world where we hadn't made any money. As we manhandled all the heavy and cumbersome flight cases of musical equipment and amplifiers up the four flights of stairs to the rehearsal room, Craig was moaning and I asked him if he had a hundred pounds' cash on him. He asked why and I said you can either pay two people to load the stuff or stop complaining.

In 1993, we moved downstairs to rehearse in the basement where other dignitaries including Creation signees Medalark Eleven rehearsed and just next door to the new kids on the block Oasis. One member of the Burnage band scrawled the anti-Manchester United jibe 'Munich 58' on Medalark Eleven's rehearsal door (it is a reference to the plane crash that killed eight of the Busby Babes in 1958). Oasis's room was festooned with pictures of their favourite Manchester City players and Burt Bacharach. It was a small cinder block room and dreams of worldwide seduction and success were cemented in it. In that regard, it is as iconic a setting as Memphis, Sun Records Studio, or The Cavern in Liverpool (which is now a car park).

On a pettier level, I returned from holiday in 1991 to find that Clint Boon had lent Oasis our Peavey PA speakers. They had put too much volume through them and, much to my annoyance, had blown up the tweeters which then had to be replaced. I remember that they always played at a tremendous volume level that would have stripped the paint and soul of anything it touched. It must at least question the narrative that Alan McGee *first* encountered them at a show in Glasgow at King Tut's in May 1993. I suspect McGee might have visited the basement rehearsal space prior to that as Medalark Eleven were on his label. If he had, the only thing that would have been louder than Oasis's backline would have been Noel and Liam's personalities. It certainly would have been hard to remain immune or unaware of them or their talent if you had been within two hundred metres of the place.

The club closed in 1999 when a bunch of dentists bought it as a property investment and converted it into private flats. There was something truly iconic and timeless about that rehearsal room where Oasis first cut their teeth. They created their own popular culture shrine to their favourite icons of popular culture: Man City players, history, The Beatles, and Burt Bacharach. The style worship of this space was part recreated on the front cover artwork for their debut album *Definitely Maybe* where the band pose in Paul Arthurs' front room which is festooned with similar pop cultural references.

Walking around the gentrified environs of Little Peter Street now, you can just about hear the ghosts of the bands that performed at the club. A thousand guitars cranked up, hundreds of lead singers hanging off the microphone stand and kicking the monitor speaker, the lines of club goers queuing up to gain entrance snaking down the street, and bands and their crew buzzing on the intercom to gain entry for sound check or rehearsal. The club full of youngsters bum-rushing the stage. The lightshow, strobing metallic points, the treble twisting your inner ear and the sub bass shocking the RSG beams and sending energy through your body. The roar of the crowd as you come onstage from the tiny, graffitied backstage room, negotiating your way round the leads, amps, floor lights (not a good look going flying in front of hundreds of baying punters, where there is always at least one who would love to see you brought down low). The slashing of a few guitar chords, bass notes, snare, bass drum, cymbal smacks, keys samples, one-two, one-two, lead and backing vocals tested out. The analogue four track spitting out scrambles of whale noise, porn movie grunts, 1970s continental shortwave radio jingles and a disgruntled Welsh promoter (who we did a runner on before playing a show) pronouncing that 'Inspiral Carpets are the biggest bunch of wankers ever'. Starting the first song and breaking the seal in the first minute as the band's collective musical visual raised the individuals in the audience into one beautiful feeling of oneness. A single beast, swaying, singing, lifted into a euphoria that no single drug, religion or football win could replace. Time standing still and rushing by so fast simultaneously. Coming off for the end of the show, wetter in sweat than a fish in stormy water, having a piss in the backstage room then going back on stage for the encore ninety seconds later, then off stage again to applause and cheers. The audience exiting the room, down the stairs and out into a cold spring night, numbers reducing like stars in the morning light. All these ghosts along with the spectres of bands, bar staff, and punters.

The Boardwalk was a shared space where we could hang out. It was a hub where we could watch others perform, steal the bits that we could use, or invert the bad stuff other bands did that was wrong or embarrassing. We'd twist it and find a way to do something cool. I was new to Inspiral Carpets when I played that seminal show there. A lot came along to see if I was any good and if the band were the same, better, or worse with their newest recruit. We proved at The Boardwalk that we could make it to the next level because the songs were the stars. We had assistance from the radio through John Peel, Meltdown and the Last Radio show as well as coverage in fanzines (the internet and social networks of the day). All this made the band much bigger than the last time they had played a home-town show.

The Boardwalk stands as a metaphor for any small venue or rehearsal space that presently sits dark due to the pandemic (and also, for all those knocked down or repurposed). In this digital world it is too easy to be lonely. This musical space brought audiences together and propelled so many artists on to music careers that ended up everything from non-existent to superstar. It was a home to music, culture and the underground. This was art that was too specific, too odd, too separate or too different to be part of the generic or formulaic nonsense of the mainstream. The Boardwalk was always a school of sorts for the destitute, the lost, and those in need of community, belief and positivity. It's a shame that the space is now a bunch of anonymous offices. They bring money and commerce but contribute little to no culture to the surrounding physical and emotional spaces of the city.

It is complex that a music space can be so much more than the simple sum of its parts. It is a physical building, bricks and mortar, tables, stage, lights, sound equipment. But the grassroots venues were also the epicentre of a community and its culture. They were somewhere where club records boomed, and bands played at way too loud a volume. A society that fails to recognise the value of cultural expression is one that risks the ruin of entropy. It will miss structures of richness and variety in which disparate distinct tributaries flow into one complex river.

Author biography

Tom Hingley is a musician and writer. He is best known for being the lead singer with Oldham indie band Inspiral Carpets during their iconic most successful period (1989–2011) where they were one of the holy triumvirate of the 'Madchester' scene, smaller brother to the more critically and commercially acclaimed Stone Roses and Happy Mondays. Tom is now a solo artist performing over a hundred shows per annum, having parted ways with Inspirals in 2011. Writing is a new string to Tom's bow. Published works include *Carpet Burns* (Route, 2012), as well as a chapter in the Bloomsbury Academic collection, *Music, Memory and Memoir*.

21 Mothers Club in Erdington

Alan Smith

Mothers Club in Erdington, an unfashionable working-class area of Birmingham, was open for only three years between 1968 and 1971, yet it made a huge impact on the progressive rock scene. The DJ John Peel, who gigged there regularly, once stated that people are 'amazed to hear that for a few years the best club in Britain was in Erdington'. And on its closure, the US *Billboard* had labelled it the 'best rock venue in the world' (Young 2015).

A troubled 17-year-old dropped in on Mothers in 1968. My father had died suddenly two years earlier. As *Coronation Street* played on the telly, Dad's face turned the colour of something forgotten in the fridge. I left school completely screwed up, failing exams, and running wild. School hadn't been going well, anyway. The Birmingham education system was experimenting. My school was labelled a 'Technical Grammar', meaning that the curriculum was shaped by science and engineering type subjects. Little time for creativity, little time for me: chemical elements, quantum mechanics and straight, straight lines.

The array of bands that came to the club was impressive. Pink Floyd visited four times, recording some of their 1969 album *Ummagumma* there. The Who played three times. I saw Led Zeppelin and a number of Brummie bands, including Black Sabbath, Traffic and the Moody Blues. Mothers also offered the opportunity for local groups to play before the big names performed. On one such occasion a band stopped in the middle of their set and launched into the theme of the TV crime series *Z Cars*, thereby announcing the arrival of four plain-clothed police – an incident that typified occurrences there. Mothers gave me hope: the music and its audience were creative with not a straight line to be seen. Readers must excuse at times my vagueness about detail, but are asked to take into account that I am referring to matters over fifty years ago and to acknowledge that even at the time I would probably have been equally vague about things that had happened. I am therefore grateful for Kevin Duffy's excellent 1997 publication *Mothers 1968–1971* for the accuracy of the dates in which the various gigs I refer to occurred.

I can't remember much about the first band I saw at Mothers, but it was probably, according to Duffy, the Bakerloo Blues Line. I can certainly recall the feelings I had on entering the club. I went with a couple of friends. We didn't really know what to expect so had dressed relatively smartly; to gain entry into most of the clubs in Birmingham at that time, you had to. After joining a queue in a dismal alleyway by the side of a furniture shop, we realised we were overdressed. My mate Pete furtively removed his tie and stuffed it into his pocket. We eventually entered the building by climbing up a staircase and joined the flow of people into a room. It was a dark room with the stage and the bar area the only illuminated spaces. The music was loud. The bass throbbed like an electric pulse to which hot bodies reacted. The bodies were everywhere. Some were sitting, a few tried to find space to dance, a few were prostrate on the ground; dark shapes to be stepped over with care. Some of the young men were stripped to the waist. Flared jeans and all that hair locked into the crowded space. This was accompanied by the strong stink of Afghan hash and the sweeter scent of cider. Unlike other clubs there were no obvious bouncers but, as we were to witness on our visits, the club's staff would appear if someone's behaviour was affecting others or if an individual was in distress, wrecked on whatever substance they had consumed.

I frequented Mothers regularly in 1969 and 1970 and never saw anything that resembled a fight there which was in contrast to so many other clubs and pubs in Birmingham. I lived in Handsworth, about five or so miles from Erdington. At that time the scene on the streets was becoming tense and agitated. To some, being a 17-year-old male was all about how hard you were and which subcultural group you belonged to. Skinheads with their shaven scalps and Doc Martens boots were starting to appear. Some of the kids, formerly Mods, associated themselves with the Jamaican diaspora and their ska, rocksteady and reggae. Others, however, were rapidly developing right-wing affiliations fed by the recently established National Front. The Conservative MP for nearby Wolverhampton was Enoch Powell. He had made his infamous 'Rivers of Blood' speech in Birmingham in 1968. On Birmingham streets the air was thick with ugly threats and hate. Stepping into Mothers, however, was like being transported to the neighbourhood of Haight-Ashbury, San Francisco, the hub of the counterculture and epicentre of the Summer of Love in 1967.

In front of the stage were five or six rows of disorganised chairs. No straight lines. Individuals were draped over them like melted fabric. To the side of the stage area lurked dressing rooms into which performers and select members of the audience would drift in and out. In my experience the 'stars' were not treated as gods. That sort of thing just wasn't cool. Steve Winwood, Jeff Lynne, Robert Plant and John Bonham were all local to Birmingham and were often among the audience. One of the first bands I saw in April 1969 was the Liverpool Scene. They were headed by the poet Adrian Henri, a lovely guy.

Before the set started, Adrian was out among us talking to everyone and freely distributing his wine. I probably accepted a drop to blend with my very rough cider (I was so sophisticated!). The band grew out of poetry readings with music at the Everyman Theatre in Liverpool. They sometimes included the poet Roger McGough who was also a member of the band Scaffold. My favourite song from that time was an amusing parody of the blues scene and its success as a musical genre titled, 'I've got the Fleetwood Mac, Chicken Shack, John Mayall Can't Fail'. I was lucky enough to be able to talk with Adrian a few years later in Yorkshire when I tried to book him for a gig in the college where I studied. We both reminisced about Mothers. In the three-year existence of the club, the Liverpool Scene had played nine times. Good times, happy times with not a straight line to be seen. Henri's poetry alongside that of Roger McGough and Brian Patten formed *The Mersey Sound* anthology of poems in 1967 and was extremely successful. The writing was witty and perceptive to the popular culture of the day and, importantly for me, was very accessible. These writers as well as others from the rock scene, particularly Bob Dylan and Leonard Cohen, certainly helped to launch my interest in poetry.

An unlikely conversation occurred just outside the club that first encouraged my interests in the visual arts. One of my favourite bands at the time was King Crimson. Their debut album *In the Court of the Crimson King* was released in October 1969 under the Island label and still has legendary status in the progressive rock genre. The Who's Pete Townshend called it an 'uncanny masterpiece' (2015). The line-up of the band was to change in April 1970 as bassist and vocalist Greg Lake left to join Keith Emmerson, formerly of Nice, and Carl Palmer of Atomic Rooster, to form Emerson Lake and Palmer, ELP. Along with half a million or so others, I'd seen them at the Stones concert at Hyde Park in July 1969 and thought they were really good. It was the Stones' first public concert in over two years and occurred two days after the death of Brian Jones. Although seeing the Stones and attending the event was great, I thought King Crimson performed the best set on the day. The band were billed to appear at Mothers later that month alongside Thunderclap Newman who had been formed by Pete Townshend of The Who and had enjoyed success with the single 'Something in the Air'.

We were all queuing in the alleyway and I was talking to a guy who I'd drunk with before at the club. An attractive woman in her mid-twenties approached and, in a very refined accent, told me that I looked like a kind guy and asked whether she could borrow me for a time. I looked at the bloke I'd been talking to. He nodded his head, raised his eyebrows and murmured something about how kind I was, perhaps the kindest guy he'd ever met. I just said 'Sure' and tried to remain cool. She told me her name was Sarah and then led me over the road to the churchyard opposite the club. The churchyard was utilised for a variety of activities by some of the Mothers customers. However, the activity Sarah had in mind wasn't the one I had imagined. Leaning against the wall of the church was a guy in his thirties and with him a frail-looking young woman of about my age. Sarah introduced me to both and said that her sister Janey, the frail one, had just taken some acid. She asked whether I'd sit with her for a time while her and the guy went somewhere. They'd only be an hour or so. She didn't say where. I agreed to babysit (being such a kind guy) and Sarah and the man walked off into the Erdington sunset.

It was more like two hours before they returned but I wasn't that bothered. Wonderous stray music crept over from the club and a number of other people littered the churchyard, talking, smoking and quietly enjoying themselves. The mood was tranquil. I hadn't known what to expect from Janey having never sat in on such an occasion and felt very awkward at first, but all was calm. We both spread out on the ground, with our legs outstretched and our backs against a wall. She updated me as to where her thoughts were journeying. She was an art student at Bournville, and her posh frail voice matched her posh frail appearance. She told me that Erdington High Street looked like it had been painted by Claude Monet. I struggled with the reference, but I was just about aware of the painter's work and tried to see the street as she did. No straight lines. We moved from Impressionism to the work of Seurat. I hadn't heard of this artist. I hadn't heard of Pointillism either, the practice of applying small strokes or dots of colour to a surface so that from a distance they visually blend. She could see the buildings, the cars, the people on the street visually constructed by dots of colour. It was fascinating and, as soon as I could, I visited Handsworth library to acquaint myself with the artist and his work. Janey was okay, a nice 'chick', as I was starting to say (adopting the term used by the 'hip' at the time). I saw her again once at her home in up-market Solihull (making sure my Brummie accent didn't leak too much). It wasn't really a date; I was more interested in her portfolio of work which was really good. No straight lines.

It is difficult for me now to think about Mothers without also including thoughts about the broadcaster John Peel. He and Pete Drummond, who also DJ'd at the club, offered frequent plugs for Mothers on their radio shows and the place obviously benefited in attracting an audience from all over the UK. Peel's Sunday afternoon radio show *Top Gear* drew a devout following from the club's punters, and he certainly played a part in both the success of the club and a number of bands on the progressive rock circuit. One of these was Tyrannosaurus Rex, who later morphed into TRex in 1970. Tyrannosaurus Rex were formed in 1967. It was a duo featuring Mark Bolan and Steve Ross

Porter. The latter adopted the stage name Steve Peregrin Took after a hobbit in Tolkien's *Lord of the Rings*. The duo appeared twice at the club in 1968. The first of these visits they were accompanied by Peel. I saw them on their second visit. Their mainly acoustic set appealed to the hippie underground fraternity because it lacked any explicit pursuit of commercial success. The evening was great fun, mystical even. Peregrin Took's bongos accompanied Bolan's strange poetic vocals. By this time, I was dressing very casually in Levi's jeans, and to the dismay of my mother (the biological one not the club), I was letting my black curly hair grow. No straight lines.

The duo released four albums before Bolan decided to change direction musically. Up to that point their music was labelled loosely as psychedelic folk, but Bolan now wanted to move towards electric. He parted company with Peregrin Took and began to produce commercially marketable material. The first single under the new name was 'Ride a White Swan', followed by 'Hot Love' which went to number one and stayed there for six weeks. Bolan at this stage was viewed as having joined the Glam Rock bands, donning themselves in make-up, platform shoes, glitter and adopting an androgynous style. TRex and other bands and individuals such as Gary Glitter, Roxy Music and David Bowie were consciously rejecting the narrative of the late 1960s rock scene. They had, in Mothers terms, become 'bread heads' and when TRex released 'Get it On' in 1971 Peel played it on his show before quipping 'Get it off'. Rumour had it that Bolan never spoke to Peel again.

John Peel was a very approachable guy who I (and a number of others) chatted to regularly when he was at the club. Those of us who regularly frequented the club were thrilled when we got a mention on *Top Gear*. This was more than likely on the Sunday after the Liverpool Scene had played there in July 1969. On the show he said something like: 'I spent most of last night in a Birmingham club trying to keep my feet warm' before making a reference to our little group: 'anyway this one's for Acker, Pete and Al Smith, I won't say nice, but it is very Nice'. Then playing, of course, a track from The Nice. What none of us could understand was why he couldn't get his feet warm. The club was renowned for being blisteringly hot. The fire escape door was often opened to let real air in with people draped dangerously over the balcony trying to take a breath full. The bands suffered too. Keith Moon of The Who collapsed over his drum kit and had to be carried off stage, only returning when he'd had water poured over him. I also remember seeing the Moody Blues again in 1969. They had just finished their rendition of 'Nights in White Satin' with a very sweaty Justin Hayward (I think) spoiling the delicate ethereal atmosphere by commenting to an unknown and unseen punter, 'Phew it's warm in here; get your knickers off, Audrey'. Poor Audrey. No, no cold feet. No straight lines.

The Nice played Mothers three times in 1969 and I saw them in the June of that year. They were another band promoted by Peel. They were exciting to listen to and exciting to watch. They fused progressive rock, jazz and classical elements and were never afraid to incorporate feedback and distortion into their overall sound. I first heard their arrangement of Leonard Bernstein's 'America', originally composed for the musical *West Side Story*, when it was released as a single in 1968. Keith Emerson on keyboard was an incredibly flamboyant showman. He treated his instrument with seeming violence. Indeed, he used daggers to jam into the keys of the organ to prolong notes. At some gigs the daggers were hurled across the stage but thankfully, given how packed the place was, that didn't happen at the gig I attended. Emerson was never still, playing his keys from all angles. No straight lines. Angry and very, very loud.

'America' is a protest piece. It is an instrumental for most of its six and a half minutes before finally a voice comes in: 'America is pregnant with promises and anticipation but is murdered by the hand of the inevitable'. The band played at the Royal Albert Hall in July 1968 at an anti-apartheid concert and upset a number of people, including the US embassy, by setting fire to the American flag. It was the era of protest and America featured highly. The struggle for civil rights was intensifying and shifting after Martin Luther King's assassination in 1968 and the country's continuing involvement in Vietnam remained controversial. Anti-war rhetoric and political satire also featured in the repertoire of two other bands I saw at Mothers in 1969: the Edgar Broughton Band and Country Joe and the Fish.

All I can recall about seeing the Edgar Broughton Band was the audience at the club chanting 'Out Demons Out' with them over and over again. The evening had started promisingly. I'd arrived fairly early and, after getting myself a drink, had started talking to this French lady. She was doing something at Birmingham University, her English was great and so was everything about her. No straight lines. The band was just setting up, so talking was possible. I bought her a drink and we talked about Captain Beefheart whose music the Broughton Band reminded me of, and (of all things) the subject of art was raised again. She started talking about the Pre-Raphaelite collection at Birmingham Art Gallery. She'd been impressed. I lied as if I knew what she was on about and said 'Yeah, yeah it's really good'. Another trip to the library was scheduled. The evening looked hopeful. The place was filling up. It was hot and we stood close together. The band came on. I went to get some more drinks. And when I came back, she'd gone. No straight lines. 'Out Demons

Out!' The whole of the building roared, chanted and leapt up in anger. Which demons were we meant to be exorcising? I wasn't too certain. The French girl had certainly exorcised hers and this poor sad demon stood all alone nursing a pint of cider and a redundant glass of Babycham.

I wasn't that in awe of the Edgar Broughton Band so consequently never saw them play again. I did, however, wish that I'd attended their gig at Mothers on 19 September 1970. This was the day after Jimi Hendrix died. Friends told me what a strange and weird evening it had been. By way of some sort of bizarre acknowledgement of Hendrix's death, Edgar had everyone in the club breathing in and out in unison and, following this, some in the audience believed that they actually saw Hendrix on stage. Were these post-bereavement hallucinations? Yes, alcohol and various other substances had been consumed and no-one I knew claimed to have seen him, but all admitted that the experience, no pun intended, had been quite eerie. Edgar also asked for two minutes' silence which was well respected. Silence at Mothers was unheard of (sorry), and, at the end of the gig, he asked all to leave quietly while the band played their last number. Some were crying as they left the building.

'Out Demons Out' was apparently an adaptation of the 1967 Fugs song 'Exorcising the Demons Out of the Pentagon'. The Fugs, a band from New York, were persistent anti-Vietnam protesters and thus played an important part in the American counterculture of the mid- to late 1960s. The Fugs name came from a euphemism for the word 'fuck' in Norman Mailer's 1948 war novel *The Naked and the Dead*. Country Joe and the Fish were another American protest band who played at Mothers in March 1969 and at the Woodstock festival later that year. The one song I remember from that time is the 'I Feel–Like–I'm–Fixin'–to–Die–Rag' commonly referred to as 'The Fish Cheer'. This always launched the crowd into sing-along mode. I also saw the band in 1970 at the Shepton Mallet festival near Bath (where the seeds of Glastonbury were planted) and again the audience, this time about 150,000 of them, sang along. Led Zeppelin also played there and did a brilliant set. I will always remember, after struggling through the crowd in search of the toilet block, the irony of hearing the band play 'Dazed and Confused' as I looked for the tent that a friend and I were dossing in. I didn't find it. It didn't matter. I lodged with someone else for the night; such were the times.

I was also dazed and confused standing in front of Julie Driscoll one night, if my memory serves me well. The club was packed, and I was at the front with some friends. The place was hot again and so was she. Throbbing and just a few feet away, her eyes locked on me it seemed; extending her arms, her long seductive fingers just in front of me, reacting to the sound. Mesmerised, the boy was completely captured. Julie sang the 'Season of the Witch' and her eyes summoned him into her spell. No straight lines. The band eventually finished their set and began to leave the stage. The boy followed her towards the dressing room, locked into the trance that she'd placed him in. But the pathway was abruptly closed off, killing the boy's dream. A heavily bearded guy, probably a roadie, emerged at the doorway. He was large, very large: 'You okay, man?' Yeah fine, fine, I mean what do you say? Dazed and confused, my friends laughed. The deluded 18-year-old male felt like a prat.

Mothers closed in 1971 and a blue plaque was unveiled in 2013. It was vandalised later but, in a sense, that doesn't really matter. The memories are still there in the heads of those who attended. The era produced incredible music. It was brave, often experimental, and always absolute magic. Seeing all of this performed in a space like Mothers was perfect. Admittedly the late 1960s and early '70s did have its victims, like Hendrix, but overall, it was a period of optimism. Naïvely, perhaps, we talked about peace. I became involved in CND activities, attended local concerts, talks, marches. The club was only up the road from where I lived, but that road widened as I approached it and showed me so very much: mixing with people who made art, made music, made time to talk, made all the difference, made me. Absolutely no straight lines.

References

Duffy, Kevin. 1997. *Mothers: The Home of Good Sounds 1968–1971*. Birmingham City Council, Department of Leisure and Community Services.
Townshend, Pete. 2015. 'Uncanny Masterpiece'. *Vinyl Connection*. https://vinylconnection.com.au/2015/01/02/uncanny-masterpiece/
Young, Graham. 2015. 'Remembering Mothers Rock Club – "the best club in Britain"'. *Birmingham Mail*. https://www.birminghammail.co.uk/whats-on/music-nightlife-news/remembering-mothers-rock-club---8673162

Author biography

Originally from Birmingham, **Alan Smith** initially trained as an art teacher, subsequently working in education for fourteen years in secondary and special schools in Essex and West Yorkshire before moving on to Higher Education advisory work with both the Open and Leeds Metropolitan University. He gained his doctorate in 2019 with a study looking at the darker stories of Thomas Hardy and creating a series of scripts intended for a TV mini-series.

22 Music Spaces and Music Memory

Anna Elias

Music has the power to reach people unlike anything else. It can reach the parts of us we often keep hidden: our emotional core, our spirit, our soul. Music is food for our senses. It transports us back to a time, a place, or the space in which we experienced it.

From playing gigs in pubs to playing music in care homes, and more recently, in a hospice setting, I have seen the ways in which music can positively impact memory and how, in this coming together of people, magic really happens. Our music memory can be relatively spared by syndromes such as dementia. There are certain songs we may hear that can trigger personal memories in which we may be able to recall quite precisely the time of year, the clothes we were wearing, who we were with, the feelings the music originally evoked or a music venue we may have been in. For many of us, these memories connect with the wider story of our lives and how we connect to other people.

My own experiences with music have taken me on an interesting path. While this hasn't been a linear journey, I can now see how the threads have all converged. I can honestly say that seeing someone with dementia finding peace when connecting to a piece of music, and the associated memory, is something I will always treasure. In this intimate moment lies true connection. It is something almost spiritual. This effect of music is something I'm personally familiar with; those moments whilst I was performing on a stage also had these transcendent qualities. Unspoken connections were made between the audience and us with any sense of separation evaporating as the performance progressed. The sound or the song would offer an escape from the mundane or perhaps open a doorway into the emotions and personal memories of all present.

I only have to close my eyes and listen to one of the songs I wrote with my teenage friend, and I'm transported back to the city of Leeds. Back to a pub and music venue named the Duchess of York on Vicar Lane. There we are, wearing cherry-red Doc Marten boots and singing on a stage, looking out on a darkened room of people who had gathered to hear and experience live music. Sadly, The Duchess is now a Hugo Boss shop (perhaps not sadly for some). However, there is a hidden history where this designer shop now sits. Instead of people buying designer suits, there were folk going to this mainstay northern gig venue to watch iconic bands like Nirvana, Pulp, Blur and Coldplay. While we may have only been a support act, it was a special time in music. Our band, Bodixa (as we pronounced it) was named after the queen of the British Iceni tribe who led a revolt against the Romans in 61 AD. A name which conjured up all sorts of images. So, there we would stand, as our own warrior queens on a sticky stage in The Duchess, the lights and cigarette smoke circling the room. There was intense quiet before our first song and then our sound proudly filled the space, our bodies full of the rush of adrenaline, the sparks of energy passing from person to person and the sense of sharing something that we had created. These memories leave me with a warm feeling but there was a darker side to the music industry, too. In retrospect, I can now clearly see how we were very much writing and performing music at a time, and within an industry, still ingrained with sexism. 'Fronted by two females' was often the local journalist's subheading under our name. This somehow made us different, quirky or 'a selling point' and highlighted in some ironic way just how misogynistic the industry was.

We were always welcomed at The Duchess and other Leeds music venues. We played at The Cockpit, Joseph's Well and then, after playing more support gigs, we had the opportunity to play at Leeds University and the City Varieties. As we started to gain respect on the local gig circuit, opportunities began to present themselves. I remember us all being a bundle of nerves and excitement travelling down to the big smoke to play on BBC Radio 6 followed by a showcase gig for representatives from the music industry. A publishing deal was on the table for us. We were enjoying playing music together and had a university tour under our belts with standout gigs including Teesside and Aberystwyth universities. We also had a support tour playing small theatre venues to look forward to: Manchester's Lowry and Brighton's Komedia were amongst these special opportunities.

While I can't recall all our gigs, there are some performances I can revisit in my mind as if they happened yesterday. The Acoustic Stage at Glastonbury Festival 2004 was one of them. The lead-up to this festival was pure joy for us as a band. We all felt proud to have been handpicked by Michael Eavis himself. I remember feeling a heady mix of no sleep and adrenaline circulating around my body as we were introduced and walked out. I had imagined a much smaller stage and a much smaller tent but after the pre first song tension we began to feel at home. The rain started to fall and weary festival goers came in looking for shelter. There was a moment in the performance when we were so lost in the music that we forgot where we were or that there was even an audience in front of us. These moments make up some of my own special memories because they remind me how music can create a 'flow state'.[1] This is a full immersion and presence, whether in the act of making music, performing or listening to it. The flow state would sometimes manifest itself in the writing process, but more often it was on the stage, blinded by lights and immersed in connecting with the emotions of the song. I found music such an honest and raw outlet for what I often kept hidden. I often found it hard to be vulnerable and honest with people in person but was able to explore this side of myself in words and through music. It was as if writing somehow released my consciousness, and through it I could piece together meaning. Perhaps this is what I wanted to explore through performing our songs, to help others connect to these parts of themselves for which they too may need an outlet.

I think my journey into working with people who also find music a helpful outlet or way of connecting with deeper emotions is by no means a coincidence. It is interesting hearing people telling their own venue stories of the night that they heard their favourite musician play, as often the place and the memory are connected in some way. I only have to listen to the band Elbow, and I can see Guy Garvey sat outside Manchester's Night and Day Café before a gig and then hearing the spinetingling 'New Born' for the first time in a venue that felt like it was birthing creative genius. It was a down-to-earth venue for gathering artists and musicians and a place in which creativity was exploding. To have been part of this creative growth for music and venues was really exciting. Looking back now from our globally connected world to the late 1990s, the difference is stark. This was a period of less global connectivity, when bands were just discovering MySpace and were still just on the cusp of being able to share with a swipe or go virtually live. It really was a special time and venues were the dominant platform for emerging talent.

After gaining a first-class honours degree in Arts Education from the University of Leeds, I became interested in the ways in which music, creativity and the arts can be taken into places and spaces and communities that otherwise would have no access to them. I started to deliver outreach sessions within day service settings. Taking music into these venues has been a huge learning experience. Working with people with different forms of dementia, and those with learning needs, and seeing the impact music can have on well-being and memory function is both fascinating and rewarding. Health and social care settings are starting to make this a part of their well-being programmes, and

---

1. For discussion of a 'flow state', see Csikszentmihalyi (1988; 1991).

there are rising numbers of singing for the brain groups popping up all over the country. There is a body of scientific evidence that, while medication may be able to reduce and manage symptoms of Alzheimer's disease, other therapies can be equally as effective when it comes to care planning and a holistic approach to the person and the disease.

My personal experiences have all supported this evidence. Pre-pandemic I was going into a day centre for the elderly in Nottinghamshire on a weekly basis. This day centre had a wonderful atmosphere, and you could tell that staff and service users genuinely wanted to be there. I got to know the staff including those in admin and the minibus drivers. I started to feel part of this community. Just as people had gathered at gigs back in my previous life, here too was a sense of coming together. I learnt so much about the everyday impact of living with different types of dementia, about the importance of living within those memories that can be recalled, and how this can allow an individual to feel safe. This in turn led to reading that revealed how music can reduce levels of the cortisol hormone and therefore decrease anxiety, stress, and agitation in a person.

I remember after a few weeks of leading music sessions at this day service, when packing up my music gear and taking it out to the car, that the minibus driver came to have a word with me. He told me that they had been having real problems trying to help one service user when it came to leaving the day service because her agitation and anxiety levels were sky high. However, he had noticed a huge difference after the music sessions. He said, 'She's just so much calmer after your music sessions. No problems at all on the way home'. Little did this driver realise that what he had observed supported years of research into the positive impacts of music and dementia. I drove away that day with a similar rush of adrenaline as I once did waiting in the wings to go on stage.

On my journey home I thought about the venues I had found myself in over the years. These music spaces were never just pubs for eating and drinking in; they offered a platform for creative expression, a meeting point for ideas and inspiration, gathering places for escapes from the everyday and where connections, memories and music were constantly being recycled. When we envisage care settings, perhaps our minds picture a group of elderly folk sitting in chairs playing bingo. They are much more than this. It is important to challenge such notions to allow more creative visions for these kinds of spaces to emerge. These venues can also be places of creativity and inspiration. They are places where memories can be explored and connections made.

When I tell people I also work at a hospice, their reactions are quite similar. The myth that hospices are simply places where you go to die needs challenging and replacing. They offer much wider services. Within the day therapy setting, there is a real awareness of human suffering but there is also joy and living for each day. My own understanding of the hospice environment has been challenged, too. There has been more laughter in this space than I could ever have imagined. There have also been some profound moments of connection for patients when memories have been recalled, relived and explored with the help of music. For some patients, certain pieces of music can trigger painful memories as they may recall a person they have lost or a time that they wish they could revisit. This time together creates a space for storytelling, for personal reflection and a sense of togetherness and gathering. For some patients, the hospice space is their lifeline, their community, their break from crippling loneliness and isolation. I think that throughout the Covid-19 pandemic we've all been reminded of our common humanity and perhaps not to take our health and well-being for granted. We have also become more aware of isolation.

Through not being able to access certain places and venues, we have realised their value and importance. When care facilities were forced to close their doors across the UK during the pandemic it exposed a previously hidden crisis. There were folks dying from social isolation. It was during the pandemic that the importance of these settings became increasingly evident. Venues, pubs, care homes, day centres, hospices, all these gathering places are so much more than just their name and a supposed function. They are a holding place, a safe place, spaces for creativity, for ideas and, more than anything, they are spaces for lives to come together and exist.

References

Csikszentmihalyi, Mihaly. 1988. 'The flow experience and its significance for human psychology'. In *Optimal Experience: Psychological Studies of Flow in Consciousness*, ed. Mihaly Csikszentmihalyi and Isabella Selega Csikszentmihalyi, 3–35. Cambridge: Cambridge University Press.

Csikszentmihalyi, Mihaly. 1991. *Flow: The Psychology of Optimal Experience*. New York: Harper Perennial.

Author biography

Anna Elias has a musical background which includes being in Leeds band Bodixa in the 1990s and the folk collective Anna Elias & the Forlorn Hope from 2008–2011. Following a degree in Arts Education from the University of Leeds in 2006, Anna went on to explore performing arts in the community. This led to a career in music and drama therapy where she works alongside people with learning disabilities and within elderly care settings.

23 Glitter, Rubber Ducks, and Dinghies: The Georgian Theatre and the Teesside Gigging Community in the Early 2010s

Amy McCarthy

It is Monday evening, early spring, in Stockton-on-Tees. My leather jacket is not protecting me from the bitterness of the northern air, nor is it making me appear cool and edgy. It is almost 8pm and I head down a urine-smelling alleyway off Stockton's deserted high street. The cracks in the pavement stones glow a variety of colours, illuminating the darkness. The LED neon lights act as a runway between the refurbished yet impoverished high street and a quaint Georgian courtyard. It is hard to believe these two worlds exist so close together. The Green Dragon Yard is a mythical land and a distant memory of a Georgian-era North East, which is slowly being eaten up by urbanisation.

In this courtyard is a small music venue called the Green Room, run by Tees Music Alliance, and that is where I am heading this evening. On weeknights and weekends, I rotate between working the box office or behind the bar for the various gigs the venue puts on. The Green Room's other purpose is to act as a recording space and practice room for bands in the Teesside area. The basement is like a bunker where various indie and alternative musicians workshop new songs and rehearse gig material. Indie, punk and psychedelic sounds wind their way up from the basement into the ground-floor foyer, and also into my teenage playlists.

Tonight, the venue has only one room open—the actual green room itself. The space holds approximately sixty people and could easily be mistaken for a living room. There is a tiny bar tucked away in the corner selling cans, and fairy lights covering every possible surface. The dimly lit room feels like an indie wonderland. The usual sofas in the middle of the space have been pushed to the corners of the room or hidden away behind the scenes. The walls are crammed with signed old gig posters, photos from past events at the venue, and the odd black-and-white photograph from the area before it was a venue. Each picture is in an antique-looking frame like the photo wall in a family home. Looking at the photos on the walls, I see artists I would never expect to visit Teesside posing after a sweaty gig. Bands and musicians I had previously seen at local festivals Stockton Calling and Stockton Weekender make up the museum of Teesside music history. The history of the venue and the local scene is everywhere, and the space almost doubles up as a museum of Teesside.

An A-board outside of the venue indicates a man named Bob is playing tonight but it is hard to know what to expect. Over the last couple of months, posters have circulated the pubs and dives of Teesside depicting a mystery figure. Doc Browns, the Princess Alice, and the various takeaway shops have this figure plastered across their walls. The poster shows a headless man on a deserted road facing away from the camera. He wears a purple jumpsuit and is clasping a guitar by the neck with his left hand. In his right hand is a slide bar. It is difficult to determine what genre of music he is playing, if he is a solo artist or a band. Judging by the Route 66 feel of the poster, he might be American. However, he could also be local as many indie bands have embraced the Americana aesthetic. Compared to the other gig posters stuck to the walls of Teesside's indie venues, this one stands out. Other posters show a group of long-haired moody boys, or a man and woman folk duo, or hardcore punks, but it is hard to make clear assumptions with Bob's poster. For weeks, my colleagues talk eagerly about this gig, but who exactly is Bob Log III? Luckily, I am scheduled to work on the box office this evening so I can find out.

At 8:30pm, approximately fifty people are squashed together like sardines facing the empty stage, waiting for the twitch of the backstage curtains. The room is full of maturing hipsters and gigging old-timers. The Green Room veterans – the middle-aged men with obscure band t-shirts and greying stubble – are here to show their support for the venue. No matter who is performing or what type of music is playing, they will be here. The audience is split in two: those who drink Newcastle Brown and those who drink Red Stripe. The younger hipster crowd drink their way through their lukewarm cans of lager whereas the older crowd stick to ale.

To have this many people already in the room is unusual. Everyone knows it is cool to arrive fashionably late to a gig. The venue regulars know the drill. The act will come through the black curtain, leading from the small backstage area, from the right-hand side of the stage. The crowd will cheer, and the musician will begin their set. Tonight, however, we are not graced with that sense of familiarity. We all want to know who the mystery person in the gig poster is. They could be in the crowd with us, or they could be the person we passed in the alleyway smoking a cigarette.

At 9pm, the lights go down. The stage is illuminated by a soft glow of light. The purple trees artfully painted on the wall behind the stage are mesmerising. However, the scene is uninterrupted. The stage remains silent. The backstage curtains do not move. After a couple of minutes, which feels like hours in gig time, people in the crowd exchange confused looks wondering what is happening.

Noise can be heard from the back of the audience; a figure in a velvet jumpsuit and glittery motorbike helmet is crowd surfing towards the stage on an inflatable dinghy. Heads are crushed and people are startled by the unorthodox entry. The chaos of the moment is incredibly entertaining. Crowd surfing would be expected during an encore or just before the big finish, but we are starting this gig at the end. Wading through a sea of people, the dinghy is eventually lowered to the front of the stage. The figure gets out of the boat and stands up to face the audience. He lifts his fist up in the air and the crowd cheers. In front of us is Bob Log III: a one-man blues band. This is the Church of Bob.

The motorbike helmet resembles a TV screen on standby. The dimness of the room makes it hard to construct a face behind the tinted glass. Upon closer inspection of the figure on the stage, an analogue telephone can be found attached to the side of the helmet. Bob towers over us and then takes a seat in the centre of the stage. Strapping a drum to his back, a harmonica to his neck and a pedal to his foot, Bob grabs his guitar and is ready to play his first song.

The first impression of Bob is difficult to describe. Trying to recollect how the songs go is near impossible. The experience is a sensory overload but in the best way possible. One man manages to make so much noise and play so many instruments at once that it is impossible to tell if he misses a beat or not. Time ceases to make sense as one song merges into another and everyone gradually becomes more drunk and in love with this surreal experience. The unpredictability of the night, the disorienting sounds and the absurdity of the performance feel like a postmodern art piece rather than a typical rock gig. The crowd is full of stunned faces. Groups of people look at each other and acknowledge the strangeness of this collective experience. No one would believe what we have seen. We only have each other.

After a few songs, Bob pauses to address the audience. The microphone inside his helmet distorts his voice and it is hard to tell how old he is or what he really sounds like. Who he is does not matter, although we all want to know. In any case, he has not stopped playing to deliver a press conference to answer our questions. He has stopped to inform us that this is an interactive concert. The audience have not entered the Green Room to be passive consumers of music: we all play a key part in the delivery of this piece.

Bob asks the audience to blow up some balloons. A pack of balloons is placed at the corner of the stage and a couple of audience members volunteer to pass out the contents of the bag. Everyone who is able to blow up a balloon does so whilst Bob plays his guitar. Once the sacks of carbon dioxide are tied, they are placed as close to Bob's feet as possible. Suddenly there is a bang and the tone of the song shifts. The balloons placed on the stage are now creating the drumbeat for the track. It lacks a beat or any sequence, but the song somehow feels like the airbags delicately rolling on the stage are specifically written into the piece.

Next, Bob asks people to climb on the stage and sit on his knee while he plays. Several drunken people ascend onto the stage and politely queue to sit on Bob's lap for five seconds. The music still flows as Bob balances two fully grown adults on each knee like a busy department store Santa Claus on an LSD trip. The men and women on Bob's lap do not contribute to the music. If anything, they make playing more difficult. There is no logical reason why these people need to sit on his lap but in the context of the gig it just makes sense.

Mid-way through the gig, members of the audience place alcoholic drinks onto the stage like an offering to the gods. Bob accepts these gifts and drinks the array of alcohol that graces the stage. Some are half-drunk pints and others are freshly bought for the man himself. Bob raises his glass to cheer the audience before spinning around on his chair to lift his helmet and take a sip. With his back to most of the crowd, he still only partially lifts his helmet to have a drink. Bob is like a superhero, lifting a portion of his mask but revealing nothing else. Eagle-eyed watchers at the corner of the stage may see a glimpse of a jawline but there is no way to determine who Bob Log is.

At 10pm I close the box office. No one else will be entering the venue now but I keep an eye on the door just in case. I stand at the back of the room leaning against the wall. Bob lunges off the stage and plays his blues sonic tunes from his electric guitar into the face of any bystander. He works his way towards me and momentarily I am in front of our leader, ready to be converted to this new religion. We are but disciples and once our saviour leaves, we must preach his word. As I stand in awe of the gangly figure in front of me, he exits the room and makes his way into the foyer and up the stairs. A band of loyal followers tail Bob into the men's bathroom. Although I don't follow him, that is the only unlocked room he could possibly enter. A few minutes later, he descends the stairs and exits the building to serenade the streets of

Stockton. He is quickly brought back inside before there is a noise complaint, but this gig is like no other. An acid-trip experience told through music and one man alone.

Over the next couple of years, the gospel according to Bob spreads across Teesside. At gigs across the local area, people mention seeing Bob Log at the Green Room. To be in the know is to be in an exclusive club and to be in on a secret. This gig becomes a local urban legend.

A year on from this legendary gig, Bob returns to the Green Room to a sold-out show and people are begging to be let in at the door. Luckily, I am working the box office again, so I have a free ticket for the headlining act. The room is so full that I struggle to see above the many heads facing the stage and end up standing on some empty beer crates behind the sound desk. A hyperactive, electric buzz fills the room as Bob is back with his old tricks. This time we know what to expect: the dinghy, the audience participation, the chaos, and we love every moment of it.

A couple of months after the second Bob Log gig, I leave Teesside and move to York for university. Although my life moves me away from my hometown, I return to the promised land for one night only just to be graced by Bob Log's presence. In 2015, Bob has upgraded to the Green Room's sister venue, the Georgian Theatre. The Georgian Theatre holds 200 gig attendees and is a Grade II Listed building. The key features of the venue are its sticky floors, dark red walls and the staircase leading to the bathrooms that everyone would successfully slip down at some point in the night. Spilt alcohol from every past gig soak into the floors and walls leaving a distinct smell of stale beer. This feels like an epic return, and I crave that familiarity and nostalgia of a space that was home to my late teen years. A lot of faces in the room are the same as last time: hungry for more. Some newcomers also join, my dad being one of them, to witness this surreal and unforgettable experience. The velvet suit is a deep purple. The helmet sparkles like a disco ball. Bob is back. The crowd are ready to enjoy a previously lived experience. However, they are wrong. This is a remix.

The quirky elements from Bob's previous gig – such as popping balloons as a substitute for a drum kit and crowd members sitting on Bob's knees as he plays – all make a guest appearance, but this time Bob has stepped it up a bit. This time we are taking communion. Bob lifts an inflatable bowl shaped like a rubber duck and a plastic dog bowl to the audience. He places them on the altar (or the front of the stage) and pours a label-less bottle of alcohol into the round surfaces. Two men volunteer themselves as altar boys grabbing each of the booze-filled plastic objects and take the first sips to christen the bowls. The inflatable duck is passed to the left and the dog bowl to the right.

The audience unite as they all share sips of what we are told is champagne. The rubber duck looks difficult to drink from, so I am thankful to be passed the dog bowl. The alcohol tastes cheap and I try not to think of the amount of other people's spit with which it is potentially mixed. If you did not feel like you were a part of a community before, you definitely do now.

As the night draws to a close, the old-timers are waiting for the grand finale: Bob crowd surfing on his inflatable dinghy. Although the electric energy is here, the crowd does not fill out the room. As Bob descends the stage with his dinghy, a sea of people forms at the foot of the stage to support the weight of Bob and his boat for smooth sailing. A group of ten to twenty attendees carry Bob and walk laps around the room until, eventually, safely transporting him back to the stage. The music lingers on as Bob faces us all before exiting stage left.

Since leaving Teesside, I moved to York, then to Sheffield, then back to York again. I have gone on to see Bob Log play five times. Three times in Stockton and twice in Sheffield at Corporation and Plug. Some of my memories may have merged and shifted. My timeline of events may not be 100 per cent accurate, but my feelings and recollection of the weird events are all clear and unwavering. I remember nothing of the setlist, or the names of the songs, or even the words. I have not even listened to his music outside of his gigs, but I will actively travel across the country to stand in a sweaty room for two hours and experience his bizarre show. What I remember from these gigs is the space and sense of community. I remember the purple trees painted on the wall like a fairy wonderland and the walls filled with pictures of gigs of the recent past. I remember the sticky floors of the Georgian Theatre and the red and black walls making the place always feel like night-time no matter what time of day it is. I remember the familiar faces from work, walking around town or at other gigs. Despite seeing Bob play at other venues and in other cities, when I think of Bob Log gigs I think of the Green Room in Stockton-on-Tees. I think of being seventeen or eighteen and wearing a leather jacket from ASDA every time I went to a gig. I think of Teesside.

Under a Conservative government, Teesside has seen significant cuts in the arts, losing community festivals such as Middlesbrough Music Live. Teesside is not known for its large venues or O2 academies; they simply do not exist. With the arena venues up in Newcastle and Sunderland (although they rarely make many bands' tour dates because the North does not exist beyond Leeds or Manchester, apparently), the rest of the North East relies on independent venues, local acts and cover bands for entertainment. The loss of independent venues would be a loss of character in the British music scene. Independent venues are embedded into their local culture. The Brudenell Social Club in

Leeds, The Cluny in Newcastle, and (I would argue) the Westgarth Social Club in Middlesbrough define the music scenes of their respective cities. It would be easy to think that to enjoy live music, you need to leave Teesside. That is far from the truth. People do not come here for the big acts; they are here for some mid-week escapism – whether that be to see some North East legends, new-risers, or a weird American one-man band.

The landscape of the Georgian Theatre has changed over the years since Bob first visited. The dark alleyway has transformed into an independent quarter with micropubs and outdoor seating. The Georgian has also had a refurb, with a brand-new family-friendly bar. The space has become more welcoming to the wider community. After years of austerity and cuts to the arts, places like Stockton need these spaces for their communities to thrive. Watching the landscape change over the years has been heart-warming and the venues have thrived.

Tees Music Alliance is a not-for-profit organisation and the cornerstone of Teesside's live music scene. The Covid-19 pandemic posed a threat to independent live music venues, and many were lost or on the brink of closure. The Georgian Theatre and its sister venue the Green Room are run by the charity organisation Tees Music Alliance and, like many independent venues across the country, rely on donations and ticket purchases to keep the venues running. To lose places like the Georgian Theatre and the Green Room would be catastrophic to Teesside. The weird and quirky, the old punk bands, and the new local bands would not have a space within which to gain an audience. It would eliminate the already sparse economy of the independent quarter in Stockton. Seeing strange and unusual acts is what makes the music scene fun. Who knew a man in a glittery motorcycle helmet playing blues music in an inflatable dinghy would be one of my most talked-about gig memories? To find something by chance, which does not depend on major labels or social media, is a special way to create regional collective memory.

Author biography

Amy McCarthy is a PhD student at York St John University (UK), researching indie music memoirs. In 2018, she was the winner of the Wilko Johnson Writing Award. Her personal essays on the Teesside area have been published in the 'zines *The Line Between Two Towns* (2017) and *Fan Club* (2019).

24 The Rock Garden: Conversations with My Dad, a Punk-Rock DJ

Thomas Jackson

For most of the twentieth century Middlesbrough was dominated by industry, specifically steelworks and industrial chemical production. Heavy industry conquered the skyline of much of Teesside, from the towering cranes at the port to the bleak cooling towers billowing out steam across the horizon. Middlesbrough entered the national lexicon as a drab, bleak and downright unpleasant place to visit or live, continuing to this day to feature on clickbait online polls of worst places to live. Inherent in this outsider's view of Middlesbrough is a classism linked to the industrial, working-class identities that built the area. The demographic of Teesside – specifically Middlesbrough, Redcar and Cleveland – has largely gone unchanged for generations. The areas that make up Teesside are predominantly populated with truly working-class people, and a lot with direct personal or family connections to the industrial fabric of the area. In the 1970s, my dad would find his own way to the beating heart of the Teesside industry, working for British Steel as a metallurgist for the next forty years until his retirement in 2010. In speaking with him about his experience DJing in the 1970s and 1980s, I wanted to consider the important role that the hidden histories of oral family archives play in offering, as Tony Whyton argues, an 'alternative [...] past' and one that 'also provides added layers of complexity to the historicising process' (2018: 1–2).

Alongside this dominating industrial identity, Middlesbrough had and continues to have a febrile and diverse creative scene. Music is littered with many of Teesside's prodigal sons and daughters, from globally recognised rock bands to emerging indie talents. Middlesbrough has a long tradition of producing recognisable music talent. International metal behemoth David Coverdale founded Whitesnake in the town. In the late 1970s, Teesside native Chris Rea would go on to sell 30 million records worldwide. Paul Rodgers would go on to front Free, Bad Company and for a short stint as the front man for the post-Freddie Mercury Queen. Billingham-born Paul Smith would front Maximo Park during the height of the 2000s indie rock scene. Growing up in Middlesbrough in the early 2000s, Evelyn Halls would go on to co-front the emerging Liverpool indie band Clean Cut Kid.

Live music is a cornerstone of my family's collective identity; it binds the generations together. The love of all things musical and a recognition of the foundational and influencing impact that live music has had upon us all is a permanent topic of conversation; from first gigs to latest gigs, to the all-important best gigs. We are a family of music lovers. Our love and adoration for music, especially live music, can be put squarely at the feet of my dad – Ian Jackson. Born in 1952 in Middlesbrough, my dad grew up during some of the most exciting and diverse eras for music. Travelling the North East during the 1960s and 1970s in search of new music, my dad racked up a dizzying collection of ripped ticket stubs, local band merchandise and, importantly, an extensive vinyl collection.

In speaking with my dad about his time DJing in a hard rock nightclub, I am aware of the importance of hidden microhistories and the role they play in developing the richness of an understood narrative. The music of the 1970s is a much researched and written-about era; however, the role that the North East played, and specifically, Middlesbrough, is mostly absent from the established history. As George Lipsitz argues, there is a need to examine the 'alternative archives of history, the shared memories, experiences and aspirations of ordinary people, whose perspectives rarely appear in formal archives' (2007: xi). In discussing this period of my dad's life, an 'alternative' history begins to emerge and one that details the aspirations of an ordinary working-class man who played his own part in the story of punk rock.

The music scene in Middlesbrough has always tipped in favour of heavier, counter-cultural genres and yet independent venues that catered to these musical outputs have been few and far between. However, for heavy metal and specifically punk rock music, one venue dominated the scene not only in Middlesbrough but arguably the wider North-East area during the 1970s. Built in 1913 as the Pavilion Theatre, this modest building has had many different identities and fulfilled many different functions across the generations, with all interactions being intrinsically linked to entertainment and performance. By 1976 the venue reopened under its most enduring and culturally significant name: the Rock Garden. Located on Newport Road, on the outskirts of Middlesbrough town centre, the unassuming, squat rectangular building gave very little away from the roadside. Inside, however, it was a truly independent local music venue, complete with bierkeller-style seating, beer-soaked sticky floors, and the all-important DJ podium.

In its earliest days, the Rock Garden hosted some of the largest and most famous rock and punk bands on the scene including The Scorpions, Iron Maiden, Def Leppard, The Clash, The Stranglers, The Dammed and Tom Robinson. Most famously, in August 1977, under a cloud of suspicion, the Sex Pistols performed to a sold-out audience under the pseudonym Acne Rabble. Due to their perceived threat to decency, decorum, and local sensibilities, councils across the country had placed a moratorium on the Sex Pistols playing music at live music venues. To circumvent these restrictions, and to avoid small independent venues from having their licences revoked by irked officials, the band performed a series of gigs across the UK under different pseudonyms, which would knowingly be dropped into their printed interviews for eager fans to pick up on and look out for in the coming weeks. Importantly, the Sex Pistols shunned the larger music cities, opting instead for small provincial locations like Middlesbrough and Doncaster as the venues for their tour of clandestine gigs.

By 1978, the Rock Garden was a huge success in the local music scene and regularly saw crowds of local teenagers and young adults flock to see bands. The teenage music scene dominated this small town-centre venue. Split into two separate venues, the Rock Garden and The Marimba occupied the same small building on the Newport Road. The two clubs catered for the different tastes of their audiences. As a former music hall, the building's size and former uses naturally allowed for a two-venue approach that brought in punters from every corner of Teesside. In 1978, the manager and DJ from the upstairs nightclub The Marimba, Ian Lister, had taken over managing the Rock Garden from its former foreman Alan Morris who had left to become Chris Rea's tour manager. Alongside managing the venue and booking bands, Lister would also man the DJ podium. After religiously visiting the venue every weekend as a punter, one evening my dad (ever curious about technology) asked Ian Lister how the DJ equipment worked. As a trained scientist, my dad was and continues to be technology obsessed and never more so than with musical gadgets. As a regular attendee, he would watch the resident DJ cycle through a stack of LPs, fading The Damned into The Clash and watching with anticipation as he queued up the next track. It was nothing more than sheer curiosity that motivated him on that evening to approach Ian and ask for a quick demo. Out of that curiosity came an opportunity and this period in my dad's life became the stuff of legend.

The friendship that resulted from my dad's curiosity afforded him an enviable place within the running of the Rock Garden, being called upon in times of need to jump into Ian's shoes and take over the decks. The demos and frequent conversations allowed him to draw on the stacks of vinyl and queue and fade in to the newest and most exciting music at the time. Over time, Ian Lister's need to manage the bar or to pay off bolshy and unpredictable bands would take him away from the decks, and quickly my dad went on to become the primary DJ and co-manager of his favourite local venue.

In reflecting on this period with my dad – which stretches for only around four years – it became apparent that his new role was more important than I had first acknowledged. Not only did it provide a much-needed additional income in a turbulent period of time in the North East, but it also offered an insight into an Ian Jackson I had never seen before. An unassuming, quiet and reserved man from a typical Teesside background, my dad recalled moments from his days at the Rock Garden that stands almost antipodal to the image I and my family have of him: from rubbing shoulders with some of the biggest musicians at the time to his one act of anarchic punk-vandalism where he plastered a passing Bob Geldof in promotional stickers for the Rock Garden. In discussing his time at the venue, my dad recalled with excitement how his role at the Rock Garden soon began to stretch outside the limits of its Middlesbrough location. In time, my dad would accompany Ian Lister to the biggest venues in London to scout out new and emerging talent for the Rock Garden and they managed to secure some of the largest punk and heavy metal bands at the time.

This remembering of the past ultimately constitutes a hidden history of a period of time in the North East where my dad's club played a key role in the growth of an entire music scene. As Tony Whyton argues, 'hidden histories [...] don't always form part of official narratives [but] can breathe new life into established discourses' and force a collective discussion on the 'connection between individuals and collectives, the past and the present, and the local and global' (2018: 8). My dad's narrative, like countless others like it, does not contribute to the official narratives of the time, but they are no less important or illuminating. For venues like the Rock Garden and for individual contributors like my dad, they forged a direct relationship with not only the local scene but the wider national one as well.

Throughout my childhood, I was surrounded by the paraphernalia and ephemera of a former punk rock DJ. Cupboards were full of vinyl records – stacked in battered Schweppes lemonade crates borrowed from the Rock Garden – and black leatherette boxes held my dad's prized punk singles, sleeves emblazoned with angular writing and song titles like 'Too Drunk to Fuck' which were quickly moved out of sight. Kept in the loft, away from prying eyes and the fingers of his three children, one by one we would all discover this treasure trove. As I became older, and my interest in my parents' musical legacies grew, the vinyl records would be ceremoniously brought down from the loft and placed in the living room where my mam and dad would slowly reminisce over long-forgotten banks. My parents would load them onto the Hi-Fi and sit pensively as they played with all the pops and fizzles, the battle scars of vinyl that have seen real use.

Also hidden away in a wardrobe is a battered *Quality Street* tin filled with homemade, slightly rusting, metal pin badges from bands long since dissolved. A mixture of graphics and stylised lettering provided a snapshot of the bands that graced the stage at the Rock Garden. Having been hidden away out of sight for thirty years, most were in good nick and were prime takings for a young teenager eager to plaster his backpack in names of obscure punk bands. Grabbing a handful of the brightest coloured badges, I would beaver away attaching them to every inch of my bag ready for my next day at school. In a time in which heavy metal, post-punk and emo music was looked down on with derision and at times aggression, these badges, though only loosely linked to the music that filled my ears, ensured that I was firmly identifiable as one of the out-crowd. In talking to my dad about his missing badges, he remembered his pride at seeing his son cutting through the school crowd wearing the badges that he'd worn back when they were still shiny and bright.

Our family stories were full of the icons of 1970s popular culture. Noddy Holder and the members of Slade stormed my dad's tiny office looking for a £1,000 payment in cash. Motörhead brought the biggest sound rig the venue had ever seen and will forever hold the title as the loudest band to play the Rock Garden. A Saturday night booking resulted in a sold-out and expectant audience who believed that Sham 69 had followed the Sex Pistol's suit and were performing under a pseudonym, only to have their dreams dashed when the Gotham City Swing band turned out to be a young and obscure punk band from London. A very young Scottish band, The Skids, ran riot around the empty club post-sound check having a water-pistol fight, soaking the stage and much of the venue. But in the pantheon of family stories, above them all is the well-worn tale of how the Rock Garden was the meeting place of my parents. My mam, Carol, was the manager of the HMV music store in Middlesbrough town centre. Obsessed with music herself, she became my dad's sole purveyor of new and exciting tunes. Her daily conversations with record labels put her firmly in the know with new and emerging music which she would pass on to my dad to play at the biggest and most important rock music venue in the area.

As the DJ, my dad was afforded a unique and enviable position – he could watch. He watched his friends and patrons lose themselves in the music, pogoing to fast drumbeats in the cramped and hot venue. He watched some of the biggest bands of the era tearing it up on a small stage in his hometown. He watched as members of the punk counterculture came together under the roof of the Rock Garden to shake off the work week and simply enjoy themselves. In that moment they were able to put aside the pressures of industrial actions, of political dogma and the poverty that continues to plague the area. In that moment they were allowed to just have fun, during a time in the North East where fun was for some a real luxury. Speaking about those heady times in the late 1970s, he remembers how factions of the alternative music scene would come together for the sake of a shared interest in new music; hostilities put aside for an evening.

For a town like Middlesbrough, dominated by hard-working, lower-working-class men and women, the Rock Garden was as much an important cultural space as it was simply a safe space for teens and young adults to come together over a much-maligned and misunderstood genre of music. For my dad and his friends, the Friday night rock nights and the Saturday punk nights were an important opportunity for a coming together over music in a town in which work was hard to come by (and what work there was, was often manual and intense). Dominated by the blast furnaces and cooling towers of what was then British Steel, Middlesbrough's industrial might was founded on the manual exertions of young working-class men. However, on 2 January 1980, workers at the Teesside beam mill would go on a thirteen-week strike over pay disputes. Recalling this long period of industrial action, my dad noted the lasting effect these strikes had on the surrounding areas that relied upon the wages of those metal workers.

The patrons who religiously attended the punk nights on a Saturday were from all over the wider Teesside area and were ultimately drawn by an exciting night of music, drinking and dancing that promised to take them away from the despair they felt. Punks from Stockton-on-Tees, Billingham, and Hartlepool would jump in cars, on buses and trains to fill the 300-capacity venue. Due to the demographic of the local area, those adherents to counter cultures were often met with suspicion, derision, and hostility from the older members of the area, confused and distrusting of these colourful and anarchic teenagers. The Rock Garden served as a safe space for self-expression, for discussion and for making friends. The Rock Garden was a beacon of hope for my dad during these difficult times. Working for British Steel, he too was forced to strike for sixteen weeks during which his only source of income came from his part-time DJing and management work. The Rock Garden kept him afloat.

Sadly, this would all end too soon in 1981 when an increasingly volatile, violent, and racist crowd led to falling revenue. In its final years as a rock venue, local National Front skinhead groups managed to infiltrate the crowds at gigs, much less interested in the music and much more focused on antagonising New Romantics and teenage punks looking for a good time. Violence quickly became a common occurrence and police presence a familiar sight. By 1981, the then owner Brian Hogg – sick of the violence the skinheads had brought to the venue and unable to make a sufficient profit – made the decision to close the venue for good, much to the sadness and disappointment of my dad and the loyal punters that had stuck with the Rock Garden. Sadly, due to the change in demographic, much of the regular crowd had drifted off to other venues that had opened in the intervening years, and so the closure of the venue happened quickly and with little opposition.

The physical building would go on to claim several more identities over the next thirty years, with most incarnations still catering to music and performance. Its most enduring identity in the mid- to late 1990s – The Arena – saw early performances from Oasis, Arctic Monkeys and The Libertines. Like the former Rock Garden, The Arena once again became the only place for young adults and teenagers to visit to see exciting and diverse music outputs in the town centre. The unassuming venue still drew scores of young music fans well into the 2000s, and by 2007 it became the main nightclub in Middlesbrough for house, dance and trance music.

This important building finally closed in 2018, ceasing to trade as an independent music venue. With nightclubs and venues in the heart of the town dominating the music and evening entertainment scene, this out-of-town venue was transformed one last time into a gym. The final death knell sounded for the building at 210 Newport Road in January 2019 when it was destroyed by a fire. For those who had attended the Rock Garden and The Arena, they had lost both an important cultural landmark and an important part of the history of music in the local area, seemingly forever.

The Rock Garden Revisited

After responding to an online post on social media about the venue, my dad was contacted by a couple of friends and former patrons who expressed their interest in putting on a one-off Rock Garden Revisited celebration night, celebrating the venue thirty years since its closure, to bring back the bands that had long since split up and to reunite friends that had long since moved away. This first Rock Garden Revisited event in September 2010 was a resounding success, with people reconnecting not only with their former friends but with a music genre that had laid dormant in the area. The promoters recognised an appetite for a regular, organised, and marketed punk-rock revival style event and got to work planning the next one.

What was once a single, stand-alone commemorative reunion night has now morphed into a regular weekly alternative music event that moves across various independent venues in Middlesbrough and Teesside. It is my contention that this original reunion event allowed those originally involved in the Rock Garden an opportunity to reengage with personal archives of the time and in doing so established, as George Lipsitz argues, 'a route to the discovery of new insights into specific historical circumstances and cultural contexts' (2007: 9). This event brought a new era of musical remembering and exploration and provided attendees with an opportunity to 'rethink' the 'microhistories' of their own past and in doing so develop and challenge the established narratives of the time (ibid.: 5).

The scope and range of the events have shifted, and the venue now features new and up-and-coming talent alongside older punk-rock bands from the original scene of the 1970s. These punk-rock events continue to have a tangible impact on local music, with bands long since dissolved having reformed and becoming regulars on the bill.

My dad's role in these newer events is more limited than before. While he retains his title as the principal DJ, the process has pivoted to a much less involved, digitised platform. His rig is now a tablet or laptop hooked up to the venue's PA system. Long gone are his Schweppes crates of 45s and the excitement of queuing up the next track, but for him, the draw of live punk rock remains. While his 45s are now digitised tracks, he mans the DJ booths of various local venues and revels in taking requests from people who would have hung around the DJ podium in the Rock Garden, thirty years prior. His knowledge and passion for music continue to grow, and his DJ sets are now more diverse. He is no longer involved in the managerial side, no longer scouting out new talent or booking local bands to play their set. However, he is the only person involved who worked at, managed, played music at, and marketed the original Rock Garden. He, therefore, holds an important role in the legacy and memorialisation of the original venue. As the manager and DJ, my dad saw behind the curtain and has stories that no one else has. And while he may hate to acknowledge it, it is his word that carries the weight of authenticity, it is he and only he that really knew what was going on all those years ago.

These most recent punk-rock events have since dropped the reference to the original Rock Garden, opting to market under their own name. Nonetheless, the reverence local music fans have towards the venue endures. The original reunion event drew people back towards a scene they had largely moved away from; thirty years had passed since they pogoed to UK Subs or The Damned. For those that continue to fill out these weekly punk events in Middlesbrough, there is more at stake than just casual memorialisation and remembrance.

These newer events attract a mixed demographic, a range of ages and identities, yet some of the Rock Garden patrons, now in their fifties and sixties, are still drawn towards a shared enjoyment of music. The original revisited events and these newer incarnations offer something entirely new in the local music scene: a serious approach to local music and a respect for bands that paved the way for some of today's bigger artists. There is a sincerity in the reaching out and booking bands that performed as teenagers back in the late 1970s; these events are not gimmicks or a rose-tinted retrospective of times gone by. Instead, they are a serious, well-intentioned attempt to bring back to the foreground talented, passionate, and authentic local musicians.

In recent years, the local area of Teesside has seen a steep decline in its traditional identity. The blast furnaces and beam mills in Grangetown and Redcar ceased operation, having a knock-on effect across the area. Middlesbrough has and continues to be the butt of many jokes, but what is often overlooked is the region's long creative and musical traditions. Since its re-emergence in 2010, the Rock Garden events continue to happen in some way, shape or form. Now sixty-nine, my dad continues to travel to independent music venues across Middlesbrough on Saturday nights and play the music he originally played back in 1980. The Rock Garden Revisited events spoke directly to a period of local history that, while at times difficult, was arguably more pluralistic and optimistic in terms of its creative output. These and the newer independent events that have spawned from that original idea have given birth to a much-needed creative outlet within the area. My dad's music tastes and awareness of emerging talent have continued to develop as a direct result of these new events and he returns home with the t-shirts, posters and pin-badges of these new acts. Many of the music venues either closed or moved wholly over to catering to the EDM and nightclub markets, creating a void in the local area for venues that specifically catered for and encouraged live music. In ignoring live music, the comradery and friendship that venues like the Rock Garden engendered were missing. With the pandemic wreaking havoc on the independent music scene, the organisers and promoters for the events have worked hard to ensure its survival post-pandemic. Slowly, the Saturday night DJ has returned and my dad is once again standing, holding court in his small DJ booth, watching bands tear up the stage.

For me, the Rock Garden is a post-memory of punk rock. For nearly thirty years, I have lived vicariously through the narratives shared and traded between family members of this renowned music venue. My understanding of punk rock and the music scene in the 1970s is vivid and exciting, filled with pogoing punks, artistic and eccentric New Romantics, aggressive and forbidding skinheads and, at the centre, my dad spinning his records.

References

Lipsitz, George. 2007. *Footsteps in the Dark: The Hidden Histories of Popular Music*. Minnesota: University of Minnesota Press.
Whyton, Tony. 2018. 'Wilkie's story: Dominant histories, hidden musicians, and cosmopolitan connections in jazz'. In *The Routledge Companion to Jazz Studies*, ed. Nicholas Gebhardt, Nichole Rustin-Paschal and Tony Whyton, 3–16. London: Routledge.

Author biography

Thomas Jackson is a PhD student examining gender in contemporary American literature. He is an avid musician, having played the drums and the guitar for several years. He is originally from Middlesbrough but moved to York in 2011. He hails from a musical family, growing up around DJs and record-shop owners.

25 ...for a Girl

Tarryn Watkins

I started my gigging life at Sheffield Arena watching Busted when I was ten years old. I went with my mum. Later that year I went to Leeds Fest and saw The Distillers. This was also with my mum. I don't remember much aside from Brody Dalle telling everyone to throw their beers in the air and the absolute drenching that followed. It was a world that I knew I wanted to be a part of. A world that I knew little about at the ripe old age of ten. Now, at twenty-eight, I'm still trying to figure some things out. Most of the gigging experience is wholesome. Most of it is waiting around for sound checks, grabbing food and drinks and sitting around with the other bands, chatting about things that don't matter; but there is a darker side. A seedy underbelly with sexism at its centre.

***

As soon as we walked into the venue, I could see that I was the only woman in there. Well, me and a painting of Debbie Harry of Blondie outside the women's bathroom door. Her hand on her hips, she was wearing the classic white dress from the *Parallel Lines* era. The pose screamed, 'Take no prisoners, and take no bullshit'. I wish that I felt the same. 'Good, innit?' said my male band mate. It was a good painting, but it made me feel terribly lonely. The guys' bathroom had a painting too. I don't remember who it was though. It didn't matter as much as the Debbie Harry painting. It was just another man to keep the fifteen men already in the building company. And I had somebody's interpretation of Debbie Harry. Nevertheless, I agreed that it was good and went to the loo.

I was at the Fiddlers Elbow in Camden in North London to play with my pop punk band One Way Street. It wasn't our first time gigging out of Yorkshire, but it was our first time gigging in London and didn't we know it! After I'd given myself a little pep talk in the bathroom mirror ('You can do this, don't let them intimidate you'), I went to the bar. My usual drink is a Jack Daniels and Coke. In Yorkshire, a JD and Coke doesn't vary in price too much. It's usually around the £4.50 mark. I expected to pay a bit more for it in the big smoke, but when the bartender said £8.50, I had to scrape my jaw off the floor. I had to pay. He'd already poured it, and I was too polite to ask him for a cheaper drink. I'd just have to drink it very slowly throughout the night. Feeling slightly robbed and quite lonely, I played the gig to a roomful of men and a handful of women.

On the six-hour drive back to Yorkshire, I had time to take in what had just happened. I'd been surrounded by men. You often hear men claiming that there is absolute equality in music. If that was true, where were all the women? It wasn't the first time that had happened either. It was only after the London gig that I'd realised that playing to a roomful of men was a regular occurrence, especially in a male-dominated scene like pop punk. I was usually the only woman on the bill. We're like unicorns. Or a total solar eclipse. A solar eclipse happens every other year or every eighteen months. You can see one depending on where you are in the world. Seeing a woman in a pop punk band is as rare as viewing a total solar eclipse. Try not to look directly at her. Not because you'll go blind (although that's not a guarantee); you'll just freak her out.

The Fiddler's Elbow gig was in 2016. Six years later, I'm still trying my best to prove my place in the Boy's Club. One Way Street was the first all-male band I'd been in and, once I'd left them in late 2017, I began to question everything. Should I wear dresses and make-up on stage? Should I be 'more of a girl'? As far as anatomy is concerned, I couldn't be any more of a girl! Wearing dresses and make-up wouldn't have sent the message I would have wanted it to. It would have been ironic. A metaphoric middle finger that I fear would have been lost on most men. They would have just seen a dress. Not the woman playing bass. Being part of an all-male band in a male-dominated scene was definitely a learning curve as far as gendered experience goes. I didn't realise I'd get treated differently because of my gender when I first started playing bass. I grew up around music and musicians. It didn't occur to me that only a handful of those musicians were women. I didn't know how to combat the inequality I felt. I'm still not entirely sure, but I am working on it. I try to channel Debbie Harry's 'take no prisoners' attitude. It's easier in front of a mirror, to a shampoo bottle, or a pillow when you're on the verge of sleep. I occasionally still find it difficult to stand my ground against men who ignore me, or sexualise me, or laugh at me.

***

'Boys be cool for once in your lives, all girls to the front!' Kathleen Hanna of Bikini Kill shouts this to a sea full of men at one of her shows. Hanna fought for girls to be seen at gigs and in music. She still does. The Riot Grrrl movement started in the tiny, sweaty, underground venues of Olympia, Washington at the start of the 1990s. Feminism, likely, did not start in those same venues in the underbelly of Olympia in the 1990s. I have no evidence for this, but I'm sure it started with the first people on earth. The first time a man told a woman she couldn't do something.

Bikini Kill formed in 1990. Their message was simple: revolution. 'Revolution Grrl Style Nooowwww!' Hanna screams as guitars fill the empty space. The band launches into their song 'Double Dare Ya'. A siren song. Calling for women everywhere to unapologetically claim a space for themselves in the world. It was the start of something big. The early 1990s saw women all over the globe forming bands, starting 'zines, creating safe spaces for each other and calling out crappy behaviour from men.

I was seventeen when I stumbled across a Bikini Kill song on YouTube. It was called 'Rebel Girl'. Now it is instantly recognisable. The second the snare drum comes in you feel like you could kick a door down. It gives you so much power. You can feel it splintering through your veins. It's the amphetamine you need after being told to smile more.

I'd been playing bass for two years when I first heard Bikini Kill. My cheap, knackered purple Benson was really put to the test after I'd discovered Riot Grrrl. I plastered it in stickers. After a while, it got all tacky where some stickers had fallen off. Some had disintegrated due to the amount that I was playing. It ended up looking pretty gross, but I liked that it wasn't a typical 'girly' bass (whatever that means).

***

In July 2017, my ska/punk/genre-hopping band Magnificent Seven had the opportunity to play with one of my dad's favourite bands. Landing the support slot was a dream come true. I'd been listening to the band in question since I was in nappies: my dad's influence. He's really into rock steady, ska and reggae. While I was growing up, my ideal band to be in would involve brass melodies and ska rhythms. Magnificent Seven was everything I wanted it to be: ska structures with a punk edge mixed with hip hop and a whole range of other things.

The gig was at Fibbers in York. Back in 2010, I had my first gig at the old site lovingly known to York locals as 'The Old Fibbers'. This gig, however, was at 'The New Fibbers'. The New Fibbers was one of the largest venues in the city; unfortunately, it has now fallen victim to Covid times and high rent. Capacity must have been somewhere in the hundreds. It could comfortably house a band having a bit of commercial success. It could definitely house a band that had enjoyed a span of at least three decades of worldwide success and a nice local support band. At first, I was so starstruck. We all were. When it was our turn to sound check, a few members of the headline band came to watch us.

When we'd finished running through some of our classics, they clapped and congratulated us on a great sounding set. They said they couldn't wait to see us perform. Beaming, I put my bass fret side down against one of my amps and headed off for the bar. A standard protocol. A pint was around £4.20 here. Not too bad at all. I saw some other Magnificent Seven members go outside with some of the headlining band so I decided to follow them once I'd got my pint. I opened a fire door that led to a long, bright corridor. I walked to the fire door at the end that was being held open with a bucket that people put their cigarette ends in. I sat down next to our saxophonist with my pint; she was happily chatting away to someone from the headline band. After a few swigs of my pint, I introduced myself. 'Hi, I'm Tarryn, I've been listening to your band since I was four!' I blurted out. They laughed, and said they appreciated it. Everyone was lovely! They say never meet your idols, but maybe they were wrong on this occasion.

Soon after, it was just me and one member from the headlining band left outside chatting. He kept commenting on my looks and how pretty he thought I was. It made me feel very uncomfortable. He was much older than me, he was older than my dad. He'd only made comments after everyone had left. Although nothing truly terrible happened, it still made me feel slimy. What should have been one of the best experiences of my life was now tainted by unwanted, unprovoked attention. This was not an isolated incident but rather a prominent part of the music industry. Perhaps the worst part is that I see myself as one of the lucky ones. All the negative encounters I've had haven't been that bad compared to some other women in music. Isn't that terrible?

***

I think there is a subtle difference between going to a gig and playing one as a woman. Whenever I've played a show, no matter the band or venue, I've always felt like I had to be twice as good as my male counterparts in order to gain their approval. Why? I know I don't need their approval, but that doesn't stop me trying to prove myself. My experiences in music are my own, but I'm not the only woman that feels slighted by most men when playing with a band. The odd comment about looks, how I can't play my instrument, that I can play it well 'for a girl', or ignoring me completely. This is not a localised problem. It is a global one. Hayley Williams of Paramore has had condoms thrown at her when they played for the first time on the Warped Tour in America. Taylor Swift constantly gets hounded with questions about past partners, current partners and future partners. This happens to most other musicians with vaginas. Sexism is a global epidemic. After all, the feminist movement and Riot Grrrl wouldn't exist if there had been longstanding equality for women in music. Haim would have probably called their album 'People in Music'.

***

It's not all doom and gloom though. The good experiences do outweigh the bad. I've had some of the best times of my life at gigs and I've met some of the best people in my life. One of my favourite venues in the UK is Temple of Boom in Leeds, Yorkshire. Although I've only been there a handful of times, I fall freshly in love with the venue every time. It looks a bit like a warehouse from the outside. The first time I went, I saw a band called RVIVR.

'We've definitely come to the wrong place', I thought as we turned the corner and I saw the big, white building. It was underwhelming. I was expecting bells and whistles. I wanted lights and music blasting through the doors. A few people were standing outside the front door smoking. They were dressed in black skinny jeans and RVIVR t-shirts. I figured this must be the place. I walked through the front door. It was a secret world. There was exposed brick and wood with fairy lights strewn everywhere. It looked like places where I used to hang out as a teenager with my friends. A secret den. Nothing and no-one with bad intentions could conquer it. It was ours.

There was a guy sitting behind a foldaway table with a grey money box asking for my ticket. I gave him my ticket and followed the corridor to the main room. It looked DIY, effortlessly cool. Posters of forthcoming gigs lined the walls with fairy lights strung up around the room. If you followed the corridor next to the stage, it led you to bathrooms and another room with a bar. More fairy lights and seating. At the bar against the wall, you could get cans of beer for less than four pounds (take that, Fiddler's Elbow). Through the door on the right, you could get outside into a little courtyard that led off to more rooms where bands occasionally play. The whole venue had the feel of going to your friend's house for a jam session and drinks. It felt communal. It felt safe and friendly. It was and is a great place to watch a band, sink a few pints and dance your feet off.

After ten to fifteen minutes of chatting over half-drunk cans of Stella, my friends had made me feel like I was wearing armour. We were sat in the little courtyard on plastic chairs, surrounded by smiling faces and chatty people. I was ready to defend myself against an onslaught of comments. Nothing came.

This is why I think gender doesn't seem to matter all that much in punk. As long as you've got a decent set of lungs to scream lyrics back to the band, a sharp set of elbows, and a good moral compass, punk will pretty much leave you alone. Pop punk on the other hand – punk's younger cousin – total sausage fest. You better be ready. You better dust off your armour and don your battle boots. Rise up to ten feet tall and stomp all over the place. You'll still be called every name under the sun, but at least it's harder to hear from way up there.

The reason I think punk is different and the reason I think it doesn't discriminate against gender is because it was built on rejection of the establishment and authority. Sure, some of the bands were manufactured (I'm looking at you, Sex Pistols), but that doesn't mean the message is manufactured too. Punk is inclusive. Punk belongs to us, and all the other millions of people around the globe, who stand up for what they believe in. There is a space for everyone.

***

In the summer of 2018, I scored a dream job behind the bar at my favourite music venue, the Fulford Arms in York. I think my employment there was kind of an adoption. I spent all my time there anyway so might as well get paid for it! I've known most of the staff since I was dumb enough to sneak into venues but old enough to know better. It was a good fit. It was my first bar job. I hadn't a clue what I was doing for the first few weeks. I accidently (and frequently) made a rancid cocktail of bitters because I'd leave a half-poured pint to settle underneath a different tap to the one I'd poured it from. I did eventually get the hang of pouring the right pints in the right glasses.

If there was a gig I wanted to see, I'd be scheduled to work behind the bar and so I would essentially get paid to see the gig. I could get into gigs for free even if I wasn't required to work. Admittedly, I am a little biased when it comes to The Fully, as it is affectionately called by the regulars. The walls are covered in scribbles, logos and band names from acts that have played at the venue. We give them a white chalk pen at the end of the gig if they're worthy (or if they ask). Magnificent Seven were almost a Fulford Arms house band at one point. Our name is on the wall several times because chalk pens were given to multiple people from the band. There is also a hole in the low ceiling above the stage that various band members keep punching through. No matter how many times we plaster and paint over it, the hole always reappears. The hole is now a part of Fulford Arms history. It was signed by London punk band (and fabulously named) Bob Vylan.

Bob Vylan played one of the first shows back during the pandemic in summer 2021. People were allowed back into the wild, and subsequently so were the venues, by August. After roughly six months of doing table service, it was a breath of fresh air to finally serve a drink to somebody whilst listening to a raw, rowdy set. All the staff were emotional that night. I certainly was. It was like coming home after a long trip away. Everything was how it should have been, as it always was. The only downside was the game of charades everyone had to play when ordering a drink. The protective screens we had fogged up after thirty minutes. The masks made it impossible to lip read what anyone wanted. Bar work in a music venue turned into guess work. I never got a drink thrown in my face in disgust throughout that time (or at the plastic screen anyway) so I reckon I did a good job.

***

From behind the bar to the front of the stage, live music is a significant part of my life and I'm not going to stop enjoying it anytime soon. There's nothing like going to see your favourite local band in a venue you love. There are not many words that can encompass the feeling of getting off stage to a sea of compliments after you know you've killed it. Even better is when a girl told me after one of my pop punk shows that I had inspired her to pick up an instrument and start her own band.

That was quite a few years ago now. I like to think she still plays in that punk band with her brilliant friends. 'Hey, you play guitar pretty well for a girl!' someone from the crowd shouts to her as her band plays. She catches their eye, winks at them, and laughs hysterically before absolutely shredding a solo. 'All girls to the front, come on!' she screams down the mic, full Kathleen Hanna style. As you look around the crowd, you can see young girls with stars in their eyes, playing air guitar, and air drumming.

The cycle of badass women continues.

Author biography

Tarryn Watkins is a Yorkshire-based musician. She has played bass for an eclectic mix of Yorkshire's finest underground bands for around twelve years. She features in the documentary 'So, What Band is Your Boyfriend in?', and has written for a few 'zines and online music publications over the years.

Final Word

Mark Davyd (Music Venue Trust)

Everyone I know, all the friends I've made, all the people I share common cause with, they all have a music story. The artist that inspired you, the song you fell in love to, the first song at your wedding, the song that meant something to you and the friend you lost. And so many of those stories have a music location; a place that the story started in, or took place at.

At Music Venue Trust, we spend a lot of time talking about the career ladder of artists, how they got where they are from where they began, and the importance of those places, dotted across the world, where those paths to the Glastonbury headline spot start. The tiny gigs, in unusual places, the doorstep opportunities in their hometowns and cities where every artist needs to put their foot on the first rung of the ladder that might take them all the way to the biggest stage in the world. The role grassroots music venues play for the multi-billion-pound UK music industry cannot be overstated. No Cavern Club, No Beatles. Every single one of our biggest selling artists of the last sixty years has an engrained connection to a grassroots music venue that inspired them, hosted them, or gave them a chance.

But those places aren't just about the stories of those artists. They mean so much more to their communities, to the people who meet there, to the stories and the lives of the people who attend them, who love them, and who want them to survive and thrive to create many more moments of magic.

At Music Venue Trust, we believe in the power of music to change lives for the better. Our mission is simple: we want these magical spaces to be protected, to feel secure, and to be supported to improve and develop. We want grassroots music venues around the world to be there for people to create those shared moments of joy and exhilaration that are essential to good health and social wellbeing. Our artists deserve the best places to play and begin their careers. Our communities need places they can gather and celebrate. We want to ensure that music is available to everyone, in their hometown or city, everywhere. Everyone deserves a home for their music story: the place where it happened.

www.ingramcontent.com/pod-product-compliance
Lightning Source LLC
Chambersburg PA
CBHW062011220426

43662CB00010B/1283

Dedication

To the people whose lives allow us to know, hear and feel what it means to be human. We cherish the varied ways we live in this world and honor the languages spoken in every part of the world. Without the deep reflections of the differences and similarities of our ways of living, the world would not be the same. We salute human diversity echoed in the wide-ranging languages spoken and written.

LANGUAGE AND LITERATURE
Vehicles for the Enhancement of Cultural Understanding

Edited By

Dainess Maganda and Karim Traoré

Adonis & Abbey Publishers Ltd
St James House
13 Kensington Square,
London, W8 5HD
United Kingdom

Website: http://www.adonis-abbey.com
E-mail Address: editor@adonis-abbey.com

Nigeria:
Suites C4 & C5 J-Plus Plaza
Asokoro, Abuja, Nigeria
Tel: +234 (0) 7058078841/08052035034

Copyright 2016 © Dainess Maganda and Karim Traoré

British Library Cataloguing-in-Publication Data
A catalogue record for this book is available from the British Library

ISBN: 978-1-909112-58-2

The moral right of the author has been asserted

All rights reserved. No part of this book may be reproduced, stored in a retrieval system or transmitted at any time or by any means without the prior permission of the publisher

LANGUAGE AND LITERATURE
Vehicles for the Enhancement of Cultural Understanding

About the Contributors

Dr. Gabriel Ruhumbika is a professor at the University of Georgia and a writer focused on Post-independence Tanzanian and Swahili literatures; a 2015 recipient of the lifetime award for greatly contributing to African literature. Dr. Lioba Moshi is a linguist specialized in language, gender, culture, discourse analysis and African language pedagogy; she is the current head of the Comparative Literature Department at the University of Georgia. Corina Mihaela Beleaua is a Ph.D. student in the Comparative Literature Department, University of Georgia. Dr. Hyangsoon Yi is a Professor of Comparative Literature and Director of the Center for Asian Studies at the University of Georgia; mainly focused on Korean literature and film, and Buddhist aesthetics. Soojin Ahn is a Ph.D. student in Language and Literacy Education and instructor of Korean language at the University of Georgia. Dr. Désiré Baloubi is a professor of English and Linguistics; he is specialized in morphophonology, applied linguistics, and TESOL—currently chair of the Department of Humanities at Shaw University in North Carolina. Adeola Agoke is a Ph.D. student and a Yoruba instructor, Department of African Languages and Literature at the University Of Wisconsin, Madison. Kazeem Kehinde Sanuth is a Ph.D Candidate in Second Language Acquisition and an instructor of Yoruba at the University of Wisconsin, Madison. Dr. Dainess Maganda is the Director of African Languages Program, Coordinator of African Studies Certificate at the University Of Georgia. Dr. Esther M. Lisanza is an Assistant Professor of Liberal Studies at the Winston-Salem State University, North Carolina, and a Visiting Scholar of African Studies at the University of North Carolina at Chapel Hill. Dr. Leonard Muaka is a linguist, Africanist, and the current head of the Department of English at Winston Salem State University. Dr. Rose S. Lugano is a linguist with interest in Swahili language pedagogy, and a Senior Lecturer at the

University of Florida. Dr. Akinloye Ojo is an Associate Professor and Director of African Studies Institute at the University of Georgia. S Satish Kumar is a doctoral student with the Department of Comparative Literature, University of Georgia where he researches and teaches courses in African Literatures. Dr. Karim Traoré is an Associate Professor of Comparative Literature and African Studies at the University of Georgia; his is specialized in literary anthropology and indigenous aesthetics in African literatures and films. Gabriel Ayoola is a Ph.D. student and the instructor of Yoruba in the Department of Comparative Literature. Dr. Odutola Kole is the president of the Southeast African Languages and Literature Forum (SEALLF), a Senior lecturer in the department of Languages, Literatures and Cultures at the University of Florida with special focus in Yoruba language and culture, media studies and participatory use of video.

Table of Contents

Dedication iv

About The Authors v

Introduction
Why and how should culture be taught?
Dainess Maganda.. 9

Chapter One
African Languages and African Development in the 21st Century
Gabriel Ruhumbika 23

Chapter Two
Sustaining the Global Visibility of African Languages and Cultures:
The Case of Kiswahili
Lioba Moshi 47

Chapter Three
Doors of Perception: Dialogues with Otherness
Corina Mihaela Beleaua 75

Chapter Four
Africa in the Selected High School World History Textbooks in Korea
Hyangsoon Yi & Soojin Ahn 93

Chapter Five
Culture Prints in African Languages: The World we Share
Désiré Baloubi 123

Chapter Six
A Literacy-Based Approach to Cultural Understanding
in African Language Pedagogy
Kazeem Kehinde Sanuth & Adeola Agoke 143

Chapter Seven
Using Music/ Songs in the African Language Classroom:
Ideas and Challenges: *Dainess M Maganda, Esther M. Lisanza,
Leonard Muaka & Rose S. Lugano* 169

Chapter Eight
Literary Translation, Cultural Understanding and Selected Translated Works Of Akínwùmí Ìsòlá
Akinloye Ojo 193

Chapter Nine
Return Of The Native? Images Of Alienation And "Outsiderhood" in Tayeb Salih's Season of Migration to the North
S Satish Kumar 219

Chapter Ten
Spatial Organization Of Mande Tales
Karim Traoré 229

Chapter Eleven
The Secret Imports of Names and its Implication for Individual in Nation Building: A Study of Yorùbá Anthroponomy
Gabriel Ayoola 243

Chapter Twelve
Teaching Languages, Literatures and Cultures: Examining Teaching Philosophies
Odutola Kole 269

Appendix I 286
Index 287

INTRODUCTION

Why and how should culture be taught?

Dainess Maganda
University of Georgia

Why this book

In an age of international movement, this book helps readers develop a global viewpoint by advancing their critical understanding of world culture in its intricacy and diversity. The authors strive to develop knowledge on the relationship between languages, literatures, and cultures. In these and other ways, the book cultivates an appreciation of foreign cultures by offering a comprehensive discussion of various aspects of African languages and literature while providing a broad range of educational models and perspectives that build African languages competence and improve the understanding of African literatures and cultures. The authors provide ways to enhance intellectual attainments of the societies involved. Through examining various methods of teaching African languages, interpreting texts and more, the authors seek to expand critical thinking that is vital to the education of good citizens.

First, we lay a foundation on the importance of teaching culture in the idea that effective communication includes not just language proficiency, but rather, comprises of the enhancement and enrichment of communicative and cultural competence respectively. While developing objectivity and cultural discernment, these elements may lead to empathy and reverence toward diverse cultures. This base also provides a background on various scholarships regarding the models of teaching culture, emphasizing prominent ways culture ought to be taught in foreign language classrooms.

In light of our focus, Africa, chapter 1 explains key issues needed in order to bring development in Africa in the 21st Century through African languages. Through a critical historical examination of Africa, right after most countries received their independence from colonial powers, the author underscores the role that African languages played and need to play in order to bring development in Africa. In chapter 2, using Kiswahili language and culture as case in point, the author brings to light the historical and current struggle to sustain the visibility of African languages in the world market despite the efforts and progress made by African and Africanist scholars.

For readers to understand the complexity of appreciating other cultures through language, chapter 3 examines how language and literature can offer a better cultural awareness through a global understanding of the otherness. In particular, because language, word, and translation constitute mechanisms that are part of understanding our reality, the author shows how knowledge of foreign languages can improve the way we approach life. As a working example, chapter 4 describes in what way Africa is represented in the selected high school world history textbooks in Korea. Before delving into pedagogical advancement on the teaching of African languages, chapter 5 re-visits what so many writers, linguists, anthropologists, philologists, and philosophers, among others, have revealed to the world about the wealth of knowledge, beliefs, attitudes, and values embedded in human languages. Based on examples of various speech acts, with specific reference to the semantic domain of body-part words and proverbs, the author examines worldviews and cultural ideologies embedded in African languages.

Pertaining to language pedagogy, African language instructors and scholars have taken up the challenge of developing effective models of integrating language and culture. In the understanding that cultural perspectives are the underlining values that connect the cultural practices, the cultural products and the linguistic activities of the community, the authors in chapter 6 argue for a language curriculum that is informed by *cultural perspectives* of target speech community. In the subsequent chapter, ideas and challenges for using songs/music to teach African languages are shared.

Because language scholars show over and over that the translation of literary works often serves as the expressive connecting bridge between languages and cultures, chapters 8, 9 and 10 present a literary examination of different writers. Even more, rendering a literary text in one language into another is critical to cross-cultural and inter-national understanding. To this end, chapter 8 examines some of the aspects of the Yorùbá society and culture which have conceivably become accessible to English readers through the translations of some of the works by the renowned Yorùbá writer, Akínwùmí Ìsòlá. The author in chapter 9 focuses on images of alienation and "outsiderhood" in Tayeb Salih's *Season of Migration to the North* as the author explores the literarization of Fanon, in Black Skin White Masks, arguing a genetic change on the phenotypic level in the native of the Antilles who returns from the "mother country" an alien to its ways- an outsider to its ethos. Chapter ten demonstrates how horizontal and vertical dimensions of African tales participate efficiently in the construction of the stories' underlying meaning. The author examines two Mande tales in which the three Sons illustrate the meaning of space at the vertical level whereas The Two Friends reflect the symbolic pertinence of the vertical dimension of African tales. To further illustrate ways in which texts offer insights about people's ways of life, an investigation of the uniqueness of Yoruba personal names as they point to the socio-psychological conditions of name-authors and their societies at large is then presented. Because all contributors in this book are teachers of languages, literatures and cultures, the last chapter examines their teaching philosophies because they serve as a window into their minds and classroom practices.

Background: Why teach culture

Knowledge and experience about people of another target community or country- culture, is merely a depository of facts and experiences to which one can have an alternative, if need be (Thanasoulas, 2001). It would rather be ridiculous to dispute that learning about another culture is a journey to discover how much flexibility the target language permits learners to control grammatical forms, sounds, and meanings, and or even break socially accepted standards at work while also reflecting upon the target culture without disowning ones' own. Teaching culture fosters cross-cultural understanding which surpasses the confines of linguistic forms—while developing and providing far unfathomable meaning to what is labelled "communicative competence"—and runs against a solipsistic viewpoint.

Before delving more into the reasons for teaching culture, we need to answer the question of what exactly is culture. Needless to say, culture has been defined differently over the years and the meaning keeps changing and getting rather complicated, partly because the world is increasingly becoming international. The definitions start as simple analysis that tag culture generally as 'the ways of a people' (Lado, 1957). This assessment, as Saville-Troike (1975, p. 83) notes, integrates the easily seen-'material' manifestations of culture as well as the ones that are not easy to observe- 'non-material'. In subsequent years, the works of Anthropologists expounded this definition to include "all the social practices that bind a group of people together while separating them from others" (Montgomery & Reid-Thomas, 1994, p. 5). Peck (1998) notes that culture signifies all of the accepted ways of a given way of people including their thinking, feeling and part of learned behavior, in addition to, their exhibited accomplishments and contributions to development.

Culture is our social heritage as juxtaposed with our organic inheritance. At every turn and opportunity in life, it is culture that controls our lives, allowing us to shape our reality while also confining how we see and participate in the world (Miles, 2008). Dismissing cognitive, behaviorist and functionalist definitions of culture, as Robinson (1988) did, we embrace a symbolic meaning which posits culture as a dynamic "system of symbols and meanings" whereby "past experience influences meaning, which in turn affects future experience, which in turn affects subsequent meaning, and so on" (p. 11). In this light, culture is like a mechanical gear that allows our every movement and interactions in this world, we then ought to accept, although it can be argued, that culture is constantly changing, never static. Pertinent to our focus, if we are to examine ways in which languages and literature serve as instruments to enhance cultural understanding, we need to identify the nature of culture. Among other frameworks, such as Straub (1999), we use Goodenough (1981, p. 62) summary of the contents of culture as follows:

1. The ways in which people have organized their experience of the real world so as to give it structure as a phenomenal world of forms, their percepts and concepts.
2. The ways in which people have organized their experience of their phenomenal world so as to give it structure as a system of cause and effect relationships, that is, the propositions and beliefs by which they explain events and accomplish their purposes.

3. The ways in which people have organized their experiences so as to structure their world in hierarchies of preferences, namely, their value or sentiment systems.
4. The ways in which people have organized their experience of their past efforts to accomplish recurring purposes into operational procedures for accomplishing these purposes in the future, that is, a set of "grammatical" principles of action and a series of recipes for accomplishing particular ends.

The above summary speaks to the inherent elements that characterize all cultures around the world. In the same notion, as it will be demonstrated in various papers in this book, to call something as reflective of a people's culture necessitates the following features to be present, namely, culture is learned, based on symbols, shared, dynamic and integrated (Thasanaulus, 2001; Gini, 2000). Culture is learned: it is not inherited because it is not biological. We acquire cultural practices often unconscious from peers, families, media and even institutions and, though we have similar biological needs, how we fulfill such needs differs cross-culturally. Culture is based on symbols: by its nature, a symbol is a depiction of something else and is rather subjective. Symbols such as money, art even language gain their meaning when a group of people agree on their use. As such, language happens to be the most important symbolic constituent of culture (Brown, 2009).

Culture is shared: there are agreeable, though sometimes unspoken rules that determine actions socially appropriate while allowing people from the same culture to predict how others will act (Hall & Hall, 2007). It is critical to note, let it not be confused, that culture is not homogenous because societies have numerous and various cultural standards (Brettell & Sargent, 2009). Culture is dynamic: as aforementioned, cultural practices involve people's actions and ways of participating in the world, by that very nature, cultures gain and change in the process of adapting to changing environments, which in turn necessitate changes based on borrowed ideas and symbols from other cultures. Culture is integrated: all parts of culture are connected, forming an interlocking system that require one who wants to participate in it to learn not just a few, but all of its parts in order to understand it. This is one of the reasons that even foreign language learners need to learn not only the face values of words, symbols, songs, and art, they have to know how such features make sense in and are appropriately used in specific contexts (Maybury-Lewis, 1998).

Evidently, culture is a pervasive force, shaping our identities and our interactions with other things and people (Dixon, 2006; Pettigrew & Tropp, 2005). It dictates how we feel and express our emotions and sensations of anger or pleasure based on cultural clues that would leave immovable somebody who has been raised in a dissimilar social convention (Shook & Fazio, 2008a). Let us declare, without hesitation, that culture can create and solve problems. For instance, if dogs are regarded as sacred animals within a specific culture but looked down upon within another culture, the way a person speaks and acts around such creatures may bring great conflict that can only be resolved upon understanding each culture on its own merits (Schneider, & Silverman, 2010).

Therefore, as Thasanaulus (2001) observes, we should teach culture in order to help students develop an understanding of the fact that all people exhibit culturally-conditioned behaviors, that social variables such as age, sex, social class, and place of residence influence the ways in which people speak and behave. Culture should also be taught to guide others become more aware of predictable behavior expected in a target culture while also increasing awareness of cultural connotations accompanying words and phrases in the target language. Teaching culture develops people's skill to assess and refine generalizations about the target culture. Even more importantly, the teaching of culture develops the necessary skills to locate and organize information about the target culture while also cultivating people's intellectual curiosity about the target culture, and to promote empathy towards its people.

At any rate, the purpose of teaching culture is to develop students' perception and to cultivate their curiosity of the target culture and their own, aiding them to make associations among cultures (Tavares & Cavalcanti, 1996). These contrasts, of course, are not meant to undervalue foreign cultures but to deepen students' knowledge and to inform them of the value of cultural diversity.

Culture in the foreign language classroom

The teaching of culture has not received much adoration as it deserves. Various methods to foreign language teaching—sociolinguistic, communicative, and pragmatic, which have undoubtedly awarded the study of language with a social "tone" (Thasanaulus, 2001); nonetheless, not attending to the social undercurrents that shape language without identifying or even trying to get insights into the very tapestry of society and culture that shape language may cause cross-cultural misunderstanding and miscommunication. In this book, the main principle in chapters that speak to African language pedagogy is that fostering "communicative competence" must take into account diverse views and perceptions of people in different cultures because such views may enrich or even constrain communication. After all, communication necessitates understanding, and understanding entails walking into the shoes of the alien and examining her cultural baggage, while always placing "[the target] culture in relation with one's own" (Kramsch, 1993, p. 205). As Politzer (1959) long ago asserted, we ought to know that teaching language without consecutively teaching the culture in which it functions is synonymous to teaching meaningless symbols to which language learners may attach the wrong meaning.

In one form or another, at any rate, learning a foreign language is foreign culture learning, and, most language teachers, for different reasons, teach culture even implicitly. As Kramsch (1993) observes:

Culture in language learning is not an expendable fifth skill, tacked on, so to speak, to the teaching of speaking, listening, reading, and writing. It is always in the background, right from day one, ready to unsettle the good language learners when they expect it least, making evident the limitations of their hard-won communicative competence, challenging their ability to make sense of the world around them (p. 1)

It is reasonable, so to speak, in this view, to assert that cultural awareness ought to be regarded as a significant element informing, and enhancing communicative competence (Kirkman, Lowe, & Gibson, 2006). This communicative proficiency we speak of, implies verbal and non-verbal communication which include gestures or/and even inability to participate with other people of a specific group. In other words, cultural consciousness enables one to know not only appropriate language but also the accurate behavior within a specific context. The question we try to answer hereafter is how then culture should be incorporated in the foreign language curriculum in ways that foster cultural understanding.

Historically, it has been agreed upon that, just as we cannot teach somebody how to breathe, likewise, we cannot teach culture (Hofstede, Hofstede & Minkov, 2010). We can, however, try to show ways in which people may learn about culture so that they not posit a particular way of viewing things. Drawing from the aforementioned elements of culture, teachers are able to educate students to dismiss such things as superior and inferior cultures by articulating the differences that exist among people even within the target culture (Hofstede & McCrae, 2004).

Evidently, the goal is to make sure teachers are not in the classroom to endorse or attack the predispositions of their students. Their task is rather to enlighten students' understanding and making the classroom "not so much as a place where the language is taught, but as one where opportunities for learning of various kinds are provided through the interactions that take place between the participants" (Ellis, 1992, p. 171, cited in Kramsch, 1993, p. 245). We therefore suggest four useful guidelines for teaching culture based on Lessard-Clouston' (1997) and Cruz, Bonissone, and Baff (1995) work.

Key elements in the teaching of culture

First, teaching culture should correspond with the active aspects of culture. Because language is alive and therefore changes overtime, so does culture. Teachers ought to instill in their students appropriate behavior that relates to the dynamic nature of the culture they are teaching. This should be done in ways that encourage constant examination of students' own culture so they behave not based on their culture but rather, in light of it. That is, students need to discuss and understand their own beliefs, values, customs, rituals and traditions unconsciously embedded in their minds before they can reflect upon and act according to the values and customs of others. For example, teachers may get students to make a list of characteristics or traits that apparently distinguish the target culture from their own on things such as music, geography, arts, clothing or food, to name just a few. By doing so, things. Drawing from the aforementioned elements of culture, teachers are able to educate students to dismiss such things as superior and inferior cultures by articulating the differences that exist among people even within the target culture (Hofstede & McCrae, 2004).

Evidently, the goal is to make sure teachers are not in the classroom to endorse or attack the predispositions of their students. Their task is rather to enlighten students' understanding and making the classroom "not so much as a place where the language is taught, but as one where opportunities for learning of various kinds are provided through the interactions that take place between the participants" (Ellis, 1992, p. 171, cited in Kramsch, 1993, p. 245). We therefore suggest four useful guidelines for teaching culture based on Lessard-Clouston' (1997) and Cruz, Bonissone, and Baff (1995) work.

Key elements in the teaching of culture

First, teaching culture should correspond with the active aspects of culture. Because language is alive and therefore changes overtime, so does culture. Teachers ought to instill in their students appropriate behavior that relates to the dynamic nature of the culture they are teaching. This should be done in ways that encourage constant examination of students' own culture so they behave not based on their culture but rather, in light of it. That is, students need to discuss and understand their own beliefs, values, customs, rituals and traditions unconsciously embedded in their minds before they can reflect upon and act according to the values and customs of others. For example, teachers may get students to make a list of characteristics or traits that apparently distinguish the target culture from their own on things such as music, geography, arts, clothing or food, to name just a few. By doing so, while always placing "[the target] culture in relation with one's own" (Kramsch, 1993, p. 205). As Politzer (1959) long ago asserted, we ought to know that teaching language without consecutively teaching the culture in which it functions is synonymous to teaching meaningless symbols to which language learners may attach the wrong meaning.

In one form or another, at any rate, learning a foreign language is foreign culture learning, and, most language teachers, for different reasons, teach culture even implicitly. As Kramsch (1993) observes:

Culture in language learning is not an expendable fifth skill, tacked on, so to speak, to the teaching of speaking, listening, reading, and writing. It is always in the background, right from day one, ready to unsettle the good language learners when they expect it least, making evident the limitations of their hard-won communicative competence, challenging their ability to make sense of the world around them (p. 1)

It is reasonable, so to speak, in this view, to assert that cultural awareness ought to be regarded as a significant element informing, and enhancing communicative competence (Kirkman, Lowe, & Gibson, 2006). This communicative proficiency we speak of, implies verbal and non-verbal communication which include gestures or/and even inability to participate with other people of a specific group. In other words, cultural consciousness enables one to know not only appropriate language but also the accurate behavior within a specific context. The question we try to answer hereafter is how then culture should be incorporated in the foreign language curriculum in ways that foster cultural understanding.

Historically, it has been agreed upon that, just as we cannot teach somebody how to breathe, likewise, we cannot teach culture (Hofstede, Hofstede & Minkov, 2010). We can, however, try to show ways in which people may learn about culture so that they not posit a particular way of viewing teachers and students are easily able to identify any preconceived ideas needing to be corrected.

Second, teaching culture should be done systematically. While teaching needs to be somewhat flexible, allowing learning to cater to students' needs and their speed of understanding, effective teaching also necessitates a structured methodology that incorporates aspects of culture that aligns with a specific linguistic topic. For example, when teaching greetings in Swahili, a teacher may intentionally plan to talk about cultural norms of respecting elders through the use of "*Shikamoo mzee*"- instead of "*Hujambo mzee*" as greetings based on age difference. Third, teaching culture should involve evaluation mechanisms of the cultural components learned. This means, as students learn culture, teachers are to give feedback and re-evaluate whether or not students' cultural understanding is advancing as their language skills develop. For instance, one area could be teachers' evaluation of ways in which language and social variables interpenetrate. Since language varies based on social variables, such as location, sex, social class age for example, teachers may evaluate how students are able to differentiate and appropriately use words and phrases suitable for women rather than male in the target culture.

Fourth, in light of Cruz, Bonissone, and Baff (1995) idea, teaching culture should underscore ways in which linguistic and cultural competence help the world negotiate and attain a sense of respect and acceptance for each other's nations' political and economic identities. Sadly however, it is hard to deny that most of our schools have not changed in many ways even though the world has indeed changed. Case in point, only a number of languages are offered to fulfil foreign-language requirements for most universities in the United States, United Kingdom and elsewhere (NCTCOL, 2015). In most foreign language classrooms, cultural awareness and competence are real global issues that are neglected although they are an absolute necessity in our global world. As Peck (1998) stated, the foreign language classroom should be a 'cultural island' where the accent will be on 'cultural experience' rather than 'cultural awareness'. History testifies over and over again that no one superpower is able to dominate without contempt from others, therefore, citizens ought to understand that they are responsible, as global citizens, to move comfortably and learn from various cultural environments. In fact, building effective relationship and communication among nations requires each party know each other's values and manners of building rapport. From this perspective, cultural competence is therefore a balancing power that maintains justice and peace stability in the world. In a sense, our knowledge and experience about other cultures should enable us to see that we cannot become members of the same mono-cultural global village but rather, we are able to simultaneously observe and be part of it.

In addition to the afore-discussed guidelines on teaching culture, we also add that literature plays a critical role in expressing culture. Literary texts are resources of authentic language and therefore expand language-learners' language competence. While teachers may use literature to present language in contextualized form, literature allows learners to see multiple applications of words based on social, political, historical and even religious contexts.

Conclusion

Readers will see that authors in various chapters in this book present ways in which literature and language teaching may enhance or inhibit people's understanding of each other's culture. Examples of struggles facing African languages and literature scholars are also shared; they include choosing appropriate songs to expand students' linguistic and cultural understanding of the target language. Through various viewpoints presented by a vibrant group of African scholars, readers will find this book to be engaging, practical and relevant to our ever changing globalized world.

References

Brettell, C. B., & Sargent, C. F. (Eds.).(2009). *Gender in cross-cultural perspective*. Upper Saddle River, NJ: Prentice Hall.

Brown, R. (2009, January 24). Nashville voters reject a proposal for English-only. The New York Times, p. A12.

Cruz, G. I., Bonissone, P. R., & Baff, S. J. (Summer, 1995). The Teaching of Culture in Bilingual Education Programs: Moving Beyond the Basics. In New York State Association for Bilingual Education Journal (v10 p1-5).

Dixon, J. C. (2006). The ties that bind and those that don't: Toward reconciling group threat and contact theories of prejudice. *Social Forces*, 84, 2179–2204;

Hall, E. T., & Hall, M. R. (2007).The sounds of silence. In J. M. Henslin (Ed.), *Down to earth sociology: Introductory readings* (pp. 109–117). New York, NY: Free Press.

Hofstede, G. & McCrae, R. R. (2004). Culture and personality revisited: Linking traits and dimensions of culture. *Cross-Cultural Research*, 38, 52-88.

Hofstede, G., Hofstede, G. J. & Minkov, M. (2010).*Cultures and Organizations: Software of the Mind* (Rev. 3rd ed.). New York: McGraw-Hill. For translations see www.geerthofstede.nland "our books".

Kirkman, B. L., Lowe, K. B., & Gibson, C. B. (2006). A quarter century of Culture's Consequences: A review of empirical research incorporating Hofstede's cultural valuesframework. *Journal of International Business Studies*, 37, 285-320.

Pettigrew, T. F., & Tropp, L. R. (2005). Allport's intergroup contact hypothesis: Its history and influence. In J. F. Dovidio, P. S. Glick, & L. A. Rudman (Eds.), *On the nature of prejudice: Fifty Years after Allport* (pp. 272–277). Malden, MA: Blackwell Pub.

Kramsch, C. (1993). *Context and Culture in Language Teaching.* Oxford: Oxford University Press.

Politzer, R. (1959). Developing Cultural Understanding through Foreign Language Study.Report of the Fifth Annual Round Table Meeting on Linguistics and Language Teaching, pp. 99 105. Washington, D.C.: Georgetown University Press.

Gini, A. (2000). *My job, myself: Work and the creation of the modern individual.* New York, NY: Routledge.

Lessard-Clouston, M. (1997).Towards an Understanding of Culture in L2/FL Education. In Ronko, K.G. Studies in English, 25, 131-150 Japan: Kwansei Gakuin University Press.

Maybury-Lewis, D. (1998). Tribal wisdom.In K. Finsterbusch (Ed.), *Sociology* 98/99 (pp. 8-12). Guilford, CT: Dushkin/McGraw-Hill.

Miles, S. (2008). *Language and sexism.* New York, NY: Cambridge University Press.

Peck, D. (1998). *Teaching Culture: Beyond Language.* Yale: New Haven Teachers Institute.

Ray, S. (2007). Politics over official language in the United States. *International Studies, 44,* 235–252.

Shook, N. J., & Fazio, R. H. (2008). Interracial roommate relationships: An experimental test of the contact hypothesis. *Psychological Science,* 19, 717–723.

Schneider, L., & Silverman, A. (2010).*Global sociology: Introducing five contemporary societies.* New York, NY: McGraw-Hill.

Thanasoulas, D. (2001). The Importance Of Teaching Culture In The Foreign Language Classroom. *Radical Pedagogy,* 3(3)

Tavares, R. & Cavalcanti, I. (July-September 1996).Developing Cultural Awareness in EFL Classrooms. *English Forum,* 34(3)

CHAPTER ONE

African Languages and African Development in the 21st Century

Gabriel Ruhumbika
University of Georgia

The need for African national languages

For the sake of clarity, this paper focuses on Sub-Saharan Africa, Africa South of the Sahara, for the simple reason that North Africa, the five countries of the African continent which border the Mediterranean Sea today, are linguistically and culturally part of the Middle East and the Arab world, and the language problems of Black Africa don't necessarily apply to them; at least not to the same extent.

First, by an African national language of an African country I mean, an African language spoken in the entire country, in other words the lingua franca of the country, and which is not used only on the "ethnic" level and then put aside when dealing with "elevated matters", but one in which the people of the entire nation write, read, think, conduct the affairs their country and all official government business, and in which they educate their children and adults at all levels of the education system, including the university.

To me, therefore, when the leaders of an African country declare ten or more of the languages of their people as their "national languages" (for example South Africa, 11, Kenya, 40) they are in effect, in spite of their good intentions, working against the development of an African national language for their people. The research on teacher belief is surely a backdoor passageway into understanding a teacher's teaching having two or even three African national languages. I also recognize that, for some particular reasons, even a small country, like Burundi, Rwanda or Zimbabwe, could have two African national languages. Otherwise the African national language of a country should be the one language of national unity, nationhood consolidation and economic and social development.

With the exception of Ethiopia, which, apart from the invasion by fascist Italy under Mussolini from the mid 1930's to end of WWII, was never colonized by Europe, Tanzania is the only Sub-Saharan African country which since its independence has developed such an African national language, Swahili, but only to a certain degree. Besides my job as a university professor, I am a Tanzanian Swahili writer, translator and editor. Before coming to the USA in 1985, I taught for 15 years at the University of Dar es Salaam. I have been writing in Swahili for over four decades. I am a non-native Swahili speaker who loves the language, which I have never stopped learning in order to know it better as I witnessed it grow and mature over the decades and as it continues to grow. As an Africanist scholar, Swahili language and literature are my main areas of research interest. It is with that background that I write about African national languages and the development of African countries today.

When discussing the need of African national languages, a number of questions arise: 1. Is it possible for the other African countries to have only one national language like Swahili in Tanzania when in almost all of them their people speak so many different languages? 2. Are African languages capable of fulfilling the needs of a developed language of the twenty-first century, including being used as the medium of instruction in universities? 3. Is it not more beneficial for the Africans to concentrate their efforts on learning and knowing well and spreading to the populations of their countries the European languages of their former colonial masters, which are the key to the Western kind of development and prosperity to which everybody in today's world aspires, instead of pursuing African national languages of no particular benefits to them? 4. Lastly, will the development of a single African language as the official and national language of the entire country not result in the decline and ultimately the death of the other languages of the people of that country! (It is important to note that this question is never asked when a European language is used as the national language of an African country!) All these are important questions which need to be answered. Hereafter, I discuss these questions as themes rather than answering them one by one since some of them are interrelated.

In 1992, I published a paper on the topic of "African languages" in *Research in African Literatures* entitled "The African-Language Policy of Development: African National Language"(Ruhumbika, 1992), and I would like to quote my opening remarks in that article, because, in my view, more than two decades later nothing has changed. I wrote:

> After more than a quarter century of independence, it is evident that both the consolidation of our nation-states and the effective development of the new African society are bound to remain mere illusions as long as we continue the futile effort of trying to make the foreign languages of our former colonial masters the national languages of our African countries. Our writers and intellectuals are fast awakening to this reality, and as a result more and more of them are advocating the use of African languages by African writers. Some are already writing in these languages and discovering in them the vehicle of their true creativity. However, those African writers and intellectuals have, in general, not yet realized that, given the linguistic fragmentation of our countries, writing in African languages alone will remain of

limited and mostly academic interest unless it is part of a larger program to develop African languages of nation-wide application, in other words African national languages. Given the social and economic reality of our countries, only such national languages can become fully developed modern African languages...

Only such languages are capable of being languages of African economic, political, and cultural development. Only such languages are capable of fostering African regional and continental cooperation and unity. And, equally important, only such languages will enable us to retain our African identity in the contemporary international arena (rightly called the Global Village in the twenty-first century) where we are belated and feeble newcomers, and where everything which matters is dictated by the same West which for centuries has been exploiting us and denigrating our humanity and our race, claiming that we are a people without civilization or culture, or, to use their own words, savages and worse!"

I further wrote:

The attempt to use the European languages of our former colonial masters has failed for the simple reason that these languages are the exclusive domain of a miniscule "educated" minority and remain incomprehensible to the masses of the African people." That was the case at the end of the last century, and it is still the case in the second decade of the new millennium. In fact things have become worse. That tiny minority of the educated *elite* in many of our countries has shrunk instead of expanding. The growing poverty of most of our countries, the near collapse of their economy, corruption, theft and mismanagement of public funds have badly affected the quality of education in our public schools and colleges, the only place where even the children of the poor could also receive a good education. As a result good secondary school and college education is increasingly available only to fewer and fewer children, the sons and daughters of the very rich! Examples of children who finish primary and middle school without knowing how to read and write and secondary school graduates who are incapable of expressing themselves intelligibly in the European national language of their particular country have become the norm rather than the exception!

I find the remarks an eminent French linguist, Pierre Alexandre makes in his book entitled *Languages and Language in*

Black Africa on the English of English-speaking Africans to be an apt description of this sad reality: "Some British academics have confessed to me that they can often understand the French spoken by a Senegalese or Ivorian better than the English of a Ghanaian or Nigerian…The case of Sierra Leonean Krio leads one to think that, unless this evolution is controlled, it might lead to the formation of new languages with no international value, whose speakers would thus be obliged to learn…English."(Alexandre, 1972, p. 98). In my 1992 article I comment on the French scholar's remark by saying that what he does not say is that the English academics found the French of the Africans good enough because they too possibly spoke French imperfectly. Otherwise the truth is that the French of an average French-speaking African is as distinctly African as is the English of the Nigerian or Ghanaian (or Tanzanian or Kenyan, etc.). Some of us who have lived in France and know the West well also know that some French "academics" are not above calling the French of an educated African from their former African colonies "petit nègre", "Nigger gibberish".

The absurdity and uselessness of such corrupted European languages to the Africans was foretold during the colonial period by an African writer, Ferdinand Oyono, in his novel *Houseboy*. Describing a scene where school children in his native Cameroon are singing for the "Commandant", the French equivalent of the District Commissioner in British colonies, who has paid a visit to the school, he writes:

> The instructor gave them the note, and then beat out the time. The children sang, without any pauses, in a language which was not their own or French but the strange gibberish which village people suppose is French and Frenchmen suppose is the vernacular. *When they finished everybody clapped*" (Oyono, 1970, p. 47). (Emphasis on the last sentence is added by me).

That incomprehensible "gibberish" was the medium by which the African children were to learn the other subjects, to get an education! That is the absurdity we Africans are still perpetuating in almost all our countries more than half a century after our independence!

Even if the number of educated people had increased, and even if there are countries where it has actually increased, still the damages to the society of those countries caused by the continued use of European languages as their national languages don't diminish, and the future of their people remains equally grim. Not only that *elites* are still cut-off from the masses of the countries they are supposed to lead, but because those European languages are so different from their native languages, even those educated Africans know them imperfectly, as is the case with most speakers of foreign languages all over the world.

For me, it was on realizing the truth that I know English imperfectly and I know Swahili much better that I began writing in Swahili. And yet I have a BA Honours degree in English from the University of London and I had received all my middle school, secondary school and college education in English. And with respect to Swahili, it is also not my native language! But it is another Bantu language with a lot in common with my native Kikerewe. Also, since the 5th grade I went to school away from my native Ukerewe, which was the usual thing in those days. And since then my language of daily use in and out of school was Swahili, except when I went home, two or three times a year, for a few days of holidays; and that was to remain the case until I went to college. I was therefore daily exposed to Swahili, a linguistic relative of my native Kikerewe since a very early age! Not less important, I had done my schooling with Swahili as the medium of instruction until the end of 6th grade. That is why I agree with

---

Chapter One — Gabriel Ruhumbika, in
Dainess Maganda and Karim Traoré (Eds.)
LANGUAGE AND LITERATURE: Vehicles for the Enhancement of Cultural Understanding
London, Adonis & Abbey Publishers

the remarks Professor Pierre Elexandre makes in his book cited above on the importance of using African languages as mediums of instruction for African children:

> ...a balancing factor was the existence in British Africa of a relatively abundant vernacular literature, and many country folk who did not know a word of English could nevertheless read and write in their own language. Besides, and especially where education was given in the mother tongue or close relative of it, there was no huge gap between family and village life and school life which proved so wasteful in the French school system" (Alexandre, 1972)

I returned home to Tanzania after my graduate studies in France and joined the University of Dar es Salaam at the beginning of 1970 having already published my first novel in English, *Village in Uhuru*, in the UK, and my intention was to continue writing in English. As an alumnus of Makerere College of the University of London of that time, with a BA Honours in English to boot, I simply could not imagine myself writing in Swahili! Fortunately for me, shortly after my return to the country I was asked by the director of the East African Literature Bureau of that time to translate into Swahili René Dumont's *L'afrique noire est mal partie (False Start in Africa)*, *Afrika Inakwenda Kombo* in my translation. It was while writing that translation that I discovered I knew Swahili much more that I could possibly know English or French; and from there on all my creative writing has been in Swahili! I have never felt as honored as when in July 2005, at the Swahili international symposium marking the 75th anniversary of the founding of the Institute of Kiswahili Research, I was awarded a certificate of excellence by the Institute of Kiswahili Research of the University of Dar es Salaam in recognition of my contribution to the development of Swahili language and literature by my "novels and translations". I was equally elated to see also honored the same way two other fellow Wakerewe, the late

Aniceti Kitereza for his novel *Bwana Myombekere na Bibi Bugonoka na Ntulanalwo na Bulihwali*, which I have translated into English from the original unpublished Kikerewe manuscript as *Mr. Myombekere and His Wife Bugonoka, Their Son Ntulanalwo and Daughter Bulihwali: the Story of an Ancient African Community*, and the novelist Euphrase Kezilahabi, my former colleague at the University of Dar es Salaam. Following in the footsteps of the Tanzanian national poets Mathias Myampala and Saadani Kandoro, we were among the non-native Swahili-speaking Bara (upcountry) Tanzanians writers who, like Kulikoyela Kahigi, Mugyabuso Mulokozi, Penina Mlama, Faraji Katalambula and many others, had contributed to the growth of our national language and its literature, and were bearing testimony to the fact that indeed one African language can become the national language of the entire nation comprising many different ethnic languages.

The multiplicity of ethnic languages and the Development of African national languages

In spite of what I have just said, it is nonetheless an undeniable fact that the linguistic fragmentation of the people of our African nations due to the multiplicity of ethnicities each speaking a different language is indeed a great obstacle to the development of one African language as the national language of the entire country. Even though we must also point out that countries which already have such lingua francas, such as Kenya (Swahili) and Senegal (Wolof), are still using the European languages of their former colonial masters as their national languages.

How then can the other African countries follow the example of Tanzania and choose a single African language as their national language in spite of the reality of the numerous languages of their people? I pointed out in my 1992 article cited above that, "As early as the 1960s, the French linguist Alexandre noted that African lingua francas are continuing to evolve," and then I wrote the following:

> Many African ethnicities are culturally and linguistically closely related; but even unrelated ethnicities living in the same country or region have often acquired an understanding of each other's languages, however linguistically different they might be. The linguistic kinship of African languages within "language families" was recognized very early by European researchers on African languages. As far back as the beginning of the twentieth century, for example, a pioneer European linguist writes the following on the Bantu family of languages: "The importance of this language family to Africa at the present day and in the near future is unquestionable. Throughout Africa, north of the Bantu border-line, you meet with a bewildering number of languages widely differing from the other and mutually quite incomprehensible. ... Further, when once one Bantu language is acquired it is not very difficult to understand the structure and even the vocabulary of the others... If, say, one started (as many an early pioneer like Livingston did) with a band of porters or canoemen from the Zambezi, one might go far and wide to the north, west, and east, and with the slow rates of travel in pre-railway days, find one's porters accustoming themselves by degrees to the changes of dialects and languages, till at length the caravan arrived at Tanganyika, the Victoria Nyanza, or the Upper Congo, with its men still able to ask their way, or to understand the drift of what was being said to them. Who that in early days explored Equatorial East Africa or Equatorial West Africa, or the very heart of the continent, has not realized the shock and interruption in easy relations when his expedition at last left Bantu Africa and arrived in a district where the languages belonged to another family -- Nilotic, Sudanic, or Nigerian?"(Johnston, 1919,p. 17).

In terms of today's African countries, Bantu-speaking Africa spreads over the entire half of sub-Saharan Africa, starting from the Cameroon and Gabon on the Atlantic coast and stretching eastward through the Central African Republic, the Congo Democratic Republic, Burundi, Rwanda and Uganda to Kenya and Tanzania on the Indian Ocean coast and then southward all the way to the southernmost tip of

South Africa, including the Comoro Islands and parts of Madagascar in the Indian Ocean (Werner 1919, p. 3; Johnston 1919, pp. 1-38; Lwanga-Lunyiigo and Vansina 1988, p. 140; Bryan 1959). The pockets of non-Bantu-speaking people which dot that large area of the continent have in most cases virtually become Bantu-speaking, by virtue of being surrounded by the Bantu-speaking majority in the midst of whom they live.

A given language might become the medium of inter-ethnic communication for a variety of reasons: it might be because it is the language spoken in the national capital (Lingala in DRC and Congo-Brazzaville), the language used by traders (as in the case of Swahili in Eastern and Central Africa), the language of soldiers-administrators (as in the case of Swahili in Uganda and Lingala in DRC), of popular music (Lingala in DRC and surrounding countries), or simply the language of the country's majority. But whenever such a lingua franca emerges, people from other ethnicities in the country or region learn it without much difficult. With the necessary political will, therefore, lingua francas can be encouraged to develop even in African countries where they do not already exist. Many countries of Black Africa in fact already have one, in some cases two or three African languages which serve as their lingua francas. Examples are: example: Somalia, Senegal, Ethiopia, Eritrea, Kenya, Tanzania, Uganda, Malawi, Botswana, Swaziland, Lesotho, Madagascar, Comoro, Burundi, Rwanda, DRC (2), Nigeria (3), Zimbabwe (2), Zambia (2). We could possibly also add the small countries of Benin, Togo, Gambia and Djibouti. Several West African countries use Hausa and Bambara (or Bamana) as regional languages; and South African linguists and other people from the region claim that Sotho and Zulu are practically lingua francas of an entire Southern Africa region,

Chapter One | Gabriel Ruhumbika, in
Dainess Maganda and Karim Traoré (Eds.)
LANGUAGE AND LITERATURE: Vehicles for the Enhancement of Cultural Understanding
London, Adonis & Abbey Publishers

just as Swahili is the lingua franca of East Africa and parts of Central Africa.

My conclusion from this situation is the following: "Africans in any given country should pull together and invest their good will, their hard work, and their economic resources in developing as their national language one of the languages of their people which is already their *lingua franca*, is virtually that, or has the potential to become that medium of their inter-ethnic communication. In cases of contending possible choices, a political decision must be made to determine which language will best serve the future needs of the nation. Some European nations of today, whose languages the Africans admire so much, like Germany and Italy, for example, are by some account still in search of their national languages as late as the nineteenth century, almost on the eve of their invasion and colonization of Africa. It is time for the Africans to take up their important historical national languages development task.

Are African languages capable of fulfilling the functions of a fully developed modern language like the major European Languages?

There are two things to consider here. One is the actual limitations of most African languages as they are today. The other one is the colonial mentality of the Africans, of a subjugated people, who had found the military power, cultural superiority, and material development of the colonizer so overwhelming that they saw everything European as not only superior but almost not of this world and, because of that, believed everything their colonial master told them, and some of them continued to do so even after independence. Many Black politicians, writers and thinkers, from Etienne Léro, Frantz Fanon, Water Rodney and Ngugi wa Thion'go to

Kwame Nkrumah and Mwalimu (Teacher) Nyerere, have in various ways written on the colonial mentality of the Africans and Black people in general, and there is nothing new I can add here. I only want to remark that the colonial mentality of the African has persisted beyond independence because our independence remains mostly what has been called "flag independence": we are still a neo-colonial people. And the African *elite*, our political leaders and the "educated" Africans, are the agents and beneficiaries of that new form of colonialism! It is therefore in their interest to perpetuate it. And the continued use of the European language of their former colonial masters is seen by them as necessary to the maintaining of their elitism, at the expense of their entire nation.

Regarding the incompetence of the African languages compared to European languages, the truth is that the denigrating of African languages by the colonial whites was nothing more than racial bias and bigotry, and the justification of their injustice in invading and colonizing the Africans. Otherwise African languages are as complete mediums of communication as any other human language, European languages included. Some Western linguists today in fact admit that some African languages are more complex and efficient vehicles of communication than European languages. In a paper on "Translations in Swahili Language and Literature in the 21st Century" I presented in 2011 at an international symposium in Frankfurt, Germany, I write:

"Until very recently, Western scholars usually dismissed African languages, each and all of them, as primitive, lacking in abstract nouns and having very few adjectives, and therefore incapable of expressing abstract thought or elevated discourse, thus transferring to African languages the prejudices out of which the European social *elite* who advocated the use of

Latin denigrated their native languages before the European Renaissance. Now Western Africanists scholars are realizing and admitting that not only are these African languages basically as complete as any of their Western languages, but that they at times express exact and subtle meanings more easily than European languages. The noun-class-based syntax of Bantu languages, for example, makes it possible for the speaker to communicate much more than what is actually said, the listener making out the rest from the affixes and suffixes and other concordants in the compressed sentence. In the epilogue of his German translation of Kitereza's novel, Professor Wilhelm J. G. Möhlig, an Africanist scholar of the University of Cologne, speaking of the challenges he encountered in translating Kitereza prose, comments on what he calls the 'sandwich structure' of a Bantu language narrative as follows:

> According to their structural type, they are noun-class-languages, characterized by a strict formal concordance between syntactically dependent elements of the sentence. As a result, the syntactical relationships even in a complex passage can always be recognized by the reader or hearer. Compared to Bantu languages, the German language possesses much fewer possibilities of expressing syntactic coherence. It is, therefore, quite impossible to imitate the structure of the (Swahili) text (Ruhumbika, 2011).

African languages are also very beautiful languages, as even pioneer European researchers had to admit. To limit myself to Bantu languages, their exceptional tonality and intricate tone patterns not only make them very melodious languages (Johnson 1919, p. 6), but, more importantly, enable them to express by the same word or phrase a multiplicity of meaning (Ashton 1947, pp. 11-34, 70-81, 110-117). I have no doubt this is equally true of the languages of the other African language families as well.

Chapter One | Gabriel Ruhumbika, in
Dainess Maganda and Karim Traoré (Eds.)
LANGUAGE AND LITERATURE: Vehicles for the Enhancement of Cultural Understanding
London, Adonis & Abbey Publishers

Finally, as languages of creative writing some African languages are simply amazing! That is what I discovered when translating from the Kikerewe manuscript Kitereza's novel mentioned above. Apart from their grammatical features, like the noun-based syntax of Bantu-languages already mentioned, and their abundant proverbs and sayings and riddles and puns, and so on, African languages have other language-enriching features not found in European languages, one of which, for example, is ideophones, which Professor Isidore Okpewho (1992) defines as "ideas-in-sound" in his book *African Oral Literature: Background, Character and Continuity*, to differentiate them from onomatopoeias. Kitereza wrote his long novel in the style of an African story-teller and uses this feature of his native Kikerewe everywhere in his narrative. AMkerewe would, for example, ordinarily signify a person's hard fall with the onomatopoeia *pu*! But if the hard fall has been caused by somebody or something, then the speaker could signal that fact by *ligiti*! The ideophone for falling down completely. A person who arrives suddenly and unexpectedly in another person's home is said to have arrived *bwaa*! Whereas the sighting of a person who simply appears as if from nowhere is signified by *kigi*! and eating and finishing food completely is signified by *fyu*!, or, for emphasis, *fyu fyu fyu*! and so on." I believe such linguistic features can enrich in a unique way the works of literature written in African languages, for they certainly are part of the beauty of Kitereza's Kikerewe novel.

All that notwithstanding, the inadequacy of most African languages in their present condition and their need for growth and development have to be admitted. What I wrote on the subject more than twenty years ago is still true:

> Swahili existed in written form long before Tanzania chose to make it the country's national language. All the same, its development from a language which is mostly only spoken to a written language capable of

Chapter One | Gabriel Ruhumbika, in
Dainess Maganda and Karim Traoré (Eds.)
LANGUAGE AND LITERATURE: Vehicles for the Enhancement of Cultural Understanding
London, Adonis & Abbey Publishers

serving the scientific, economic, educational, and other needs of a modern state will require a concerted national effort lasting several generations. English, French, Spanish, and other languages that are today considered world languages underwent the same process of growth and development. Problems of standardization have already been solved in the case of Swahili in Tanzania, but they would have to be addressed for most African languages that are developing into the national languages of their countries. Vocabulary development (especially the development of scientific and technical terms), the continuous standardization of spelling and the rules of grammar as the language expands and grows, the preparation of dictionaries and school manuals, and the dissemination of new information about the language as it grows and expands call for the mobilization of all the human and finance resources that an African country can put aside for the endeavor. As a Swahili writer and translator, I do not underestimate the magnitude of these problems, but I know that they alone rule out the possibility of developing all the ethnic languages of an African country as national languages, even if a single African national language (or two or three at most) wasn't absolutely necessary for the forging of national unity and the development of the country.

More than a decade later, in a paper I presented at a Swahili international symposium at the University of Dar es Salaam in 2005, I was still writing about what Swahili in Tanzania lacked, notably good and complete dictionaries capable of serving the needs of the language at its current level of development as well as good grammar books (Ruhumbika, 2005, p. 231).

African national languages and the need for European world languages

In my 1992 article I wrote:

> Won't we be isolating ourselves from the world, especially the Western world of science and technology and economic development, by making the African national languages the medium of instruction in all our schools and universities?" The answer to this question is simple. We will continue to learn and teach the languages of world communication such as English in our schools. But, as in many other nations of the world, they will be treated as foreign languages needed for external communication and academic research only. The Africans who equate European languages with higher education, knowledge, culture, and civilization need only to ask themselves what the fate of

those languages and their nations would have been, if the admirers of Latin in England, France and Spain and other European countries had prevailed and Latin had remained the medium of education in those countries at the crucial moment in the development of those nations? I think we can say with certainty that the European Renaissance, even if it had taken place, would not have been of the same magnitude, and likewise the age of Enlightenment. Above all, the spread of education which was so essential to launching in Europe an era of unprecedented expansion of literacy and advances in knowledge in every field and an explosion of scientific discoveries and inventions of all kinds, and the industrial revolution of the eighteenth and nineteenth centuries which resulted from those inventions would most likely not have taken place, at any rate not at the time they did.

It is also my conviction that had European nations not cast aside the use of Latin and began using their people's languages; those languages would not have developed and become the world languages of today with their rich literatures. As I write in my 1992 article:

> A thriving literature is a literature which forms part of a people's living culture. It is a literature written for the people, reflecting their endeavors and aspirations, and reaching a significant number of them so as to have a meaningful impact on the public. That is why the Latin-language literatures of England, Spain and France never thrived; instead were esoteric writings for a small group of individuals, the aristocracy and other members of the *elite* of that time. The thriving literatures of those countries were only born when their writers turned to the use of their native languages. It is perhaps not by accident that the period of the most rapid growth of the national languages of those countries, between 1500 and 1650, (Baugh, 1954, pp. 245 – 312) coincided with the emergence of their greatest writers: Shakespeare and Milton in England, Corneille, Molière and Racine in France, and Lope de Vega and Cervantes in Spain. European literature in European national languages achieved in a relatively very short time what writing in Latin in those countries had failed to achieve in more than a millennium!" Africans cannot afford to ignore this important historic lesson about the importance of their languages in their cultural development.

The African countries have the example of the small countries of Europe, like the Scandinavian countries, and even Iceland, which use their national languages are the language instruction all the way to the university while also teaching English and other European world languages to the students of their institutions of learning. Even the examples of Asian countries like South Korea, and Japan, and even China have something African countries can learn from. We can even learn from the pitfalls of the language policies of India. What we can no longer afford to do is to let the status quo continue.

African national languages and the other languages in the country

Again let me quote what I wrote some twenty years ago:

> Depending on the needs and abilities of the country in question, those other ethnic languages can also be given be a place in the national education system alongside the new African national language, which should remain the medium of instruction in all schools and at all levels. In Tanzania Swahili is still at the beginning of the historical process of becoming a fully developed national language of the country, but because it is closely related to the other languages in the country, a new people is beginning to emerge everywhere, a people with two mother tongues, their own ethnic language and Swahili, the new national language. In other words, the new national language in gradually becoming the native language of everybody in the country, following a process which has taken place in many other nations in the world at similar stages in the development of their national languages. At the same time Swahili itself is being influenced a lot by the other languages of the country as it grows, especially regarding the expansion of its vocabulary. After more than fifty of using Swahili as the national language, the Tanzanian example also shows that the other ethnic languages of the country are resilient and don't die easily, especially in the rural areas. The bilingual young child of today's rural Tanzania switches very easily from Swahili to the ethnic language as the occasion demands. However the situation in the urban areas also indicates that eventually some of the a hundred or so ethnic languages of Tanzania

will die and disappear and be replaced by Swahili, the new native language of every Tanzanian. And to me that is not something to fear or regret, just as the English or Germans or Italians or Spaniard who speak only their national language don't regret the disappearance of their particular area's former languages or dialects which no longer exist.

Conclusion

I must first of all say that the situation which existed in Tanzania (Tanganyika of the time) at independence with regard to Swahili is unique to Tanzania, and the leaders of other African nations who want to develop African national languages would most likely be facing a more difficult task. Swahili spread in today's Tanzania (and neighboring parts of East and Central Africa) first of all with the Arab slave trade, which climaxed in the first half of the nineteenth century. The language was further spread in the country first by the Germans and then the British, who used it as the language of their colonial administration and as a medium of instruction in primary schools. At independence, therefore, even though not everybody in the country spoke Swahili, the language was, nevertheless, already the country's lingua franca. All that was needed was a national leadership which saw the need of Swahili in the building of their new nation, which the country had under Julius Kambarage Nyerere, the father of the nation and fist president of Tanzania (and which Kenya, which was in a similar situation lacked). The other African countries would have to start with the different realities of their countries. However, as we have shown, today lingua francas, or potential lingua francas, exist practically everywhere in Black Africa and, with the correct political leadership; those countries too can start developing their African national languages. And they have to do so, because the status quo has failed.

Chapter One	Gabriel Ruhumbika, in Dainess Maganda and Karim Traoré (Eds.) LANGUAGE AND LITERATURE: Vehicles for the Enhancement of Cultural Understanding London, Adonis & Abbey Publishers

More than fifty years after the use of Swahili as the national language of independent Tanzania, all I could say above is that in Tanzania Swahili is still at the beginning of the historical process of becoming the country's fully developed African national language. In fact, in one crucial way, we are still exactly where we were when I began writing in Swahili at the beginning of the 1970s. Unless the situation has changed recently and I am not aware of it, Swahili is still the medium of instruction in the country only up to the end of primary school, which in Tanzania is the 7th grade! The crucial move of teaching all subjects in Swahili in secondary schools and, shortly after that, at the university and other institutions of higher learning is still pending! We actually have taken a backward step: private English-medium primary schools have sprung up in the capital and other cities, where the rich who can afford it prefer to send their children! To me that is the undeniable evidence of the colonial mentality of our national leaders, who equate English with education and everything European with civilization. It is also evidence of the selfishness our country's *elite*, to whom the continued use of English as the medium of instruction in secondary schools and the university is a way of consolidating their *elitism* and perpetuating their role as agents and beneficiaries of neo-colonialism. Otherwise the Swahili of Tanzania today is a fully developed modern language which can be used as a medium of instruction in secondary schools and at the university without any difficult, as the department of Kiswahili of the University of Dar es Salaam has been demonstrating for decades by offering undergraduate and graduate studies using the language. The cost of making Swahili textbooks and other teaching materials available is easily met once the nation sees that need. May be it would help our national *elite*, who insist on equating education with English, to know that the richest country on earth, the USA, which happens to be the English-speaking, is lagging behind some Asian countries like South Korea and some small European countries like Finland in education!

On the positive side, Swahili has given Tanzanians a united nation in a way which perhaps is not found anywhere else in Sub-Saharan Africa. In human history anything can happen anytime, and we are not out of danger by any means. For example, religious tensions of the kind we had never known since independence have in recent years threatened to disrupt our people's unity, just as they are threatening to disrupting peace in many other parts of the world. Let us hope that we have enjoyed our unity for so long that we will fight and defeat such dangers and continue to be the nation of a united people.

Also, the transformation of Tanzania into a bilingual nation, people who speak two native languages, continues to accelerating and has reached even the villages of my remote native Ukerewe island, judging from what I witnessed when I was home last a few years ago, and most likely that is true in the other parts of the country too! And that is great news to all those who advocate the growth of African national languages. But to me the real evidence that Tanzania of the twenty-fist century has become a Swahili-speaking nation is when I am in the country and listen to the debates in the Bunge, the National Assembly, or to a cabinet minister presenting in superb and fluent Swahili the budget of his or her ministry, or when I hear a medical doctor, a university professor or some other expert talk about his or her area of technical or scientific expertise on the radio or television in Swahili which is understandable to a person who does not know a word of English! Even more than that, though our so called "educated" people send their children to English-medium primary schools (some even to England and South Africa!), when it comes to those Tanzanian parents themselves, it would appear Swahili has irreversibly become their language of daily use! Even when they are among their fellow educated Tanzanians, they speak principally in Swahili, and not in English. The same appears to be true even when they are among people of from the same ethnicity. The only question we must ask therefore is how much longer can the selfish leadership of the country continue to deny the people of Tanzania the right to receive a sound education in their African national language all the way to the university?

Regarding the rest of our African nations, as democratic countries of the twenty-first century, the development of African national languages for their people's unity and development is a task which cannot be postponed any longer. To do so is to prolong blatant neo-colonialism and underdevelopment, with the masses of their countries becoming poorer and poorer, uneducated and forgotten, except once in four or five years when they asked to vote again for their "leaders", and only a tiny group of the people enjoying whatever little wealth is left behind in the country, after foreign investors and other exploiters of their people have taken to their countries their lion's share of the loot. Such social injustice is not only unacceptable but also very dangerous. It has already, directly or indirectly, caused grave social unrest and even civil wars in some of our countries, and things could get worse

Finally, African national languages and African inter-state languages are essential for the Africans' cultural survival. The prospect of the Africans being the only people on earth who have no languages of their own in today's "global village", or whose languages are some corrupt versions of so-called world languages which nobody understands, to me should be unacceptable to all Africans as well as to all those who wish us well.

References

Alexandre, P. (1972). *Languages and Language in Black Africa.* Evanston, IL: Northwestern University Press,

Ashton, E.O. (1947). Swahili Grammar (Including Intonation). Harlow: Longman.

Baugh, A. C. (1954). *A History of the English Language.* London: Routledge and Kegan Paul, Ltd.

Bryan, M. A. (1959).*The Bantu Languages of Africa.* London: Oxford University Press.

Lwanga-Lunyiigo and J. Vansina.(1988).The Bantu-speaking People and Their Expansion".InM. Elfasi (Ed) & I. Hrbek (Assistant Ed) *UNESCO General History of Africa.Vol. 3. Africa from the Seventh to the Eleventh Century.* Paris and Berkeley: UNESCO & University of California Press.

Johnston, Sir Harry H. (1919). *A Comparative Study of the Bantu and Semi-Bantu Languages.*London: Oxford University Press.

Möhlig, Wilhelm J. G. (1991). *Nachwort des Übersetzers"*. Kitereza, Aniceti. *Die Kinder derRegenmacher: Herr Myombekere und Frau Bugonoka.* Trans. Wilhelm J. G. Möhlig.Wuppertal: Peter Hammer Verlag

Okpewho, I. (1992). *African Oral Literature: Background, Character and Continuity.* Bloomington and Indianapolis: Indiana University Press

Oyono, Ferdinand. (1970). *Houseboy.* London: Heinemann – African Writers Series.

Ruhumbika, G. (2005) "Mwandishi wa Kiswahili na Lugha yake katika Tanzania Huru. ("TheSwahili Writer and His or Her Language in Post-Independence Tanzania"). In Makala ya Kongamano la Kimataifa la Jubilei ya TUKI -2005

(Proceedings of the International IKR Jubilee Symposium - 2005). Dar es Salaam: Taasisi ya Uchunguzi wa Kiswahili, ChuoKikuu cha Dar es Salaam, 2006, page 231. (Translation from Swahili by the author.)

Ruhumbika, G. (1992). African-language Policy of Development: African NationalLanguages. *Research in African Literatures*, 23 (I),73-82

Werner, Alice. (1919). *Introductory Sketch of the Bantu Languages*. London & New York: KeganPaul, Trench, Trubner & Co. & E. P. Dutton.

CHAPTER TWO

Sustaining the Global Visibility of African Languagesand Cultures: The Case of Kiswahili

Lioba Moshi
University of Georgia

Introduction

At an African Studies meeting, a graduate student complained that it was very difficult to find a challenging African language program beyond the first two semesters unless you are able to go to the target country and spend a semester or a year to strengthen the skill already acquired and to experience the culture. When pressed to say more, the student indicated that many institutions are wary of funding a class that has less than ten students because it is not cost effective. Also, many students, especially undergraduates, take an African language to fulfill graduation requirements and have no intention of going beyond the required sequences. In many institutions, the requirement ranges between one and three semesters. Consequently, the graduate students who would like to take more classes, and who are out-numbered by the undergraduates in the class, receive the 'short end of the stick' in so far as their needs are concerned. The predicament of the African languages on college campuses is not unique because other less commonly taught languages face similar challenges. However, the African languages are more endangered compared to Asian and European languages in the same category. As the graduate student explained, the African languages have not succeeded in establishing a business or a political need despite the global security challenges that African countries are currently facing. Historically, the status of a particular less commonly taught language depended on world events. For example, during the cold war, Russian and German were very popular. Currently, they are at their lowest points. In recent times, Arabic and Hebrew have gained a lot of popularity in college campuses because of the prevailing conflicts in the Middle East. The status of Arabic has been further enhanced due to the "war on terror" which is associated with Islamic and Arabic speaking countries. Chinese, Japanese, and Korean have both a political and an economic implication. Recently, Hindi has joined their ranks of languages that have a high demand on college campuses. Many of the students taking these languages are in business school, international affairs, and a small number in literature and philosophy, especially where a department of comparative literature exists and offers courses on Asian literature. Many of these units also receive support from the corporate world in anticipation to recruiting the graduates to join the business world to enhance their global business advantages. African languages do not possess these advantages. Kiswahili, which made a lot of advancements in the 60s, 70s, and part of the 80s, is slipping. The end of the cold war could be used to explain this loss of momentum, but one would have thought that it would have been neck to neck with Arabic, considering that the initial acts of terrorism were committed on the soil of Kiswahili speaking countries and to date those states are considered areas of close watch for a variety of reasons. Some of these reasons include their close cultural and economic ties to the presumed perpetrators, and poverty, which considered an attractive motive for an individual to be lured to assist a planned terrorist act. Furthermore, Tanzania and Kenya have a strong link with the business world due to their rich tourist attractions and more so for Tanzania because of its minerals, diamonds and tanzanite. Tanzania is also very favorably viewed due to its peaceful political stance, espouses democratic governance that has allowed peaceful transitions from one regime to another through free and fair elections over the years. So, the question is why?

The Demise of Kiswahili

There are three factors that contribute to the demise of African languages, namely historical, prevailing world politics, and the African consciousness. Not only did these factors contribute and continue to contribute to the marginalization of the African languages but also are the stumbling blocks that the languages continue to face in the age of globalization.

Historical Factors

Imperialism and colonialism did not encourage the development of local languages in Africa. As such, Kiswahili was affected by this. For a long time, scholars debated the origins of Kiswahili, taking a stand in defense (e.g. Stigand,1913; Kirkman, 1964 and others) or in opposition (e.g. Kusimba,1999; Fitzgerald, 1898; Horton, 1996; Wilding, 1989; Muturo, 1987; Nurse & Spear 1985; Nurse, 1983; and Hinnenbusch, 1976), to the 'external origin theory', which essentially stated that the Coastal people of Eastern Africa did not exist prior to the arrival of outsiders, bringing with them the culture, civilization, and language. There was a tendency to believe that African cities were built by foreigners, that the civilization which developed on the Kiswahili Coast was a by-product of the migration of people and ideas from the Near East, and that the role of indigenous people (Kirkman1964, p. 22) was largely irrelevant to the question of understanding the origins of social complexity.

The existence of a Bantu people in the coastal states also establishes that Kiswahili is an old language. The earliest known documentation of this fact dates back to the 2nd century AD. As Kusimba (1999) notes, merchants visiting the East African coast at that time from Southern Arabia, found natives speaking the language, spreading from southwards of Somalia and Kenya to all the way to Zanzibar and Kilwa. It is also believed that the Kiswahili civilization carved out a small territory even further south around Sofala in Zimbabwe. Visitors to this area, the Arabs, Persians, and the Portuguese played a significant role in the growth of Kiswahili civilization. They destroyed successful polities that were highly respected by the people and nobilities that were African in origin and enslaved the indigenous people. They also disrupted a vibrant trade that had established them as sophisticated merchants who traded with other coastal people and those who lived near and far. They played a prominent role in the triangular mercantile trade, establishing cultural and commercial relations with the East African interior, the Persian and Arabian Gulf, the Indian subcontinent, and Indonesia. As such, they were very important in the world trade as early as 1 B.C. As such, if the Kiswahili coast had been left untouched, their savvy trading skills would have served them well, become conduit for language development, perhaps placing Kiswahili in the ranks of global languages earlier than other world languages, including English. Without doubt, the 'external origin theory' affected the way the Coastal States have been viewed throughout history. The distinctive cultural and ethnic character of the Kiswahili people who are urban, literate, and Islamic, and seemingly unlike the other others who are rural, farmers, non-literate, and traditionally African in their beliefs, was and still is regarded as evidence of their separate identities and cultural origins, reinforcing the class system that we will

Chapter Two | Lioba Moshi, in
Dainess Maganda and Karim Traoré (Eds.)
LANGUAGE AND LITERATURE: Vehicles for the Enhancement of Cultural Understanding
London, Adonis & Abbey Publishers

discuss shortly. Because the origin of the Kiswahili civilization was not rightfully accorded to the indigenous people, the debate on the origin of Kiswahili continues to negatively impact the views about the language and its speakers. As such, Kiswahili continues to struggle for its visibility due to its placement on the margins of world history. Such a history has destroyed the ability for Kiswahili to claim its ability to deal with scientific matters and allows science to be viewed through the lenses of western languages. This claim is also true for many other African languages. The African people are at best viewed as the receptors of ideas rather than innovators.

But it is important to bring to bear that before it was infiltrated, the Kiswahili culture was vibrant and later became multi-textured because of a number of factors including an extensive and dynamic interaction between the indigenous people of the Coastal States and towns with the majority culture, the cultures of the rural people who traded and interacted with them, and non-Africans who ventured into the coastal states from across the oceans.

The decline of the coastal city-states began in the 16th century; the advent of the Portuguese who caused the most disruption of the trade routes, making the Swahili peoples' commercial centers obsolete. The Portuguese were not interested in integrating the native Africans in the early free trade practices. Because the Arabs had enslaved and converted the locals into Islam, the Portuguese set out with a mission to defeat the established Islamic city-states along the eastern coast of Africa. Although the Omans (from south of Arabia) returned in the 17th Century and conquered the Portuguese and took back the cities the natives did not fare any better under their control. Slavery and subjugation played a major role in destroying individual and collective creativity that had existed prior to the arrival of the foreign forces. It also destroyed the local cultural diversity that preceded the invasions, trade, friendship, and alliances between many different communities that led to the exchange of ideas, information, and genes through shared language and cultural beliefs. The invasion created a forced occupation of the land and the colonization of the people.

However, it is important to note that despite the undesired destructions, the language benefited by borrowing from the language of the rulers of different periods. This is evident in the rich lexicon. For example the numbers as used in Kiswahili: *moja* 'one', *mbili* 'two', *tatu* 'three', *nne* 'four', *tano* 'five', *nane* 'eight', *kumi* 'ten', are considered to be of Bantu origin. *sita* 'six' *saba* 'seven' and *tisa* (that replaced the Bantu word *kenda* which is still used) 'nine' are considered borrowed words from Arabic. Furthermore, the Kiswahili words: *serikali* 'government', *diwani* 'councilor', and *chai* 'tea', are among some of the words considered borrowed from Persian. Borrowings from Portuguese include *meza* 'table' *gereza* 'prison', and *pesa* ('peso'), 'money'. The German rule introduced into the language words like *shule* 'school' and *'hela'* a German coin. Likewise, English (British) introduced words like *baiskeli* 'bicycle', *basi* 'bus', *penseli* 'pencil', *mashine* 'machine', and *koti* 'coat', and continues to influence the language to date.

Needless to say, new languages were the windows through which cultural behavior, cultural values, cultural attitudes, and perspectives were introduced to the people. While the coast was influenced heavily by Islam and the Islamic culture, the hinterland adhered more to the western culture. With Arabic came Islam and Islamic schools that emphasized the Koran and strict observances of the Islamic culture. It also introduced a social class system that valued those who were direct descendants of the rulers and demeaned those who were note.

There were four main social classes (Kusimba, 1999, pp. 140-141):

a) *waungwana* 'elite' (the ethic of possessing high culture) which included the free, or nobly born--- descendants of the Sultan (Arab ruler)
b) *wazaliwa* 'free-born' usually the descendants of freed slaves or at least one of their parents (often the mother);
c) *watumwa* 'slaves' those who were enslaved;
d) *wageni* 'visitors' which included recent immigrants and other inhabitants from thenon-Coastal States.

Rights and privileges depended on one's social status. The *waungwana* were predominantly in the urban areas and led an urban life and controlled the social, political, and economic structure of the community. Because they were considered to possess the high culture, intellectual, and artistic sensitivity, they also acquired the ideological support to their control of wealth-creating activities, including land and labor; had exclusive ownership of the fertile land, stretches of beach, and mangrove swamps. They had a right to slaves who worked these lands and had a right to make policy decisions in the affairs of the town. There were also membership restrictions to the *uungwana* social group it was limited to those who demonstrated blood ties to a well-respected ancestor, who could supplement their kin-based claims to status with wealth, especially ownership of a stone house located in an elite section of the town. This is an important aspect that I will revisit in the next discussion on African consciousness. As Kusimba (1999) notes, *Uungwana* privileges include the right to: religious scholarship; own property such as fertile farmland, stretches of beach land, mangrove forests, and fishing areas; own cattle; build and live in stone houses in one's own *mtaa*(neighborhood); receive, entertain, and trade with foreign merchants; elect town and mosque officials; hold hereditary offices of *Mkuu wa Jela* (prison warden), *Mweka Hazina* (keeper of the town treasury) and *Mkuu wa Pwani* (warden of the sea).

The British, who introduced the English language, also introduced a British governing system, an educational system, and its cultural values. English was given a priority, in the urban cities and slowly infiltrated the rural areas through schooling. During the colonial period, schools offered at least three classes of English a day and only one class of Kiswahili a week. The medium of instruction was also English in the Middle Schools, High Schools, and Colleges. Emphasis was placed on excelling in English as a prerequisite to excelling in other subjects. Consequently, an attitude was developed in the minds of the learners that their local languages and Kiswahili that linked them as a nation were inferior to English. As it will be shown later, to change this attitude is a major challenge, even in a country like Tanzania where there was great after independence to eliminate this colonial mentality from the citizenry.

Mastery of the English language created comparable social class system, although rights and privileges were not mandated. However, there was nothing to stop one from feeling superior because they had a mastery of English. In fact, fluency in English, to date, is considered a sign of 'being educated/the road to success which is one's chance of securing a good job, promotion, or landing on the good life at home or internationally.

Prevailing world politics

It was noted in the introduction that the gain or lose the status of prestige for some languages was a consequence of the politics and world events of the time. Examples of such world events include the cold war and the rise and fall of the popularity of the Russian and German language instruction in many institutions. Another example would be the current popularity of Arabic and Hebrew due to the prevailing conflicts in the Middle East and the "war on terror".

Evidence of Kiswahili's role as a lingual Franca in east Africa is in the way it fostered the spread to other parts of sub-Sahara Africa. Furthermore, the rapid nature of its spread and the ease at which it was accepted by other communities stems from adopted role in the early 50s when it assumed a political function of fostering nationalism. It was the language the new breed of African political leaders used to impel for African nationalism and the African right to self-determination and independence.

An even bigger role was assumed by Kiswahili in the armed forces of both colonial and post-colonial East Africa. The Uganda's experience is interesting because of the relationship between who ruled the country and who dominated the armed force. Both Milton Obote and Idi Amin come from the northern part of Uganda and were linked to the Nilotes. Consequently, the armed forces recruited mostly from the Nilotes who were very conscious of their separateness from the Bantu groups that were predominantly settled in the southern parts of Uganda. The Nilotes were especially alienated from the Baganda (Mazrui & Mazrui, 1999). This relationship created ethnic rivalry among the groups (Acholi, Langi, Kakwa, Lugbara, Baganda, and Nilotes). It is also interesting to note that the rivalry necessitated the use of a common language for communication between them. Kiswahili became the language of choice across ethnic boundaries and even when Idi Amin came to power and eliminated many of the Acholi and Langi members of the armed force, Kiswahili remained the lingua franca of the army.

Outside the Ugandan army, Kiswahili gained political importance, especially during Idi Amin's reign despite the hostility and political decline associated with his brutal regime. This is because the Baganda saw wisdom in changing their resistance to Kiswahili and became the propagators of Kiswahili and its integrative functions in the army. The society responded well to this change and warmed up to the use of Kiswahili. The increasing functional role of Kiswahili in Kenya and Tanzania, its neighboring states, was also a factor that assured the Ugandans that it was not just a military language.

Kiswahili as also penetrates areas like the Francophone countries of the Democratic Republic of the Congo (DRC), Rwanda, and Burundi, where French was introduced through the Belgians. To understand the mitigating factors, one has to look at the linguistic implications of the Belgians and not the French introducing French to the people of these countries. Belgians have two languages, French and Flemish. At the onset, it was not clear in Belgian Congo whether French or Flemish would be the language to be adopted. The Belgians revered and feared French because of its association with autocracy. The Flemish cultural affiliations with German afforded the Belgians the linguistic distance between the masters. This attitude allowed French to thrive even though it was sandwiched, in some parts, between indigenous African languages and Flemish. It was important, therefore, to instill it in the schools that were largely controlled by the Flemish Belgians. The attitude that prevailed among the Flemish Belgians at the time allowed Kiswahili to penetrate the Eastern and Southern parts of the Congo. Kiswahili provided the bond that the subjects needed. By the time the DRC achieved its independence a substantial number of Congolese spoke Kiswahili with reputable proficiency. Kiswahili has since remained one of the important languages in the DRC in addition to Lingala, and Kikongo.

A more recent evidence of the expansion of Kiswahili can be found in its integrative role in migrant labor communities in sub-Saharan Africa, states that achieved independence after a period of liberation struggle, and misplaced communities in refugee camps in Eastern Africa, and those who have been settled overseas after spending a number of years in refugee camps in Eastern Africa (these include Somalis, Rwandans, Burundians, and Congolese). These groups learned Kiswahili and now use it as a lingua franca in their new communities. Often, these groups select Kiswahili as the language of their identity when requesting an interpreter in England and America and also as a medium of communication with other displaced peoples from these four ethnic groups when they find themselves in the same communities abroad. Mazrui and Mazrui (1999) note that while Kiswahili has been used to influence ethnic loyalties it has also been an instrument for changing ethnic behavior, creating social classes and religious affiliations, and for providing racial identity and national consciousness.

In Tanzania, Kiswahili gained prominence in the 60s, shortly after the country's independence from the British. It was the language of politics and governance. In 1967, it was declared the language of instruction at elementary and middle school levels. Julius Nyerere, the first President of Tanzania championed the change and in identifying an indigenous language as the national language. His efforts were supported by those of the other leaders in East Africa in developing Kiswahili. Their enthusiasm stemmed from a national patriotic understanding and belief in specific ideals. Citizens of Tanzania, for example, believe that nationalism and cultural-revolution rely heavily on the development of Kiswahili, the single unifying language. It is no secret that Kiswahili is the preferred language of the home, especially among the younger generation despite a heavy competition from local and other indigenous languages. There are those who would argue that promoting Kiswahili creates a grave yard of other indigenous languages (including associated cultures) in East Africa, particularly in Tanzania.

African consciousness

It is not the intension of this paper to cast blame but rather to awaken an academic discourse that would lead to less compliance and more actions, forcing the African consciousness to be re-directed to the problem of shielding cultural insecurity, one that accepts the 'receptor' status rather than the 'innovator' status.

It is true that colonization followed by neo-colonization leaves a lasting impact on a people, strips them of their sense of worthiness and a trust that they can do for themselves, speak for themselves, and act on behalf of themselves. As noted in the preceding discussion, the people of the Swahili States were stripped of their culture, rights, privileges, and wealth; they also lost their dignity and sense self-worth through slavery. Undoubtedly, this accounts for the development of self-doubt with respect to their abilities to achieve and sustain achievements. They have, for the most part, believed that they do not possess any expertise and that true expertise comes from foreign lands and their role is that of a 'recipient'. We can best understand this attitude by looking Henri Tajfel's (1974, 1978, 1981) theory of social grouping.

Within the preview of the theory of inter-group relations and social change Tajfel discusses how perceived inferior/minority groups operate in comparison to the superior/majority group. He notes that, a minority/inferior group is often viewed in negative terms when comparing them with other groups. Because they are aware of this negative perception, members within the inferior group always look for ways to stay visible and to coexist within the social structure. Tajfel suggests two strategies available to the inferior group: (1) to accept the minority/inferior status or (2) to reject the minority/inferior status. Each strategy yield different outcomes.

Tajfel notes that, when a group or an individual accepts the perceived inferior status, they attempt to assume an individualistic stance. This means that they get out of the group circle in order to achieve a personal positive image. They also attempt to measure themselves against members of their own group. In a sense, they create their own in relation to the group they isolate themselves from.

When the second strategy, namely rejecting the inferior/minority status, is selected, an attempt is made to change the status by seeking equality with the superior (majority) group and by adopting the values of the majority/superior group, a process known as assimilation. An individual or group that adopts the rejection strategy would try to redefine the negative characteristics that characterize them by creating positive characteristics. There is also an attempt to create new dimensions that could be used for comparison with the superior group as a way to create an identity for themselves.

How does this apply to the African consciousness? Based on the prevailing status quo among African scholars and leaders, it is not unreasonable to claim that for the most part, the first strategy is selected when confronted with that choice. Both Ali Mazrui (1986) and Henry Louis Gates (1999) in their documentaries about Africa (The Africans and Wonders of the

African World respectively) have alluded to this tendency. It is not uncommon to hear someone say that the Ivorians, Congolese, and Algerians are more French than the French. Also, in the 70s, one Kenyan politician refused to fly in an aircraft whose pilot was not English speaking, meaning an African from Kenya was incapable of serving him as a pilot in the plane he was on. In his documentary, Henry Louis Gates was shocked when he found out that in Lamu and Zanzibar, a good percentage of the people did not consider themselves *Waswahili* but rather Persians or Shiraz. Cognizant of the "consciousness" factor, Gates, laughingly, commented in the documentary that African Americans in America have issues with identity too, and that some claim ancestry from many places except Africa and presumably for the same reasons, the need to distance themselves from slavery. Like some of their brothers and sisters in Lamu and Zanzibar, some African Americans do not want to be considered descendants of slaves. A good example is Tiger Woods who claimed ancestry that does not include Africa when some African Americans wanted to claim him as one of their own has made them proud.

Considering the earlier discussions on the social status that was accorded to different groups inhabiting the Swahili coastal states, I do not see why anyone should be shocked. Admitting that they are *Waswahili*, Gate's interlocutors would have also admitted that they are not *Waungwana* 'elites'. They did not want to accept membership in the class of inferiors and by pulling themselves outside of the circle they are able to create a superior social group of their own. As *Waungwana* they can compare themselves with the *watumwa* 'slaves' or the *wazaliwa* 'free born/offspring of the slaves'. A Persian and Shirazi identity also includes Arabic as the language of identity while eliminating Kiswahili. It is without doubt that Kiswahili as the language of the more inferior members cannot emerge as a respected language in the eyes of the superior/majority group (non-Africans). The place of Arabic in the world is much higher than that of Kiswahili and allows the *waungwana*, individually or as a group, to try to join the superior/majority group.

The Lamu and Zanzibar people who shocked Gates by identifying with the Persians/ Shiraz and Arabic also wanted to emphasize their affiliations with the acceptable scholarship since knowledge of Arabic also meant membership in the class of scholars who can read and interpret the Koran and the possibility to claim themselves as direct descendants of the Prophet Mohamed unlike the converts to Islam which are the *wazaliwa* and *watumwa*. It is important to note that, this is not unique to Islam. Catholicism was closely associated with Latin until Vatican II in 1965 when the Council of Catholic Bishops resolved that churches around the world could use their local languages for religious services. Until then, knowledge of Latin was used to claim a superior status in the church as well as a requirement for all clergy who were entrusted with the power to interpret the Bible 'Word of God' to the heathen.

The need to break out of the circle in order to represent self is also evident among Swahili people whose language of identity if Kiswahili. Because they consider Kiswahili to be inferior to European languages, they have found a way to stay visible but not the language. As noted earlier, during the colonial period, the education system in Swahili speaking areas (include Tanzania, Kenya, and Congo), emphasized the European language at the expense of the local language (English in Tanzania and Kenya and French in the Congo). In the case of Tanzania, for example, the school curriculum mandated at least three classes of English a day and only one class of Kiswahili a week. The medium of instruction for the other classes was also English in Middle Schools, High Schools, and Colleges. Emphasis was placed on excelling in English as a pre-requisite for advancement from one class to another, and certainly a guarantee for further education such as going to college or vocational training school. Consequently, an attitude was developed in the minds of the learners that their local languages and Kiswahili that linked them as a nation were inferior to English. This attitude has not changed in the minds of the affluent, even in a country like Tanzania where a lot of effort was made after independence to eliminate it. In Tanzania (also Kenya), there is a growing interest in English medium schools that has the interest of affluent and elite parents. Their interest sends a negative message about Kiswahili to the rest of the Swahili community, that proficiency in Kiswahili is not as important as English which identifies its speakers as a superior group within the perceived inferior group of Kiswahili speakers and that fluency in English places the group closer to the superior/majority social group.

It goes without saying that scholars from Kiswahili speaking communities are in the elite group. How many scholars publish their works in Kiswahili? In the early stages of his presidency, the late President Nyerere, the first President of the Republic of Tanzania, sought to move Africa in a different direction after many years of colonialism by advocating a government that empowered its people and embraced self-reliance, a means to ensure human dignity. His policy was called *Ujamaa*, a Swahili word that meant Fairyhood. Unfortunately, the west translated to it 'socialism' and later equated it to 'communism'. Those who liked his African philosophy appreciated what Ujamaa meant to a nation emerging from colonialism. Nyerere need to create a sense of familyhood in order to institute a conscious nation, one with a strong sense of nationalism to wade the possibility of tribal conflicts. Nyerere knew that he came from a very small tribe and the larger tribes had very powerful leaders, some of whom were just or more educated than him. He sought the power of a national language policy to contain that consciousness and to downplay the ethnicity card. By empowering Kiswahili, Nyerere created a following of admirers who also developed a very strong interest in Kiswahili that allowed it to be elevated to an international recognition. In the United States, this period marked the initiation of Kiswahili in College campuses and the appreciation of the concept of Pan-Africanism.

The first steps he adopted to make Kiswahili a powerful languages in the world the late President Nyerere minimized the power of English by removing the stigma that was placed on those who could not speak or read English. A command in the English language was no longer viewed as the prestige of the educated but rather a mark of someone who is snobbish. In fact if one tried to express themselves in English rather than Kiswahili in the late sixties and parts of the seventies, he or she was said to have *kasumba* 'colonial mentality' (now his detractors claim that this was the sole reason for the gradual erosion of English proficiency among many Tanzanians who received their primary or higher education after independence). Nyerere also wanted to lead by example. To demonstrate his scholarship, he authored several books in Kiswahili (with an English version): *Ujamaa* 'Familyhood/Socialism', *Uhuru na Umoja* 'Freedom and Unity', *Uhuru na Maendeleo* 'Freedom and Development'. In addition, he translated plays written in English that he considered influential in the way he articulated the policies of his young nation emerging from colonialism: The Merchants of Venice '*Mabepari wa Venice*', Julius Caesar '*Julius Kaisari*'.

Thus, in addition to emphasizing Kiswahili to meet the post-independence mission statement of the Ministry of Education in his country, Nyerere challenged other scholars to do likewise. Many scholars in Tanzania and Kenya have done so, enhancing literary publications in Kiswahili. Language textbooks as well as textbooks for other disciplines are in abundance in Kenya and Tanzania for elementary and secondary schools. A few can be found for linguistics study and literature at the college level. Very few scholars can follow his footsteps by publishing in both Swahili and the other languages that made their career (French or English).

There are obstacles to this, we understand, but by not doing so, scholars are perpetuating the perceived inferior status instead of rejecting it. Crystal (2005, pp. 508-514) enumerates the risks of accepting one language and rejecting others as viable to serve the world. These include:

1. *Elite monolingual linguistic*: where one group assumes the monopoly of the language encouraging the development of complacent and dismissive attitudes towards other languages and cultures.
2. *Manipulative tendencies*: where the privileged group use their competitive edge to manipulate the system at the expense of those who have less power and lack theability to use it. Consequently the gap between the poor and the rich would increase.
3. *Marginalization*: where somelanguages become marginalized and rendered not worth learning.
4. *Language death*: when a language is considered not worth learning, it becomes irrelevant and its ultimate death is hastened. This is a real danger for small languages and languages spoken in less powerful nations. This also perpetuatesthe mentality of "survival of the fittest".

There is no doubt that presently, Africa is confronted with these risks because of its dependency on foreign languages for communication, education, and trade.

Schmied (1991) correctly observes that there are persistent inequities in practice and application of resources available to L-2 English speakers. Specifically African scholars face sociolinguistic or grammatical problems as they try to express their ideas in English in an English only academy. Furthermore, despite the claim for global English, many written works in English around the globe remain unpublished due to sociolinguistic stereo-typing of both the authors and the texts. Often times, research by Africans that is enhanced by firsthand knowledge of linguistic phenomena that is particular to their first language is considered intuitive. This is an effort to distinguish between 'mainstream' researches from 'other' research practices. Such categorizations reinforce Crystal's concern of manipulative tendencies by the custodians of the designated global language. The categorizations also explain why large amounts of works by non-L1 English speakers have limited access to English-based publications. Obviously when scholars are confronted with the mainstream academia realities, they have no choice but to succumb to the subscribed inferiority status and cultural timidity. Schmied correctly observes that when scholars limit as well as discriminate the avenues through which they share or acquire knowledge they are missing valuable opportunities afforded by the exchange of ideas in written form between scholars of diverse cultures and linguistic backgrounds. This is also core in the attempt to reverse the prevailing African consciousness that is reflected cultural insecurity and timidity.

Language reflects its power in the way it is exploited by its speakers. Accepting the role of a non-powerful participant, through constraining contents of usage, relations entered into, and subject position occupied will remain the major impediment to the efforts of establishing and maintaining a visible status of African languages and more so of Kiswahili whose advancements to global status surpasses those of other African languages. Institutions will not continue to consider the need to encourage the teaching of African languages if scholars and speakers downplay their significance in the world market. Crystal (2005) has pointed out to us the dangers of accepting one language and consciously or sub consciously rejecting others. Downplaying the power of a language contributes to the limitations imposed on other sources of knowledge from and about the target nations. It is not uncommon, for example, to find an institution that has one faculty member who is expected to represent the teaching of the history of the entire continent of Africa. A scholar with expertise in economics or the sciences at institutions in the United States rarely teaches about Africa. Furthermore, the amount of Africa covered is less than 25% of the course content, even if they are themselves African. Linguistics and Literature departments used to be the champions on teaching about Africa and attracted a lot of students with an interest to study one or two of the African languages to a level where they could use it for research purposes. The number of linguistics publications on Africa has dwindled over the years and graduate students are afraid of developing a full-fledged interest in the study of Africa for fear that they will not be marketable upon graduating. Considering the mushrooming of NGOs in Africa, especially those associated with public health, one would expect that institutions would see this as a ready market for their graduates. Of course they would but no one is marketing it in the same way as other areas with superior status are marketed. African scholars, governments, and businesses are extremely handicapped when it comes to advocating for Africa, a consequence of long periods of accepting the inferior status even where the expertise is evident.

Implications for Africans and Africanists

Based on our discussions above, the demise of African languages and cultures and for that matter Kiswahili is not just a result of foreign forces. The Africans themselves are as much responsible especially where they have lost pride in their language and the culture associated with it. In the case of Kiswahili, there is no doubt that it has gained ground as a language of choice by millions of people in East Africa and its neighbors. It has also been transported to different parts of Africa and the West due to migration, both voluntary and as a consequence of ethnic wars, including the fight against colonialism and apartheid. Refugees from neighboring countries learn Kiswahili during their short stay in Kenya or Tanzania and keep the language when they finally immigrate to England, the United States, or other western countries. This is evident in the increase in demand for Kiswahili translators for agencies like the American based Language Line Incorporated and Pacific Interpreters Inc. that offer services to law enforcement, hospitals, legal services, immigration services, airline companies, and schools. Furthermore, the number of people learning Kiswahili at institutions of higher education in the United States has also attained impressive numbers but the enrolments are only high at the elementary and in special cases intermediate levels. Scholars in a position to advocate for serious language learning, in the likes of the commonly taught languages, should seize that opportunity.

It is also encouraging when we look at Europe and Asia where the enthusiasm in teaching and using African languages is strong and their objectives better defined. For example, many European institutions of higher education, including private organizations, teach Kiswahili more intensely and purposefully. Their programs are usually tied to development projects that are sponsored by the European Economic market, and specific agencies such as DANIDA and NORAD, to name only a few. The United States institutions could exploit this opportunity for programs such as Peace Corps, UNCEF and UNESCO, various NGOs associated with projects on global health, the World Bank, USAID, other independent agencies and missionary organizations. Currently, most institutions focus on academic related programs for the purposes of research projects that relate to the publication of books and graduate theses. This is a very narrowly defined market for the purposes of advocating for African languages especially the popular ones like Kiswahili.

Available examples that demonstrate that Kiswahili is attaining prominence are ample as we experience the growing use of Kiswahili in world media such as the Voice of America, and Radio Deutsche Welle, BBC radio and Television, and Asia radio and TV programs that come to many homes in East Africa. Some of these programs are broadcasted to East Africa (especially Kenya, and Tanzania) on a regular basis (in some cases twice a day). In addition, Kiswahili has been identified by Microsoft for the development of scanner OCR that would identify Kiswahili text. The Nairobi Microsoft office (cf. Majira Newspaper, June 2004:2) noted that Kiswahili was selected because of its status, a strong African language that can stand a global test as a language of business and communication in East Africa. Other African languages that are being targeted include: Yoruba, Hausa, Somali, and Amharic. The growing interest to expose Kiswahili to technology is also demonstrated in the move by Vodacom and Celtel phone companies to regularly place advertisements in newspapers in both English and Kiswahili to advertise their services. Both companies have seen the wisdom of reaching all sectors of the public since the buying power or usage does not reside in the affluent only. The challenge is to prevent these signs from remaining as signs only that make us feel good for the moment. Establishing a sustainable global need and importance among other global languages is what Kiswahili needs (also other African languages), and this can only be done by scholars and speakers. They should be the champions of establishing the need rather than discouraging it by inadvertently demonstrating that fluency in Kiswahili (or other key African languages) is unnecessary and therefore a low priority.

The burden is also on the leaders. The only leaders, who give their speeches abroad in languages other than their own, even where they run a risk of embarrassing themselves because of limited fluency, come from Africa. Other leaders take pride in their language and culture and are provided with translators when they need them. If African leaders are provided with translators when they need to speak to an English audience and the language of use is also foreign (French, Portuguese), why not use their own languages? For the most part, they know they are more fluent in the foreign language than their own. But, those who speak Kiswahili, especially from Kenya or Tanzania have no excuse because that is the language of official business in their home countries. The example of cultural pride and appreciation was set by President Joachim Chisano of Mozambique at the African Union (AU) Assembly in Addis Ababa in 1995. He offered a model for what is expected from African leaders, namely leading by example. President Chisano showed the hidden power of African languages by, unexpectedly, deciding to address the Assembly using Kiswahili. The Assembly was not prepared for this bold move and there was a brief moment of panic as the delegates scrambled to get translators to provide simultaneous translation. Needless to say, President Chisano was not swayed and continued with his remarks without worrying about the inability of the delegates to comprehend what he was saying. President Chisano's bold move, prompted President Obasanjo of Nigeria to follow suit by greeting the delegates in Kiswahili and thanking President Chisano for his bold move. Though symbolic, this move was both bold and commendable. President Chisano demonstrated the uniqueness of Kiswahili, reminding the delegates that they have been debating on the use of African languages at the assembly for over a decade and yet they had not moved to implement it. He wanted to show that this was the time to implement it, at the birth of a new organization, the African Union (that replaced the Organization of African Unity – OAU). President Chisano wanted to emphasize that the organization should change to reflect the world as it changes in the 21st Century. Africa and Africans should not continue to do business as usual. Rather, Africa and Africans have to assume their place in the global world and that language is one avenue through which they can assert their authority and cultural power. President Chisano demonstrated the power of Kiswahili and its prospective global use. Needless to say, other delegates at the assembly who could have used Kiswahili did not follow suit. Like African scholars, African leaders should overcome cultural insecurity and timidity when it comes to rejecting perceived inferiority/minority status.

Conclusion

Langer (1953, 1979) notes that language transforms speakers from biological creatures, who respond to the concrete world as it exists, into thinking beings that interpret, interact with, and remake the world through symbols. The symbols used shape our understanding of the world and our own places within it. The power of symbols lies in the kind of thought and action they enable. Symbols allow us to define, organize, and evaluate experiences and people. At the same time, they enable us to think hypothetically and to reflect on ourselves. Thus, the language that we use, selectively, shapes our perceptions and the names we apply emphasize particular aspects of reality and neglect others. Language names what exists and those with power name and define the world in their own terms. Furthermore, those with power to name the world use names and words rooted in their language to acknowledge what affects them. Therefore, when we talk about "the power of language" we are talking about how it reflects its speakers and how the speakers exploit that power. It is also important to note that language conventions and acceptance replicate and validate the existing power structures. Powerful participants (attempt to) control and constrain the distribution of non-powerful participants, through constraining contents of usage as well as relations entered into and the subject positions occupied. Therefore, what becomes of a language depends on its users and advocates. It is incumbent upon speakers and scholars to look for ways to grow the languages that are the root of the African symbolic place in the world. In order to make a language visible, one should expose its existing powerful achievements and global role.

References

Ali, H. O. & Mwikalo, R. (2000).*Kompyuta.jifunze na ielewe*. Ottawa: Commoners'Publication.

Anyanzwa, J. (2004). Computers to go Ki-Swahili, compliments of Microsoft. Business Times, 841:1.

Batibo, H. (2000). The linguistic situation in Tanzania. In Kahigi, K., Kihore, Y. and Mous, M. (eds.). *Lugha za Tanzania*, pp. 5-18. Leiden: CNWS Publications, 89.

Bhagwati, J. (2004). *In defense of globalization*. New York: Oxford University Press.

Chuwa, A. R. (2003). *Jifunze kompyuta WP5.Hatua ya kwanza*. Dar Es Salaam: IKR.

Coates, J. (1986). *Women and men and language*. London: Longman House, Burnt Mill, Harlow.

Crystal, D. (2005). Globalizing English. In Keith Walters and Michal Brody (eds.). *What'sLanguage Got to Do with it?* 504-514. New York: W.W. Norton and Co.

David D. (1999). The future of African language programming in the United States: The conceptof national African language center. *Journal of African Language Teachers Association*1, 17-24.

Dwyer, D., &Wiley D. (1981).*Directions and Priorities for the 1980's.*Michigan State University, African Studies Center.

Dwyer, D., & Moshi L. (1994).*The Field of African Language Programming* (Manuscript).

Fairclough, N. (1989). *Language and Power*. Longman Inc., New York.

Hancock, I. (Ed.).(1979). *Readings in Creole studies*. Gent: Story-Scientia.

Kiango, J. D. (2004). *Tanzania's historical contribution to the recognition and promotion of Swahili*. A paper read at the LASU Conference, University of Mauritius, August 11-13, 2004.

Kusimba, C. M. (1999). The rise and fall of Swahili States. Walnut Creek, California, AltamiraPress.

Langer, S.K. (1953). *Feeling and form, a theory of art.* New York: Scriber's.

Langer, S.K. (1979). Philosophy in a new key: A study in the symbolism of reason, rite and art. Cambridge: Harvard University.

Legere, K. (2005). *Uwezeshaji wa Kiswahili siku hizi, mafanikio na matatizo*. A paper read at the 2005 Annual Conference on African Linguistics, Savannah, Georgia.

Mazrui, A. A.' & Mazrui, A. M. (1998). *The Power of Babel: Language & governance in the African experience.* IGCS Publications: Binghamton University. Binghamton.

Mazrui, A. A., & Mazrui, A. M. (1999). *Political culture of language. Swahili, society, and state.* IGCS Publications. Binghamton University, Binghamton.

Middleton, J. (1992). *The World of the Swahili: An African Mercantile Civilization.* New Haven, Connecticut: Yale University Press.

Moshi, L. (1988). *Tuimarishe Kiswahili chetu* (Building proficiency in Kiswahili). A textbook for second and third year students. Lanham: University Press of America.

Moshi, L. (1994). *The teaching of African languages.* Penn Language News, Spring Issue.

Moshi, L. (1996). KiSwahili Lugha na Utamaduni: A 23 Lesson Video Series for the teaching KiSwahili language and culture. University of Georgia, OISD.

Moshi, L. (1998). KiSwahili, lugha na utamaduni (Swahili, language and culture). Hyattsville MD: Dunwoody Press.

Moshi, L., & Omar, A. (2003).*Kiswahili kwa Kompyuta (KIKO)*: a series of computer assistedlessons for Kiswahili learners at the elementary, intermediate, and advanced levels.Accessable at http://www.africa.uga.edu/Kiswahili/doe/.

Mwita, A.M.A & Mwansoko, D.N. (1998).*Kamusi ya Tiba*. Dar es Salaam, GTZ.

Ohly, R. (1987). A Primary technical dictionary English-Swahili. Dar es Salaam, Tanzania.

Schleicher, A., & Moshi, L. (2000).*The pedagogy of African languages: An emerging field*.Pathways Series: Ohio State University.

Schmied, J. (1991). *English in Africa: An introduction*. New York: Longman.

Scotton, C. M. (1979). The context is the message: morphological, syntactic, and semanticreduction in Nairobi and Kampala varieties of Swahili. In Ian Hancock (Ed.), *Readings in Creole studies* (pp. 111-128). Gent: Story-Scientia.

Stiglitz, J. (2003). *Globalization and its Discontents*. New York: W.W. Notron & Company.

Tajfel, H. (1974). Social Identity and Intergroup Behavior.*Social science information,13*(2),65-93.

Tajfel, H. (1978). Differentiation between social groups: studies in the social psychology ofintergroup relations. London: Academic Press.

Tajfel, H. (1981). Human groups and social categories. Cambridge: Cambridge University Press.

Walters, K. and Brody, M. (2005). What's language got to do with it? New York: W.W. Norton and Company.

Whitely, W. H. (1969). Swahili: the rise of a national language. London: Methuen.

CHAPTER THREE

Doors of Perception: Dialogues with Otherness

Corina Mihaela Beleaua
University of Georgia

The limits of my language mean the limits of my world.
Ludwig Wittgenstein

Thesis

The focus in the present paper is the concept of education and how knowledge of foreign languages can improve the way we approach life. Language, word, and translation constitute mechanisms that are part of the processing of our reality. Polysemy, metaphor and rhetoric manage to give us a broader perspective, surpassing the immediate understanding and reaching a metaphysical dimension of our grasp of reality. A better understanding of how we use language and the richness of the semantic assembly increases the chances of creating an educational system that might provide students with an almost holistic understanding of the world.

Therefore, in the first part of the essay I will focus on language that will be considered from several points of view. On one hand, the fact that it facilitates a certain approach to reality is undeniable. On the other hand, language and culture create a bridge between people/peoples. They allow interpersonal connections to happen and transform the relation between me and the other, thus allowing access to a better self-awareness.

In the second part of the essay I will mostly focus on how the process of translation opens new doors of perception. I will try to prove how important it is for the educational system to be based on a program that encourages an encounter with the other through a better linguistic awareness, through translation, through cultural exchange and through encouraging the learning of a second or third language. In doing so, the student would be able to erase linguistic and cultural fences and eventually prepare himself/herself for a dialogue at a global level.

This analysis is framed by the journey of the word toward the metaphor and toward its partial linguistic equivalents in a different language. Based on the bibliographic material gathered so far, I will conduct a cumulative analysis with visible effects in education. The power of speech, language and translation is essential for students' capacity to adapt to new cultural contexts in a globalized world where social inclusion and international dialogue are basic elements.

Word as a metaphor exists everywhere and can be approached from three different perspectives: linguistic/scientific, mythical/biblical (as a sacred phenomenon) and educational/literary (product of creative human mind.)

Linguistic approach

From a linguistic, scientific and physical perspective, the word is a particular medium between things and their unchanging content. Each of us possesses the most powerful instrument that natural selection provided; it is a piece of neuro-audio technology used to wire other people's minds. Language allows us to implant a thought from one mind directly into another's mind. Language can be used to alter the settings inside someone else's brain, the same as a remote control would alter the entire settings of a television.

There are several linguistic perspectives about language and the way in which it relates our thoughts to our reality. Ferdinand de Saussure finds 3 terms to define the relation between words and things. His theory is based on the linguistic sign defined by the combination of signifier, signified and referent.

Signifier—the shape of a word
Signified—the mental image or concept of an object
Referent—the object in reality

That is why, for instance, an object- or referent can have one signified, but several signifiers. "Every object is a room, you walk words into" (Ricardo Pau-Llosa).

Noam Chomsky, the father of modern linguistics introduces the transformational' generative grammar that states that there are similarities between languages because of their deep structure (phrase structure rules). Similar to Plato's theory of recollection, Chomsky's idea is that most of our knowledge is innate, with the result that a baby can have a large body of prior knowledge about the structure of language in general, and he/she only needs to *learn* the idiosyncratic features of the language(s) he/she is exposed to.

In terms of language acquisition, Chomsky considers that there is a window of opportunities we all have access to during the first years of life. This window allows us to learn any language due to the flexibility of our vocal cords. We start losing this ability close to the age of seven when our phonetic system is already well defined. If during that period we are in contact with other languages besides our native language, that window of opportunity will remain open and the process of language acquisition will be much more easily facilitated in the future.

In order to address the question—Does language intervene in shaping one's reality? We will use a sequence of different answers, coming from writers, philosophers and linguists, who agreed with the idea that language can determine the manner in which we might approach the part of reality we have access to through our limited experience:

"A completed isolated word would be meaningless because a word is a transaction between contexts"(Richards, [1936]1965; p. 134).The same mental image of a reality can be perceived differently in different cultures, so words without culture are *forms without content* (Maiorescu).

WORDS "The old idea that words possess magical powers is false; but its falsity is the distortion of a very important truth. Words do have a magical effect- but not in the way that magicians supposed, and not on the objects they were trying to influence. Words are magical in the way that they affect the minds of those who use them." *Words and Their Meanings* (Huxley, 1940)

"Language is not simply a body of knowledge to be learnt, but a social practice in which to participate" (Kramsch, 1994).

Not only do language learners need to know how language is used to create and represent meanings (as parts of reality), they also need to know how to communicate with others. Each language comes with a different type of mentality, depending on the reality/lifestyle certain peoples might have access to. Both language and culture are frames of reference for grasping reality. There is a fundamental relationship between language and culture because language is not only a thing to be studied; it is a way of seeing, understanding and communicating about the world. Once a new language is acquired there is an explosion of creativity. The Romanian artist Brancusi writes "You have to climb very high to see very far"[1], which is a good argument that encourages the study of a second language and, implicitly, of a new culture."Most people are principally aware of one culture, one setting, one home; exiles are aware of at least two, and this plurality of vision gives rise to an awareness of simultaneous dimensions, an awareness that, to borrow a phrase from music—is *contrapuntal*"(Edward, [2000] 2001; p.186). Eduard Said uses the word contrapuntal to refer to the two melodic lines that a person living a liminal experience will certainly experience. By separating oneself from the native country and language and having access to a second culture, the capacity to compare, to contrast and the analytical view are sharpened. This inbetweenness is a privileged context that gives access to a greater grasp of reality and a better understanding of it. Learning a new language and discovering a new culture means to reconcile two views and get to a third one which is superior because of a more experienced perspective. "The man who comes back through the Door in the Wall will never be quite the same as the man who went out. He will be wiser but less sure, happier but less self-satisfied, humbler in acknowledging his ignorance yet better equipped to understand the relationship of words to things, of systematic reasoning to the unfathomable mystery which it tries, forever vainly, to comprehend"(Huxley, 1954; p. 191). There are several ideas that spring out from Huxley's quotation:

- Language acquisition allows us to have access to the concepts we need in order to understand reality.

---

[1]Translated from Romanian: "Trebuie să încerci necontenit să urci foarte sus, dacă vrei să poți să vezi foarte departe." https://ro.wikiquote.org/wiki/Constantin_Brâncuși

- Our "doors of perception" are opened through language because we adjust our conception of reality taking into account the linguistic loops we are exposed to.
- Literature widens our frames of reference, increasing our cultural convictions and improves our perception of reality.
- Teaching literature or language means having the flexibility to move from one system of reference to another and make the student understand the benefits of the cultural enrichment he/she is exposed to.
- By having access to another culture, we are lead to a different reality through new doors of perception.
- Language can shape the perception of reality because reality is what we put into.
- Different types of mentalities, different cultures would look at reality from different perspectives.
- Language and culture give us the frames of reference we need to understand reality.
- Literatures or any type of art are vehicles for what is way beyond the individual. They expand the understanding of reality through a different emotional coloring and a different perception of the same experience.

Social learning -which is the ability to learn from others by copying (Carel, 2011) is very important in acquiring language. We can benefit from others' ideas. We can build on their wisdom. Our evolutionary path leads us to develop a system that can help us share ideas and cumulative knowledge. Language is used for reaching agreements, for sharing feelings and thoughts, emotions and experiences. Not having language or a common language would prevent us from interacting or connecting with other people. The simplest act of exchange we might be involved in is based on language. There are approximately 7000 languages around the world (Anderson, 2010). The greatest densities of languages on earth are where people are living very close together. In Papua Guinea for instance, there is a new language every two or three miles. As we diverge, languages will diverge. Different languages slow communication.

In the Greek mythology, Hermes confused the languages, causing Zeus to give his throne to Phoroneus. The tower of Bable in the Christian tradition warns us about the power of language. Bable means the "Gate of God" in Akkadian, the language spoken in Mesopotamia and in the Hebrew balal, meaning to jumble. The daring of people, blinded by the mentality of power and their wish to create this tower that could reach the sky and implicitly God, determined the punishment. God seems to separate humankind on the basis of language. He scattered the people by giving them different languages. Therefore, there is a legitimate question that one can ask: Do languages exist to prevent us from communicating, or, on the contrary, are they and always will be the main human-connection we can think of?

Spiritual approach

In the beginning was the Word, and the Word was with God, and the Word was God. All things were made through him, and without him was not anything made that was made(John 1:1-3). One can start talking about words and language by using one of the most important quotations from the Bible. The Book of John portrays the Trinity explaining what Logos means, from a Christian perspective. Words are the *sine qua non* of our existence, of our understanding of the world and of our approach to reality. The metaphorical dimension they can reach is emphasized in the differences between languages, in daily talk or in artistic creations. The Bible includes an explanation for the existence of words, together with a rhetorical language that can give birth to several interpretations and discussions.

The creation of the Earth was possible through the articulation of God's words. God gave Adam and Eve the chance to name the things in paradise from trees to animals and that is how they received identity. Their names empowered them with identity. *Things have no proper names except in God* (Benjamin, 1996, p. 73) *The making of man did not take place through the word: God spoke: and there was, but this man, who is not created from the word, is now invested with the gift of language and is elevated above nature*(pp. 67-68).

The role of words and metaphors is obvious now. We need rhetoric in order to get to a higher understanding of the world. Words are open windows toward otherness, toward the world. Our access to reality is intermediated by words, but the mental images of certain elements belonging to reality are linked to specific words. Conceptualizing our reality is our path to understanding it and this can be done only through words that, in a Christian perspective, come from God.

John the Evangelist uses the word "Word" to underline the materialization of God on Earth, through His Son: *"And the Word became flesh and dwelt among us, and we beheld His glory, the glory as of the only begotten of the Father, full of grace and truth."*(John 1:14) This sentence clarifies the manner in which the Son and Word of God came to us through Incarnation. The Word became fully human without ceasing to be fully God. It is hard to accept and understand this idea that can be grasped only at a linguistic level. Semantically, it might reach a superior level that implies the presence of faith and revelation in order to be internalized. Rudolf Bultmann observes that the Bible uses objective language in speaking of God's acts. What we can do is to "*retain the original experiential meaning by translating passages into the language of human Self-understanding...*"(Barbour, 1997, p. 86).

Another fragment that emphasizes how important God's words are is the following: *God spoke the world into being by the power of His words* (Hebrew 11:3). Here, the world seems to be the consequence of the articulation of words, the same as in the beginning of time. Genesis bears a contradiction. Even if we are aware of the fact that there was chaos and God made light out of it, still there was language that helped God create: "Let there be light; and there was light...God called the light day." All God's creation had to be named in order to become. It is written, *"Man shall not live by bread alone, but by every word that comes from the mouth of God."* (Matthew 4:4) Words become source of life through their metaphorical power.

Carlo Ginzburg uses references to the Bible in order to show the importance of the word: "Dixit Deus Fiat et factum est" (Ginzburg, 1999,p. 14). Quoting Nietzsche, Ginzburg agrees with the fact that language cannot give a satisfactory image of reality, (p. 12) Gerber's and Humboldt's perspective, that: "language is spirit (Die Sprache ist Geist)"(p. 15) also shows Augustine's view that man-made things are called true in relation to our mind. This thought confirms again that language can say things about our reality and our way of approaching it.

Literary approach

Any literary discourse has the potential to create a vision that sparkles between the lines. Writing can postulate things that do not exist: *Aixo era y no era*. Metaphor has a re-descriptive power because when used in literature what it says is always different in kind or degree from what it means (Ricoeur, 1997, p. 234). "The power of the metaphor is to reorganize our perception of things because...all symbolism consists in remaking reality" (p. 236) Ricoeur's definition of metaphor is illuminating: METAPHOR is that strategy of discourse by which language divests itself of its functions of direct description in order to reach the mythic level where its function of discovery is set free (p. 237). We cannot say what reality is, only what it seems to be to us. Our words define our understanding of the world.

In poetry, the language of metaphor manifests itself in its wholeness because of the connotative dimension. Paul Valery masters the use of metaphors and sustains that like sculpture, poetry converts language into matter (p. 232) The unity of a poem is the unity of a mood, state of soul (état d'âme)- a way of finding oneself among things(Heidegger). The poetic experience expresses the ecstatic moment of language (going beyond itself) (p. 237) Turbayne's metaphor belongs to the order of manipulable, but there is a reality that comes to language beyond the control of the poet. "Poetry is what gets lost in translation" (Frost, 1959).

The word 'translate' comes from the Latin for 'to move from one place to another'. Schlegel said about translators, that they *'should have traveled through all the three or four continents of humanity, not in order to round off the edges of individuality, but to broaden [their] own vision...* When it comes to translation, there are certain aspects that need to be taken into consideration, so as to avoid misleading interpretations. Because of the imperfect semantic superposition of words, and because of the diverse grasps of reality, it is impossible to have a perfect translation. As the Italians would say: *traduttore traditore*, which means that the translator is a traitor since he loses a part of the initial message that he is only able to convey in part. A good example would be the word "hypostases". The Greeks refer to

---

Chapter Three | Corina Mihaela Beleaua, in
Dainess Maganda and Karim Traoré (Eds.)
LANGUAGE AND LITERATURE: Vehicles for the Enhancement of Cultural Understanding
London, Adonis & Abbey Publishers

the Father, Son and Holy Spirit as being the three "hypostases" but in Latin it does not sound correctly to say that there are three, although the term "hypostasis" in Greek means the same as "substantiae" in Latin. The truth is that "substantiae" in Latin is commonly used to describe the essence. Greeks claim that there is only one essence in God. Therefore, when the Greeks speak of three "hypostases" Latins speak of three "persons" as Augustine was mentioning, in the seventh book of the Trinity (Augustine, 2012).

Another aspect involved in the translation process is the potential direct contact that the translator might have with the object he might want to talk about. Jakobson says that "no one can understand the word 'cheese' unless he has a nonlinguistic acquaintance with cheese" (Jakobson, 1) Humboldt touches upon the reception theory mentioning that the *unprejudiced reader*' (Berman, 1992, p. 154) can draw the line between the foreign and the strangeness. *As long as one feels the foreign, but not the strangeness, the translation has reached its highest goal...* (p. 154). He also underlines that a good translator should master language very well because he has to have *love of the original* (p.154) and the target language. He definitely considers translation "not a science, but an exact art" and finds the means to combine the *intimacy of thinking and language* (p.152) for a translation to *smack of translation* (p.155).

Educational approach Formational effects of linguistic mediation.

By combining these approaches we can come up with a productive educational method by paying attention to the language. Every single approach deals with the idea of metaphor because the word does not mean what it says.

Language used in literature and translation makes us aware of the sublime and ineffable power of words. Metaphor is at the height of this power because of the freedom it imbues in interpreting and finding meaning. The word is not concrete or carved in stone, but the word is indication and manifestation of the self, of the one articulating a message, of the one speaking. This manifestation of the self is always caused by the connection with the other, by the encounter with nature, or by a self-mirroring which has the purpose of a personal encounter toward the ideal *nosce te ipsum*, know thy self (through language again).

From birth, children's brain processes experiences, codifying them into electrical impulses. In time, those impulses receive linguistic constructions and every time sensory perceptions or the visual perceptions encounter an object, let's say "hair brush," the brain activates a path to the neuro-connection in the brain map.

Knowing several languages offers a person the possibility of multiple paths to the same neuro-connection. What at first sight seems to be complicated misleads expectations because paradoxically the whole process simplifies the manner in which these connections happen. In fact, what we achieve is the exact opposite, which is a simplified way. The brain exercises itself into thinking faster and into recognizing there is never a singular way of looking at things. When talking about interacting with different cultures, a polyglot will have a higher tolerance for accepting the others, because he/she already knows there are multiple ways of looking at the same thing. That is why learning another language in schools is something that should continue being addressed because it leaves an open gate toward the other, the foreigner.

Now let us see how words and language can be used in the educational field. The awareness of the other, of *alterity* or in Buber's terms the I-*Thou* relation is fundamental for the teaching process. (Berman, 1992, p. 143) If we teach, we use language not as a tool or instrument to convey ideas, but as actual material which makes people experience their ideas rather than communicate them. It is not important what you convey but the way you convey it. It is not the idea that finds the followers, or the persuaded ones, but the way it is expressed gives itself its value and its persuasive force. The main focus should be on how convincing, how applicable and how the words resonate with someone's feelings, about a particular issue. I convey not the knowledge itself, but my feeling about it. Language is between things and their sublime part. At a spiritual level, we can talk about a sharing of souls which only language can access. Language is a sound-euphony for which reason it may reach the soul through its physical vibrations.

Teaching is important because teaching is communication. We can use facts, but facts do not speak to anyone. In order for them to resonate, they have to reach sensitive cords, inwardness; hence the need for metaphors, for literature and for personal approach is important. When two souls meet and use language because of a vivid interest they have in common, they project themselves toward a certain fact that receives a new value.

What we teach is a material for us to connect with others. The same as water is a good electrical conductor, by using language and naming a thing we electrify the connection and the word that resonates with our tuning gets a new approach based on the slice of reality we refer to. It is hard to approach each other directly, but when using words it is easier for us to express ourselves because words express what is objectively perceivable by both sides. The word does not mean what it says. It gives an idea and relates a mental image to a sequence of phonemes that address a referent from the physical world. All possible approaches to a certain idea manifest themselves through the approach of the real things. The problem is that one thing can have different names. It can have different understandings, beside a universal idea that might be accepted everywhere, as a collective agreement. By comparing its different connotations, by contrasting it, so that it can be seen in its small details, we reach a wholeness of that specific object. The game between the denotative and connotative semantic aspect of a certain word gives language its richness. Metaphor and rhetoric are there to enforce this superior dimension of language for increasing chances to a greater understanding of the other and of the world we live in. We do not want the idea of the word; the ultimate goal is to go beyond the fact that the word is a connector and to have access to the other through this linguistic mediation.

If language is the basis of our cooperation, toward a free form of exchange of ideas, then would a universal language bridge the gap between people of different nationalities? We are genetically specified for talking, for using language. Being bilingual is cognitively beneficial. The connected world of Facebook friendship raises a problem because languages impose a barrier to cooperation. A good example is the EU, where the 27 countries speak 23 official languages. There is the need of 253 translators to anticipate all the possible dialogues. Measuring methods for time and distance are going towards being standardized. The modern world is confronted with a dilemma. Chinese is the most widely spoken language in the world, however Chinese people learn English. There were people who took into consideration the possibility to have only one language. For instance, Volapük is a borrowed word, of German origins. It was invented by Johann Martin Schleyer, a Roman Catholic priest from Baden, who dreamt that God asked him to create an international language. The word refers to Schreyer's constructed language.

The idea of a universal language is not as exotic as it may seem. Educational systems all over the world encourage students to acquire linguistic competence in a second language. Of course, what is at stake in many of these systems is the will to power of some rich countries and their colonizing attitude toward the poor ones. However, as mentioned previously, knowing a second language is cognitively beneficial. Elevation of language refers to what Chomsky understood by universal/pure language. The same idea was resumed by both Bellos and Benjamin—*Belief in the existence of a transcendent form of human expression- pure language- is really just the same as believing in God* (Bellos, 2010, p. 218), or *release in his own language the pure language which is under the spell of another… for a reconciliation and fulfillment of languages* (Benjamin, 1996; p. 216) Might history play with us and determine a revival of the lingua franca from centuries ago, into a unique universal language that might answer our new global needs of connection and dialogue? This is a question that only time might give an answer to. Meanwhile, we can take advantage of all the cognitive benefits that the process of acquiring a new universal language might imply.

References

Anderson S. R. (2010). *How Many Languages are there in the World?* http://www.linguisticsociety.org/files/how-many-languages.pdf

Barbour I. G. (1997).*Religion and science*. Historical and Contemporary Issues, A Revised and Expanded Edition of *Religion in an Age of Science*. New York: Harper Collins Publishers.

Benjamin W. (1968).*Illuminations.The task of the translator...* l: James Hynd, E.M. Valk (Trans).Frankfurt: Suhrkamp Verlag.

Benjamin W. (1996).On Language as such and on the language of man.In Marcus Bullock, M. and Jennings, M. W. (Eds.). *Selected Writings*, Volume 1, 1913-1926., Cambridge: Harvard University Press. Retrived from http://users.clas.ufl.edu/burt/chaucer'swake/LanguageofMan.pdf

Blumenberg H. (2010). *Paradigms for a metaphorology*. Robert Savage (Trans). New York: Cornell University Press.

Derrida J. (1986).*Margins of Philosophy*, Alan Bass (Transl). Chicago: The University of Chicago Press.

Frost, R. (1959/1995).*Conversations on the Craft of Poetry.Collected Poems, Prose and Plays*. Ed. R. Poirier and M. Richardson, New York: Library of America.

Ginzburg C. (1999). *History, rhetoric and proof*. London: University Press of New England.

Gisel P. (1990). *Le Christ de Calvin*. Paris: Desclé.

Huxley A. (2014) *The Doors of perception*. New York: Harper Collins Publishers

Man P. de (1986). *The resistance to theory, conclusions*: Walter Benjamin's 'The Task of the Translator.' In *Theory and history of literature*, Volume 33, Minneapolis: University of Minnesota Press.

Richards I.A. ([1936]1965). *The philosophy of rhetoric*, New York: Oxford University Press.

Ricoeur P. (1997). The Rule of metaphor, multidisciplinary studies of the creation of meaning in language, Toronto, Buffalo, London: University of Toronto Press.

Said E. (2000] 2001). *Reflections on exile and other essays*. Cambridge: Harvard University Press.

Saint Augustine de Hippo, W. G. T. Sheed D.D., P. A. Boer Sr., Rev. A. W. Haddan B. D. (2012). *On the trinity, de trinitate*. Charleston: CreateSpace Independent Publishing Platform.

van Schaik, C.P. & Burkart, J.M. , (2011). Social Learning and Evolution: The Cultural Intelligence Hypothesis. Phil. Trans. Royal Society B, (366), 1008–1016 doi:10.1098/rstb.2010.0304 Retrieved fromhttp://rstb.royalsocietypublishing.org/content/royptb/366/1567/1008.full.pd

CHAPTER FOUR

Africa in the Selected High School World History Textbooks in Korea

Hyangsoon Yi
University of Georgia

Soojin Ahn
University of Georgia

Introduction

Until recently, Africa remained psychologically and practically a continent of little interest to Koreans. Although the Chosŏn dynasty (1392-1910) produced the world's oldest map of the African continent in 1402[1]—about a hundred years earlier than Europe's "discovery" of the Cape of Good Hope,[2] no known cases of direct contact between Korea and Africa are found in official documents from the premodern period, except for a brief mention in the *Annals of the Chosŏn Dynasty* of the four African divers who came to Korea in the late 16th century as part of the Ming navy.[3] Korea's major exposure to Africans took place for the first time in the early 1950s when the Ethiopian Kagnew Battalions (3158 troops; Varhola, 2000)

---

[1] The full name of this map is: "Honilkangniyŏktaeguktojido" (Map of the capitals of the historical kingdoms). Made in the second year of King T'aejong's reign in the early Chosŏn dynasty (1392-1910), this map marks thirty seven place names in the African continent, including River Nile, Lake Victoria, and Mt. Kilimanjaro.
[2] It was in 1488 that Bartolomeu Dias (1450-1500) rounded the Cape of Good Hope for the first time as a European.
[3] The *Annals of King Sŏnjo*, May 26, 1598.

came to aid South Korea as part of the UN forces during the Korean War.

As South Korea emerged as a new economic powerhouse in the late 1980s, however, her contact with Africa has become more active and diverse. It was Christian missionaries who first traveled to different parts of Africa, followed by businessmen.[4] Since the 1990s an increasing number of Africans have visited South Korea to study or work.[5] They have formed a community of their own in Seoul.[6] This new community is bound to grow given the rapid multi-culturalization and multi-ethnicization of South Korea (henceforth Korea), a nation which has for a long time been one of the most homogeneous countries in the world in terms of race, ethnicity, language, and culture.[7]

Despite the distinct changes in the recent Korea-Africa relations, their interactions are still deplorably meager compared with Korea's robust economic ties and cultural exchanges with North and South Americas, Middle East, Europe, and other Asian countries. One of the main reasons for this unfortunate situation can be found in the ideological and military confrontation between South and North Koreas. Many African nations established diplomatic relationships with the communist North soon after their independence from European colonizers in the 1950s and 1960s. The ideological

---

[4] Korea is close to the U. S. A. in terms of the number of Christian missionaries sent overseas (Kim, 2008). As of December, 2013, the total number of Korean missionaries in Africa was 1,876 (Cho, 2014).
[5] As of March, 2002, the number of African workers in Korea was 2,272. As of August, 2003, the total number of foreign migrant workers in Korea was 410,000 (Han, 2003, p. 160, 161, 176, 177).
[6] Africans tend to concentrate in It'aewŏn, an area of Seoul traditionally known for foreign expatriate communities. Specifically, Pogwang-ro 69 Gil (69 Pogwang Street) in It'aewŏn has been known as "Nigeria Street." As of June, 2011, 549 Nigerians and 131 Africans of other nationalities were living in this area (Song, 2011).
[7] As of January, 2011, the number of foreign residents constituted 2.5 % of the total population in Korea, which is 1,265,006 (Cha, Kim, & Ham, 2013).

barrier discouraged the staunch anti-communist South Korean government to engage in affairs relevant to Africa during the Cold War era. Although the political and economic situations have changed greatly in both Africa and Korea in recent decades, the general level of understanding is inadequate with regard to African history, society, and culture.

This problem raises a fundamental question: "What do Koreans learn about Africa in school?" Except for the mass media and overseas travel, formal education is the single most important source of information about the outside world for the majority of Koreans. Therefore, as a way of answering the above question, this article reports our content analysis of the three most widely adopted high school world history textbooks. Although the three selected textbooks share the same title, *Kodŭnghakkyo segyesa* (High School World History), they were published in 2011 by Kyohaksa, Kŭmsŏng Publishing Company, and Chihaksa, respectively (K 1, K 2, and C hereafter).[8] In addition to their titles, the three books also have a commonality in their authorships; each text was written by a group of experts on history and history education.[9]

Our content analysis investigated the amount and type of the information on African history that is presented to Korean high school students through these textbooks. A similar attempt was made on African geography in elementary and

---

[8] The sequence of the books follows the order of the Korean alphabet (Han'gŭl), not English; hence, K 1, K 2, and C.
[9] The authors of the three textbooks are: Ŭnsuk Kim, Hanuk Cho, Myŏngch'ŏl Chu, Chunch'ae Choe, and Hanho Nam (K 1); Kŭmsŏng O, Kyŏngjun Yu, Hwayŏng Im, Munhwan Kang, and Yŏn Chŏng (K 2); and Ch'anghun O, Chonggŭn Chang, Tuho Chang, and Ch'ansŏk Pak (C).

middle school textbooks.[10] Only a small number of scholars have studied education on Africa in the Korean school system. This situation clearly reflects the relative novelty of research interest in Africa by Korean academics. There are only a handful of studies on the portrayal of Africa in high school textbooks.[11] It is our intention to address and remedy this lacuna.

This article is organized into three parts. The first part provides a brief explanation of the current Korean high school curriculum. This task is primarily to identify where Africa is situated in the overall curricular organization, but it also justifies the scope of the present study as well. The second part, which constitutes the main body of the paper is devoted to a content analysis of the textbooks. This analysis part is organized into five sections according to the broad periodization and thematization of African history by the Ministry of Education. In the third part of the article, the analysis will be concluded by recapitulating overall patterns in handling Africa in the three books and proposing ideas for improving history texbooks.

The Place of Africa in the Korean High School Curriculum

Currently, the Korean Ministry of Education requires all high school students to study four core areas, according to the

---

[10] For a detailed analysis of the problematic treatment of African geography in the Korean middle school textbooks, see Da-Won Kim and Geon-Su Han (2012), "'Sasil' kwa 'chaehyŏn' ŭi kwanjŏm esŏ Ap'ŭrik'a tasi pogi - Ch'ojunghakkyo sahoe kyogwasŏ Ap'ŭrik'a sŏsul naeyong ŭl chungsim ŭro [Reviewing Africa from the points of view of "fact" and "representation": Focusing on the contents on Africa in the elementary and middle school social studies textbooks]. *Taehan chirihakoeji, 47*(3), 440-458.

[11] Han (2007) investigated the representations of Africa in high school world geography and world history textbooks, and Park and Woo (2009) analyzed stereotypes on Africa in high school social studies textbooks. Kim and Cho (2010) scrutinized ideological biases on Africa embedded in middle school social studies textbooks.

latest national school curriculum revised in 2009.[12] The first and most important core area covers three subjects: Korean, math, and English. The next core area includes: social studies and science. The third core area consists of: physical education and the arts. The fourth core area is general education. It includes: a second foreign language, technology and home economics, Chinese characters, and cultural studies.

The guidelines of the Ministry of Education further specify a list of topics that they recommend each school cover in each subject. In social studies, for example, topics are divided into two groups: basic, and in-depth research topics. The basic topics include: society, Korean geography, world geography, Korean history, East Asian history, world history, economics, law and politics, society and culture, social life and ethics, and ethics and ideology. The in-depth research topics are: international politics, international economy, international relations, international organizations, global issues, comparative cultures, social science methodologies, Korean society and culture, international law, regional understanding, and future society.

The above topics in social studies are not taught with equal weight. Individual schools can prioritize and select topics for their students to concentrate on. Consequently, the amount of time allotted to each topic can differ, depending on its significance within the curriculum of a particular school.

---

[12] Technically, the overall outline of the 7th revised national curriculum was published in 2009, and the specific details of the new curriculum became available in 2011. The entire document of the revised curriculum can be accessed online at the National Curriculum Information Center (http://ncic.kice.re.kr).

Where is African history situated in the above curricular configuration? Africa is introduced in social studies under world history. This means that Africa is treated as one of the basic topics in social studies classes in all Korean high schools. In theory, diverse aspects of the African continent can and should be addressed in multiple subjects catalogued above. Indeed, pieces of Africa-related information crop up in certain subjects, including world geography. In reality, however, world history is virtually the only subject that treats Africa systematically as an integral component of the instructional contents.

For the analysis of the textbooks, we first read each book to identify content on Africa. We then developed a coding system to categorize recurrent themes. Since the chapter division of the Ministry of Education already set large categories, our coding focused on those categories with attention to key phrases in each chapter and its subsections. Although unquantified, we believe that a considerable degree of consistency was maintained across the three textbooks due to a list of themes predetermined by the national curriculum.

A Content Analysis of the African Sections in the World History Textbooks

A survey of the parts in the three textbooks that are devoted to Africa demonstrates that all three organize the history of the African continent in chronological order, using major socio-political upheavals as critical milestones on the temporal axis. In addition to the traditional linear development model of the historical timeline, the three books deal with similar themes and materials in alignment with the chapter divisions of the world history textbook that the government has established. Below are the specific chapter headings set by the Ministry of Education[13]:

(1) Time, Space, and Humans; (2) The Dawn of Civilization and the Ancient Civilizations; (3) The Expansion of Asia and East-West Contacts; (4) Feudal Society in Europe; (5) The Development of Asian Society; (6) The Emergence and Expansion of Modern Society in Europe; (7) The Modernization of Asia; (8) Imperialism and the Two World Wars; and (9) Global Development in the Post-World War Era

African history is taught in certain chapters in the above list. Although scattered in different chapters, the Africa-related contents tend to form five clusters of information in terms of important historical periods and thematic foci:

(1) African civilization in the ancient period; (2) Slave trade; (3) Imperialism and the division of Africa; (4) Births of African nations; and (5) Challenges faced by Africa today

In what follows, the results of the analysis of the three books are discussed in the order of the five clusters of information. In each of the five sections, notable subheadings will be examined first. This will be followed by a list of main points addressed in the three texts. Afterwards, comments are offered on the salient aspects of the instructional materials and pedagogical approaches of the textbook writers.

---

[13] For more information on the 6th and 7th national curricula for history education and the two editions of the textbooks produced according to the curricular guidelines, see Kim (2006).

African Civilization in the Ancient Period

In the world history textbooks, Africa is first introduced in the second chapter: "The Dawn of Civilization and the Ancient Civilizations." Although the chapter titles are nearly identical among the three books, the amount of information contained in each differs[14]: "Early Civilizations of America and Africa" (K 2) and "American and African Worlds" (K 1 and C).

Below are the chief points of lesson addressed by the three books.

- Africa as the birthplace of humanity
  This statement is borne out by fossil evidence, Eve of Africa, etc.
- Tassili pre-historic rock art in the Sahara Desert
  Photos of the Tassili paintings accompany the linguistic descriptions.
- Sahara before its desertification
- Carthage, the Poeni War, and the Roman occupation of North Africa
- Major kingdoms and empires in West, East, and South Africa
  Kushite Empire, Axum Empire, Ghana Empire, Mali Empire, Songhai Empire, Luba Empire, Lunda Kingdom, and Congo Kingdom are mentioned. Timbuktu is highlighted as the intellectual and cultural center of ancient Africa. All three books display a map marking the locations of these empires and kingdoms in

---

[14] The sizes and the fonts of the three books are identical because they have to conform to the government guidelines. As to the length of a textbook, however, the guidelines allow slight flexibility. Therefore, the three selected textbooks show different page numbers.

the continent. Book C even quotes a passage from al-Bakri's *Book of Roads and Kingdoms*, which is concerned with King Tenkamenin of Ghana. Book C further engages students in the study of the economic basis of King Tenkamenin's rule. In the in-depth research section, this book also introduces three trade terms widely used in the Islamic world: *bari, dinar,* and *mitokar.*

- Introduction of Islam to Africa and its spread in the sub-Saharan regions

While the three textbooks cover nearly the same contents, small differences are also noted. For instance, they all treat the introduction of Islam to Africa as an essential topic. However, K 2 summarizes it only in a couple of sentences as part of ancient African history; whereas K 1 and C assign one full page and revisit the topic again in Chapter 3: "The Formation and Expansion of the Islamic World."

In several respects, K 1 is the most extensive and balanced among the three books in handling Islam in Africa. K 1 supplies more details than the other two books. Moreover, it invites students to challenge stereotypical ideas on Africa by directing their attention to the underlying assumptions of such ideas that are often based on bias. In this way, students are encouraged to read the subtext of the historical text and the implicit ideological underpinnings of the given information. In K 1, for instance, the text explains that Swahili emerged in East Africa under the influence of the Arabic language, and that the Mali and Songhai empires were founded as the results of the introduction of the Islamic religion. In a separate box, the book introduces King Mansa Musa of the Mali Empire against the backdrop of a map, along with his famous image of showing off his gold. This textbook also incorporates visual materials related to the topic, such as the photos of the Obelisk of the Axum Empire and the pyramids of the Kushite Empire.

Specifically, K 1 opens the topic of Islam in Africa with thought-provoking statements that are aimed at forcing students to critique widespread misconceptions and misnomers of the continent:

> "We often call America and Africa 'New Continent' and 'Dark Continent,' respectively. However, these expressions only reflect the perspective of the West. These days, rich pieces of evidence are unearthed one after another, proving that surprisingly unique cultures and civilizations of their own were developed in ancient America and Africa" (p. 80).

As a way of reinforcing the above statements, K 1 juxtaposes the historical timelines of America, Africa, and Korea for the purpose of comparing the developments of civilizations in the three places. The parallel timelines show that farming and the use of money began far earlier in America and Africa than in Korea. In addition, the book offers special food for thought:

> "We often hear from newspapers and the television that ethnic conflict in African society results in a number of victims. Such news can easily mislead us to develop a biased view that Africa remains in an uncivilized state characteristic of tribal society. However, Africa has witnessed diverse kinds of historical development from the time of the appearance of the human race to the

contemporary period. What kind of ancient civilization did Africa achieve?" (p. 84)

The above question is accompanied by the photo of an elaborate bronze artwork from ancient Africa, which illustrates the advanced civilization on the continent in the pre-historic period. The authors also describe international trade relationships that Africa had with China, India, and Mediterranean states.

Slave Trade

The second cluster of materials on African history is concerned with the slave trade. In each book, the content on the slave trade is placed in Chapter 3 under the title of "Europe's Expansion, and America and Africa." The chapter subheadings slightly vary among the three textbooks: "Africa before Europe's Expansion" and "Slave Trade by Europeans" (K 1); "The Ordeal of Africa" (K 2); and "Africa before Europe's Expansion" (C). Regardless of the minor differences in the subheadings, the slave trade functions as the overarching theme in all three texts.

Before examining major characteristics of the treatments of the slavery, it is useful to look at the brain storming questions raised at the outset of the section. These questions provide an insight into the authors' perspectives on the topic as well as their educational objectives.

(1) K 1: "Although we do not know since when, Africa tends to conjure up the image of starvation and disease.

In most cases, the [main] reason for us to imagine Africa with such a prejudice is our lack of appropriate understanding and knowledge of the continent. Was Africa really the 'Land of Darkness'?"

(2) K 2: "Roughly 12% of the U. S. population are Afro-American. When and through what channels did they enter the U. S. A.?"

(3) C: "This is an Afro-American spiritual sung by black slaves. The song reflects their pain at being forced to work in a large farm and their hope for freedom from the shackle. . . . How many Africans were sold from Africa to America?"

It is interesting to note that K 2 and C commonly link the topic of the slave trade with American history. This reveals that for many Koreans, slavery is primarily an issue associated with American, not African, history. K 2 begins the section with the phrase, "Africa Fallen as the Supply Camp of Slaves," stressing the centrality of Africa in understanding the international operation of the slave trade.

The authors of C employ unique content about slavery by including lyric spirituals that we think are likely to move students to be horrified when realizing the brutality experienced by many slaves. This textbook attempts to elicit affective responses from students to the topic of slavery.

K 1 opens the lesson on African slaves by posing the following rhetorical question:

"Since some unknown point in history, Africa has been associated with hunger, disease, and civil war in our minds. The reason for which this prejudice has been formed in spite of its geographical importance and infinite potential for development is mostly due to our lack of precise understanding or knowledge of Africa. Was Africa really the Land of Darkness?" (p. 235)

The authors encourage students to critique the conventional, biased interpretation of the Euro-centered color symbolism of "darkness" as "backwardness."[15]

All three books attempt to account for the historical context and development of the slave trade in four stages.

- Africa prospered before Europeans arrived there in the 15th century. Examples for this claim include: King Mansa Musa of Mali, Songhai Empire, large stone structures in Zimbabwe, Africa-China trade, etc.
- People in West Africa began to sell slaves to Arab merchants. This trade formed a market for Europeans later.
- A large demand for sugar canes in Europe caused the expansion of the slave market.
- Portugal and Spain monopolized the trade in the 16th century. The Dutch took it over in the 17th century, and England expanded the trade further to the Caribbean Islands and South America in the 18th century.

---

[15] According to Pierterse (1992), the implication of blackness as backwardness in European cultures originated in the early Christian period when the color black, which had nothing to do with skin color began to be associated with sin and darkness as opposed to spiritual light. Thus, "[b]lack became the color of the devil and demons" (p. 24). Such a negative connotation of blackness permeated into the dominant view of Africa in Europe.

The three books commonly condemn the slave trade by quoting, among others, a large number of African men and women—12 millions—who were transported to Europe between the 16th and the 18th centuries. The appalling conditions of their maritime transportations are also depicted.

However, the three books adopt different strategies to underscore the inhumanity of the slave trade. In K 2 and C, the cruelty is vividly illustrated by the pictorial representations of a typical slave ship. They also explain the Triangular Trade among Europe, America, and Africa by means of flow charts that demonstrate how trade items, such as cotton, ivory, guns, sugar, tobacco, etc., along with slaves, were circulated among the three continents. The charts pointedly attest to the dehumanization of slaves as material goods.

As a concrete case of the slave market, the authors of C focus on the American South. In a separate box, they describe the Underground Railroad and the historical background of Harriet Beecher Stowe's fiction *Uncle Tom's Cabin*. An illustration from Stowe's classic novel is included.

The authors of K 1 take a distinct approach to the given topic by presenting a small photo of two children in a peaceful African village. At a first glance, the image appears to be irrelevant to the slave trade. The bright and innocent faces of the children, however, illustrate everyday African life before the slave trade, and as such, the photo inspires students to imagine the depth of tragedy that slave captors, traders, and owners caused to the families and communities of those captured, transported, and sold in faraway lands.

K 1's soft approach to the slavery is balanced with its more rigorous intellectual attention to the problematic of historiography itself. The authors explicitly state that much of African history prior to the advent of Europeans was buried and erased because no script was available to record it, except for a very few tribes. Thus, students are led to ponder the complex relationship between language, literacy, and history. By recognizing the key role that literacy plays in producing and propagating discourse on historical experience, memory, and record, the authors cogently reiterate what Gayatri Spivak calls the "voice of the subaltern," in an appropriate manner to high school students.[16]

K 1 closes the section on the state of Africa before the European invasion by underlining that Africa was never an isolated continent but maintained contact with various groups of outsiders, including Admiral Zheng He's fleet from Ming China.[17] In general, the K 2 authors seem to have made conscious efforts to avoid sensational visuals that would instantly capture students' attention and stir up their emotional reactions to the brutalities of the slavery. In particular, the opportunity to reflect on the problematic of historiography can induce a deeper level of comprehension in the student with regard to subjectivity and agency in narrativizing and interpreting history in general.

Imperialism and the Division of Africa

The third major topic on Africa is centered on the political and economic impact of European Imperialism on Africa. The

---

[16] Gayatri Spivak (1988), Can the subaltern speak? In C. Nelson & L. Grossberg (Eds.), *Marxism and the interpretation of culture* (pp. 271-313). Urbana, IL: University of Illinois Press.

[17] The Chinese treasure fleet under the command of Zheng He (1371-1433) made several expeditionary voyages to South and Southeast Asia, the Arabian Peninsula, and East Africa between 1405 and 1433. Zheng He's fleet visited Africa for the first time in their 5th expedition (1417-1419), and in their 7th and last voyage (1431-1433), they reached the Swahili coast in East Africa.

section titles are formulated similarly in the three books, involving key phrases, such as "imperial power," "nationalist movements in Africa," "division of the world," and "fights for colonies."

Unlike the first two topics analyzed earlier—"African Civilization in the Ancient Period" and "Slave Trade," the theme of Imperialism and Africa receives a relatively uniform treatment across the three texts. Their common thread can be summed up in three points.

- Imperialism emerged in Europe, U. S. A., Russia, and Japan in the 19th century.
- David Livingstone's and Henry Stanley's journeys into African inlands accelerated the European invasion and territorial division of the "Dark Continent."
- Imperialism eventually caused the First World War.

The three books emphasize two factors as crucial to the rise of imperialism in Europe: the development of capitalism since the Industrial Revolution; and the emergence of nationalism. To these two, C adds the influence of Social Darwinism as well. The authors of C cite the infamous statements made by Cecil Rhodes and Heinrich von Treitschke who advocated the British and the German colonial expansionisms respectively, as a way of solving their own "domestic" problems, including the high unemployment rates.

In mapping the territorial division of the African continent by the European nations, the three books pay much attention to continued clashes between Europeans. In K 2 and C, the Fashoda Crisis in 1898 is described as the most notorious instance of the European nations' fights over Africa.

As indicated above, the textbooks stress the breakout of World War I as the ultimate self-destructive consequence of Europe's imperialist projects. In this way, the textbooks address the broad impact of imperialism on the international community.

Lastly, the discussions of Europe's colonial domination of Africa are illustrated with maps and drawings. The maps show the partition of Africa by the European colonizers. One of the intriguing visual aids used in K 2 and C is a cartoon that satirizes political manipulations, Christian mission, and military campaigns that coalesced into Europe's maximum economic exploitation of Africa. The cartoon depicts an African man bound on a press machine, around which three Europeans position themselves. A politician in British tweed pours a whisky bottle into the mouth of the black man. Another European in a military uniform turns the large wheel of the machine to squeeze gold coins out of the African body. On the opposite side of the politician stands a priest piously holding up the Bible with his two hands. This German cartoon, published in the early 20th century, is entitled: "Thus Colonize the English" (Austin, 1900). The comic illustration caricatures the vicious collaboration, implicit and explicit, among the political, religious, and military institutions in Europe to extract every possible resource out of the African continent. The graphic parody is echoed by the caption:

"Hey, pour more whisky."
"Try to squeeze hard for more gold coins."

A Catholic priest stands next to the colonialists who squeeze the skinny crushed man, reading the biblical passage diligently: "Thou shalt love thy neighbor." Drunk with whisky, the African man has no idea of what is happening now.

The caption especially indicts the church that turns a blind eye to the colonialist undertaking. Interestingly, K 2 urges students to compare this cartoon and Aesop's fable on a hen that lays golden eggs. This textbook also presents two additional materials: a cartoon of Cecil Rhodes' ambition to connect a telegraph line between North and South Africa; and a short passage on the political outcome of Henry Stanley's exploration of the African inlands. The authors of K 2 then instruct students to contrast the imperialist's perspective on the colony and the colonial subject's perspective on imperialism.

The Births of the African Nations

Starting from the late 19th century, independence movements against European rule swept various parts of Africa. These movements call due attention in all three history textbooks because Africans' persistent resistance merits a significant treatment. The instructional core of the section focuses on nationalism as a prime ideological force that shaped modern Africa. Proliferating throughout much of the Cold War era, African nationalism was a watershed in their history, ushering the continent into the contemporary world order. Africa's efforts to achieve independence are presented in the section subheadings in the textbooks: "Emergence of the Third World" (K 1); "Births of African Nations and Pan-

Africanism" (K 2); and "Nationalists Movement in Africa" (C).

Despite the importance of the emergence of African nations, wide discrepancies are observed in the amount of textual space assigned to this topic in each book: K 1 (half page); K 2 (3 pages); and C (half page). The wide variance in the quantity of textbook information invites a comment. Although it is not easy to discern precise reasons for the uneven lengths of the sections, two possibilities can be considered as responsible for the difference. Some authors might have viewed European invasion and Africa's resistance as two separate topics; whereas others defined them as one interrelated subject. The other viable explanation can be found in the increased international media coverage of African issues in recent decades. Thanks to newspapers, radio, television, and the Internet sources nowadays, educational materials on 20th-century Africa are relatively easily obtainable. These abundant information sources could have led the writers of K 1 and C to reduce the information volume to the essential. In both books, African nationalism is subsumed by the more encompassing topic of the fundamental changes in international politics that led to the emergence of the Third World. Consequently, the African nationalist movement receives a less amount of text than the topic of European imperialism.

Below is the survey of the main contents on the births of modern Africa in the three textbooks.

- As WWI ended, Africans' anti-colonial resistance activities developed into organized independence movements in various regions.

- Africans formed political organizations, such as the Wafd Party in Egypt that played a vital role in putting an end to European rule.
- Pan-Africanism spread in the sub-Saharan regions.
- Seventeen nations were founded in 1960, the "Year of Africa," and many more ensued until 1963.
- African countries actively participated in the Third World Movement.

The salient elements in each book's handling of African nationalism can be discussed briefly. Although limited to less than a page, K 1's contents highlight relatively less known facts about Africans' own efforts for independence rather than Euro-centered landmark events in international politics. For background knowledge, K 1 attributes the influence of Woodrow Wilson's idea of self-determination on the nationalist movements in Africa. Starting with the Wafd Party, the book provides representative anti-colonial struggles: the first Pan-African Congress organized in 1919 by W. E. B. Du Bois; the armed revolt in 1929 by Aba women in Nigeria; and the inspirational poetry composed by the Senegalese writer, Léopold Senghor. In a separate box, K 1 quotes Jomo Kenyatta's famous court statement from Robert July's *A History of the African People*. This passage is presented side by side with an African map showing the names and sites of the independence movements. In the following section, the book introduces the Third World Movement. To illustrate Africa's strong support for this alternative international political order, the book emphasizes that many newly independent states on the continent sent their delegations to the 1955 Bandung Conference in Indonesia.

K 2 spends nearly four pages on the liberation of Asia and Africa from the imperial powers and the formation of the Third World non-alliance. It mentions Egypt's independence, the armed rebellions in West and Southwest Africa in the 1880s and 1890s, and the births of African countries between 1957 and 1963. But at the same time, the book comments on the unresolved problem of the Suez Canal and the failures of the majority of Africa's independence movements due to their lack of proper organizations.

K 2 takes one more step, pointing out that the new African nations experienced political instability due to ethnic conflict, illiteracy, chronic poverty, disease, and hunger. Most importantly, the authors identify the principal cause of this instability in the arbitrary borders that Europe forced upon the African states along the lines of their colonial territories. The new national borders were irrelevant to the socio-political, economic, and cultural traditions of the local people themselves. This explanation elucidates the source of the continued post-colonial tribal tension in subsequent years. K 2 concludes the section with a brief passage on the establishment of the Organization of African Unity in 1963 and the active participation of the African nations in the Third World Movement from 1974. Unlike K 1 and C, K 2 presents a photo in which Algerians celebrate their independence from France in 1962.

Compared with K 1 and K 2, C offers a cursory look at Africa's struggle against colonialism and the emergence of the new nations. As with the other two textbooks, C describes the rise of the Wafd Party and its contribution to Egypt's independence. C's treatment of African nationalism tends to focus on North Africa, such as Tunisia, Algeria, and Libya. As for the sub-Saharan regions, the book only touches on Du Bois' Pan-Africanism.

Challenges Faced by Africa Today

Among the five clusters of Africa-related materials in the three textbooks, the last one is the shortest and the least satisfactory in its focus and presentation methods. In fact, the topic of contemporary Africa is covered only in K 1 and K 2, not in C. Even in K 1 and K 2, the chapter titles reveal their vague pertinence to Africa: "20th-century Conflict that Needs Urgent Solutions in the 21st Century" (K 1); and "The World Today" (K 2). While Africa is mentioned in a scattered manner here and there, no specific regional issues are addressed. Ironically, however, both books use photos of African people plagued by political, economic, and health problems. The following issues are the focus of the last chapters in the two books as major challenges in today's world, including Africa.

- Many newly independent countries experience social unrest and armed conflict over national borders, tribal interests, and religious sectarianism.
- The growing North-South economic disparity, population explosion, and environmental damages seriously threat the quality of our lives. Food shortage is the most pressing consequence of these problems.
- Terrorism is becoming a serious world-wide concern.
- The root cause of terrorism is often hunger and poverty.

Although the problems pointed out above are not unique to Africa, the majority of photos in the texts are set in Africa as if the continent is the dominant site of such trouble. For instance, K 1 presents a Liberian boy soldier holding a machine gun. In the subsequent section on the "Characteristics of the 21st Century and Our Tasks," K 1 examines a close link between poverty and terrorism. The book then shows the picture of a dying child and his/her crying mother. Below the picture is written: "Severe Starvation in Africa."

K 2 displays a photo of refugees during the Rwandan Civil War. The accompanying caption says, "The tribal conflict between the Tutsi and the Hutu resulted in the killings of more than a million people in three months." To underscore the degrees of poverty and starvation, K 2 cites an article on Somalia from a Korean magazine. Entitled, "Land of Starvation," the article argues: "Although Somalia has land three times larger than Korea, and rich natural resources, one and a half million people there died of hunger in 1991 only... Greedy politicians and the political interventions of the neighboring countries turned the impoverished country into hell on earth" (p. 315). This quote is juxtaposed with the picture of an emaciated child and his/her helpless young mother. In the "in-depth thinking" corner, K 2 throws light on environmental issues, referring to them as "nature's attack on humans." The textbook sharply contrasts today's scientific and technological advancement with the mass destruction of nature. As evidence, the book shows an unidentified place in

Chad where the desertification of farming land is in progress due to the global warming.

Conclusion

The analysis of the contents on Africa in the three high school world history textbooks demonstrates a few notable patterns.

(1) All three books are slightly over 300 pages in length, but the African parts total a maximum of 6 pages in each, occupying less than 2% of the entire book.

(2) The chapter divisions of the books are centered on European history and Western perspectives. The amount of text assigned to Europe also far exceeds that to Africa, making their quantitative comparison nearly meaningless.

(3) The section on ancient Africa is packed with the kingdoms and empires, but their descriptions sometimes ignore the precise periods of their existences. Some empires appeared in the 14th century, but they are mentioned in the pre-historic chapter. Similarly, factual errors are found. Book C misspells "Tenkamenin," the king of Ghana, as "Tenkaminen."

(4) K 2 and C tend to reify the negative perceptions of African people and their cultures by using stereotypical images. The mass media portrayals of starving children and civil wars are quoted and reiterated without a critical assessment of their accuracy. For instance, the sensational descriptions and depictions of the slave trade can mislead the student to conjure up the image of Africa locked in their helpless past forever.

The contents of the three selected textbooks are based on the 7th revised national curriculum for Korean secondary schools. Compared with their previous editions, the current books show several changes. The most important revisions are reduced emphasis on the history of the Western superpowers and the inclusion of smaller countries. A representative example is the newly introduced sections on the ancient and medieval histories of sub-Saharan Africa and North and South Americas. Furthermore, the present editions of the world history textbooks begin with a chapter on "Time, Space, and Humanity." The instructional objective of this opening chapter is to engage the student in thinking about what it means to study and research history.

While the new components strengthened the textbooks significantly, there are still areas that need improvement. The result of our content analysis leads to the following recommendations. Firstly, more of African views on their own historical experience should be incorporated into the textbook contents. Although the three books occasionally quote statements from well-known Africans, they are not sufficient to convey insiders' views on African society and culture.

A related problem is that none of the authors of the three textbooks are experts on Africa. The references they consulted do not include works representing an "emic" perspective on the continent. Many of the information sources listed in the books are Western in origin. An ideal and ultimate solution to this problem would be producing Korean educators specializing in African history. But for a more immediate way of redressing the current flaws, reference materials for textbook writers should be diversified.

Secondly, Africa is a large continent that comprises many tribes and nations. Treating them as if they are one entity creates serious flaws in the textbooks. More local and regional history should be brought to light. Presently, much space is allocated to North Africa. Various sub-Saharan areas deserve a more detailed treatment.

Thirdly, positive aspects of African history should receive more attention, such as the resilience of African people against natural disasters and socio-political predicaments. Diverse efforts they have made for environmental conservation should also be recognized. Contents on the brighter side of African society and culture will help develop a sense of balance and objectivity in the student in handling the continent's tumultuous history. The success stories of local Africans with regard to their education, health, and economic development should be given due credit in the textbooks.

Another important recommendation for textbook writers is the use of the political, historical, and economic ties between Korea and Africa for educational purposes. The aforementioned Chosŏn Korea's map of Africa can function as an effective pedagogical apparatus for diminishing the student's psychological distance from the continent. But neither the map's cartographic contents nor the rich educational implications of the premodern global knowledge exchange are utilized in the current books. An awareness of the Korea-Africa connections will increase the student's curiosity about African history and make his/her learning more meaningful.

Lastly, world history is often organized in terms of major socio-political events, economic development, and industrialization processes. This type of approach inevitably puts Africa in an inferior position vis-à-vis Europe, North America, and East Asia. An alternative method for organizing world history should be explored to enhance cross-cultural understanding. In such an endeavor, the theory and practice advocated by the Annales School of historians may lend an insight. Only when we conceptualize and interpret history as a form of narrative with more rigor and objectivity, the deep-seated prejudice against Africa and similarly "backward" regions of the world can be overcome.

References

Austin, O. P. (1900). Does colonization pay? *Forum, 28*, 621.

Cha, Y., Kim, S., & Ham, S. (2013). Multicultural education and Asian immigrants in Korea: Current status and evolving issues. *Multicultural Education Studies, 6*(1), 105-126.

Cho, M. (2014). The Korea World Missions Association website. *2013 Han'guk sŏn'gyosa p'asong hyŏnhwang* [The 2013 state of Korean overseas missionaries]. Retrieved from http://kwma.withch.kr/bbs/board.php?bo_table=sub7_1&wr_id=1602&sfl=wr_subject&stx=%EC%84%A0%EA%B5%90+%ED%98%84%ED%99%A9&sop=and

Han, G. (2003). T'aja mandŭlki – Han'guk sahoe wa ijunodongja ŭi chaehyŏn [Making other: The representation of foreign migrant workers in Korea]. *Pigyomunhwa yŏn'gu, 9*(2), 157-193.

Han, G. (2007). Korean imagining and representing of Africa. In O. Yi, J. Yi, T. Yi, P. Yi, H. Yi, & G. Han, *Oryu wa p'yŏn'gyŏn ŭro kadŭkch'an segyesa kyogwasŏ paro chapki* [Correcting the world history text books full of errors and prejudice] (pp. 241-299). Seoul, Korea: Samin.

Kim, D., & Han, G. (2012). Sasil kwa 'chaehyŏn' ŭi kwanjŏm esŏ Ap'ŭrik'a tasi pogi - Ch'ojunghakkyo sahoe kyogwasŏ Ap'ŭrik'a sŏsul naeyong ŭl chungsim ŭro [Reviewing Africa from the points of view of "fact" and "representation": Focusing on the contents on Africa in the elementary and middle school social studies textbooks]. *Taehan chirihakoeji, 47*(3), 440-458.

Kim, H. (2006). *Yŏksagyoyukkwajŏng kwa kyogwasŏ yŏn'gu* [The history education curriculum and textbook analysis]. Seoul, Korea: Sŏnin.

Kim, S., & Cho. C. (2010). Chunghakkyo sahoe kyogwasŏ e nat'anan ideollogi mit p'yŏn'gyŏn punsŏk – Sŏnam Asia mit Ap'ŭrik'a tanwŏn ŭl chungsim ŭro [The analysis of the ideology and the bias in the middle school social studies textbooks: Focusing on Southwest Asia and Africa]. *Chungdŭnggyoyuk yŏn'gu, 58*(3), 87-112.

Kim, T. (2008). Christian webzine. *Segye sŏn'gyo ŭi yŏksa wa hyŏnhwang* [The past and present of the world mission]. Retrieved from http://www.cry.or.kr/news/articleView.html?idxno=730

Park, S., & Woo, S. (2009). Sahoe kyogwasŏ e nat'anan kukkabyŏl sŭt'ereot'aip – 7ch'a kodŭnghakkyo sahoe kyogwasŏ chung ilbansahoe yŏng'yŏk ŭl chungsim ŭro [The national stereotypes in the social studies textbooks: Focusing on the 7th high school social studies curriculum]. *Sahoegwa kyoyuk, 48*(4), 19-34.

Pierterse, J. (1992). *White on black: Images of Africa and blacks in western popular culture.* New Haven, CT: Yale University Press.

Song, H. (2011, October 23). "Kat'ŭn p'ibusaek, tarŭn kukchŏk" Ch'ian ŭi sasaekchidae ["Same skin color, different nationality," the dead zone of public security]. *Han'guk kyŏngje*. Retrieved from http://www.hankyung.co m/board/view.php?id=nagija_newsman_paper&no=349& page=1&sn=&ss=&sc=&old_no=347&old_id=nagija_ne wsman_paper&skin=&keyword=&category=3&tag=&pag enum=&sel_order=&desc=desc&cmt_page=1&cmt_order =&cmt_desc=asc

Spivak, G. (1988). Can the subaltern speak? In C. Nelson & L. Grossberg (Eds.), *Marxism and the interpretation of culture* (pp. 271-313). Urbana, IL: University of Illinois Press.

Varhola, M. J. (2000). *Fire and ice: The Korean War, 1950-1953*. Cambridge, MA: Da Capo Press.

CHAPTER FIVE

Culture Prints in African Languages: The World we Share

Désiré Baloubi
Shaw University

Introduction

The primary objective of this paper is to re-visit what so many writers, linguists, anthropologists, philologists, and philosophers, among others, have revealed to the world about the wealth of knowledge, beliefs, attitudes, and values embedded in human languages (See Labov, 1973; Lakoff, 1973; Boon, 1972; Lakoff and Johnson, 1980; MacLaury, 1989; Wolfram and Schilling-Estes, 2006; Irvine, 2006; and Warner-Lewis, 2009a). It is a call for the revival of African languages and dialects, for now is the time to break away once for all from the myth that African languages, in particular, express "folk culture [that] was valued more as a matter of performance for public display than as a subject of serious scholarly study" (Warner-Lewis, 2009b, p. 1)" Indeed, Wole Soyinka won the Nobel Prize for his command of the English language, which he still demonstrates throughout his great contributions to African literature. But Chinua Achebe, who does not deserve any less than his compatriot Soyinka, has also exposed the whole world time and again to the rich traditions, culture, ideology, and philosophy of his Igbo ancestry through his writing. Both Soyinka and Achebe, together with Amos Tutuola, Ayi Kwei Armah, Ngugi, Bernard Dadie, Cheikh Anta Diop, Camara Laye, Olympe Behly Quenum, and Aimé Césaire, to name just a few, have certainly paved the way from

Africanizing English and French to actually celebrating our indigenous languages: Dendi, Idaacha, Igbo, Pulah, Wolof, Yoruba, and Zulu, among others. Based on examples of various speech acts, with specific reference to the semantic domain of body-part words and proverbs, this article serves as a starting point of what could be a lifelong study of the worldviews and cultural ideologies embedded in African languages. In a larger perspective, as the paper argues, finding our voices again and promoting African languages and cultures would certainly be the least we can do in a shrinking world we now call "our global village."

With special reference to Dendi and the Idaacha dialect of Yoruba, this paper shows how both languages reflect theories on language and culture, cultural ideologies, or linguistic culture in greetings, idiomatic phrases, and sentences. It also demonstrates that, indeed, different languages may express similar worldviews, beliefs, and attitudes via similar or identical symbols. Additionally, the paper looks at examples of Igbo proverbs in Achebe's works to further prove the wealth of symbolic meanings in African languages.

Theoretical framework

The theoretical framework of this article is the literature that defines the concepts of culture, language and culture, language ideology, cultural ideology, linguistic culture, cultural symbols, and symbolic meanings. According to Boon (quoted in Varenne), "Culture pertains to operations which render complex human phenomena communicable" (Varenne, 1987; p. 369). One could also say that all human endeavors are cultural experiences, and so is human communication, just as Varenne suggests: "[C]ulture is an activity that human beings perform on what is given to them in the course of their lives: biological needs . . . and, last but not least, the language of their contemporaries and coparticipants in everyday life scenes" (p. 369).

Schiffman rejects the phrase language ideology and prefers 'linguistic culture', which he defines as

> ...the sum totality of ideas, values, beliefs, attitudes, prejudices, myths, religious strictures, and all the other cultural `baggage' that speakers bring to their dealings with language from their culture. Linguistic culture also is concerned with the transmission and codification of language and has bearing also on the culture's notions of the value of literacy and the sanctity of texts. And of course language itself is a cultural artifact and must be counted as a part of linguistic culture (Schiffman. 2005).

Culture embedded in the transmission or codification process of messages in African languages is the main focus of this paper. Cultural ideology is the rationale behind culture-loaded words, phrases, and proverbs that speakers of other languages may have to understand in order to communicate effectively in the languages discussed in this article. This rationale confirms that language is indeed a cultural artifact, and, as such, it reflects parts of the native speaker's worldview and the ways he or she may interpret a number of complex human phenomena. Linguistic anthropology elaborates quite extensively on this subject in Indo-European languages, and it warrants special attention in African languages as well, at least for the sake of cross-cultural communication that is so important in this era of globalization. As Bonvillain argues, "In some domains of vocabulary, cross-cultural comparisons uncover basic difference in the ways that people perceive their universe" (Bonvillain, 2008; p. 52). While some people may say that understanding this basic difference can result in better cross-cultural communication, others may argue that the world which languages and cultures share is more likely to facilitate such communication rather than what separates them. Studies in that regard include Eibl-Eibesfeldt (1972) and Schneller (1988).

Areas that are worth exploring to uncover similarities are cultural presuppositions, extended and transferred meanings, and metaphors or symbolic meanings. Bonvillain recognizes the role that shared assumptions and cultural symbols play in communication processes: "In order to gain insights into a people's worldview or system of values, it is necessary to ascertain the cultural symbols embedded in their words" (Bonvillain, 2008; p. 67). In fact, not all words are assigned arbitrary meanings; some are associated with cultural beliefs, attitudes, and values shared sometimes across speech communities. That is exactly what Bonvillain claims in the following terms:

> The vocabulary of a language is not merely an inventory of arbitrary labels referring to objects, entities, or events. Words also convey many kinds of cultural meanings that add to, transform, or manipulate basic senses of words. Research into these areas of meaning and usage includes investigation of cultural presuppositions, assosciational or extensional meanings, and uses of words to carry symbolic or ideological content (p. 67).

An Overview of Dendi, Idaacha, and Igbo languages

Dendi

Dendi is a Gur and Nilo-Saharan language spoken in the northern regions of Benin; it is also spoken in Nigeria and is related to Zarma and Songai with which it forms a dialect cluster. A 15-year old census indicates that approximately 30, 000 people speak Dendi in Benin and about 32,050 speakers in all countries (See Gordon, 2005).

Idaacha

Ede Idaacha is a Benue-Congo, Defoid, and Yoruboid language spoken by approximately 100, 000 people, according to SIL 2002 census, mainly in the Collines Province/Department, formerly northern Zou Province. Administrative territories where Iddaacha is spoken include Dassa-Zoume and Glazoue *Sous-Prefectures*. Idaacha is "One of 8 languages that make up the Ede language cluster (Yoruboid) that spreads over southwestern Nigeria, southern and central Benin, and into southern and central Togo" (Gordon, 2005; p. 43). For more details on Idaacha, see Baloubi (2005).

Igbo

Igbo is a Benue-Congo, Igboid language spoken by probably over 18,000,000 people across various states, with at least 30 dialects, in the Federal Republic of Nigeria. Igbo is being standardized, and it is the official language in the southwest of Nigeria. It is also "The main trade language of Abia, Anambra, Ebonyi, Enugu, and Imo states" (Gordon, 2005; p. 163).

Symbolic meanings and cultural ideologies in Idaacha and Dendi greetings

Both Idaacha and Dendi use similar symbolic meanings and rationales or cultural ideologies in everyday greetings. It is usually about good wishes, congratulations, thanks, good existence or survival, good health, good luck, comfort, happiness, and encouragement—among other forms of wishful thinking.

Upon Meeting

In both Idaacha and Dendi cultures, people usually inquire about each other's state of health at the first encounter—whether they are strangers, acquaintances, families, or friends. These greetings, in examples (1) and (2), are most appropriate in the morning. The focus is on **being well** and **in good health**.

- (1) **Idaacha (I) and Dendi (D)**
    (I) *E ji* **ire?** [Did you wake up **well—in good health?**]
    (D) N*oo tunu* **baani?** [Did you get up **well—in good health?**]
- (2) **(I) and (D)**
    (I) *E sun ire?* [Did you sleep **well?**]
    (D) *Noo kani baani?* [Did you sleep **well—in good health?**]

In the next five examples, (3), (4), (5), (6) and (7), being **in good health** is associated with the general concept of existence. The greeter expresses gratitude or compliments to the one being greeted. In that case, a person is complimented even if he or she is doing something that benefits him or her alone. This reflects selflessness and a deep sense of altruism. Indeed, caring or showing concerns more about others than about one's self—at least at the surface level—is a sign of good upbringing among the Idaacha and Dendi. Cultural ideologies, as expressed in both Idaacha and Dendi languages, support the existentialist approach to life according to which what you say and what you do determine your nature. But unlike existentialism, the teaching of Sartre, Hiedeger and Kierkegaard, African or Idaacha and Dendi cultural ideologies portray human life as a collective responsibility in a purposefully meaningful world. The following examples are a token of the ideologies mentioned above:

- **(3) (I) and (D)**
    - (I) Greeter: *Ira yin an fe?* [How about your relatives?]

Respondent: A wa [They are/exist.]
- (D) Greeter: *Mete noo boro yo?* [How about your people?]
    Respondent: *ŋ gonon (baani)*.
    [They are/exist (well).]

- **(4) (I) and (D)**
    - (I) *E waa re?* [Are you well?]
    - (D) *Noo gonon baani?* [Are you/do you exist well?]

Greeting someone who has returned from a trip, irrespective of the means of transportation (on foot, by bicycle, or on a plane):

- **(5) (I) and (D)**
    - (I) *E ku u rin* [Thanks for walking.] "Greetings for a successful trip"
    - (D) *Foo naa zure* [Thanks for running/rushing.]
- **(6) (I) and (D)**
    - (I) *E k'aabo* [Thanks for returning/coming back.]

"Greetings on a successful return trip"
- (D) *O foo naa kayo* [Thanks for coming.]

How does one greet a person who may be working, say, cutting grass in his or her own backyard? The answer is that it does not make any difference whether the work (being) done benefits the worker, the greeter or someone else:

- **(7) (I) and (D)**
    - (I) *E k'uche* [Thanks for the work.]
    - (D) *O foo naa gbei* [Thanks for the work.]

As examples (5) through (7) demonstrate, the greeter thanks, compliments, or expresses gratitude.

Departing:

When departing, people wish to see each other again. They wish each other good luck and pray so that they may meet again in good health. Therefore, the predominant ideology or rationale is the constant need and feeling of togetherness in peace and happiness.

- **(8) (I) and (D)**
  - (I) *O d'abo* ['Until arrival' (Until you/I come)]
  - (D) *A chi kayo* ['Until arrival' (Until you/I come)]

- **(9) (I) and (D)**
  - (I) *Ipade e wa ko d'ayo* [May we meet in peace/happiness!]
  - (D) *Iri n di chere naa alaafia* [May we see each other in peace!]

- **(10) (I) and (D)**
  - (I) *Ese e re* ['May you have good feet' (good luck!)]
  - (D) *O zummu baani* ['Get down well' (May you arrive safely!)]

Metaphorical language use and idiomatic expressions (referring to body parts)

Bonvillain (2008), Cruse (2004), Irvine(2006), Labov (1973), Lakoff (1972), Lakoff and Johnson (1980), and MacLaury (1989), among other studies, discuss quite extensively language, culture, the meaning of messages in context, meaning in language, speech community, language community, boundaries of words and their meanings, meaning criteria and the logic or rationale of fuzzy concepts, symbolic meanings of body parts, metaphors, metaphorical language use, prototypes and metaphoric extensions. As the following examples of language use and idiomatic expressions demonstrate, the concepts listed above also apply to Idaacha (I) and Dendi (D) speech communities.

- (11) (I) and (D)—The eyes and metaphoric extensions:

It is common belief among the Idaacha and Dendi that red eyes, burning eyes, and a sweaty nose are signs of struggle and hardship. Thus, someone who is struggling, making great efforts physically and/or psychologically, may exclaim as follows:
- (I) *Oju wa pan!* ['The eyes are getting red'] or *Imu wa be* ['The nose is shining']
- (D) *Mon koŋnu!* ['The eyes are hot']

- (12) (I) and (D)

Just as many people across languages and cultures do, the Idaacha and Dendi show signs of anger and bitterness through the eyes.
- (I) *Oju è é koro* [Your eyes are bitter]
- (D) *A na mon dibi* ['He or she has mixed up/stirred up his or her eyes.']

- (13) (I) and (D)

Similarly, impatience and laziness may be detected in a person's eyes.
- (I) *Oju wa ro m* ['The eyes are hurting me' or 'My eyes are hurting' (I am impatient/feeling lazy.)]
- (I) *Oju le m* ['My eyes made me feel tense' (I was impatient)]
- (I) *M'oju ro!* ['Make your eyes endure' or 'Make your eyes strong/resistant' (Be patient/tolerant or endure to the end!)]
- (D) *Mon naani!* ['Press your eyes' (Be brave!)]

- (14) (I) and (D)—The neck

The neck symbolizes responsibility and awareness. If something is hanging around your neck, it means you are in charge or responsible. It also means you are giving it serious thought.

- (I) *O wa l' èké e* ['It is around your neck' (It is your responsibility)]
- (D) *A gonon ŋjinde* ['It is around your neck' (It is your responsibility)]
- (I) *O wa sere èké* ['He or she is thinking the neck' (He or she is thinking)]
- (I) *E è gbagbe èké* ['He or she forgets the neck' (He or she is forgetful)]

- (15) (I) and (D)—The heart

In everyday communication, people refer to the heart when they want to convey messages related to peace, happiness, and anger. It is also the body part that symbolizes sincerity; it serves as storage for very important ideas and resolutions. In short, the heart is considered a very precious human organ, and no one should mess with it.

- (I) *O wa l'okan m* ['It is in my heart' (I am thinking about it; I am giving it serious consideration)]
- (I) *Okan yin bale* ['Your heart has gone down' (You are calm/at peace)]
- (D) *Noo bine zobu* ['Your heart has gone down' (You are calm/at peace)]
- (I) *Okan m dun* ['My heart is sweet' (I am happy/delighted)]

- (D) *A bine yei* ['My heart is wet/cool' (I am happy/delighted)]
- (I) *O b'okan m baje* ['He or she messed up my heart' (He or she got on my nerves)]
- (D) *A na a bine sara* ['He or she messed up my heart' (He or she got on my nerves)]

- (16) (I) and (D)—The stomach and the heart

In the examples below, *inun*—the stomach, belly, or, more broadly speaking, the inner part of the human body is used as a substitute for *okan*—the heart. In most cases both body parts can be used interchangeably.

- (I) *Inu m tutu* ['My belly is wet/cool' (I am a calm/worry-free/nice person)]
- (D) *A sinna gunde konni* ['I do not have a hot stomach' (I am not a bad/wicked person)]
- (I) *Inu un yin ko san* ['Your stomach belly/inside is not good' (You are not a loving/good- hearted person)]
- (D) *Noo bine su boori* ['Your heart is not good' (You are not a loving/good-hearted person)]
- (I) *Inu m baje* ['My belly is messed up' (I am angry/upset)]
- (D) and *A bine sara* ['My belly is messed up' (I am angry/upset)]
- (I) *Inu m dun* ['My belly is sweet' (I am happy)]
- (I) *Inu m koro* (I am mad/bitter-My belly is bitter)

- (16) (I) and (D)—The back and the head

References are often made to the back and the head to express support and good luck respectively. When the Idaacha and Dendi say literally you have a good head, they mean you are lucky or fortunate. In order to show support, as is the case in English, they stand behind you. The examples below illustrate those symbolic meanings:

- (I) *O wa l'eyin m* ['He or she is behind me' (He or she got my back; he or she is supporting me; he or she is behind me)]
- (D) *A gonon a banna* ['He or she is behind me' (He or she got my back; he or she is supporting me; he or she is behind me)]
- (I) *E ku eewo re* ['Thanks for a good head' (Congratulations!)]
- (D) *O foo na boŋwon kaani* ['Thanks for a good head' (Congratulations!)]

All the examples above confirm the use of very similar symbolic meanings in the Idaacha and Dendi languages. In expressing important thoughts and critical ideas, and even in discussing trivial issues, the Idaacha and Dendi utilize these symbols quite naturally in their daily communication transactions. Now it may be worth pointing out that, as far as African languages and cultures as concerned, the power to transmit connotative meanings is not restricted to idiomatic expressions that refer to human body parts. On the contrary, as is the case in most speech communities where oral literature outweighs written discourse, people use parables and proverbs as the norm in sharing and passing their ancestral wisdom from one generation to the next. As Schipper argues, "[using a proverb] allows the speaker to broach sensitive matters in an abstract and indirect manner [...] As a matter of fact, indirectness is a highly esteemed quality in many oral societies. Thus, the speaker is not held personally responsible for his/her statement" (Schipper, 1991; p. 3). Not only do these proverbs linguistically represent very interesting instances of indirect speech acts, but they also embody cultural values and ideologies that sometimes cut across various geographic boundaries in Africa. Special attention is now directed towards Igbo proverbs as rendered in English by Chinua Achebe's works.

Igbo Proverbs in Achebe's Works

It might be interesting to begin with what Ravenscroft says about language use in *Things Fall Apart*, the earliest and most widespread piece of African literature by Achebe:

> The language of the people of Umuofia is full of Ibo proverbs (which Achebe renders into English) that allow well-tested traditional wisdom to be applied to problems of the present. If the nub of a contemporary situation can be seen to correspond to the generalized truth contained in a proverb, then present perplexity and past experience are made congruent, and language remains an effective instrument for coping with life (Ravenscroft, 1969; p. 15).

The proverbs below, cited in Lindfors (1973), are classified by theme as they appear in Achebe's novels and short stories:

1. Things Fall Apart (Achebe, 1958)

Proverbs (1) and (2) are about status and achievement; one deals with self-praise or self-esteem, while the other indicates that appearances matter. If you do not praise yourself or believe in yourself, who else will? In our modern society the second proverb also makes sense; we dress up for job interviews because we strongly believe that first impressions count.

> "The lizard that jumped from the high iroko tree to the ground said he would praise himself if no one else did" (Lindfors, 1973, p. 6).
> "You can tell a ripe corn by its look" (p. 18).

2. No Longer At Ease (Achebe, 1960a)

These proverbs are about the importance of kinship, unity, togetherness. More specifically, proverb (3) supports the Igbo belief that human resources as more valuable than material and financial wealth. In the novel, the Umofians raise funds to send their son Obi to study in England. Also, after Obi Okonkwo had been charged with bribery and corruption, the Umofia Progressive Union raised funds again on his behalf, but he lost his trial. That is clearly an action of solidarity and unity, as proverb (4) explains. Proverbs (5) and (6) teach us that no one can be happy alone and also warn against "foolish and unworthy actions." The last proverb (7) in this section compares Obi with the rat who went swimming with his friend lizard and died from cold. The implicature is that Obi did what everybody else was doing, but he did not really know how to shield himself from public eyes.

(1) "He who has people is richer than he who has money" (p. 79).
(2) "If all snakes lived together in one place, who would approach them?" (p. 81).
(3) "When there's a big tree small ones climb on its back to reach the sun" (p. 96).
(4) "A person who has not secured a place on the floor should not begin to look for a mat"(60)
(5) "[…] the house rat who went swimming with his friend the lizard and died from cold, for while the lizard's scales kept him dry the rat's hairy body remained wet" (p. 7).

3. Arrow Of God (Achebe, 1969a)

The following proverbs from this novel highlight the importance of doing the right thing. They focus on helping the helpless (8), setting priorities (9), and making no enemies (10):

"An adult does not sit and watch while the she-goat suffers the pain of childbirth tied to a post" (p. 21).

"Let us first chase the wild cat; afterwards we can blame the hen" (p. 122).

(10) "A traveler to distant places should make no enemies" (p. 208).

4. Girls At War (Achebe, 1973)

As one can tell, the symbols in proverbs do not by themselves help to understand the meanings of the messages they convey. In all cases, the meanings are context-based and deeply rooted in the beliefs, values, and cultures of the people who use them. Furthermore, proverbs may be used in many ways, even as incantations. In one of the stories in *Girls At War* (Achebe, 1973), "Chike's School Days," when Elizabeth consults the oracle because her son insists on marrying an Osu girl, an outcast in any Igbo community, the Ifa priest remarks very sarcastically:

(11) "Those who gather ant-infested faggots must be prepared for the visit of lizards"(Lindfors, 1973, p. 39).

Because they have been converted to Christianity, Elizabeth and her son Amos have thus gathered ant-infested faggots according to the diviner. Therefore, they should not be surprised now that the son is turning his back on the traditional ways of his own people. In the pre-colonial period, nobody would dare marry an Osu girl in any Igbo community. As a new Christian convert, Amos challenges this, and his mother is visited by lizards; she is tormented. She eventually gives up Christianity and returns "to the faith of her people" (Lindfors, 1973, p. 44).

Proverbs are a form of indirect speech, which tends to be the norm of language use among adults in African cultures, especially in traditional settings in rural areas. Bennett alludes to this oblique language by referring to a conversation between a group of American students and a Nigerian student: "Does that mean in your culture nobody ever tells anybody the point? Well, that's not exactly true. You have to tell little kids the point because they're not sophisticated enough to use this adult style of communication" (Bennett, 1996; p. 6). In short, all the examples above show that the use of proverbs can be viewed as a linguistic strategy, among other alternatives, to express a worldview, to interpret social phenomena, and to define individual and collective attitudes to social realities.

Conclusion

I hope this paper has achieved what it set out to do, which is to expose the wealth of knowledge, beliefs, attitudes, and values embedded in human languages. It is a call to keep on working on the revival of African languages and dialects. Research and findings on African languages have made significant contributions to linguistics and related disciplines; therefore, any assumption that they are "more valued as a matter of performance for public display than as a subject of serious scholarly study" (Warner-Lewis. 2009b; p. 1), is simply untenable.

Chinua Achebe has never missed any opportunity to show and elaborate on the rich traditions, the culture, the ideology, and even the philosophy of his Igbo ancestry in his novels and short stories. Joseph Ki-Zerbo, Felix Iroko, Toyin Falola, and many more African history scholars have helped better understand Africa, one of the oldest continents, whose history is yet to be fully reconstructed. Kwame Nkrumah, Julius Nyerere, Leopold Senghor, Paulin Hountondji, Kwasi Wiredu, Odera Oruka, Peter Bodunrin, John Mbiti, among other African scholars, have paved the way and shed light on African philosophy. African linguists, such as Akinbiyi Akinlabi, Hounkpati B. C. Capo, John Mugane, Salikoko S.

Mufwene, Ayo Bamgbose, and others have attracted so many to African linguistics, which has definitely established itself as an academic discipline of great interest.

Finally, this paper is not the voice of another ideologue; it is not a piece of political writing to the left or to the right. It is not "essentialist", "relativist", or "particularist"; neither does it presume to be "universalist" (Hammond, 1999b). In fact, while some cultural, philosophical, anthropological, and historical studies may focus on emphasizing who did what the best, or what features or achievements set some peoples or species apart, this paper celebrates the beauty of the common ground on which we all stand in terms of our frames of references and the way language use projects our cultures, our beliefs, our attitudes, and our values. Without proclaiming the Whorf-Sapir hypothesis, this paper purports that even if different peoples in different cultures hold different worldviews, they may sometimes think alike (See Baloubi, 2003) and express their thoughts in different languages that utilize similar metaphors and symbolic meanings. In that regard, this study concurs with Saussure's view that in language, there are only differences without any positive terms (See Saussure, 1966), but it strongly argues that between two languages there may be similarities with positive terms.

Reference

Achebe. C. (1973).*Girls at War and Other Stories*. New York: Doubleday & Co. Inc.

Baloubi.D. (2005).*The Morphophonemics of the Idaacha Dialect of Yoruba*. Charlotte, NC:Conquering Books

Baloubi.D. (2003, October).*Language in the era of globalization: Old wine in new bottles*.Paper presented at the American

Society of Geolinguistics International Conference. Baruch College, NY.

Bennett. M. (June/July, 1996).Intercultural communication in a multicultural society.*TESOL Matters, 6* (3), 6.

Bonvillain, N. (2008). *Language, Culture, and Communication: The Meaning of Messages, 5th ed.* Upper Saddle River, NJ: Pearson Prentice Hall.

Boon, J.A. (1972). From*Symbolism to Structuralism*: Lévi-Strauss in a Literary Tradition. NewYork: Harper and Row.

Cruse. A. D. (2004).Meaning in language: An introduction to semantics and pragmatics, 2nd ed.Oxford: Oxford University Press.

Eibl-Eibesfeldt, I. (1972). Similarities and differences between cultures in expressivemovements.In R. Hinde (Ed.). *Nonverbal Communication* (pp. 297-312).New York:CUP.

Gordon, R. G. (Ed.) (2005). *Ethnologue: Languages of the World, 15th ed.*Dallas, TX: SILInternational.

Hammond, P (1999b) Cultural Identity and Ideology. Retrieved fromhttp://myweb.lsbu.ac.uk/philip-hammond/1999b.html

Irvine. J. (2006).Speech and Language Community.In K.Brown (Ed), *Encyclopedia ofLanguage and Linguistics, 2nd ed., (pp.* 689-696). Oxford, Elseiver.

Labov.W. (1973).The boundaries of words and their meanings. In C. Bailey and R. Shuy ed.*New Ways of Analyzing Variation in English*, (pp. 340-373). Whashington, DC:Georgetown University Press.

Lakoff.G. (1972). Hedges: A study in meaning criteria and the logic of fuzzy concepts.*Papersfrom the 8th Regional Meeting of the Chicago Linguistic Society.*Chicago:ChicagoLinguistic Society.

Lakoff, G. & Johnson.M. (1980).*Metaphors We Live By*. Chicago: University of Chicago Press.

Lindfors.B. (1973).*Folklore in Nigerian Literature*. New York: African Publishing Company.

MacLaury, R. (1989). Zapotec body-part locatives: Prototypes and metaphoric extensions,*International Journal of American Linguistics* 55, 119-154.

Ravenscroft.A. (1969).*Chinua Achebe*. Essex, England: Longman Co. Ltd.

Saussure, Ferdinand de & Bally, Charles, 1865-1947 & Riedlinger, Albert & Sechehaye, Albert(1966).*Course in general linguistics* (1st McGraw-Hill pbk.Ed). McGraw-Hill, NewYork.

Schiffman.H. (2005).Problems with Language and 'Ideology.' Retrieved fromhttp://ccat.sas.upenn.edu/~haroldfs/540/handouts/ideology/ideology.html

Schipper.M. (1991) Source of All Evil: African Proverbs and Sayings on Women. London:Allison & Busby.

Schneller, Raphael. (1988).The Israeli experience of cross-cultural misunderstanding: Insightsand lessons. In F. Poyatos (Ed.). *Cross-cultural Persspectives in NonverbalCommunication* ed. (pp. 153-171). Lewiston. NY: CJ Hogrefe.

Warner-Lewis.M. (2009).*Trinidad Yoruba: From Mother-Tongue to Memory*. UniversityAlabama Press.

Varenne. H. (Aug., 1987).Talk and Real Talk: The Voices of Silence and the Voices of Power inAmerican Family Life, *Cultural Anthropology*, 2.(3), 369.

Warner-Lewis.M. (2009a).Affirming the Subaltern: The Contribution of J. D. Elder.*Research in African Literatures*, 40, 1.

Wolfram, W. & Schilling-Estes, N. (2006).*American English: Dialects and Variation*, 2nd ed.Malden, MA: Blackwell.

CHAPTER SIX

A Literacy-Based Approach to Cultural Understanding in African Language Pedagogy

Adeola Agoke
PhD Student, Department of African Languages andLiterature, University of Wisconsin, Madison.

Kazeem Kehinde Sanuth
PhD Candidate in Second Language Acquisition, University of Wisconsin, Madison.

The cultural content of our textbooks is limited and overshadowed by a strong emphasis in grammatical analysis. The argument has been that our students can acquire the necessary cultural knowledge by taking courses in anthropology, other African studies programs, or by traveling to country where the African language is spoken. (Folarin-Schleicher and Moshi 2000, p. 114-115)

Introduction

The excerpt above is from one of the seminal publications to date in the field of African language teaching, *The Pedagogy of African languages: An Emerging Filed*, by Folarin-Schleicher and Moshi (2000). The quote is over a decade old but the condition it references still enjoys strong currency: A majority of textbooks that the scholars analyzed in the book are still in active use in African language classes. However, the argument for seeking cultural knowledge beyond the language classroom has so far declined. It is widely accepted that language and culture are not discrete and that "cultural understanding is an important part of world languages education" (ACTFL, 1996, 2000). Thus, over the course of the years, African language instructors and scholars have taken up the challenge of developing effective models of integrating language and culture (Folarin-Schleicher & Moshi 2000; Schleicher 1997.) In this article, we offer a Literacy text-based approach to instruction, which hinges on an integration of *Performance-Based Assessment* (PBA) and the *pedagogy of multiliteracies*.

Our goal in this paper is to argue for a language curriculum that is informed by *cultural perspectives* of target speech community, in the understanding that cultural perspectives are the underlining values that connect the cultural practices, the cultural products and the linguistic activities of the community. We hold strongly that cultures are inextricably connected to language, and both are encapsulated in *texts* of various forms; thus neither should be privileged over the other in language teaching. And drawing from contemporary works such as Kramsch (2012; 2014), we seek to advance a curriculum that, by factoring in the cultural productions, bridges the divides between the classroom instruction and actual practices in the social context.

With the changing linguistic configurations of societies globally, signified by fast-pacing social mobility, seamless cross-border communications, and globalization, foreign language pedagogy, in this case, teaching "target cultures", requires equivalent models that is sensitive to the sociolinguistic dynamics of contemporary societies. Claire Kramsch, in a dedicated volume of Modern Language Journal to the discussions of foreign languages in an era of globalization affirms that globalization "has changed the conditions under which foreign languages (FLs) are taught, learned, and used" (Spring 2014.) She also noted that:

> …there has never been a greater tension between what is taught in the classroom and what the students will need in the real world once they have left the classroom. In the last decades, that world has changed to such an extent that language teachers are no longer sure of what they

are supposed to teach nor what real world situations they are supposed to prepare their students for (p. 296).

Kramsch's quote underscores the disparity between foreign language classroom contents and the sociocultural practices in the supposedly target language community. It highlights the dilemma of language instructors resulting from the complex use of language varieties and the dynamic cultural practices that permeate the contemporary societies. Her argument also, necessitates a befitting model for language teaching in this evolving era.

The new sociolinguistic formations, characterized by diversity of languages and complexity of speech communities might have serious implications for foreign language pedagogy in general. However, additional challenges have earlier been identified for African language pedagogy. Folarin-Schleicher and Moshi (2000) identified that, "most African language students cannot read authentic materials at the advanced level by the time they are ready to leave the program. This is usually at the end of the 2nd or 4th semester of language learning." (p. 93). They also observed the deficit of authentic content for teaching of culture, noting that:

> If cultural information is so poorly presented in most of our African language first-year textbooks, the immediate concern will be to develop a cultural curriculum that could guide African language first year textbook writers to prepare texts that will overtly present cultural information and integrate these informations into language learning activities (p. 120).

Although the above observation is valid in terms of African language instruction especially in the first year nevertheless, creating a separate culture curriculum to guide textbook writing may not offer an ultimate solution, but further makes bifurcation of language and culture more profound. In order to bridge this gap, it requires a teaching curriculum that emphasizes active integration of language and culture, starting from the beginning level; a curriculum that is built on authentic linguistic resources and cultural practices, thereby serving as an intervention for the identified challenge.

In this article, we propose a literacy-based curriculum that is constituted by integrating the principles of *pedagogy of multiliteracies* (Kern, 2000; New London Group 1996) and *Performance-Based Assessme*nt (PBA) (McTighe, 1994). On the one hand, we use pedagogy of multiliteracies as an instructional framework for language teaching, which allows for integrating language and culture in African language curriculum. On the other hand, we integrate PBA to foster a formative assessment that is capable of ensuring a holistic and effective assessment of language learners' capabilities. With this combination, we argue that cultural products and practices do not only provide access to authentic language codes and cultural norms but actually engender effective use of linguistic resources based on the understanding of cultural practices of language users in the target community. In the next section, we describe pedagogy of multiliteracies and Performance-Based Assessment as the two main frameworks for our proposal. We then followed the discussions with a description of a sample curriculum design.

Pedagogy of multiliteracies

The pedagogy of multiliteracies is a relatively new introduction to the collegiate foreign language education. It has been copiously discussed in relation to college-level foreign language teaching, mostly as an intervention to the concern on what has come to be known as the *bifurcation of language and culture teaching* in many foreign language departments (Allen & Paesani, 2010; Byrnes, 2002; Maxim, 2009; 2007; Paesani &Allen, 2012). This concept of bifurcation describes a system whereby the language departments create programs that distinguish between language and culture-related contents, such as literature. In this system, the curriculum at the beginning levels are heavily focused on language teaching, such as grammar, pronunciation and fluency, mostly using graded materials. The teaching of authentic cultural creations and contents are differed to later levels. We find this situation similar to the challenge identified above in relations to African language pedagogy, in which many student do not continue to the upper-level classes.

The pedagogy of multiliteracies is based on the broadened, pluralistic view of literacy and the understanding that various forms of literacy are key to achieving a bridge between language and cultural contents in L2 instruction. It was presented by the New London Group (1996), a group of scholars who collectively worked to refine the scope of literacy pedagogy. According to these scholars, "multiplicity of communications channels and increasing cultural and linguistic diversity in the world today call for a much broader view of literacy than portrayed by traditional language-based approaches." Thus, language teaching, according to this approach, is considered to be beyond the traditional teaching and learning of reading and writing in "page-bound, official, standard forms of the national language" or "project - restricted to formalized, monolingual, monocultural, and rule-governed forms of language." Instead, literacy and literacy teaching and learning is broadened to encompass "a multiplicity of discourses" which "now must account for the burgeoning variety of text forms associated with information and multimedia technologies" (New London Group, 1996, p. 60).

The reconceptualization of literacy expands its traditional meaning beyond the limited process of reading and writing in a specific language. According to Kern (2000), literacy consists of Sociocultural, linguistic, and cognitive/metacognitive dimensions. Thus, he defines it as:

> The use of socially-, historically-, and culturally-situated practices of creating and interpreting meaning through texts. It entails at least a tacit awareness of the relationships between textual conventions and their contexts of use and, ideally, the ability to reflect critically on those relationships …It draws on a wide range of cognitive abilities, on knowledge of written and spoken language, on knowledge of genres, and on cultural knowledge (p. 16).

From this definition, literacy is construed as a practice of meaning making from variety of textual materials. The ability to make meaning from a text is tied to the way language is socially and culturally used in a given society; it depends on the time and context in which the text materials is produced and it hinges on understanding much more than the words, but also visuals or images in focus. Furthermore, Kern adds that literacy "involves communication" (p. 17), and this comprises of seven principles, namely: Interpretation of texts; a collaboration between reader and writer; conventions relating to how texts are written and read; cultural knowledge; problem solving, to figure out relationships between texts, meaning and worlds; reflection & self-reflection about language, and language use, beyond writing systems, vocabulary & grammar. All these not only complicate the hitherto understanding about literacy, but also stretch the understanding of literacy to accommodate various modalities that are contemporary and emergent.

A Pedagogy of Multiliteracies is conceptually presented using the term "Design." *Design* used in this regard simply defines the process of meaning making, through reading and writing. The New London Group further explicate the concept thus: "We propose to treat any semiotic activity, including using language to produce or consume texts, as a matter of Design involving three elements: Available Designs, Designing, and The Redesigned" (p. 73-74). The first element, *Available Designs* refers to the existing resources, such as linguistic, social and cultural knowledge that a reader brings to a text, and draws on, consciously or unconsciously, to create meaning when they approach the texts. A text, in a Multiliteracies approach, is understood to mean a variety of genres. Genre, according to Swaffar & Arensia "an oral or written rhetorical practice that structures culturally embedded communicative situations in a highly predictable pattern, thereby creating horizons of expectations for its community of users" (2005, p. 99). Thus, genre includes books, essays, poetry, songs, newspaper, television shows, advertisement, cartoon, comics etc. The second element, *Designing* involves working on the texts in focus. In other words, *Designing* is the process whereby the reader draws from the available design to make sense of the text at hand. The reader, at this stage, engages in the "process of shaping emergent meaning [that] involves re-presentation and recontextualization" through reading, viewing, or listening (New London Group, p. 75). This stage is similar to the process of recycling existing concepts to fit new use. The third element, *Redesigned* emerges as a result of the process involved in the second element. It is the "transformed representation of Available Designs" (Allen & Paesani, p. 123). In other words, it is the outcome of the prior element that becomes the third element, Redesigned. These elements of meaning making are interrelated and feed into one another to achieve the goals of literacy.

For curricular application to language teaching, the elements of multiliteracies design are further reorganized by the New London Group into four curricular components, described as:

[A] complex integration of four factors: Situated Practice based on the world of learners' Designed & Designing experiences; Overt Instruction through which students shape for themselves an explicit metalanguage of Design; Critical Framing which relates meanings to their social contexts & purposes; and Transformed Practice in which students transfer & re-create Designs of meaning from one context to another (p. 83).

Unpacking the definition above, *Situated Practice* is the process where the learner is made to experience the language without conscious reflection on the structure of the language. According to Allen & Paesani, it the stage where learners are provided the opportunity to immerse themselves in spontaneous language use, and focusing on learner's expression, thoughts, opinions and feelings. The next stage, *Overt Instruction* is when, through scaffolded activities, learners begin to think about the language and developing an explicit metalanguage of the activities they are involved in. Allen & Paesani (2010) assert that at this stage, "students explicitly build upon existing Available Designs" *Critical Framing* is the process analyzing the texts. At this point, learners are guided to develop a critical awareness of language use. They relate the content of the text to social context and draw comparison where possible. Activities at this stage encourage learners to reflect on the relationship between design of meaning and communicative, social, and cultural contexts (Allen & Paesani, p. 123). The last stage, *Transformed Practice* is mainly the stage of application. Here, the learner uses the knowledge that was gathered along the way to create "new texts on the basis of existing ones, or [reshape] texts to make them appropriate for contexts of communication other than those for which they were originally intended" (Kern, p. 134). This last stage is where the learner demonstrates competence in the use of the language.

Performance based assessment

Performance Based Assessment (PBA) is an approach to teaching where pedagogy is informed by assessment (McTighe & Ferrera, 1994). Although PBA has been viewed from different perspectives using various models, the central idea in this approach argues for close relationship between teaching and learning. (Marzano et. al 1993; Eddy 2010; McTighe, 1994.). Within this framework, teaching and learning have a bidirectional relationship; assessment therefore, is an ongoing process that forms an important aspect of classroom instruction. In view of this, PBA takes a diverging turn from the traditional assessment of students. Rather than the traditional method which mostly targets conventional forms of testing like multiple choice questions, or other kinds of assessment that elicit very narrow responses from learners, it employs multiple strategies for assessing learners such as:

- Creates formative assessment before the start of instruction to evaluate students' previous knowledge about the task in focus,
- Forms part of learning process using different kinds of classroom activities that help learners to clearly relate with the subject topic and internalize some concept of the lesson,
- Develops an open ended assessment where students utilize ample materials and or information to transform the knowledge acquired into real life context and practices. Based on these features, classroom assessment calls for integration of different sources of information that would engage learners in the learning process.

Thus, McTighe and Ferrara proposed the *Principle of Multiple Sources*, a process where multiple evaluative criteria are deployed to ascertain evidence of learning in various forms. This principle of multiple sources therefore connects Performance Based Assessment to thepedagogy of multiliteracies. They feed into each other because they advance a flexible use of multiple and varied types of genre materials for evaluating and teaching language respectively.

Furthermore, PBA emphasizes interconnectivity of teaching and learning processes, and it draws from the framework of backward curriculum design for foreign language instruction as articulated by Mctighe &Thomas (2005). The backward curriculum design emphasizes a non-text book driven curriculum. Its main components include that, teachers: (a) Identify the pedagogical end goal; (b) Determine the activities that will attest to learners' mastery of the goal, and (c) Utilize relevant teaching materials that facilitates achieving the set goals. This implies that the end goal is the overall drive for curriculum design. Eddy (2007) builds on the connection between PBA and backward curriculum design to critique language instructors' inability to adequately implement the ACTFL National Language Standards in foreign language instruction, a challenge she describes as "coverage without pity." This is a practice in which teaching is basically focused on the communication goal of the Standards, and often driven by the textbook. Eddy argues that the communication standards are mostly emphasized by teacher but its application in classroom practice does not give room for learners' performance in relation to the perspectives of the target culture and practices of the language speakers. Rather, the classroom practices are laden with contents that bifurcates language practice from cultural understanding. To this end, Eddy proposes a reordering of the Standards to enhance productive performance and assessment of the student. She suggested a new acronym, called UC ADAPT which means *Uncovering Content: Assessment Design Aligning Performance and Transfer*. In this new ordering, she posits that "cultural response to those topics in the syllabus drive the curriculum". She places culture as the pillar that connects all the 5Cs together. First, Culture drives the themes and essential questions of the language curriculum; Communication determines modes of assessment while Connection, Comparison and Community demonstrate learners' knowledge and how the knowledge is put to use in cultural context (p. 3). From this perspective, culture is construed as the most important component of the standards that allows for effective use of language in a way that embraces understanding of the cultural practices and perspectives of the language users in the target community. From the foregoing, PBA enhances learners' performativity when instructors use multiple assessment rubrics that are based on the target culture.

In sum, PBA does not dichotomize teaching from learning. It positions the students at the center of both practices, and allows them to engage objectively with the subject matter through communication. To achieve such an effective communicative practice in the African language classrooms, we need a language curriculum that will encourage some levels of engagement with products from target culture. The use of multiple texts will give room for classroom participants to generate conversations that reflect their own perspectives of the target cultures. Pennycook (2001) refers to this spiral relationship of the curriculum and its sensitivity to the learners own perspective as *critical pedagogy*.

Building on the robust principles that underlie PBA and pedagogy of multilitercies described above, our take is the idea that, learning goals should cut across wide spectrum of experiences, in terms of what is taught, how it is taught and the material with which they are presented. In other words, on a given topic, learners would be provided with a variety of contents, presented in various ways. Placing culture as the overall umbrella for curriculum design, it redirects the classroom practices to reinforce language use that exhibits cultural understanding. Texts will offer language learners authentic format of the desired linguistic and cultural contents and, in the processes of acquiring the relevant forms of literacy that correspond to each genre, learners will be able to gain understanding of the varied ways that language users in the target community conduct communicative endeavors. In this vein, grammar teaching will shift from rote learning and be strategically incorporated into the instruction, such that leaners are able to use language to demonstrate their understanding of the practices and perspectives of the target culture. The teacher becomes the facilitator of learning by synthesizing the culturally-motivated ideas in the lesson and creating assessment rubrics that can engage the students in meaningful classroom practices. As a result, the learning activities can enhance learners' creativity.

In this framework, assessment is not singular, but conducted at multiple times, using variety of means and incorporating multiple genres throughout the duration of the course. Teachers evaluate students in relation to multiple evaluative criteria that provide evidence of learning in various forms using different modalities and targeting various competences. As a result, evaluation gives a holistic representation of the learner's capability, and so, such assessment is assumed valid, reliable and fair.

By integrating all the ideas discussed above, we maintain that the step-by-step processes indicated in pedagogy of multiliteracies and the dynamism of PBA present an operative model for African language pedagogy. This Literacy-Based

Curriculum is not only capable of enhancing culturally-oriented language learning but also allows for the possibility of achieving an important priority of the language curriculum—closing the gaps between language and cultures, such as between language codes and linguistic productions of the target community, and also between classroom instructions and communicative practices of the language users.

Sample course curriculum (beginning Yorùbá language)

As Gee (2012) asserted, literacy is beyond the ability to read and write. Rather, it involves being able to read specific types of texts within particular socially situated contexts. This sociocognitive view of literacy (Kern, 2003) has three dimensions, namely linguistic (knowledge of the interrelationship between words, phrases, discourse and the world), sociocultural (idea that textual meaning depend and derive from the worldviews, beliefs, practices and sociocultural context of a community) and cognitive (critical thinking to read and write). Through these multiple dimensions of literacy, the course will train students to draw connection between literature from the target culture, the language it is composed of, and culture it is embedded in; and in this way provide learners the opportunity to draw and create personal meanings of their own.

In essence, this curriculum is for a course designed to develop language acquisition of Yorùbá through literacy, based on textual products from the Yorùbá cultures. Unlike traditional curriculum that treats topics in language and literature as separate enterprises, it has the capacity to connect the face-to-face verbal interaction with the development of learners' ability to read, discuss, think and write critically about texts (Kern, 2002;p. 21). Consequently, in this curriculum, we present a course that departs from the popular presentations of African language courses in two main ways. First, this course has a theme-based title; not like the usual courses that present a blanket area of coverage of an African language. Secondly, we depart from the hitherto pattern of ordering of lessons for beginner-level classes which, in most cases, begin with topics that are considered highly important to African cultures and also easier to learn, such as greetings and family, talking about oneself, etc. This decision is based on the principle that the literacy- based approach privileges texts over topics. Although literacy- based approach does not oppose the ordering of topics, it however, encourages the use of multiple genres right from the start as a means to integrating language and culture. Thus, this curriculum presents modules that demonstrate the teaching of cultural content from the beginning level, using the authentic text materials. Although it equally presents those same topics, it does so in a different order.

Each module corresponds to sub-themes that are drawn out from the main topic. Contents of each module are created from a combination of most relevant textual materials to the subtopic. Each subtopic of the lessons is generated with the pedagogical objectives in mind, and are outlined to provide models of expected learning outcome. We believe that these texts will not only offer a good exposure to the written and spoken forms of Yorùbá but they will also springboard students attempt at becoming creative users of the language.

Furthermore, the course is performance-based. It presents pedagogical contents to students through a variety of texts— that is, different genres—and as well adopts a varied means of assessment that correspond to learners' levels. As such, it will imbue students with functional linguistic and culturally appropriate skills needed to adapt in Yorùbá communities. Ultimately, language learning is meaning-making or "design of meaning" from our list of texts. Learners are only able to make these meaning through "available designs" (i.e. the nature of discourse in the respective texts) and the process of reflecting on connection between form and meaning of the texts. By combining a variety of genres, this course will provide varied opportunities for learners to make contextualized sociocultural meanings.

Course Title: Contemporary Yorùbá Political Systems
Level: Beginning Level

Course Objective: The primary objective of this course is to expose beginning level learners to the use of Yorùbá language. It will also assist students to reach intermediate level proficiency in presentational, interpersonal and interpretive communication, in oral and written forms, through study of authentic Yorùbá texts that present the perspective and practices of the culture. In this course, students will be guided to engage with the content of different genres of texts in ways that will help them construct and communicate their personal meanings of the texts in both written and oral modes suitable to their levels. Through this course, students will gain confidence in expressing their thoughts and opinions, and be able to sustain casual conversations with any Yorùbá language speaker.

Course Description: This course is designed around the main topic, *Contemporary Yorùbá Political Systems*. As a literacy-based curriculum, lesson modules are ordered along the sub-themes that are derived from the main topic, and they will be taught through the study of various authentic literary texts mostly in Yorùbá, including movies, oral and written poetry, news broadcast, newspapers, advertisements, as well as existing Yorùbá textbooks. These genres will constitute the primary texts to study Yorùbá language. Through them, learners will acqiuire the skill to read and negotiate understanding of texts written for native speakers of Yorùbá.

Specific Learning Objectives

By the end of the course, students will be able to:

- Read, watch and discuss contents of various texts/genres from Yorùbá communities and attempt basic analysis of the perspectives suggested by the authors of the texts.
- Identify and analyze at basic level the language forms in the Yorùbá texts
- Identify and analyze at the basic level cultural values and perspectives contained in each text.
- Identify and describe attributes of concrete cultural products among Yorùbá people that reflect their life activities in relation to each sub-theme of the course.
- Compare themes, ideas, and perspectives from Yorùbá cultures to their own.
- Express their comprehension of linguistics forms and cultural perspectives contained in Yorùbá textual genres and recreate contents to demonstrate mastery of the forms.
- Engage in basic interaction and in a culturally appropriate manner with Yorùbá speakers of various backgrounds in a variety of contexts.
- Document and discuss about language learning experiences, such as their development, challenges and perspectives

Course Resources, Materials, & Texts

- Newspaper: Akéde Àgbáyé; Aláròyé.

Short excerptsof relevant sections from these papers will be beposted on the course website at the begining of each module.
- Yorùbá Films:

  Ṣaworo Idẹ; Agogo Èèwọ̀; Wúrà àti Fàdákà; Tí n bá táyé wá. (links to these films would be shared on the course website)
- Others: Pictures, magazines, image cuts outs etc.
- Textbook:

  Colloquial Yorùbá by Antonia Schleicher (Routledge Press, London)

  Aláwíyé by J. F. Odunjo (Book 1and 2)
- Yorùbá Dictionary (there is a free online version)
- Online community (E.g Lino)

  Using *Lino*, students will create an internet community as a way to collaborate and share resources, such as useful vocabulary and language experiences.

Portfolio: In addition to short answer write-ups during each lesson, every student will write an essay at the end of each module. Every essay will comprise of two parts: The first will focus on the topic of the module and second will be individual student's reflection on their language learning progress. The essays will be graded and returned to students to modify accordingly. After modifying the essays, the final drafts will be compiled in the portfolio of the students writings, and would also be uploaded online to *Lino* under the section, entitled "students work."Also, students will create an audio-visual documentary of their language learning experience and connect this to topics related to their academic interest or research. Students will collaborate to write the script and make this video at the end of class.

Course Calendar

Module with Date	Theme/Topic
Module 1: (2-3 weeks)	**Learning about the socio-political organization of the Yorùbá people:** *City, town, village, and suburbs.* **Grammar:** **Vocabulary:** Ìlú, abúlé, abà, àdúgbò, agbègbè, alábàágbé, baálẹ̀ etc. **Using basic functional verbs** such as ni, lò, gbé wọ etc…. **Descriptive adjectives:** ńlá, tóbi, fẹ́ lẹ́wà, gbòòrò etc…. − Describing the features of a village and suburbs, − Talking about a city in Yorùbá land − What I like/dislike about my city **Genre /Texts:** Film: Ṣaworo Idẹ Àláwìíyé Ẹ̀kọ́ kíìní Ìwé ìròyìn Akéde
Module 2: (2-3 weeks)	**Learning about family and community building:** *Family*, relatives, *Inlaws* **Grammar:** **Vocabulary:** Ilé, agboolé, ẹbí, ará, ìbátan, ọ̀rẹ́, ojúlùmọ̀, àna, ìyàwó ọkọ etc… Using basic Functional words: Gbé, ní, fẹ́ràn, pẹ̀lú, wà, jẹ etc.. • Describing people who constitute a family in the Yorùbá culture • Talking about a Yorùbá family house • Expressing the role of age and gender in the family hierarchical structure • How household chores are shared among male and female **Genre/Texts:** Film: Ṣaworo Idẹ

		Àláwíiyé Èkọ́ kííní Ìwé ìròyìn Akéde
Module 3: (2-3 weeks)		**Meeting People and Salutations:** *Greetings, establishing relationships, Age, and respect* **Vocabulary:** ikíni, ibọ̀wọ̀, ìjúbà, iwúre, dọ̀bálẹ̀, kúnlẹ̀, tẹríba etc.. **Basic functional words:** Kí, wólẹ̀, wúre, ki, etc.... − Greetings among peers − Greeting the elderly − Introducing oneself − Paying homage to kings, queens, high chiefs and parents. **Genre/Text** **Film:** Tí m bá tayé wá Ṣaworo idẹ Colloquial Yorùbá
Module 4: (2-3 weeks)		**Learning about Leadership and Government:** *King, chief, governor, and president* **Grammar** **Vocabulary:** ọba, olórí, aṣojú, olóyè, olú ìlú, ìpínlẹ̀, ìletò, ìbò, ifá, gómìnà ààrẹ etc. **Basic functional words:** Jẹ, di, jọba, ṣojú, yàn, dìbò, kéde, du, díje dá etc.. − Describing the royal dynasty of a Yorùbá king − Naming and describing various positions of leadership in the Yorùbá community. − Talking about what the governor does as the ruler of a state − Describing the leadership titlessuch as King, chief, president and governors etc... − Comparing the role of a King, governor and president in a

		community
		Genre/Text
		Film:
		Tí m bá tayé wá
		Agogo Èèwọ̀
		Aláwìíyé ẹ̀kọ́ kejì
		Akéde Agbáyé
Module 5: (2-3 weeks)		**Leadership and Politics:** *History, lineage, selection...*
		Grammar:
		Vocabulary: ìran, ìtàn, orúkọ, yíyàn, ìbò, ifá, etc....
		Basic Functional words: wádìí, yan, náwó, dìbò, pólówó, etc...
		– Talking about the names of people in my family
		– About my family history
		– How to select a king
		– How to elect a governor
		Genre/Text
		Film:
		Tí m bá tayé wá
		Arugbá
		Àláwìíyé ẹ̀kọ́ Kejì
		Akéde
Module 6: (2-3 weeks)		**Social events and Celebrtions:** *Coronation and Installation, inauguration and swearing-in ceremony*
		Grammar
		Vocabulary: aṣọ, ìmúra, ijó àṣẹ, ounjẹ, ètò, ayẹyẹ, ìnáwó etc...
		Basic functional words: Wọ, lò, dé, jó, ki, etc....
		– Talking about Yorùbá clothing for ceremonies such as king's attire and other ceremonial clothings
		– Talking about a coronation ceremony in my community: attendance, food, etc...
		– Talking about entertainment in a social event: Dance, drum, praise poetry etc..

Genre/Text
Film: Tí m bá tayé wá Arugbá Àláwíìyé ẹ̀kọ́ Kejì Agogo èèwọ̀ Colloquial Yorùbá

Sample Lesson Plan

General description of module

Ideally, each module will be further broken down into a number of lessons and each lesson will correspond to a classroom encounter. In this section, we developone of the modules further by illustrating a lesson plan for a classroom encounter. For illustration purpose, we chose module 6, entitled *Social Events and Celebrations: Coronation and Installation, inauguration and swearing in*.In the sequence of the curriculum, this moduleadvances the main goal of the course by presenting the social aspect of the Yorùbá Political system. Like other modules, this topic subsumes several possible topics that could be explored in further detail when designing the lessons. Social celebrations are traditionally one of the important values among the Yorùbá people. Celebrating landmark events and achievement connects to several other social practices, such as rites of passage, marriage, burial ceremony, and several others. Such events sometimes serve as avenue to disperse common societal knowledge, and they form the platform for displaying numerous cultural practices and products, such as hair styling, dressing and making up, event-specific chants, and songs etc. Many of the traditional practices have been retained, and a few modified to fit into the contemporary system of governance.

This sub-theme is intended to generate discussions about various social events, with political events, such as coronation of a King and inauguration of a state governor, as the starting point. For instance, a very important aspect of many Yorùbá ceremonies is the AṣọẸbí (Family matching attire). It is a practice by which, for important events such as coronation and marriage, the families and friends of the celebrant would buy and wear a matching attire. In addition to these matching attires, other cultural items that would become relevant in developing this section will include food, dances, songs, social affiliation, age-group etc.

The texts that we chose to carry out instruction in this lesson present variety of dialogues relating to the topic, as well as cultural-specific images, gestures, etc. A particular example is on the process of buying clothes in the market and taking it to the dressmaker. This might be a good starting place to introduce the topic; it is followed up with the relevant scenes in the movies. All the three movies present a fussion of both modern and contemporary aspects of Yorùbá political institutions. Precisely, each of them presents the process involved in selecting a leader, king, president or governor and they all highlight the role of the various arms of governance, including the involvement of the public. Lastly, the magazines, *Akéde*, and *Aláròyé* have regular columns that provide commentaries on Nigerian politics in Yorùbá.

The different kinds of texts in this module do not only contextualizeinstructions on politics among Yorùbá people, but they more importantly, introduce students to sociocultural practices of Yorùbá , mainly relating to social events. The module will make learners to access, acquire and utilize the socioculturally-appropriate linguistic and cultural knowledge relating to coronation ceremony and celebration of social events. Furthermore, the texts will springboard learners' use of the Yorùbá language extensively, through critical reading (watching) and presentation on the materials we would study in this module. Thus the immediate objectives of the module are for students to be able to:

1. Use appropriate register of Yorùbá social events
2. Discuss and analyze the practices involved in a Yorùbá political event
3. Learn about and compare the activities involved in traditional political event and contemporary ones.
4. Discuss commonalities between Yorùbá socio-political event and similar event in their culture
5. Write a role-play skit about Yorùbá king coronation (collaboratively)

In each class session, instructions will follow the pattern of the New London Group's cycle, namely, situated practice (SP), overt instruction (OI), critical framing (CF), and transformed practice (TP). Each class will feed into the other; the assignments from one class would open the discussion in the next class, while current class discussion will be connected to prior class activities as well.

Lesson Plans

Lesson 1
Objectives: Introduce the Yorùbá *Social Events and Celebrations: Coronation and Installation, inauguration and swearing in* by situating it as one of the several social events among the Yorùbá people Acquire the linguistic resources for beginner level discussion on the Coronation and Installation, *inauguration and swearing ceremony* and social events in general
Materials: 1. Colloquial Yorùbá, chapter 5 2. Two pictures each of four different ceremonies popular among the Yorùbá people (e.g. naming ceremony, burial ceremony, coronation, graduation from school, etc. 3. Vocabulary list: names of the events, event-specific roles and practices, foods, type of cloth/fabrics for event etc. 4. Handout (matrix)
Activities: Teacher will begin by asking students to mention the social events they had taken part in or know of but have not taken part in (SP) Teacher will present two short video clips of different Yorùbá events (including political events, e.g. coronation ceremony for a new king), without any accompanying commentary but ask students to make note of the striking features of each photograph. (SP) After watching the video clips, student will be grouped in pairs, and asked to list their observations. At this point they can ask and answer questions about the cultural and communicative events in the video, as an indication of their conscious engagement with the dialogues and images. (SP/CF) In the process, teacher will present a model instruction of communicative goal. Teacher will provide help with certain vocabulary relating to social events, as well as introduce coronation ceremony and pronunciations. (OI) Student will now discuss their takes on the events in the video, by comparing the events using the physical actions and clothing of the people in the picture (CF). With this, the teacher will gradually turn attention to the coronation ceremony. Using the matrix below the students will describe and compare the content of the video: (CF/OI)

Video	Event	Main people in the picture	Aṣọẹbí present?	Describe clothings	Greetings?
1					
2					

After the comparisons, student will be guided to read the dialogues in their textbook/handout, relating to choosing a rightful individual for king.
They will discuss the content of the reading, answering basic Yes/No questions about the personality of the protagonist (SP)
Guide students to identify and list the recurring themes that appear frequently across texts (video and reading). (CF)
Ask students to compose and write out four to five questions they would like to ask a king-elect (TP) and then ask students to pair up and role-play the scenario with each other's questions.

Chapter Six	Kazeem Kehinde Sanuth & Adeola Agoke, in Dainess Maganda and Karim Traoré (Eds.) LANGUAGE AND LITERATURE: Vehicles for the Enhancement of Cultural Understanding London, Adonis & Abbey Publishers

References

Allen, H. W., & Paesani, K. (2010). Exploring the feasibility of a pedagogy of multiliteracies in introductory foreign language courses. *L2 Journal, 2*, 119-142

Childre, A., Sands, J., & Pope, S. (2009). Backward design. *Teaching Exceptional Children, 41*(5), 6-14.

Eddy, J. (2007). From Coverage without Pity to Performance: World Language Curriculum and Assessment Exposed in the Light of Backward Design.

Eddy, J. (2007). Uncovering Content and Designing for Performance. *Academic Exchange Quarterly, 11*(1), 233.

Eddy, J. (2010). BECOMING DESIGNERS. *World Language Teacher Education: Transitions and Challenges in the Twenty-First Century*, 87.

Eddy, J. (2015) Uncovering Curriculum: Language performance through culture by design. *Journal of Less Commonly Taught Languages*, 17, p. 1-22.

Gee, J. (2012). Social Linguistics and Literacies: Ideology in Discourses, 4th Edition.

Kern, R. (2000). *Literacy and language teaching.* Oxford: Oxford University Press.

Kern, R. (2003). Literacy as a new organizing principle for foreign language education. In P. C. Patrikis(Ed.), *Reading between the lines: Perspectives on foreign language literacy* (pp. 40-59). New Haven, CT: YaleUniversity Press.

Kramsch, C. (2012). Authenticity and legitimacy in multilingual SLA. *Critical Multilingualism Studies 1*(1), 107-128.

Kramsch, C. (2014). Teaching foreign languages in an era of globalization: Introduction. *The Modern Language Journal, 98*(1), 296-311.

Lotherington, H. (2007). Book and software review [Review of the book *Remapping the Foreign Language Curriculum: An Approach through Multiple Literacies*, by J. Swaffar & K. Arens]. *Canadian Modern Language Review,63*(3), 429-431.

Marzano, R. J., Pickering, D., & McTighe, J. (1993). *Assessing Student Outcomes: Performance Assessment Using the Dimensions of Learning Model.* Alexandria, VA: Association for Supervision and Curriculum Development.

McTighe, J., & Ferrara, S. (1994). Performance-based assessment in the classroom. *Pennsylvania Educational Leadership,* 4-16

McTighe, J., & Ferrara, S. (1996). Performance-based assessment in the classroom: A planning framework. *A handbook for student performance assessment in an era of restructuring,* 1-9.

McTighe, J., & Thomas, R. S. (2005). Backward Design. *Educational Leadership.*

New London Group. (1996). A pedagogy of multiliteracies: Designing social futures. *Harvard EducationalReview, 66*(1), 60-92.

Pennycook, A. (2001). *Critical applied linguistics: A critical introduction.* Routledge.

Richards, J. R. TS (1986). Approaches and Methods in Language Teaching. *A Description and Analysis.*

The New London Group. (1996). A pedagogy of multiliteracies: Designing social futures. *Harvard Educational Review,* 66 (1): 60-92

Wiggins, G. P., McTighe, J., Kiernan, L. J., & Frost, F. (1998). *Understanding by design* (pp. 0-87120). Alexandria, VA: Association for Supervision and Curriculum Development.

CHAPTER SEVEN

Using Music/ Songs in the African Language Classroom: Ideas and Challenges

Dainess M Maganda
University of Georgia

Esther M. Lisanza
University of North Carolina, Chapel Hill
University of Winston Salem State University

Leonard Muaka
Winston Salem State University

Rose S. Lugano
University of Florida

Introduction

The 21st century has been characterized as an era of decreasing enrollments in foreign language and literature departments nationwide (Tworek, 2013). The need to reverse the slow depletion of our departments and classrooms is among a plethora of the challenges facing language instructors today. Less commonly taught languages (LCTL) in particular, face even bigger challenges. In fact, according to the National Council of Less Commonly Taught Languages (NCOLCTL), nearly ninety-one percent of Americans who study foreign languages in schools, colleges, and universities choose French, German, Italian, or Spanish, while only nine percent choose to study Arabic, Chinese, Japanese, Yoruba, Russian, Swahili and other languages (http://www.ncolctl.org/). Furthermore, theories in second language acquisition have complicated this matter due to placing more emphasis on the mode by which we learn a first language over how we assimilate a second language. As such, there is a great need for foreign language (FL) teachers to use more acquisition-based comprehensible input (i.e., pictures, authentic texts, realia) rather than using traditional learning-based activities such as workbook exercises, vocabulary quizzes, dialogue-memorization drills, to name just a few (Richards & Rodgers, 2001).

First, we highlight the significance of this study, after which a definition of music and brief background on this topic is presented. A selection of literature on benefits of using music and songs for language learning comes next. Some ways in which teachers of African languages- (AFLANG hereafter) may incorporate music and songs in their classrooms as well as some challenges which instructors face in their efforts to use music/songs to teach AFLANG are examined thereafter. Kindly note, music and songs are used interchangeably in this paper.

Significance of the study

Studies show many advantages of using music and songs in language classes (Kelly, 1969; Jolly, 1975; Steiner, 1988; Murphy, 1990; McCarthy, 1985; Matondo 2005). Most scholars examining this topic have focused on the use of music and songs in teaching European and Western languages as foreign languages in the US. For instance: Hahn (1972) on German; Gatti-Taylor (1980) Italian; Jolly (1975), Japanese as well as Arellano and Gatti-Draper (1972), on Spanish. However, except for a few articles like Matondo's (2005) who examines the use of rap music in teaching Swahili and Kezilahabi's, who briefly touches on the subject in his article "Aesthetics and the Teaching of Foreign Languages," in

JALTA, spring 2005, articles on the use of music to teach African languages are almost non-existent. Therefore, we see a great need to further investigate the numerous ways in which music and songs can be integrated in the African language classrooms.

Definition of Music/Songs

According to American Heritage Dictionary, 2nd Edition (1985), Music "is the art of organizing tones in a coherent sequence so as to produce a unified and continuous composition". While Webster Collegiate Dictionary explains that "Music is the science or art of ordering tones or sounds in succession to produce a composition having unity and continuity". In both definitions there is a consensus that music utilizes words. While we acknowledge that there is instrumental music which has no words, the music or songs we are concerned with in this paper is the one with lyrics (i.e., words or language).

Background

The author of *Language Acquisition and Language Education*, Stephen D. Krashen (1989) attests that we acquire language by understanding messages or by gaining understandable input. He writes:

> The best hypothesis now, the one that fits data the most accurately, is that we acquire in just one way- by understanding messages or by obtaining comprehensible input. More specifically, we acquire a new rule by understanding messages that contain this new rule. This is done with the aid of extra linguistic context, knowledge of the world, and our previous linguistic competence. This Input Hypothesis explains why pictures and other realia are so valuable to the teachers; they provide context,

background information that helps make input comprehensible (Krashen, 1989, p. 9).

This hypothesis, known as Input Hypothesis, implies that we gain any new rule by comprehending messages that contain this new rule with the help of several things including, knowledge of the world, past linguistic competence and extra linguistic context. This occurs because we do not just acquire language, a subconscious procedure; rather, we undergo a learning process, the conscious knowledge or "knowing about" language, which propels us to only understand and retain input that makes sense. As such, this explains why we find pictures and other realia to be valuable in teaching language as they provide background information and context that helps make input understandable.

Based on this theory and drawing from our experience as language instructors, appropriately selected songs, like pictures, can serve as a kind of understandable input or a type of realia that puts together language rules (i.e, phonological, semantic, syntactic, pragmatic, prosodic, and idiosyncratic-rules that shape how language is written, spoken, and interpreted) into contextualized language packages for students. Songs have micro narrative-like structure that contain intelligible context more suitable for making sense of vocabulary. In addition, song texts, when appropriately selected comprise understandable messages that include the new rules which aid students' understanding of target language's linguistic structure. Rather than using isolated dictations or substitution drills, songs allow instructors to appeal to a larger student body's interest because they have a broad range of selection which span from pop to rap or classical to folk, to name only a few. Additionally, songs are easily convertible to any type of latest technology or even

Web-based format, and in turn, they enable teachers keep up with technological advances in education.

Benefits of Using Music

Many researchers and scholars agree that music is available in abundance and that it is used for different purposes such as reducing stress and anxiety (Patricia Richard-Amato, 2003). Pertinent to our study, the varied uses of music in different contexts are not presented; we therefore highlight scholarship pertaining to language learning.

Language educators and researchers agree that using music to teach language has great advantages. Music improves retention of texts, aids in language acquisition (Keskin, 2011) and facilitates learning a foreign language in particular (Jolly, 1975; Richard-Amato, 2003; Sposet, 2008; Ajibade & Ndububa, 2008; Enghs, 2010). Murphey (1990), who has conducted extensive research on this topic has documented his findings in *Song and Music in Language Learning*, argues that extensive use of music in language instruction is not a new phenomenon at all; it dates as far back as the middle ages in Greek and Latin schools. He explains that the "first introduction to Latin was given to students in the 'song school' or 'school of liturgical music' (p. 137)". Therefore, historically, music and songs were an integral part of language acquisition. It seems they gradually fell out of use in language instruction as the discipline of linguistics began focusing on new theories of language learning, making it a more formal undertaking (Kelly, 1969). Teachers of foreign languages, especially those teaching less commonly taught languages, such as Swahili and other African languages need to rediscover the invaluable use of music once again.

The advantages of using music in the language class are many. From our own experience in the language classroom and that of other teachers and scholars (e.g. Jolly, 1975;

Kramer, 1997; Ludke, 2009; Nuelssel & Cicogna, 1991), properly selected songs just like pictures can serve as a strategy for comprehensible input. Songs provide a context more suitable for understanding new grammar rules, vocabulary, and culture. Also, use of songs or music reduces stress and anxiety in a learner and lowers their affective filter (Krashen, 1989), which in turn increases their motivation to learn the language. In fact, music evokes students' interest to learn a language while creating an enjoyable authentic reading material which may have vocabulary unlikely to be encountered through regular textbook reading passages.

Scholars point to the memorability of songs and how they are useful in teaching vocabulary and culture. The repetitive nature of music and songs also aid and stimulate memory while enabling easy recalling of information after a lapse of time. The vocabulary and grammar rules learnt through drills can easily be forgotten, but a song remains in the students' minds. Sometimes, recalling the song may trigger a memory of language learnt in the past. Several other learning activities and bridging exercises can be generated from one song to allow students transfer and retain language. Osman (1979) for example, underscores that:

> Groups of words are easily retained in the mind when they are fixed in the framework of melody, rhythm, and rhyme. Many examples can be cited of foreign language students who are able to remember whole songs in a language they studied but perhaps not able to speak more than a few words freely (p. 2).

Music is didactically useful in teaching the rhythm and flow of the language. For example, Swahili basic word-structure being 'consonant-vowel-consonant-vowel' (CVCV) demands syllabic pronunciation. This differs from that of the English language, where some sounds are elided or silent. Since most Swahili learners come from this background; it takes them some time to get their pronunciation and rhythm of Swahili words right. Music can facilitate this, as Murphey (1990) explains in his statement that singing is a great way of teaching pronunciation. Murphy further quotes Walker (1987) who reinforces this when he states that "Reading, like singing is, to a certain degree, is much more easily learned by ear than by notes…" (68-69).

Both Murphey and Walker seem to suggest that acquiring musical qualities of a language will not only facilitate pronunciation but are a prerequisite for efficient reading. By singing a piece of music or song, students will acquire the proper pronunciation and rhythm of the language with much ease compared to them using language drills. The beats of music makes them particularly attractive and appealing to students and later, the music can easily serve as introduction to poetry, an important aspect of African cultures. For example, Swahili has a long history of poetry which dates as far back as the Arab occupation of the East African coast (Knappert, 1979). Traditionally, Swahili poetry was written to be sung and today, a popular form of Swahili music known as *Taarab* that is basically poetry in song can be easily taught and learnt as music.

Music can be utilized in the classroom simply to brighten up and add variety, the same way it functions in theatre and film. Using a genre that is loved by most of the students encourages more participation and collaboration. Today one does not need to go too far to find music for every occasion. The media through You-Tube has made it easy to access music online. When music is incorporated in a language class, the instructor is utilizing almost everyone's love of music to create a fun-learning, relaxed and non-threatening atmosphere. Most students, mostly youth, (and a few adults) love music and therefore "relate to songs as part of entertainment rather than work and find learning vocabulary through songs amusing rather than tedious" (Shtakser, 2001). Music is a great morale and motivation booster because of its power to make tasks seem effortless. Maybe it is because learning is made fun, emotionally stimulating and entertaining. On a similar note, music keeps students' attention as Murphey (1990, p. 135) notes, "The ability of music to excite emotional-cognitive interest is extremely useful for anyone who wishes to have audience stay attentive for any length of time".

In our own classes we have observed that music has the power of melting-off any vestiges of inhibition and shyness between instructor and students so that even the most reserved students will open up and become active participants in the act of learning. Music thus creates an instant valid rapport between a teacher and students by removing barriers and initiating a friendly, two-way open communication. In addition, the use of music in class promotes group spirit, a necessary ingredient in a language class, especially because of the need for students to work in groups during skit presentations or role-plays.

We have realized that, besides the entertainment aspect, songs and music deal with themes and address problems that greatly interest people of all age groups, such as love and romance, family relationships, loneliness, self-esteem, youth, ambitions, etc. Since most themes center on these universal social issues, students are able to relate and identify with the singers and are curious to understand what they are saying. Therefore, finding the meaning of words becomes an exciting exercise, especially when they can follow the singer. Discovering different perspectives of dealing with social issues is an added bonus resulting from cultural exchange, discussions about attitudes and behavioral differences that stem from words or phrases used in songs.

Music is also accredited with the power to convey the culture of the target language as well as ingrain ideological content (Osman, 1979). Musicians have great cultural influence over a population and sometimes their creativity in conjugating words can become part of everyday language use within their community. Students are more likely to encounter this form of language when they visit the geographic location of the target language and interact with the native speakers.

Many would agree that most songs have a story, a hidden message or a theme (Iudin-Nelson, 1997). For example, "*Malaika*" the popular old Swahili song of the 1960s can lead to discussion on why the boy cannot marry the girl and what is the societal expectation of a prospective suitor in that culture etc.

Introducing music or songs from the target language also sheds light on the interesting musical traditions in the countries where the language is spoken and cultivates appreciation of other cultures among students (Callahan, 2013). For instance, African languages come from cultures endowed with a rich variety of music or songs for every aspect of life, such as weddings, funerals, love, festivals, and celebrations of the seasons and so on. Music is also a great way to learn slang and idioms of the target language (Matondo, 2005). The abundance of songs on religious, political and cultural ideas in many societies and their promotion by those in authority is a testament to their effectiveness in inculcating and reinforcing ideas deemed desirable.

How to incorporate music in the teaching of African languages

There are several approaches and ways music can be used in a foreign language classroom. For example, Osman (1979) suggests three possible approaches in the use of songs in language learning. To use songs as an introduction to grammar before the structure is taught, as a learning tool to illustrate structure in an authentic and contextualized passage; and at the end of teaching the structure, as enforcement of language structure. Drawing from these ideas, we highlight some ways African language teachers may incorporate songs/music in their teaching. First and foremost, it is crucial for the AFLANG teachers to select appropriate songs, which reflect the linguistic and cultural topics being studied in the language classroom. A song should put emphasis on a particular grammatical element or a theme. Also, it is very important to keep the proficiency level of the students (i.e. novice, intermediate, advanced, or superior) in mind. The song should match the students' proficiency level. For instance, for novice, the lyrics must be simple and singer's diction must be clear. Also, songs should not have too much new vocabulary or grammar items, because this can cause confusion and frustrations to students. Moreover, to avoid boredom and to make the class more entertaining, it is important to make use of different musical styles (e.g. classical, pop, Jazz etc).

Introducing a new song

How should AFLANG teachers introduce a song in the target language? Though not prescriptive, we suggest that instructors take into account the theme and grammar focus of that particular unit and the proficiency level of the students. Teachers are not to just get a song without thinking through its identified use in their teaching. Second, we suggest that teachers decide which features of the song will be the primary focus of the lesson (e.g., grammar, vocabulary or culture). After that, they may want to prepare a short description of the singer or the group of the song. As already mentioned, it is important to use appropriate vocabulary and grammar depending on the level of the students. For, example in a Swahili class for beginners, when teaching the conditional tense (*nge*) and object markers, the Swahili teacher may decide to use *Malaika* song by Fadhili Williams Mdawida. So, the teacher may give his or her students the following brief biography of Fadhili Williams Mdawida who was the original composer of *Malaika* song, which has been performed by various groups and artists across the globe (e.g. Miriam Makeba, Boney M):

> Fadhili Williams Mdawida alizaliwa tarehe kumi na moja mwezi wa kumi na moja mwaka wa elfu moja na thelathini na nane. Yeye alizaliwa katika Taita-Taveta, Kenya. Yeye alirekodi wimbo wa Malaika katika mwaka wa elfu moja sitini na tatu. Alirekodi zaidi ya nyimbo mia mbili. Yeye alikufa tarehe kumi na moja mwezi wa pili mwaka wa elfu mbili na moja.
> [Fadhili Williams Mdawida was born 11/11/1938. He was born in Taita-Taveta, Kenya. He composed Malaika song in 1963. He composed more than 200 songs. He died 02/11/2001.]

Then, to ensure comprehension, the teacher can ask 3-5 questions after the description. For instance:

1. Jina la mwimbaji wa *Malaika* ni nani? (What is the name of the singer who composed *Malaika*?)
2. a) Mwimbaji alizaliwa lini? (When was the singer born?)
   b) Mwimbaji alizaliwa wapi? (Where was the singer born?)
3. Mwimbaji alirekodi wimbo wa *Malaika* lini? (When did the singer record the *Malaika* song?)
4. Mwimbaji alirekodi nyimbo ngapi maishani mwake? (How many songs did the singer compose during his lifetime?)
5. Mwimbaji alikufa lini? (When did the singer die?)

This background information is important because it helps the learners to have an opportunity to comprehend the target language. Also, it gives the learner an opportunity to learn or to review grammar in context. This brief description makes use of the third person singular subject marker (e.g. alizaliwa, alikufa). In addition, this kind of description is a good model on how to write short biographies of people. As a follow up activity, the students can write biographies of different singers from the target culture or from their own culture.

After the introduction of the song, the next would be the focus of the lesson. For example, teaching vocabulary through songs; first, it is important for the foreign language teacher to identify a song that contains several vocabulary items that he/she is currently teaching. Then, she/he presents the new words on the board or on the projector. We suggest that teachers use different comprehensible input strategies to help learners understand the meaning of the new words (e.g., photos, pictures, realia, gestures, etc.). After introducing the new words, then the teacher can play the song and also she/he may use fill in the blanks exercise to focus on the vocabulary items.

Apart from using songs to teach vocabulary in AFLANG classroom, teachers may also use songs to teach grammar. Just like focusing on vocabulary, the teacher should select a song that has grammatical structures she/he is teaching in that unit. Teachers may use a modified cloze activity to focus on a particular grammatical point. In this exercise students may be asked to fill in a blank with an appropriate grammatical element after listening to the song at least twice. For example, in a Swahili class the Swahili teacher may use Mama Rhoda song by Chameleon to teach object markers and then have a fill in the blank exercise. This exercise would facilitate a connection of Mama Rhoda song with object markers presented in the classroom.

Songs are also important resources for practicing pronunciation. It is thus crucial to choose a song that is not too fast. Teachers need to remember that pronunciation focus can also be combined with other practice activities like grammar, vocabulary, listening, etc. The song should be played and then students asked to chorally repeat the key words of the unit. The teacher should pay close attention to the students' pronunciation especially on the sounds that students struggle with (e.g., the first sound in the word *Ng'ambo* in Swahili.)

The AFLANG teacher may also use songs to teach listening comprehension. For the teacher to be able to meet his/her objective for listening comprehension, it is very important to choose a song with clear diction. Also, it is important to avoid a song with many new grammatical items and words. To develop listening skills, the teacher can ask students to fill in the blanks focusing on a particular grammar item as the song plays. The teacher may also ask listening questions (written or oral/in writing or orally) based on the lyrics of the song. Additionally for advanced students, a dictation exercise where students write out the lyrics of the chorus or the first verse of the song is a good way to practice listening skills.

In addition, songs can be used to teach reading skills. As a matter of fact, songs are authentic reading materials. In foreign language pedagogy, authentic materials are treasured. Based on the lyrics of the song, the teacher can develop reading comprehension questions. Then, the teacher presents the lyrics of the song to the students as a written text, alongside the reading questions. Also, when students have become familiar with the song, they can play matching games. For example, the teacher can ask students to put lines of the song in the right order. Then play the song so that the students can check their responses.

Chapter Seven | Dainess M Maganda, Esther M. Lisanza, Leonard Muaka & Rose S. Lugano, in Dainess Maganda and Karim Traoré (Eds.)
LANGUAGE AND LITERATURE: Vehicles for the Enhancement of Cultural Understanding
London, Adonis & Abbey Publishers

Furthermore, songs are a resource for enhancing speaking. For instance, after listening to a song in the classroom, the teacher can write a number of questions for the students to discuss in the target language. For example, advanced Swahili students may be asked to discuss the messages that emerge from the following songs: *Malaika, Mama Rhoda,* and *Stella Wangu.* Specifically, students can compare and contrast marriage and separation in the Swahili culture and their own.

Songs can also be used as a tool for teaching writing. However, writing activities should come when the students are familiar with the song. One of the ways teachers may incorporate songs to practice writing is, for instance, asking students to write a short story based on the song. For example, for the *Malaika* song a teacher may ask students, "Do you think the young man in the song will eventually marry his sweetheart? Why?" The complexity of the response will depend on the proficiency level of the students. For beginners, this can be a very simple paragraph, while for the advanced students this can be a one-page long essay.

As already mentioned, songs are authentic materials of the target culture. Therefore, depending on the theme being covered in class, the teacher should search for a song which focuses on that week's cultural theme (e.g. marriage, education, work etc.). For example, besides using *Malaika* song to teach about conditional tense and object markers, Swahili teachers can use *Malaika* song to teach about marriage, especially the importance of bride price in East Africa.

In conclusion, songs are a great teaching tool. It is very likely that students will sing songs beyond the classroom walls. In fact, many of our students report that they have taught their friends and family Swahili songs. As a matter of fact, songs are more likely to stick in students' minds after a lesson than a paragraph read or written in class. In the many years we have used music in our Swahili classes, we have noticed that the days designated for music record full attendance as students do not want to miss out. In fact, on a few times when we have had to cancel lessons with music due to unavoidable circumstances, students complain bitterly. This is a testament that using music in the language classroom works.

Challenges in using music in the AFLANG classroom and strategies to overcome them

In this section a brief survey of some of the challenges that the use of music to teach African languages could present, is offered.

Scarcity of Resources

In general, resources for teaching African languages as foreign languages are scarce. In cases where such materials are available, they are usually in formats that are not ready for teaching purposes. More importantly, in some cases African language instructors may be teachers who have taught their languages to native speakers but not necessarily to foreign language learners. As a result, the ability to convert their material to suit new leaners in a foreign language context becomes another layer of challenges. New African language instructors therefore need models that they can follow in converting songs or music to serve as teaching aids.

Online Resources: how suitable are they?

Although music can enhance speaking, reading, listening, and writing skills in the target language, and more importantly culture - one of the five components within the overall foreign language standards commonly known as the 5Cs, the biggest challenge is getting level appropriate songs/music. Music represents the richness of a people's culture with an authentic language structure that requires a careful, deliberate, and intentional selection of appropriate song(s) so that learners can fully benefit linguistically, culturally, and pedagogically. Cakir (2006, as quoted in Feskin, 2011) states that music and audio-visuals can have a positive effect on the learner as long as they are used appropriately. Consequently, although music is available and can be used to enhance language proficiency skills, the right kind of music for the right level remains a challenge. Music can be in the target language but if the structure or vocabulary is too advanced, the possibility of a breakdown in communication might be inevitable (see also Jolly Yukiko, 1975). If on the other hand the content is comprehensible but does not offer anything new to the learner either due to the simplistic nature of the content or a lack of any cultural or linguistic significance, the learner could easily get disengaged.

The Consistency of Material in target language

Music is in abundance, however, due to globalization, modernity, and language contact between African languages and former colonial languages, younger artists prefer to codeswitch. Codeswitching is a natural phenomenon in multilingual settings; however, if learners are to benefit fully from authentic material, then that material has to adhere to traditional norms of the target language. Most artists who capture the audience's attention are of the younger generation and to them codeswitching is trendy. Consider for example, musicians such as Vanessa Mdee, Ali Kiba, Kidum, Juliana Kanyomozi, Alicios Theluji, Diamond Platnumz aka Nasibu Abdul Juma, who sing in Swahili. Although their music appeals to the younger generation who form the majority of today's learners, it incorporates English, French, and other

African language phrases that interfere with the learning process while using some of the music as authentic material for foreign language learners. Some instructors may be able to address this issue by clipping the songs into smaller chunks and editing out the portions that contain non target language expressions. However, for the less creative instructors, this remains a challenge because they cannot edit the raw authentic data that they have to work with. For the technologically savvy instructors this may not be a problem just as for the more advanced learners who already have the basic knowledge of the target language.

Teachers' and Learners' Personalities

Teachers and learners have what may be considered their comfort zone in the teaching and learning processes respectively. Learners who are uncomfortable singing may use their comfort as an excuse to not participate in class activities. Learners may feel uncomfortable singing and this could increase their affective levels thus negatively impacting language acquisition in general. Teachers are supposed to model and then facilitate the learning process in the classroom. However, if the teacher is unable to model for the learner, the text will not be different from any other text that does not have a melody and rhythm associated with it. It is however different if the teacher uses a piece of popular music recorded and available via video, Internet, or other forms of media. For the student, passive participation via listening is not enough. Recall through reproducing a similar tune, is a more effective way of retaining what was learned and making it applicable in daily life. This supports the school of thought that believes in differentiated learning styles. Music and songs should therefore be additional aids for the learners but not the primary avenue through which students are expected to acquire the foreign language. Therefore, instructors must carefully think of how music will be incorporated in their lesson plans for it to be pedagogically relevant.

Old School Music and a Changing Clientele

Depending on where the music originates, it is possible that the music that is played represents the preference of the instructor and not necessarily what the learners will find appealing. The biggest challenge could be a generational gap where learners view what could have been a favorite song during the instructor's time as being out of touch. An instructor should therefore provide a variety of songs or music and solicit students' opinion on what they like. Failure to do this could lead to a disconnection between the teacher and his or her audience.

Mismatch between Content and Learning Outcomes

Successful learning emerges from a well-planned lesson with clear objectives. Language and culture are intertwined in a way that when language is taught, cultural nuances of the target language emerge and students easily make connections. In a situation where these two elements are not integrated well enough, the intended pedagogical objective may not be achieved and learners may not retain it. Music should enhance the acquisition of language in a way that learners make a clear connection between music and a grammatical element. This approach helps learners to use a similar form in their own language. Here is an example from Diamond Platnumz: Nimpende nani? "Whom should I love?" The grammatical objective of the lesson could be to enhance the use of the subjunctive mood or questioning in Swahili. The thematic objective of the lesson could be friendship, marriage, or simply relationships. The cultural aspects portrayed in the song then reinforce the acquisition of these two aspects.

Differences in Cultural Beliefs

Although foreign language entails the culture of the speakers of the target language with cultural artifacts such as music, food, and, films, it is important for teachers to be aware of students' own beliefs. Music and songs may contain content that conflict with religious beliefs and ideologies of some of the students in a given class. Instructors must double check to ensure that such content does not negate the benefits already attributed to the use of music and songs in foreign language teaching. Also, although foreign language instructors may claim that certain aspects are a reflection of a given culture, variation and differences within cultures must be acknowledged. It is not uncommon for a portion of the population to generalize cultural elements only for another section to claim that such elements do not represent them.

Strategies that can alleviate challenges in the use of music/songs

Songs and music chosen must be relevant to the topic of the day and the students' needs or experiences. This ensures that as students listen to the music, it is relevant to what they go through in their own lives and therefore learning becomes meaningful and enjoyable (Ajibade & Ndububa, 2008).

In a student-centered classroom, learners should always be given opportunities to lead in class activities. Although it has already been pointed out that due to different learning styles and levels of anxiety, some students may be uncomfortable singing in class, instructors can request volunteers who can then lead the rest of the class in singing a song they like. If students like a certain tune, they are likely to listen to it later on their own. Using Swahili as an example, the popular "Jambo Bwana" song usually gets students quickly engaged due to its simple but relevant message. It is a song that allows the lead singer to start to sing and then have the rest of the people join in as a group. In this case therefore, students can repeat what the soloist says to a point where they are able to do it on their own. Also, since students do not view their own peers as authority figures, they do not feel intimidated. In fact, as Ajibade & Ndububa (2008) observe, "such activities are student centered; hence by using them we give learners a chance to express themselves, enjoy themselves during learning, and use the resources of their own minds" (p. 33).

Due to the stage where African languages are, it would be beneficial to the field if African language instructors can collaborate and share their music. Sharing ensures that students learn similar cultural aspects and it also promotes higher proficiency standards in the target language. Examples are songs that celebrate special occasions such as birthdays, Valentine Day, Thanksgiving, etc. These events may not have special songs in many African cultures, but concerted efforts can lead to the creation of short verses/songs that can be sung. This should not be the opportunity to impose a different cultural practice onto the African culture, but it should be viewed as one way of enhancing proficiency by connecting the two cultures and making the learner express something she or he already knows, in a different language.

Before incorporating any song in a lesson, as already mentioned, careful planning must be undertaken. The instructor must be aware of the level of the learners, their grammar knowledge and how useful the input from song could benefit the students. The instructor should then have pre listening, listening, and post listening activities associated with the song. These activities allow students to focus on certain aspects of the song in a more meaningful way.

Clearly what emerge from the foregoing discussion are several layers of pedagogical considerations. Although music and songs are important cultural artifacts, not every learner or student will embrace them. The old adage reminds us that what is music to one person's ears may actually be noise to another person's ears. Despite the challenges, music and songs reflect a people's culture and transmit cultural values between people, societies and generations. Therefore, while learning a foreign language, a person can learn about a society and its culture through songs. What is critical is to acknowledge that as music presents an additional option to the teacher and learners, it also presents challenges and therefore the authenticity of such cultural artifacts must be carefully evaluated so that cultures are not misrepresented or certain aspects of it overgeneralized as cultural values of an entire community.

Conclusion

Using music to teach African languages is not only relevant, it is necessary to assure an engaged, practical, relaxed, participatory and well-grounded language-learning practice. Music was used for language pedagogy many decades ago and the benefits were astounding then and still are today. This paper has outlined specific steps AFLANG teachers may take to begin or continue using music in their classrooms. Despite the many challenges facing AFLANG instructors in their quest to incorporate music in their teaching, we have provided ways for teachers to overcome such challenges. Nothing changes overnight but eventually everything changes. Our concern is that AFLANG teachers take it upon themselves to make positive changes in their classrooms to maximize students' learning.

References

Ajibade, Y., & Ndububa, K. (2008). Effects of Word Games, Culturally Relevant Songs, and Stories on Students' Motivation in a Nigerian English Language Class. *TESL Canada Journal/Revue TESL du Canada, 25* (2), 27-48.

Arellano, A & Draper, J. (1972). Relations Between Musical Aptitudes and Second-Language Learning. *Hispania 55,* 11-121.

Callahan, J. (2013). Teaching about other Cultures through Music. Accessed from http://www.ocala.com/article/2013 0401/ARTICLES/130409983

Engh, D, W. (1975). Why use Music in English Language Learning? A Survey of the Literature. *English Language Teaching, 6*(2), 113-27.

Gatti-Taylor, M. (1980). Songs as Linguistic and Cultural Resource in the Intermediate Italian Class. *Foreign Language Annals.6,* 465-69.

Hahn, S.M. (972).*The effect of music in the learning and retention of lexical items in German.* Education Resources Information Center (ERIC Document # ED 119455). Retrived fromhttp://files.eric.ed.gov/fulltext/ED119455.pdf

Iudin-Nelson, L. J. (1997). Songs in the L2 Syllabus: Integrating the Study of Russian Language and Culture.Diss. University of Wisconsin, Madison.

Jolly, Y. S. (1975). The use of Songs in Teaching Foreign Languages.*The Modern Language journal,* 59(1/2), 11-14.

Keller, M. (1988).Teaching Grammar Through Songs. *English Teachers Association,* Switzerland Newsletter 5 (3), 30-31.

Kelly, L.G. 1969). *25 Centuries of Teaching language*. Mass: Newberry House Publishers.

Keskin, F. (2011).Using Songs as Audio Materials in Teaching Turkish as a Foreign Language. *TOJET: The Turkish Online Journal of Educational Technology, 10*(4), 378-83. Kezilahabi, E. (2005). Aesthetics and the Teaching of African Languages.*Journal of African language Teachers Association,* 7, 33-46.

Kramer, D. J. (1997).Teaching Foreign Languages through Music.*Consortium News Autumn* 1997: 22–24.

Krashen, S. D. (1989). *Language Acquisition and Language Education.*2nd ed. Language Teaching Methodology Ser. New York: Prentice.

Ludke, K. (2009). Teaching foreign languages through songs (workbook). Retrieved from http://ww.academia.edu/97895 1/Teaching_foreign_languages_through_songs_workboo_

Matondo, M. (2005). Rap Music in the Language Classroom: The Case of Kiswahili. *Journal of African language Teachers Association,* 6, 67-82.

Murphey, T. (1990).*Song and Music in Language Learning.* New York: Peter Lang.

Nuessel, F., & Cicogna, C. (1991).The integration of songs and music into the Italian curriculum.*Italica,* 68, 473-486.

Osman, A. (1979). *A Program of Songs as a Mode for Learning EFL.* Professional Diploma Report, Columbia University Knappert, J. (1979). *Four Centuries of Swahili Verse*. Nairobi:Heinemann.

Richard-Amato, P. A. (2003). *Making it happen: from interactive to participatory language teaching: theory and practice* (3rd ed.). White Plains, NY: Longman. Richards, J. C., & Rodgers, T. S. (2001). *Approaches and methods in language teaching* (2nd ed.). Cambridge: Cambridge University Press.

Matondo, M. (2005). (Rap) Music in the Language Classroom: The Case of Kiswahili.*Journal of African language Teachers Association,* 6, 67-82.

Shtakser, I. (2001). Using Music and Songs in the Foreign Language Classroom. Available at: http://www.laits.utexas.edu/hebrew/music/music.html

Sposet, B. A. (2008). *The role of music in second language acquisition: a bibliographical review of seventy years of research, 1937-2007.* Lewiston, NY: E. Mellen Press.

Steiner, E. (1988). The Interaction of language and Music as Semiotic System: The Example of a Folk Ballad.In *Linguistics in a Systemic Perspective.* Eds. Benson et al. 393-441.Amsterdam: John Benjamins.

Tworek, Heidi. (2013). The Real Reason the Humanities Are 'In Crisis.' In *The Atlantic,* Dec. 18, 2013: Retrived from. http://www.theatlantic.com/education/archive/2013/12/the-real reason-the-humanities-are-in-crisis/282441/

Walker, J. (1987). *The Melody of Speaking Delineated; Or Elocution Taught Like Music.* Menston: England. Scolar Press Ltd.

CHAPTER EIGHT

Literary Translation, Cultural Understanding and Selected Translated Works of Akínwùmí Ìsòlá

Akinloye Ojo
University of Georgia

Introduction

The translation of literary works often serves as the expressive connecting bridge between languages and cultures. It is regularly perceived as a purely linguistic exercise of rendering a literary text in one language into another contributes whereas, in reality, it is critical to cross-cultural and inter-national understanding. As noted by Schulte & Bigunet (1992), *"in the act of literary translation, the soul of another culture becomes transparent and the translator recreates the refined sensibilities of foreign countries and their people through the linguistic, musical, rhythmic, and visual possibilities of the new language."* The most fundamental description of what translators do is that they write or as some others would define it, rewrite in language B a work of literature originally composed in language A. This they do with the hope that readers of the second language (i.e. readers of the translation) will perceive the text, emotionally and artistically, in a manner that parallels and corresponds to the esthetic experience of its first readers (Edith Grossman, 2010). This paper will examine some of the aspects of the Yorùbá society and culture which have conceivably become accessible to English readers through the translations of some of the works by the renowned Yorùbá writer, Akínwùmí Ìsòlá.

The translated works to be considered are *Efunsetan Aniwura, Iyalode Ibadan and Tinuubu, Iyalode Egba: Two Yorùbá Historical Dramas by Akínwùmí Ìsòlá* translated from the Yorùbá by Pamela J. Olubunmi Smith (these two historical plays were written in Yorùbá by Akínwùmí Ìsòlá with the titles; Efunsetan Aniwura and Olu Omo respectively); and *Àfàimò àti Àwon Àrofò Míràn by Akínwùmí Ìsòlá* translated into English by Akinloyè Òjó. In examining these translated texts, the paper seeks to achieve three objectives. The first is fairly instrumental as the paper discusses one of the identified linguistic challenges acknowledged by the two decoders in translating these particular works by Ìsòlá. The second and most critical objective is identifying and reflecting about specific aspects of the Yorùbá culture and society which have conceivably become accessible for English readers through these translations. Understandably, in the course of the discussion, the paper will achieve its third objective of highlighting some inherent values of literary translation and its contributions to cultural understanding.

The paper recognizes that the goal of these two translators (Pamela Smith and Akinloyè Òjó) in translating the three selected Yorùbá works by Ìsòlá into English is akin to the intention of other literary translators which is to provide access for the readers of the text in English into the social, cultural and linguistic world of the Yorùbá people, who unquestionably, were the conceivable inspirations and intended consumers of the original text. To paraphrase Schulte & Bigunet (1992), in their act of literary translation of Ìsòlá's work to the English language, Smith and Ojo have recreated the refined sensibilities of the Yorùbá people and culture through the linguistic, cadenced, and illustrative possibilities of the English language. The paper therefore concludes with a succinct commentary on noted instances where aspects of the

---

Chapter Eight   Akinloye Ojo, in
Dainess Maganda and Karim Traoré (Eds)
LANGUAGE AND LITERATURE: Vehicles for the Enhancement of Cultural Understanding
London, Adonis & Abbey Publishers

Yorùbá culture, history and society have plausibly become more accessible for English readers through these translations.

The value of literary translation

Edith Grossman in her 2010 influential essay, *"Why Translation Matters,"* actually argued that translators are more than just the humble, anonymous literature servants of the publishing industry but rather, translators are 'writers.' Quite candidly, one would harken to somewhatsupport this position and further posit that, irrespective of what translators think of themselves, they must, at the most minimum be considered as rewriters or re-workers of the text. Unlike the original writers in the source language, the translator has to develop a keen sense of style in both languages as Grossman instructed, *'honing and expanding our (their) critical awareness of the emotional impact of words (in both languages), the social aura that surrounds them, the setting and the mood that informs them, the atmosphere they create.'* In addition, *"the translators have to sharpen and elaborate our (their) perception of the connotations and implications behind basic denotative meaning in a process not dissimilar to the efforts writers make to increase their familiarity with and competence in a given literary form."*

As controversial as it might seem, in the process of translating a text into another language, the text becomes the translators' but then it remains, concurrently and inexplicably, the work of the original author as it is transformed into a second language (Grossman, 2010). There is no better situation that exemplifies this mystery of ephemeral ownership than in the situation of translating literary works written in African languages into other languages (such as English). Particularly in the situation that the original authors of these works in the African languages could arguably be said to be translators or decoders themselves- captivatingly as they have worked hard, in their creative geniuses to transform oral literary materials into modern literature. As Akinyemi & Falola (2008) noted, the functions performed by such literary materials in oral society are sustained in the modern literary production into which they are transferred or translated. We will return to this interesting idea and how it relates centrally to the works of Akínwùmí Ìsòlá but first, let us conclude with our introductory discussions on the worthy task of translation which Grossman argues is not magic as in the altering of base metals into precious ones but rather, translation is the result of a series of creative decisions and imaginative acts of criticism.

However we consider the history of translation theories and its impact on the creative process, we cannot escape the tangible task of refining that takes place in the different aspects of the translation process in which there is the transferal of texts from one language to another. If the Linguistic Ethnologue (2013) now in its seventeenth edition is to be believed, there are over 6,000 distinct languages in the world but only about 1/6th or about 1000 of these are written. Of course, there is a limit to the number of languages in which a person can acquire a worthy reading ability. It therefore means that when we say World Literature and celebrate it as a discipline fit for academic study, we are acknowledging the availability of translations. There is no denying the variation that exists in the quality of translations but there is also no denying the centralized position that translation occupies in our conjecturing of a universal, enlightened civilization.

Studies such as Friedrich (1965), Schulte & Bigunet (1992) and more recently, Grossman (2010) have argued that it is translation that almost defines the European Renaissance. According to Grossman (2010), "the 'rebirth' we have all studied at one time or another began as the translation into Latin and then the vernacular languages of the ancient Greek philosophy and science that had been lost to Christian Europe for centuries." A critical appraisal of Friedrich's historical overview of translation theories, starting with the Roman Empire becomes exceedingly suggested. In this overview, it appears apparent that over the years and decades, the basic premise of any good translation was not only to render the text in the second language but also to move the translated text close to the original as much as possible. Translation expands and deepens our world, our consciousness, in countless, indescribable ways. In addition to this basic premise, Friedrich's historical overview begs the question of how would literary studies and even the world of enlightenment be without translation.

As expressed in the works of Schulte & Bigunet (1992), Grossman (2010), and Bassnet (2002, 2014), translation expands our ability to explore through creative works, the thoughts and feelings of people from another society and time. It permits us to enjoy the transformation of the foreign into the familiar and for a brief moment, we are able to locate ourselves outside our immediate environment. Translation promises writers across the world a significant increase in readership and it increases the number of people that they communicate and affect around the world. More than any other language, it is generally accepted that translation into the English language ensures both commercial success and visibility for a writer. In essence, translation helps a literature to be less insular and less ignorant of others and the rest of the world.

In spite of all the noted benefits and value of translation, one is not blind to the challenges and controversies that go along with the process. Primary is the concern for the loss of intended and expressed meaning in translation. If nothing else, there is to be expected a great linguistic and poetic loss that will (and must) occur when a text is translated. As Robert

Frost once opined, *'the poetic is what is lost in translation,'* and as Miguel de Unamuno also posited, *'an idea does not pass from one language to another (through translation) without change.'* J. Ortega's 2006 *Transatlantic Translations* provide a worthy discussion of some of the notable challenges and controversies inherent in the translation process. Here is a quote from the work, *"translating is the possibility of constructing a scene of mediation that frames interpretation as a dialogic exercise [...] It is the first cultural act that places languages and subjects in crisis, unleashing a redefinition of speakers, a debate over protocols, and a struggle over interpretation"* (p. 26).

One can also not forget the controversies inherent in the colonial write up about Africa in which authors such as Conrad and company were attempting to 'translate' Africa for their fellow Europeans. These authors engaged in the production of highly well written racist representation of the continent as well as the prejudiced representation of others in the process of translation within the postcolonial context. Tymoczko (1999) in her discussion of *Early Irish Literature in English Translation* explains this inherent challenge very well, *"translation is paradoxically the means by which difference is perceived, preserved, and proscribed. Translation stands as one of the most significant means by which one culture represents another"* This is a representation that is often mapped as differences and which, as Frantz Fanon stated, is often motivated by the need *'to show the totalitarian character of the colonial exploitation- the settler painting the native as a sort of quintessence (embodiment) of evil- insensible to ethics and representing the absence and negation of values.'*

Is there anyone that can deny that translation carries with it its own racial, political, cultural, and pragmatic baggage? These challenges notwithstanding, the translators must continue to engage in the craft. As Pamela Olubunmi Smith pointed out in the introduction to her translation of two of historical plays by

Akínwùmí Ìsòlá, translation (particularly of works in Yorùbá into other languages) must continue to ensure greater reach of the inherently indigenous ideologies of the Yorùbá people. As she stated, "it is increasingly acknowledged that these contemporary works need not remain shrouded by the politically fueled debate 'to translate or not to translate,' especially when some of the writers, such as Ìsòlá, are fully capable of writing in English but choose to write in Yorùbá."

Translation from one language into anotherconsistently enables the kind of artistic discovery that is profoundly important to the health and vitality of any language and any literature. In fact, we must support the claim by Grossman (2010) that *"translation asserts the possibility of a coherent, unified experience of literature in the world's multiplicity of languages. At the same time, translation celebrates the differences among languages and the many varieties of human experience and perception they can express."* We must not see the assertion of unity and the celebration of exceptionalism as a contradiction but rather, we must see the existence of both as a testimonial to the complete and all-encompassing embrace of both literature and translation.

The conversation gets more interesting and colorful regarding the African continent. With about 3,000 plus languages spoken and many of which have their own multiple dialects, Africans are significantly multilingual speakers with most people speaking at least two languages. The value of translation increases be it between the different indigenous African languages or between the African languages and the highly impactful but non-indigenous African languages such as English, French and Portuguese. More remarkably, most of these over 3,000 languages are virtually oral with no writing systems. There is therefore a significant impact and importance of the oral tradition. And as we noted earlier, there is an unbroken continuity between oral and written literature in most of the continent. According to Gyasi in his 2003 work (*The African writer as translator: writing African Languages through French*), in which he studied the implications of the use of European languages on African written works and attempted to resolve the difficulty of rendering African ideas, thoughts and feelings in a foreign language, '*the point to note ... is that African writers tend to have been inspired by oral literature and traditions for stylistic and ideological reasons. Thus, oral tradition is undoubtedly one of the abstract commanders of modern African writing; it is a living tradition that has both literary and moral consequences. It is a tradition that has helped to shape the writer's conceptions of the world and his/her relationship to the external world.*'

The importance of the oral literature and traditions to modern written literature of Africa was concisely stated by Irele (1993), "*the major forms of the African oral tradition are employed in modern African writing to project structures of the collective mind that serve as explicative narratives of the world.*" According to Gyasi (2003), the "*transportation, transformation or, if you will, transmutation of African oral traditional elements – imagery, proverbs, wise sayings, myths, folktales, dramatic factors, and lyrical language – into the written Europhone African literature*" is what he refers to as creative translation. So the question would therefore be about what to call that which has been indemnified in the works of Akínwùmí Ìsòlá and other Yorùbá writers who have transported, transformed and, if you will, transmuted elements of Yorùbá oral traditions such as imagery, proverbs, and lyrical language- into the modern written Yorùbá literature. Akinyemi and Falola (2008) included these in their consideration of translation- in that the "*concept of translation here* (their work) *is the transformation of oral literary materials, first, into modern literature written by Akínwùmí Ìsòlá in Yorùbá or English, and second, into the English and French versions of some of Ìsòlá's titles "transliterated" from Yorùbá.*"

Summarily, it is our opinion (as someone engaged in the process of translating works written originally in Yorùbá language into the English language) that there is more in the process of translation than just merely expressing written ideas from one language to another and that it also includes the transfer of cultural ideas and ideals from one society into the other. As we translate literary text, we decode the represented culture- both the culture of the society that produced the author of the text and which includes, for all intents and purpose, the individual culture of the author that is situated and well enshrined within his society's larger culture.It would be interesting to note that the multilayered 'transmutation' that is being done by African writers such as Akínwùmí Ìsòlá is of critical value to not only foreigners (i.e. non Yorùbá natives) but also to Yorùbá citizens who, due to circumstances of colonialism and economic development are in great need of works by writers such as Ìsòlá for multiple reasons.

The first form of this need concerns those that are literate in the Yorùbá language but are not very conversant with Yorùbá oral traditions – Ìsòlá's engagement (or translation) of the oral tradition in his creative works therefore serves their need very well. The second form of this need concerns the few but interestingly growing population of *bi-cultural monolingual Yorùbá citizens* (these are proficient in Yorùbá and English/western cultures but are speakers of only the English language). These are neither literate in the Yorùbá language nor conversant with the oral traditions – for this group, it is the translation of Ìsòlá's work into English being done by Smith and Òjó serves their purpose very well.

The Writer, Playwright, and Poet, Akínwùmí Ìsòlá

Akínwùmí Ìsòlá has been noted as *"one of the very few highly productive African authors writing in indigenous languages whose works are original, creative, imaginative, and satisfying"* (Akinyemi & Falola, 1). Ìsòlá, who writes in all the three genres of drama, fiction and poetry, has significantly contributed to the African language promotion efforts by producing most of his literary works in his mother tongue, Yorùbá. A Professor of Yorùbá language and literature and a Fellow of the prestigious Nigerian Academy of Letters, Ìsòlá has contributed immensely to the development of the Yorùbá language and its literary traditions particularly in the areas of drama and novel. In addition, he has written as a literary critic about various areas of Yorùbá literature including the Yorùbá novel as well as the contents and performance of Yorùbá oral poetry, especially *Sàngó Pípè* (Sango Worship poetry). He has however gained more significant recognition for his creative works as a novelist, playwright, stage director, and poet.

Ìsòlá is also celebrated as one of the few courageous African writers that chose to write in indigenous African languages at a time in the 1970s when it was very difficult to get any national or international recognition for writing in the indigenous African languages. Ìsòlá produced all of his initial creative writings in his indigenous language, Yorùbá. Among his earlier works is the historical play, *Efúnsetán Aníwúrà*. This was written in 1970 and based on the life of one of the strongest female political leaders to emerge from Yorùbá land. There is also the novel *Ó Le Kú*, written in 1974. A modern day Yorùbá love story of passion, deceit, hope, and betrayal. He also published, in 1981, the play *Kòseégbé*, which he had written and produced for stage in 1976. The play is on corruption and other common vices in the society. It later became a television drama and recently produced as a movie. These examples of Ìsòlá's works are significant signposts in the chronology of Yorùbá literature at their publication and are presently categorized as classics in the Yorùbá literary tradition. Over the years, Ìsòlá has excelled in all the genres of Yorùbá literature and has earned himself the reputation of being one of Nigeria's most productive and talented Yorùbá writers. In addition to this, he has provided excellent leadership in Yorùbá studies within and without the Yorùbá nation. In his singular poetry anthology, *Àfàimò*, he continues this practice of excellence and leadership.

Writing in 1997 about how Yorùbá literary writers have constructed or invented Yorùbá heroes, the historian scholar, Toyin Falola noted that the legendary D.O. Fagunwa enhanced the status of Yorùbá creative fiction while Akínwùmí Ìsòlá had dominated Yorùbá literature. This elevated status has been reaffirmed recently by another renowned Nigerian playwright, Femi Osofisan in his description of Akínwùmí Ìsòlá as *"unarguably the most accomplished and the most hardworking writer in the Yorùbá language of our time"* (Akinyemi & Falola x). The hard work, accomplishments, and dominance saw Ìsòlá's works featured, reviewed, and critiqued in Nigeria and beyond. Akinyemi and Falola (2008) reported that Ìsòlá's extraordinary ability continues to be widely recognized by *"scholars, critics, and students of Yorùbá Studies, for he is featured prominently in nearly every serious appraisal of modern Yorùbá drama, poetry, fiction, and film."*

Translating Ìsòlá: The Language Dilemma

This section will concisely consider the enigmatic issue of language and language use in Ìsòlá's works and in the process of translating these works to English. This consideration will necessarily provide an enhanced understanding of Isola's dexterity with the use of the language and the challenges that this deftness raised for the translators. Moreover, an appreciation of the use of the Yorùbá language in Isola's writing will aid our discussions in subsequent sections about aspects of the Yorùbá culture which have conceivably become more accessible to English readers through the translations done by Pamela Smith and Akínlóyè Òjó. Much has been written about Akínwùmí Ìsòlá's use of the Yorùbá language in his creative works both from the standpoint of language choice as well as the use of language as a tool for generating meaning. In terms of his choice of the Yorùbá language, many of his contemporaries have noted that Ìsòlá's mastery of the language is simply beyond compare; and that his insistence on using Yorùbá for his writing is a courageous choice aimed at sustaining and promoting the Yorùbá culture particularly against the eroding pressures of globalization. This has meant that Ìsòlá's creative works raise questions about both language theory and aesthetic policy.

On the other hand, in terms of Ìsòlá's use of the Yorùbá language in his creative works, the best description is provided by Arohunmolase (2008). According to him, *"the high level of Ìsòlá's creative sensibilities has largely been responsible for his ability to recognize materials gathered from his pool of experience in such a way that the interconnections between them and the whole from which they are abstracted are revealed"* (151). Ìsòlá's use of language therefore shows that he *"is a master craftsman in his creative use of language. He uses Yorùbá idioms, euphemisms, irony, similes, metaphors, personification, and historicopoetic and institutional materials copiously."* This should not be too surprising to us as Ìsòlá himself noted in his discussion of the expected level of Yorùbá use in contemporary Yorùbá novels *"that the musical quality of this verbal dexterity presented by the language's drum-like rhythm is the measure of a writer's creativity.... This love of rhetoric, this preoccupation with beautiful words, this delight in verbal celebration, is a feature of the Yorùbá novel..."* Similar to the performance of the Yorùbá oral poet, Akínwùmí Ìsòlá has displayed his linguistic capabilities and the depth of the paralinguistic resources available to him.

In terms of linguistic capacity, Ìsòlá has consistently used his writings for Yorùbá linguistic expansion in the face of the dominance of English in the national life and the educational curriculum of Nigeria. Both translators, Smith and Ojo affirm the beauty in Ìsòlá's use of the language in his creative works. As Smith noted, Ìsòlá along with other contemporary writers such as Adebayo Faleti and Femi Fatoba have taken up the 'Fagunwa tradition' which invariably involves making the language 'sing,' imbuing it with a musicality that is at the core of a distinctive legacy. "The Fágúnwà tradition" places the Yorùbás sheer love of rhetoric above choice of material in creative writing and oral art. Contemporary writers, particularly Ìsòlá, have continued this tradition of verbal celebration and extended it with linguistic contributions of their own, thereby honing some of its tested qualities. Due to the musical qualities inherent in the language, the linguistic, aesthetic, and cultural value of sound in Yorùbá literature and speech cannot be overlooked in translation. It was a challenge that both translators had to devise means of overcoming in the process of translating Isola's works to English.

Other concerns were in the translation of Yorùbá idioms into English. As Smith noted "what would therefore be the strategy of translating the idiom without changing the shape of the metaphor" as the Yoruba text is transmuted into English? "And in choosing alternate English idioms, what choices are to be made, should the language be elevated or conventional, conversational or austere yet contemporary. Interestingly, how does one reproduce the sound of the Yorùbá ideophones in English, especially when so much meaning is implanted in such ideophonic uses?" As Akinyemi & Falola (2008) noted, *"Smith calls attention to the problem of maintaining a semblance of the rhythm and sound effects in the numerous allusions, hyperboles, repetitions, word plays, and figurative language designed to delight aurally,* and to give "psychological satisfaction" to the owners of the praise poetry." In Ojo's case, he posited that a significant and compelling feature of Ìsölá's work as a versifier is his use of both antiquated and modern Yorùbá in a manner that is relatively comprehensible while still highlighting the stunning proverbial elements of the language.

The poems in Àfàimö essentially have more of the texture of spoken words, i.e., oral poetry. Good-humoredly, one can say that the beauty of the language makes these poems best spoken and heard rather than read. It is safe to hypothesize that this is a prevailing element in the works of many published contemporary Yorùbá poets. The adaptation of the familiar oral form of the language translates into enhanced comprehensibility for the work and better access to the poet's ideas for the reader. This feature renders each of the poems quite memorable. Similar to the performance of the Yorùbá oral poet, Akínwùmí Ìsòlá has displayed his linguistic capabilities and the depth of the paralinguistic resources available to him. Ìsòlá's opinion based on his recognition of the uses of language in modern Yorùbá poetry is also given in the poetic foreword, "Òrò Àkóso" to his translated anthology, *Afaimo*:

1) *Àmó bó sàná, bó sòla,*   18 Whether yesterday or be it tomorrow

Ìrònú akéwì a móo joraa won.   Poets' thoughts are always similar

Ìrònú nìkan kó   20 Not only the thoughts,

Èdè akéwì bí àwòrán aláràbarà ni The poets' language is like a magnificent picture

Èdè tó wuyì ní i satókùn férò(p 1) Eloquent language is the usher for thoughts

Interestingly, the beautiful use of language in Ìsòlá's work and the nature of the Yorùbá language itself would subsequently constitute a challenge for the translators. The apparent "best-spoken" characteristic and the remarkable inclusive use of language do not make for easy translation into English for rather palpable reasons. The concentration of vivid but mixed images in Ìsölá's poetry from both traditional and modern Yorùbá socio-cultural milieu as well as the heavy reliance on Yorùba idiomatic language prohibits a bookish or literary translation. On the other hand, the integrated pattern of language use in the poetry makes certain that the translation of these verses cannot be done verbatim.

The discovery that Smith made in her translation of the two historical plays was that Ìsòlá found in *Oríkì* (Yorùbá praise poetry) the means by which to display his love of "beautiful language," his delight in verbal celebration, and his marvelous competence in language use. Therefore, due to the musical qualities inherent in the language, the linguistic, aesthetic, and cultural value of sound in Yorùbá literature and speech could not be overlooked and could become altered in translation. As with every tonal language (TL), capturing and preserving sound, in translation into a less tonal language is problematic. Providentially, the two translators found exciting and meaningful ways to address the two sided nature of Ìsòlá's dexterity in Yorùbá language use as exemplified in the translated works.

The translated works and aspects of the yorùbá society and culture highlighted

Finally in this section, we turn our attention to the translated works and aspects of the Yorùbá society and culture highlighted for English readers. The first translated work is *Efunsetan Aniwura* translated from the Yorùbá with the same title but with the added suffix- *Iyalode Ibadan* and the second is *Olu Omo* also translated from the Yorùbá with the title *Tinubu, Iyalode Egba*. The two plays were translated together by Pamela Smith 'two Yorùbá Historical Dramas and published in 2005 by African World Press. *Efunsetan Aniwura*, written by Ìsòlá in 1966 is the dramatization of the life of the Yorùbá woman, Efúnsetán Adékémi Ògúnrìn known in Yorùbá history as Efúnsetán Aníwúrà, Ìyálóde Ìbàdàn. She was a woman of great wealth, bold, brave and brazen. She was also a woman of controversial historic and political stature in her time. The dramatized story was said to have been largely based on Ìsòlá's creativity from the limited details of Efúnsetán's life contained in the works of Yorùbá historians such as Revered Samuel Johnson, A.K Ajisafe and Isaac Delano.

Olu Omo, the second play was published in 1983 and chronicles the earlier, more chaotic Abeokuta years of Efúnporóyè Osúntinúubú who would famously be known as Madam Tinubu. It was the Yorùbá sequel to Isola's play written in English titled *Madam Tinubu* which chronicles the later Lagos years of Madam Tinubu. Unlike Efunsetan, the stories of Tinubu contained in both the English and Yorùbá plays were based on documented historical records and products of Ìsòlá's detailed research in the life of the prominent Yorùbá leader. She was a highly successful, politically astute, bright and hardheaded stalwart to be reckoned with in an all-male political milieu of then Yorùbá land.

In the introduction to the two translated plays provided by the translator, it was well articulated that Efunsetan Adekemi Ogunrin (Efunsetan Aniwura) and Efunporoye Osuntinuubu (Madam Tinubu) were two powerful, nineteenth century female political leaders in Yorùbá land. They both occupied the titled position of *Ìyálóde* (the political women leaders within the Yorùbá society) in their respective domains during the seventy-year protracted internal Yorùbá wars. The story of these two gallant Yorùbá women underscores the point that besides the known important male historical figures during this period, there were also a number of change agents who were very distinguished women. Interestingly, many of these women have been largely excluded from Yorùbá historiography. In addition to being remarkable, it is beyond debate that the historical trajectory of these women went beyond the nineteenth century. *Efúnsetán Aníwúrà* tells how the focused Iyalode administered an act of terrible cruelty to a slave, and was subsequently removed from power at the hands of the powerful, while *Olú Omo* explores how Tinúubú carried the Egba people to victory against Dahomey, and was awarded the Ìyálóde title as a result.

It is therefore apparent that in depicting the stories of *Ìyálóde Efúnsetán* and *Tinuúbu* in play form, Ìsölá speaks on behalf of the collective who make up the vast list of distinguished women in Yorùbá (and African) history whose life stories and contributions to the economic, social, and political development of their respective societies are waiting to be told for posterity and for scholarship (Smith, 2005). This is a notion made more accessible by Smith's translation. It becomes quite apparent through first the play and subsequently through the translation (even more importantly for the English reading audience) that Yorùbá women have and continue to pray critical roles in the socio-cultural and political lives of the Yorùbá people. The two translated texts serve as works of literature but more importantly, they highlight the gendered aspects of the political and social existence within the historical Yorùbá society and by extension, the contemporary society. More than a work of literature, *the two translated works* affords the modern reader a primer of Yorùbá culture (Smith, 2005).

The modest as well as the somber lives of Yorùbá women becomes highlighted to the English language audience. The struggles and achievements of the Yorùbá women are exemplified not only in the characters of the two female leaders but also in the other female characters. The English language audience is able to gain access to the common and unique challenges facing both the lowly placed women (such as the servants in the compounds of the two Iyalodes) and the highly placed women found in both Ibadan and Abeokuta- the sojourns of the two female leaders. More particularly, the stories of these two Iyalodes include the mundane elements of their lives such as managing the domestic or household economy as shared with other Yorùbá women and the exciting or unusual elements peculiar to the lives of highly successful economic and political women such as the management of expansive economic ventures and the administration of servants and slave labor. Adeleke Adeeko, in his forward to the two translated plays distinctly stated this cogent point, "the translation of these works bring to the English language audience a sumptuous cultural and intellectual package that can only enlarge our historical understanding of the lives of women in precolonial African/Yorùbá societies."

The final work is the translation of the solitary collection of poems by Akínwùmí Ìsòlá, *'Àfàimò Àti Àwon Àròfò Mìíràn'* published in 1978. Majority Of the 27 poems in the anthology have been translated and variously published in different collections over the years, the most recent being three published in *Imagine Africa*, the collection of translated literary works in English from different African languages published in 2014 by Archipelago Books. The manuscript won the 2010 PEN Translation Fund Grant, and it is scheduled for publication in 2015. The poems are classifiable into three categories by their contents and represented notions (Love and dedication; Warning and admonition and General Opinions). The poems, individually and collectively as anthology, serve as the medium for the poet to directly express his outlook on varied themes such as cultural preservation, delinquencies of youth, the virtues of patience, endurance and cooperation, marriage, death, justice, and love.

In actual fact, it is still possible to consider other common elements of his poetry such as the poet's incessant allusion to nature, particularly animals and plants and his embracing of the popular and populated environment of the market as the setting for his poems. These two elements alone speak volumes to the Yorùbá traditional essence inherent in Ìsòlá's poetry. As an agrarian society, the Yorùbá people have significant value for the environment. The relationship of the Yorùbá people with the environment from time immemorial has been that of mutual interdependence. Their oral tradition is dominated with evidence of this relationship. On the other hand, the market is central to daily life in most Yorùbá societies. It is often considered the heart of the town where socio-economic relationships that form the backbone of the society are formed and nurtured. More particularly, the night market, in most Yorùbá communities, is traditionally the setting for the beginning of most amorous relationships amongst young men and women.

Finally, to further underline aspects of the Yorùbá society and culture highlighted for English readers in the translated poetry of Isola, we turn our attention to the widely acclaimed and celebrated Yorùbá social element of age and respect for elders. The Yorùbá people are renowned for possessing a social structure in which younger people remain in deference of those older. In this culture, the young is expected to provide aid and assistance to those who are older, particularly the elderly. As such, it will be uncommon to find an elder in Yorùbá society doing chores or for example, carrying a load when younger people are around. A rare exception to this social rule will be in the situation when the elder or older person has committed an act of social 'perversity or self-disrespect.' Even in such a situation, the injury to the younger person by the older person is expected to be significant. One of the motivations for this reality for the Yorùbá people is captured by the maxim, *esin iwaju ni teyin n wo sare* (the leading horse provides the example for the trailing horses). This expresses the demand on all older and/or elder Yorùbá people to model good behaviors and serve as good role models in the society.

Remarkably, the Yorùbá people also has another maxim that highlights the enormous benefit that 'naturally' accrues to the older person, especially in their dealings with younger people or youths. The saying, *Ko si ohun ti a n fagba se ju ka fi yomode je'* says that the only accruing benefit for old age is the opportunity to take advantage of the young. This was the case in the poem, *A kì í láhun ká níyì* (there is no respectable miser) in which the selfishness and greed of an elder leads a young(er) man to completely disrespect the elder by not relieving the elder of his luggage on the way back from the farm. In the poem (partial translations provided below), as in the anthology, Ìsòlá confirms many aspects of the treasured and respected socio-cultural values of the Yorùbá people. Nevertheless, in some instances, he also attempts to illustrate and explain the unlikely exceptions to these social rules, even if they often appear quite comical and inadvertent. Ojo's translation of this humorous but contentious poem ensures that these confirmed values and their balanced representation are accessible to non-native readers. Below in (2) is the entire poem by Akinwumi Isola along with Ojo's translation into English:

2. A kì í láhùn ká níyì	**There is no respectable miser**
Ọ̀rọ̀ tí í bàgbà jẹ́	The matters that disgrace the elder
Kò tó okòó	Are not up to twenty
Arábánbí, ohun kínnkin	Brethren, the least of things
Níí sọni dahun.	Is what turns one into a miser.
Ló dífá fọmọdé tó tẹlágbà	This apprises the youth following the elder
Tí ò gberù l'órí àgbà.	And did not assist in bearing the elder's load
Mo wá bèèrè ọ̀rọ̀:	I then inquired on the matter:
Mo fẹ́ẹ́ mọ̀dí abájọ	I wanted to find out the cause.
Ọmọdé ní 'A kì í rí kékeré erù	The youth noted 'There is no frothy luggage
Bó mọ kínnkín	Even if it is the tiniest,
Orí ní fi í ta ni'	It will still discomfort the scalp.'
B'ọ́rọ̀ bá rújú,	Whenever matters become befuddling,
Àlàyé ni ò tí ì tó.	It is the clarifications that are insufficient.
Ọ̀rọ̀ ò pọ̀, àlàyé ẹ̀ ló pọ̀.	The matter is simple, but the clarification is much
Ṣebí irẹ̀ lásán ló fa sábìbí	Isn't it ordinary crickets that caused the situation,
Ọ̀kúndùn àgbà tí í bọ́mọdé pàrẹ̀,	Habituated elder that kills crickets with the youth,
Babá pàrẹ̀ tán,	The elder finished killing crickets
Babá sùnrẹ̀ jẹ.	The elder roasted and ate the crickets
Ọmọde wojú títí.	The youth looked on yearningly
Baba ò kúkú wobẹ̀ lẹ́ẹkan	The elder refused to even peer once in his direction
O ní, 'A kì í rí kékeré irẹ̀,	He says, 'there is no tiny cricket,
Bó mọ kínnkín,	Even if it is the tiniest,
Inú eegun ló n lọ.'	It is going inside the bones.'
Àgbà tó jàjẹ-i-wẹyìn,	The Elder that ate-without-sharing
Ni yóò r'ẹrù ara rẹ̀ délé.	Will bear his luggage home.

Through the poem and the rather humorous situation described, Isola provides an explanation of seemingly conflicting cultural tenets of the Yorùbá. According to Yorùbá society's communal structure, the young man in the poem is culturally bound to carry the load for an elder and not follow barehanded as the elder carries his own luggage. Interestingly, the rare exception to the 'rule' which frees the young man from this cultural requirement is the matter of the elder that 'ate crickets without sharing' and basically broke the 'other' cultural requirement for an elder to be the model of good behavior for the young. Isola's poem, as written originally in the Yorùbá language serves to regale and educate native speakers including those literate in the language but are not very conversant with Yorùbá proverbs focused on age group responsibilities. The poem rendered, via translation by Ojo, in the English language continues to do the task of regaling and informing non-native speakers of the Yorùbá language including the English speaking readers and the earlier identified bi-cultural monolingual Yorùbá citizens that are neither literate in the Yorùbá language nor conversant with Yorùbá proverbs. Remarkably, the access provided to these two latter groups of English language audience will essentially provide an increased understanding of the Yorùbá culture and society.

Conclusion

This paper has examined some of the elements of oral traditions, society and culture of the Yorùbá people which have conceivably become accessible to English readers through the translations of some of the works by the renowned Yorùbá writer, Akínwùmí Ìsòlá. In showcasing the access provided by these translations, the paper concretely highlighted the inherent values of literary translation and its significant contributions to cultural understanding. The paper focused on a limited number of illustrations from three translated works of Akínwùmí Ìsòlá including two historical plays translated by Pamela Smith and an anthology of poems translated by Akinloye Ojo. The paper highlights how the translation of these works into the English language has abetted in conveying Isola's commitment to the promotion of Yorùbá culture and the development of Yorùbá language. The transmission of the author's linguistic and cultural commitment to the Yorùbá language and culture inherently exposes the refinement and value of Yorùbá oral traditions.

The access provided to English speakers in the translated works, particularly the two historical plays, included the cognizance of two outstanding Yorùbá historic female political leaders as well as the leadership roles that women have historically played in the Yorùbá society. More critically, the paper establishes that the translated works bring the different world in which the Yorùbá people reside closer for the speakers of the English language reading the works in translation. As Adeeko (2005) noted in reference to Smith's translations of the two historical plays by Isola, 'the translations bring to vivid life Isola's sense of Yorùbá speech, spectacle, and their relationship to power.' Sapir (1956) noted that "no two languages are ever sufficiently similar to be considered as representing the same social reality." The three translations of Yorùbá works by Ìsòlá- two historical plays and a poetry anthology- provide access for readers of the text in English into the social, cultural and linguistic world of the Yorùbá people, the conceivable inspirations and intended consumers of the original text.

References

Achebe, C. (1975). *Morning yet on creation day: Essays*. London: Heinemann.

Akinyemi, A. and Falola, T. (2008).*Emerging perspectives on Akínwùmí Ìsòlá*.Trenton: Africa World Press.

Akinyemi, A. (2008). Proverbs, creativity, and language use in *Madam Tinuubu*. In A. Akinyemi and T. Falola (Eds), *Emerging Perspectives on Akínwùmí Ìsòlá*. (pp. 161-176). Trenton, NJ: Africa World Press.

Arohunmolase, L. O. (2008). Language and meaning in the creative works of Akínwùmí Ìsòlá. In In A. Akinyemi and T. Falola (eds), *Emerging Perspectives on Akínwùmí Ìsòlá*.(pp. 149-160). Trenton, NJ: Africa World Press.

Bassnet, S. (2014).*Translation Studies*. New York: Routledge.

Conrad, J. (1910). *Heart of Darkness*. New York: New American Library.

Falola, T. (1997).Yorùbá Writers and the Construction of Heroes. *History in Africa, 24*, 157-175.

Grossman, E. (2010). *Why Translation Matters*. New Haven: Yale University Press.

Gyasi, K. A. 2003. The African Writer as Translator: Writing African Languages through French. *Journal of African Cultural Studies16*(2), 143-159.

Howland, D. (2003). The Predicament of ideas in culture: Translation and historiography. *History and Theory,42*(1), 45-60.

Irele, A. (1987). In Praise of alienation: An Inaugural, lecture delivered on the 22nd of November, 1982 at the University of Ibadan. University of Ibadan.

Irele, A. (1993). Narrative, history, and the African imagination. *Narrative, 1* (2), 156-172.

Ìsòlá, Akínwùmí. (1992).The African writer's tongue.*Research in African Literatures,23*(1), 17-26.

Ìsòlá, A. (1978). *Àfàimò àti Àwon Àròfò Mììràn*. Ibadan: University Press Limited.

Lewis, M. P. et al. (Eds). (2013)*Ethnologue: Languages of Africa and Europe*. Texas: SIL International, Global Publishing; 17 edition

Ngugi wa Thiong'o, (1986). *Decolonising the mind: The politics of language in African literature*. London: James Currey Ltd.

Ojo, A. (2011). Abinibi produces the best ability: Yorùbá Language splendor and the poetry of Akínwùmí Ìsòlá.' In A. Akinyemi (Ed.).*African creative expressions: Mother tongue and other tongues,* (pp. 121-136). Bayreuth: Bayreuth African Studies Series89

Ojo, A. (2008). From oral to contemporary: Praise singing in Akin Ìsòlá's Poetry. In A. Akinyemi and T. Falola (Eds.).*Emerging Perspectives on Akínwùmí Ìsòlá,* (pp 385-394). Trenton, NJ: Africa World Press.

Ojo, A. (2002). From oral to contemporary: Praise-singing in *Afaimo, a collection of Yorùbá poems* by Akínwùmí Ìsòlá." *Metamorphoses, 10*(1), 199-221.

Okpewho, I. (1992). *African oral literature: Backgrounds, character, and continuity*. Bloomington: Indiana University Press.

Okpewho, I. (Ed.) (1985). *The heritage of African poetry: An anthology of oral and written poetry*. New York: Longman.

Olabode, A. (2008). Akínwùmí Ìsòlá's *Afaimò*: A prolegomena." In A. Akinyemi and T Falola (Eds.), *Emerging Perspectives on Akínwùmí Ìsòlá,* (pp.217-228).Trenton, NJ: Africa World Press.

Olatunji, O. (1984). *Features of Yorùbá Oral Poetry*. Ìbàdan, Nigeria: University Press Limited.

Ortega, J. (2006). *Transatlantic translations: Dialogues in Latin American Literature*. London: Reaktion Books.

Owomoyela, O. (1996). *The African difference: Discourses on Africanity and the relativity of cultures*. New York: Peter Lang Publishing.

Smith, P. J. O. (2005). *Efunsetan Aniwura Iyalode Ibadan & Tinubu Iyalode Egba: Two Historical Plays*. New Jersey: Africa World Press.

Schulte, R. and J. Bigunet. (1992). *Theories of translation: An anthology of essays from Dryden to Derrida*. Chicago: University of Chicago Press.

Tymoczko, M. (1999).*Translation in a postcolonial context: Early Irish literature in English translation*. Manchester, UK: St. Jerome Publishing.

CHAPTER NINE

Return of the Native? Images of alienation and "Outsiderhood" in Tayeb Salih's Season of Migration to the North

S Satish Kumar
University of Georgia

The act of locating one's scholarship has become, in recent times, imperative within the discourses of academe in the humanities. Thus in aid of locating this present study it is important that one locate oneself. Jadavpur University in Kolkata, where I trained as a graduate student for four years before coming to the University of Georgia, has had a long association with African Studies. The Centre for Studies in African Literatures and Cultures at Jadavpur University is in its tenth year of research and teaching; it has successfully hosted a number of national and international annual conferences and currently has three publications to its name. "PALAVER", the title of both the Centre's annual conference and publication truly embodies the spirit in which it was founded. The Centre functions in close association with the Department of Comparative Literature at Jadavpur University and aims at facilitating a 'South-South dialogue' through its scholarly endeavours. It is this context that shapes my understanding and interest in African Studies. As a Masters' student at the Department of Comparative Literature at Jadavpur University I completed the Area Studies component of my program with the Centre. It was here that my attention was constantly and inadvertently drawn to convergences, and I refrain from using the term 'similarities' consciously, in our Histories. Interactions with a rich body of literature from both the African "Mainland" and the "Diaspora", brought to my attention not only of the convergences but also the divergences in cultural and literary histories of Africa and South Asia. It is from this located understanding of the literatures and cultures of Africa that one endeavours to explore the themes of alienation and outsiderhood in Tayeb Salih's *Season of Migration to the North*.

K.M George (1992) in his magnum opus- *Modern Indian Literature, An Anthology*- comments on the theme of alienation in "Modern Indian writing" (p. 116). The appearance of this theme in the Indian literary expression could certainly be linked to the exposure to and the reception of western literatures. However, asserting that such literary expressions in both Indian English writing and literatures in Indian languages were entirely imitative of western literary models would entirely inaccurate (George, 1992; p. 116). The theme of alienation is common to most Post-Colonial literatures. The specifications of the expression or manifestation of course vary from one literary culture to another. The specificity of the manifestation does not, however, take away from the generality of this theme in Post-Colonial literatures. One could think of several theorizations, contexts and texts for the study of this theme. Homi Bhabha (2004) explains the subject position of Post-Colonial modernity in terms of "cultural hybridity" (p. 9). Cultural hybridity can be understood as a liminal position in Post-Colonial cultures located at the interstices of the cultures of the colonizer and the colonized. The angst of outsiderhood is experienced on both ends of the spectrum, because the subject position of an individual located in this liminal space does not allow for a sense of complete belonging in either the colonizing culture or the culture of the colonized. This becomes even more apparent in the figure of the western-educated individual in Post-Colonial literary cultures- all the more so if the individual receives this education in the "mother country" (to borrow from Fanon's turn of phrase). The returning native is, as Frantz Fanon (2008) argues in *Black Skin, White Masks*, transformed beyond recognition: "The black man who has lived in France for a certain time returns home radically transformed. Genetically speaking, his phenotype undergoes an absolute, definitive mutation" (p. 3). The returning native, as evidenced by Fanon's analysis, seeks to shed all nativity. This abandonment of all things native comes with its own set of problems. The problems of abandoning nativity coupled with the inability to secure a sense of belonging through assimilation into the colonizing culture, makes inhabiting this liminal or hybrid space simultaneously complex and problematic. Therefore in speaking of the retuning native, one is not speaking of a happy homecoming. We clearly this sentiment echoed in Césaire's *Cahier*, "My far distant happiness which makes me aware of present misery", says Césaire (1969) in his *Notebook of a Return to the Native Land* (p. 42).

Not all pictures of a return are painted as grimly as the *Cahier*... The unnamed narrator of Tayeb Salih's novel *Season of Migration to the North* uses the image of something cold-frozen—at the very core of his being melting in the warmth of the sun and the people of his community in the first few days of his return from a seven year long stay in Europe (1991; p. 1). He was slowly re-familiarizing himself with the sights and sounds of his 'once familiar' home. This takes long because, as he says, "something like a fog had arisen" between him and his people through his absence—through his remembrance of them in absentia (ibid.). The fog disperses, but there is a reminder in the very beginning of the story that he had learnt much and much had passed him by (ibid.). Images of change surround him at every step of this journey to recovery of remembrances past. "From my position under the tree I saw the village slowly undergo a change: the water-wheels disappeared to be replaced on the bank of the Nile by pumps, each doing the work of a hundred water-wheels."(Salih,199, 1 p. 4).

Simultaneously, he also seems much comforted by the idea of being back amidst his native people, his family—his home. One understands the urgency in a statement like, "I want to take my rightful share of life by force" (p. 5). However one cannot also help but wonder about the location of this life that our narrator envisions. As a man of letters—as the possessor of a distinguished degree from a University in the "mother country"—would he be satisfied with mere clerical labour in his "native land"? Would being reduced to mundaneness of a steady income from a job (that despite carrying a prestigious title) would not sate his wanderlust—a desire that infected him during his travels in the colonial tabernacle?

The predicament of the unnamed narrator in *Season of Migration to the North* presents a classic example of the condition Fanon explains in *Black Skin White Masks*. Fanon's critique of colonization as a psychological process is, one can infer, directed at the essentially flawed premise of the colonizer's need to assimilate the colonized subject into their own culture. The incontrovertible reality of this process or policy of assimilation is that it can never be complete or absolute. The realization of this reality, in a certain sense, is the tension at the core of Fanon's own enterprise. His critique of the French colonial policy of *assimilation* stems undeniably from a position or location that lies inside rather than outside the process itself. If one carefully observes the referential locus of Fanon's critique, one will realize that it is specifically French and generally European. It is perhaps this location that makes his critique so uncompromising in its interrogation of assimilation and the explication of its effects. The effects for Fanon, considering his trade, are psychological. It is psychological in the sense, that it occludes and obscures the colonized subject's sense of self to a zone that can only be described in terms of an absence of being or a zone of Non-Being. Being defined by constant negation the black man's sense of self is emptied of culture, civilization and history (Fanon, 2008; p. 17). In writing on National Culture Fanon states that the enterprise of assimilation is not just satisfied with mere cultural estrangement—not just satisfied with emptying the "native brain" of all things "native", but with instilling an insecurity that justifies the indispensability of the colonizer's continued presence. Being a product of the enterprise of assimilation, Fanon understands the failure of this project in the cruel horror of the native's encounter with his own blackness. This is in a certain sense, for Fanon (2001), the predicament of the native intellectual (pp. 175-180). Horrified by his own blackness when the "white mask" of European civilization— that he has been trained to don— shatters and the subsequent discomfort of inhabiting his "black skin", relegate the black man's sense of self to a zone of "Non-Being". This is, of course, only the condition- the symptoms present in a variety of ways. The prodromal phase, however, almost always presents with symptomatic discomfort and unease.

Our unnamed narrator in *Season of Migration to the North* is no different. As stated, the contidtion of outsiderhood does manifest in a variety of ways. In the case of our narrator, the discomfort presents itself in the very beginning of the narrative where he states that much had passed him by (Salih, 1991; p. 1). While what has passed him by, as he states, is "another story", the seasoned reader will conclude and correctly so, that the narrative will reveal precisely that which has passed him by. All the changes that happened in the seven years of his absence manifest themselves in subtle ways through the length of the narrative—the pumps that replace the water-wheel or the mass-produced iron doors that replace the fine art of fashioning doors out of wood- are all signifiers of change and the narrators unease. The most substantial manifestation of this discomfort with change in the novel, however, is our unnamed narrator's fascination with Mustafa Sa'eed. Though our narrator emphasizes that Mustafa Sa'eed is not an obsession, we observe the story of Mustafa Sa'eed taking up nearly the entire narrative. Our narrator's obsession with the life of Mustafa Sa'eed rivals perhaps Marlow's obsession with Kurtz in Conrad's *Heart of Darkness*. The beginnings of this obsession become apparent in our narrator's very first apprehension of Mustafa Sa'eed. The man is an outsider in the village. Our narrator spots him as an unfamiliar face amidst his welcome party. A better understanding of the narrator's obsession calls for a Fanonian reading.

Mustafa Sa'eed becomes a character of interest primarily because, despite being an outsider in the village, he seems to have very comfortably claimed his place in the village society. He seems to have transitioned and settled rather easily in his place as an insider in the village. One might even say that he is more at home in our narrator's home than the narrator himself. While our narrator is still finding his bearings in his home, Mustafa Sa'eed is already at home despite having been an outsider not too long ago. He presents in the narrative as a Doppelgänger—a heautoscopic alter ego to the narrator. This is hinted at in an instance of recognition when Mustafa Sa'eed in an alcohol induced daze recites in perfect English lines from a poem that our narrator later finds in a World War I anthology (p. 14). This process of recognition finds completion at the very end of the novel. One assumes our narrator has emerged from Mustafa Sa'eed's library. The last section of the novel is not in reported speech, as indicated by the absence of inverted quotes. It is as though our narrator is experiencing Mustafa Sa'eed's death. We know for certain that the last section cannot be from any of Mustafa Sa'eed's letters or journals for it narrates the experience of his death by drowning.

Our narrator's obsession with Mustafa Sa'eed is comparable to Marlow's obsession with Kurtz in the *Heart of Darkness*. Kurtz, in many ways, is a story gone horribly wrong. Similarly Mustafa Sa'eed represents the worst-case-scenario of the outcomes of colonial assimilation. Kurtz is both fascinating and horrifying to Marlow because he represents the realisation of a fate not very far from home. Achebe (1978) in his critique of Conrad's novel explains that the fear (almost to the point of a psychosis) that dominates *Heart of Darkness*, stems not from an apprehension of difference but from the horror of perceiving a similarity (p. 3). Marlow's obsession, then, finds justification in the fact that he could have just as easily met the same fate as Kurtz. One finds a similar tension at the heart of *Season of Migration to the North*. Our narrator and Mustafa Sa'eed are more similar than they are different. They are both products of the grand colonial enterprise of assimilation. Both studied in the "mother country" and both returned to the colony. The difference lies in the fact that one found a homecoming while the other did not. The circumstances of Mustafa Sa'eed's return and his fate in the "mother country" are realities our narrator, perhaps, missed by the skin of his teeth: "You, Mr. Sa'eed, are the best example of the fact that our civilizing mission in Africa is of no avail. After all the efforts we've made to educate you, it's as if you'd come out of the jungle for the first time." (Salih, 1991; p. 93) This could just as well been the fate awaiting our narrator. The words, "I am no Othello. Othello was a lie." could just as well been his, had he been as entrapped by the allures of the "mother country" as Mr. Sa'eed was (p. 33).

The two stories—the narrator's and Mustafa Sa'eed's- do not run as parallels but rather in chiasms—even more so when our narrator is called upon to fill Sa'eed's absence. Mustafa Sa'eed implores not to encourage wanderlust in his sons. He knew what the lures of a wanderer's life had done to him (p. 65). In putting our narrator to fill his absence, he, in a sense, implores the narrator to learn from his mistakes. These chiasms point towards the fate that lies before Fanon's 'native intellectual'. Mustafa Sa'eed presents the worst scenario imaginable from the ones outlined in *Black Skin White Masks*— of the tragic failures of the grand colonial enterprise of assimilation. His calm and composed outward demeanour conceals a core of frustration and deep-seated unrest. This does intermittently come to the surface, particularly in his interaction with our narrator. The fact that Mustafa speaks English in his sleep and of his past 'loves' is perhaps indicative of a deep-seated neurosis (p. 91). This is an unrest that ultimately consumes him.

In the last section of the novel, our narrator too is consumed by the very same unrest as he emerges from Mustafa Sa'eed's library. In an almost somnambulistic trance he begins to walk towards his own death. The ray of hope comes at the very end of the novel when the drowning narrator cries out for help. This is where an optimistic reading of this novel would suggest that the vicious cycle of psychoses and neuroses perpetuated by the enterprise of assimilation is broken. The image of drowning and emerging from the water carries with it the most obvious allusion to rebirth, but also simultaneously the possibility of a "complete lysis" of the "morbid universe" that defines the post-colonial subject position (Fanon, 2008; p. xiv).

References

Achebe, C. (1978). An Image of Africa. Research in African Literatures 9(1), 1-15.

Bhabha, H. K. (2004). The Location of Culture. New York: Routledge. Print.

Césaire, A. (1969). Return to my native land. Harmondsworth: Penguin Books Ltd.

Fanon, F. (2001).The Wretched of the Earth. (C. Farrington, Trans.). London: Penguin Books.

Fanon, F., (2008).Black Skin White Masks. (Richard Ph., Trans.). New York: Grove Press.

George, K.M. (1992). Modern Indian literature, an Anthology: surveys andpoems. New Delhi: Sahitya Akademi.

Salih, T. (1991).Season of Migration to the North. (Denys Johnson-Davies, Trans). Harlow: Heinemann.

CHAPTER TEN

Spatial Organization of Mande Tales

Karim Traoré
University Of Georgia

The meaning of space in African tales

Tales are known to be generally authorless. They are passed down from one generation to the other. This form of transmission has prompted many people to think that tales never change; in reality, every retelling of the tale transforms it, negatively or positively. What most retellings do contribute to the tale is paradoxically to confirm its basic organizational principles, its canvas. It is this canvas that anthropologist Sory Camara (1981) refers to as schème narratif, "narrative pattern" of the story.

Working on stories collected in Eastern Senegal, Sory Camara proposed a method of tale interpretation based on their narrative pattern. Camara's approach is the result of empirical observations that he made while he listened to the storytellers in the course of numerous years. Camara noticed that whenever storytellers hesitated or lost the thread of their narration, they would draw imaginary lines simulating the movements of the protagonists. Because of the iterative nature of this way to remember, Camara formulated the hypothesis that movements are meaningful structuring elements. Movements always imply a direction and a destination, which suggests that fixed places may also contribute to the construction of the story's spirit.

This contribution will look at one tale and study in what ways movements and relevant stations and places mentioned in the stories bear symbolic meanings suggesting that listeners consider giving further thoughts to the symbols. Possibly, this may even lead to developing and proposing an alternative understanding of the tale.

The mythical space, narrative patterns meaning construction

According to Sory Camara, the specific types of tale under scrutiny in this essay develop a theme including actions taking place in a bipolar (mythical) world. The protagonists move between the poles of this imagined world. This patterned commuting is essential as it is the origin of the stories' dynamism. Each movement brings about a psychological change of the character that implements the movement. Indeed, Camara suggests that stories are designed according to specific conventions known to the community that tells or hears these tales. Each story can be classified under a specific narrative pattern. A narrative pattern consists of the totality of the movements that the protagonists operate in the mythical space. Whenever a protagonist goes from one pole to another, he/she operates a movement. Each movement results in a new situation, which depicts an evolution of the story as well as a psychological maturing of the protagonist. Let us observe that these movements are all horizontal. Another dimension needs to be taken into account, namely the vertical movement that usually the main protagonist makes after having reached a specific location. Horizontal movements lend to the tales their dynamic allure. As for the vertical movement, it mostly signal that the protagonist is about to make a specific discovery or observation at a specific time and place.

Suffice this very brief description to convey the basic ideas that need to be taken from Camara's approach to tales. They suggest that the spatial organization of stories convey possible understanding or interpretation of the tales if one pays attention to the configuration of the protagonists involved at a specific location. Let us illustrate these statements by carrying out a more detailed study of the spatial organization entailed in the tale, The Two Friends.

This tale is a common story that mothers like to tell their sons. Some variations replace the friends with twins. My first memory of this story goes far back to the year I had to leave my little town for a boarding school. On the eve of my journey, my mother formally called me into her house and requested that I listen to a story, "keep it in my belly and make it my own." Decades later, in 1995, the story came back to my mind when I was manifesting my frustration in front of Sory Camara for never having provided me with any satisfactory answer whenever I asked to know the meaning of a story. Camara simply referred me to a passage that he reported several years in his masterpiece, Paroles très anciennes (1982:8). When he wished to understand a story, his teacher Kidugu Mahan simply declared:

Les paroles très anciennes	The very ancient words
C'est comme les grains	Are like seeds
Tu les sèmes avant les pluies	You sow them before the rains
La terre est chauffée par le soleil	The sun warms the earth
La pluie vient la mouiller	The rain comes and wets it
L'eau de la terre pénètre dans les graines	The water of the earth penetrates the seeds
Les graines se changent en herbes	The seeds change into grasses
Puis deviennent des épis de mil	Then they become millet ears
Ainsi, toi à qui je viens de dire la	Thus, you to whom I just told

parole très ancienne	the very ancient words
Tu es la terre	You are the earth
J'ai semé en toi la graine de la parole	In you I have just sown the seed of the word
Il faut que l'eau de ta vie pénètre en la graine	The water of your life must penetrate the seed
Pour que la germination de la parole ait lieu	Before the germination of the word can take place

Kidugu Mahan's words echo the recommendation of my mother. I eagerly looked forward to Sory Camara's enlightening interpretation of the strange story. Instead, he simply suggested to me that I tell him more about the second friend by the end of my six-week visit at his department. The following can be viewed as a very late answer to Sory Camara's request. My response will build on the configuration of space in the tale.

Spatial organization of The Two Friends

Summary of The Two Friends

The story of The Two Friends can be summarized as follows. Two children were born on the same day. As children they did everything together. When they reached the age of circumcision, the two boys were cut on the same day. They had an agreement: the two friends should never contradict each other or argue with one another. Several years after their circumcision, they decided to go Senegal to make some money and found their own family. Our young adults spent a few seasons in Senegal, working hard and saving money. They finally returned to their hometown. One day, they discussed how they would get married. One friend suggested that they should marry only one wife who would sleep between them.

As the other friend tried to argue against such an idea, his friend simply reminded him that they were not allowed to argue with each other. So, our friends married one woman who shared their bed every night. One day, the two friends heard of an initiation festival being held in a neighboring city. The first friend suggested that they should attend this festival with their wife. Our friends and their wife set out to the town of the initiation festival. It was a longer trip and the sun was burning, soon the wife of the two friends complained about thirst. As she would not stop requesting water, the first friend asked the other one to poke one of his eyes and give its liquid to their wife, promising to do the same later. The liquid could not really quench the woman's thirst because she soon asked for water. Immediately, the same first friend declared that his friend should offer the "water" of his other eye. Of course, there could be no discussion because of the agreement. The second friend sacrificed his second eye to please their wife. As soon as the second friend was blind, the first friend offered him a walking stick and disappeared with their wife. The blind man could only complain about his misfortune and try to find his way to the festival town. He could not follow the path and ended in the brushes. He wandered about until he hit the opening of a baobab tree. Our blind man entered in the rather spacious hole of the baobab tree and decided to spend the night there and try to recover. In the middle of the night, the blind man heard voices: a vulture came to perch on the baobab and started a conversation with a jinn who lived in the baobab. The vulture reported to his friend that the initiation festival was not going well because the town could not provide enough water to the attendants. And the vulture added that if the head of the town were not dumb, he would have asked that the tree in the middle of the town be uprooted to provide water for everybody. Moreover, the vulture said, the dumb head of the town would complain about missing the gold and silver that his father left him. The vulture told his friend that in fact, these riches were underneath the stone on which the town leader sat every time he took his shower. Finally, the jinn's visitor concluded his report by stating that if one leaves the hole of this baobab, one could find a plant on the right hand that can cure blindness; on the left hand one could harvest leaves that heal all types of diseases. Early in the morning the blind man went out of the hole of the tree, used the plant of the right hand to recover his sight, took some leaves on his left hand and hurried to the festival town where he saved the thirsting community, healed many ill people and retrieved the gold and silver of the town leader. The town leader rewarded the young man by giving him his daughter in marriage and by granting him 100 of each item available in his town.

The formerly blind man took his rewards and set out to return home. Underway, he met with his friend who was coming back from Senegal. The first friend could not believe his eyes. His friend simply told him that all this happened while he was sitting blind in the hole of the baobab. The first friend quickly poked both of his eyes and asked to be led to the baobab. In the middle of the night, the vulture came to visit with his friend. He reported that the initiation festival was going well because they have found water and… The jinn interrupted his friend and declared that he needed to make sure that nobody was overhearing them. The jinn discovered the first friend and struck him to death with a heavy iron rod. The tale misleadingly states that one should not betray one's friend. As we will show, this moral concern does not represent the most important aspect of the story.

Spaces in the tale

The spatial organization is rather simple. We can identify the following major sites: the town of the two friends, Senegal, the location of the baobab tree and, finally, the town of the initiation festival. The noticeable movements are the travel to Senegal and return, the trip to the town of the initiation festival. While we can assume that the first trip to Senegal took place following the "beaten path," the itinerary to the festival town seems to be more problematic. Indeed, we need to be specific about the travelers. The two friends went together to Senegal; their trip to the town of the initiation festival starts with all three protagonists and becomes more complex. Indeed, after the second friend lost both of his eyes, we need to observe exactly the movements and locations of the protagonists.

The blind friend tries to stay on course and finishes nonetheless to go off the path and he interrupts his journey for one night that he spends in the hole of the baobab tree. We can figure his itinerary as entailing a detour, namely the leg during which he was blind. He strayed off course, marked a pause and came back on track, as it were. With respect to the symbolism of space and movement, this part of the story clearly suggests that some detours may reveal themselves as shortcuts. Indeed, the apparently forced break was what expedited the traveler's journey. We can come to such a conclusion only when we try to account for the destination of the other characters. We remember that the first friend simply took off with their wife. While we know that the two friends' initial destination was the town of the initiation festival, we are not told the destination of the first friend when he disappeared with their wife.

When the two friends meet again almost at the place where the second friend lost his sight, the story does mention that the second friend encountered the first friend who was returning from Senegal. Only now we understand that the first friend had opted for another destination: Senegal. This precision allows us to carry out a new evaluation of the space/place that Senegal represents in the tale. We know that Senegal provided the two young men with the wealth that allowed them to marry a woman. Accordingly, the woman can be regarded as a product from Senegal. It is therefore not surprising that the first friend is alone when he is momentarily reunited with his friend. While we could speculate more about what happened to the woman, it seems more important to pay close attention to the language that the tale displays.

The tale says basically that two friends decided to attend an initiation festival in a neighboring town; however, only a friend stuck to the initial plan; the other friend kept his eyes wide open and missed to see the village of the festival. Here may be the place to observe that our friends did not set out to go to any frivolous enjoyment; they wanted to attend an initiation festival. This detail grants the journey a totally different significance. The travelers were meant to achieve an additional education that would enhance their level of knowledge. Indeed, what an initiation brings about consists of accessing a higher level of spiritual sophistication; and this is even more so as the journey takes place after our friends took a wife.

Mande culture considers that each child's growth until to marriage is accompanied with the assistance of his family and community. This specific tale does not mention parents but it does sketch the typical "curriculum vitae" of young men. After marriage, it is the responsibility of each man to launch a new phase of his life that will make out of him a knowledgeable, respectable and useful member of his community. This phase is a continuing education that takes place under the guidance of a freely chosen master.

These sociological assumptions known to culturally competent community members confer to our story its hidden side: The Two Friends is a tale of initiation into how to become a fulfilled member of Mande community. What is admirable about this tale is that even as a tale of initiation, it offers complex and multiple possible interpretations.

For instance, an interpretation may insist on the encoded twinhood principle. The insistence of the story on the fact the two friends would do everything together may be interpreted as either that the friends are twins or—more likely—as the two contradictory components of an individual's identity. This understanding would suggest that each person struggles against the painful need to improve on oneself and the attractiveness of easy pleasure and lack of thoughtfulness. The disappearance of the first friend would corroborate such a stance.

However, the interpretation that I see in the text concerns its powerful pleading for acquiring a great wealth of knowledge in order to offer it to the people, selflessly. This knowledge acquisition can take place only under the guidance of a master who monitors one's evolution. From this perspective, a totally new and different light is cast on the first friend.

Be recalled that the contradiction between the two friends comes about only with the marriage. As noted before, marriage marks the beginning of a new life span. The second friend rigorously plans this new part of his life, refusing to succumb to any easy solution, rejecting to follow the beaten path and welcoming every testing hardship that will contribute to making out of him a well-tried community member whose selflessness suffers no doubt. This take on the story insinuates that the first friend is the spiritual guide that the second friend has chosen to lead him to his ultimate self-fulfillment.

Sometimes, the acquisition of a higher form of knowledge involves renouncing many forms of convenience; hence the return of the woman from Senegal to the place that allowed to "acquire" her; the second friend's mind is clearer with her disappearance. This "acquisition" does not suggest that women can be bought; it merely suggests that sexuality may interfere with the search for higher knowledge. In the ethics of the hunters, sexuality and the search for means of power are mutually exclusive. Similarly, while the second friend intends to reach the town of the initiation festival, he must put all of his energy in focusing on his goal. This attitude makes him blind to all worldly preoccupation and receptive to spiritual inspiration by fully emptying himself and his mind.

The journey of the second friend to the baobab tree marks the end of his initiatory search for the location of empowering knowledge. In the baobab, our seeker of more knowledge undergoes his true initiation, his veritable transformation. After the stay in the baobab, the second friend can see clearly now, and he knows how to cure diseases. Indeed, the second friend cures the sick in the town, helps the town leader recover his pots of gold and silver. These items represent another manifestation of individual self-fulfillment. Indeed, in Mande culture, silver does not represent mere wealth; it also bears the symbolic meaning of knowledge. The second friend possesses enough knowledge to impart it to those who need some, such as the ignorant community leader. Thanks to the second friend, we can perceive the community of the initiation festival as an empowered one that will enjoy good health—thanks to the healing plants—and learn more. The second friend also helps the town leader recover the gold that his father left him as inheritance. Like the silver, gold carries a hidden meaning in stories such as this one. Gold, a precious metal that cannot rust stands, for wisdom.

The community that the second friend visits is now a viable one: it has found water, symbol of life and rebirth or regeneration. More importantly, the community has now a leader who is knowledgeable and wise. Its future is therefore promising. As for the second friend, we learn that he is given one hundred of each item that can be found in the town of the initiation festival. Receiving so many items and being married to the daughter of the community leader equates to providing for all things necessary to start a new community. In other words, the second friend set out to learn more and improve on himself. He returns home, owner of much wealth and credentials allowing him to launch a new striving community.

What the story implies is that true leadership comes about once you acquire the needed knowledge. It also suggests that such a leadership never aims at controlling people; on the contrary, it inspires to promoting the prerequisites for fulfilled life accessible to anybody willing to undertake the initiatory journey.

This quick analysis would be incomplete if we did not mention the vertical dimension of our spatial organization. Indeed, the site of the baobab allows us to discuss the relevance of the vertical perspective in the construction of the story's meaning. Entering the hole of the baobab represents the first vertical component. Here, the verticality of the space in the baobab hints more to a dimension underneath of the earth than in the sky. One can even see the place of asylum of our blind friend as some return in the motherly womb for a rebirth to sound fulfilled life.

In addition to this aspect combining vertical dimension and being buried in the womb, the position of the vulture and the jinn is undoubtedly celestial. One can mention the baobab itself that represents an erected position. That the vulture and the jinn congregate in a baobab is very meaningful. The baobab is regarded as the tree in which spirits and jinns live. Jinns are considered owners of diverse forms of knowledge that they impart to those to whom they appear. A baobab illustrates the polyvalence of some "beings" in the world. Indeed, there is no single part of the baobab that is not useful. Its barks give fiber to make clothes; its leaves are a highly appreciated source of iron. The baobab's fruits serve to make different sorts of drink with varied healing properties. The baobab in this story also symbolizes the longevity or permanence of sound knowledge. Baobabs can reach 2000 years of age. The vulture also symbolizes the notion of oversight and anticipation. In Mande mythology, vultures and hyenas are the embodiment of sophisticated knowledge, premonition and cautiousness.

The concentration of these beings who all point to the vertical dimension of the story is the mythical language helping us to identify the real nature of the first friend. Indeed, my claim that he is the spiritual guide that the second friend freely chose to be led to more complete forms of knowledge, can be verified in the apparent tragic end of the story: the tale says that the jinn kills the second friend in the very hole of the baobab in which the first friend recovered his sight and discovered the healing virtues of many plants. One may wonder if the second friend's death is indeed a punishment, as the storyteller seems to suggest.

Because of the striking accumulation of the symbols of knowledge that the vulture, the jinn and the baobab represent, I would suggest that we consider the second friend as another member of the congregating knowledgeable beings. Accordingly, we will see in the so-called death of the first friend an evident homecoming of the master. Indeed, the first friend made sure that the second friend underwent all sorts of tests and trials; and he prevailed, earning the deserved rewards that patience and knowledge bring. Since the second friend can stand alone, there is no need for the first friend and mentor to be around: he simply goes back home to his peers, the jinn and the vultures, his "roommates" in the residence of the "knowers."

References

Camara, S. (1981). Paroles de nuit ou l'univers imaginaire des relations familiales chez les Mandenka. Lille: Service de reproduction des thèses.

Camara, S. (1982).Paroles très anciennes.Grenoble : La pensée sauvage.

Traoré, K. (2000). Le jeu et le sérieux. Essai d'anthropologie littéraire sur la poésie épique des chasseurs du Mande (Afrique de l'Ouest). Köln: Rüdiger Köppe Verlag.

Traoré, K. (forthcoming). "The Duty to Dissent: Community and Individual Responsibility in a Mande Tale." In Traoré, K., Sotunsa, M., and Ojo, A., Eds. Expressions of Indigenous Knowledge in Africa and Its Diaspora. London: Cambridge Scholars Publishing Ltd.

CHAPTER ELEVEN

The Secret Imports of Names and its Implication for Individual in Nation Building: A Study of Yorùbá Anthroponomy

Gabriel Ayoola
University of Georgia

Introduction and scope

Scholars in philosophy, religion and linguistics have, over the years, been fascinated by, have pursued and continue to pursued, the subject of onomastics across cultures. One paramount question that has been at the center of most of these works is the question: What is in a name? In literature, attempts have been made in defining what name is, who names who or what, and why do people name both human, places, animals or things. The Yorùbá people like other cultures place great value on names. However, while in the West, name like Anderson means 'son of Andrew', Johnson 'son of John' and Williams 'son of Will', Yorùbá personal names mean more than that (Nuessell, 1992, p.14). They are unique in that they point to the socio-psychological conditions of name authors, and their societies at large, and are the very expression and construction of Yorùbáness such that it can be argued that Yorùbá personal names are not just arbitrary labels.

Method of data collection

The method of data collection in this paper is first the intuitiveness of the researcher as a native speaker and teacher of the language in question. Secondly, names are collected from the Yorùbá dictionary of personal names by Babalola and Alaba (2006). The dictionary is an alphabetically ordered listing of Yorùbá personal names. It is a reliable source for some personal names used in this paper. No interview or other methods of data collection is used in this paper.

Significance of the study

This work attempts to dissect the secrete imports in Yorùbá personal names by looking at those personal names as signs and further examines their implications for the individual bearers in nation building. The scholarly gaps it sets to fill would bother on the cultural information about Yorùbá society and ability to view those names as verbal signs. It is also very important to this study to indicate that the classifications of names done in English or the Western world may not apply to all languages of the world as it is proved in Yorùbá through this study. This work examines the principles that underline the name of a person in the Yorùbá socio-cultural context, and semantic fields which are covered in Yorùbá naming practices and the rationale for such coverage. The work reveals personal names as socio-cultural artifacts that are revealing of the past, present and the future – the means by which the Yorùbá people document their experiences and also construct their future.

Related literatures

There is no human being so wretched as to have no name of his own and the largest class of names is that of personal names (Gardiner, 1954). As long as there is no statistical proof for this assertion, one may wonder though if other things and places are not much more in number compare to the humans as places, things and animals also have their own names. This keen observation on why almost everything is named allows an inquiry into the origins of names. Philosophers, onomasticians and linguists through the ages have attempted to make a list of the origins of names. These include, but not limited to Mill, Hilka cited in Pulgram (1954), Algeo (1973), Bosmajian (1974), Nuessell (1992), and Anderson (2007).

Naming system in Yorùbá tradition

There is a great difference in the naming system of the Yorùbá in comparison to that of the West. Naming among the Yorùbá is an important affairs and it is accompanied with a lots of cultural ceremonies. The sex of a child determines when it would be named. If it is a boy child, it is named on the 9th day after birth, on the 7th day if it is a girl. Female twins are named on the 7th day after birth, on the 8th day if they are male and female twins, while on the 9th day if they are male twins (Akinyemi, 1987, 2005; Johnson, 1921). One reason it takes the Yorùbá people days before naming a child is that during this period, the parents are busy ruminating over the circumstances that surround the birth of the new baby and the events that has been going on in the family as at when the baby was born. By taking time to put together all these events they would be able to come up with names that would not only describe the experience of the parents but also project into the future of the child. In the Western world, it is a baby shower which is done before the baby is born. A new born baby is introduced and initiated to the culture of its people from the day it is named. This means every name of Yorùbá child has within it some embedded cultural information. It is so informed that once a person mentions his or her name, there is a quick recognition of the person's family background in terms of occupation, religion or royalty. This is evident in the names like Odeniyi 'game hunting is noble', Agbedeyemi 'Smithy befits me 'Ifalere 'divining pays off'.From the name Odeniyi, it becomes evident that *hunting* is the family occupation of the bearer of such a name. Cultural information about the world view of the people is clearly expressed in the name an individual is called.

Babalola (2003) identifies sixteen patterns and opines that on the basis of the meanings cohering in Yorùbá personal names, a variety of patterns can be identified and appreciated. On the other hand, Akinyemi (2005) classifies Yorùbá personal names into five major groups:

a) Names that some children are said to be born with because they described the physical condition and posture of the name bearer at birth or the newborn's position in the sequence of other siblings in the family.
b) Names expressing child-parent-family relationship
c) "Death prevention" names,
d) One-word descriptive praise names
e) Nicknames adopted as personal names.

These names equally reveal some of the socio-cultural ideologies and circumstances of the Yorùbá people. These personal names are not arbitrary labels but reflect the viewpoints, the history, the aspiration, the circumstances of their authors or their ideological beliefs and those often times of their immediate community. It has been argued that the name an individual bears has a potential influence on the pattern or kind of life he or she lives. This explains the reason for the Yorùbá proverb in the oral tradition which says "*Oruko a maa ro ni, apeje a si maa ro eniyan*" lit. "The act of what one does or the kind of life a person lives is a reflection of what his or her name is". This view point is also corroborated by Dansei (2008) when he asserts on the Roman notions and believes on the subject of name. He asked, would the Romans' view explain names such as Cecil Fielder who was a fielder, Rollie Fingers who was a pitcher, William Wordsworth who was a poet, Francine Prose who was a novelist, and Mickey Bass who was a musician? He then summits that, perhaps such occurrences simply indicate that some people are inspired subliminally by their names to gravitate toward occupations suggested by them.

Sebeok (1994) argues that, there is one kind of sign that merits separate consideration - the *name*, the sign that stands for a person, place, or by connotative extension, a brand, an animal, a tropical storm, and so on. He claims that names are identity signs and that it is impossible to think of human-being who are without a name. This is why namelessness may not be tolerated by the society, hence, if an individual is not given a name by his or her family, the society steps in to do so. Names define the human person in more ways than one. This may account for why children or an adult become upset when someone calls them by a name other than their birth name, or else makes fun of that name. The personal name, known as an *anthroponym*, constitutes truly significant part of being human. Throughout the world, a newly born child is not considered a *person* until he or she is given a name.

Sebeok explains further that people also name things other than human beings. Throughout the world, they give names to deities, vehicles, geographical spaces and formations-countries, states, islands, rivers, streets and so on. Naming has also been applied to identify products (brand names), aware that a product with a name has a more personal quality to it; marketing and advertising people pay a close attention to the choice of a brand name.

Names are perceived typically to belong to the realm of the sacred. In many cultures, including Yorùbá, giving a child the name of an ancestor will bestow on that child the ancestor's spirit, protection, nobility and or wealth, and thus guarantee familial continuity and tradition. This spiritual dimension is the reason why name-giving ceremonies are found throughout the world, many of which are linked to religious rites (Danesi, 2008). This view point may perhaps have informed the reason behind some cultures and religious practices in believing that names are so important both in life and after life. The Ancient Egyptians believed that if an individual's name was forgotten on earth, the deceased would have to undergo a second death. To avoid this danger, names were written multiple times on walls, tombs, and papyri. In Hebrew culture, the ancient art of *gematria* was based on the belief that the letters of any name could be interpreted as digits and rearranged to form a number that contained secret messages encoded in it. The Romans, too, thought names were prophetic, claiming in one of their proverbs that *nomen est omen*-a "name is an omen". The Puritans also believed that one's name was a self-fulfilling prophecy. This may account for why they choose names like Obedience for their child, hoping that the child would exemplify the virtue.

Yorùbá personal names as signs

Here, this paper analyzes Yorùbá personal names as pointers to some semantic fields, by assessing the socio-cultural and psychological significance of these semantic fields in the construction and expression of Yorùbáness. This semantic fields based is subdivided thus: (1) Religion/belief, (2) Bravery, (3) Wealth and Nobility, (4) Association, (5) Ownership and Possession, (6) Events, (7) Joy and Happiness, (8) Gendered Names.

1. Religion/Belief

The Yorùbá cosmos contains Olorun or Olodumare, the supreme deity; the orisa or lesser divinities; ancestral spirits, and a number of other categories of spiritual beings. Man is made up of both corporeal and spiritual elements, the latter having a variety of functions. These are related to Yorùbá beliefs about destiny and reincarnation. Olorun is to the Yorùbá a rather distant figure, apparently playing little part in the day-to-day affairs of men. Idowu (1962) uses the analogy of the Yorùbá *oba* (king) who is responsible for the affairs of his kingdom, but who has little contact with his subjects, as most of his dealings with them are through the *orisa* (deities). He argues that the orisa are, nevertheless, only the ministers of the deity, whose supremacy is clearly recognized. He is the creator, the final arbiter of heavenly and worldly affairs, omniscient, immortal and pure, and the source of all benefits to mankind.

From the foregoing, Yorùbá believes in gods, goddesses and deities. This shows their belief system and the reasons for several of their names having theo-prefixes, theo-infixes and theo-suffixes. . Some of the names in the above category could have a referential, appreciative, and expectation attribute to a god or deity. It is obvious to see expression of god or deity mentioned either as a prefix, infix or suffix. This category is recognized with the form 'Olu' 'Oluwa' or 'Olorun' for God and numerous names of other deities like; Ogun 'god of iron', Sango 'god of thunder,' ifa 'divinity god' Osun 'sea goddess' and so on as illustrated in sections 1.1 to 1.3 below:

1.1 Names with theo-phoric prefixes.

a. Oluwaseun 'God be thanked'
b. Oluwasanmi 'God pays me'

c. Oluwasola 'God does (me) noble
d. Olutayo 'God worths the joy'
e. Olugbile 'God fills the home'
f. Oloruntoba 'God worths being king'
g. Oloruntobi 'God is great'

1.2 Names with theo-infix
   a. OlaOluwayemi 'God's wealth fits me'
   b. IniOluwani 'it (the child) is God's heritage'
   c. Toluwani 'it (this child) is God's'
   d. AnuOluwapo 'God's mercy is limitless'

1.3 Names with theo-suffix.
   a. MoriireOluwa 'I found God's goodness'
   b. MogbotOluwa 'I obey God's (instruction)'
   c. AdeOluwa 'God's crown'

The semantic import covered under this category of personal name expresses the religion belief system, the high esteem with which the Yorùbá society holds the gods and deities. Sometimes they express their appreciation to gods and deities, at some other times they make a plea, or request for long life, wealth and prosperity and sometimes they declare the might and awesomeness of gods and deities through these personal names.

1.4 Reincarnation and Abiku names as a sub-category under semantic field of religion belief.

   a. Babatunde 'the dead father has returned'
   b. Yetunde 'the dead mother has returned'
   c. Ta a ní mọ̀ ọ́n wò→ Tanímọ́ọ̀wò? 'Who is it that knows how to watch him'
   d. Ta a ní mọ inú un rẹ̀→Tanímọnúrẹ́? ' who is he that knows what is in its mind'

e. Ta a ní mọ̀ọn ọ̀la→ Tanímọ̀la? 'who is he that knows tomorrow'?'
f. Ta a ní tó Ọlọrun→Tantọ́lọ́run 'who is he that is equal to God'
g. Kí ni a rí í bẹ̀ ẹ́ → Kíaríbẹ̀ẹ́? ' What is it we can beg him with'
h. Ayedun *'life is good'*
i. Durosinmi *'stay and bury me'*

Many Yorùbá are identified through resemblance, dreams or divination as being reincarnations of particular ancestors, and are given names such as (1.4a) *Babatunde* 'the dead father has returned' or (1.4b) *Yetunde* 'mother returns'. However, even after this 'reincarnation', these ancestors may still be invoked to help their descendants. An abiku may be born in a child on earth, but it soon leaves for heaven again, and the child dies. The abiku spirits have their own egbe (society) in heaven, and when one of them leaves for earth, he promises to return quickly to his companions. If a woman gives birth to a succession of children who die in infancy, it may be divined that it is an abiku at work, and the next child is given special treatment. Abiku children are given special names examples are (1.4h) Ayedun, 'life is good', implying that the child should stay to enjoy it, or (1.4i) Durosinmi, 'stay and bury me', implying that the child should outlive its parents. It also shows the importance the Yorùbá cultural view attached to funeral. It is believed in the culture and a wish of the parents that their children buried them when they die. Hence, name like (1.4i) above becomes a plead to the child who has been *'coming and going'* to stay and live longer to be able to bury the parents when they die. The appearance of these children is often neglected, and they might even be disfigured to make them less attractive to their companions in heaven. It is normal to postpone the circumcision or scarification of an abiku child until it appears likely that it will survive.

2. Bravery

There were great accounts about wars and heroism among the Yorùbá dated back as far as pre-colonial era till present. Any titles are bestowed on some of the warriors who fight with the last blood in their veins in defense of their people and or sometimes in carving out dynasty or kingdom for themselves. Following are examples of Yorùbá personal names of bravery:

2.1 Names for bravery
a. Balogun *father at war*
b. Ologbenla *one who inflicts deep wounds*
c. Anikulapo *one who carries death around in his pouch!*
d. Akintunde *the brave one has come*
e. Akinlabi *it is the brave one we give birth to*

Name like (2.1a) is a chieftaincy title confers on a warlord. It means '*father at war*' and has become last name for some people over a period of time. Names like 2.1b that is 'one who inflicts a very deep wound on his enemy at war. The wound is so deep that it caused the death of the inflicted. 2.1c is the one who has or carries death around in his pocket. This name is said to belong to a family or lineage of warriors. A child or family bearing this name are said to be fearless and be at all times bold in the face of any kind of situations. This may be evident, that bearer of such name may not necessarily go to battle by firing guns at their supposed enemies but often times in the modern Yorùbá society they may become a political activist or a social critic. Example of this is noticed in the legendry of Fela Anikulapo Kuti, a renowned and god of Afrobeat music in Nigeria who opposed every government dictatorship and sang to the liberation of human minds. On several occasions the Nigerian government imprisoned him as his music was always about critiquing bad leadership and corruption in Nigeria system. Although this legend is dead but his sons also take after the legacy of their father in the music industry. They sing to criticize any government of the day without fear of incarceration.

The underline projection for the child is that they want him to live with the idea sternly imprinted on his mind that he is a brave one who is not expected to be afraid or run from challenges in life. As it is often assumed that life could be ups or downs sometimes, the name author expects the name bearer to understand the down side of life is a test of his bravery which is associated with his resilience. One of the important parts of the naming culture among the Yorùbá is the fact that there are good expectations from the individual name bearer, the family (name author) and the society in which the name bearer belongs. This is why in the Yorùbá society whenever a person does something ignoble in the society the first question the elders ask is about the name of the perpetrator. It can be assumed that they want to know whether there is a symmetrical relationship between the name and the acts committed. If they noticed any asymmetrical relationship between the act and the name, the first rehabilitating process begins with orientating the offender about his or her own name. This has often times proved productive as the offender may have a change of attitude henceforth and start to live a life worthy of the name he or she bears. Some of the names that have to do with bravery are often associated with male children and not female children. This however does not suggest that there are no brave female or feminine warriors in the Yorùbá society. In fact, there are a number of female heroes in the historical account of the

Yorùbá nation. Women like Moremi, a princess who delivered the Ife people from Ugbo people, the invaders on Ife around the 1500 BC.

3. Wealth and Nobility

Wealth and nobility are great concepts in the Yorùbá worldview. These terms form the basis for Yorùbá various occupational endeavors. However, the Yorùbá ideas and the way they view wealth in the traditional society might be different from the way it is viewed in the modern Yorùbá society. In (3.1) are Yorùbá personal names of wealth and nobility.

3.1 Names of wealth and nobility

a. Ogunniyi the god of iron is noble
b. Olaniyi wealth is noble
c. Ayanniyi drumming is noble
d. Ifatola oracle equals wealth
e. Fiowowe child whom the royal lineage sire has bathed with money
f. Ajewole the goddess of commerce has arrived our home
g. Inaolaji the fire of wealth has awakened or rekindled

In the traditional Yorùbá society wealth is not considered in term of money and/or houses a person has but it is rather measured in terms of lives a person is able to affect positively and influenced to achieve their heights. To them, money is just a micro aspect of wealth. To the Yorùbá society, nobility is considered superior to wealth and riches. This is reflected in their maxims, *O n wa owo lo o pade iyi lona, ti o ba lowo tan iyi naa lo maa fi ra;* which literarily means, *you are all out in search of money but meet honor on the way, you rather grab honor because honor can never be bought with the money after all.* The semantic import in this maxim is rather on the fact that money is good for living but it is not as good as being a noble person. A noble person can get whatever he or she needs both human and materials but sometimes a rich man may not always have his way. So it is assumed that nobility is a father to wealth and riches if put on relativity scale.

In naming therefore, it is sometimes difficult to translate the nobility aspect of someone's name as oppose to the wealth aspect of it. That is they are so interwoven. This is why there are names like: Ọlá ní iyì → ọláníyì'wealth has honor'. The bearer of this name lives with the impression that to be wealthy is to be noble but the kind of wealth in question does not necessarily bother on the amount of money have, fleet of cars and numerous houses built. But rather within the frame of nobility, that is having good testimonial and being in right standing with everybody.

Names that fall within this semantic field are reflections about the worldview of the Yorùbá in the ways and manners they view wealth in relation to being noble. This explains the reason why in the Yorùbá society a wealthy person whose riches cannot be traced to hardwork but rather to fraud or money ritual is treated with scorn and disrespect. The fact is that, it is possible to be wealthy at the same time to be noble provided the wealth comes from a clean slate of hard-work and good behavior. The Yorùbá society is built on hard-work, truthfulness and nobility.

The Yorùbá society takes dignity in their occupations; they see their jobs as noble and source of wealth. They also esteem their gods and deities, they see them as noble. This is reflected in names like Ogunniyi, 'the god of iron is noble'. This accounts for reasons for various names that reflect the kind of occupation a family or lineage does –for instance 3.1c, that is 'drumming profession is noble'. 3.1d, 'divining equals wealth'. 3.1a, 'the iron god is a noble god'. The import here is the professing of the nobility in their gods and deities.

The declarative name 3.1e (omo-ti-a-fi-owo-we "child whom the royal lineage sire has bathed with money") is one of such names that explain expectations and aspiration parents place on their child when he or she is named. The import is that this child is born with a silver spoon and he or she is expected to grow and live the life of affluence and influence because of the wealth. They picture the child in a bigger mirror of abundant riches that could be likened to bathing with money. Metaphorically, the money is imagined here as water with which the child is expected to bath. The name author is like prophesying to the name bearer that he or she would be so rich that money will be to him like water meant for bathing. Once again this kind of name explains the socio-psychological functions behind naming a person. As it is expected of the bearer to live up to the name he or she bears.

Name like 3.1f (Aje – wo – ile) means the goddess of commerce has arrived our home. Aje, is the guardian goddess for wealth, profit, wealth creation and sustenance among the Yorùbá people. Aje is responsible for profit making in the market place, and in fact, supervises the entire aspects of life that relates to money. Within the Yorùbá calendar, Monday is a day referred to as 'ojo aje' – the day for making wealth and reaping profits. Therefore on two different stances the name author can name a child Ajewole. One stance is if the child is born on Monday and another stance is if the name author is a business mogulthat holds Aje goddess in a high esteem. The first stance explains the socio-cultural notion of the Yorùbá society regarding the days of the week and how important Monday is to them. In the actual fact, Monday is sacred to them as whatever happens to their business on Monday could either have a negative or positive impact on the rest of the week. The Yorùbá people dare not joke with Monday as it is the day Aje blesses or prospers their business and this has a great influence on their business for that week.

The semantic import behind this name is that, if a name bearer who bears this kind of name goes into businesses, he/she is expected to be an outstanding and successful person because s/he bears the mark of the goddess of wealth by the name he bears. However, it not automatic or necessary for the name bearer to be successful in business if he or she fails to work hard, prudent and having good business plans and strategies and or otherwise as believed among the Yorùbás that destiny plays a vital role in whether or not a person succeed at chosen profession or business. As religion permeates all facets of traditional Yorùbá life, Aje in traditional Yorùbá religion is a goddess that must be venerated; thus fortunes smile on whoever venerates her. An individual's effort towards amassing wealth could be both physical and spiritual since it is believed that Aje is the guiding force for seeking and amassing wealth.

The name, Inaolaji: (ina-ti-ola- ji) *the fire of wealth has been relighted or rekindled.* For a fire to be rekindled it must have been that at one time or the other it was glowing but suddenly got smothered. The name author gives such name to a child born at the awakening of the wealth of the parent which at one time they have lost. This name implies that the child marks the beginning of good life for the family he is born into and it is also a reminder for the name bearer that his wealth when he grows up is not expected to dwindle or quench. At the psychological level, the child is growing with the consciousness that he must build an enduring wealth that would outlive him for generations. The bearer is expected to build a dynasty of an unquenchable wealth rooted in hard work and honesty. At another stance, in 3.1g, the name author assumes that the arrival of such child signals prosperity for the family.

4. Association

It is important to understand the nature of existence among the Yorùbá society. The uniqueness of communal society comes to fore in the names Yorùbá people bear. Man, as conceived by Africans, is created a being in-relation in relation to God, his creator, and his fellow men (Awolalu, 1976). Society is defined in terms of distinct person who finds fulfillment by living for one another. The parts are neither subsumed by the whole nor are they paramount. In other word, the focus is neither on the individual nor the community but on the interaction, the in-between, the society relations or the commitment to the well-being of all. The self is a being-in-relation and the community is relational (Faniran, 2008). Names that show association in (4.1) attest to these facts.

4.1 Yorùbá personal names of association

   a. Olaore 'the reflected glory of the friend'
   b. Olaiya 'the reflected glory of the mother'
   c. Olababa 'the reflected glory of the father'
   d. Owoiya 'the mother's money or wealth'
   e. Egbedeyi 'the ancestor masquerade divinity has resulted into this child'
   f. Ebiyinka 'I am surrounded by family members

The collectivist society downplays the self and stresses the importance of the community, which is seen as a complex organism with interdependent organs. But the communalistic society is based on the principle of maturity. The communality is based on mutuality. The mutuality or affinity may be between friends, parents to children, and or associationto which someone belongs.

The semantic imports of this type of personal name may be of the following: First, the name author that is the father of the name bearer may just have had a major financial breakthrough through the help or assistance of a friend as at when the baby is born. At another instance, the name author might have had infertility problem of which he got solution through his friend at that instance, the name author, as a sign of appreciation may give this kind of name that depicts communality or association. At another stance, a matured man may be assisted at wooing a woman in marriage by his friend(s) hence as a token of appreciation, he authors a name like Olaore for his child.

Thus, if a mother has been incessantly appealing to her son on the subject of marriage, and such a son decides to take a wife or the mother marries a wife for him, the fruit of that union, which is the new born baby, is named to reflect the glory of the mother. Also, a man is considered manly when he has good job and his own apartment before he marries a wife, some men do not have to work for another man or look for a job as long as their own mother has a good business, the benevolence of which they have enjoyed that make them to marry a wife without necessarily work too much. The child born under this kind of circumstance is named Olaiya, meaning 'I only ride in the glory of my mother to be able to achieve to this point'. Same thing apply to the name Olababa, *the reflected glory of the father*. In fact this associative benefits is engrained in a Yorùbá maxims 'Ola abata ni modo san, ola baba omo ni mu omo yan' '*A river flows its course through the help of the mire, and a child is proud through the nobility of his father*'

The name, Owoiya, *"it is the mother's money that I am enjoying"* denotes that the mother of the child is rich and shares her wealth with this child, the name-bearer. The socio-function of this name is that the society at hearing the name must acknowledge the fact that the child has a rich mother and at the other hand it is meant to humble the bearer as much as he is expected to be proud of his mother's wealth. It should serve as a reminder at all times to the bearer to be cautious and not be extravagant in spending since the riches is not what he works for all by himself. At another instance, this kind of names exhibits the kind of family structure which could mean that perhaps the child is raised by a single mother or that the family is a polygamous family in which wives or mothers are largely responsible of their children. This could suggest that father is not responsible or that the father is dead as so the mother is the only one that cares for the child without any help from the extended family.

There are associations and age groups which forms different societies among the Yorùbá community. The father of a new child may decide to name his new baby Egbedeyi, *the ancestor masquerade divinity has resulted into this child* so as to express his profound affinity to the group he belongs. The semantic signification about this kind of name is that it expresses 'togetherness' and endearing love to the spirit of association the name author belong.

Personal name like Ebiyimika, *'my family surrounds or supports me'* implies that the father of the child might have decided not to have any child again but the family put pressure on him to give birth to one more child at least. Hence, the father who is the name author named the child, Ebi-yi-mi-ka to show that the child is born not as he wishes but as the family wishes.

5. *Ownership and Possession*

There is a very great joy in possessing something of noble value and it makes the possessor to be very proud. Yorùbá personal names that fall under this category express the ownership or possessive tendency.

5.1 Names that show ownership and possession

a. Oloko *owner of a boat or a means of transportation*
b. Onibon *owner of gun*
c. Toluwanimi *I am owned by God*
d. IyanuOluwa *I am a wonder of God*
e. Onigbinde *the owner of Igbin has arrived*
f. Olopade *the owner of drumsticks has arrived*
g. Ololade *the owner of wealth has arrived*
h. Oniyide *the owner of honor has arrived*

Yorùbás have great desire to express what they possess for the world in order to show their greatness and prowess. Ololade, for instance, at the socio-psychological functional level is a declarative statement by the name author with an impression that the child grows up with the consciousness that s/he is in possession of wealth. The name author predicts wealth for the bearer at the same time affirms that the child is in no way expects to be poor. Sociologically, the family and the society do not want to be disappointed at the child, they want to see the child becoming wealthy.

The personal name, Oniyide, *the owner of the nobility has arrived* is also a projection that engrafts onto the psychic of the bearer to live as a noble individual. The society expects such a bearer to live up to every societal ethos and by no means fall short of good behaviors. S/he is expected to live up to the societal moral codes of conduct like the concept of *omoluabi*, a person of personal and good integrity.

6. Events

Names under this scope explain certain circumstances, festival, historical events or circumstantial events surrounding the birth of the name bearer.

6.1 Names that reflect certain events

a. Adeodun *a crown (child) given me during an annual festival.*
b. Adagunduro *he who stopped a host of enemies during a war*
c. Badiya *father has compensated me/ made it up to me for my past suffering.*
d. Odunitan *the year of history*
e. Abijaro *child whose birth belies (his father's) detractors [Literally: child born who knocks the bottom of falsehoods peddled about (concerning the father)]*
f. Abisogun *a child born during an outbreak of war*
g. Abioro *child born during the Oro annual festival*
h. Abifarin *child born during the Ifa annual festival*
i. Ogunde *the god of iron has arrived*
j. Abogunde *child born during the outbreak of war*
k. Odunitan *a festival marked by an untoward incident, subsequently memorable*
l. Enitan *a child of story*
m. Abidemi *child born while the father was away on a journey, child born in my absence awaiting my home coming*
n. Ige *a breech child*
o. Ojo *a child born with its placenta around its neck*

There are numerous circumstances that surround the day to day life of people at different place and at different time. Such circumstances that surround the Yorùbá life and people include wars, famine, festivals and voyages. In the traditional

Yorùbá society, children born during the inter-tribal war are commonly named as 6.1e Abisogun or 6.1i Abogunde. During the time of annual traditional festivals like *Ifa, Oro, Ogun* and so on, children who are born during these times are named Abioro, Abifarin, and Ogunde respectively. The name author decides to name this kind of name to serve as memorial. Names like these help to keep record of certain events that happened in the history of the people.

There had been question of paternity of a child since the time immemorial. Whenever there is such a situation or circumstances, such child born is named Abijaro, *child whose birth belies (his father's) detractors [Literally: child born who knocks the bottom of falsehoods peddled about (concerning the father)]*. As there was no DNA test in the traditional Yorùbá society, there are two different ways to authenticate the paternity of a child. First, certain family rite is done and if the child does not belong to the acclaimed father, the child may die after the family rite is done. Secondly, the elders in the family into which the child is born may observe certain physical semblance of the child to see who the child resembles among men who were fighting over the child. This kind of name signifies the fight over the paternity and it keeps such memory in the mind of the family and the community. When a father of the new born child is not around as at when the mother gives birth, Abidemi is given to such a child whether the child is a male or a female.

Odunitan, *a festival marked by an untoward incident, subsequently memorable*. At the time a child named Odunitan is born certain communal festival during that period is highly memorable for the parents of the child though the feelings about such memory may be relative. Enitan *'a child or person of story'* is another name that comes with it a unique historical experience which varies from one name author to another. The point here is that no two women are likely to have the same experience before and during the child birth. Basically, Enitan is a person who has stories behind his/her birth. Different bearers of names like this may have different stories behind their names as no two individuals are likely to have the same life experiences. Certain names also reveal the position of birth of a child, names like Ige, a breech child, Ojo, a child born with its placenta around its neck. These names express events and situational circumstances behind the birth of a child.

7. Joy and Happiness

Having children is considered a thing of joy and happiness among the Yorùbá. When a child is born, joy and happiness fills the hearts of family members and the community. Often when a child is born there is a popular expression as *ayo abi ara bintin*, that is joy with a slender body.

7.1 Names that denote joy and happiness

a. Omotayo 'having a child is equal to joy'
b. Ayomide 'my joy has come'
c. Ayokunle 'joy feels the home'
d. Ayoyemi 'joy fits me'
e. Omolayo 'child is a joy'
f. Ayotunde 'joy has come again'
g. MoyinOluwa 'I praise God'
h. Opeyemi 'I am thankful'
i. Titilopemi 'forever is my thanks'

The new child is considered as a joy that has slender body. There is greetings of congratulations and expression of joy on the faces of everyone as they visit the family of the new born baby. In order to express this joy, names given to a child often have joyful expression as an undertone. Names like 7.1a- *having a child is equal to joy*, 7.1b- *my joy has come*, 7.1c- *joy feels the home*, 7.1d- *joy fits me*, 7.1e- *child is a joy*, 7.1f- *joy has come again*.

The socio-psychological functions behind names mentioned here are first to express the grateful attitude to God who they believed has given the child to them. Secondly, it is to suggest to the name bearer that joy is the ultimate and that s/he is not expected to experience sorrow or sadness in his or her lifetime. This same scope of joy and happiness underline some other names that reflects thanksgiving or appreciation to god for example, 7.1g- I praise God, 7.1h –I am thankful, 7.1i – forever is my thanks.

8. *Gendered Names*
   Female

   a. Ajoke meant to be taken care of by all
   b. Alake to take care of her as a result of victory over circumstance
   c. Anike to have (a property) -and – to cherish.
   d. Arike meant to be spoiled on sight.
   e. Aduke people will fight over the privilege to spoil her.

Male

   f. Ajani 'fought to have this child'.
   g. Ajagbe *'fought to carry this child'* Male and female children have different kind of Oriki, praise name.

Praise name is an attributive name, a praise intended to have a stimulating effect on the individual. Although not very common today among the educated Yorùbá elite, it used to be a day to day form of showering praises on children by their parents when they greet them in the morning. Examples of female praise name include, (8a) Àjo**ké** - *meant to be taken care of by all*. (8b) Àlà**ké** - *to take care of her as a result of victory over* circumstance.(8c) Àníké – *to have (a property) -and – to cherish.* Àshàké - *selected to be spoiled (with good things).* (8d) Àríké - *meant to be spoiled on sight.* (8e) Àdùké - *people will fight over the privilege to spoil her.*

The female oriki is predominantly evident with the verb *ke* which is translated as cherished or pampered. The idea here is that Yorùbá society sees the female folks as objects that can be possessed cherished or pampered. Perhaps this explains the belief of the Yorùbá that women are to be cared for and never to be mistreated. However, male oriki names like (8f) *Àjàní - fought to have this child.Àjàgbé - fought to carry this child* have certain significance which is depicted by the activity verb '*ja*' '*fight*'. This semantic import is that male oriki carry with them a sense of responsibility which signals they have a lot of responsibilities to family including women and the society.

Conclusion

The various semantic fields and their secret imports considered in this paper are based on socio-cultural relevance of Yorùbá personal names. It is, for clarity sake to mention that, the categorizations made in this paper do not in any way exhaustive of the personal names of the Yorùbá nation.

Also, the semantic fields discussed do not rank one field over the other. The cultural relevance that each field portrays could be relative to name author and or name bearer. The family and the society expect every individual to live up to its name and consequently make the society proud. Hence, the nation is built and developed as an individual reflects the good names bear.

The paper has also emphasized that Yorùbá personal names are meaning-based with a lot of socio-cultural information embedded in them. That is, they are not arbitrary labels. Thus, calling or mentioning a Yorùbá personal name is as good as asking for a story. Having demonstrated that Yorùbá names are meaning based, it is however expected of the name author to live in accordance to the meaning of his or her name. The supposedly implication about this ideology of living up one's name is that the Yorùbá nation values a united society as it is believed that a united society is a developed society. Hence, the self-realization of who an individual personality within the society is, through the name he or she bears is expected to resonate in making his or herself values the society in which he or she is born into or migrated into and is ready to contribute positively to develop such society. Thus, nation building may be said to start from an individual understanding the imports behind his or her name.

References

Akinyemi, A. (2005). Integrating culture and second language teaching through Yorùbá personal names. *Journal of African Languages Teachers Association, 89* (1).115-126.

Algeo, J. (1973). *On defining the proper name.* Gainesville: University of Florida Press.

Anderson, J. M. (2007). *The grammar of names.* New York: Oxford University Press Inc.

Atkinson, F. (1977). *A dictionary of pseudonyms and pen names.* 2d ed. London: Linnet Books.

Awolalu, J. O. (1979). *Yorùbá beliefs and sacrificial rites.* London: Longman

Babalola, A., & Alaba, O.(2006). *A dictionary of Yorùbá personal names.* Lagos: West African Book Publishers Limited.

Bamgbose, A. (1962). Journal of African Languages and Linguistics, 10 (2).

Barnard, M. (1996). Orderly fashion: A sociology of markets. London: Routledge.

Bosmajian, H. (1974). *The language of oppression.* Washington, D.C.: Public Affairs Press.

Cameron, C. (1983). *The name givers. How they influence your life.* Englewood Cliffs: Prentice-Hall.

Daniel, C. (2007). *Semiotics: the basics.* New York: Routledge.

Eco, U. (1976). *A theory of semiotics.* Indiana: Indiana University Press.

Faniran, J.O. (2008). Foundation of African communication: with examples from Yorùbá culture. Ibadan: Spectrum Books.

Gardiner, A. (1954). The theory of proper names: a controversial essay. New York: Oxford University Press.

Idowu, B. (1962). *Olodumare: God in Yorùbá belief.* London: Longman.

Lakoff, R. (1975). *Language and woman's place.* New York: Harper Colophon Books.

Langendonck, W. (2007). *Theory and typology of proper Names.* Berlin: Mouton de Gruyter.

Marcel, D. (2008). Of cigarettes, high heels, and other interesting things: an introduction to semiotics. Michigan: Palgrave Macmillan

Modupe, O. (1972). Yorùbá names: their structure and their meanings. Nigeria: Daystar Press.

Nuessel, F. (1992). The study of names: a guide to the principles and topics. London: Greenwood Press.

Olatunji, O. (1984). *Features of Yorùbá oral poetry.* Ibadan: University Press Limited.

Pulgram, E. (1954). *Theory of names.* Berkely: American Name Society.

Sebeok T, A. (1994). Signs: an introduction to semiotics. Toronto: University of Toronto.

CHAPTER TWELVE

Teaching languages, literatures and cultures: Examining Teaching Philosophies

Odutola Kole
University of Florida

Introduction

If the eye is the window to the soul, a teaching philosophy is like the light that shines on inner workings of the mind. In the case of teachers, a systematic comprehension of the inner workings of their minds allows for better understanding of what happens in college classrooms and why. It is the statement of teaching philosophy that acts as a learning/teaching barometer both for the teacher and the taught. Though not always consciously, teachers continuously create and evaluate their instruction and instructional activities based upon their individual philosophy of teaching. Statements of teaching philosophy have the potential to become seeds for fruitful dialogue among peers during formal and informal discussions regarding teaching. A central point of focus during such discussions happens to be how the intricate act of teaching transforms concepts and information into knowledge on the part of the learner. The question needing our attention and hence a great aspect of this study is what then does it mean to teach? Or when can it be said that learning has taken place? J. F O'Connell (2000) frames teaching as binary opposites. In one breath the act of teaching can be "...both fun and frustrating, energizing and disheartening, simple and complex" (p.243)

In effect teaching can be said to be both a science and a creative enterprise that has built-in codes and conventions. Also, other scholars talk about teaching metaphorically, as such, the metaphor of teaching as a journey comes up in literature quite often such as in a book by Savory, Burnett and Goodburn (2007) titled *"Inquiry into the College Classroom: A Journey Toward Scholarly Teaching"* where they present their model of the intricacies of teaching based on a large sample of instructors at the University of Nebraska-Lincoln. If we stick to the metaphor of teaching as a journey, then teaching philosophies act as drivers, road maps, and milestones needed to guide travelers as they navigate the twists and turns on the metaphorical roads and highways that lead to understanding.

The flip side of teaching, which is learning (or how learning takes place), should not also be neglected in a gathering of teachers; it needs to be included in teaching deliberations. Without too much elaboration on how learning takes place, I will briefly refer to Mathew Lieberman's (2014) classification of human nature as it relates to learning. One of the views he presents is the classic view which suggests "classroom learning is motivated by carrots and sticks. The carrot is the desire for a better material life in the future. The stick is the fear that doing poorly, leads to harsh evaluations from the teacher, embarrassment in front of peers and potential punishments from parents" (p.4). It can be observed that there are many contestable points of view in the way the "carrot and stick" concept have been elaborated upon, especially when taken into a language class where learning is not necessarily for material betterment but as part of the requirement by a department within a university or a college as a whole.

The other view which Lieberman terms the social view resonates more with language teaching in that there is a social motivation to learning. According to this view, learning is a strategy that involves peer-to-peer teaching. To be sure, this strategy has empirical grounding in neuroscience based on participants in a study who were subjected to functional magnetic resonance imaging fMRI. Based on this study, it was discovered that "[a] network of brain regions involved in social thinking was more active when participants were seeing a show idea that they would later pass on so successfully that the producer (i.e., another participant) would deem it worth passing on to a third party" (p.5). This empirical evidence supports the idea that learners understand their subject better when they are aware of possibilities of sharing what they have learned with others.

This paperfocuses upon what happens in the minds of those who intend to use language and literature to enhance cultural understanding. There are two parts to this paper: The first section looks briefly at current literature on the subject. The second part presents an analysis of data gathered from a survey from non-representative sample as well as five randomly selected teaching philosophy statements written by language instructors at the University of Florida.

Literature review

There is a limited amount of articles published about statements of teaching philosophy but in the last decade and half there has been various research projects on the intersection between teachers' beliefs and classroom practice. About 19 years ago, Zhihui Fang (1996) was one of the opinions that teacher education research had a long record of looking at the complex relationship between what teachers believed and what they practiced. According to Fang,

"Teachers' thought processes occur inside teachers' heads and are unobservable" (p. 48). Could what teachers believe about teaching be what gets encrypted into statements of teaching philosophy? Dona Kagan (1992) defined a teacher's belief "as tacit, often unconsciously held assumptions about students, classrooms, and the academic material to be taught" (p. 65). The research on teacher belief is surely a backdoor passageway into understanding a teacher's teaching philosophy. Dona Kagan (1992) argues further that "[t]eacher belief is a particularly provocative form of personal knowledge that is generally defined as pre-or in-service teachers' implicit assumptions about students, learning, classrooms, and the subject matter to be taught" (p. 66).

In the same vein, a statement of teaching philosophy can be a projection into a future or a reflection based on what has been done. Whichever way, both projection and reflection constitutes "critical thinking of a more or less systematic kind about general nature of the world" (Korn, 2003, p. 51). Critical reflections are in essence what philosophy as a subject proposes to do. Just as the statement reflects a teacher's ability to think critically, the notion also shows up in classroom teaching. Rezaei, Derakhshan & Bagherkazemi (2011) concluded that teachers' " in-class application of critical thinking skills and attitudes, and [their provision of] explicit explanations of the importance of critical thinking could also help students enhance [their] critical thinking" (p. 775).

A lot can be said regarding statements of teaching philosophy written by teachers of languages, literatures, and cultures in that, teaching of any language requires careful planning and methodical execution. As stated earlier, if the theory of mind as enunciated by Keith Oatley (2011) is applied, teaching statements then present a window into the minds and practice of the writers. Oatley submits that "Theory of Mind has a projective quality: we cast a model onto another person in ordinary life, or onto a character in fiction" (p.16). For instance four scholars, Schönwetter, Sokal, Friesen and Taylor (2002) did a meta-analysis of teaching statements and came to the conclusion that a "teaching philosophy statement reflects not only personal beliefs about teaching and learning, but also disciplinary cultures, institutional structures and cultures, and stakeholder expectations as well (p.83).Along the same lines,Goodyear and Allchin (1998), submitted that "[t]eaching is a scholarly activity when it is purposeful, reflective, documented, and shared in an evaluative forum" (p.103).Furthermore, I agree with Chism (1997) statement that "the best philosophy of teaching statement examples for most college teachers are those of peers who teach in similar settings or disciplines."

It is on the basis of creating an evaluative forum that this exploratory study on Teaching Languages, Literatures and Cultures examined 10statements of teaching philosophy of experienced teachers and professors. The exercise allows readers to gain insight into the submission of McKeachle, Pintrich, Lin and Smith (1986) when they concluded that "[w]hat we choose as goals depends upon our understanding of learning and of what teaching can produce" (p.1). Hence, the objective of this chapter as stated earlier is to stimulate a much needed dialogue about what goes on in African languages, literature and cultures classrooms by exploring various perspectives from those presently in practice.

Methodology

To access teachers' teaching cognition, a survey instrument was designed to be administered to a very small convenient sample, five to be exact, of language teachers at the university level. The choice of some of the questions in the survey is predicated on Goodyear and Allchin (1998), who stated that "[a]rticulating an individual teaching philosophy provides the foundation by which to clarify goals, to guide behavior, to seed scholarly dialogue on teaching, and to organize evaluation" (p.103). There are questions to be raised from what Goodyear and Allchin expressed in the quote above when they alluded to the fact that a teaching philosophy can be a foundation; but it is unclear how to move from that foundation to a metaphorical completed structure. In my view the metaphor of a building may be misleading here but an alternative metaphor would be that of a tree with leaves and branches. The authors mentioned dialogue as one of the anticipated seeds from the root of a teaching philosophy. It was on that premise that the survey I distributed sought to harvest fruits that are already in the public domain. So my guiding question sought to uncover what others think a statement of teaching philosophy should be. The survey sent to teachers of languages and literatures used two email contact lists.

To find out if any discussion goes on about statements of teaching philosophy, I sent out a five-question survey to two different list-serves of teachers of languages and literatures. Though the response rate was very low, I was still able to collect data from twelve respondents which will be analyzed in the next section. Prior to sending out of the survey instruments, ten samples of teaching philosophy statements were collected from language instructors at the University of Florida, from which only five were randomly selected. These samples form the basis for my review of content in the next section. Results of the survey will also be discussed in the next section below.

Data Collection: There were only 10 respondents to the questionnaire sent out to a convenient sample. The table below shows the response to some of the questions.

Question 1- Have you ever discussed the content of a statement of teaching philosophy with colleagues?	Question 2- Have you ever revised your statement of teaching philosophy?	Questions 3 /4 If yes why? 4) What does a statement of teaching philosophy mean to you? Please define what a 'statement of teaching philosophy' should entail	Question 5- Do you think there is a correlation between a well written statement of teaching philosophy and actual teaching practice?
N 1-No Ass Professor	Yes	Evolution/approach	No
N2-No	Yes (regularly)	Feedback/communication	It depends….
N3-No	No	personal belief	No (with reasons)
N4-Yes (but only 1)	Yes	Teaching objective	No
N5-Yes	Yes (to meet career needs)	Learner/Teacher interaction	Yes-should be evident in the outcomes
N6-Yes	Yes (emphatic yes)	Impart knowledge	Not sure
N7-No	Yes (a couple of times)	Dynamics of teaching	There should be
N8-No	Yes (type of course/Students	explains what teaching entails	Not sure
N9- Yes	Yes	theoretical rationale/ solid control of latest trends in learning and teaching methods/strategies,	No evidence
N10- Yes	No (but may do when needed)	A constant guide	No
N-11 No	Yes	Yes for a job/ reflection of classroom planning	Maybe, not necessarily
N-12 No	No	Personal convictions	Not sure
Total- 5 yes/ 7 No	Yes 10—No 2	Divergent views	No 7, other views 5

Findings

Review of five statements of teaching philosophy:

This section takes a look at a sample of statements of teaching philosophy collected from Languages Literatures and Cultures department at the University of Florida. A total of 10 statements were obtained, but 5 were randomly selected for content analysis. There were no criteria attached to the 5 statements chosen for the content analysis. One of the statements states that "My primary teaching goal is to **develop in students** the skills and basic knowledge that will allow them to continue to acquire language and cultural competence throughout their lives, linking the instruction I provide with their other studies and interests." The second sample indicates that language learners are fearful of learning a new language. Her "approach to teaching is to first tap into and deepen their curiosity about these cultures, then to help them **develop the learning skills** necessary to successfully engage them, while at the same time modeling the courage it takes to learn a second language, as well as the humility, perseverance, critical thinking, and sense of humor that will make them better learners of everything there is to learn in this life." The writer of the statements also indicates that connection to a community is very essential.

The third sample is not far removed from the first two in that she too stays her goal and her intention for teaching the language she teaches. "My primary goal when beginning any new semester is to create a learning environment in which students have the opportunity to immerse themselves in Italian language and culture. The first step towards this goal is the **development of a sense of community** that is instilled on the first day of class." The fourth sample does not explicitly describe a goal for teaching but instead mentions teaching style and the theory from which it is based. She states that her teaching style is "proficiency based and communicative in nature. I believe language is a tool used for real world communication. Hence any of the classroom activities I develop [is] to focus on the fours skills—listening, speaking, reading and writing—require interaction among the students" Here again the concept of a learners' community is implicit. The last sample does not state his teaching goal(s) but delves into his attitude to learners and how a professional learning atmosphere can aid effective classroom learning. He indicates that he tries to be "sensitive to the needs of each class as a group, and the needs of individuals in the class. And I try to challenge students while being available to them, and to provide them with tools to learn, while attempting to create a professional atmosphere in the classroom that will give students a sense of responsibility. I believe that a sense of freedom needs to be combined with a clear framework, and a leadership that an instructor must provide. I give a great deal of thought to the creation of a friendly atmosphere while being clear, and setting boundaries when necessary."

There are chords linking these five samples from totally different individuals who may never have spoken to each other about their philosophy of teaching. All the narratives are written from a first person perspective and each turns attention to what has been tried in class. None of the samples make projections into what may be done in class. One of the sample states explicitly the number of years she has taught at the College level. "Despite having taught at the college level for over ten years, every class I teach feels novel and fresh" she asserts. These opening lines could be said to set the tone for a reflexive statement of teaching philosophy. It would be instructive to read her earlier versions before now.

Discussion

The result of the survey indicates that 58% of the teachers in this study have not discussed the content of their statement of teaching philosophy with any other instructor or professor. Part of the 41.67% who indicated 'yes' did so with qualification. One of the respondents indicated that discussions were held with only one person while a few others self-reported that the discussions were with either a graduate student or with administrators during the review process of application packets or tenure and promotion packets. In response to the question of whether the respondents have ever had to revise a course based on their statement of teaching philosophy, 83% responded in the affirmative while 16.67% indicated that they have never revised or written a philosophy of teaching.

As a way to better understand why the decision for revising a philosophy of teaching statement was taken, the third question probed the respondents to state the reason(s) for the revision. Their views were divergent. One language teacher stated that the statement was modified "to meet local and teaching conditions (all depends on the prevailing teaching and learning environments, on the type of learners.... [and] their level of motivation. One other respondent who teaches literature submitted that he keeps revising his statement continuously having chosen to privilege his 'African' perspective on passing good practices of teaching literature and culture by trying to reflect on what and how he teaches. . . " It is interesting to note that there are very slight differences of teaching philosophies for those who teach literature as compared to those who teach different languages.

In addition, the literature teacher I referred to previously further stated that "the frustrating part is that it is very tedious to develop an alternative philosophy that may have little to do with US American convention. For instance, one of my principles is to teach NOT for grades... When students are not threatened with grades, their participation is mild. My major reason to permanently amend my philosophy is to try to find common ground with the "American" culture of teaching and learning. I have taught for 15 years in Europe and the approach is completely different from the one I deal with now." Another professor of literature revealed a different perspective; in his case the teaching philosophy is theory driven like Paulo Freire's concept of theory informing practice and practice informing theory. That professor stated that "my teaching philosophy is informed by my educational background, training, experiences, learning theories, and instructional technologies. These parameters, especially the last three are not static; therefore, I must adapt to any new paradigm that I believe will best serve my students and produce optimal student learning outcomes."

Based on the aforementioned data, one of the reasons teachers revise their teaching philosophy statements has to do with career advancement and change of teaching environments. This view is captured by one of the teachers who sadly wrote, "I revised them at different turns in my academic journey (i.e. reappointment, tenure, promotion, etc.), as each occasion gave me an opportunity to take a second look at, rethink and refine my teaching philosophy to bring it current with the reality of what I was already doing in the classroom with some degree of success." Apart from career advancement, it appears cross-fertilization of ideas is another motivation for the revision of a statement of teaching philosophy. This point is succinctly made by another professor who shared his reason for revising a statement of teaching philosophy, "I have also revised it after reading other people's teaching philosophy and discovering on my own as my own philosophy evolved based on the types of students I was teaching."

The first three survey questions help us understand how statements of teaching philosophy are used while the fourth question is meant to interrogate how each respondent conceptualizes the concept of teaching. One of the respondents, while stating what her teaching philosophy entails presented four bullet points which are made up of two observations and two suggestions for other instructors. She begins with dualities by asserting that "there is no learner who cannot learn" and follows that up with a pronouncement that "there are a lot of teachers who cannot teach." The next point in her submission is the role of the teacher. She ascribes that teachers need to take a facilitating role in learning. Her next point appears to be an advice to others which she stated as follows: "do not assume that the learner is like an empty vessel that needs to be filled." Finally she charges teachers to tap into the knowledge students bring to class, she wrote, "the knowledge learners come with to class need to be tapped to ensure experiential learning."

The final and fifth questions asked the participants to show whether or not a correlation between a well written statement of teaching philosophy and actual teaching practice exists. One person stated that it is a 'mere' document that shows ones' "teaching style, techniques and how you approach the material and students. It's what defines you; however, it is a text that's remote from the experience itself." In line with the idea of self-definition, another respondent put it succinctly that "a teaching philosophy should entail one's personal belief of what teaching and learning is about." These perspectives are in line with Palmer's (year) perspective that "the personal cannot be removed from the professional. We teach what we are" (p.?). Though the views are different, communication appears to be a link between them all. Another respondent states that his statement of teaching philosophy encompasses "[h]ow I intend to **communicate** my ideas to students so that they can **think right** and formulate opinions on issues discussed in class."

There has been over 36 years of academic research on the relationship between mission statements of corporate organizations and their performances. The results according to Christopher Bart and Mark Baetz (1998) from their study are provocative, they "suggest that most of the previous writings extolling the virtues of having a mission statement appear to be wrong or incomplete" (p. 848). Likewise, my study seems to support such claims.

Furthermore, the last survey question focused on the relationship between theory and practice to explore whether statements of teaching philosophy had any direct bearing to what happens in the classroom. Thus, this last question asked the respondents if they thought there is a correlation between a well written statement of teaching philosophy and actual teaching practice. The responses ranged from a definite yes to a few respondents who thought there should be such a correlation. One of the respondents submitted that "I don't think so since I have seen over-inflated statements that people use from others, and that does not mean much until you see the actual person teaching. It is words, and it can be beautifully written as for a contest." Another argues that "Honestly, I think the statement writing and actual practice are two different things. The classroom teaching is dynamic while the statement may be static. So, I don't see the two as being correlated." On the one hand, another professor actually stated that no such correlation exists. "I believe every teacher has his/her principles that guide their teaching endeavor which are not necessarily written down in a statement. I don't think there is necessarily a correlation between a well written statement of teaching philosophy and actual teaching practice."

Another respondent believes both should correlate; explained it this way. "I believe there should be (although I know that this is not always the case). My teaching ought to be driven by my philosophy about teaching, and vice versa. There should always be constant interaction/"communication" between both. In other words, the philosophy and the actual classroom practice should constantly be "talking" to each other." Along the same premise another teacher suggested that "There should be a correlation if the teacher revisits what s/he believes in. However, please note that just as one strives to do well when applying for a job, a true correlation between the two does emerge when one knows s/he is being observed. However, good teachers should be consistent with what they have stated in their statements. Sadly this doesn't always occur."

One of the literature teachers took a middle ground on the above question regarding teaching philosophy and teaching practice, "I see no evidence that a well-written statement of teaching philosophy is always the reflection of actual practice. If you could call this a correlation, I would say, **yes**, the statement of my teaching philosophy, as a theory, guides me while I am teaching, and the results of my teaching, which is practice, actually helps me better formulate or modify that statement or theory. For that reason, I may agree that there should be a relationship between the statement and actual practice. After all theory is the child of practice; it is practice that helps develop better and more accurate theories. It's also a two-way street in which theories influence practice, and practice also enlightens theories."

These results are not too far from those which Bart and Baetz (1998) obtained when they looked at the relationship of mission statements and the performance of the companies. Their conclusion raised the question about why bother writing one if there is no empirical data to support the hypothesis that a well written mission statement has a direct correlation to company performance. However, it can be deduced from online articles that a statement of teaching philosophy, without being judgmental, fulfils a number of things:

(1) Goal clarification;
(2) Provision of behavioral guidance in class and out of it;
(3) Basis for further scholarly discussion on teaching; and finally
(4) Organization of evaluation by all the stakeholders connected to what is taught and how it is taught.

Conclusion

The section on literature review shows that it is easier to locate research findings on how to construct acceptable teaching philosophy but difficult to come across one that takes a look at the content of statements and lessons that can be learned from them. To buttress this point, Dieter Schönwetter, Laura Sokal, Marcia Friesen and Lynn Taylor (2002), provided an overview of what they found from literature on the subject examined, "Each teaching philosophy statement reflects not only personal beliefs about teaching and learning, but also disciplinary cultures, institutional structures and cultures, and stakeholder expectations as well. This synergy among self, discipline, and institutional context guided the development of a conceptual model for constructing a teaching philosophy statement." The conceptual framework consists of six dimensions which are listed as "[t]he purpose of teaching and learning; the role of the teacher; the role of the student; the methods used; evaluation and assessment of teaching and learning; and also includes two framing devices – a metaphor or a critical incident and a device for acknowledging the impact that contextual factors have on teacher decision making" (p. 83). These six dimensions were uncovered in the five samples examined. It could be seen that each of the statements made mention of two or more of the dimensions listed above.

If statements of teaching philosophies are taken purely as texts to be analyzed, there are at least three issues a researcher would have to contend with. One of those would be to uncover the primary audience for the text; next would be the decoding strategies to be used in interpreting the text; and finally what the text expresses about the writer and approach to teaching/ learning.

Since findings from the survey have been stated and this paper has also presented ideas from statements of teaching philosophy written by others, I presume a few words about how I conceptualize teaching statements would be in order. In my view and that of a few scholars (Korn, 2003, Coppola, 2002); a statement of teaching philosophy is one of the very reliable road maps which is a condensed perspective of how a teacher conceptualizes what goes on in his or her mind after a few years in the classroom. A statement of teaching philosophy would represent the rudder or the roadmap for long trips that go on for extended miles. The committing of ideas according to Brain Coppola "requires an added degree of reflection on your purpose and intents." In my opinion eventually what gets to be written usually starts from the experience of the teacher or based on the experiences of others who have been in the profession longer than a new instructor.

References

Bart, C.K., &Baetz, M.C. (1998).The relationship between mission statement and firm performance and exploratory study.*Journal of Management Studies*, 35(6), 823-852.

Chism, N. V. N. (1998). Developing a philosophy of teaching statement.Essays on Teaching Excellence. Professional and Organizational Development Network in Higher Education, 9 (3), 1-2.

Coppola, B. (2002). Writing a statement of teaching philosophy. *Journal of College Science Teaching*, 31(7), 448-453.

Fang, Z. (1996). A review of research on teacher beliefs and practices.*Educational Research*, 38(1), 47-55.

Goodyear, G.E., & Allchin, D. (1998).Statements of teaching philosophy.In M.Kaplan (Ed.).*To improve the Academy*, (pp.17,103-122). Stillwater, OK: New Forums Press and theprofessional and organizational Development Networking Higher Education.

Kagan, D. M. (1992).Implication of research on teacher belief.*Educational Psychologist*, 27(1), 65-90.

Korn, J. H. (2003).Writing a philosophy of teaching."Excellence in Teaching" e-column in the PsychTeacher Electronic Discussion List.

Lieberman, M. D. (2014). Learning from others.*Chronicle of Higher Education*, LX (31), B4.

McKeachie, W. J., Pintrich, P. R., Lin, Y.-G., & Smith, D. A. F. (1986).*Teaching and learning in the classroom: A review of the literature*. Ann Arbor, MI: University of Michigan.

Oatley, K. (2011). Theory of mind and theory of minds in literature.In Leverage, P.; Mancing, H.; Schweicket, R.; and William, J. M. *Theory of mind and literature*.West Lafayette, Indiana; Purdue University Press.

O'Connell, J. F. (2000). Reflections.*Journal of Cancer Education,* *15*(4), 243.

Rezaei, S.; Derakhshan, A., & Bagherkazemi, M. (2011).Critical thinking in language education.*Journal of Language Teaching and Research,* 2 (4), 769-777.

Savory, P., Burnett, A., & Goodburn, A. (2007).*Inquiry into the College Classroom: A Journey Toward Scholarly Teaching.* San Francisco: Jossey-Bass/Anker Publishing.

Schönwetter, D. J., Sokal, L., Friense, M., and Taylor, K.L. (2002). Teaching philosophies reconsidered: A conceptual model for the development and evaluation of teaching philosophy statements. *The International Journal of Academic Development,* *7*(1), 83 96.

Appendix I

Questions:

(1) Have you ever discussed the content of a statement of teaching philosophy with colleagues?
(2) Have you ever revised your statement of teaching philosophy?
(3) If yes why?
(4) What does a statement of teaching philosophy mean to you? Please can define what you believe a "statement of teaching philosophy" should entail
(5) Do you think there is a correlation between a well written statement of teaching philosophy and actual teaching practice?

Index

A
Abeokuta, 208, 210
Addis Ababa, 69
Africa South of the Sahara, 23
African language instructors, 11, 144, 183, 188
African Union, 69
Africanizing English, 124
Afrobeat music, 252
Agoke, Adeola, v, 143
Ahn, Soojin, v
Akkadian, 81
Amharic, 68
Amin, Idi, 55, 56
Arabian Gulf, 50
Armah, Ayi Kwei, 123
Ayoola, Gabriel, 243

B
Baganda, 55, 56
Baloubi, Désiré, v, 123, 127, 139
Bambara, 32
Bamgbose, Ayo, 139, 267
Bantu, 28, 31, 35, 36, 44, 45, 50, 52, 55
Beleaua, Corina Mihaela, v, 75
Belgians, 56
Black Africa, 23, 27, 32, 40, 44
Bodunrin, Peter, 138
Bultmann, Rudolf, 82
Burundi, 24, 31, 32, 56

C
Camara, Sory, 123, 229, 230, 231, 232, 241
Cameroon, 27, 31
Central African Republic, 31
Césaire, Aimé, 123, 227
China, 39
Chisano, Joachim, 69, 70
Chomsky, Noam, 77, 89
Codeswitching, 184

Comoro Islands, 32
Coppola, Brain, 284, 285
Council of Catholic Bishops, 61

D
DANIDA, 68
Diop, Cheikh Anta, 123
Djibouti, 32

E
East African Literature Bureau, 29
Elexandre, Pierre, 29
Equatorial East Africa, 31
Equatorial West Africa, 31
Ethiopia, 24, 32
European Economic market, 68
European languages, 25, 26, 27, 28, 30, 34, 35, 36, 37, 47, 61, 125, 200
European Renaissance, 35, 38, 196

F
Fagunwa, D.O., 203, 205
Falola, Toyin, 138, 196, 200, 202, 203, 205, 216, 217
Fanon, Frantz, 11, 33, 198, 221, 222, 223, 226, 227
France, 27, 29, 38, 221
Frankfurt, 34, 90

G
Gabon, 31
Gates, Henry Louis, 59, 60, 61
Genesis, 83
Germany, 33, 34
Ginzburg, Carlo, 83, 90

H
Hausa, 32, 68
Heart of Darkness., 216, 224, 225
Historiography, 209, 216
Holy Spirit, 85

I
Igbo, 123, 124, 126, 127, 135, 137, 138
Imperialism, 49

Indian Ocean, 31
Islamic city-states, 51
Ìsòlá, Akínwùmí, 11, 193, 194, 214, 216, 217

J
Jadavpur University, 219

K
Kenya, 23, 30, 31, 32, 40, 48, 50, 56, 60, 61, 64, 67, 68, 69, 179
Kikerewe, 28, 30, 36
Kikerewe., 28
Kikongo, 57
Kiswahili language, 10
Kole, Odutola, vi, 269
Korea, 10, 39, 42
Kumar, S Satish, vi, 219

L
Langi, 55
Language pedagogy, v, 11, 16, 144, 145, 147, 154, 181, 189
Laye, Camara, 123
Léro, Etienne, 33
Less commonly taught languages, 169
Lingala, 32, 57
Lingua franca, 23, 32, 33, 40, 55, 57, 89
Lisanza, Esther M, 169
Literary texts, 20
Lugano, Rose S, 169

M
Maganda, Dainess, ii, iii, v, 9, 169
Makeba, Miriam, 179
Malawi, 32
Mazrui, Ali, 55, 57, 59, 73
Mbiti, John, 138
Mediterranean Sea, 23
Mesopotamia, 81
Metaphor, 83, 86, 88
Middle East, 23, 48, 55
Möhlig, Wilhelm J. G, 35, 44

Moshi, Lioba, v, 47, 72, 73, 74, 143, 144, 145
Muaka, Leonard, 169
Mulokozi, Mugyabuso, 30

N
New London Group, 146, 147, 148, 149, 165, 168
Nilotes, 55
Nkrumah, Kwame, 34, 138
Non-Being, 223
NORAD, 68
Nyerere, Mwalimu Julius, 34, 40, 57, 62, 63, 64, 138

O
Obasanjo, Olusegun, 70
Obote, Milton, 55
Ojo, Akinloye, vi, 193, 194, 205, 206, 212, 213, 214, 215, 217, 241, 262, 264
Okonkwo, Obi, 136
Okpewho, Isidore, 36, 44, 217
Organization of African Unity, 70
Osu, 137
Oyono, Ferdinand, 27, 44

P
Pan-Africanism, 63
Papua Guinea, 81
pedagogy of multiliteracies, 144, 146, 147, 154, 167, 168
Performance Based Assessment, 151, 152
Persians, 50, 60, 61
Post-Colonial literary cultures, 221

R
Radio Deutsche Welle, 68
Rodney, Water, 33
Ruhumbika, Gabriel, v, 23, 25, 35, 37, 44, 45
Rwanda, 24, 31, 32, 56

S
Said, Edward, 79, 91

Senegal, 30, 32, 229, 232, 234, 235, 236, 238
Somalia, 32, 50
Sub-Saharan Africa, 23, 42
Superior and inferior cultures, 18

T
Tajfel, Henri, 58, 59, 74
Tanzania, 24, 29, 30, 31, 32, 36, 37, 39, 40, 41, 42, 44, 48, 54, 56, 57, 61, 62, 64, 67, 68, 69, 72, 73, 74
Tower of Bable, 81
Traore, Karim, ii, iii, 229
Tutuola, Amos, 123

U
Uganda, 31, 32, 55
Uhuru na Umoja, 63
Ukerewe island, 42
UNESCO, 44, 68
University of Cologne, 35
University of Dar es Salaam, 24, 29, 37, 41
University of London, 28, 29
Upper Congo, 31
USAID, 68

V
Valery, Paul, 84
Vatican II, 61

Victoria Nyanza, 31
Vodacom, 68

W
wa Thion'go, Ngugi, 33
Waswahili, 60
Wolof, 30, 124
Woods, Tiger, 60
World Bank, 68

Y
Yoruba, v, 12, 68, 124, 139, 141, 169, 205
Yorùbá, 11, 155, 156, 157, 158, 159, 160, 161, 162, 163, 164, 165, 166, 193, 194, 199, 200, 201, 202, 203, 204, 205, 206, 207, 208, 209, 210, 211, 212, 214, 215, 216, 217, 243, 244, 245, 246, 248, 249, 250, 251, 252, 253, 254, 255, 256, 257, 258, 259, 260, 261, 262, 263, 264, 265, 266, 267, 268

Z
Zambezi, 31
Zanzibar, 50, 60, 61
Zeus, 81
Zimbabwe, 24, 32, 50
Zulu, 32, 124

www.ingramcontent.com/pod-product-compliance
Lightning Source LLC
Chambersburg PA
CBHW062005220426
43662CB00010B/1233